HANDBOOK OF INFANT, TODDLER, AND PRESCHOOL MENTAL HEALTH ASSESSMENT

Handbook of Infant, Toddler, and Preschool Mental Health Assessment

EDITED BY

Rebecca DelCarmen-Wiggins, PhD
Alice Carter, PhD

OXFORD

UNIVERSITY PRESS

2004

OXFORD
UNIVERSITY PRESS

Oxford   New York
Auckland   Bangkok   Buenos Aires   Cape Town   Chennai
Dar es Salaam   Delhi   Hong Kong   Istanbul   Karachi   Kolkata
Kuala Lumpur   Madrid   Melbourne   Mexico City   Mumbai   Nairobi
São Paulo   Shanghai   Taipei   Tokyo   Toronto

Published by Oxford University Press, Inc.
198 Madison Avenue, New York, New York 10016

www.oup.com

Library of Congress Cataloging-in-Publication Data

Handbook of infant, toddler, and preschool mental health assessment /
edited by Rebecca DelCarmen-Wiggins, Alice Carter.
p. cm.
ISBN 978-0-19-514438-3
1. Mental illness—Diagnosis.   2. Psychodiagnostics.   3. Behavioral
assessment of children.   4. Child psychiatry.   5. Infant psychiatry.
I. DelCarmen-Wiggins, Rebecca.   II. Carter, Alice (Alice S.)
RJ503.5 .H375   2004
618.92'89075—dc22   2003024325

Printed in the United States of America
on acid-free paper

Preface

This volume is quite possibly the first published handbook on assessment of mental health in infants, toddlers, and young preschool children. As such, it signals that this young field is growing up. Despite rapid growth in recent years, there is not to our knowledge a comprehensive volume reviewing conceptual, methodological, and research advances on early identification, diagnosis, and assessment of disorders in this young age group that could be used for teaching, research, and clinical practice. It is our hope that offering this collection of chapters will facilitate conceptual and methodological integration, and provide an opportunity to disseminate some of the very exciting recent developments within the young child assessment field. Our goal is to promote further advances within the research community and to promote changes in best practice (i.e., adoption of new, empirically based methods of assessment) within the clinical community.

ISSUES AND ADVANCES THAT INFORM THIS BOOK

The impetus for compiling this handbook is derived from the following concerns or developments within the young child assessment field:

1. *Challenges in applying existing diagnostic approaches to young children.* There is a consensus that traditional diagnostic approaches, such as the *Diagnostic and Statistical Manual of Mental Disorders* (*DSM*) system, have not been shown to be reliable or valid for young children. In addition, they do not incorporate research on infants and young children that highlights the importance of developmental and relational issues in diagnostic formulations. Modifications to criteria for a variety of disorders including depressive, anxiety, posttraumatic stress, and disruptive behavior disorders in young children have been proposed and are currently under investigation.

2. *The need for early identification of risk and disorder for available programs and services.* Public policy and legislative efforts have led to new opportunities for programs and services that target this young population. In addition, a growing empirical literature on a variety of disorders in very young children, such as autism, suggests that early, appropriate intervention (possibly capitalizing on the neuroplasticity of the young brain) can achieve better outcomes than treatment commencing in the later years. Despite a consensus regarding the value of early intervention and prevention efforts, most psychiatric disorders are not easily diagnosed before 3 years of age and, with the excep-

tion of a few disorders (e.g., autism, ADHD), diagnostic tools for preschoolers are still in the development stage. Parents and researchers together are actively seeking earlier and more sensitive diagnostic assessment tools, given the close linkages between early diagnosis, treatment, and prognosis. It can also be argued that although the typical threshold for referral to services among adults and older children is diagnosis (i.e., the presence of sufficient symptoms to meet criteria for a disorder along with associated impairment), the infancy, toddler, and preschool periods need a different threshold for referral. Specifically, it would be wise to invest intervention dollars in children who may be subthreshold for diagnostic caseness, but who, in addition to a concerning number of symptoms, experience the additional threat to normative developmental progress of significant child, family, and community-level risk factors for psychopathology.

3. *New instrumentation.* Several new diagnostic and assessment approaches have been proposed for use with infants, toddlers, and young children. These remain largely underutilized, including assessments of child functioning (e.g., behavioral problems, competencies, and diagnostic symptoms) as well as parent or relationship functioning (e.g., the parent-child relationship and early relationship disturbances).

4. *Contextual factors.* Though the study of context has long been important in developmental theory, there is now consensus within the young child assessment field that contextual factors, including relationship (see chapter 3) and culture (see chapter 2), need to be incorporated into our clinical understanding of psychopathology in young children.

5. *Regulation.* Another important theme to emerge recently in the young child assessment literature is the importance of assessing temperament and regulatory functioning. Some researchers and theoreticians now view many mental health problems in the first two years as closely tied to regulatory or sensory-related functioning. These problems may manifest in infants as sleep disturbances, eating difficulties, problems in organized play, or uncontrollable emotional outbursts (see chapter 13). This represents a shift in thinking with respect to the manner in which prob-

lems in young children are conceptualized and a recognition that psychopathology in young children may need a different framework than psychopathology in older children and adults. In particular, we believe that it is crucial to understand how various temperamental, regulatory, sensory, and neurophysiological factors may increase risk for or protect against mental health disorders. In addition, further study of normative and atypical courses of emotion and behavior regulation may aid in disentangling the role of temperament versus other nontemperamental regulatory factors that may combine to influence mental health outcomes. We believe that a greater understanding of developmental linkages between temperamental and regulatory domains will lead to a better characterization of early emerging core deficits of mental health disorders and the complex developmental pathways that lead to the development of disordered states. Moreover, better developmental characterization of mental health disorder phenotypes will aid in genetic studies that aim to identify susceptibility genes.

6. *Impairment.* The issue of impairment comes to the fore when considering diagnostic assessment of psychopathology in infants and young children. Documenting impairment or level of impaired functioning is an essential component of assigning a diagnosis to an individual. Within older children and adults, impairment is located within the individual, and individual functioning is assessed. The diagnostician must carefully verify not only that the individual meets the appropriate symptom criteria but also that the individual is unable to perform and adapt to expectable work, school, relational, and self-care activities and demands.

For infants and young children, this approach may not always work. At times, it may be possible to identify specific ways that a young child's social-emotional or behavioral difficulties interfere with (a) adaptation to developmentally appropriate demands or specific contexts (e.g., a child is expelled from several day care centers because his or her behavior is too challenging and is seen as atypical within the day care context), (b) the acquisition of new developmental capacities and skills (e.g., a child's tactile sensitivities or fears interfere with his or her exploration of toys and fine motor skills begin to lag), (c) relationship and interpersonal functioning (e.g., a child's problems with impulsivity and attention lead to difficulties with peers), or (d) health (e.g., a child's inability to regulate arousal during feeding leads to significant weight loss or failure to thrive). At other times, however, clear markers of impaired functioning may not be present despite the presence of risk or disorder because parents and other caregivers are providing protective scaffolding (for example, appropriate structure, limits, regulatory strategies, and support) to minimize the impact of a problem. We believe that given the embedded nature of child behavior within the family context (along with the gradual shift from dependence to autonomy) in the first years of life, it is important to locate impairment not only within the very young child (i.e., as evidenced by failure to acquire developmentally expected competencies) but also within the family context, as evidenced by parental distress or a child's needs interfering with the parent's ability to maintain family routines (e.g., eating together as a family in a restaurant), household activities (e.g., making a phone call to family members or friends), or employment (e.g., stopping work or changing work settings because of difficulty obtaining appropriate child care). From a developmental perspective, therefore, it is important to evaluate the individual child's functioning as well as family functioning in determining level of impairment in the first few years.

Given the very small numbers of infants, toddlers, and preschoolers who are identified as having social-emotional and behavioral disturbances relative to the large number of children who enter school with significant mental health impairment, it is critical to enhance early identification and to develop new strategies to assess impairment and risk such that targeted interventions can be effectively employed to minimize suffering for very young children and their families and to decrease the number of children who, due to behavioral and social-emotional concerns, enter school without the necessary skills to adapt to the demands of the classroom setting.

7. *Next steps in diagnostic nosologies for very young children.* There is continued controversy about whether an independent diagnostic nosology is required for infants and toddlers or whether a downward extension or adaptation will be sufficient. It is important to place this controversy within the broader context of the growing debate concerning core issues of the validity of nosology of adult psychiatric disorders, which poses a unique challenge to the relatively new and emergent field of infant and young child mental health assessment. On the one hand, we appreciate the clinical utility of more seasoned older child, adolescent, and adult diagnostic approaches as vitally important, particularly as they allow for increased and effective communication for focused intervention. The success of the downward extension approach within the field of autism is evidence of the utility of this approach. On the other hand, mounting scientific criticism concerning central issues of validity, particularly for this young population, reinforces attempts to develop and utilize distinctive, theoretically derived, and empirically based diagnostic approaches for young children that address the greater role of relationship, temperamental, and regulatory influences. For this young field to develop more fully, we need to identify lessons learned from previous historic attempts at psychiatric nosology as well as to understand the unique conceptual contributions of the infant and young child assessment field. In so doing, we may not only provide fresh, developmentally based perspectives that can address the difficult questions of how to incorporate context, including relationships and culture, in the assessment and treatment of disorders in young children, but we may also have something to offer the broader scientific debate about psychiatric diagnosis in older children and adults.

ABOUT THE WORK REPRESENTED IN THIS VOLUME

For the chapters in this book, we include mostly work funded by the National Institute of Mental Health (NIMH). Therefore, most of the work presented here has undergone the scrutiny of the peer review system within NIMH as well as expert review when the proposal was submitted to Oxford University Press and again when the chapters were finalized for publication. Though the field is young and some instruments still are not yet well utilized, researchers are making rapid advances in this important area. This is reflected in the increased number of applications submitted and funded by NIMH for diagnostic assessment in young children. We believe that the work presented here is state of the art in terms of both methodological and conceptual advances.

This book was written with several potential readers in mind. First, researchers concerned with advancing diagnostic assessment for infants and young children may use it as a review and a resource. Second, it is intended for professionals conducting clinical work with infants and young children, to bring to them empirically based approaches to identifying and assessing problems. Third, the book is for those in advanced training including psychiatry fellows, child psychiatrists, clinical psychology interns, and advanced students.

ACKNOWLEDGMENTS We wish to thank our contributors for their willingness to share their work in this venue. We want to thank NIMH for encouraging and supporting the development of this volume. We also wish to acknowledge and thank our families for their support, including Steve, Daniel, and Elizabeth (RDW) and Dave, Rachel, and Zack (ASC).

We hope that the following chapters inform the future development of valid diagnostic approaches and lead to research advances in our understanding of the role of parenting and cultural context, regulatory functioning, and impairment in the assessment of mental disorders in infants and young children. More broadly, our hopes for this volume are that it may integrate empirical findings, introduce fresh concepts, and stimulate a rich, generative discussion that advances not only the field of young child assessment but mental health nosology more generally.

Contents

Contributors

Thomas M. Achenbach, PhD, Department of Psychiatry, University of Vermont

Thomas F. Anders, MD, Department of Psychiatry, University of California, Davis

Adrian Angold, MD, Center for Developmental Epidemiology, Duke University Medical Center

Kathyrn E. Barnard, PhD, Department of Psychology, University of Washington

Jeanne Brooks-Gunn, PhD, Center for Young Children and Families, Teachers College, Columbia University

Alice S. Carter, PhD, University of Massachusetts, Boston, Department of Psychology

Anil Chacko, BA, Center for Children and Families, University of Buffalo

Irene Chatoor, MD, Department of Psychiatry, Children's National Medical Center, Washington, DC

Katarzyna Chawarska, PhD, Yale Child Study Center, Yale University School of Medicine

Michelle Christensen, PhD, University of Colorado Health Sciences Center, Division of American Indian and Alaska Native Programs

Roseanne Clark, PhD, Department of Psychiatry, University of Wisconsin Medical School

Barbara Danis, PhD, Preschool Behavior Problems Clinic, Department of Psychiatry, University of Chicago

Rebecca DelCarmen-Wiggins, PhD, Developmental Psychopathology and Prevention Research Branch, Division of Mental Disorders, Behavioral Research, and AIDS, National Institute of Mental Health

Helen Link Egger, MD, Developmental Epidemiology Center, Division of Child and Adolescent Psychiatry, Duke University Medical Center

Robert Emde, MD, Health Science Center, University of Colorado

Ruth Feldman, PhD, Department of Psychology, Bar-Ilan University

Candace Fleming, PhD, American Indian and Alaska Native Programs, University of Colorado Health Sciences Center

Nathan A. Fox, PhD, Department of Human Development, University of Maryland

Kathleen Cranley Gallagher, PhD, Early Childhood Intervention and Family Studies, University of North Carolina, Chapel Hill

Jody Ganiban, PhD, Department of Psychology, George Washington University

Walter S. Gilliam, PhD, Yale University Child Study Center

Beth L. Goodlin-Jones, PhD, Department of Psychiatry and Behavioral Sciences, University of California, Davis, School of Medicine

Magdalena Hernandez, Center of Children and Families, Columbia University

Lynne C. Huffman, MD, Department of Pediatrics and The Children's Mental Health Council, Stanford University School of Medicine

Miri Keren, MD, Geha Mental Health Center, Tel-Aviv University

Ami Klin, PhD, Yale Child Study Center, Yale University School of Medicine

Alicia F. Lieberman, PhD, Infant-Parent Program, San Francisco General Hospital

Joan L. Luby, MD, Department of Psychiatry, Washington University School of Medicine

Linda C. Mayes, MD, Yale Child Study Center, Yale University School of Medicine

Lisa A. McCabe, PhD, Cornell Early Childhood Program, Cornell University

Susan C. McDonough, PhD, School of Social Work, University of Michigan

Lucy Jane Miller, PhD, Department of Rehabilitation Medicine and Pediatrics, University of Colorado Health Sciences Center

Debra Moulton, PhD, Sensory Processing Research and Treatment (STAR) Center, Children's Hospital, Denver

Mary Nichols, PhD, Children's Health Council, Palo Alto, California

William E. Pelham, Jr., PhD, Center for Children and Families, State University of New York at Buffalo

Cindy P. Polak, BS, Department of Human Development, University of Maryland

Pia Rebello-Britto, PhD, National Center for Children and Families, Teachers College, Columbia University

Leslie A. Rescorla, PhD, Bryn Mawr College

JoAnn Robinson, PhD, Prevention Research Center, Denver

Emily Rubin, MS, CCC-SLP, Yale Child Study Center, Yale University School of Medicine and Communication Crossroads

Arnold Sameroff, PhD, Center for Human Growth and Development, University of Michigan

Michael S. Scheeringa, MD, Department of Psychiatry and Neurology, Tulane University Medical Center

Ronald Seifer, PhD, Bradley Hospital, Brown University

Cynthia A. Stifter, PhD, Department of Human Development and Family Studies, The Pennsylvania State University

Audrey Tluczek, PhD, Department of Psychiatry, University of Wisconsin Medical School and School of Nursing, Madison

Fred Volkmar, MD, Yale Child Study Center, Yale University School of Medicine

Lauren S. Wakschlag, PhD, Preschool Behavior Problems Clinic, Department of Psychiatry, University of Chicago

Susan L. Warren, MD, Center for Family Research, George Washington University

Serena Wieder, PhD, International Council of Developmental and Learning Disorders, Washington, DC

Crystal N. Wiggins, MS, Department of Psychology, The Pennsylvania State University

Brian T. Wymbs, MA, Center for Children and Families, State University of New York at Buffalo

Marina Zelenko, MD, Child and Adolescent Services, Kaiser Permanente Medical Center, Santa Clara, California

HANDBOOK OF INFANT, TODDLER, AND PRESCHOOL MENTAL HEALTH ASSESSMENT

1

Introduction

It is now widely recognized that the signs and symptoms of social, emotional, and behavioral disorders are apparent and measurable as early as infancy and toddlerhood, and that an early age of onset, without intervention, may have important clinical implications concerning prognosis. The prevalence estimates for mental health problems in young children are substantial and similar to those for older children, roughly 17 to 20%. Helping infants and very young children, along with their parents, overcome these early difficulties offers the compelling possibility of derailing disorders before they become entrenched and possibly treatment resistant. A mounting empirical literature suggests that early, appropriate intervention, possibly capitalizing on the neuroplasticity of the young brain, can achieve better outcomes than treatment commencing in the later years. In order to provide appropriate treatment or early intervention that is tailored to specific problems, valid and reliable diagnostic assessment tools for infants and young children are required.

Despite the growing consensus on the importance of early intervention, diagnostic assessment of psychopathology in infants and young children lags far behind work with older children and adults. The lack of readily available tools to assess mental health disturbances in the very early years has interfered with referrals to and the development of intervention services for children and families who are suffering. Researchers (for example, Angold and Egger, chapter 7) studying the assessment of disorders in infants and young children have suggested that their field is 30 years behind work with older children. Reasons for this lag include the following: (1) a general reliance on the pediatric adage, "It is just a stage; the child will grow out of it"; (2) an emphasis on treating severe symptoms; and (3) focusing on the here and now rather than viewing problems from a more developmental perspective with an emphasis on prevention.

This book is designed to address that gap. In particular, its purpose is to bridge clinical work and research and to advance research in the following areas:

- Developmentally and empirically based approaches to identifying and assessing disorders in infants and young children

- Validity of current diagnostic criteria for disorders that emerge during the infant, toddler, and preschool years
- New criteria or conceptualizations of dysfunction in the early years
- Ways to incorporate parental and cultural context into the assessment process
- The role of regulatory functioning in psychopathology in infants and young children
- The issue of impairment in making recommendations for assessment in infants and young children

Recently, methodologically sound research on the diagnostic assessment of disorders in early childhood has begun. Although preliminary, it provides a useful base for both young child clinical researchers and for practitioners. For example, in the last few years the National Institutes of Mental Health has funded studies examining the validity of diagnostic criteria across a variety of disorders in the preschool years, such as affective disorders, PTSD, and ADHD. Studies examining promising new assessment tools and instruments in this area have also been funded. Diagnostic interview scales, parent rating scales, and observational approaches are being successfully employed in the assessment of socioemotional functioning, emotion regulation, and clinical disorders in the early years. There is also preliminary evidence that incorporating relational assessments and impairment can increase the validity of our diagnostic work with young children.

As they look toward the future and begin to assess developmentally appropriate diagnostic approaches, researchers in the young child area are encouraged by the growing consensus in this field concerning the importance of relationship and cultural contexts, regulation, and impairment in understanding and assessing early problems.

ORGANIZATION OF THIS VOLUME

This book is arranged in seven parts. The first part includes three chapters highlighting the important aspects of a contextual assessment: development, culture, relationship, and ecology. The second part addresses the role of individual differences in temperament and regulation in assessing disorders in infants and young children. The third part examines the broader conceptual issues involved in diagnostic assessment in young children. The fourth addresses methodological issues involved in observation and developmental assessment. The fifth addresses problems in early state regulation, development, and disorders with an onset in infancy and toddlerhood. The sixth part contains chapters that focus on assessment of specific major disorders commonly seen in clinical practice with preschoolers. The goal of this substantial part is to advance diagnostic criteria of various disorders in preschool children. Each of the chapters in this important disorder-focused part is based on NIMH-funded work. The final part addresses applied issues and measurement across a variety of settings including community-based, primary care, and preschool/Head Start settings.

Our goals for this volume are to disseminate the empirical findings and promising conceptual models on assessment of mental disorders in infancy and early childhood, to bridge research and clinical work on early assessment, and to generate increased linkages among specialists working in different areas within the field to advance science. We hope that you will find the following chapters conceptually stimulating and clinically useful in your own assessment work with infants, toddlers, and preschoolers.

I

CONTEXTUAL FACTORS
IN EARLY ASSESSMENT

For the infant or young child who has not yet achieved autonomy or self-regulation, emotional and behavioral patterns are inextricably woven into the immediate relationship context. Our appreciation of this relationship context has grown out of the many theories, traditions, and perspectives central to developmental psychopathology, including attachment, ethology, psychodynamic, family systems, and transactional ecological theories. As we continue to advance in our understanding of how contextual factors influence development, the parenting or caregiving context (at least for very young children) continues to emerge as a central construct.

In a groundbreaking chapter that addresses the role of culture in assessment, Michelle Christensen, Robert Emde, and Candace Fleming present an outline of eight defining features of culture and its influence. These guidelines provide the framework for their recommended revisions of the Outline for Cultural Formulation in the *DSM-IV*.

An illustrative case example is also presented. Their work not only highlights the importance of culture in assessment, but also makes the linkages between culture and child outcome via the par-

enting relationship. In discussing the eighth feature of cultural influence, they make the important point that culture is mediated through the parenting relationship. They go on to consider the far-reaching clinical implications of that influence for assessment of infants and young children.

The parental and relationship context in understanding mental health difficulties is now well recognized. Although relationship functioning is highlighted throughout this volume for a variety of mental health issues in young children, how best to include the relationship perspective in assessment practices continues to elude researchers and clinicians. Roseanne Clark, Audrey Tluczek, and Kathleen Cranley Gallagher present a comprehensive approach for incorporating the relationship and parenting context into the process of infant and young child assessment. They review the rich theoretical foundations and empirical support for employing a parent-child relationship paradigm when assessing the mental health of the infant or young child and describe structured clinical evaluation procedures and domains for assessment when evaluating parent-child relational quality and determining relational diagnoses or attachment classifications. They propose that an assessment of the parent-child relationship should be the centerpiece of an infant/toddler mental health assessment and should consist of both objective observational assessment of parent-child interactions across contexts and a subjective interview assessment of the parent's experience of the child. Clark and colleagues address the importance of involving parents in the process of assessing their relationship with their child and the implications of this collaborative assessment approach for relationally focused treatment and research. The core relationship issues offered in this chapter represent fundamental principles upon which a developmentally based approach to assessment in infant and young child mental health can be successfully built.

Arnold Sameroff, Ronald Seifer, and Susan McDonough have long been proponents of examining the transactional processes that exist between the multiple layers of influence in child development. Given that the infant lives in the context of the family, the neighborhood and community, the peer group, and a variety of caregiving arrangements, they emphasize that it is important to assess all these subsystems of the child's ecology. In their work, they have been examining how environmental risk is predictive of mental health throughout childhood. To increase the specificity of assessment of risk and move toward a greater specification of environmental influence, they present an innovative way to produce and assess multiple-risk scores that are relevant to young children. The authors note the importance of measuring demographic features in any study of risk and raise the question of whether risk scales must be sample specific.

The authors in this introductory section present a number of approaches for integrating contextual factors into assessment procedures. They unanimously note the need for research and clinical approaches to assess the multiple influences on child development, particularly the parental relationship, in assessing infants and young children. Although the perspective is more broadly acknowledged, future research needs to incorporate these core contextual issues and the relationship perspective more systematically. This integration will benefit not only the infant/young child mental health field, but also mental health assessment more generally.

2

Cultural Perspectives for Assessing Infants and Young Children

Michelle Christensen
Robert Emde
Candace Fleming

Culture is acknowledged as a significant factor in the assessment of psychological functioning and treatment of mental disorders (American Psychiatric Association, 1994; American Psychological Association, 1993; U.S. Department of Health and Human Services, 1999). Regarding infant mental health, the *Diagnostic Classification of Mental Health and Developmental Disorders of Infancy and Early Childhood* (DC:0–3; Zero to Three, 1994) states that any intervention or treatment program should include an assessment of family functioning and cultural and community patterns in addition to developmental history, symptoms, and assessment of the child's current functioning.

According to the members of the work group charged with developing the Outline for Cultural Formulation in the *Diagnostic and Statistical Manual of Mental Disorders*, Fourth Edition (*DSM-IV*; American Psychiatric Association, 1994), there has been growing recognition that psychiatric diseases need to be understood not *only* as biological processes, but rather, in the context of an illness experience, which is in part determined by cultural interpretations of the disease (Good, 1996). Kleinman (1988) was one of the first authors to

discuss the concepts of disease and illness in this way (Castillo, 1997). By considering disease in the context of an "illness experience," there is an acknowledgment that the experience of disease—that is, its symptoms, its remedy, and so on—is unique to a particular individual who is situated in a particular sociocultural context.

While the inclusion of the Outline for Cultural Formulation in *DSM-IV* has made a significant contribution to the assessment of adult psychological functioning in the context of culture (Manson, 1995), the field of infant mental health assessment has lagged behind (Yamamoto, 1997). This is not surprising, considering the newness of the field and the fact that appreciation of cultural factors in development in general has lagged behind other approaches (Shonkoff & Phillips, 2000; Super & Harkness, 1986). It is also not surprising that the need to understand culture has come increasingly into our awareness, given the changing demographics of the U.S. population. According to the U.S. Census Bureau (2000), minority and foreign-born groups are expected to constitute increasingly large segments of the total U.S. population over the next 50 years, while the current majority of non-Hispanic Whites is expected to decrease from 72% of the total population in 1999 to 53% in 2050.

Despite current acknowledgment of the importance of culture in our work as psychologists, psychiatrists, and other mental health providers, the concept of culture has remained abstract and therefore difficult to apply in real-world situations. Certain advances, such as the inclusion of a cultural case formulation in Appendix I of *DSM-IV*, are conducive to making culture a more routine element in the assessment, diagnostic, and treatment process. However, as Garcia Coll and Magnuson (2000) highlight, academicians and clinicians alike have had what they call an uneasy relationship with culture as it influences the lives and well-being of young children. In this chapter, our goal is to discuss the relevance of culture for, and the influence of culture on, infant mental health and, more important, to provide a practical framework to aid in the oftentimes ambiguous task of taking culture into account in the assessment of young children's psychological functioning.

CULTURAL DEFINITION AND INFLUENCE: EIGHT GENERAL FEATURES THAT FORM A BACKGROUND FOR ASSESSMENT

Culture can be defined as meaning that is shared by a group of people. These shared values, assumptions, beliefs, and practices are transmitted across generations and are brought to life through the daily behavior and interactions of people within a group. Culture supports early development in varied ways, most often operating silently in the background through the mediation of parenting. The supportive aspects of culture are often not appreciated by clinicians, who typically become aware of cultural influences among peoples when they see differences (e.g., in practices, behavior, etc.) from their own cultural expectations. In addition to reviewing the particulars of cultural difference that contribute to development, we believe it is useful to identify some general features about cultural definition and influence.

Culture as Shared Meaning

First, it is useful to distinguish culture—as shared values, beliefs, and practices among members of a group—from the terms *ethnicity*, *race*, and *minority status*. Ethnicity refers to an identity that is assumed, and to some extent chosen, by individuals within a group (Lewis, 2000). Race, although there is controversy over the current usefulness of this term, generally refers to the genetically influenced physical appearance of individuals, while minority status is a descriptive population term often invoked for considerations of social policy. Following others, we advocate that culture is especially important to include in the assessment and treatment process (Betancourt & Lopez, 1993; Garcia Coll & Magnuson, 2000).

Culture Occurs in an Ecology

Second, culture occurs in a setting. As such, it is useful to bear in mind that culture not only occurs in an ecology but also contains adaptations to it. The importance of setting or ecology for culture, and its influence on human development, has been conceptualized in some detail by Bronfenbrenner (1977, 1979) and by Sameroff and Fiese (2000) and given instantiation in the separate studies of rural African caregiving practices by Super and Harkness (1982, 1986) and by LeVine and colleagues (1994). For example, infants' sleeping and feeding patterns are apt to be shorter but more frequent in a context where mothers engage in culturally supported daily routines that include the continuous carrying of their infants on their backs to soothe and quiet them. Similarly, the environmental demands of work for mothers in rural Africa, along with culturally derived expectations for childbearing and the availability of large family networks, are apt to be associated with routines in which infants and toddlers are cared for by siblings who are not much older. Thus, customs of child care such as how infants are carried and the type and amount of supervision infants receive are governed by assumptions about development espoused by cultures in particular environmental contexts (Harkness & Super, 1996). Furthermore, as Lewis (2000) points out, customs of child care influenced by setting also include the ways in which parents respond to infant cues, determinations about the amount and type of stimulation (tactile, verbal, and social) an infant should receive, routines of infant care, and the teaching of skills valued in a particular culture (e.g., smiling, vocalizing, and play).

Culture Is Transactional

Third, culture is dynamic and transactional. Evolving history, with its changing norms, roles, and values, contributes to the dynamic and transactional nature of culture. Moreover, shared meaning changes in the midst of adaptations to technology, influences from other cultural groups, and influences from developing individuals. These factors represent important transactional processes in which culture is both influencing settings and people and is itself being influenced and changed.

Culture Is Experienced Subjectively

Fourth, culture is experienced subjectively by individuals. More specifically, culture guides early development by means of subjective experiences that are shared, that is, *intersubjectively* experienced, especially between caregivers and children (Stern, 1985). Culture not only influences the physical setting and context for parents and young children but also influences attitudes, expectations, and perceptions of safety and appropriate behavior. Parents share meaning in an intuitive manner with their children as they engage them in everyday learning activities. But parents also share meaning in such activities (i.e., engagement in intersubjectivity) in a special way. Contemporary thinking in the field of child development, following Vygotsky (1978), portrays the parent as providing a psychological scaffolding for the child's learning, pulling the child forward in development according to what is sensed as appropriate in a "zone of proximal development." There is an active process of "guided participation" or "apprenticeship" between adult and child, as Rogoff (1990) puts it. That such a process is reflective of cultural support and variation is indicated by the work of Rogoff, Mistry,

Goncu, and Mosier (1993), who observed mothers and their toddlers in a rural Mayan village of Guatemala (San Pedro) and in an urban city of the United States (Salt Lake City, Utah). Guided participation of mothers in San Pedro occurred in a courtyard setting with a number of mothers watching a number of toddlers as mothers engaged in weaving and other tasks. While mothers in this setting provided fewer vocabulary lessons to their children and engaged in less praise than did mothers in Salt Lake City, San Pedro mothers were more available and ready to help any of the children, as opposed to just their own, if there were concerns of safety. Rogoff and Mosier (1993) interpreted these differences to be part of a more general cultural respect for autonomy in learning under these particular circumstances in San Pedro as well as more of an orientation to interdependence among San Pedro mothers (also see discussion in Emde & Spicer, 2000).

Culture Operates Silently and With Voices

Fifth, culture operates silently as well as with voices. Rather than being obvious or talked about, much of cultural influence involves procedural knowledge and mental activity. We have come to understand the importance of procedural knowledge as the form of knowledge that refers to information underlying a skill or set of behaviors but that does not need to be represented in conscious awareness in order for the skill or behavior to be exercised (Clyman, 1991; Cohen & Squire, 1980). Knowledge organized procedurally contrasts with knowledge that can be accessed in awareness via processes of recognition or recall (usually referred to as *declarative knowledge*). Most rules that guide behavior in everyday circumstances have been learned in the course of development through many participatory experiences and are organized procedurally. Common examples include the rules of grammar of a learned first language and the many rules that guide basic moral conduct such as turn taking and reciprocity in social interactions (Emde, Biringen, Clyman, & Oppenheim, 1991). Thus, while some knowledge about one's culture can be talked about and can be accessed consciously and declaratively, for example in interviews, much culturally guided knowledge exerts its influence through internalized rules that govern routines and social interactions, silently, without reflection and without awareness. Anthropologists have long known that participant observation and immersion in a culture—often by someone from outside the culture—are needed to supplement interviews of key informants in order to access this form of knowledge. In a similar vein, anthropologists have known that cultural models contain rules that regulate behavior through values, attitudes, and beliefs that are largely assumed by members of a particular group, rather than being explicit or formalized (D'Andrade, 1992; Weisner, Matheson, & Bernheimer, 1996).

The cultural construct *amae*, introduced by Takeo Doi (1973, 1992), illustrates the above point. Amae refers to a form of intimacy in Japanese culture that is pervasive and typically operates outside of conscious awareness. It involves procedures wherein one monitors the feelings and sensitivities of another according to what feels right. While a prototypic form of amae is particularly prominent in the mother-infant relationship, it describes a process of behavioral organization that is motivational throughout life, guiding actions in many social circumstances, most notably when caring is involved (Doi, 1992; Emde, 1992). Amae carries with it a sense of dependency, reciprocity, and obligation, and, according to Doi, it operates "sweetly." Processes of amae guide a good deal of what outsiders see as the routines of courtesy, generosity, and mutuality in Japanese social interactions. Again we are reminded that much of Eastern cultural practice has emphasized mutuality in development and the overlapping connections between the person and the other, whereas much of Western practice and thought, in contrast, has tended to emphasize individuality in development and the separability of the person and the other. Interestingly, recent concepts from infancy research have emphasized the development of mutuality and connectedness as well (e.g., Emde et al., 1991; Sroufe, 1995; Stern, 1985). Clinical implications of amae for assessment have been discussed in a special section of Volume 13, Number 1 of the *Infant Mental Health Journal* (1992, pp. 4–42).

Culture Provides a View of Reality and Experience

Sixth, culture provides multiple views of reality and the world. In addition to everyday reality, most cultures support a variety of spiritual experiences that often contain alternative views of reality. These may be important for understanding variations in health behaviors in families with young children (e.g., related to diet, exercise, provisions for safety, and protections from toxins and abusive substances) as well as for understanding variations in opportunities for social connectedness and support. Thus, for example, Native American parents who participate in sweat lodges, ritual dancing, and related spiritual affirmation experiences may be protected from the risk of substance abuse, and hence may be more available for caring activities with their infants and toddlers. Similarly, Latino parents who participate in organized religious activities or other alternate belief systems about protection from evil spirits, curses, or illness may find support and benefit. The forms of play and types of stories that parents tell young children within a given culture also allow for alternative views of reality and, to varying degrees, allow for important "intermediate zones of experience" (Winnicott, 1971) in which child and parent can try out different cultural views, values, and worlds of belief and "make believe."

Cultural influences on general views of the world may also be important in clinical assessment of families with young children. That such influences may change in relation to time and context may make such assessments challenging but no less important. We can illustrate using a cultural dimension for guiding development already discussed, namely the view of individuality versus social connectedness or, in other words, the view of self in relation to others. Although Western views of self have typically been described as "self-contained" (Sampson, 1988) and "self-reliant" (Spence, 1985) in contrast to Eastern views of self as more other oriented (Doi, 1973; Shweder, 1991), there is now substantial appreciation in the West of the self as connected, social, and dialogical (Gilligan, 1982; Hermans, Kempen, & van Loon, 1992; Sampson, 1988).

Moreover, as one might expect, within North America there is now appreciation of significant variations on this cultural dimension. Many Latino families, for example, may feel that maintaining a network of family connections and respect is more important than personal achievement (Falicov, 1998). In a related vein, families also differ on cultural beliefs and practices concerning infant sleeping arrangements. Wolf, Lozoff, Latz, and Paludetto (1996) found that cultural differences in cosleeping practices were connected to different values about autonomy, independence, and interrelatedness. Japanese, Italian, and African American families were found to cosleep with their infants more regularly than a U.S. White sample, with the former groups emphasizing the importance of the child learning a sense of interdependence in family and other relationships in contrast to an emphasis on autonomy.

Culture Influences Expressions of Distress

Seventh, culture influences the ways individuals express distress and difficulty. The current version of the *Diagnostic and Statistical Manual of Mental Disorders* takes this aspect of culture into account by including a glossary of culture-bound syndromes. Descriptively, many of these syndromes involve the dysregulation of emotions and seem to be supported by cultural forms of belief in the power of strong emotions, such as in the syndrome of *ataques de nervios* in Puerto Rican and related groups. Expressions of grief and depression in some cultures (e.g., Asian) may occur in somatic forms such as gastrointestinal disturbances rather than emotional forms such as crying or mood changes (Kleinman & Good, 1986; Kleinman & Kleinman, 1986).

Culture Is Mediated Through the Parenting Relationship

The eighth general feature of cultural influence is at the center of clinical assessment. This feature acknowledges that in early development, culture is mediated through the parenting relationship. All of the above-mentioned influences occur via parenting. Moreover, the field of infant mental health makes explicit that understanding the caregiving relationship and evaluating its qualities and variations is essential for the prevention and treatment of disorder (Fraiberg, 1980; Fraiberg, Adelson, & Shapiro, 1975; Sameroff & Emde, 1989; Shonkoff & Phillips, 2000; Zero to Three, 1994). We have mentioned how cultural influences result in parent-mediated variations in infant feeding, sleeping, security, and soothing. We have also mentioned how cultural influences result in parent-mediated variations in closeness inclinations, caring practices, feeling states, and what is communicated. Next we consider some of these matters in terms of clinical assessment.

CURRENT INTEGRATION OF CULTURE AND CLINICAL ASSESSMENT

The Relationship Context

Perhaps more than in any other field of assessment, the assessment of infant mental health acknowledges the inextricability of the individual from the context in which he or she functions, placing a central focus on evaluating the parenting relationship. The relationship context as a focus for assessment has dual origins. One origin is clinical experience. It finds itself echoed in the oft-repeated clinical phrase of Winnicott (1971) "there is no such thing as a baby" (i.e., there is only baby with mother) and in the equally famous phrases of Fraiberg of "ghosts in the nursery" (Fraiberg et al., 1975) (characterizing the haunting effects of conflicted internalized relationships across generations) and "it's like having God on your side" (1980, p. 53) (when working in parent-infant psychotherapy while benefiting from seeing the rapid development of the infant). This clinical tradition of infant mental health has led, in a relatively short time, to the creation of parent-infant psychotherapy with both psychodynamic/systems approaches (Lieberman, Silverman, & Pawl, 2000) and interaction guidance/educational approaches (McDonough, 1995, 2000). Another origin of the focus on early relationships is the developmental sciences and considerations of mental disorder in infancy and early childhood.

A multidisciplinary study group of scientists and clinicians proposed that, based on current knowledge, all mental disorder in the earliest years should be evaluated and treated in the context of evaluating caregiving relationships (Sameroff & Emde, 1989). The task group proposed a scheme of relationship disturbances and disorder, which then became influential in the formation of a separately designated axis for this purpose later included in the new diagnostic classification system for ages 0–3 (see next section).

Cultural variation in the caregiving relationship is therefore a logical topic for us to consider in assessment. Before moving to our suggestions in this area, however, and specifically to our proposed modifications of the cultural formulation as it currently exists in *DSM-IV*, it is important to review our thoughts about diagnosis as a process and the schemes that are available in the current diagnostic classification systems.

The Diagnostic Process

It is useful to recognize that the diagnostic process consists of two aspects: (1) assessment of individuals and (2) classification of disorder. The assessment of individuals involves a variety of evaluations of symptoms, suffering, and functioning, and it is considered within the context of family relationships, culture, and stresses that are both biological and environmental. The classification of disorder, on the other hand, involves a way of ordering knowledge about symptom patterns and linking these patterns to what is known in general about etiology, prognosis, and treatment. Disorder classification may also provide a link to services. In other words, such classification allows for communication among professionals about general knowledge, and it is important to remind ourselves that we classify disorders, not individuals (Rutter & Gould, 1985).

The *DSM-IV* is used primarily for classification of disorder. It is also, however, a multiaxial system, with the first three axes dealing with disorder and the fourth and fifth axes dealing with individual assessment (psychosocial and environmental problems and global assessment of functioning). The International Classification of Mental and Behavioral Disorders (ICD-10; World Health Organization, 1992) is also multiaxial and similar in many respects to *DSM-IV*.[1] Both systems have evolved from initially being concerned with classification only to adding axes dealing with the assessment of individuals. It is therefore noteworthy that both systems, by being multiaxial in this way, have evolved to provide a guideline for clinical formulation. In the applications of *DSM-IV*, Axes IV and V have received little attention—although there are indications that in future schemes, increased attention will be paid to the assessment of stressors, adaptive functioning, and the degree of impairment. Along these lines, a substantial innovation of *DSM-IV*, in contrast to earlier *DSM* schemes, is the inclusion of an appendix suggesting a cultural formulation for assessment of disorder within individuals. The appendix includes an emphasis on assessing adaptive functioning, stressors, symptoms, and impairment in culturally relevant terms. Although not designed for children (let alone for early childhood), the formulation is appropriate for assessment of parents and is worth reviewing, prior to our suggested modifications.

The *DSM-IV* Approach

The Outline for Cultural Formulation consists of two parts. The first concerns individual assessment and contains a guideline for inquiry that highlights four areas: (1) cultural identity of the individual; (2) cultural explanations of the individual's illness; (3) cultural factors related to the psychosocial environment and levels of functioning; and (4) cultural elements of the relationship between the individual and the clinician. In addition to learning about the individual's cultural reference group and language use, it is important to understand the predominant idioms of distress, explanatory models for illness, and culturally relevant perceptions of social stressors, available supports, sources of care and interpretations of disability. The cultural formulation also acknowledges that differences in culture and social status between clinician and client can introduce challenges for diagnosis and treatment and therefore implicitly recommends that the clinician reflect on this in terms of awareness of his or her own cultural origins and perceptions. In such cases of cultural difference between staff and clients, we recommend the use of cultural sensitivity discussions and workshops to supplement reflective supervision.

The second part of the appendix on cultural formulation makes suggestions for classification, by supplementing the regular *DSM-IV* disorders with a glossary of what are referred to as culture-bound syndromes. The term *culture-bound syndrome* is intended to refer to patterns of "locality-specific patterns of aberrant behavior and troubling experience" (American Psychiatric Association, 1994, p. 844) that often have local names and connote localized meanings of importance. The appendix points out that some of the syndromes may seem exotic or strange but that there are many subcultures and widely diverse immigrant groups in North America and that the glossary documents syndromes and idioms of distress that may be encountered in clinical practice among these groups.

Cultural Formulations
With Children

As mentioned, the *DSM-IV* cultural formulation is clearly aimed at the assessment of adult functioning. As we move to a consideration of children, other schemes are important to review, as they pertain to context and culture. The DC:0–3 was developed in response to the need for classification of syndromes experienced in the early years that were not covered in the existing *DSM* system. Similar to the *DSM* scheme, it is multi-axial, with the first three axes dealing with classification of disorder and the fourth and fifth axes dealing with individual assessment (psychosocial stressors and functional emotional and developmental level). Axis I of DC:0–3 contains an array of regulatory and other disorders that represent particular syndromes for this age period. Axis II is innovative in classification and deals with relationship disorders between caregiver and child. That Axis II in DC:0–3 is useful is clearly indicated by a number of reports of trials which indicate that a substantial number of referrals are classified within this axis in a way that is meaningful for provision of services (Guedeney et al., 2003; Keren, Feldman, & Tyano, 2001). In setting forth a relationship disorder axis, DC:0–3 targets the evaluation of the child-caregiver relationship as central and goes a step further than *DSM-IV* in assessing context in that sense, but it does not provide a cultural formulation or guide for assessing cultural context.

Two contributions offer suggestions for cultural assessments of children. Novins et al. (1997) suggest adaptations to the *DSM-IV* cultural case formulation for use with culturally diverse children and adolescents. Additions to the *DSM-IV* outline are exemplified with four American Indian children (ages 6 years and older). Novins et al. suggest accounting for the developmental aspects of cultural identity, the cultural identity of the parents and/or other caregivers, the impact of a biracial heritage, and cultural aspects of the relationship between the parents and/or other caregivers and the therapist. In another effort to promote culturally relevant assessment of children and adolescents, Johnson-Powell (1997) proposes a "culturologic interview," and includes the following: country of origin, reason for migration, language use, kinship support, beliefs about causality, child-rearing practices, sex roles, a description of community, life, and home space, reasons for seeking help, description of help-seeking behavior, educational attainment, occupation, experiences with rejection, degree of acculturation, and degree of cultural conflict.

While Johnson-Powell's culturologic interview and Novins et al.'s adaptations to the *DSM-IV* Outline for Cultural Formulation offer useful starting points, both remain limited in their utility for use in clinical practice with infants and toddlers; the former by its lack of detail (as in the *DSM-IV* outline) and the latter because of its lack of attention to issues relevant to infancy and toddlerhood. Considering both the promise and the limitations of existing systems, we propose an outline that represents modifications to the *DSM-IV* outline, which extends features proposed by Novins et al. (1997) and Johnson-Powell (1997). As with the *DSM-IV* outline, its purpose is to provide a framework that will guide both the collection and structuring of culturally relevant information so that an assessment of infant and toddler mental health can be culturally situated, relevant, and useful.

A CULTURAL ASSESSMENT FRAMEWORK FOR USE WITH INFANTS AND TODDLERS

To date, we have no knowledge about the extent to which the existing *DSM-IV* Outline for Cultural Formulation is routinely implemented by clinicians. However, we regard it as a useful guideline to frame clinicians' thinking about culture and assessment. In this spirit, we present our proposed revision to the *DSM-IV* Outline for Cultural Formulation (see table 2.1) for use with infants and toddlers.

Proposed Revision to *DSM-IV*

Our revision heavily reflects the eighth general feature of cultural influence discussed previously—that culture is mediated through the parenting relationship. In general, we conceive of this revision as both an extension of previous work and also the beginning of an effort to make cultural assessment a formal part of current diagnostic schemes for infancy and early childhood (e.g., DC:0–3). As is implicit in current multiaxial schemes, we also view this revised formulation as a helpful guideline for clinical inquiry and formulation. Following a discussion of our proposed revisions, we conclude with a case example, utilizing the revised outline.

The *DSM-IV* Outline for Cultural Formulation contains five areas for inquiry, as mentioned previously. The first directs the clinician to describe the individual's cultural identity, noting the individual's ethnic or cultural reference group and the extent to which the individual is involved with both the culture of origin and the dominant culture. The individual's language ability, use, and preference are also noted here. For infants and toddlers, the parents' cultural reference group and degree of involvement with host and dominant culture can be noted. More important, the parents' intentions for raising the child with respect to the culture of origin and the dominant culture are discussed. Following Novins et al. (1997), we suggest including, where relevant, a discussion of issues of biculturality that may arise for an infant or toddler whose parents come from, and identify with, different cultural backgrounds. Finally, we suggest a discussion of generational is-

sues, such as those that might arise as the infant or toddler grows older and may serve as a cultural mediator or negotiator for the parents (e.g., in terms of language, especially for immigrant groups).

The second area outlined in the *DSM-IV* Cultural Formulation addresses cultural explanations of an individual's illness. The unique ways in which the individual expresses distress are noted here, along with a discussion of how the symptomatic expression compares to normative behavior in the cultural reference group. Any cultural explanations for the individual's experience of distress are discussed, as well as the individual's past experience with and current preferences for care. For infants and toddlers, we suggest beginning with a discussion of who first noticed the child's symptoms of distress (e.g., the parents or someone outside the family, such as a doctor or day care provider) and the extent to which the parents or caregivers agree that the child's behavior is indicative of distress. This may be especially important in terms of help-seeking behavior, because if the parents do not also see a problem, they will be less motivated to seek services for their child. Following this can be a discussion of the parents' perceptions of the child's distress, how the child's behavior is viewed relative to other children's behavior in their cultural group, any cultural explanations for the child's distress, and the parents' experiences with and preferences for treatment. The extent to which others are expected to be involved in treatment can also be noted, acknowledging that for certain cultural groups, children are frequently cared for by an extended network of kin.

The third area outlined by the *DSM-IV* Cultural Formulation addresses cultural factors in the psychosocial environment that impact the expression, experience, and treatment of distress and disorder. Our suggested revision for this part of the outline is the most extensive and the most heavily influenced by our view that culture is mediated through the parenting relationship for infants and toddlers. In this section, we suggest addressing three domains: the child's life space and environment, the child's caregiving network, and parental beliefs about parenting and child development. The child's life space and environment refers largely to his or her physical life space in both the home and the larger community. This

Table 2.1 *DSM-IV* Outline for Cultural Formulation Text and Revised Text for Use With Infants and Toddlers

1. *Cultural Identity of the Individual*
   Current *DSM-IV* Text
   "Note the individual's ethnic or cultural reference groups. For immigrants and ethnic minorities, note separately the degree of involvement with both the culture of origin and the host culture (where applicable). Also note language abilities, use and preference (including multilingualism)" (o, 843).
   Proposed Revised Text
   Cultural Identity of Child and Caregivers. Note the ethnic or cultural reference group for the child's parents and, if relevant, other significant caregivers. Note how the parents/caregivers intend to raise the child with respect to their own ethnic or cultural reference group and, in particular, whether there are potential issues of biculturality for the child. For immigrants and ethnic minority families, note the degree of involvement with both the culture of origin and the host culture, and whether they anticipate any generational issues with respect to the involvement of the child in the culture of origin and host culture. Note here parent/caregiver language abilities, use, and preference (including multilingualism) and what language(s) they intent to teach the child.

2. *Cultural Explanations of the Individual's Illness*
   Current *DSM-IV* Text
   "The following may be identified: the predominant idioms of distress through which symptoms or the need for social support are communicated (e.g., "nerves," possessing spirits, somatic complaints, inexplicable misfortune), the meaning and perceived severity of the individual's symptoms in relation to norms of the cultural reference group, any local illness category used by the individual's family and community to identify the condition (see "Glossary of Culture-Bound Syndromes" below), the perceived causes or explanatory models that the individual and the reference group use to explain the illness, and current preferences for and past experiences with professional and popular sources of care" (p. 843).
   Proposed Revised Text
   Cultural Explanations of the Child's Presenting Problem. Note here who first noticed the problem (e.g., parent, other relative, daycare provider, physician), and if referred by someone else, the extent to which the parents/caregivers also see a problem. Identify what the parents/caregivers observed to be the signals of distress displayed by the infant/toddler (i.e., how did the parents/caregivers know there was a problem); the meaning and perceived severity of the infant's distress in relation to the parents'/caregivers' expectations for the behavior and/or development of other infants/toddlers in their community/cultural group; whether there are any local illness categories to describe the child's presenting problem; the parents'/caregivers' perceptions about the cause of, or explanatory models for, the child's presenting problem; and parents'/caregivers/ beliefs about treatment of the child's presenting problem (including previous experiences with Western and non-Western forms of treatment; current beliefs about and preferences for Western and non-Western forms of treatment; and beliefs about who should be involved in the treatment).

3. *Cultural Factors Related to Psychosocial Environmental and Levels of Functioning*
   Current *DSM-IV* Text
   "Note culturally relevant interpretations of social stressors, available social supports, and levels of functioning and disability. This would include stresses in the local social environment and the role of religion and kin networks in providing emotional, instrumental, and information support" (p. 844).
   Proposed Revised Text
   Cultural Factors Related to the Child's Psychosocial and Caregiving Environment.
   A. Infant's Life Space and Environment. Note description of child's physical life space, including community factors (e.g., ethnic/racial composition, urbanicity, crime, and cohesion) and home factors (e.g., people living in the home, their relationship to one another and the child, and extent of crowding in the home), infant's sleeping arrangements, and parents'/caregivers' culturally relevant interpretations of social supports and stressors (e.g., role of religion, community, and kin networks).
   B. Infant's Caregiving Network. Note here the significant caregivers in the child's life, including the role and extent of involvement of primary (e.g., mother, father) and secondary (e.g., grandparents, siblings, aunts/uncles) caregivers. Note significant continuities and disruptions in the child's caregiving network (e.g., child's mobility between caregivers and the extent to which this mobility is fluid, predictable, and consistent versus the extent to which this mobility is unpredictable, inconsistent, and/or disrupted) and the extent to which these continuities or disruptions are normative within local culture.

(continued)

Table 2.1 Continued

C. Parents'/Caregivers' Beliefs About Parenting and Child Development. Note here any beliefs about parenting and child development not noted elsewhere, such as: ceremonial practices (e.g., naming), beliefs about gender roles, disciplinary practices, goals and aspirations for child, cosmological views related to children and child development, sources parents/caregivers turn to for advice about parenting, beliefs about parenting/caregiving role, etc.

4. *Cultural Elements of the Relationship Between the Individual and the Clinician*
Current *DSM-IV* Text
"Indicate differences in culture and social status between the individual and the clinician and problems that these differences may cause in diagnosis and treatment (e.g., difficulty in communicating in the individual's first language, in eliciting symptoms or understanding their cultural significance, in negotiating an appropriate relationship or level of intimacy, in determining whether a behavior is normative or pathological" (p. 844).

Proposed Revised Text
Cultural Elements of the Relationship Between the Parents/Caregivers and the Clinician. Indicate differences in culture and social status between the child's parents/caregivers and the clinician and any problems these differences may cause in diagnosis and treatment (e.g., differences in understanding the child's distress, communication difficulties due to language differences, communication styles such as issues of privacy or understandings about the involvement of others such as extended kin in the diagnosis and treatment process). Also note how the parents'/caregivers' past experience with clinicians or treatment/service systems impacts the current clinical relationship.

5. *Overall Cultural Assessment for Diagnosis and Care*
Current *DSM-IV* Text
"The formulation concludes with a discussion of how cultural considerations specifically influence comprehensive diagnosis and care" (p. 844).

Proposed Revised Text
Overall Cultural Assessment for Child's Diagnosis and Care. The formulation concludes with a discussion of how cultural considerations specifically influence comprehensive diagnosis and care of the child.

Source: Reprinted with permission from the *Diagnostic and Statistical Manual of Mental Disorders*, Fourth Edition. Copyright 2000 American Psychiatric Association.

includes issues such as individuals in the home and their relationship to one another, and community factors such as racial composition and crime. Parental interpretations of social stress and social support within this physical environment are also addressed here. The child's caregiving network is especially critical for placing the child and his or her distress in context. This domain should inventory the significant caregivers in the child's life, acknowledging, as stated earlier, the importance of the entire network of both kin and nonkin caregivers involved in raising a child. The child's experience within this network of caregivers should also be described—such as the child's mobility within the network, noting in particular both continuities and disruptions within this network of care. The final domain addresses parents'/caregivers' beliefs about parenting and child development not discussed elsewhere—such as any ceremonial practices, beliefs about gender

roles, and disciplinary practices. Also noted here are parents' goals and aspirations for their child, which can suggest a positive point for intervention as it provides the clinician with an understanding of potential strengths within the family.

The fourth area outlined by the *DSM-IV* Cultural Formulation address cultural elements of the relationship between the individual and the clinician. Our revision here largely reflects a reframing from the individual perspective to the parents'/caregivers' perspective. In this section, the clinician is directed to identify cultural differences between the clinician and the child's parents that may impede the clinical relationship—because of difficulties in either communication (e.g., language) or understanding (e.g., different interpretations of the child's distress). In addition, once identified, the clinician must reflect on the significance of these differences for diagnosis and treatment of the child. The fifth and final part of the *DSM-IV* Cultural Formulation calls for an overall cultural assessment for diagnosis and care that is based on the preceding four sections. We made no revision to this section, except to frame the overall assessment in terms of diagnosis and care of the child.

CLINICAL PRESENTATION AND CASE DESCRIPTION

Presented here is a hypothetical case of an American Indian toddler, intended to demonstrate the utility of the cultural formulation presented above.

Background

Reason for Referral

Thomas was a 15-month-old American Indian boy referred for a psychological evaluation by his pediatrician. Thomas was asthmatic and had been seen regularly by the same pediatrician since birth. Thomas's mother brought him in because he was having difficulty sleeping and was increasingly fussy about what he ate. She thought these difficulties might be due to the new medication prescribed by the pediatrician. During the office visit, the pediatrician noted Thomas's lethargy, relative lack of social engagement, and an apparent language delay. Because the pediatrician could not account for the changes in Thomas's sleeping and eating medically, and because of the additional behavioral concerns noted during the office visit, it was recommended that Thomas's mother seek a psychological evaluation for Thomas.

Developmental History

Thomas's mother described a normal pregnancy and birth, without complications. She described, however, feelings of ambivalence about the pregnancy and about the idea of having a third child after her other children were grown and in school. The ambivalence also arose out of the fact that Thomas's father left the family when Thomas's mother became pregnant and that before he left, he had been physically abusive with her. Thomas's mother had just started school and worried that the pregnancy and having an infant to care for would interfere with her progress in school. She considered several options in order to continue school uninterrupted—including having Thomas live with a classmate for a year until she was finished with school, or having Thomas live with relatives on the reservation. She ultimately arranged for subsidized day care through social services.

Since birth, Thomas had spent a great deal of time with his day care provider, who cared for Thomas in her home. Throughout his first year of life, Thomas would spend weeks at a time with his day care provider, without seeing his mother. At most, Thomas would spend weekends with his mother, having spent the entire week, including nights, with the day care provider. Several months prior to the evaluation, Thomas's mother finished school and decided to sharply curtail his time with the day care provider because she not only had more time to spend with him, but because she was also concerned that he was becoming "too attached" to the day care provider and needed to spend more time with his family. The clinician was impressed with the likelihood of attachment problems between Thomas and his mother, and was concerned about the consequences of a disrupted attachment relationship for symptoms of regulation and affect.

Cultural Identity of Child and Caregivers

Thomas's mother was American Indian and had grown up on a Northern Plains reservation. She maintained strong ties with her tribal community. Even though she had moved away ten years previously, she returned to the reservation frequently to visit family and to attend powwows and other community gatherings, such as ceremonies. She enrolled Thomas as a member of her tribe when he was born. She intended to introduce Thomas to his American Indian culture by having him dance at powwows when he was old enough, by having him spend time with extended family on the reservation, and by having a naming ceremony. Thomas's father was Mexican American. Thomas's mother acknowledged his Mexican American heritage by giving Thomas his father's last name, and hoped that one day he would know his father's side of the family and learn about his Mexican heritage. Thomas's mother spoke English as her first language but knew some of her tribal language and would occasionally speak to Thomas in their native language. She hoped that Thomas would learn more of the tribal language than she had, by spending time with family elders on the reservation.

Cultural Explanations of the Child's Presenting Problems

Thomas was referred for a psychological evaluation by his pediatrician subsequent to the pediatrician noticing Thomas's lethargy, relative lack of engagement with his physical and social world, and apparent delays in language acquisition. At home, Thomas's mother noticed a change in his behavior, observing in particular that he was sleeping more and was more "fussy" about eating. Though Thomas's mother was the first to notice the changes in his sleeping and eating, she noticed little of the lethargy, lack of engagement, and language delay noted by the pediatrician. She believed that what the pediatrician observed was, in actuality, evidence of Thomas's easy and nondemanding nature. In her family and home community, she said that children were taught to learn through quiet observation of their surroundings and by listening to adults and elders. Thomas's quiet nature, she believed, was evidence that he was a "respectful" child—a quality highly valued in her reservation community. When asked what she thought the effect of Thomas's separation from his day care provider might be, Thomas's mother stated that she had been around many different adults as a child, and that whatever reaction Thomas might have would pass because he was "strong, and would grow out of it." She believed in general that facing some challenges was good for a child's character. Furthermore, she respected Thomas's ability to "be on his own," to respond as needed to what he faced in life.

Cultural Factors Related to the Child's Psychosocial and Caregiving Environment

Infant's Life Space and Environment

Thomas was living in a three-bedroom apartment with his mother and two older half siblings, in a low-income urban housing complex designed specifically for families with parents who were either working or in school full-time. Parents were also required to volunteer for one of the complex's programs, such as evening child care or tutoring other children. The complex was situated in a racially diverse community; however, there were few other American Indian families nearby. Thomas's older siblings had their own bedrooms, while Thomas shared a room and a bed with his mother. Thomas's mother valued this sleeping time with Thomas, and said that it made her feel closer to him. During times of hardship, her relatives would stay with the family. Most recently, Thomas's maternal uncle came from the reservation to escape legal trouble. However, he was causing problems for Thomas's family because of his disruptive behavior and because his residence there was in violation of the complex rules, jeopardizing the entire family's ability to remain in the apartment. Thomas's mother struggled with her sense of duty to her extended family versus her duty to her own family, because these duties often pulled her in opposite directions. Growing up on the reservation, and as the oldest daughter in her family, Thomas's mother was raised with a sense of obligation to help family members in their times of need. This was a heavily ingrained value, and when she considered asking her brother to leave, she felt conflicted and feared being judged negatively by other family members, especially her mother. She worried that the stress she felt about this situation made her more impatient and irritable with her own children.

Infant's Caregiving Network

Thomas's day care provider had cared for him most of the time since he was born. This woman took care of Thomas in her home, and would keep him for weeks at a time, during which he did not see his mother. Thomas's mother trusted this woman and readily agreed to let Thomas stay for extended periods of time because she felt her time was already consumed with work, school, and her other two children. As mentioned, she was so busy when Thomas was born that she considered letting a classmate take Thomas to live with her until she was finished with school. She decided against this, however, when subsidized day care became available. Thomas was also cared for by a maternal aunt who lived nearby, who would occasionally keep him over weekends. Thomas's older siblings provided some care for Thomas; however, the pediatrician expressed concern about their ability to care for him, having observed them handling him roughly several times during office visits. Just prior to being referred for an evaluation, Thomas's mother decided to put him in the child care facility located in the complex where they lived. She did this because her child care subsidy had been eliminated, the location was more convenient, and also because she wanted to have Thomas with her on a regular basis. At the time of referral, Thomas's mother had made no arrangements for him to see his previous day care provider. Thomas's mother stated that during her childhood she was often cared for by people other than her biological mother, staying variously with her grandparents, her aunt, and a family friend. She also stated that when she was growing up, little distinction was made between cousins and siblings, or between aunts and uncles and parents. Additionally, close family friends were often considered family and at times were ceremonially adopted into the family—rendering their relationship the same as if they were biologically related. Thus, the fact that Thomas was variously cared for by herself, the day care provider, and her sister was not unlike her own experience growing up. In fact, she saw it as a positive experience that Thomas had a close relationship with three "mothers."

Caregiver Beliefs About Parenting and Child Development

When observed with Thomas, Thomas's mother seemed to engage in a hands-off style of parenting. She stated that this reflected a general respect for the fact that her children were autonomous and separate individuals, free to learn about the world through exploration and direct experience. She believed it was her duty to tell her children something once, but that it was up to them to follow that guidance after that—learning "the hard way" if they chose not to heed her advice. Her greatest aspiration for Thomas was that he would one day go to college, have his own family, and lead a drug- and alcohol-free life. She also

hoped that he would be respectful and strong. Her belief that children were largely autonomous and separate individuals who needed to find their own way in life stemmed in part from what she said was a tribal belief that children, before birth, had been taught many things about life by the spirits, and also chose their families based on what they needed to accomplish on their path here on earth. Thomas's mother said her family elders had taught her these things about children, and that when she needed advice about parenting she turned to these elders as well as to other elders in her home community.

Cultural Elements of the Relationship Between the Parents or Caregivers and the Clinician

In Thomas's mother's tribe, discussing problems from the past is believed to give them new energy in one's present life. Thus, there are prohibitions against speaking of past problems lest they be brought to life again. In collecting a family history, which involved the discussion of some past trauma that Thomas's mother experienced (e.g., domestic violence), additional care was taken to gather only the most pertinent information in this regard. When asked about previous experiences with therapy, Thomas's mother said that she had some mistrust of psychologists because she had heard stories that if they did not agree with how a mother was raising her children, they would take her children away. She also remembered how, in her reservation community, word would get out if one was seeing a mental health specialist. She was thus concerned about confidentiality. She and the clinician espoused different views of attachment relationships and Thomas's strength to endure the challenges he faced on his own. This was an area in which the clinician needed to bring her understanding and expertise about child development to bear in a way that respected the mother's cultural beliefs but also served the needs of the child, who seemed clearly to be reacting to a disruption in his network of attachment relationships.

Overall Cultural Assessment for the Child's Diagnosis and Care

The foremost issue in Thomas's case was to support his mother in her culturally derived belief that an extended network of kin (whether biological or "fictive") would benefit both her and her child. The challenge, however, was to help her understand the importance of continuity in this network of care and the relevance of Thomas's attachment to individuals in this caregiving network. The other challenge was to help Thomas's mother find ways that she could maintain her respect for his "being on his own" but also intervene and provide stimulating engagement for Thomas.

Cultural Case Formulation: Overview

The case presented above is intended to highlight several issues in conducting a mental health assessment of an infant or a toddler that is not only culturally sensitive but, more important, is culturally relevant and meaningful to the point that it enhances the care that is delivered. First and foremost, cultural assessment places the presenting concern within the larger cultural context that provides for greater understanding of the disorder and also suggests points for interventions. The case formulation presented above also points out that for clinicians, there are several important issues to consider in conducting a cultural case formulation, often involving the balancing of two apparently opposite poles. First, clinicians must balance cultural sensitivity on the one hand with useful concepts from Western psychological practice on the other. In Thomas's case, the clinician needed to be sensitive to the fact that Thomas's mother believed that her son's mobility within his network of caregivers not only made him "stronger" but provided him with the advantage of having several "mothers." To the clinician, however, it seemed clear that Thomas was having an emotional reaction to his curtailed involvement with one of the attachment figures within this network of care, which made sense from the perspective of attachment theory. The challenge, as stated in the overall assessment, was to help Thomas's mother understand the importance of continuity in this network of care and the relevance of his attachment to individuals in this caregiving network, while still respecting the fact that she saw this as an experience that would strengthen his character.

The case also highlights that, on the one hand, cultural assessment requires a general working knowledge about the process of assessment, while on the other, it requires specific knowledge about a given culture. General knowledge about process involves the "how" of assessment—that is, how one approaches a situation of cultural differences in a way that transcends the particulars of any one cultural group. General knowledge about process involves not only a basic acknowledgment and respect for the relevance of culture but also the utilization of such tools as the *DSM-IV* Outline for Cultural Formulation, which can be applied to the spectrum of cultural groups that one might encounter in practice. In order to address the relevance of culture to a particular case, however, one must also possess specific knowledge about the cultural group from which the child and his or her family comes. However, this specific cultural knowledge must be held loosely, as parents may or may not espouse those particular beliefs, which also points to the fact that not all parental beliefs are culturally supported—and that there will always be individual differences in the understanding of broader cultural constructs (which speaks to culture's dynamic, transactional, and to some extent subjective nature).

CONCLUSION

The undertaking of cultural sensitivity is not an insignificant exercise in the field of mental health. As Good (1996) warns, the danger of cross-cultural misunderstanding in the psychiatric process means that "at stake is not only the integrity of psychiatry's claims to knowledge as a science of the human mind but also, more importantly, the care of many of the most disadvantaged members of American society—psychiatric patients who are recent immigrants, members of minority populations, or persons who are poor and living on the margins of our society" (p. 349). Good further points out that such misunderstandings can have deleterious consequences for those who are misunderstood—such as inappropriate intervention, the withholding of effective interventions, or even greater social injustices.

In this chapter, we presented an outline of eight general features of culture that provide a background for understanding the role of culture in the assessment of infants and toddlers. Those eight features define culture as shared meaning, distinct from ethnicity, race, and minority status, as occurring in a setting or ecology, as dynamic and transactional, as experienced subjectively, as operating silently as well as with voices, as providing multiple views of reality and the world, as influencing the ways in which individuals express distress, and, for infants and toddlers in particular, as mediated through the parenting relationship.

We distinguished the classification of disorder from the assessment of the individual, and the role of current systems such as *DSM-IV* and DC: 0–3 in these pursuits. Both *DSM-IV* and DC:0–3 are multiaxial systems, which allow for the classification of disorder and the assessment of the individual. By including a specific relationship axis, DC:0–3 acknowledges that to understand the infant, one must understand the context of his or her development and experience. In this chapter, we argue that to understand the infant, it is also necessary to understand the larger cultural context in which the infant's development, and development in relationship, takes place. As a cultural tool, *DSM-IV* has made a significant contribution to the assessment of the individual with the inclusion of the Outline for Cultural Formulation; the thrust of this chapter is to adapt this outline for use with infants and toddlers. By presenting a cultural case formulation based on these revisions, we hope to demonstrate the relevance of culture for infant mental health assessment as well as to highlight the challenge for clinicians to apply general knowledge about the classification of disorder in the process of assessing a particular individual who is situated in a particular sociocultural context.

Note

1. We focus on *DSM-IV* rather than ICD-10 in our subsequent discussion because of its inclusion of the Outline for Cultural Formulation in its appendix and our proposed modification of it.

References

American Psychiatric Association (1994). *Diagnostic and statistical manual of mental disorders* (4th ed.). Washington, DC: Author.

American Psychological Association (1993). Guidelines for providers of psychological services to ethnic, linguistic, and culturally diverse populations. *American Psychologist, 48,* 45–48.

Betancourt, H., & Lopez, S. R. (1993). The study of culture, ethnicity, and race in American psychology. *American Psychologist, 48,* 629–637.

Bronfenbrenner, U. (1977). Toward an experimental ecology of human development. *American Psychologist, 32,* 513–531.

Bronfenbrenner, U. (1979). *The ecology of human develoment.* Cambridge, MA: Harvard University Press.

Castillo, R. J. (1997). *Culture and mental illness.* Pacific Grove, CA: Brooks/Cole.

Clyman, R. B. (1991). The procedural organization of emotions: A contribution from cognitive science to the psychoanalytic theory of therapeutic action. *Journal of the American Psychoanalytic Association, 39*(Suppl.), 349–382.

Cohen, N. J., & Squire, L. R. (1980). Preserved learning and retention of pattern-analyzing skill in amnesia: Dissociation of knowing how and knowing that. *Science, 221,* 207–210.

D'Andrade, R. (1992). Schemas and motivation. In R. D'Andrade & C. Strauss (Eds.), *Human motives and cultural models* (pp. 23–44). New York: Cambridge University Press.

Doi, T. (1973). *The anatomy of dependence.* New York: Harper and Row.

Doi, T. (1992). On the concept of *amae. Infant Mental Health Journal, 13,* 7–11.

Emde, R. N. (1992). *Amae,* intimacy, and the early moral self. *Infant Mental Health Journal, 13,* 34–42.

Emde, R. N., Biringen, Z., Clyman, R. B., & Oppenheim, D. (1991). The moral self of infancy: Affective core and procedural knowledge. *Developmental Review, 11,* 251–270.

Emde, R. N., & Spicer, P. (2000). Experience in the midst of variation: New horizons for development and psychopathology. *Development and Psychopathology, 12,* 313–331.

Falicov, C. J. (1998). The cultural meaning of family triangles. In M. McGoldrick (Ed.), *Revisioning family therapy: Race, culture, and gender in clinical practice* (pp. 37–49). New York: Guilford Press.

Fraiberg, S. (1980). *Clinical studies in infant mental health.* New York: Basic Books.

Fraiberg, S., Adelson, E., & Shapiro, V. (1975). Ghosts in the nursery: A psychoanalytic approach to the problems of impaired infant-mother relationships. *Journal of the American Academy of Child Psychiatry, 14*(3), 387–421.

Garcia Coll, C., & Magnuson, K. (2000). Cultural differences as sources of developmental vulnerabilities and resources. In J. P. Shonkoff & S. J. Meisels (Eds.), *Handbook of early childhood intervention* (2nd ed., pp. 94–114). New York: Cambridge University Press.

Gilligan, C. (1982). *In a different voice: Psychological theory and women's development*. Cambridge, MA: Harvard University Press.

Good, B. J. (1996). Epilogue: Knowledge, power, and diagnosis. In J. E. Mezzich, A. Kleinman, H. Fabrega, & D. L. Parron (Eds.), *Culture and psychiatric diagnosis: A DSM-IV perspective* (pp. 347–351). Washington, DC: American Psychiatric Association Press.

Guedeney, N., Guedeney, A., Rabouam, C., Mintz, A., Danon, G., Huet, M., & Jacquemain, F. (2003). The Zero-to-Three diagnostic classification: A contribution to the validation of this classification from a sample of under-threes. *Infant Mental Health Journal, 24*, 313–336.

Harkness, S., & Super, C. M. (Eds.). (1996). *Parents' cultural belief systems: Their origins, expressions, and consequences*. New York: Guilford Press.

Hermans, H. J. M., Kempen, H. J. G., & van Loon, R. J. P. (1992). The dialogical self. *American Psychologist, 47*, 23–33.

Johnson-Powell, G. (1997). The culturologic interview: Cultural, social, and linguistic issues in the assessment and treatment of children. In G. Johnson-Powell & J. Yamamoto (Eds.) and G. E. Wyatt & W. Arroyo (Associate Eds.), *Transcultural child development* (pp. 349–364). New York: John Wiley and Sons.

Keren, M., Feldman, R., & Tyano, S. (2001). Diagnoses and interactive patterns of infants referred to a community-based infant mental health clinic. *Journal of the Academy of Child and Adolescent Psychiatry, 40*, 27–35.

Kleinman, A. (1988). *The illness narratives: Suffering, healing, and the human condition*. New York: Basic Books.

Kleinman, A., & Good, B. (Eds.). (1986). *Culture and depression: Studies in the anthropology and cross-cultural psychology of affect and disorder*. Berkeley, CA: University of California Press.

Kleinman, A., & Kleinman, J. (1986). Somatization: The interconnections in Chinese society among culture-depressive experiences, and the meanings of pain. In A. Kleinman & B. Good (Eds.), *Culture and depression: Studies in the anthropology and cross-cultural psychology of affect and disorder* (pp. 429–490). Berkeley, CA: University of California Press.

LeVine, R. A., Dixon, S., LeVine, S., Richman, A., Leiderman, P. H., Keefer, C. H., & Brazelton, T. B. (1994). *Child care and culture: Lessons from Africa*. Cambridge: Cambridge University Press.

Lewis, M. L. (2000). The cultural context of infant mental health: The developmental niche of infant-caregiver relationships. In C. H. Zeanah, Jr. (Ed.), *Handbook of infant mental health* (2nd ed., pp. 91–107). New York: Guilford Press.

Lieberman, A. F., Silverman, R., & Pawl, J. H. (2000). Infant-parent psychotherapy: Core concepts and current approaches. In C. H. Zeanah, Jr. (Ed.), *Handbook of infant mental health* (2nd ed., pp. 472–484). New York: Guilford Press.

Manson, S. M. (1995). Culture and major depression: Current challenges in the diagnosis of mood disorders. *Cultural Psychiatry, 18*, 487–501.

McDonough, S. C. (1995). Promoting positive early parent-infant relationships through interaction guidance. *Child and Adolescent Psychiatric Clinics of North America, 4*(3), 661–672.

McDonough, S. C. (2000). Interaction guidance: An approach for difficult to engage families. In C. H. Zeanah, Jr. (Ed.), *Handbook of infant mental health* (2nd ed., pp. 485–493). New York: Guilford Press.

Novins, D. K., Bechtold, D. W., Sack, W. H., Thompson, M. D., Carter, D. R., & Manson, S. M. (1997). The DSM-IV outline for cultural formulation: A critical demonstration with American Indian children. *Journal of the American Academy of Child and Adolescent Psychiatry, 36*, 1244–1251.

Rogoff, B. (1990). *Apprenticeship in thinking: Cognitive development in social context*. New York: Oxford University Press.

Rogoff, B., Mistry, J., Goncu, A., & Mosier, C. (1993). Guided participation in cultural activity by toddlers and caregivers. *Monographs of the Society for Research in Child Development, 58*(8 Serial No. 236).

Rogoff, B., & Mosier, C. (1993). Guided participation in San Pedro and Salt Lake. *Monographs of the Society for Research in Child Development, 58*, 59–100.

Rutter, M., & Gould, M. (1985). Classification. In M. Rutter & L. Hersov (Eds.), *Child and ado-

lescent psychopathology (pp. 437–452). New York: Guilford Press.

Sameroff, A. J., & Emde, R. N. (Eds.). (1989). *Relationship disturbances in early childhood: A developmental approach.* New York: Basic Books.

Sameroff, A. J., & Fiese, B. H. (2000). Transactional regulation: The developmental ecology of early intervention. In J. P. Shonkoff & S. J. Meisels (Eds.), *Handbook of early childhood intervention* (2nd ed.). New York: Cambridge University Press.

Sampson, E. E. (1988). The debate on individuality. *American Psychologist, 43,* 15–22.

Shonkoff, J. P., & Phillips, P. A. (Eds.). (2000). *From neurons to neighborhoods: The science of early childhood development.* Washington, DC: National Academy Press.

Shweder, R. A. (1991). *Thinking through cultures: Expeditions in cultural psychology.* Cambridge, MA: Harvard University Press.

Spence, J. T. (1985). Achievement American style: The rewards and costs of individualism (presidential address). *American Psychologist, 40,* 1285–1295.

Sroufe, L. A. (1995). *Emotional development: The organization of emotional life in the early years.* New York: Cambridge University Press.

Stern, D. (1985). *The interpersonal world of the infant.* New York: Basic Books.

Super, C. M., & Harkness, S. (1982). The infant's niche in rural Kenya and metropolitan America. In L. L. Adler (Ed.), *Cross-cultural research issues* (pp. 47–55). New York: Academic Press.

Super, C. M., & Harkness, S. (1986). The developmental niche: A conceptualization at the interface of child and culture. *International Journal of Behavioral Development, 9,* 545–569.

U.S. Census Bureau (2000). United States Department of Commerce News: Census Bureau Projects Doubling of Nation's Population by 2100. http://www.census.gov/Press-Release/www/2000/cb00-05.html.

U.S. Department of Health and Human Services (1999). *Surgeon General's report.* Rockville, MD: Office of the Surgeon General, SAMHSA.

Vygotsky, L. (1978). *Mind in society: The development of higher psychological processes.* Cambridge, MA: Harvard University Press.

Weisner, T. S., Matheson, C. C., & Bernheimer, L. P. (1996). American cultural models of early influence and parent recognition of developmental delays: Is earlier always better than later? In S. Harkness & C. M. Super (Eds.), *Parents' cultural belief systems: Their origins, expressions, and consequences* (pp. 496–531). New York: Guilford Press.

Winnicott, D. O. (1971). *Playing and reality.* New York: Basic Books.

Wolf, A. W., Lozoff, B., Latz, S., & Paludetto, R. (1996). Parental theories in the management of young children's sleep in Japan, Italy, and the United States. In S. Harkness & C. M. Super (Eds.), *Parents' cultural belief systems: Their origins, expressions, and consequences* (pp. 364–384). New York: Guilford Press.

World Health Organization (1992). *ICD-10: The ICD-10 classification of mental and behavioural disorders: Clinical descriptions and diagnostic guidelines.* Geneva: Author.

Yamamoto, J. (1997). Culture and psychopathology. In G. Johnson-Powell & J. Yamamoto (Eds.) and G. E. Wyatt & W. Arroyo (Associated Eds.), *Transcultural child development* (pp. 34–57). New York: John Wiley and Sons.

Zero to Three, National Center for Clinical Infant Programs (1994). *Diagnostic classification of mental health and developmental disorders of infancy and early childhood.* Arlington, VA: Author.

3

Assessment of Parent-Child Early Relational Disturbances

Roseanne Clark

Audrey Tluczek

Kathleen Cranley Gallagher

The parent-child relationship provides the primary context for the development of the child's sense of self and self in relation to others (Stern, 1985, 2002; Winnicott, 1965), that is, the child's beliefs about what can be expected in relationships (Bowlby, 1982; Bretherton, 1985; Main, Kaplan, & Cassidy, 1985). Lieberman and Zeanah (1995) underscore the importance of the early mother-child relationship when they suggest that "the infant-mother relationship has the power to promote mental health or serve as the genesis of psychopathology in the young child" (p. 571). Understanding the quality of the parent-infant relationship within which the infant or young child is developing plays an important role in the assessment of social and emotional functioning and in formulating a diagnostic profile for infants and young children. Cicchetti (1987) asserts that "disorders in infancy are best conceptualized as relational psychopathologies, that is, as consequences of dysfunction in the parent-child environment system" (p. 837). The Committee on the Family of the Group for Advancement of Psychiatry (1995) has argued that, in general, important and common relationship conditions can

exist independent of severe individual psychopathology, and that these conditions should be described in relational terms, with specific diagnostic criteria. Furthermore, the Practice Parameters for the Psychiatric Assessment of Infants and Toddlers developed by the American Academy of Child and Adolescent Psychiatry (1997) recommend a "developmental, relational, and multidimensional" approach to assessment of psychiatric disturbances in infants and toddlers. More recently, a research agenda for the proposed *Diagnostic and Statistical Manual of Mental Disorders*, Fifth Edition calls for a three-part approach to assessing relationship disorders including: "1) standardized procedures for evoking and observing interactions within the dyad; 2) questionnaires for each member to delineate his or her individual perceptions of the relationship; and 3) a structured clinical interview to supplement questionnaires and observations and integrate additional clinical information" (First et al., 2002, p. 171).

In the field of infant mental health, the parent-infant relationship is often the focus of therapeutic work (Clark, Paulson, & Conlin, 1993;

Fraiberg, Adelson, & Shapiro, 1980; Lieberman, 1985). Thus, it is important to conceptualize primary relationships as entities to be assessed and, when indicated, diagnosed. Including assessment of the parent-child relationship as part of the evaluation process can inform and focus intervention approaches (Sameroff & Emde, 1989).

Parent-child relationship problems are characterized by perceptions, attitudes, behaviors, and affects of either the parent, the child, or both that result in disturbed parent-child interactions. If disturbances in the parent-child relationship interfere with the functioning of the child or parent and continue over a period of time, a diagnosis of a relationship disorder may be warranted. An assessment of the affective and behavioral quality of the parent-child interaction can reveal significant relationship difficulties. If the relational disturbance has a long duration and/or high intensity, the disturbance may be evidenced by the parents' perceptions of the child or the meaning they ascribe to their child or their child's behavior and can affect the nature of parental involvement with the child (Zero to Three: National Center for Clinical Infant Programs [Zero to Three], 1994).

This chapter reviews the theoretical foundations and empirical support for employing a parent-child relationship paradigm when assessing the mental health of an infant or toddler. It describes domains of functioning for assessing the parent, child, and dyad that may contribute to relational disturbances. Although "parent" is used throughout the chapter, another significant caregiver who holds a parenting role may be substituted as needed, such as a grandparent or foster parent. This chapter also describes structured evaluation procedures for evaluating parent-child relationships, cultural considerations, and relational diagnoses for infants and young children and implications for treatment. Finally, considerations for future research are recommended, linking assessment research to practice.

CONCEPTUAL AND THEORETICAL FOUNDATIONS

Using a relational approach to assessment integrates theoretical application of developmental

and psychiatric disciplines (Sameroff & Emde, 1989). Foundations for assessing child mental health at the parent-child relational level can be supported by several compatible theoretical paradigms that share prioritization of the importance of early experience and context in examining development. Foundational contributions of the following perspectives are reviewed: attachment/ethological theory, psychodynamic/object relations theory, social learning theory, family systems theory, and multiple systems theories, including bioecological and transactional approaches.

Attachment/Ethological Theory

John Bowlby (1982) conceptualized the parent-child relationship as an *attachment behavioral system* that represents the foundations of the child's psychological development. Bowlby (1969) observed that infants who did not form securely attached, intimate relationships with a primary caregiver often developed psychological and behavioral problems. Drawing on ethological theory, Bowlby posited that infants produce behaviors to elicit protective and sustaining behavior from caregivers . Infants cry when hungry and coo to attract attention. Later, babies maintain proximity to their parents and turn to parents frequently for assistance and approval, as well as for confirmation of safety. When a parent responds quickly and appropriately to the child's cues, the child learns to rely on the support of the parent. This "secure attachment" allows the child to develop a sense of efficacy, as the child feels safe to explore the world.

According to attachment theory, the child constructs "internal working models," (Bretherton, 1985) or mental and emotional representations of these early parent-child interactions. The child projects qualities of the parent-child relationship onto other relationships. Beliefs about the self, about the relationship, and about the world are categorized, much as other cognitive and emotional data might be. For example, the child may internalize "I am lovable" or conversely "I am not lovable" as a result of these interactions. These internalizations have been linked with developing social cognition and social competence (Sroufe, 1979, 1988). Indicators of relationship quality are found in the behavior of the child, the caregiver, and the dyad, and in narratives describing these relationships (Hesse, 1999).

Psychodynamic/Object Relations Theory

Freudian psychoanalytic theory provides a perspective for understanding how an individual's developmental trajectory, including personality structure, may be shaped by the quality of the early parent-child relationships one experiences. This theory posits that the seeds of personality are sewn during children's early interactions with their parents and suggests that unresolved intrapsychic conflicts that arise from how early stages of child development are negotiated or experienced can lead to neurotic symptoms in adulthood. Anna Freud (1970) described the quality of the early mother-infant relationship as paramount to the child's subsequent psychological development. When a mother consistently reads her infant's cues and sensitively responds to her child's physical and emotional needs, providing an "auxiliary ego" for the young child, her infant feels satisfied. With the infant's needs gratified, the infant turns his or her emotional interests from the self to the proximal environment, which includes the mother. When the infant initiates expressions of affection toward the mother and she responds in kind, the pair form an emotional bond. These early relational patterns characterized by emotional reciprocity become the template for the young child's future relationships and are likely to foster a healthy progression along developmental lines through subsequent developmental stages (Freud, 1963). In contrast, the "rejecting mother," described as being incapable of or unwilling to identify and respond to her infant's needs, has been associated with subsequent developmental psychopathology in the child.

Spitz (1965), Mahler (1975), Winnicott (1968), and others have suggested that the abilities of the human being to establish healthy social relations are acquired early in the mother-child relationship. Winnicott (1965) described the parent-child relationship as a psychological "holding environment" for the developing child. The assumption is made that if this relationship is disturbed, the child will lack the adaptive abilities necessary to effectively interact with the environment. A sense of effectance and competence is the result of the ongoing experience of interacting with an empathic, consistent, and responsive caregiver who helps the child to understand and structure his or her world.

Object relations theory represents a more contemporary view of psychodynamic theory. The "object" of the infant's desire is the mother. This early relationship becomes the template for future relationships. Mahler (1968), through extensive observations of infants, toddlers, and mothers, proposed stages of early development in which the relationship between the infant and the mother progresses from an undifferentiated state during the first few weeks of the infant's life to a close symbiotic relationship, to attempts at separation and rapprochement or an exploration of the environment and touching base with the parent for "emotional refueling," to a psychological state of individuation when the child is about 3 years old. According to this model, the parent's feelings of rejection, ambivalence, and inability to help the toddler to complete this early developmental task can contribute to borderline or narcissistic personality organization, in which the individual lacks a consolidated sense of self as separate from others. Winnicott (1970) emphasized the importance of "mutuality" in the early parent-infant relationship as "setting the emotional tone of interpersonal experiences and their intrapsychic coloring throughout life" (p. 245) and suggested that the child who experiences inconsistent or unpredictable care becomes "a reaction to impingements from the environment."

Social Learning Theory

Bandura (1977) theorized that social behaviors are learned either through direct experience with subsequent reinforcement of those behaviors or through observing others modeling certain behaviors that are rewarded. Behaviors that are contingently rewarded continue while behaviors that are ignored cease to be performed. The parent-child relationship becomes the primary environmental influence shaping the child's behavior. Thus, for example, the toddler whose parents tend to respond to him primarily when he is hitting his younger brother is likely to continue this negative behavior. Although the parent's reprimands may seem like a negative consequence, for the child this is still experienced as parental attention.

Bandura (1989) later incorporated the concept of self-efficacy as a motivational factor in the development of behavioral patterns. Children who believe that they are capable of performing certain tasks are more likely to attempt those tasks and perform them successfully. This sense of efficacy may be derived from previous experience in which the behaviors have been reinforced by parental encouragement or a history of successfully accomplished tasks.

Based upon the tenets of social learning theory, Patterson (1982) elucidated a pattern of "coercive" parent-child interactions that lead to the development of conduct disorders in children and antisocial behavior in adulthood. This model consists of a pattern of escalating negative interactions between the child and parent associated with the parent's attempt to set limits, a particularly salient issue during toddlerhood. For example, a parent gives the child a directive to do or not to do something; the child attempts to avoid the directive by engaging in negative behavior such as noncompliance or tantrums; the parent responds with criticism or threats; the child returns with an increase in the negative behavior; the parent increases the threats. This interaction often ends in the child receiving physical punishment. The parent in this scenario unwittingly reinforces the child's negative behavior.

Another social learning theory of parenting and its influence on child development is that of noted that warm parental support incorporates behaviors that convey supportive presence, acceptance, positive affect, sensitivity, and responsiveness to the child's needs and are generally thought to enhance children's positive social and emotional development.

Family Systems Theory

Family systems theories, such as structural family therapy (Minuchin, 1974; Minuchin & Fishman, 1981), offer a framework for assessing parent-child interactions. According to this theory, a family consists of parental and child subsystems that function interdependently as a single unit. The parental subsystem possesses the responsibility of caring for and raising those within the child subsystem. Within a healthy system, parents establish family rules and behavioral expectations that maintain clear boundaries between the parental and child subsystems in a way that meets the socioemotional needs of all members. Pathology occurs when there is a disturbance in the family system. For example, when a parent's capacity to meet the needs of the children is compromised by physical or mental illness, one of the children, usually the oldest child, may assume parental responsibilities, which may result in ambiguous boundaries or cross-generational alliances, as well as conflicts within and/or across subsystems. This is observable even in 2- or 3-year-olds who become focused on their parents' emotional states. Thus, observations of the whole family interacting during an evaluation may inform the clinician about patterns of interactions that preclude the optimal functioning of the family system.

Multiple Systems Theories

Contemporary theories have extended consideration of the child's developmental milieu to include multiple synergistic systems. Transactional systems theory (Sameroff, 1975) and bioecological systems theory are two complementary models that support a relational approach to clinical assessment and treatment in infant mental health. In transactional theory, development depends on the complex interdependent interactions of the child, parent, and environment over time. Development is dynamic, and children's mental and emotional health depend upon multiple factors, including nutrition, responsive caregiving, parental mental health, safety of neighborhoods, and quality schooling (Sameroff, 1975).

Similarly, Bronfenbrenner elaborate on the interaction of the individual child with multiple environmental systems. In bioecological systems theory, nested hierarchical systems both influence and are influenced by the developing child. However, it is the proximal processes, or the daily interactions of life, that bear the most importance for development. For the infant, daily activities with the parent are most influential. Bronfenbrenner contends that the quality of these proximal processes matters more than any individual contribution of the child (e.g., temperament, medical condition) or parent (e.g., pathology, education) alone. The degree to which the infant and parent can contribute to and participate in high-quality proximal processes predicts the adjustment of the child and dyad.

Reasons for Looking at Relationships

In the context of normal development, the parent-child relationship plays a critical role in the infant's emergent behavioral and emotional regulation (Cohn & Tronick, 1989; Emde, 1989; Field, 1997; Schore, 2001). Recent research integrating neurobiology and attachment suggests that the infant brain develops in response to regulating social interactions with a caregiver, engaging in a circular feedback system of increasingly complex interactions (Schore, 2001). These developing regulatory processes are influential in the infant's developing attachment (Cassidy & Berlin, 1994; George & Solomon, 1996) and subsequent sense of self and social competence outside of the parent-child relationship.

An early caregiving environment characterized by physical safety, satisfaction of physiological needs, empathic responsiveness, mutual enjoyment, learning opportunities, and age-appropriate limit setting helps the child develop a consolidated sense of self and prepares the child for future social interactions (Sameroff & Emde, 1989). A supportive parent-child relationship has been found to serve as a buffer for children living in stressful urban environments (Kilmer, Cowen, & Wyman, 2001). A parent-child relationship that fails to meet the child's needs may place the child at risk for developmental delays, emotional dysregulation, behavior problems, and psychopathology later in life. For example, Carlson (1998) found that disturbances in the early parent-child relationship, specifically disorganized attachment behavior identified in infants ages 12 or 18 months, were associated with behavior problems and psychopathology during middle childhood and the adolescent years. Lyons-Ruth, Easterbrooks, and Cibelli (1997) reported that infants who demonstrated disorganized insecure attachment behaviors at 18 months had externalizing behavior problems at age 7 years, while infants with avoidant insecure attachment behaviors showed internalizing behaviors at age 7 years. Research has also shown that interventions directed toward at-risk parent-child relationships can decrease maternal depression, improve the child's cognitive development and emotional regulation (Cohen, Lojkasek, Muir, & Parker, 2002), and improve mothers' perceptions of their infants' adaptability and reinforcement value, as well as increasing maternal positive affect and verbalization with infants (Clark, Tluczek, & Wenzel, 2003).

CONTRIBUTIONS OF PARENT

Nurturing Parenting

Empirical studies of parenting and attachment theory underscore the importance of examining the context within which the child is developing when evaluating the young child's mental health. The quality of the parent-child relationship or *optimal parental care* provides for the infant's physical and emotional needs as well as sensorimotor stimulation and physiological and emotional regulation (Ainsworth, 1969; Clarke-Stewart, 1973). The mother's ability to demonstrate affection has been linked to enhanced infant development and involvement with mother and other caretakers (Stern et al., 1969). Maternal contingent reinforcement of an infant's signals has been found to be important to the development of the infant's sense of effectance and competence (Ainsworth & Bell, 1975). From her study of infant-mother interaction in the home, Clarke-Stewart (1973) described quality maternal care, which results in optimal, secure attachment, as socially responsive and affectionate but not necessarily excessively physical. Apparently, while holding and physical contact can be very important in the early months of life, this type of contact can become restrictive as the child matures (Clarke-Stewart, 1973). Maternal attention must be paid to the infant's changing developmental needs, such as readiness and need for autonomy. Sander (1962) suggests that the manner in which these developmental issues are negotiated is extremely important in determining the continuing nature of the relationship.

From her observation in the home and experimental studies in the lab, Ainsworth (1969) suggested the following five variables as most important to a high-quality parent-infant relationship: (1) responding sensitively and empathically to the infant's signals; (2) providing frequent physical contact; (3) allowing the infant freedom to explore; (4) helping the infant derive a sense of consequence of his or her actions; and (5) engaging in mutually enjoyable and reciprocal activities. Through these early interactions, not only does the mother teach the child about the self and the self in relation to others, but also the quality of this early interaction allows for optimal development in capacities for organization (Sroufe, 1979), linguistic and problem-solving skills (Bruner, 1974; Epstein & Evans, 1979; Vygotsky, 1978), and cognitive abilities (Clarke-Stewart, 1973).

In addition to the mother's provision of nurturant, responsive care, developmental psychologists such as Bruner (1975) and Vygotsky (1978) view the adult's role as important for communicating and translating the culture for the young child. The structure, modeling, and focused joint attention with the child allows the child to first observe and then internalize the adult's approaches, communication, and problem-solving strategies. This process of *scaffolding* leads to the growth and development of higher mental processes and attentional abilities. Through focusing, encouraging, and assisting, parents provide a "zone of proximal development" in which young children can do more than is possible independently, thus helping them learn what they can do (Vygotsky, 1978).

Disturbed Parenting

The grave effects of maternal deprivation or disturbed parenting on a child's personality and intellect are well documented (Bowlby, 1951; Rutter, 1974; Spitz, 1965). Children of parents with psychiatric disorders may experience a type of deprivation. Psychiatric hospitalizations require long separations between mothers and young children, and psychotic symptoms may also serve to separate mother and child.

Several factors that may influence a parent's contribution to the early parent-child relationship are the parent's expectations, values, and attitudes toward the infant's or child's needs, the parent's own history of being cared for, and perception of the self as a parent (Sameroff, 1975).

These are further influenced by the parent's personality and level of cognitive development. If a mother is under pressure of urgent and unsatisfied needs of her own, she will tend to behave inconsistently, being influenced by fluctuating moods or needs (Bromwich, 1976). The mother who is functioning at a lower cognitive level, either due to genetic endowment, environmental deprivation, or psychotic delusions may not be able to perceive her child as a separate individual (Sameroff, 1975). She is not able to attribute a level of complexity to the child's behavior. Sameroff speculates that "the cognitive level from which the mother viewed the child was another complicating factor in the manner in which early differences get translated into later deviancies" (p. 289). For example, the cognitively impaired mother who approaches her infant from a sensorimotor perspective might demand that her own physical needs be met. Beckwith (1976) suggests that if the mother's needs for success or effectance are not met, either because the infant is not alert due to prematurity or a medical condition or because the infant has a challenging temperament and is difficult to comfort, the mother may become distant and negativistic. Because she may feel rejected, she may turn around and reject her child. This process has been implicated in nonorganic failure to thrive and child neglect and abuse.

Numerous studies have documented adverse effects of maternal depression on mother-infant interactions, although the mechanisms are still in need of theoretical and empirical elucidation (Goodman & Gotlib, 1999). Women who are depressed have been characterized as either withdrawn or rough, insensitive, and intrusive in their handling and care of their infants (Field, 1997). Depressed mothers have been found to more often mirror the negative affective expressions or behaviors of their infants than their positive affective states (Field, Healy, Goldstein, & Guthertz, 1990). Maternal depression disrupts the process of mutual regulation, including mother-infant interaction and intersubjective experiences that contribute to the child's social-emotional and internal working models, thereby leaving the child vulnerable to emotional and behavioral dysregulation (Tronick & Weinberg, 1997). Maternal depression also has been found to be a risk factor for delays in cognitive development, and it increases risk for subsequent major depression and behavioral problems (Beardslee, Bemporad, Keller & Klerman, 1983; Cummings & Davies, 1994; Weissman et al., 1987). Infants of depressed mothers have been found to exhibit more dysregulated behavior and to be more difficult to read (Field, 1997). Cohn and Tronick (1989) noted that infants as young as 3 months exhibited heightened distress levels, increased protests, and gaze aversion in response to observations of their mother's still-faced simulated depression. Maternal depression has been associated with insecure attachments in 1-year-old infants (Lyons-Ruth, Zoll, Connell, & Grunebaum, 1986), cognitive-linguistic delays in preschool children (NICHD Early Child Care Research Network, 1999), and depressive mood and behavioral problems in young children (Radke-Yarrow, Nottelmann, Martinez, Fox, & Belmont, 1992). However, the quality of mother-child interactions, specifically maternal sensitivity, was found to mediate the association between chronicity of maternal depressive symptoms and child outcomes (NICHD Early Child Care Research Network, 1999).

More recently, a meta-analysis of six studies examining the effects of maternal depression on infant-mother attachment concluded that maternal depression was significantly associated with insecure infant-mother attachment (Martins & Gaffan, 2000). Lyons-Ruth and colleagues (2002) identified two specific patterns of behavior among depressed mothers interacting with their infants that seem to be associated with disorganized attachment behaviors in infant-mother interactions. Some mothers display "hostile, self-referential" interactions characterized by rough or intrusive handling of the infant, while other mothers show a "helpless, fearful" pattern marked by withdrawn or less involved interactions with their infants.

CONTRIBUTIONS OF CHILD

Temperament

Thomas, Chess, and Birch (1968) suggest that constitutional variability in children has tremendous influence on parents' attitudes and caretaking styles. Infants' arousal level, rhythm, response

threshold, capacities, and weaknesses play important roles in shaping parents' perceptions about and feelings toward their infant. The parent and the child influence each other's ability or desire to relate. Therefore, problems in the early parent-infant relationship may develop when there is a mismatch in the goodness of fit between parent and child. For example, an active infant with a high need for stimulation may become frustrated and irritable in the care of a parent whose rhythm or tempo is much slower.

An infant's temperament, specifically mood, emotional reactivity, and behavioral regulation, all impact the quality of the child's participation in the parent-child relationship Crockenberg, 1981). The term "difficult" was coined by Chess and Thomas to describe a cluster of child temperament characteristics that challenged caregivers. Infants who exhibit these difficult behaviors were more likely to (1) elicit less sensitive parenting and (2) require more sophisticated parenting skills. Therefore, infants requiring the most skilled parenting may, in fact, elicit parenting that fails to meet their greater needs.

The interaction of child temperament and parenting style has been examined in studies of parental limit-setting. Kochanska (1997) reported that fearful toddlers tended to develop better social conscience over time when mothers used gentle discipline (psychological and de-emphasizing power) as compared with children whose mothers used negative discipline (coercive and/or angry). On the other hand, Arcus (2001) in her work with Kagan found that inhibited children had more favorable outcomes when parents used stronger forms of limit setting. Parents who report that their children are temperamentally fearful or reactive to limit setting also describe the parenting process as less pleasurable (Leve, 2001). Thus, certain infant temperament characteristics are associated with risk for relational disturbance.

Gender may affect the parent's responses to the infant. Six-month-old boys have been found to be more emotionally reactive (expressing both more positive and negative affect) than girls. Girls tend to show more curiosity and capacity for self-soothing than boys (Weinberg & Tronick, 1992). Mother-son dyadic interactions have been found to be more organized than mother-daughter interactions (Tronick & Cohn, 1989). However, boys may be more vulnerable than girls to the negative consequences associated with maternal depression on cognitive development (Sharp et al., 1995).

Medical Conditions

Children with chronic illnesses are two to three times more likely to experience emotional maladjustment or behavioral disturbances than their healthy peers (Northam, 1997; Wallander & Varni, 1998), and the risk for psychopathology seems to increase with the severity of the disability (Cadman, Boyle, Szatmari, & Offord, 1987). A series of studies have implicated chronic illness as a potential risk factor for parent-child relationship disturbances and subsequent emotional and behavioral problems in childhood. The findings showed that children diagnosed in infancy with congenital heart disease and cystic fibrosis demonstrated higher rates of insecure attachments at 12 to 18 months as compared with a healthy comparison group (Goldberg et al., 1990). Insecure-avoidant attachment behaviors in preschool children with cystic fibrosis were associated with poor nutritional status and poor growth (Simmons, Goldberg, Washington, Fischer-Fay, & Maclusky, 1995). Other researchers (Carson & Schauer, 1992) have documented that mothers of children with asthma tended to view their children as more demanding, less reinforcing, and less acceptable than mothers who had healthy children. The mothers of children with asthma also reported higher levels of parenting stress and tended to demonstrate more rejecting, overprotective, or overindulgent parenting styles as compared with mothers in the control sample, underscoring the potential risk to the parent-child relationship when a serious illness is diagnosed.

Premature birth has been recognized as a risk to the quality of the parent-child relationship for over 40 years (Kennell & Rolnick, 1960; Klaus & Kennell, 1970; Klaus et al., 1972; Leve, Scaramella, & Fagot, 2001). Several pathways accounting for these relational problems have been proposed. Infants who are born prematurely have been found to have a higher incidence of attentional problems and difficult temperaments than peers who were born at term (Chapieski & Evan-

kovich, 1997). It appears as though multiple risk factors (e.g., negative emotionality and health problems) may increase the likelihood that an infant will experience lower quality parent-child interactions (Fiese, Peohlmann, Irwin, Gordon, & Curry-Bleggi, 2001). More recently there has been recognition that parent-child attachment is influenced by a complex interaction of both parent and child variables. Poehlmann and Fiese (2001) reported that the premature birth of a child was found to be a moderating factor for maternal depressive symptoms and the quality of the mother-infant relationship. Premature infant birth in combination with maternal depression was predictive of insecure attachment behaviors in infants at 12 months. Other research (Cox, Hopkins, & Hans, 2000) has shown that the mother's representations of her infant were more predictive of the presence of secure infant attachment behaviors at 19 months than the child's health history, which included prematurity and intracranial hemorrhage. However, the presence of neurological impairments in infants was associated with a specific insecure attachment, that is, disorganized attachment, in children.

ASSESSMENT OF THE PARENT-CHILD RELATIONSHIP: BEST PRACTICES

The American Academy of Child and Adolescent Psychiatry (1997) Practice Parameters for the Assessment of Infants and Toddlers recommend that the psychiatric evaluation of children under 3 years of age include an assessment of the parent-child relationship. The goal of this assessment is to obtain a comprehensive picture of the parent-child relationship within its sociocultural context. The findings from such an assessment can assist the clinician in formulating an intervention plan and in evaluating progress during the therapeutic process. Sources of information should include the parents and other primary caregivers, the child, the extended family when indicated, day care providers, and the pediatrician. If the family is involved in other services, such as social services or mental health services, information should also be obtained from these collateral sources. The University of Wisconsin Parent-

Infant and Early Childhood Clinic's relational assessment model involves a diagnostic evaluation that uses a multimodal approach and actively involves the parents through interviews, observations, and parent report assessment instruments. Observations of parent-child interactions are conducted across developmentally salient situations. Assessment procedures are structured to address particular domains appropriate to the child's level of development. For example, infants need emotionally available parents who are capable of reading their cues and responding in a sensitive and timely fashion (Ainsworth, 1969; Stern, 2002), whereas toddlers need caregiving that is respectful of their emerging autonomy and provides cognitive and emotional scaffolding, clear expectations, consistent limit setting, and assistance in managing transitions and with affective and behavioral regulation. Note that an observation of interactions should be considered to be just "one snapshot in time" while the parent-child relationship represents the child's and parent's "sense and quality of connectedness" over time and across settings (Clark, 1985). The parent's mood and parenting capacities, the family's stress, and the family's access to and need of social supports and resources should also be evaluated as part of the parent-child relationship assessment.

Interview With Parents

Developing a therapeutic alliance with the parents is critical to the assessment process. Taking a collaborative approach with parents throughout the assessment may build such an alliance. At the onset of the interview, parents should be asked about their concerns about their child and what they would like to get out of the assessment. By empathically listening to parents' experiences of their child and their struggles in parenting, the clinician can begin a parallel therapeutic process with the parents that may have a positive effect on their relationship with their child. Several elements of the parent interview that are particularly salient to an assessment of the parent-child relationship include the following:

1. Demystify the assessment process by explaining the multimodal nature of the assessment procedures and the parents' significant role in the assessment process.

2. Ask parents what information and assistance they would like to receive from the assessment.

3. Provide a safe, comfortable, developmentally appropriate environment for children and parents. Ideally, all members of the family household as defined by the parents should attend the initial evaluation. Having the whole family present provides the clinician information about family dynamics, including sibling relationships and cross-generational alliances.

4. Assess the parents' optimal parenting capacities across several developmentally salient situations (e.g., routine tasks of daily living such as feeding, limit-setting, play, separation/reunion).

5. Involve the parents in assessing their child's regulatory capacities and behaviors and their capacity to see their child as a separate individual by observing the child together and discussing what you and they are observing.

6. Learn the parents' perspectives and meaning of the child and his or her behaviors by asking parents to describe their child and their impressions about the source or cause of the presenting problem.

7. Include a perinatal history about the pregnancy, labor, and delivery. This time represents the critical beginnings of the child's relationship with each parent. An unplanned or symptomatic pregnancy or a complicated labor or delivery may have profound implications for the parent-child relationship. Ask open-ended questions (e.g., "What was the pregnancy like for you?") to allow parents to share those aspects of the experience that are important to them.

8. Involve parents in assessing their relationship by reviewing a videotape of the parent and child interacting together. Help them focus on strengths as well as on reading their child's cues. "Wonder along with" the parents about who their child reminds them of in general and when the problem behavior is present. This information may help to elucidate parents' projections of negative intentionality attributed to their child.

9. Assess the sociocultural context of the parent-child relationship, respecting and appreciating the family's beliefs and values. Recognize the parents as the experts in their personal sociocultural environment and ask them to educate you about their life experiences and worldviews. Seek additional consultation from cultural experts to address the clinician's cultural knowledge deficits or biases.

10. Provide parents feedback about the assessment findings with a caring attitude, void of judgment about the parents or their parenting style. This approach will facilitate a therapeutic joining with the parents vital to the development of a collaborative treatment plan.

Observations of Parent-Child Interactions

When conducting an assessment using observational methods to assess the quality of the parent-child relationship, there are several key points to remember:

1. Note the intensity, frequency, and duration of the affect and behavior between parent and child. This information may differentiate normal interactions from pathological interactions and assist the clinician in determining the seriousness of a relationship problem. For example, the DC:0–3 Axis II system uses this information to classify the relationship problem as "a perturbation, a disturbance or a disorder" (Anders, 1989, p. 134).

2. Assess the quality of interaction within the context of the situation. For example, differentiate parental directives or conversation related to structured tasks from those intended to join with or engage the child in a mutually enjoyable social interaction.

3. Consider parents' responses relative to the child's age and developmental level. Examples of reading cues and responding sensitively include a mother who adjusts the way she holds her infant after noticing the child's discomfort in a particular position or the father who responds to his toddler tugging at his arm by touching, talking to, or picking up his child.

4. When the child engages in negative testing or oppositional behavior, note whether the parent responds to the child in a way that suggests he or she experiences the child's behavior as resistant or "bad."

5. Note whether the rapidity and regularity with which the parent responds to the child helps the child feel that his or her actions have an effect on the parent.

6. Differentiate a genuine sense of "connectedness" from "going through the motions." An emotionally connected parent is aware of and involved with the child even when not actively interacting with the child. The parent is attentive to the child, subtly monitoring the child with an empathic awareness of the child's emotional state. Connectedness may also include seeing the child as a separate individual.

7. Assess the parent's capacity to reflect the child's affect and/or behavior through echoing (with infants), gazing, confirmation of affect, behavior, approval, encouragement, and praise, as well as labeling of the child's internal feeling states. This process of "mirroring" represents the parent's emotional availability and affective attunement to the infant or young child.

8. Assess the parent's capacity for "scaffolding" by looking at the amount and way in which the parent gains, helps to focus, and sustains the child's attention to the relevant aspects of the situation. Scaffolding is a process in which parents recognize their child's developmental capacities and provide a physical and socioemotional environment that gives the child an opportunity to expand his or her capacities. Just as a metal scaffold allows construction workers to build taller buildings, parents' emotional and cognitive scaffolding helps their child reach higher levels of cognitive, social, and motor skills as well as emotional and behavioral regulation. Scaffolding with a younger infant may be manifested by protective caregiving. With an older child, this process may include assistance such as teaching, demonstrating, stating expectations clearly, and setting limits with a sensitivity to the child's affective and cognitive status.

9. After the observations, ask the parents how typical the interaction was. If the parents indicate that it was different from

usual, inquire about how it was different and what attributions parents make about the differences. For example, parents may state that the child was much more cooperative than usual and that they rarely have the opportunity to play with their child one on one. Such information informs the diagnostic process and the planning for therapeutic intervention.

10. Observe from the child's perspective as well. Ask the question, "If I were this child, what would I see/experience when I look up at my mother or father?"

A systematic approach to assessing parent-child interactions is central to identifying the areas of strength as well as areas of concern that may contribute to disturbances in the parent-child dyad. Researchers (e.g., Ainsworth, Blehar, & Waters, 1978; Barnard, 1979; Clark 1985, 1999) have identified specific characteristics of the child, the parent, and the parent-child interaction that deserve attention during a relational assessment. The Parent-Child Early Relational Assessment (PCERA), a method that incorporates both an objective assessment of strengths and areas of concern across situations and a subjective component that involves parents in assessing their relationship with their child and the meaning of their child's behavior through video replay interview, is described below. This is followed by descriptions of several other empirically validated methods for assessing the quality of the parent-child relationship. See table 3.1 for an overview of these instruments.

PARENT-CHILD EARLY RELATIONAL ASSESSMENT

The PCERA (Clark, 1985) attempts to capture the child's experience of the parent, the parent's experience of the child, the affective and behavioral characteristics that each bring to the interaction, and the quality or tone of the relationship. The PCERA may be used as part of an initial diagnostic evaluation to formulate relationship issues and focus intervention efforts, for monitoring progress in therapy and to assess outcomes in treatment efficacy studies. The quality of the parent-child relationship is assessed from videotaped

observations of the child interacting with the parent during four 5-minute segments that include feeding, structured task, free play, and separation/reunion (Clark, 1985, 1999; Farran, Clark, & Ray, 1990). The rating scales are based on empirical developmental studies and attachment, psychodynamic, and Soviet cognitive-linguistic theories and informed by clinical observations of those aspects of functioning seen as important for differentiating parents experiencing difficulty in parenting from well-functioning parents (Ainsworth, 1969; Clarke-Stewart, 1973; Musick, Clark, & Cohler, 1981; Sander, 1964; Vygotsky, 1978). The PCERA identifies areas of strength and areas of concern in the parent, the child, and the dyad. Relational profiles may be developed for use in focusing clinical intervention efforts, program evaluation, and research with families at risk for early relational disturbances.

Ratings are made on a 5-point Likert scale for 29 domains of parental functioning, 30 domains of child functioning, and 8 of dyadic functioning, described in table 3.2. The amount, duration, and intensity of affect and behavior exhibited by the parent, the child, and the dyad are rated:

1. Items assess aspects of parental behavior and affect including parental positive and negative affect, mood, sensitivity and contingent responsivity to child's cues, flexibility/rigidity, and capacity to structure and mediate the environment, genuine connectedness, mirroring, and creativity/resourcefulness.

2. Child items include positive and negative affect, somber/serious mood, irritability, social initiative and responsiveness, interest/gaze aversion, assertion/aggressivity, persistence, impulsivity, and emotional regulation, important aspects of infant functioning vulnerable to stress and family functioning.

3. Dyadic items include mutual enjoyment, tension, reciprocity, and joint attention.

The parent, child, and dyadic scales were initially developed on an NIMH-funded clinical intervention project studying maternal psychiatric disorders and the quality of the mother-child relationship (Musick et al., 1981). The PCERA has been further developed for use with normative and other at-risk populations (Clark et al., 1993).

Table 3.1 Parent-Child Relationship Assessment Instruments

Instrument	Age	Domains	Reliability/Validity	Comments
Parent-Child Relational Assessment (Clark, 1985)	Birth to 5 years old	Observations *Parent Subscales:* Positive affective involvement and verbalization Negative affect and behavior Scaffolding, sensitivity, and consistency *Infant Subscales:* Positive affect, communicative and social skills Quality of play, interest, and attentional skills Dysregulation and irritability *Parent-Child Dyad Subscales:* Mutuality and reciprocity Disorganization and tension *Video Replay and Interview:* Meaning of child and child's behavior Parent's perception of self in parenting role	High interrater reliability Good face validity Good construct validity Discriminates high-risk from normative dyads	Theoretically and empirically derived scales rated from video-taped observations and parent interview using video replay to identify areas of strength and concern for treatment planning and evaluations Widely used for research and clinical purposes
Still-Face Paradigm (Tronick et al., 1978)	<12 months	Parent-child interactions are characterized by initiation of interaction, mutual orientation, greetings, exchange of affect, and mutual disengagement through behavioral observations *Parent:* Vocalizations, head and body position, quality of handling infant, direction of gaze and facial expression *Infant:* Vocalizations, direction of gaze, head orientation and position, facial expression, amount of movement, blinks and tongue placement	High interrater reliability and some predictive validity for attachment security at 12 months	Research paradigm useful in studies of clinical and normative infants

Instrument	Age range	Constructs	Psychometrics	Comments
Nursing Child Assessment Satellite Training NCAST Teaching and Feeding Scales (Barnard, 1979)	Infancy (including premature infants) through 3 years	*Mother:* Sensitivity to the child's cures Response to the child's distress Fostering social-emotional growth Fostering cognitive growth *Child:* Clarity of cues Responsiveness to caregiver	Good reliability Good validity Discriminates high-risk from normative dyads Parent total score has predictive validity for child IQ at 3–5 years	Ratings of home observations widely used for clinical and research purposes
Home Observation for Measurement of the Environment (Caldwell & Bradley, 1978)	Birth to 3 years	*Mother:* Responsivity Acceptance Organization of the infant's physical environment and provision of appropriate play materials Involvement with the infant Opportunities for variety in the infant's daily stimulation	Good concurrent and predictive validity with Stanford-Binet and Illinois Test of Psycholinguistic Abilities at 3 years	Administered in the child's home at a time when the child is awake and present
Emotional Availability Scales (Biringen, 2000; Biringen et al., 1998)	Infancy/early childhood	*Parent:* Sensitivity Structuring Nonintrusiveness Nonhostility *Child:* Responsiveness to the parent Involvement of the parent	Good reliability Very good concurrent and predictive validity associated with attachment security and child development	Grounded in attachment and emotional availability theories; although primarily used in research, may be useful for assessing intervention programs
Clinical Problem-Solving Procedure (Crowell & Feldman, 1988)	24–54 months (with modifications as young as 12 months, see Zeanah et al., 2000)	*Parent:* Emotional availability Nurturance/empathic responsiveness Protection Comforting/response to distress Teaching Play Discipline/limit setting Instrumental care/structure/routines	Good reliability. Parents should be interviewed in order to establish ecological validity	9 episodes—well suited for clinical use

(continued)

Table 3.1 Continued

Instrument	Age	Domains	Reliability/Validity	Comments
		Infant: Emotion regulation Security/trust/self-esteem Vigilance/self-protection/safety Comfort seeking Learning/curiosity/mastery Play/imagination Self-control/cooperation Self-regulation/predictability		
Strange Situation (Ainsworth et al., 1978)	11–20 months	Attachment security of infant with parent/caregiver: Secure Anxious-resistant Anxious-avoidant Disorganized	High reliability, stability, and predictive validity with U.S., Western European mothers	Grounded in Attachment theory Better suited for research than clinical purposes Research paradigm that is well suited for studies of attachment security in clinical and normative populations
Parenting Stress Index (Abidin, 1986)	1 month to 12 years	*Parent Domain:* Competence Isolation Attachment Health Role Restriction Depression Spouse Life Stress *Child Domain:* Distractibility/hyperactivity Adaptability Reinforces parent Demandingness Mood Acceptability	Good internal consistency for child domain subscales and parent domain subscales Good test-retest reliability for child domain, parent domain subscales, and total stress score Good construct validity Discriminates high-risk from normative dyads	Self-report paper-and-pencil instrument used clinically and in research

38

Working Model of the Child Interview (Zeanah & Barton, 1989)	Infant and toddlers	Richness of perception Openness to change Coherence Intensity of involvement Caregiving sensitivity Acceptance/rejection Infant difficulty Fear of loss Affective tone Narrative organization	Concurrent and predictive validity with Strange/Situation, infant attachment behavior and quality of mother-infant interaction	Grounded in Attachment theory Well suited to research and clinical purposes
Insightfulness Assessment (IA; Koren-Karie et al., 2002; Oppenheim, Koren-Karie, & Sagi, 2001; Oppenheim & Koren-Karie, 2002)	Infants, toddlers, preschoolers	*Parent Domain:* Insight into child's motives Openness Complexity in description of child Maintenance of focus on child Richness of description of child Coherence of thought Acceptance Anger Worry Separateness from child	Growing evidence of concurrent validity and reliability	Well suited to research and clinical purposes
Adult Attachment Interview (George et al., 1996)	Adult	Narrative/adjectives re early relationships with parents, rated: Secure/autonomous Dismissive Preoccupied Unresolved/disorganized	Associated with child attachment behavior; predictive validity has been established AAI scores correspond with their infants' attachment classification in the Strange situation	Semi-structured interview used for research purposes Maybe promising as a clinical tool

Table 3.2 Parent-Child Early Relational Assessment

Domains	Behavioral Observations	Indicators of Strengths in Relationship	Indicators of Areas of Concern in Relationship
Parent Domains			
Expressed affect and mood	Pervasive and sustained emotional state inferred by quality, intensity, and durations of: Facial expressions Behavior Tone of voice Content of verbalizations Posture	Warm, kind, and loving voice Cheerful and lively expression of positive affect Relaxed demeanor Expressions of affectionate exchanges (such as touching, smiling, or hugging)	Depressed mood (flat or constricted range in affect, withdrawn, few or sluggish movements, little energy, expressed helplessness or hopelessness, self-absorption, negative perceptions or preoccupations of rejection, anhedonia, and/or little interest in activities or interactions) Anxious mood (worried facial expression, heightened motor activity, agitation, vigilance, verbal expressions of anxiety, and/or an edgy or staccato tone of voice) Hypomania Voice may be flat, lacking in emotion or warmth *or* may be angry or hostile, including shouting
Expressed attitude toward child	Content, intensity, duration, and frequency of verbalizations to the child: Tone of voice Facial expressions Parent's actions	Encouraging statements to child Taking delight in being with child Positive and accepting attitude toward child	Harsh tone of voice, critical comments, cynical and/or taunting remarks that communicate displeasure and disapproval of the child and/or his or her behavior Negative attributions about child Rejecting behavior (turning away, harsh or abrupt-sounding voice or behaviors, and scowls, frowns, or other negative facial expressions)
Affective and behavioral involvement with child	Parent's physical contact Visual contact with the child Verbalizations and social initiatives Contingent responsivity Capacity to structure and mediate the environment Capacity to read child's cues Sense of connectedness Capacity to mirror child's emotional experience	Frequent gentle touching child Gazing at the child with genuine regard Frequent and meaningful verbalizations and social initiatives Imitating and expanding infants' vocalizations or the young child's verbalizations Questioning and answering the child, elaborating on the child's verbalizations, and commenting on the child's activities Using "motherese" cadence to regulate the mood state of young infants Initiating vocalizations, making faces, gesturing or playing with child	Little physical contact or rough, restraining touch Little or no verbalization or social initiation Blank stare at child Does not typically respond to child's cues, or does so inappropriately Ineffective at structuring child's environment Distant, uninterested in child Emotionally unavailable

	Definition	Adaptive	Concerning
Parenting style	Manner in which the parent looks, touches, talks, holds, initiates, and responds to the child including: Flexibility Creativity Resourcefulness Intrusiveness Consistency, predictability In clinical populations, evidence of behavioral disturbance	Making conversation relevant to the child's interests Prompting social play with child Responding quickly and appropriately to the child's cues Responding positively to child's positive age-appropriate behavior Ignoring or redirecting negative behavior Providing structure for child, helping the child to focus and sustain attention Involved and interested in child Engaged and connected Emotionally available to the child Mirroring and labeling the child's emotional state Helping child focus and sustaining attention Protective caregiving Uses scaffolding to expand child's capacities Flexible, spontaneous, and creative Following the child's lead Adapting to the changing circumstances Respecting child's autonomy Consistent and predictable Behavior is contextually and developmentally appropriate	Rigid, inflexible and shows little creativity Intrusive and controlling Inconsistent Behavior is extremely inappropriate, possibly indicative of psychopathology

Infant/Child Domains

	Definition	Adaptive	Concerning
Mood/affect	The child's overall range, intensity, and duration of affective expressions, not just toward the parent, and range from positive to negative expressions	Expresses enthusiastic/cheerful affect easily and regularly Characteristically happy and relaxed Smiles, laughter, or positive excitement, playful Very young infants may brighten their eyes, smile, coo, wave their arms and legs, and increase their respiratory rate	Withdrawn or disinterested, or appears depressed Anxious or fearful Jumpiness, watchfulness, hesitancy, rocking, motor tension Thumb-sucking, baby talk, stuttering, nervous laughter, persistent questioning Irritable, crying, whining, scowling, tantrums

(continued)

41

Table 3.2 Continued

Domains	Behavioral Observations	Indicators of Strengths in Relationship	Indicators of Areas of Concern in Relationship
		Toddlers may clap their hands, share playfulness, exchange kisses and hugs, and/or display a sense of pride in their accomplishments	Serious or somber Frustration, anger, or extreme negativity Throwing objects, hitting, biting, banging, or obstinacy Shifts of affect or mood may be frequent, or expression of affect may be inappropriate
Behavior/adaptive abilities	Social initiatives and responsiveness Compliance Assertiveness Exploratory play Persistence Focus on parent's emotional state	Frequently initiates interaction with parent and responds to the parent's initiatives Typically compliant—infrequent disruptive behavior Communicates needs while accepting parent's limit setting Age-appropriate interest in play and activities Maintains goal-directed behavior (6+ months) Recognizes parent's affect but continues in activities	Disinterested in or unresponsive to parent's initiations Noncompliant with parent's structure or requests Demanding of parent's attention—becomes disruptive if not immediately gratified Little interest in exploring or manipulating objects in play Leaves task if not immediately successful Overconcerned about parent's emotional state
Activity level	Passivity/lethargy Hyperactivity	Energetic and not easily exhausted Activity level is appropriate for age and situation	Tires easily Over- or underactive for age and situation
Regulatory capacities	Child's capacity to organize and regulate his or her state in response to external stimuli or frustration: Alertness/interest Attention Robustness Impulsivity Self-regulation Consolability	Generally alert and focused Able to attend and focus on persons or objects Energetic High frustration tolerance Resilient to stressful situations Generally content and easily soothed	Lackluster, disinterested Distractible, unable to focus and sustain attention Tired, low energy Low frustration tolerance and poor impulse control Becomes disengaged and disorganized easily Frequently distressed and inconsolable
Communication	Expressive and receptive communicative skills: Visual contact Communication competence Readability	Generally seeks and/or maintains visual contact with parent Effectively uses gestures, vocalizations, or words to express wants Age-appropriate receptive skills Cues are easy to read	Little or no eye contact with parent Delayed expressive or receptive skills Signals are difficult to read
Motoric competence	Age-appropriate gross and fine motor skills	Gross and fine motor abilities are age-appropriate and coordinated	Delayed or uncoordinated motor ability

Parent-Child Dyad

Affective quality of interaction	The emotional tone of the dyad	Dyad is marked by expressive, relaxed, joyful, enthusiastic interactions	Dyad is characteristically angry or flat, or highly anxious Little enjoyment in interactions
Mutuality	The general rhythm of interactions: Joint attention Reciprocity Organization and regulation of interactions Similarity of state	Dyad engages in frequent joint attention Turn-taking, dialogues Contingent responsivity in interactions Order, timing, and pace of interactions are harmonious Frequently matched or complementary affective and arousal states	Each attends to different activity Dyad may appear out of sync, lacking in reciprocity Interactions are disorganized or discordant Emotion and arousal states may frequently be mismatched
Sense of security in relationship with parent	Pattern of interactions based upon history of trust and affective bond between parent and child	Child explores environment while intermittently making visual or physical contact with parent Child seeks proximity of parent when distressed Child reaches for and seeks comfort from parent following brief separation/reunion Parent is emotionally responsive in comforting distressed child Parent shows developmentally appropriate monitoring of child's activity and attention to child's physical and emotional safety	Child shows indiscriminant affection-seeking from strangers Child clings to parent, protests, does not let parent leave or freezes when parent leaves; child shows subdued affect, little curiosity or exploration of environment Child averts gaze from parent Child is inconsolable by parent after brief separation/reunion Child shows contradictory behaviors—reaching for and pushing parent away after brief separation/reunion Parent is inconsistent or insensitive in response to child's distress Parent shows disregard for child's physical and/or emotional needs

Clark (1983) and Goodman and Brumley (1990) found that PCERA scores differentiate patterns of mothers with depression and mothers with schizophrenic disorders from well-functioning mothers. Both construct and predictive validity have been established. PCERA ratings of early mother-infant interactions have been correlated with both concurrent measures of child temperament and behavior and parenting stress and with later quality of mother-child interactions and security of attachment behaviors at 12 months and has been found to document change following therapeutic intervention (e.g., Mothander, 1990; Teti, Nakagawa, Das, & Wirth, 1991; see review, Clark, 1999).

Each of the four situations in the PCERA provides a window for understanding what has been shared in the parent-child relationship. Each situation is experienced differently, with some eliciting conflictual feelings and others allowing for feelings of competence in the parenting role. After the procedure has been explained to parents, written consent is obtained for videotaping. The clinician explains that the videotaping is for the family's benefit so that the parent and clinician can view the tape together in a reflective manner during a subsequent session. Parents also are told, "We understand that this is just a snapshot of one point in time. We'll be interested in your sharing with us how it [the interaction] is like or different from how things usually go." The videotaping procedure involves placing the camera at a 45-degree angle to the parent and child, who are seated together at a small table, and using a medium shot to capture the facial expressions of the parent and the child.

During the feeding situation, the parent and young child are provided a snack of juice, raisins, and crackers and told, "We are interested in seeing you and [child's name] during feeding or a snack time together. Please be with [child's name] as you usually would." If the mother is breastfeeding, she is asked if she is comfortable being videotaped during a feeding. If she is not comfortable or if the infant is bottle fed, parents are asked to bring a bottle. The feeding situation allows for an assessment of the parent's capacity for nurturing and social interaction as well as sensitivity to the child's cues and need for regulation. The child's readability, affect regulation, social initiative, and

responsivity during feeding may also be assessed. Comfort, tension, and regulation of the dyad in this situation is observed.

The instructions and nature of the structured task are determined by the age of the child. For example, parents of infants under 7 months are asked to change their baby's diaper and attempt to get the baby interested in shaking a rattle. Parents of children between 8 and 12 months are given two cups and a toy and asked to hide a toy under one cup and alternately hide it under the second cup within the child's sight and have the child try to find it. At 8 to 12 months, they are also told, if time permits, to read a book together. For children 13 months and older, they are asked to build a tower of three cubes and have the child do the same. With a child of 19 months and older, the task includes building a tower with more cubes and having the child make a design with colored blocks that matches the block design cards. This task is always a little difficult for the child to complete on his or her own. This situation allows for an assessment of the parents' capacity to structure and mediate the environment according to the child's developmental and individual needs. Some of the tasks tap the child's emerging abilities and require adult cognitive scaffolding and emotional availability in order for the child to complete the task successfully. The child's attentional skills, persistence, and interest in complying with parental expectations in a structured situation are observed. The dyad's capacity for joint attention to an activity, reciprocity in negotiations, and mutuality may be assessed.

The introduction to the free play situation explains, "This is a free play time for you and your child. You or [child's name] may choose the toy or toys that you would like to play with together." These toys may include rattles, plastic keys, a cloth diaper or small blanket (for peek-a-boo), a busy box, two toy telephones, a ball, two small stuffed animals or puppets, a doll and bottle, small cars/trucks, and bristle blocks. The free play allows for an assessment of the parents' capacity to be playful with and enjoy their child, to facilitate their child's capacity for exploratory and representational play. In addition, the dyad's capacity for social interaction, mutuality, and reciprocity can be observed.

At the end of the instructions for the free play, parents also are given instructions for the separation/reunion episode. They are told, "We'd also like to see how things go for [child's name] when you leave the room. After 5 minutes of play I'll knock on the door but won't come in. Let [child's name] know that you're going to be leaving the room for a few minutes. Then please come stand outside the room for a few minutes with me." This situation allows assessment of the parents' ability and level of comfort in preparing the child for a brief separation. The child's capacity for self-regulation and quality of mood and exploratory play during the parents' absence is assessed. The dyad's quality of affect and engagement at reunion may also be observed.

Confirmatory factor analyses of 12-month free play interactions revealed eight subscales: Parent Subscale I, Parental Positive Affective Involvement and Verbalization; Parent Subscale II, Parental Negative Affect and Behavior; Parent Subscale III, Parental Intrusiveness, Insensitivity, and Inconsistency; Infant Subscale IV, Infant Positive Affect, Communicative and Social Skills; Infant Subscale V, Infant Quality of Play, Interest, and Attentional Skills; Infant Subscale VI, Infant Dysregulation and Irritability; Dyadic Subscale VII, Dyadic Mutuality and Reciprocity; Dyadic Subscale VIII, Dyadic Disorganization and Tension. Internal consistency of factors, interrater reliability, and predictive and discriminant validity have been established for the PCERA (Clark, 1999; Clark et al., 1993; Clark, Hyde, Essex, & Klein, 1997) in a number of studies with normative and high-risk populations. Training is recommended.

A video replay session, in which brief segments of the videotaped interactions are played back and viewed with the parents, is an important part of the assessment process. In a semistructured interview, the parents' perceptions, attitudes, and goals during the interactions with the child are assessed. Objective assessments often fail to answer questions about what parents are experiencing with the infant/child. The video replay interview allows parents to share what they were seeing, doing, and feeling in relation to the child and their perceptions of the child and themselves as parents. By "wondering along with the parents" about their perceptions, attitudes, and feelings about their child, the clinician can gain insights about parents' phenomenological experience of the parent-child relationship that influence their behavioral interactions with the child. Before the tape is replayed, parents are asked, "How was this interaction like or different from how things usually go at home for you and [child's name]?" "What was the most enjoyable part of this session for you?" "What part was the most difficult or did you like the least?" "Do you have any questions or comments about the taping?" During the replay, the clinician encourages the parents to share their subjective perception of the child's behavior and of themselves in the parenting role.

First, the meaning of the child to the parent is assessed by stopping the tape at a point when the child's face can be seen clearly on the screen. The clinician asks the parents, "I wonder who [child's name] looks like or reminds you of [physical features, temperament, behavior]?" "How did you select your child's name?" "How would you describe that person?" Then, parents' capacity to read their child's cues may be assessed by stopping the tape at a point when the parent is not responding to the child's cues, misinterpret cues, or has difficulty responding empathically. In addition, parents' capacity for reflective functioning is assessed, that is, the ability to reflect upon the internal affective experience of their child and themselves (Slade, 1999; Fonagy & Target, 1998). The clinician asks parents, "How were you feeling during that interaction?" "What do you think was going on for your child?" "What do you imagine your child may have been feeling then?" This process helps the clinician to assess parents' capacity to see the child as a separate individual and their ability to empathically read their child's cues. Parents' capacity for reflective functioning, that is, their ability to reflect upon the internal affective experience of their child and themselves, is assessed (Slade, 1999). In addition, the clinician can also help parents to expand their perceptions of their child and his or her behavior and increase their ways of being with their child by wondering with them about alternative explanations for the child's behavior.

To assess the reinforcement value of the child and parents' sense of competence in the parenting role, the clinician stops the tape at a point when parent and child are experiencing a mutually satisfying interaction and asks, "How do you think [child's name] felt at that moment?" Then the clinician asks parents what they think they did to elicit this positive response. The clinician offers additional observations that amplify parents' strengths in reading their child's needs and responding in a developmentally sensitive manner. Additional questions in this video replay interview to inform the clinician about parents' experience of parenting this child include, "How would you describe yourself as a parent?" "In general, what have you found most difficult or frustrating about being a parent?" "What have you found most enjoyable about being a parent?" "When do you feel best, or that you have done well as a parent?" "Did becoming a parent change you as a person in any way? How?"

Finally, it is extremely valuable to obtain a relational history from each parent to better understand their own template of being parented, or, their internal working model of relationships. The following questions may be asked during the video replay session or at a subsequent session: "How would you compare yourself to your own parents?" "What do you remember about being parented by your mother or father when you were young?" "What words would you use to describe your mother or father? Please give specific examples of these." "How was discipline handled in your family?" "Who was available/responsive to you?" "Who kept you safe, physically and emotionally (or did not)?"

REVIEW OF OTHER PARENT-CHILD INTERACTION ASSESSMENT METHODS

Still-Face Paradigm

The still-face procedure was developed to assess the synchronous nature of parent-child interactions. In the still-face procedure (Adamson & Frick, 2003; Tronick, Als, Adamson, Wise, & Brazelton, 1978), a parent is instructed to withdraw from interacting with the infant (by making a still or affectless facial expression) for a short period of time. The infant's affective and regulatory responses to the parent's affective withdrawal are observed. Based on the infant's re-

sponse, judgments are made regarding the infant's typical affective responding and history of experience with the parent. The Still-Face evaluates the reciprocity and achievement of mutual goals of mother-infant interactions, which are central to the infant's sense of well-being. These interactional goals include initiation of interaction, mutual orientation greetings, exchange of affect, and mutual disengagement.

According to Cohn and Tronick (1989), face-to-face interactions between parents and children are regulated mutually, with parent and child each contributing to the interaction. Infants learn to adjust their own affective and regulatory states to match those of the parent, and vice versa. Ideally, over time, these exchanges become increasingly synchronous, with each member reading and responding to the other's cues. In less than ideal circumstances, the parent may not participate successfully in the affective interchange, and may send poorly matched emotional and reactive messages to the child. The child may respond by engaging in regulation that is more self-directed than relational, finding comfort in sucking, turning away, and rocking. While the domains assessed have relevance for clinical intervention, the Still-Face procedure is primarily a research paradigm.

Nursing Child Assessment Satellite Training

The Nursing Child Assessment Satellite Training (NCAST) Teaching and Feeding Scales assess mother and child behaviors on 149 variables: 76 in the Feeding Scale and 73 in the Teaching Scale (Barnard, 1979; Kelly & Barnard, 2000). Designed for use with infants and yhoung children up to 36 months of age, the NCAST scales have been widely used with infants at risk due to such circumstances as prematurity, failure to thrive, and maltreatment (Farran, Clark, & Ray, 1990). The NCAST has also been used to measure the quality of mother and child interactions in samples of children with developmental delays and social-economic disadvantages (Barnard, 1994). During feeding and teaching activities, the absence or presence of behaviors are rated, indicating the mother's sensitivity to the child's cues, responsiveness to the child's distress, and ability to foster of social-emotional and cognitive growth.

Half of the items in each scale tap into the dyad's capacity for reciprocity and contingent responsiveness, considered central to learning developmental tasks. Children's behaviors are rated for clarity and responsiveness to the caregiver. The teaching scales are more strongly correlated with cognitive development than the feeding scales, and have predictive validity when examining children's language and cognitive outcomes at 3 and 5 years of age. Although the domains of parental functioning in the NCAST are central to positive parent-child interactions and early childhood social-emotional development, use of the NCAST scales in mental health settings may be limited by presence/absence ratings, reducing the possibility of measuring incremental change with therapeutic intervention. Training is recommended.

HOME Inventory for Families of Infants and Toddlers

The HOME Inventory for Families of Infants and Toddlers (Caldwell & Bradley, 1978) was developed to examine the quality of stimulation and interaction in the young child's home environment. In particular, the measure focuses on cognitive and social-emotional stimulation with materials and the quality of parent-child interaction. The protocol is completed by a single observer interview in the child's home. The observer-interviewer asks the parent questions and observes aspects of the setting and parent-child interaction. The interview is not standardized, to allow parents to feel more at ease in the process. The assessment needs to be administered while the child is awake and at least one parent is available. The HOME takes approximately an hour to administer, and items are scored "yes" or "no."

While the HOME was not standardized on a diverse sample, subsequent use with varied samples has established its utility with children and families from a variety of backgrounds. The HOME correlates substantially with measures of cognitive development (.72 with the Stanford-Binet at 36 months) and has sufficient test-retest reliability. Strengths of this assessment include its ease of use and predictive validity of cognitive development.

Emotional Availability Scales

The Emotional Availability Scales (EAS), Third Edition (Biringen, Robinson, & Emde, 1998), assesses the emotional availability of the parent for the child, and the child for the parent. Parental sensitivity, structuring, nonintrusiveness, and nonhostility are assessed in the context of a parent-infant interaction. Children are observed for their responsiveness and involvement with parents. The EAS uses global ratings, taking the context into account, to make clinical judgments about the quality of behavioral interactions.

Contemporary theory sets forth two main adaptive roles for emotion: approach/avoidance motivation and signaling intent/communication (Emde, 2000). Regulation is needed to optimize emotional functioning. Emotional availability emerged as a relationship construct, in which members of dyadic interchange (e.g., parent and child) engage in reciprocal interactions, which, ideally, become smoother over time. The EAS has been found to be associated with security of attachment (Biringen, 2000).

Clinical Problem-Solving Procedure

The Clinical Problem-Solving Procedure, developed by Crowell and Feldman (1988), is based on the "tool-use task" (Matas, Arend, & Sroufe, 1978). Crowell asserts that mental health problems are not found "within the infant" (Crowell & Fleischmann, 1989). In examining parent-child interaction problems, she cites several essential elements: It is important that the behavior of the parent and child be observed directly, and that the child's age and developmental level be taken into account. The assessment needs to be short and simple, with an uncomplicated scoring scheme. Finally, it should allow parental match to child developmental level to be observed, and the activities should reflect everyday life. The Crowell procedure consists of nine episodes consisting of free play, cleanup, bubbles, four teaching tasks, separation, and reunion. In this procedure adapted for infants, the parent is given a variety of common toys and activities and instructed to play with the child. The teaching activities are increasingly difficult, and the last two are technically beyond the child's developmental capacities.

Strange Situation

The Strange Situation (SS) was developed by Ainsworth (Ainsworth et al., 1978) to assess the quality of the security of the child's attachment to the parent, and its use as a reliable research instrument is widely accepted. However, as a clinical assessment tool, the SS has several limitations. The SS makes its determination of attachment security entirely from the child's behavior, primarily from the child's behavior during reunion with the mother. Additionally, because the SS capitalizes on fear of strangers, which becomes salient at about 6 months of age, use of the SS is limited to the end of the child's first year and about halfway through the second year. While the concept of the SS is to activate the attachment system using a moderately stressful situation, for some children the scenario is very stressful, possibly highlighting differences in temperamental proneness to distress and not solely attachment (Kagan, 1998). For others, who have been in large-group day care from an early age, being left by the parent and the introduction of a stranger may not be novel at all and thus not experienced as very stressful (Clarke-Stewart, 2001).

Parenting Stress Index

The Parenting Stress Index (PSI) is a 120-item, self-report inventory measuring the parent's perception of specific areas of stress in the parent-infant relationship (Abidin, 1986). The PSI measures variables of stress within the child domain, parent domain, and other life circumstances domain. Child domain subscales include measuring to what extent the child is experienced as acceptable, reinforcing, demanding, adaptable, unhappy, and distractible/hyperactive. Parent domain subscales measure to what extent the parent feels stress associated with attachment to the child, feeling competent in the parenting role, restricted in roles, depressed, socially isolated, healthy, and satisfied with the spousal relationship. The other life circumstances domain assigns a stress value to situations such as divorce, changes in income, and pregnancy. Except for the Life Stress Scale, items are scored on a 5-point scale (from 1 = strongly agree to 5 = strongly disagree). For the other life circumstances items, the respondent simply indicates whether a specific life event has occurred within the past 12 months. A total stress score is calculated by combining the scores from the child and parent domains. Scores within the clinical range on the Attachment Scale indicate that the parent may not feel emotionally connected to the child or that the parent has difficulty reading the child's cues and meeting his or her needs. The other subscales provide additional information about child and parent factors that may contribute to disturbances in the parent-child relationship.

Working Model of the Child Interview

The Working Model of the Child Interview (WMCI; Zeanah & Barton, 1989) systematically examines parental perceptions of their infant. An hour-long interview, the WMCI has been found to be correlated with the child's behavior in the Strange Situation and with mother-child interactive behavior (Benoit, Parker, & Zeanah, 1997; Zeanah, Benoit, Hirschberg, Barton, & Regan, 1994; Zeanah & Barton, 1989) and has been adapted for use in clinical settings (Zeanah & Benoit, 1995; Zeanah, Larrieu, Heller, & Valliere, 2000). Narrative features emerge that are considered to be clinical indices of the nature of the parents' experience of the child. These include richness of perception, openness to change, coherence, intensity of involvement, caregiving sensitivity, acceptance/rejection, infant difficulty, and fear of loss. The parents' affective tone and organization of the narrative are also considered and are classified as either balanced, disengaged, or distorted (Zeanah et al., 2000).

The Insightfulness Assessment

The Insightfulness Assessment (IA; Koren-Karie, Oppenheim, Dolev, Sher, Etzion-Carasso, 2002; Oppenheim, Koren-Karie, & Sagi, 2001) evaluates parents' capacity to empathically understand their children's internal experiences of the world. The IA involves videotaping the child and parent during a play activity. Subsequently the parent views segments of the videotape during an interview designed to assess his or her perspective about the child. Transcribed interviews are coded using 10 scales: insight into child's motives, openness, complexity in description of child, maintenance of focus on child, richness of description of child, coherence of thought, acceptance, anger, worry, and separateness from child. The scales provide the basis for 4 classifications: Positively Insightful, One-Sided, Disengaged, and Mixed. Although IA is a relatively new instrument, there is growing evidence to support its validity and reliability in differentiating securely attached parent-child dyads from insecurely attached dyads. Mothers classified as Positively Insightful have been associated with securely attached children while mothers identified as One-Sided tended to have insecure/ambivalent children and mothers in the Mixed classification had children with insecure/disorganized attachment patterns. Furthermore, these classifications have been found to be independent of parental educational level (Oppenheim & Koren-Karie, 2002). Finally, change in parental classification from noninsightful to insightful has been associated with improvement in preschool children's behavior following a therapeutic treatment program (Oppenheim, Goldsmith, & Koren-Karie, in press).

Adult Attachment Interview

The Adult Attachment Interview (AAI; George, Kaplan, & Main, 1996) is a semistructured hourlong interview method consisting of 18 questions used to classify a parent's state of mind with respect to attachment. Parents are asked to describe their salient early childhood relationship experiences, and to give five adjectives that best describe their relationship with each parent, then specific memories to support each adjective. Hesse (1999) describes the central task on this interview to be "producing and reflecting upon memories related to attachment while simultaneously maintaining coherent discourse with the interviewer" (pp. 396–397). The narrative is classified as either secure/autonomous, dismissive, preoccupied, or unresolved/disorganized. Parents' attachment classifications on the AAI have been found to be associated with their child's attachment behavior with that parent (VanIjzendoorn, 1995). Training in the coding of the AAI is required.

DIAGNOSIS OF RELATIONAL DISORDERS

Understanding the quality of the parent-infant relationship is an important part of developing a diagnostic profile for infants and young children. The primary relationships of infants and young children contribute not only to the development of children's personality and structure of psychological defenses but also to young children's beliefs about what is possible to expect in relationships with others.

The *DSM-IV* and Medical Diagnoses

The *Diagnostic and Statistical Manual of Mental Disorders* (*DSM-IV*; American Psychiatric Association, 1994), a multiaxial classification system developed to assist clinicians and researchers in the identification, study, and/or treatment of individuals with mental health problems, includes Axis I, clinical disorders; Axis II, personality disorders (used only for adult clients) and/or mental retardation (developmental delays in children); Axis III, general medical conditions; Axis IV, psychosocial and environmental stresses; and Axis V, global assessment of functioning. Several Axis I diagnoses address disturbances in the parent-child relationship. Reactive attachment disorder is defined as "markedly disturbed and developmentally inappropriate social relationships in most contexts that begins before age 5 years and is associated with grossly pathological care" (p. 116). The two subtypes include inhibited type and disinhibited type. The *DSM-IV* also describes rumination disorder as recurrent vomiting and feeding or eating disorder of infancy and early childhood as failure to eat adequate amounts of food without physiological causes; both are associated with lack of environmental stimulation and/or child neglect that constitute a disturbance in the parent-child relationship. Other *DSM-IV* diagnoses that may be associated with problems in the early parent-child relationship include separation anxiety, sleep disorders, oppositional defiant disorder, and expressive language disorder, as well as the V code of a parent-child relational problem. Although not found in the *DSM-IV* system, the medical diagnosis of a nonorganic failure to thrive has been associated with a disturbance in the parent-child relationship. This disorder is usually recognized by the child's pediatrician when a child who shows no other signs of illness demonstrates poor growth patterns that cannot be accounted for by parental growth patterns or further medical testing. Such patterns have been associated with caregiver deprivation and neglect. These children often manifest other signs of child neglect or maltreatment such as poor hygiene and/or frequent accidental injuries (Tunnessen, 1999). Table 3.3 illustrates several classification systems used for describing attachment disorders. Although these systems vary in their classification, each system describes a disturbance in the balance between the child's proximity seeking and exploration of the environment.

DC:0–3

The *Diagnostic Classification of Mental Health and Developmental Disorders of Infancy and Early Childhood* (DC:0–3; Zero to Three, 1994) is a multiaxial classification system designed to provide clinicians and researchers a diagnostic profile of an infant's or young child's functioning within the context of his or her caregiving environment. The axes include Axis I, primary classification; Axis II, relationship classification; Axis III, physical, neurological, developmental, and mental health disorders or conditions described in other classification systems; Axis IV, psychosocial stress; and Axis V, functional emotional developmental level.

Axis II describes parent-child relationship disorders as perceptions, attitudes, behaviors, and affects of the parent, the child, or both that result in disturbed interactions in a specific parent-child relationship. The parent may relate to the infant from the beginning in light of his or her own personality dynamics, including projections and defenses. These may interact with distinct infant characteristics and lead to relationship difficulties or disorders.

Diagnoses of relationship disturbances or disorders should be based not only on observed behavior but also on the parent's subjective experience of the child as expressed during a clinical interview. Where there are difficulties in the relationship, the intensity, frequency, and duration of the disturbance are the factors that guide the cli-

nician to classify the relationship problem as a perturbation, a disturbance, or a disorder (Anders, 1989). Within the DC:0–3 system, Axis II is used only to diagnose significant relationship difficulties. Infants with a primary diagnosis (Axis I) need not have a relationship diagnosis (Axis II). The relationship axis does not address the full range of relationships, from well adapted to disordered. Some parents may have tendencies in the directions described in Axis II—toward, for example, overinvolvement or hostility. Milder forms of relationship disorders may be triggered by the child's temperament or behavior, family dynamics, or other stresses that challenge parents' usual balance between nurturance and more problematic parental functioning. Clinicians are cautioned not to overdiagnose a relationship disorder when such milder and transient forms related to stress are observed. The clinician may want to keep the described categories in mind when they appear in milder or transient forms in order to understand the dynamics of the family and to guide intervention. Classifications include Overinvolved, Underinvolved, Anxious-Tense, Angry-Hostile, Mixed, or Abusive (Verbally Abusive, Physically Abusive, or Sexually Abusive Relationship).

The Parent-Infant Relationship Global Assessment Scale (PIR-GAS) is a rating scale used to determine the level of disturbance in a parent-child relationship on Axis II of the DC:0–3. The PIR-GAS covers a range of parent-infant relationship quality over time and can be used to describe the strengths of a relationship as well as to capture the severity of a relational disorder. These ratings range from well-adapted (90) to grossly impaired (10). A rating below 40 includes disordered, severely disordered, and grossly impaired relationships. These qualify for a relationship diagnosis based on the severity and pervasiveness of the dyad's difficulties. At these levels, the majority of the behaviors must be in evidence in an intense, ongoing, and persistent manner. For ratings between 70 and 40, the relationship tendencies or features may be usefully described, but are not severe enough to be considered a disorder.

Three aspects of a relationship are used in deciding whether a relationship disorder is present: (1) the behavioral quality of the interaction, (2) the affective tone, and (3) the psychological involvement of the parent with the child. When a

Table 3.3 Attachment Disturbances Classification Systems

System of Classification	Types	Manifestations
Strange Situation (Ainsworth et al., 1978; Main & Solomon, 1986)	Secure Insecure-avoidant Insecure-resistant Insecure-disorganized/disoriented	Securely attached infant explores environment while intermittently making visual or physical contacts with parent; seeks proximity of parent when distressed; reaches for and seeks comfort from parent following brief separation/reunion. Insecure-avoidant infants are upset when left with an unfamiliar person or in a strange setting. During the reunion, they may actively resist any attempts to be comforted by turning away and squirming to get down if picked up. Insecure-resistant infants have difficulty feeling comfortable in a strange situation; are more wary of strangers and tend to get more upset when the parent leaves the room; during separation/reunion show ambivalence to the parent, first approaching, then pushing the parent away. Insecure-disorganized/disoriented infants show an inconsistent mix approach and avoidance behavior when reunited with parents after a brief separation.
DSM-IV (American Psychiatric Association, 1994)	Reactive attachment disorder: Inhibited type Disinhibited type	Inhibited infants may appear apathetic, lack reciprocity in interactions, fail to visually track objects or faces, and/or fail to initiate or respond to social interactions. Disinhibited infants may indiscriminately express affection with strangers.
DC:0-3 (Center for Clinical Infant Programs)	Reactive attachment deprivation/maltreatment disorder of infancy and early childhood	Persistent neglect or abuse of a physical or psychological nature Inconsistent availability of primary caregiver Other environmental compromises that interfere with care of the child and stable attachment Infant/child fails to initiate social interactions; shows contradictory or ambivalent social responses; or shows inappropriate/indiscriminate social relatedness

(continued)

Table 3.3 Continued

System of Classification	Types	Manifestations
Zeanah & Boris (2000)	Nonattachment Disorders: Emotional withdrawal Indiscriminate sociability Self-endangerment Clinging/inhibited exploration Vigilance/hypercompliance Role reversal	Nonattached children with emotional withdrawal show little comfort-seeking behavior or environmental exploration; show no preference for a primary caregiver; may have depressive symptoms; found among institutionalized children. Nonattached children with indiscriminant sociability show no preference for a primary caregiver; seek comfort from any adult, including strangers; lack self-protection skills; found among institutionalized children. Attachment disorder with self-endangerment is seen in children who do not seek the protective proximity of a primary caregiver; engage in impulsive, aggressive, or risky behavior; and is associated with family violence Attachment disorder with clinging/inhibited exploration is seen in children who appear anxious and do not explore their environment when with primary caregiver in a novel environment. Attachment disorder with vigilance/hypercompliance is seen in children who show little or no exploration of the environment, have a constricted mostly serious affect, and demonstrate fear of and excessive compliance to parental directives. Associated with harsh or intrusive parenting practices Attachment disorder with role reversal is seen in children who focus on taking care of the parent/caregiver. These children may present as excessively solicitous or excessively demanding with parents.

disorder exists, it is specific to a relationship (Steele, Steele, & Fonagy, 1996). The categories of relationship disorders described in Axis II of DC:0–3 are used only to diagnose significant relationship difficulties. The relationship axis does not address the full range of relationship quality, from well adapted to disordered. In other words, readers should be aware that an Axis II diagnostic classification is appropriate only when a clinician would rate the relationship being assessed as below 40 on the PIR-GAS.

The behavioral qualities and affective tone are required criteria for making a relational diagnosis, since these are observable and of sufficient concern to assess and treat. The quality of psychological involvement is presented to elaborate and guide the user to the possible dynamics related to the behaviors worthy of further exploration and treatment and is determined through an interview process with the parent, such as the ERA Video Replay Interview (Clark, 1985), the WMCI (Zeanah & Benoit, 1995), or the AAI (George, Kaplan, & Main, 1996) through identification of a parent's internal working model of relationships or "ghosts in the nursery" (Fraiberg, Adelson, & Shapiro, 1980).

Behavioral quality of the interaction is reflected in the behavior of each member of the parent-infant dyad. The behavior of the parent, the child, or both may be disturbed. Sensitivity or insensitivity in responding to the infant's cues, contingent or noncontingent responsivity, genuineness of involvement or concern, regulation, predictability, and the quality of structuring and mediating of the environment are parental behaviors that contribute to the quality of the interaction. Averting, avoiding, arching, lethargy, nonresponsiveness, and defiance are examples of behaviors that infants and toddlers may bring to the interaction. At times it is not clear whether the behaviors of concern are initiated or reactive. For instance, a mother or father may look depressed, uninvolved, or unresponsive with the young child. However, this may in part be a result of the unfocused gaze or other unresponsive, nonreinforcing behavior of a medically ill infant. Disturbances in infants and young children may also appear as delays in development (language, motor, cognition, or social-emotional) and may constrict the child's interactive capacities. These delays may be both the result of and contribute to the relationship disturbance.

Affective tone refers to the emotional tone characteristic of this dyad. Intense anxious/tense or negative affect (e.g., irritable, angry, hostile) on the part of either member of the dyad or both may contribute to the characteristic affective tone of the dyad. The concern here is the dysregulating function of intense or flat affect and the uncertainty as to what may happen next that is conveyed when intense affect is present.

Psychological involvement is focused on parental attitudes and perceptions of the child (i.e., the meaning of the child's behavior to the parents). The parents' image of a caregiving relationship developed from past experiences in early childhood relationships often influences their perceptions of a particular child and what can be expected in a relationship. Disturbing or adverse past relationship experiences may result in a parent misinterpreting and projecting these feelings onto the infant; for example, the parent may misinterpret certain behaviors of the infant as demanding, negative, or attacking (Zero to Three, 1994).

INTEGRATING CULTURALLY SENSITIVE APPROACHES

The integration of culturally sensitive approaches into the assessment of the parent-child relationship is critical to obtaining an accurate picture of the child in the context of his or her family, community, and larger sociocultural environment. The meaning of the child and his or her behavior to the parents as well as the parents' response to the child will be colored by the parents' cultural lenses. Most multicultural experts agree that culturally competent clinical assessments and interventions include examining one's own cultural beliefs and biases, acquiring knowledge about the family's culture, and developing culturally congruent clinical skills (Johnson-Powell, 1997). For more information about cultural issues, see chapter 2.

CONCLUSION

In conclusion, assessment of the parent-child relationship and, when indicated, diagnosis of a relationship disturbance or disorder is an important component, if not the centerpiece, of a clinical assessment of mental health in the infant or young child. Involving parents in the process of assessing their relationship with their child allows parents to become collaborative partners in the intervention process. Parents who take an active role in the assessment process and who feel their concerns have been heard and understood by the clinician are more likely to engage in the assessment and therapeutic process. By conducting interrelated assessments of each member of the parent-child dyad as well as the dyadic unit, the clinician obtains information that is essential to developing treatment goals and intervention strategies. Goals should be developed collaboratively with parents for the child and each parent-child relationship. When assessing the infant or young child in the context of the caregiving environment, it is critical that the process include the acquisition of information from others such as day care providers, pediatricians, parents' mental health providers, early intervention programs, social services, alcohol and other drug addictions treatment providers, and the court system. It has been our experience that the most successful interventions involve coordination of services across settings with regular communication. Depending upon the needs of the particular dyad, focused intervention strategies may be incorporated into the therapeutic education process. Empathically listening to the parents' own struggles and reflecting their feelings and concerns enhances the therapeutic relationship between clinician and parent. Finally, assessing the quality of the parent-child relationship should be an ongoing process, because early childhood is a time of rapid change, and the needs of the parent-child dyad will change as the relationship evolves.

As identified by First and his colleagues (2002), there is a need for universally accepted procedures for assessing relationship disorders across the life span, such as parent-infant, parent-toddler, and so on. Future research efforts should establish the validity and reliability of these methods in differentiating normative relational patterns from pathological relationship patterns as well as categorizing symptomatology and behavioral observations to define various syndromes of relationship disturbances (Lyons-Ruth, 1995).

A universally accepted nosology will facilitate research in the etiology and developmental trajectory of the disorders as well as the effectiveness of various intervention approaches.

References

Abidin, R. R. (1986). *Parenting stress index manual* (2nd ed.). Charlottesville, VA: Pediatric Psychology Press.

Adamson, L. B., & Frick, J. E. (2003). The still-face: A history of a shared experimental paradigm. *Infancy, 4*, 451–473.

Ainsworth, M. (1969). Object relations, dependency, and attachment: A theoretical review of the infant-mother relationship. *Child Development, 40*(4), 969–1025.

Ainsworth, M. D. S., & Bell, S. M. (1975). Mother-infant interaction and the development of competence. In K. Connolly & J. Bruner (Eds.), *The growth of competence* (pp. 97–118). New York: Academic Press.

Ainsworth, M. D. S., Blehar, M. C., & Waters, E. (1978). *Patterns of attachment: A psychological study of the strange situation*. Hillsdale, NJ: Lawrence Erlbaum.

American Academy of Child and Adolescent Psychiatry (1997). Practice parameters for the psychiatric assessment of infants and toddlers (0–36 months). *Journal of the American Academy of Child and Adolescent Psychiatry, 36*(10, Suppl.), 21S–36S.

American Psychiatric Association (1994). *Diagnostic and statistical manual of mental disorders* (4th ed.). Washington, DC: Author.

Anders, T. F. (1989). Clinical syndromes, relationship disturbances and their assessment. In A. J. Sameroff & R. N. Emde (Eds.), *Relationship disturbances in early childhood: A developmental approach* (pp. 125–144). New York: Basic Books.

Arcus, D. (2001). Inhibited and uninhibited children: Biology in the social context. In T. Wachs & G. Kohnstamm (Eds.), *Temperament in context* (pp. 43–60). Mahwah, NJ: Lawrence Erlbaum.

Bandura, A. (1977). *Social learning theory*. Englewood Cliffs, NJ: Prentice-Hall.

Bandura, A. (1989). Human agency in social cognitive theory. *American Psychologist, 44*, 1175–1184.

Barnard, K. E. (1994). What the Feeding Scale measures. In G. S. Sumner & A. Spietz (Eds.), *NCAST: Caregiver/parent-interaction feeding manual* (pp. 98–121). Seattle: University of Washington NCAST Publications.

Barnard, K. E. (1979). *Instructor's learning resource manual.* Seattle: NCAST Publications, University of Washington.

Baumrind, D. (1971). Current patterns of parental authority. *Developmental Psychology Monographs, 4*(1, Part 2), 1–103.

Beardslee, W. R., Bemporad, J., Keller, M. B., & Klerman, G. L. (1983). Children of parents with major affective disorder: A review. *American Journal of Psychiatry, 140*(7), 825–832.

Beckwith, L. (1976). Caregiver-infant interaction and early cognitive development in preterm infants. *Child Development, 47*(3), 579–587.

Benoit, D., Parker, K. C. H., & Zeanah, C. H. (1997). Mothers' representations of their infants assessed prenatally: Stability and association with infants' attachment classifications. *Journal of Child Psychology and Psychiatry and Allied Disciplines, 38*(3), 307–313.

Biringen, Z. (2000). Emotional availability: Conceptualization and research findings. *American Journal of Orthopsychiatry, 70*(1), 104–114.

Biringen, Z., Robinson, J., & Emde, R. N. (1998). *The Emotional Availability Scales* (3rd ed.). Unpublished manual. Colorado State University, Fort Collins.

Bowlby, J. (1951). Maternal care and mental health. *Bulletin of the World Health Organization, 3,* 355–533.

Bowlby, J. (1969). Disruption of affectional bonds and its effects on behavior. *Canada's Mental Health Supplement, 59,* 12.

Bowlby, J. (1982). *Attachment* (2nd ed., Vol. 1). New York: Basic Books.

Bretherton, I. (1985). Attachment theory: Retrospect and prospect. In I. Bretherton & E. Waters (Eds.), *Growing points of attachment theory and research. Monographs of the Society for Research in Child Development,* Vol. 50 (1–2, Serial No. 209, pp. 3–35). Chicago: University of Chicago Press.

Bromwich, R. (1976). Focus on maternal behavior in infant intervention. *American Journal of Orthopsychiatry, 46*(3), 439–446.

Bronfenbrenner, U., & Morris, P. (1998). The ecology of developmental processes. In R. M. Lerner (Ed.), *Theory* (5th ed., Vol. 1, pp. 993–1028). New York: Wiley.

Bruner, J. (1974). Continuity of learning. *School Psychology Digest, 3*(3), 20–25.

Bruner, J. (1975). From communication to language: A psychological perspective. *Cognition, 3*(3), 255–287.

Cadman, D., Boyle, M., Szatmari, P., & Offord, D. R. (1987). Chronic illness, disability, and mental and social well-being: Findings of the Ontario Child Health Study. *Pediatrics, 79*(5), 805–813.

Caldwell, B. M., & Bradley, R. H. (1978). *Manual for the home observation for measurement of the environment.* Little Rock: University of Arkansas.

Carlson, E. A. (1998). A prospective longitudinal study of attachment disorganization/disorientation. *Child Development, 69*(4), 1107–1128.

Carson, D., & Schauer, R. (1992). Mothers of children with asthma: Perceptions of parenting stress and the mother-child relationship. *Psychological Reports, 71*(3, pt 2), 1139–1148.

Cassidy, J., & Berlin, L. J. (1994). The insecure/ambivalent pattern of attachment: Theory and research. *Child Development, 65,* 971–991.

Chapieski, M. L., & Evankovich, K. D. (1997). Behavioral effects of prematurity. *Seminars in Perinatology, 21,* 221–239.

Chess, S., & Thomas, A. (1990). Continuities and discontinuities in temperament. In L. N. Robins & M. Rutter (Eds.), *Straight and devious pathways from childhood to adulthood* (pp. 205–220). New York: Cambridge University Press.

Cicchetti, D. (1987). Developmental psychopathology in infancy: Illustration from the study of maltreated youngsters. *Journal of Consulting and Clinical Psychology, 55*(6), 837–845.

Clark, R. (1983). *Interactions of psychiatrically ill and well mothers and their young children: Quality of maternal care and child competence.* Unpublished doctoral dissertation, Northwestern University.

Clark, R. (1985). *The parent-child early relational assessment.* Instrument and manual. Madison, WI: Department of Psychiatry, University of Wisconsin Medical School.

Clark, R. (1999). The parent-child early relational assessment: A factorial validity study. *Educational and Psychological Measurement, 59*(5), 821–846.

Clark, R., Hyde, J. S., Essex, M. J., & Klein, M. H. (1997). Length of maternity leave and quality of mother-infant interactions. *Child Development, 68*(2), 364–383.

Clark, R., Paulson, A., & Conlin, S. (1993). Assessment of developmental status and parent-infant relationships. In C. H. Zeanah, Jr. (Ed.), *Handbook of infant mental health* (pp. 191–209). New York: Guilford Press.

Clark, R., Tluczek, A., & Wenzel, A. (2003). Psychotherapy for postpartum depression: A preliminary report. *American Journal of Orthopsychiatry, 73*(4), 441–454.

Clarke-Stewart, K. A. (1973). Interactions between mothers and their young children: Characteristics and consequences. *Monographs of the Society for Research in Child Development, 38*(6–7, Serial No. 153).

Clarke-Stewart, A. (2001). Day care and the strange situation. In A. Goncu & E. L. Klein (Eds.), *Children in play, story, and school* (pp. 241–266). New York: Guilford Press.

Cohen, N. J., Lojkasek, M., Muir, E., Muir, R., & Parker, C. J. (2002). Six-month follow-up of two mother-infant psychotherapies: Convergence of therapeutic outcomes. *Infant Mental Health Journal, 23*(4), 361–380.

Cohn, J. F., & Tronick, E. (1989). Specificity of infants' response to mothers' affective behavior. *Journal of the American Academy of Child and Adolescent Psychiatry, 28*(2), 242–248.

Committee on the Family, Group for the Advancement of Psychiatry (1995). A model for the classification and diagnosis of relational disorders. *Psychiatric Services, 46*(9): 926–931.

Cox, S. M., Hopkins, J., & Hans, S. (2000). Attachment in preterm infants and their mothers: Neonatal risk status and maternal representations. *Infant Mental Health Journal, 21,* 464–480.

Crockenberg, S. B. (1981). Infant irritability, mother responsiveness, and social support influences on the security of infant-mother attachment. *Child Development, 52,* 857–865.

Crowell, J., & Feldman, S. (1988). Mothers' internal models of relationships and children's behavioral and developmental status: A study of mother-child interaction. *Child Development, 59,* 1273–1285.

Crowell, J., & Fleischmann, M. A. (1989). Use of structured research procedure in clinical assessments of infants. In C. H. Zeanah, Jr. (Ed.), *Handbook of infant mental health* (pp. 210–221). New York: Guilford Press.

Cummings, E. M., & Davies, P. T. (1994). Maternal depression and child development. *Journal of Child Psychology and Psychiatry, 35,* 73–112.

Emde, R. N. (1989). The infant's relationship experience: Developmental and affective aspects. In A. J. Sameroff & R. N. Emde (Eds.), *Relationship disturbances in early childhood* (pp. 33–51). New York: Basic Books.

Emde, R.N. (2000). Next steps in emotional availability research. *Attachment and Human Development, 2*(2), 242–248.

Epstein, A. S., & Evans, J. (1979). Parent-child interaction and children's learning. *High/Scope Annual Report, 4,* 39–43.

Farran, D., Clark, K., & Ray, A. (1990). Measures of parent-child interaction. In E. Gibbs & D. Teti (Eds.), *Interdisciplinary assessment of infants: A guide for early intervention professionals* (pp. 227–247). Baltimore: Paul H. Brooks.

Field, T. (1997). The treatment of depressed mothers and their infants. In L. Murray & P. J. Cooper (Eds.), *Postpartum depression and child development* (pp. 221–235). New York: Guilford Press.

Field, T., Healy, B., Goldstein, S., & Guthertz, M. (1990). Behavior-state matching and synchrony in mother-infant interactions of nondepressed versus depressed dyads. *Developmental Psychology, 26*(1), 7–14.

Fiese, B. H., Poehlmann, J., Irwin, M., Gordon, M., & Curry-Bleggi, E. (2001). A pediatric screening instrument to detect problematic infant-parent interactions: Initial reliability and validity in a sample of high- and low-risk infants. *Infant Mental Health Journal, 22*(4), 463–478.

First, M. B., Bell, C. C., Cuthbert, B., Krystal, J. H., Malison, R., Offord, D. R., Reiss, D., Shea, T., Widiger, T., & Wisner, K. L. (2002). Personality disorders and relational disorders: A research agenda for addressing crucial gaps in DSM. In D. J. Kupfer, M. B. First, & D. A. Regier (Eds.), *A research agenda for DSM-V* (pp. 123–199). Washington, DC: American Psychiatric Association.

Fonagy, P., & Target, M. (1998). Mentalization and the changing aims of child psychoanalysis. *Psychoanalytic Dialogues, 8*(1), 87–114.

Fraiberg, S., Adelson, E., & Shapiro, V. (1980). Ghosts in the nursery: A psychoanalytic approach of impaired infant-mother relationships. In S. Fraiberg (Ed.) in collaboration with L. Fraiberg, *Clinical studies in infant mental health: The first year of life* (pp. 164–196). New York: Basic Books.

Freud, A. (1963). The concept of developmental lines. *The Psychoanalytic Study of the Child, 18,* 245–265.

Freud, A. (1970). The concept of the rejecting mother. In E. J. Anthony & T. Benedek (Eds.), *Parenthood: Its psychology and psychopathology* (pp. 376–409). London: Little, Brown.

George, C., Kaplan, N., & Main, M. (1996). *Adult attachment interview protocol* (3rd ed.). Unpublished manuscript. University of California, Berkeley.

George, C., & Solomon, J. (1996). Representational models of relationships: Links between caregiving and attachment. *Infant Mental Health Journal, 17*(3), 198–216.

Goldberg, S., Washington, J., Morris, P., Fisher-Fay, A., & Simmons, R. J. (1990). Early diagnosed chronic illness and mother-child relationships in the first two years. *Canadian Journal of Psychiatry, 35*(9), 726–733.

Goodman, S. H., & Brumley, E. H. (1990). Schizophrenic and depressed mothers: Relational deficits in parenting. *Developmental Psychology, 26*(1), 31–39.

Goodman, S. H., & Gotlib, I. H. (1999). Risk for psychopathology in the children of depressed mothers: A developmental model for understanding mechanisms of transmission. *Psychological Review, 106*(3), 458–490.

Hesse, E. (1999). Adult attachment interview. In J. Cassidy & P. R. Shaver (Eds.), *Handbook of attachment: Theory, research and clinical applications* (pp. 395–433). New York: Guilford Press.

Johnson-Powell, G. (1997). The culturologic interview: Cultural, social, and linguistic issues in the assessment and treatment of children. In G. Johnson-Powell & J. Yamamoto (Eds.), *Transcultural child development: Psychological assessment and treatment* (pp. 349–364). New York: John Wiley & Sons.

Kagan, J. (1998). Biology and the child. In N. Eisenberg (Ed.), *Handbook of child psychology: Vol. 3 Social, emotional and personality development* (5th ed., pp. 177–236). New York: John Wiley & Sons.

Kelly, J. F., & Barnard, K. E. (2000). Assessment of parent-child interaction: Implications for early intervention. In J. P. Shonkoff & S. J. Meisels (Eds.), *Handbook of early childhood intervention* (pp. 258–289). New York: Cambridge University Press.

Kennell, J. H., & Rolnick, A. (1960). Discussing problems in newborn babies with their parents. *Pediatrics, 26*, 832–838.

Kilmer, R. P., Cowen, E. L., & Wyman, P. A. (2001). A micro-level analysis of developmental, parenting, and family milieu variables that differentiate stress-resilient and stress-affected children. *Journal of Community Psychology, 29*(4), 391–416.

Klaus, M. H., & Kennell, J. H. (1970). Mothers separated from newborn infants. *Pediatric Clinics of North America, 17*, 1015–1037.

Klaus, M. H., Jerauld, R., Kreger, N., McAlpine, W., Steffa, M., & Kennell, J. H. (1972). Maternal attachment: Importance of the first post-partum days. *New England Journal of Medicine, 286*, 460–463.

Kochanska, G. (1997). Mutually responsive orientation between mothers and their young children: Implications for early socialization. *Child Development, 68*(1), 94–112.

Koren-Karie, N., Oppenheim, D., Dolev, S., Sher, E., & Etzion-Carasso, A. (2002). Mothers' insightfulness regarding their infant's internal experience: Relations with maternal sensitivity and infant attachment. *Developmental Psychology, 38*(4), 534–542.

Leve, L. D., Scaramella, L. V., & Fagot, B. I. (2001). Infant temperament, pleasure in parenting and marital happiness in adoptive families. *Infant Mental Health Journal, 22*(5), 545–558.

Lieberman, A. (1985). Infant mental health: A model for service delivery. *Journal of Clinical Child Psychology, 14*(3), 196–201.

Lieberman, A. F., & Zeanah, C. H. (1995). Disorders of attachment in infancy. In K. Minde (Ed.), *Infant psychiatry: Child and adolescent psychiatric clinics of North America* (pp. 571–587). Philadelphia: Saunders.

Lyons-Ruth, K. (1995). Broadening our conceptual frameworks: Can we reintroduce relational strategies and implicit representational systems to the study of psychopathology? *Developmental Psychology, 31*(3), 432–436.

Lyons-Ruth, K., Easterbrooks, M. A., & Cibelli, C. D. (1997). Infant attachment strategies, infant mental lag, and maternal depressive symptoms: Predictors of internalizing and externalizing problems at age 7. *Developmental Psychology, 33*(4), 681–692.

Lyons-Ruth, K., Lyubchik, A., Wolfe, R., & Bronfman, E. (2002). Parental depression and child attachment: Hostile and helpless profiles of parent and child behavior among families at risk. In S. H. Goodman & I. H. Gotlib (Eds.), *Children of depressed parents: Mechanisms of risk and implications for treatment* (pp. 89–120). Washington, DC: American Psychological Association.

Lyons-Ruth, K., Zoll, D., Connell, D., & Grunebaum, H. U. (1986). The depressed mother and her one-year-old infant: Environment, interaction, attachment, and infant development. *New Directions for Child Development, 34*, 61–82.

Mahler, M. (1968). *On human symbiosis and the vicissitude of individuation.* New York: International Universities Press.

Mahler, M. (1975). On the current status of the infantile neurosis. *Journal of the American Psychoanalytic Association, 23*(2), 327–333.

Main, M., Kaplan, N., & Cassidy, J. (1985). Security in infancy, childhood, and adulthood: A move to the level of representation. *Monographs of the Society for Research in Child Development, 50*(Series No. 209), 66–104.

Main, M., & Solomon, J. (1986). Discovery of an insecure-disorganized/disoriented attachment pattern. In T. B. Brazelton & M. Yogman (Eds.), *Affective development in infancy* (pp. 95–124). Westport, CT: Ablex.

Mangelsdorf, S., Gunnar, M., Kestenbaum, R., Lang, S., & Andreas, D. (1990). Infant proneness-to-distress temperament, maternal personality, and mother-infant attachment: Associations and goodness-of-fit. *Child Development, 61,* 820–831.

Martins, C., & Gaffan, E. A. (2000). Effects of early maternal depression on patterns of infant-mother attachment: A meta-analytic investigation. *Journal of Child Psychology and Psychiatry and Allied Disciplines, 41*(6), 737–746.

Matas, L., Arend, R. A., & Sroufe, L. A. (1978). Continuity of adaptation in the second year: The relationship between quality of attachment and later competence. *Child Development, 49*(3), 547–556.

Minuchin, S. (1974). *Families and family therapy.* Cambridge, MA: Harvard University Press.

Minuchin, S., & Fishman, H. C. (1981). *Family therapy techniques.* Cambridge, MA: Harvard University Press.

Mothander, P. R. (1990). The first year of life: Predictive patterns of infant development, maternal adjustment, and mother-infant interaction. Unpublished doctoral dissertation, Uppsala University, Uppsala, Sweden.

Musick, J. S., Clark, R., & Cohler, B. J. (1981). The Mothers' Project: A clinical research program for mentally ill mothers and their young children. In B. Weissbourd & J. Musick (Eds.), *The Social and Caregiving Environments of Infants* (pp. 111–127). Washington, DC: National Association for the Education of Young Children.

NICHD Early Child Care Research Network. (1999). Child care and mother-child interaction in the first 3 years of life. *Developmental Psychology, 35*(6), 1399–1413.

Northam, E. A. (1997). Psychosocial impact of chronic illness in children. *Journal of Pediatrics and Child Health, 33,* 369–372.

Oppenheim, D., Goldsmith, D., & Koren-Karie, N. (in press). Maternal insightfulness and preschoolers' emotion and behavior problems: Reciprocal influences in a therapeutic preschool program. *Infant Mental Health Journal.*

Oppenheim, D., & Koren-Karie, N. (2002). Mothers' insightfulness regarding their children's internal worlds: The capacity underlying secure child-mother relationships. *Infant Mental Health Journal, 23*(6), 593–605.

Oppenheim, D., Koren-Karie, N., & Sagi, A. (2001). Mother's empathic understanding of their preschoolers' internal experience: Relations with early attachment. *International Journal of Behavioral Development, 25*(1), 16–26.

Patterson, G. R. (1982). *Coercive family process.* Eugene, OR: Castalia.

Poehlmann, J., & Fiese, B. (2001). The interaction of maternal and infant vulnerabilities on developing attachment relationships. *Development and Psychopathology, 13*(1), 1–11.

Radke-Yarrow, M., Nottelmann, E., Martinez, P., Fox, M. B., & Belmont, B. (1992). Young children of affectively ill parents: A longitudinal study of psychosocial development. *Journal of the American Academy of Child and Adolescent Psychiatry, 31*(1), 68–77.

Rutter, M. (1974). Parent-child separation: Psychological effects of children. *Psychiatrie de l'Enfant, 17*(2): 479–514.

Sameroff, A. (1975). Early influences on development: Fact or fancy? *Merrill-Palmer Quarterly, 21*(4), 267–294.

Sameroff, A., & Emde, R. (1989) *Relationship disturbances in early childhood: A developmental approach.* New York: Basic Books.

Sander, L. (1962). Issues in early mother-child interaction. *Journal of the American Academy of Child Psychiatry, 1,* 141–166.

Sander, L. (1964). Adaptive relationships of early mother-child interaction. *Journal of the American Academy of Child Psychiatry, 3,* 221–263.

Schore, A. N. (2001). Effects of a secure attachment relationship on right brain development, affect regulation, and infant mental health. *Infant Mental Health Journal, 22*(1–2), 7–66.

Sharp, D., Hay, D. F., Pawlby, S., Schmucker, G., Allen, H., & Kumar, R. (1995). The impact of postnatal depression on boys' intellectual development. *Journal of Child Psychology and*

Psychiatry and Allied Disciplines, 36(8), 1315–1336.

Simmons, R., Goldberg, S., Washington, J., Fischer-Fay, A., & Maclusky, I. (1995). Infant-mother attachment and nutrition in children with cystic fibrosis. *Journal of Developmental and Behavioral Pediatrics, 16*(3), 183–186.

Slade, A. (1999). Attachment theory and research: Implications for the theory and practice of individual psychotherapy with adults. In J. Cassidy & P. R. Shaver (Eds.), *Handbook of attachment: Theory, research and clinical applications* (pp. 575–594). New York: Guilford Press.

Spitz, R. (1965). *The first year of life: A psychoanalytic study of normal and deviant development of object relations.* Oxford, England: International Universities Press.

Sroufe, L. A. (1979). Socioemotional development. In J. D. Osofsky (Ed.), *The handbook of infant development* (pp. 462–515). New York: John Wiley & Sons.

Sroufe, L. (1988). The role of infant-caregiver attachment in development. In J. Belsky & T. Nezworski (Eds.), *Clinical implications of attachment* (pp. 18–38). Hillsdale, NJ: Lawrence Erlbaum.

Steele, H., Steele, M., & Fonagy, P. (1996). Associations among attachment classifications of mothers, fathers and their infants: Evidence for a relationship-specific perspective. *Child Development, 67*(2), 541–555.

Stern, D. (1985). *The interpersonal world of the infant.* New York: Basic Books.

Stern, D. (2002). *The first relationship: Mother and infant.* Cambridge: Harvard University Press.

Stern, G., Caldwell, B. M., Hersher, L., Lipton, E. L., & Richmond, J. B. (1969). A factor analytic study of the mother-infant dyad. *Child Development, 40*(1), 163–181.

Teti, D. M., Nakagawa, M., Das, R., & Wirth, O. (1991). Security of attachment between preschoolers and their mothers: Relations among social interaction, parenting stress, and mother's sorts of the attachment Q-set. *Developmental Psychology, 27*(3), 440–447.

Thomas, J. M., Chess, S., & Birch, H. G. (1968). *Temperament and behavior disorders in children.* New York: New York University Press.

Tronick, E. Z., Als, H., Adamson, L., Wise, S., & Brazelton, T. B. (1978). The infant's response to entrapment between contradictory messages in face-to-face interaction. *Journal of the American Academy of Child Psychiatry, 17,* 1–13.

Tronick, E. Z., & Cohn, J. F. (1989). Infant-mother face-to-face interaction: Age and gender differences in coordination and the occurrence of miscoordination. *Child Development, 60*(1), 85–92.

Tronick, E. Z., & Weinberg, M. K. (1997). Depressed mothers and infants: Failure to form dyadic states of consciousness. In L. Murray & P. Cooper (Eds.), *Postpartum depression and child development* (pp. 54–81). New York: Guilford Press.

Tunnessen, W. W. (1999). *Signs and symptoms in pediatrics* (3rd ed.). Philadelphia: Lippincott, Williams & Wilkins.

Van Ijzendoorn, M. (1995). Adult attachment representations, parental responsiveness, and infant attachment: A meta-analysis on the predictive validity of the adult attachment interview. *Psychological Bulletin, 117,* 387–403.

Vygotsky, L. S. (1978). *Mind in society: The development of higher psychological processes.* Cambridge, MA: Harvard University Press.

Wallander, J. L., & Varni, J. W. (1998). Effects of pediatric chronic physical disorders on child and family adjustment. *Journal of Child Psychology and Psychiatry, 39*(1), 29–46.

Weinberg, M. K., & Tronick, E. Z. (1992). Sex differences in emotional expression and affective regulation in 6-month old infants. [Abstract]. *Society for Pediatric Research, 31*(4), 15A.

Weissman, M. M., Gammon, G. D., John, K., Merikangas, K. R., Warner, V., Prusoff, B. A., & Sholomskas, D. (1987). Children of depressed parents: Increased pathology and early onset of major depression. *Archives of General Psychiatry, 44*(10), 847–853.

Winnicott, D. W. (1965). *The maturational processes and the facilitating environment: Studies in the theory of emotional development.* New York: International Universities Press.

Winnicott, D. W. (1968). Playing: Its theoretical status in the clinical situation. *International Journal of Psychoanalysis, 49*(4), 591–599.

Winnicott, D. W. (1970). The mother-infant experience of mutuality. In E. J. Anthony & T. Benedek (Eds.), *Parenthood: Its psychology and psychopathology* (pp. 245–288). London: Little, Brown.

Zeanah, C. H., & Barton, M. L. (1989). Internal representations and parent-infant relationships. *Infant Mental Health Journal, 10*(3), 135–141.

Zeanah, C. H., & Benoit, D. (1995). Clinical applications of a parent perception interview. In K.

Minde (Ed.), *Infant psychiatry: Child and adolescent psychiatric clinics of North America* (pp. 539–554). Philadelphia: W. B. Saunders.

Zeanah, C. H., Benoit, D., Hirshberg, L., Barton, M. L., & Regan, C. (1994). Mothers' representations of their infants are concordant with infant attachment classifications. *Developmental Issues in Psychiatry and Psychology, 1,* 9–18.

Zeanah, C. H., Jr., & Boris, N. W. (2000). Disturbances and disorders of attachment in early childhood. In C. H. Zeanah, Jr. (Ed.), *Handbook of infant mental health* (2nd ed., pp. 353–368). New York: Guilford Press.

Zeanah, C. H., Jr., Larrieu, J. A., Heller, S. S., & Valliere, J. (2000). Infant-parent relationship assessment. In C. H. Zeanah, Jr. (Ed.), *Handbook of infant mental health* (2nd ed., pp. 222–235). New York: Guilford Press.

Zero to Three: National Center for Clinical Infant Programs (1994). *Diagnostic classification of mental health and developmental disorders of infancy and early childhood.* Arlington, VA: Author.

4

Contextual Contributors to the Assessment of Infant Mental Health

Arnold Sameroff
Ronald Seifer
Susan C. McDonough

In this chapter, we examine a model for predicting child mental health based on an assessment of the child's social environment. Although it is important to understand the specific processes that lead to specific maladjustment, from an epidemiological standpoint the best predictor of problem behaviors seems to be a cumulative risk score that reflects statuses of the full range of ecological subsystems of the child. Moreover, the specific kind of risk appears to be secondary to the quantity of negative factors. When social risk is contrasted with indicators of infant competence, the context of the child is a better indicator of future functioning.

Although scientists usually see their task as a search for causes, research on risk factors may appear to be a substitute for a more basic understanding of why individuals succeed or fail. Risks are probabilistic, whereas causes are thought to be deterministic. The history of research into the etiology of biological disorders has demonstrated that there are no single sufficient causes. The phrase *risk factors* itself arose from epidemiological research seeking the cause of heart disease (Costello & Angold, 2000). In the most compre-

hensive of these efforts, the Framingham Study, it was found that no single factor was either necessary or sufficient (Dawber, 1980). Hypertension, obesity, lack of exercise, and smoking all made significant contributions to heart disease at the population level, but for any single affected individual there was a different combination of these factors. We shall discover a similar result in our search for the causes of developmental problems in children and adolescents. It will not be any single factor that causes such difficulties, but an accumulation of adversity that reduces developmental competence.

The emerging field of prevention science (Coie et al., 1993; Mrazek & Haggerty, 1994) is much concerned with the universality of risk factors. Common findings are that the same risk factors affect multiple outcomes, such as depression, conduct disorder, or substance abuse, and that each disorder has multiple risk factors (Coie, Miller-Johnson, & Bagwell, 2000). In studies of single risks and single outcomes, this fact would be missed. The comprehensiveness and the unity of the developmental process require studies of multiple risks and multiple outcomes to avoid a distorted view of the importance of any single risk.

ASSESSING RISKS

Let us turn for a moment to research aimed at identifying representative risk factors in the development of cognitive and social-emotional competence. Such child competencies have been found to be strongly related to family mental health and especially social class. In an investigation of a sample of families with a high level of maternal psychopathology, children were followed from birth through high school in the Rochester Longitudinal Study (RLS). When the effects of mothers' mental health and social status on children's preschool intelligence and mental health were compared, socioeconomic status (SES) had the greater influence (Sameroff, Seifer, & Zax, 1982). Although socioeconomic status was the best single variable for predicting children's cognitive competence and an important predictor of social-emotional functioning, the circumstances of families within the same social class differed quite markedly. SES impacts on parenting, parental attitudes and beliefs, family interactions, and the availability of service programs in the surrounding community.

To better understand the role of SES, more differentiated views of environmental influences needed to be taken. The measures of parents' educational level and occupational prestige that constituted SES scores (Hollingshead, 1975) needed to be transformed into variables that would have a conceptually more direct influence on the child and would illuminate the differences in experiences of children raised in different socioeconomic environments.

From the early data available in the RLS, a set of 10 psychological and demographic variables were chosen that were related to economic circumstance but were not the same as SES (Sameroff, Seifer, Barocas, Zax, & Greenspan, 1987). The definitions of the 10 environmental risk variables were: (1) a history of maternal mental illness; (2) high maternal anxiety; (3) parental perspectives that reflected rigidity in the attitudes, beliefs, and values that mothers had in regard to children's development; (4) few positive mater-

nal interactions with the child observed during infancy; (5) stressful life events; (6) minimal maternal education; (7) head of household in unskilled occupations; (8) single parenthood; (9) large family size; and (10) disadvantaged minority status. Each of these risk factors has a large literature documenting its potential for deleterious developmental effects (Cicchetti & Cohen, 1995; Damon & Eisenberg, 1998; Sameroff, Lewis, & Miller, 2000, Zeanah, 2000).

To establish a risk condition, we dichotomized each variable into a high- and low-risk condition. For the demographic variables, there was usually a documented split (e.g., less than a high school education or father absence). For the psychological variables, this was not the case except for the presence of a psychiatric diagnosis. Scales for anxiety, parental perspectives, mother-child interaction, and stressful life events were continuous variables that required some decision rule for creating high- and low-risk groups. We arbitrarily decided to use 25% as the cutoff for the high-risk condition. Such a decision is clearly sample dependent, and the 25th percentile in one study may be quite different than in another study. This continuing problem is discussed in greater detail in a later section.

Once the dichotomy for each variable was made, we then tested whether poor cognitive and social-emotional development was related to the risk factors when the children in the sample were 4 years old. Indeed, each of these variables was a risk factor for preschool competence. For both cognitive and mental health outcomes, the high-risk group for each factor had worse scores than the low-risk group, validating our dichotomies. However, these group differences were not of sufficient size to provide the specificity necessary to identify specific individuals as needing intervention; most children with only a single risk factor did not have a major developmental problem.

CUMULATIVE RISK STUDIES

To increase specificity of assessment, it is necessary to take a broader perspective when examining the risk for mental health problems. Multiple systems must be examined simultaneously because risk factors tend to cluster in the same individuals (Bronfenbrenner, 1979, 1994). Conversely, indices of successful adaptation also tend to cluster (Carnegie Council on Adolescent Development, 1995). As children often experience many risks and recurring stressors, focusing on a single risk factor does not address the reality of most children's lives.

As a way of improving predictive power, Rutter (1979) argued that it was not any particular risk factor but the number of risk factors in a child's background that led to psychiatric disorder. Psychiatric risk for a sample of 10-year-olds rose from 2% in families with zero or one risk factor to 20% in families with four or more. The six risk factors considered included severe marital distress, low socioeconomic status, large family size or overcrowding, paternal criminality, maternal psychiatric disorder, and admission of the child to foster care. Similarly, Williams, Anderson, McGee, and Silva (1990) related a cumulative disadvantage score to behavioral disorders in 11-year-olds based on number of residence and school changes, single parenthood, low SES, marital separation, young motherhood, low maternal cognitive ability, poor family relations, seeking marriage guidance, and maternal mental health symptoms. For the children with less than two disadvantages only 7% had behavior problems, whereas for the children with eight or more disadvantages the rate was 40%. Even more risk factors were used by Ferguson, Horwood, and Lynsky (1994) in a study of the effects of 39 measures of family problems on the adolescent mental health of a sample of New Zealand children. In each study, the result was the more risk factors, the more behavioral problems.

To increase explanatory power in the Rochester study, we created a multiple-risk score that was the total number of risks for each individual family (Sameroff, Seifer, Barocas, et al., 1987). Using this strategy, major differences were found on mental health and intelligence measures between those children with few risks and those with many. Four-year-olds in the high-risk group (five or more risk factors) were 12.3 times as likely to be rated as having clinical mental health symptoms (Sameroff, Seifer, Zax, & Barocas, 1987). On the intelligence test, children with eight or nine risk factors scored more than 30 points lower than children with no environmental

risks. No preschoolers in the zero-risk group had IQs below 85; 26% of those in the high-risk group did. On average, each risk factor reduced the child's IQ score by 4 points.

Utility of Multiple-Risk Scores

Statistically, use of the multiple-risk score strategy sacrifices a degree of predictability within a sample. Maximal explanatory power usually is attained by regression analyses of raw scores where the whole distribution for each risk variable is used and they are differentially weighted in the regression equation. An intermediate strategy is to use dichotomized risk factors in a regression where the variance in the full distribution of each variable is lost but individual risks still can be differentially weighted. In the multiple-risk strategy, explained variance is reduced further because (1) information is lost when the continuous distribution of each risk factor is converted into a dichotomized 0 or 1 score, and (2) each factor is equally weighted when they are added up to produce the risk score. The multiple-risk score does have advantages in that it does not capitalize on the uniqueness of risk variables that are sample dependent, that is, the risk score is determined by regression equations. A clearly defined risk scale should have generality across studies, which would validate its usefulness.

Despite the loss of explanatory power, the multiplerisk strategy has been useful in both large-sample studies, where one is seeking to describe the level of developmental adversity, and small samples, where one is trying to reduce the degrees of freedom in multivariate analyses. We proposed that it was most useful when there was a small sample with a large number of variables and the main concern was other constructs (Sameroff, Seifer, Baldwin, & Baldwin, 1993). If the primary interest is in some developmental process relating single predictors and outcomes, then the multiple-risk score provides a good summary of background variables without sacrificing degrees of freedom. An example of this is the Ackerman, Izard, Schoff, Youngstrom, and Kogos (1999) study examining the relationship between contextual risk and problem behaviors of 6- and 7-year-old children from economically disadvantaged families. Eleven indicators were used to index background contextual risk excluding specific family variables of specific interest in a search for interacting factors. Using this method, they found a protective factor where more positive caregiver emotionality buffered the influence of higher cumulative risk.

Burchinal and her associates have explored this issue in several samples. First they found support for accumulating scores when they examined the long-term effects of low family income and stressful life events on math and reading achievement test scores (Pungello, Kupersmidt, Burchinal, & Patterson, 1996). Using a cumulative risk consisting of only three factors—low family income, stressful life exposure, and minority ethnic status—they found European-American children with no risk factors had the highest achievement test scores, and these scores increased over time. African American children with high risk had the lowest achievement test scores, and these scores decreased over time.

Developmental issues became apparent in studies of infants. In a group of 12-month-olds, Hooper, Burchinal, Roberts, Zeisel, and Neebe (1998) found relationships between a larger multiple-risk score based on Sameroff, Seifer, Barocas, et al.'s (1987) 10 variables and language scale outcomes but not developmental quotients. For at least one outcome, the multiple-risk score was a better predictor than a regression equation. The young age of the sample may have been a problem because outcomes are measured less accurately during infancy (Neisser et al. 1996). Other studies also found it difficult to demonstrate SES effects (highly correlated with social risks) before the second year of life (Sameroff et al., 1982; Wilson, 1985). In another study with children assessed at 12, 24, 36, and 48 months, Burchinal, Roberts, Hooper, and Zeisel (2000) again compared regression and multiple-risk strategies. As expected, the regression analyses were better predictors of outcomes at a single age, but the multiple-risk score strategy was better at relating risk to developmental patterns.

Quality versus Quantity

Another question about the multiple-risk strategy is whether the negative effects on developmental outcomes are the result of the accumulation of risk factors or the action of a specific risk factor. We examined this question in an analysis of the 4-year IQ data in the Rochester study (Sameroff, Seifer, Barocas, et al., 1987). Data from the families that had a moderate multiple-risk score (3 to 5 out of 10) were analyzed to determine which risk factors occurred together and whether specific combinations had worse effects than others. The families fell into five groups with different combinations of high-risk conditions. Despite these differences, developmental competencies were the same for children in the five groups. If the number of risks was the same, it did not matter which ones they were. No single factor was regularly related to either poor or good outcomes. It was not the quality of specific risks but the quantity that was affecting the development of children. Moreover, as in the Framingham study of heart disease (Dawber, 1980), no single variable was either a necessary or sufficient determinant of good or bad outcomes.

In another study contrasting regression and additive strategies, Deater-Deckard, Dodge, Bates, and Pettit (1998) found that multiple-risk scores were successful outcome predictors, but explained about two thirds of the variance predicted by regressions. In addition, they followed up on the quantity versus quality issue and found that different combinations of risks led to similar outcomes. What this means is that it is unlikely that the same interventions will work for all children. For every family situation, a unique combination of risk factors will require a unique set of intervention strategies embedded within a developmental model.

Multiple Outcomes and Multiple Risks

To provide an adequate risk assessment instrument, one would need to know the prevalence of risk factors and their association with developmental outcomes. This would require a study with a large representative sample and a clearly conceptualized model of risk. Unfortunately, no such epidemiological study has been performed as yet. Moreover, most studies of the effects of risk on development have not applied an ecological perspective in their conceptualization. As a consequence, ecological analyses are post hoc rather than a priori. The planning of most studies has not included attention to family, school, peer, and community variables at the same time. It is usually after the fact that risk analyses are considered.

An example of such a study is an analysis of the progress of several thousand young children from kindergarten to third grade using community samples from 30 sites (Peck, Sameroff, Ramey, & Ramey, 1999). From the data collected, 14 risk factors were chosen that tapped ecological levels from parent behavior to neighborhood characteristics. The number of risk factors were summed and a linear relation was found between the multiple environmental risk score and school outcomes of academic achievement and social competence, supporting the findings from the RLS. Although this study used a large sample in multiple sites, the children were not a representative sample of the community, and the risk factors were selected from available data rather than planned in advance.

Philadelphia Study

A set of data on the effects of multiple environmental risks in multiple contextual subsystems was provided by a study of adolescents in Philadelphia (Furstenberg, Cook, Eccles, Elder, & Sameroff, 1999). Mothers, fathers, and offspring were interviewed in close to 500 families that included a youth between the ages of 11 and 14. Although not a representative sample, the families varied widely in socioeconomic status and racial composition.

An advantage of the Philadelphia project was that it took a more conceptual approach to the design so that environmental measures were available at a number of ecological levels. For the analyses of environmental risk, variables were grouped and examined within subsystems that affected the adolescent, from those microsystems (Bronfenbrenner, 1979) in which the child was an active participant to those systems more distal to the child where any effect had to be mediated by more proximal variables.

To approximate an ecological model, 20 environmental risk variables were categorized in six groupings reflecting different subsystems of the adolescent world (Sameroff, Seifer, & Bartko, 1997). The intention was to be able to have multiple factors in each of the six ecological subsystems. Family Process was the first grouping and included variables in the family microsystem that were directly experienced by the child and would fit into a category of parent-child interaction. The group included support for autonomy, behavior control, parental involvement, and family climate. The second grouping was Parent Characteristics and included mental health, sense of efficacy, resourcefulness, and level of education. The third grouping, Family Structure, included the parents' marital status and socioeconomic indicators of household crowding and receiving welfare payments. The fourth grouping, Family Management of the Community, was composed of variables of institutional involvement, informal networks, social resources, and adjustments to economic pressure. The fifth grouping, Peers, included indicators of another microsystem of the child, the extent to which the youth was associated with prosocial and antisocial peers. Community was the sixth grouping, representing the ecological level most distal to the youth and the family. It included census tract variables reflecting the average income and educational level of the neighborhood the family lived in, a parental report of the number of problems in the neighborhood, and the climate of the adolescent's school.

In the Philadelphia study, in addition to the larger number of ecological variables, a wider array of youth assessments was available for interpreting developmental competence. The five outcomes used to characterize successful adolescence were Psychological Adjustment, Self-Competence, Problem Behaviors with drugs, delinquency, and early sexual behavior, Activity Involvement in sports, religious, extracurricular, and community projects, and Academic Performance as reflected in grades.

To examine the effect of the accumulation of risks, scores were calculated for each adolescent. The resulting scores ranged from a minimum of 0 to a maximum of 13 of a possible 20 risk factors. When the five normalized adolescent outcome scores were plotted against the number of risk factors, a very large decline in each outcome was found with increasing risk (see figure 4.1; Sameroff et al., 1998).

Whether cumulative risk scores meaningfully increase predictive efficiency can be demonstrated by an odds-ratio analysis, a comparison of the odds of having a bad outcome in a high-risk versus a low-risk environment. For the typical analysis of relative and attributable risk, the outcome variable is usually discrete, either succumbing to a disease or disorder or not. For children, there are few discrete negative outcomes. They are generally too young to have many pregnancies or arrests, and the rate of academic failure is not particularly high. In the Philadelphia study, bad outcomes were artificially created by identifying the 25% of adolescents who were doing the most poorly in terms of mental health, self-competence, problem behavior, activity involvement, or academic performance.

The relative risk in the high-risk group (eight or more risks) for each of the bad outcomes was substantially higher than in the low-risk group (three or fewer risks). The strongest effects were for Academic Performance, where the relative risk for a bad outcome increased from 7% in the low-risk group to 45% in the high-risk group, an odds ratio of 6.7:1. The odds ratios for Psychological Adjustment, Problem Behavior, Self-Competence, and Activity Involvement were 5.7, 4.5, 3.4, and 2.7, respectively. For the important cognitive and social-emotional outcomes of youth, there seem to be powerful negative effects of the accumulation of environmental risk factors.

SINGLE RISK FACTORS REVISITED

It is difficult for some to believe that the quantity rather than the quality of risks is more predictive.

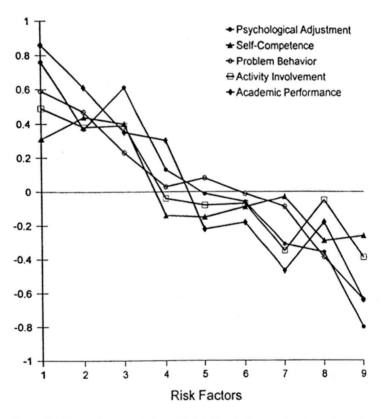

Figure 4.1 Five outcomes of the Philadelphia study as a function of multiple-risk score.

Rather, there are disciplinary and political investments in believing that specific single variables have overriding importance. We examined this issue with data from the Philadelphia study (Sameroff et al., 1998).

Income and Marital Status

On the environmental side, we examined the effect of some single risk factors in the Philadelphia study that economists and sociologists have been very concerned about, low income level and single parenthood. Although these factors should have powerful effects on the fate of children, we did not find such differences when these single variables were put into a broader ecological framework. Differences in effects on child competence disappeared when we controlled for the number of other environmental risk factors in each family. To test the effects of different amounts of financial resources, we split our sample of families into those with high, middle, and low income levels. For the family structure comparison, we split the sample into groups of children living in two-parent and single-parent families. In each case, there were no differences in the relationship to child competence when we compared groups of children with the same number of risk factors raised in rich or poor families or in families with one or two parents (Sameroff et al., 1998). Poor children did as well as wealthier children in low-risk contexts and children with two parents did as poorly as those with single parents in high-risk contexts. There are many successful adults who were raised in poverty and unsuccessful ones who were raised in affluence. There are many healthy and happy adults who come from broken homes, and there are many unhappy ones who were raised by two parents.

Again, what our analyses of these data reveal is that it is not single environmental factors that make a difference but the constellation of risks in each family's life. The reason that income and marital status seem to make major differences in child development is not because they are overarching variables in themselves, but because they are strongly associated with a combination of other risk factors. For example, in the Philadelphia study, whereas 39% of poor children lived in high-risk families with more than seven risk factors, only 7% of affluent children did. Similarly, whereas 29% of single-parent families lived in high-risk social conditions, only 15% of two-parent families did.

Gender and Race

Personal characteristics should be important ingredients in each child's development. Personal variables can be divided into demographics, like gender and race, and behavioral domains, like efficacy. To give some perspective on the individual contribution to the effects of risk, some child characteristics were included in the Philadelphia study (Furstenberg et al., 1999). The correlations between risk scores and outcomes for separate groups of boys and girls and African Americans and Whites were examined, and no differences were found (Sameroff et al., 1997). When the relationship between our summary competence measure and risk factors was compared for different gender and racial groups, the curves were essentially overlapping: the more risk factors, the worse the developmental outcomes.

MENTAL HEALTH

For this volume, our concern is with the assessment of mental health in young children. From a person-oriented perspective, the best predictors of mental health would be other psychological aspects of the individual. A personality variable that is given great importance in discussions of successful development with mental health consequences is resourcefulness. Is it possible that despite social adversity, children with high levels of resourcefulness are able to overcome minimal resources at home and in the community to reach levels of achievement comparable to children from more advantaged social strata?

In the Philadelphia study, we were able to measure this construct of resourcefulness with a set of questions asked of the parent and child about the youth's capacity to solve problems, overcome difficulties, and bounce back from setbacks. We divided the sample into high- and low-efficacy groups and looked at their adolescent outcomes. Indeed, high-efficacy youth were more competent than those with low efficacy on our measures of adolescent competence. A sense of personal resourcefulness did seem to pay off.

But what happens to this effect when we take environmental adversity into account? When we matched high- and low-efficacy children for the number of environmental risk factors, the difference in general competence between youth in the high and low environmental risk conditions was far greater than that between highly resourceful and less resourceful groups. High-efficacy adolescents in high-risk conditions did worse than low-efficacy youth in low-risk conditions (Sameroff et al., 1998).

We did the same analysis using academic achievement as an indicator of competence and examined whether good work at school was related to better mental health, more engagement in positive community activities, and less involvement in delinquent problem behavior. Again, for every outcome, academically high-achieving adolescents in high-risk conditions did worse than youth with low school grades in low-risk conditions

For current purposes, the Philadelphia study is deficient in two respects: (1) the data are cross-sectional and (2) the sample is adolescents, not infants. Finding causal factors is impossible without longitudinal developmental data, and difficult even then. The Rochester study was about infants and did have a series of developmental assessments, which permitted a longitudinal view of the contribution of individual factors to developmental success. We could see how infant competence affected preschool competence, and then how preschool competence affected middle and high school competence.

From the Rochester data collected during the first year of life, we created a multiple competence score for each child during infancy that included 12 factors. These were scores from newborn medical and behavioral tests, temperament assessments, and developmental scales. We then divided the sample into groups of high- and low-competency infants and examined as outcomes their 4-year IQ and social-emotional functioning scores. We found no relation between infant competence and 4-year IQ or social-emotional problems. We could not find infant protective factors (Sameroff et al., 1998).

At later assessments at 13 and 18 years of age, we did find continuities in competence from the preschool years. More resourceful children did better on average than less resourceful children but, as in the Philadelphia data, when we controlled for environmental risk, the differences between children with high and low levels of early competence were much less than the differences in performance between children in high- and low-risk social environments. In each case we found again that high-competency children in high-risk environments did worse than low-competency children in low-risk environments.

PREDICTIVE POWER OF ENVIRONMENTAL RISK SCORES

Within the RLS, our attention was devoted to the source of stability and instability in child performance. The typical statistic reported in longitudinal research is the correlation between early and later performance of the children. We too found such correlations. Mental health and intelligence at 4 years correlated .41 and .72, respectively, with mental health and intelligence at 13 years. The usual interpretation of such numbers is that there is a continuity of competence or incompetence in the child. Such a conclusion cannot be challenged if the only assessments in the study are of the children. In the RLS, we examined environmental as well as child factors. We were able to correlate environmental as well as child characteristics across time. We found that the correlation between composite multiple-risk scores at the two ages was .77, which was as great or greater than any stability within the child. The children had poor family and social environments when they were born (Sameroff, Seifer, Barocas, et al., 1987), still had them when they were 13 (Sameroff et al., 1993), and probably would continue to have them for the foreseeable future.

GENERALIZING THE MULTIPLE-RISK ASSESSMENT MODEL

We have discussed how environmental risk is highly predictive of mental health throughout childhood. Moreover, the multiple-risk score is a simple and robust method for summarizing contextual risk. The task in this handbook is to produce assessments related to infant mental health. The remaining task for this chapter is to offer a method to produce multiple-risk scores that are relevant to young children.

We have argued that a multiple-risk score has advantages in that it does not capitalize on the uniqueness of risk variables that are sample dependent; that is, the risk score is determined by regression equations. A clearly defined risk scale should have generality across studies, which would validate its usefulness. In an attempt to test this assumption, we applied the Rochester Longitudinal Study risk scale in two later studies, the Providence Family Study and the Michigan Family Study. In both of these studies, one of the preschool mental health outcome measures was the Child Behavior Checklist (CBCL; Achenbach, 1992), at 48 months in the Providence study and at 33 months in the Michigan study. We then examined the relationship between risk score and CBCL scores in each study. A comparison of risk factors in the three studies can be seen in table 4.1.

The Providence Family Study (Seifer, Sameroff, Dickstein, Keitner, & Miller, 1996) is similar to the Rochester study in that it was a longitudinal investigation of infants and toddlers at risk for psychopathology because their mother had a diagnosed mental illness. About two thirds of the mothers had a psychiatric disorder, primarily major affective disorder. Families entered the study when their child was 14 or 30 months of age, and were followed longitudinally at 30 and 48 months of age. The overall focus of the project was to examine the early development of at-risk children within both their family and larger social context. The 4-year data was used for the risk analysis reported here.

The Michigan Family Study (McDonough, Rosenblum, DeVoe, Gahagan, & Sameroff, 1998) is different from both the Rochester and Providence studies in that the recruitment strategy was based on infant rather than mother characteristics. A community sample of families of babies with regulatory problems was recruited at pediatric 6-month well baby clinics. Infants varied in their crying, sleeping, and feeding behavior such that 55% of mothers were concerned and 28% reported that infant problems in these domains affected their feelings about the child. The infants and their families were assessed in the laboratory and at home at 7 months, 15 months, and 33 months. The 33-month data were used for the risk analysis.

The primary difference between the Providence and Rochester studies was in the social status of the families. Unskilled occupational status characterized 17% of the Providence families compared to 27% of the Rochester families. High school degrees were obtained by 95% of the mothers and 93% of the fathers compared to 78% of mothers in the RLS. Only 13% of the families did not have the child's father present in the household at the time of the study, although 6% of the sample had another partner living with the family compared to 24% in the RLS. Families with more than three children living at home represented 7% of the sample, compared to 16% in the RLS. Whereas in the RLS African Americans and Hispanics comprised 35% of the sample, in Providence they were only 11%.

The primary difference between the Rochester and Providence studies on the one hand and the Michigan study on the other was in the men-

Table 4.1 Percentage of Families in 10 Risk Categories for Three Samples: The Rochester Longitudinal Study (RLS), the Providence Family Study (PFS), and the Michigan Family Study (MFS)

	RLS	PFS	MFS
Sample size	212	182	258
Psychological risks			
Mental health	47	76	25
Psychological distress	23	35	30
Family functioning	20	49	22
Child interaction	19	12	6
Stressful life events	23	29	21
Demographic risks			
Mother education	33	6	7
HH occupation	27	17	17
Father absent	24	20	15
Family size	16	7	6
Disadvantaged minority	35	11	27
Mean number of risks	2.6	2.6	1.3

tal health of the mothers. In the first two studies, families were selected to overrepresent maternal psychopathology, whereas in Michigan the families were a community sample. In the Michigan study, there was no information on psychiatric diagnoses. Otherwise the demographics were similar for the Michigan and Providence samples in that both were more affluent than the Rochester sample. All but 15% of the Michigan mothers had more than a high school education and only 7% had not completed high school. The number of families with head of household occupational status as unskilled or less and with four or more children at home were the same in both samples. Father absence was somewhat lower, 15% compared to 20%, and number of minority families was higher, 27% compared to 15%.

Common Risk Variables

Although the five demographic risk variables were the same across the three studies, the psychological risk variables differed. Because the studies were not designed to replicate each other, the measures in each study were chosen according to the specific aims of each. Yet there was enough overlap in the constructs to permit the utilization of similar variables.

Mental health risk in the Rochester and Providence study was based on psychiatric diagnoses, which automatically provided a dichotomous variable. For Michigan there was no psychiatric evaluation, so a mental health assessment score of the mother's behavior during a 60-minute home visit was used, the Psychological Impairment Rating Scale (Baldwin et al., 1993), and a 25th percentile cutoff point was used.

The psychological distress construct was assessed with the Rutter Malaise Scale (Rutter, 1976) in Rochester, the Symptom Checklist-90 (SCL-90; Derogatis, 1992) in Providence, and the Center for Epidemiologic Studies Depression Scale (CES-D; Radloff, 1977) and State-Trait Anxiety Index (STAI; Spielberger, Gorsuch, & Lushene, 1983) in Michigan. These scores are highly intercorrelated and provided comparable measures and there were clinical cutoff points in the literature, except for the Malaise Scale, for which a 25th percentile cutoff point was used.

Measures of family functioning and child interaction constructs varied the most across the three studies. Family functioning was measured with the Concepts of Development Scale and the Parent Attitude Research Instrument in Rochester, the McMaster Clinical Rating Scale (Epstein, Baldwin, & Bishop, 1982) in Providence, and the Dyadic Adjustment Scale (Spanier, 1976) in Michigan. Child interaction risk in Rochester was based on a negativity score from ratings of a laboratory observation of mother-child interaction (Barocas et al., 1991) and the Caldwell and Bradley (1984) Home Observation for Measurement of the Environment (HOME) Scale in Providence and Michigan. Deciding on the cutoff point for high risk was an example of the sample dependency of risk definition. Using a cutoff score based on the 25% rule would have resulted in a score at the 75th percentile based on HOME norms. To use the bottom 25th percentile of the norms would have only put a small part of the sample in the risk category. Our pragmatic decision was to use the 50th percentile, which still left only 12% of the sample in the risk category for the Providence study and 6% in the Michigan study.

Stressful life event risk was based on the Life Events Questionnaire (Garmezy & Tellegan, 1984) in Rochester and Providence and the Life Event Scale from the Abidin (1986) Parent Stress Index in Michigan. Again, a comparable cutoff score was difficult to find. A cutoff of more than 10 out of 64 events on the Garmezy and Tellegan measure placed 23% and 29% of the Rochester and Providence samples in the risk category, respectively. But on the 22-item Abidin measure, only 20% of the Michigan sample had more than two stressful events and only 3% had more than four. Is this difference because different scales were used or because there was less risk in the Michigan sample?

We have provided the detailed description above to illuminate the problems in developing a standard assessment for environmental risk. Once we have made the assessments, the question is whether they relate to anything. The 10 risk factors were summed in each study to produce a multiple-risk score, which was related to the CBCL outcome in the Providence Family Study and the Michigan Family Study.

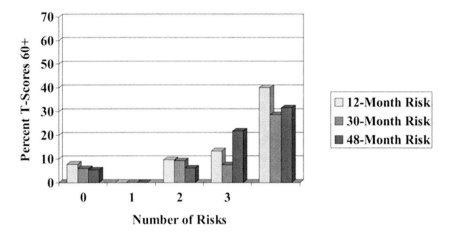

Figure 4.2 Percentage of 4-year-olds in the Providence Family Study with CBCL total T-scores of 60 or more as a function of number of risk factors at 12, 30, and 48 months.

Predicting Early Mental Health
From Multiple-Risk Scores

When we examined the relationship between environmental multiple-risk scores and the mental health of 4-year-olds in the Providence study, we found results similar to those of the Rochester study. The use of T-scores is an easy way of determining who is well above the mean on CBCL scores. Figures 4.2 and 4.3 show the relation between multiple-risk scores from the 12-, 30-, and 48-month family assessments and 48-month

CBCL T-scores above 50 and above 60. There is no significant difference in CBCL scores based on predictions from the three assessment ages. Predictions are as accurate from the 12-month score as from the contemporary 4-year score. There are clear differences in predictions at each age based on the number of risk factors. For the children with T-scores above 50, there is an increase from 10% in the zero-risk group to 60% in the group with four or more risk factors, a relative risk of 6:1. For the children with T-scores above 60, moving into the clinical range, there is an increase

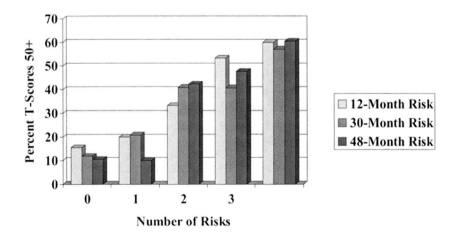

Figure 4.3 Percentage of 4-year-olds in the Providence Family Study with CBCL total T-scores of 50 or more as a function of number of risk factors at 12, 30, and 48 months.

from about 5% in the zero-risk group to 30% in the group with four or more risk factors, again a relative risk of 6:1.

When creating an assessment measure, important factors are sensitivity, which is the ability to identify a large proportion of the individuals who have the problem, and specificity, which is the ability to identify as few individuals as possible who do not have the problem. In this instance, the problem is a high CBCL score. Table 4.2 shows sensitivity and specificity for predicting 4-year CBCL T-scores of 60 or more using risk scores from 12, 30, and 48 months. The numbers from the three risk scores are quite similar. The use of a criterion of four or more risk factors is not better than using three or more risk factors. The sensitivity with fewer criteria is in the 75 to 85% range, compared to 55 to 65% using more criteria, which is not surprising. But there appears to be no difference in specificity, which is somewhat surprising. In either case the specificity is low, misclassifying approximately 70% of the high-risk children, although when the percentage correctly identified was calculated, it was about 80% using four or more risk factors and 60% using three or more risk factors. The use of the multiple-risk scale has statistically significant correlations with mental health outcomes in the Providence study, but is far less successful at identifying specific children with poor mental health.

The results from the Providence study are the good news about generalizing the use of the Rochester multiple-risk scale. The results from the Michigan study are the bad news. There was no relationship between the multiple-risk score

and CBCL score at 33 months. In figure 4.4 one can see that there is roughly the same proportion of high T-scores for each of the Michigan risk groups. An explanation for the difference can be found in the nature of the samples. Both the Rochester and Providence samples had an overrepresentation of mothers with psychiatric diagnoses and were less affluent than the Michigan sample. The Michigan study had the highest HOME scores, the fewest stressful life events, the smallest family sizes, the highest level of education, and the fewest families with an absent father. In short, the Michigan sample had the fewest risk factors, half as many as in the Rochester and Providence samples (see table 4.1).

Other analyses from the Michigan study found variables that have stronger relations to child mental health scores than the 10 in the risk scale, such as parenting stress and social support. We could have constructed a risk scale unique to the sample that would have done better at predictive classifications but that would undercut the point of this presentation.

THE FUTURE

We have made an effort to test a multiple-risk assessment across several samples of infants and found that in different samples the use of similar cutoff points does not maximize predictability. The Rochester Longitudinal Study sample had a full range of SES, a large proportion of minority group members, and a full range of family mental health situations. The Providence Family Study

Table 4.2 Sensitivity and Specificity of 12-Month, 30-Month, and 48-Month Multiple-Risk Scores for Predicting 4-Year CBCL T-Scores Above 60 in the Providence Family Study

	Number of Risk Factors			
	0–3 versus 4+		0–2 versus 3+	
	Sensitivity (%)	Specificity (%)	Sensitivity (%)	Specificity (%)
12-Month	55	20	73	27
30-Month	67	29	80	19
48-Month	60	32	85	27

Note: 15% of the CBCL T-scores were 60 or more.

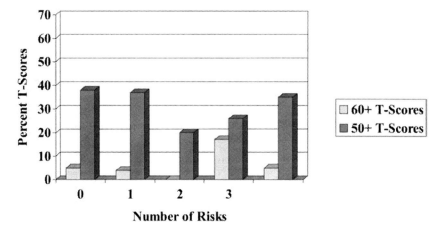

Figure 4.4 Percentage of 33-month-olds in the Michigan Family Study with CBCL total T-scores of 60 or more and 50 or more as a function of number of risk factors.

and, especially, the Michigan Family Study were constricted on one or more of these dimensions. One must also consider historical issues. When the early childhood data were collected at Rochester almost 30 years ago, families were different in many ways from the current families in Providence and Michigan. In 1975, a parent who did not have a high school degree was placing his or her child at risk. Today, not having more than a high school degree may be placing a child at risk, a matter to be settled by empirical work. In any case, including parents who have only a high school degree or GED in the educational risk category along with those who have not completed high school would increase the size of the risk group.

Within studies, many measures related to mental health outcomes are not represented in the multiple-risk scale we tested here. The Providence study had a major emphasis on family functioning that plays an important role in child development (Dickstein et al., 1998; Hayden et al., 1998). Such measures should be part of a risk scale with a full ecological perspective. Adding variables would enhance the efficacy of the measure. Using 20 risk factors in the Philadelphia study was quite effective. But consider the difficulty in an ecological model. Child- or family-focused assessments eventuate in a single instrument that can readily be transported from study to study. The risk score requires assessments in

all areas, a task greater than the resources of most research projects

CONCLUSION

Pervasive Effects of Multiple Risks

We have examined the effects of multiple risk across a wide range of studies and have found the accumulation of social risks across the family, peer group, school, and neighborhood to have a consistent negative effect. The more risks, the worse the outcomes.

Nonspecificity of Risks

A variety of developmental problems and disorders have been studied, and in each case different risk factors have been found to produce the same negative results. Moreover, a similar set of risk factors affect a number of different disorders (Coie et al., 1993; Mrazek & Haggerty, 1994).

Small Effects of Single Risks

Single variables, such as income level and marital status on the family side, and gender, race, and mental health on the personal side, taken alone may have statistically significant effects on children's behavior, but their effects are small in comparison with the accumulation of multiple negative environmental influences that characterize high-risk groups. The overlap in children's outcomes is substantial for low-income versus high-income families, families with one or two parents, boys versus girls, Blacks versus Whites, and highly resourceful and less resourceful youth when the number of social risks is controlled. More competent children in high-risk conditions consistently do worse than less competent children in low-risk conditions.

General versus Sample-Specific Risk Scales

Efforts to produce a general risk scale are difficult when research samples are so different. Identifying a high-risk condition in one sample may find few families meeting the criteria in another sample. Using a sample-specific high-risk group often may include individuals who score above norms in order to get a large enough proportion of the sample in the risk group. The objective of including measures in multiple domains of the child's social ecology may make a comprehensive assessment unwieldy.

Necessity of Multiple Interventions to Counter Multiple Risks

A systems perspective requires attention to the multiple influences on child development, ranging from individual competencies to the characteristics of the many social settings in which the child participates. A focus on single characteristics of individuals or families has never explained more than a small proportion of variance in behavioral development. Those children at the most risk for poor outcomes are those with problems in the most settings. Interventions designed to change the fates of such high-risk children will have to operate in the multiplicity of these contexts. The proverbial magic bullet may need to be a cadre of special forces. The major implication of multiple risk models is that assessments and interventions need to be as complex as development itself.

References

Abidin, R. R. (1986). *Parenting Stress Index manual.* Charlottesville, VA: Pediatric Psychology Press.

Achenbach, T. M. (1992). *Manual for the Child Behavior Checklist/2–3 and 1992 profile.* Burlington, VT: University of Vermont Department of Psychiatry.

Ackerman, B. P., Izard, C. E., Schoff, K., Youngstrom, E. A., & Kogos, J. (1999). Contextual risk, caregiver emotionality, and the problem behaviors of six- and seven-year-old children from economically disadvantaged families. *Child Development, 70*(6), 1415–1427.

Baldwin, A. L., Baldwin, C., Kasser, T., Zax, M., Sameroff, A., & Seifer, R. (1993). Contextual risk and resiliency during late adolescence. *Development and Psychopathology, 5,* 741–761.

Barocas, R., Seifer, R., Sameroff, A. J., Andrews, T. A., Croft, R. T., & Ostrow, E. (1991). Social and interpersonal determinants of developmental risk. *Developmental Psychology, 27,* 479–488.

Bronfenbrenner, U. (1979). *The ecology of human development.* Cambridge, MA: Harvard University Press.

Bronfenbrenner, U. (1994). Ecological models of human development. In T. Husten & T. N. Postlethwaite (Eds), *International encyclopedia of education* (2nd ed., Vol. 3, pp. 1643–1647). New York: Elsevier Science.

Burchinal, M. R., Roberts, J. E., Hooper, S., & Zeisel, S. A. (2000). Cumulative risk and early cognitive development: A comparison of statistical risk models. *Developmental Psychology, 36*(6), 793–807

Caldwell, B. M., & Bradley, R. H. (1984). *Home Observation for Measurement of the Environment.* Little Rock: University of Arkansas.

Carnegie Council on Adolescent Development. (1995). *Great transitions: Preparing adolescents for the new century.* New York: Carnegie.

Cicchetti, D., & Cohen, D. (Eds.) (1995). *Developmental psychopathology, Volume 2: Risk, disorder, and adaptation.* New York: Wiley.

Coie, J. D., Miller-Johnson, S., & Bagwell, C. (2000). Prevention science. In A. Sameroff, M. Lewis, & S. Miller (Eds.), *Handbook of developmental psychopathology* (pp. 93–112). New York: Plenum.

Coie, J. D., Watt, N. F., West, S., Hawkins, J. D., Asarnow, J. R., Markman, H. J., Ramey, S. L., Shure, M. B., & Long, B. (1993). The science of prevention. *American Psychologist, 48,* 1013–1022.

Costello, E. J., & Angold, A. (2000). Developmental epidemiology: A framework for developmental psychopathology. In A. Sameroff,

M. Lewis, & S. Miller (Eds.), *Handbook of developmental psychopathology* (pp. 57–73). New York: Plenum.

Damon, W., & Eisenberg, N. (Eds.) (1998). *Handbook of child psychology: Vol. 3. Social, emotional, and personality development* (5th ed.). New York: Wiley.

Dawber, T. R. (1980). *The Framingham study: The epidemiology of coronary heart disease.* Cambridge, MA: Harvard University Press.

Deater-Deckard, K., Dodge, K. A., Bates, J. E., & Pettit, G. S. (1998). Multiple risk factors in the development of externalizing behavior problems: Group and individual differences. *Development and Psychopathology, 10*(3), 469–493.

Derogatis, L. R. (1992). *SCL-90-R: Administration, scoring, and procedures manual II.* Towson, MD: Clinical Psychometric Research.

Dickstein, S., Seifer, R., Hayden, L. C., Schiller, M., Sameroff, A. J., Keitner, G., Miller, I., Rasmussen, S., Matzko, M., & Magee, K. D. (1998). Levels of family assessment. II. Impact of maternal psychopathology on family functioning. *Journal of Family Psychology, 12*, 23–40.

Epstein, N. B., Baldwin, L. M., & Bishop, D. S. (1982). *McMaster Clinical Rating Scale.* Available from Brown/Butler Family Research Program, 345 Blackstone Blvd., Providence, RI 02906.

Fergusson, D. M., Horwood, L. J., & Lynsky, M. T. (1994). The childhoods of multiple problem adolescents: A 15-year longitudinal study. *Journal of Child Psychology and Psychiatry, 35*, 1123–1140.

Furstenberg, F. F., Jr., Cook, T., Eccles, J., Elder, G. H., & Sameroff, A. J. (1999). *Managing to make it: Urban families and adolescent success.* Chicago: University of Chicago Press.

Garmezy, N., & Tellegan, A. (1984). Studies of stress-resistant children: Methods, variables, and preliminary findings. In F. Morrison, C. Lord, & D. Keating (Eds.), *Advances in applied developmental psychology* (Vol. 1, pp. 231–287). New York: Academic Press.

Hayden, L. C., Schiller, M., Dickstein, S., Seifer, R., Sameroff, A. J., Miller, I., Keitner, G., & Rasmussen, S. (1998). Levels of family assessment. I. Family, marital, and parent-child interaction. *Journal of Family Psychology, 12*, 7–22.

Hollingshead, A. B. (1975). *Four factor index of social status.* Unpublished manuscript. Available

from author, Yale University, New Haven, CT.

Hooper, S. R., Burchinal, M. R., Roberts, J. E., Zeisel, S., & Neebe, E. C. (1998). Social and family risk factors for infant development at one year: An application of the cumulative risk model. *Journal of Applied Developmental Psychology, 19*(1), 85–96.

McDonough, S. C., Rosenblum, K., DeVoe, E., Gahagan, S., & Sameroff, A. (1998, April). *Physiologic regulatory problems during infancy.* Paper presented at International Conference of Infant Studies, Atlanta, GA.

Mrazek, P. G., & Haggerty, R. J. (Eds.) (1994). *Reducing risks for mental disorders: Frontiers for preventive intervention programs.* Washington, DC: National Academy Press.

Neisser, U., Boodoo, G., Bouchard, T. J., Jr., Boykin, A. W., Brody, N., Ceci, S. J., Halpern, D. F., Loehlin, J. C., Perloff, R., Sternberg, R. J., & Urbina, S. (1996). Intelligence: Knowns and unknowns. *American Psychologist, 51*(2), 77–101.

Peck, S., Sameroff, A., Ramey, S., & Ramey, C. (1999, April). *Transition into school: Ecological risks for adaptation and achievement in a national sample.* Paper presented at the biennial meeting of the Society for Research and Development, Albuquerque, NM.

Pungello, E. P., Kupersmidt, J. B., Burchinal, M. R., & Patterson, C. J. (1996). Environmental risk factors and children's achievement from middle childhood to early adolescence. *Developmental Psychology, 32*(4), 755–767.

Radloff, L. S. (1977). CES-D scale: A self-report depression scale for research in the general population. *Applied Psychological Measurement, 1*, 385–401.

Rutter, M. (1976). Research report: Isle of Wight studies, 1964–1974. *Psychological Medicine, 6*, 313–332.

Rutter, M. (1979). Protective factors in children's responses to stress and disadvantage. In M. W. Kent & J. E. Rolf (Eds.), *Primary prevention of psychopathology: Vol. 3. Social competence in children* (pp. 49–74). Hanover, NH: University Press of New England.

Sameroff, A., Lewis, M., & Miller, S. (Eds.) (2000). *Handbook of developmental psychopathology.* New York: Plenum.

Sameroff, A. J., Bartko, W. T., Baldwin, A., Baldwin, C., & Seifer, R. (1998). Family and social influences on the development of child competence. In M. Lewis & C. Feiring (Eds.), *Fam-*

ilies, risk, and competence (pp. 161–186). Mahwah, NJ: Lawrence Erlbaum.

Sameroff, A. J., Seifer, R., Baldwin, A., & Baldwin, C. (1993). Stability of intelligence from preschool to adolescence: The influence of social and family risk factors. *Child Development, 64,* 80–97.

Sameroff, A. J., Seifer, R., Barocas, B., Zax, M., & Greenspan, S. (1987). IQ scores of 4-year-old children: Social-environmental risk factors. *Pediatrics, 79*(3), 343–350.

Sameroff, A. J., Seifer, R., & Bartko, W. T. (1997). Environmental perspectives on adaptation during childhood and adolescence. In S. S. Luthar, J. A. Barack, D. Cicchetti, & J. Weisz (Eds.), *Developmental psychopathology: Perspectives on risk and disorder* (pp. 507–526). Cambridge, MA: Cambridge University Press.

Sameroff, A. J., Seifer, R., & Zax, M. (1982). Early development of children at risk for emotional disorder. *Monographs of the Society for Research in Child Development, 47* (7, Serial No. 199).

Sameroff, A. J., Seifer, R., Zax, M., & Barocas, R. B. (1987). Early indices of developmental risk: The Rochester Longitudinal Study. *Schizophrenia Bulletin, 13,* 383–394.

Seifer, R., Sameroff, A. J., Dickstein, Keitner, G., & Miller, I. (1996). Parental psychopathology, multiple contextual risks, and one-year outcomes in children. *Journal of Clinical Child Psychology, 25,* 423–435.

Spanier, G. B. (1976). Measuring dyadic adjustment: New scales for assessing the quality of marriage and similar dyads. *Journal of Marriage and the Family, 38,* 15–28.

Spielberger, C. D., Gorusch, R. L., & Lushene, R. E. (1983). *State-Trait Anxiety Inventory.* Palto Alto, CA: Consulting Psychologists Press.

Williams, S., Anderson, J., McGee, R., & Silva, P. A. (1990). Risk factors for behavioral and emotional disorder in preadolescent children. *Journal of the American Academy of Child and Adolescent Psychiatry, 29,* 413–419.

Wilson, R. S. (1985). Risk and resilience in early mental development. *Developmental Psychology, 21,* 795–805.

Zeanah, C. H. (Ed.). (2000). *Handbook of infant mental health* (2nd ed.). New York: Guilford.

II

TEMPERAMENT AND REGULATION IN ASSESSING DISORDERS IN YOUNG CHILDREN

Although researchers have not yet established consensus definitions of emotion regulation and dysregulation, there is considerable agreement that emotion regulation involves the modulation of the internal aspects of emotion (including physiology and experience) as well as its outward expression. A variety of constructs have been considered in characterizing both the internal and external aspects of emotion regulation including effortful control, delay of gratification, temperament, colic, behavioral noncompliance, attentional processes, reactivity, and neuroendocrine functioning. The way these various factors interact to produce risk for disorder is continuing to evolve. Researchers generally believe that the processes involved in emotion regulation are constitutionally based and can be reliably measured in early life. It is thought that such indices may be useful in identifying children at risk for disorder, but the empirical bases for these assumptions have not yet been clearly established.

In that vein, Cynthia Stifter and Crystal Wiggins present work on the assessment of colic, difficult temperament, and noncompliance in relation to poor outcomes. They consider these problems to be regulatory in nature and review the historic and current conceptualizations along with data on developmental course. They discuss the various methods for assessing each of these behavioral constructs in hopes of both advancing research on regulatory functioning in relation to early disorders and more effectively addressing parental concerns of these ubiquitous problems in the early years.

Temperament and regulatory functioning also involve the ability to adapt comfortably to the demands or requirements of each situation and adjust behavior in flexible ways. This adaptability and flexibility may be enabled or constrained by the way an individual reacts to sensory stimulation. Reactivity or responsivity to sensory stimulation is thought to be biologically based, stable over time, and influential in cognition, emotion, and behavior. Some researchers (e.g., Miller and colleagues, chapter 13, this volume) even propose that it relates to attentional processes. While reactivity is thought to underlie problems in a variety of areas, a sensory battery assessing reactivity is not yet part of a standard assessment protocol for infants and young children.

Nathan Fox and Cindy Polak provide an overview of basic research on sensory reactivity in relation to infant temperament and review approaches to assess sensory reactivity within clinical settings. They highlight the importance of assessing reactivity, not in an effort to label the child as over- or underreactive, but to provide information on "goodness of fit" that will inform clinical recommendations regarding adjustments to children's living environments to match their temperamental constitutions and promote optimal functioning. While assessment tools are available within specific modalities, they suggest the need to develop a more standardized protocol for assessing sensory reactivity.

The chapters in this part emphasize the need for research to develop more standardized behavioral measures to evaluate both the underlying components of temperament, such as reactivity, and associated behavioral outcomes, such as noncompliance. A comprehensive assessment of these internal and external manifestations of temperament and regulation will allow clinicians to make appropriate, problem-specific recommendations to parents for environmental adjustments. Authors of chapters in this part (as well as in part V on state-related disorders of infancy and toddlerhood) highlight the importance of parental understanding and adjustment of environmental demands to accommodate children's temperamental constitutions in order to promote optimal functioning and to minimize the risk for negative outcomes.

5

Assessment of Disturbances in Emotion Regulation and Temperament

Cynthia A. Stifter
Crystal N. Wiggins

Two predominant behavioral complaints that parents bring to clinicians during infancy are infant colic and difficult temperament. Infant colic, or unexplained inconsolable crying occurring during the first 3 months of life, can be found in approximately 10% of the population. The intensity of crying and the inability to soothe the crying infant creates a host of parental reactions and concerns about the behavioral development of these infants. Similarly, an infant who fusses frequently and is hard to settle, characteristics of a difficult temperament, can affect family interactions. In contrast to infant colic, temperament is conceptualized as a relatively stable construct and, as such, a difficult temperament can have implications for more negative, persistent outcomes. During the toddler years, often called the "terrible twos," parental concerns revolve around issues of compliance. Interestingly, this focus comes at the same time that toddlers are discovering and asserting their autonomy. Such conflicting goals can produce tense and coercive interactions that, if persistent, may put the child at risk for later problem behavior.

In this chapter, infant colic, difficult temperament, and toddler noncompliance are discussed within a developmental context. While these three constructs constitute the primary behavioral complaints of early childhood and have received some "bad press," a closer look at the empirical evidence suggests that poor outcomes are conditional. In this chapter, the historical and current conceptualizations of each of these problems are presented along with their developmental course. In addition, the empirical findings regarding the outcomes for infant colic, difficult temperament, and compliance are presented and discussed. Finally, in keeping with the theme of this handbook, we discuss the various methods for assessing each of these behavioral constructs. As there is considerable overlap among these behavioral manifestations, several important issues consistent to all three will be raised. Understanding the developmental basis for infant colic, difficult temperament, and toddler noncompliance may guide clinicians in their assessment efforts and alleviate parental concerns about their effect on later development.

INFANT COLIC

All infants cry, and all cry for a reason. Indeed, the attributions applied to early infant crying range from pain to anger to boredom (Wolff, 1987). In the first months of life, crying is particularly salient as infants have relatively few effective methods of communicating their needs and states. Developmentally, crying in early infancy is distinguished by its temporal qualities. Over 40 years ago, Brazelton (1962) demonstrated that infants typically increase their crying across the first 3 months, with a peak at around 6 to 8 weeks of age. This finding has been replicated in other samples (see Barr, 1990, for a review) although a 2-week peak for fussing was found in a British sample (St James-Roberts & Plewis, 1996). Importantly, crying decreases significantly around 3 to 4 months of age, coinciding with important developmental changes in affect (social smiling), nonnegative vocalizations (cooing), and motor behavior (voluntary grasping). However, some infants exceed this developmental pattern of crying, by crying long, hard, and inconsolably. In this section, we consider the condition often referred to as infant colic. We discuss the incidence and developmental outcome of infant colic. We also consider the current debates on the conceptualization of colic and its measurement. Finally, we review techniques for assessing colic with recommendations for professionals working with parents of infants with colic.

Definition

Whereas it is expected that crying increases in early infancy, some infants cry significantly more during this time. Although there has been a healthy debate about how to define infant colic, the most popular definition was provided by Wessel in his classic 1954 study of infants in the Yale Rooming-In Project (Wessel, Cobb, Jackson, Harris, & Detwiler, 1954). He defined colic as "paroxysms of irritability, fussing or crying lasting for a total of more than 3 hours a day and occurring on more than three days in any one week" (p. 426) in an otherwise healthy young infant. Studies have begun to include other behavioral descriptions such as inconsolability, a distinctive cry sound, evening clustering, and hypertonia

(Lester, Boukydis, Garcia-Coll, & Hole, 1990; St James-Roberts & Haili, 1991; Stifter & Braungart, 1992). For example, although Wessel and others focused on the total amount of crying, the inability to soothe or be externally regulated may be a more important but related characteristic of infant colic (Barr, St James-Roberts, & Keefe, 2001).

Incidence

The incidence of infant colic varies from study to study, and ranges from 10–20% of the population. Infant colic does not appear to be specific to gender, and only a few studies report socioeconomic differences in colic (e.g., educated, white-collar workers were more likely to report infant colic) (Crowcroft & Strachan, 1997; Hide & Guyer, 1982), likely because the majority of colic samples are homogeneous (white, middle class). Parity has also been shown to be a factor when reporting colic, with parents of firstborns reporting colic more often (Crowcroft & Strachan, 1997; St James-Roberts & Haili, 1991). This finding contrasts with that of a number of studies, which found no difference in incidence between first- and later-borns. With regard to ethnicity, many of the studies of infant colic have been in Western societies. In the few studies that have examined non-Western populations (African, Indian), a similar crying peak was identified (Barr, Korner, Bakeman, & Adamson, 1991; St James-Roberts, Bowyer, Varghese, & Sawdon, 1994). The duration of crying for these infants, however, was significantly reduced compared to infants from Western communities because of differences in the caregiving practices of the non-Western societies studied, such as more carrying and sleeping together. These results suggest that the crying peak may be a universal phenomenon but that the length of crying in early infancy is due to culturally accepted methods of child care. However, since many of the Western samples used in studies of colic were predominantly Caucasian, it would be important to continue to examine the developmental crying curve by expanding samples to other ethnic groups.

Etiology

The causes of colic are as diverse as the methods for measuring this condition and can be categorized as either residing in the infant or the parent-infant dyad. Historically, the cause of infant colic has been primarily due to problems with the gastrointestinal tract. The term *colic* is derived from the Greek *kolikos*, the adjective of *kolon*, which implies a disturbance in the colon (Carey, 1984). Dietary causes of infant colic are the most predominant explanations, likely because of the number of studies dedicated to understanding the relationship between either lactose or protein found in breast milk to infant colic (for review see Treem, 1994). Methodological concerns regarding subject selection, timing of intervention, and lack of crossover effects, however, suggest that protein and lactose intolerance may be rare in infants with excessive crying. Other gastrointestinal causes such as malabsorption, intestinal motility, and gastroesophageal reflux have been less studied, and the evidence thus far is inconclusive. Taken together, the available data on organic causes has led researchers to conclude that "colic is a syndrome describing a heterogeneous group of disorders of which the minority represent specific dysfunctions of the gastrointestinal tract" (Treem, 1994, p. 1122). Indeed, the current perception is that only 5 to 10% of infants who cry excessively suffer from some organic disease (Gormally & Barr, 1997).

Prolonged infant crying has often been attributed to poor parenting practices. Bowlby and his associates (Bell & Ainsworth, 1972; Bowlby, 1982) suggested that increased infant crying signals the parents' failure to meet the biological and affectional needs of their infant. Alternatively, parents may overstimulate their infants, resulting in increased crying. Because infants with colic are characterized by excessive crying, it has been proposed that it may be in part due to insensitive parenting (Carey, 1984; Taubman, 1984). This highly controversial hypothesis is supported by evidence which shows that when parents are given instructions on when and how to respond to their infant's cries, crying decreases (Taubman, 1984). Also in support of this hypothesis are the few studies that have found a link between prenatal and/or early postnatal parental characteristics such as anxiety and depression and the development of colic (Carey, 1968; Rautava, Helenius, & Lehtonen, 1993). While this evidence would indicate that parenting style is related to colic,

there were some methodological weaknesses such as sample bias, assessment of colic, and the timing of the studies that limit forming a conclusion about the role of parenting in infant colic. Furthermore, while new parents are more likely to report colic, the fact that later-born infants develop colic in families in which the firstborn did not have colic belies this claim. Finally, these findings contrast with those of studies which have shown parents of infants with colic to be no different in parental characteristics and behavior when compared to parents of infants who did not have colic (Paradise, 1966; St James-Roberts, Conroy, & Wilsher, 1998a; Stifter & Braungart, 1992). In summary, the evidence that parenting behavior may account for excessive crying in early infancy is inconclusive. However, such parental characteristics may explain why some parents refer their children for problematic crying.

Current Conceptualizations

A Johnson & Johnson roundtable was held to address the nature, consequences, and management of infant colic (Barr et al., 2001). The meeting was dominated by discussion of the term *colic* and its appropriateness in defining a behavioral syndrome. It was agreed that colic was likely conceived by medical practioners and parents alike as having an organic origin (Stifter, Bono, & Spinrad, in press). But reviews of the existing research have led colic researchers, many of whom participated in the roundtable, to conclude that infant colic is a developmental phenomenon having to do with individual differences in reactivity and regulatory function. Indeed, Barr and Gunnar (2000) have hypothesized that infants with colic have "transient responsivity." That is, such infants are proposed to be more reactive and to have more difficulty regulating themselves than infants who did not have colic, but only during the colic period (1–4 months of age). Several studies provide empirical evidence for this conclusion:

1. Inconsolability or resistence to soothing is a characteristic of infants with colic (St James-Roberts, Conroy, & Wilsher, 1995; Stifter & Braungart, 1992; Prudhomme White, Gunnar, Larson, Donzella, & Barr, 2000).

2. Colicky infants' crying bouts were found to be longer but not more frequent than crying bouts of infants without colic (Barr, Rotman, Yaremko, Leduc, & Francoeur, 1992).
3. Whereas carrying reduced crying in non-colicky infants, it was ineffective for infants with colic (Barr et al., 1991).
4. Finally, a longitudinal study that examined infant reactivity before and after the colic period demonstrated that while infants with colic cried significantly more during the colic period, they were no more reactive either at birth, prior to the onset of colic, or at 5 and 10 months of age, shortly after the offset of colic (Stifter & Braungart, 1992).

The evidence is mounting that infant colic may be a function of delayed regulatory capacity, and that only a small portion of infants who cry excessively in the first 3 months of life do so because of some underlying organic condition. Differences in study methodologies, however, indicate that this conclusion should be treated cautiously until more definitive studies are conducted (see next section).

Assessing Colic

Much of the variation among the studies in definition, etiology, and incidence is likely due to differences in how colic was operationalized and the methods for obtaining the incidence data. For example, whether an infant had colic has been assessed retrospectively anywhere from 3 months of age (Lehtonen & Korvenranta, 1995) to 9 months after the colic has resolved (Rubin & Pendergast, 1984) and was determined by simply asking the question "Did your child have colic?" Interviews with either health visitors (Crowcroft & Strachan, 1997) or research assistants (Stifter & Braungart, 1992) have also been used to assess the presence of colic. In the study by Stifter & Braungart (1992), researchers telephoned parents when their infants were 3, 4, and 5 weeks of age and asked a series of questions regarding the children's crying behavior. In contrast to methods described previously, parents were never asked whether their child had colic in this study.

In all of the above cases, parents were entered into the study regardless of whether the child had colic. In other studies, the method for identifying colic relied more on self-referral, either to the researchers for "problematic" crying (Barr et al., 1992) or to a physician (St James-Roberts & Haili, 1991). Typically, these children were compared to children who were not identified by parents as having colic or worrisome crying behavior.

Each of these assessment methods has its limitations. Clearly, retrospective methods are problematic as they rely on parent memory and can be biased by current circumstances. For example, a parent of a difficult child might think back and recall incorrectly that the child was colicky based on the child's current behavior. In this case, any data that examines the outcome of colic using the retrospective method would need to be interpreted with caution. Moreover, simply asking whether a child had colic or not, even at 3 months of age, requires the parents to agree on what colic is. In a more recent study, we asked new parents to describe their conceptualization of infant colic (Stifter et al., 2002). While the majority of parents endorsed the characteristic "cries for long periods of time" (63%), over 50% of the parents also said colic was a gastrointestinal problem and 48% said colic was "inconsolability." Interestingly, 8% of the parents thought colic was "crying for no reason" and 1% had never heard of the term. Thus, there is some confusion among parents about what excessive crying in infancy represents. Unfortunately, disagreements also exist among researchers of infant colic.

Relying on parents to refer their infants for problematic crying or colic introduces a different bias. Considering a child's crying as problematic suggests that this difficulty is a product of an interaction between the characteristics of the child and those of the parent. For example, a parent who is young, inexperienced, and prone to anxiety may view fussing for 30-minute periods as excessive and problematic, while a less anxious, multiparous parent may view this behavior as normative. Indeed, such crying would be normal if the child were less than 3 months of age. This confound is further demonstrated by a study that compared infants referred for problematic crying to those for whom crying was not a problem. Barr and colleagues (1992) had all parents, problematic and nonproblematic, complete cry diaries. Using the Wessel (Wessel et al., 1954) definition of 3 or more hours of crying/fussing in a day, they found that not all infants referred for problematic crying fit the definition. In fact, 65% of the problematic criers did not meet the standard definition of colic. Moreover, these infants cried as much as the control infants and significantly less than the infants who met colic criteria. While these data point to the importance of validating infants referred for colic, they also demonstrate that excessive crying may be in the eye of the beholder.

The most current and accepted method for assessing infant colic is through the use of a parental diary. Briefly, the cry diary consists of a 24-hour day broken up into 5-minute segments (Barr, Kramer, Boisjoly, McVey-White, & Pless, 1988). Parents are asked to track the crying, fussing, sleeping, awake/content, and feeding periods of their infants. Some diaries also allow the reporting of "colic" bouts (St James-Roberts et al., 1995). In most cases, the researcher will define for the parent what is meant by each of these behaviors, particularly the difference between fussing and crying. The number of days of diary keeping needed to assess the presence of colic depends upon the purpose of the assessment. According to Barr (Barr & Desilets, n.d.), at least 6 days are required to obtain a reliable assessment of excessive crying. Researchers interested in questions of development and individual differences will want to have parents complete diaries for this length of time. However, given that maintaining a diary can be a difficult, time-consuming task for parents, clinicians may want to use fewer days. See figure 5.1 for an example of a diary recording day. As can be seen, this diary also includes who was with the child during each of the five behavioral states.

In summary, a parental diary that tracks infant crying is the most preferred method of assessing infant colic for several reasons. First, while the differences between crying and fussing may be influenced by the characteristics of the parent, diaries appear to reduce much of the bias associated with the retrospective method. Indeed, a study which applied prospective and retrospective methods to a community sample showed that the incidence rate for all infants regardless of method was 9.3% using the Wessel definition (Canivet, Hagander, Jakobsson, & Lanke, 1996). However,

only 5.3% came from the prospective cry diary, while 12.1% came from the postcolic interview. Second, although diaries depend upon parental reporting, by breaking down crying and fussing into 5-minute periods, parents do not have to recall whether their child cried for a total of 3 or more hours in a day. In a rigorous test of the validity of parental reports, two studies showed strong correlations between parental diaries of infant crying and voice-activated audiotaped crying during the same period (Barr et al., 1988; St James-Roberts, Conroy, & Wilsher, 1996). Finally, the diary can be used to validate parental complaints of excessive crying. However, whereas the assessment of colic that depends upon parental self-referral is less preferred, it does not mean such reporting should be ignored. Self-referrals may indicate a dynamic within the parent-child relationship that may be of interest to the researcher and clinician.

Concurrent and Developmental Outcomes

Although the research indicates that infant colic may be transitory, that does not preclude its immediate effect on the family environment nor its long-term outcome. Indeed, since colicky infants cry excessively and inconsolably, it is expected that such behavior would have a negative impact, particularly on parents. If one takes a transactional perspective, the outcomes for the infant should also be affected. Taking methodological limitations discussed earlier into consideration, the majority of the research data suggest that infant colic does not negatively affect the infant but rather has significant short-term and long-term consequences for parents.

The effects of colic on infant outcome have not been researched extensively; however, the few studies that have examined temperament or behavioral outcomes of infants with and without colic have been relatively consistent. Contemporaneous assessments of temperament and behavior of colicky infants during the first 3 months of life reveal differences that are consistent with the assessment of colic. Infants with colic were rated as having more difficult temperaments (more negative, less adaptable) and as more inconsolable than infants who did not have colic (Lehtonen,

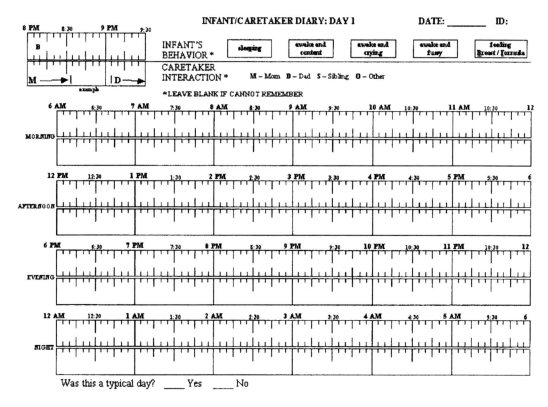

Figure 5.1 Infant/caretaker diary: day 1.

Korhonen, & Korvenranta, 1994; St James-Roberts et al., 1998b). Longitudinal observations and parent ratings of temperament show that infants with colic may continue to be more negatively reactive shortly after the colic has resolved (Roberts et al., 1998b; Stifter, 2001; cf. Stifter & Braungart, 1992). However, long-term assessments of temperament have revealed few differences (Lehtonen et al., 1994; St James-Roberts et al., 1998b; Stifter, 2001; Stifter & Braungart, 1992). Interestingly, Stifter's (2001) data suggest that this early difference in reactivity may be due to a delay in the development of regulatory strategies. In one follow-up study, mothers reported more temper tantrums in their 3-year-olds who had colic, although there were no differences in reported behavior problems between the colic and noncolic groups (Rautava, Lehtonen, Helenius, & Sillanpa, 1995). Finally, several studies have also examined mental development in infants with colic and, likewise, have demonstrated

no effect of colic (Rautava et al., 1995; St James-Roberts et al., 1998b; Stifter & Braungart, 1992). In one study, although a significant difference between infants who had colic and those who did not on the Bayley MDI was revealed at 6 months, both groups were within the normal range and no differences were found at 12 months of age (Sloman, Bellinger, & Krentzel, 1990).

As might be expected, the impact of infant colic is felt more by the parents, particularly mothers who have the burden of caring for the excessively crying child. During the colic period, mothers report more stress and greater separation anxiety (Humphry & Hock, 1989), while also manifesting symptoms of psychological distress (Pineyard, 1992). In a prospective study that examined both prepartum and postpartum affective distress, mothers of infants with colic were more likely to increase in their distress across this period while mothers of infants without colic decreased in distress (Miller, Barr, & Eaton, 1993).

The few studies that have examined the consequences of having a colicky child, thus far, indicate that there are no negative outcomes for parent behavior and, importantly, for the parent-child relationship. However, having cared for an infant with colic appears to have affected parents' feelings about their own ability to parent as well as their perceptions of how their family is functioning. In two separate studies (St James-Roberts et al., 1998a; Stifter & Braungart, 1992), mothers of colicky and noncolicky infants were observed to be alike in maternal sensitivity shortly after the colic resolved (5 months of age) and 7 months later. These findings may explain why no long-term effects of infant colic on the parent-child relationship have been found. Infants who developed colic were not more likely to be insecurely attached than infants who did not have colic (Stifter & Bono, 1998). On the contrary, the number of securely attached colicky infants was well above the norm found in other studies of noncolicky infants. While there appears to be no negative effect for infant colic on maternal behavior, there is some evidence that mothers are affected personally by their interactions with an inconsolable child (Stifter, 2001; Stifter & Bono, 1998). In two studies, mothers of infants who had colic rated themselves as less competent than mothers of infants who did not have colic. What is remarkable about these findings is that mothers of colicky infants continued to feel lower self-efficacy even after the colic had resolved. These findings are not surprising when one considers the intensity and duration of the crying exhibited by colicky infants and that the ability to respond with success to an infant's needs is the basis of maternal self-efficacy. The long-term effect may be explained by other follow-up results, which showed mothers (and fathers) of colicky infants to be dissatisfied with their marriages (Stifter, 2001) and with the distribution of responsibilities within the home (Rautava et al., 1995).

It is important to note a study that deals with excessive crying in infancy that occurs after the colic period. The findings are in contrast to what has been reported on infants with colic and suggest some significant negative developmental outcomes for these infants and their families (Hofacker & Papousek, 1998). While these infants are referred by their parents for problematic crying, like infants in the first 3 months of life, they do not fit the criteria of colic and therefore are not presented here.

Summary of the Research on Infant Colic

Infant colic continues to be an enigma to parents, clinicians, and researchers. Thus far, research has produced such varied and conflicting results that investigators are beginning to conclude that colic is a complex condition that has many causes. Given the methodological weaknesses of many of the studies on infant colic, this action may be premature. However, when taken together, the findings clearly suggest that infant colic is a transient condition characterized by intense crying of long duration that is stressful for the family. Although the origins of colic continue to be debated, the evidence is growing that it does not have a profound long-term effect on the child. On the other hand, whereas infant colic may not affect maternal behavior toward a child, it does appear to affect a mother's perceptions of her ability as a parent and her satisfaction with her family and marriage. Such perceptions may have further consequences for the child, but this outcome requires more research.

Because of the disparateness of the approaches to the study of infant colic, more research is necessary. Future research should build upon the consensus that currently exists, including, first, the operationalization of infant colic. Studies that use an agreed-upon definition such as that of Wessel (Wessel et al., 1954) are more easily compared than those that rely on parents to diagnose their infant's condition. Second, parents' complaints of excessive crying should be validated with diary data or observational data. The use of diaries has greatly improved the assessment of infant colic, but such studies continue to rely on parents' perceptions. Advances in technology may make it easier for families to maintain a video record of their infants' activities for assessment by less biased researchers. Third, more comparisons are needed between clinical (self-referred) and community samples to verify differences within and between these samples. Fourth, few studies have assessed infant and parenting characteristics prior to the onset of colic. Such research would be important toward confirming or disconfirming the biological, temperamental, and social causes of colic. Finally, the proposal that colic is a condition of "transient responsivity" (Barr & Gunnar, 2000) requires further study. Assessment of regulatory capacity before, during, and after the colic period is needed.

DIFFICULT TEMPERAMENT

Infants exhibit individual differences in their responses to both internal and external stimuli. For example, the same toy that elicits interest and cooing in one infant may induce crying and withdrawal in another infant. Additionally, the duration and intensity of emotional reactions may vary from infant to infant. These individual differences in emotional and behavioral responses can be explained by the psychobiological concept of temperament. Infant temperament has been associated with later social, emotional, and cognitive development. In particular, the concept of difficult temperament has perpetuated a significant amount of empirical research, likely due to its relation to negative child outcomes. The following sections review both seminal and contemporary definitions of difficult temperament, as they evolved in the temperament literature. In describing past research defining difficult temperament, this section addresses measurement concerns and developmental outcomes. We take the position that eventual negative outcomes are the product of many confluent factors that combine and interact with difficult temperament. Future research ideas are also presented.

Defining Temperament

There are several conceptualizations of temperament (Buss & Plomin, 1975, 1984; Goldsmith & Campos, 1982; Rothbart & Derryberry, 1981; Thomas & Chess, 1977), most differing on the importance of emotional valence and the preeminence of physiology in temperament. Since these distinctions are not central here, only the commonalities are discussed (see Goldsmith et al., 1987 for in-depth discussion of these positions). Simply stated, temperament can be defined as in-

dividual differences in reactivity and self-regulation (Rothbart, 1981). Although there is empirical research to support the contrary, temperament is assumed to have a constitutional basis (DiPietro & Porges, 1988; Goldsmith, Buss, & Lemery, 1997; Porter, Porges, & Marshall, 1988), to be relatively stable (Lemery, Goldsmith, Klinnert, & Mrazek, 1999), and to be influenced by the environment (Bates, Wachs, & VandenBos, 1995; Wachs, 1994).

Original Conceptualization of Difficult Temperament

Thomas, Chess, and Birch introduced the concept of difficult temperament in 1968. Data from their longitudinal study, which relied on parental report of infant behaviors assessed through an interview format, yielded at least three constellations or types of infant temperament, labeled easy, slow-to-warm, and difficult. These three temperament types were derived from their nine dimensions of infant behavior. According to Thomas et al. (1968), the "difficult" type of temperament, which represented 10% of their sample, was characterized by five categories of functioning: (1) prevalence of irregular biological functioning (low rhythmicity); (2) initial aversion to environmental changes (low approach); (3) slow or low adaptability to environmental changes; (4) high intensity in affect expression; and (5) negative mood. The most popular assessment tool that mirrors the conceptual archetype is the Infant Temperament Questionnaire (ITQ) and the Revised Infant Temperament Questionnaire (RITQ) developed by Carey and McDevitt (Carey, 1970; Carey & McDevitt, 1978).

Subsequent Definitions of Difficult Temperament

Other definitions of difficult temperament can be found (Buss & Plomin, 1975; Kagan, 1982; Rothbart, 1982; Rowe & Plomin, 1977; Thomas, Chess, & Korn, 1982). Some of these definitions pay more attention to the influence social perception plays on the formation of difficult temperament. For example, Bates, Freeland, and Lounsbury (1979) introduced the concept of the fussy-difficult dimension, measured using the Infant Characteristic Questionnaire (ICQ). Within this alternative definition, the negative mood and the high intensity of affect dimensions represented in Thomas et al.'s (1968) conceptualization were maintained; however, the concept of infant soothability was introduced. Soothability emphasizes the degree to which parents feel that they can modulate the negative affect of their infant. Bates's concept of infant soothability appears to contain both the within-infant characteristics and elements outside the infant. The infant's physiological and behavioral response to external regulation attempts is an important component of soothability. However, infant soothability also depends upon factors outside of the infant like parental efficacy, parental competence to regulate infant distress, and parental expectancies of infant's emotional states. Thus, Bates's assessment of difficult temperament may contain elements of subjective perception, as well as objective components.

Additionally, Thomas and Chess, two of the three originators of the difficult temperament conceptualization, have revised their definition. According to Thomas and Chess (1982), the category of difficult temperament has now evolved into a continuous easy-to-difficult dimension. After conducting a second-order factor analysis with the nine original categories, difficult temperament no longer resembles a five-factor structure mentioned previously, but a three- or four-factor model, which includes mood, approach, adaptability, and sometimes distractibility. Rhythmicity and intensity, which were originally present, are now absent.

Grappling With the Definition: Consolidation and Implications

As one can observe, there is no unitary definition of difficultness. To many, the concept of difficult temperament may seem like a work in progress. Despite the fact that difficult temperament has been defined numerous ways and has withstood several revisions (Thomas & Chess, 1982), the core characteristics remain consistent. The central aspects of difficult temperament appear to be frequent fussing or crying and longer time required to regulate negative affect.

At first glance, the definition of difficult temperament appears strikingly similar to the concept of infant colic. However, the stability of these infant conditions serves as a prominent distinction. Infant colic, or excessive/persistent crying and inconsolability in early infancy, ends around 3 to 4 months of age (see above). On the other hand, empirical evidence suggests that the concept of difficult temperament is moderately stable (Bates, 1986; Rothbart, 1986; Worobey & Blajda, 1989). For example, Riese (1987) reported that irritability, a major aspect of difficult temperament, was modestly consistent from the neonatal period to 24 months of age. Although modest relations can be detected from the neonatal period onward, stronger and longer-term stability coefficients can be found when difficult temperament is measured after 6 to 9 months of age (Lee & Bates, 1985; Lemery et al., 1999; Pettit & Bates, 1984).

Although difficult temperament in infants is relatively stable, many theorists and researchers have asked the question "What makes difficult temperament stable?" (Wachs, 1999). Some theorists believe that an infant's underlying biology contributes to the constancy of difficult temperament. Others have suggested that the stability of difficult temperament may stem from the measurement process rather than from infant characteristics (Lemery et al., 1999). This assumption is revisited and emphasized in the following section, which addresses current measurement techniques and their benefits and limitations.

Assessing Temperament

If a researcher desires to assess the temperament of an infant, numerous tools are available. Researchers have identified three major ways of measuring infant temperament and difficult temperament in particular: (1) parental report, (2) home observation, and (3) laboratory assessment (Rothbart & Goldsmith, 1985). Furthermore, within each category there are a variety of questionnaires, procedures, and coding systems from which to choose. As mentioned previously, different definitions of temperament have given rise to many measurement techniques. However, each measurement technique—parental report, home observation, and laboratory assessment—

has its advantages and disadvantages. Although one cannot eliminate all error from the assessment of difficult temperament, employing multiple measures may reduce bias associated with any single method.

Parental report is the most utilized method for assessing difficult temperament, and temperament in general. Of the numerous infant temperament questionnaires presently available, the ICQ (Bates et al., 1979), the Infant Behavior Questionnaire (IBQ; Rothbart, 1981), the Revised Infant Temperament Questionnaire (RITQ; Carey & McDevitt, 1978), and the EAS Temperament Survey (Buss & Plomin, 1984) are the most popular (see Slabach, Morrow, & Wachs, 1991 for in-depth synopsis of available questionnaires). Recently, new temperament questionnaires like the Early Infancy Temperament Questionnaire (EITQ; Medoff-Cooper, Carey, & McDevitt, 1993) and the Pictorial Assessment of Temperament (PAT; Clarke-Stewart, Fitzpatrick, Allhusen, & Goldberg, 2000) have emerged and may be found useful. Some of the questionnaires conceptualize difficult temperament on a continuum (e.g., the ICQ Difficulty Scale), while others categorize infants into "difficult" or "nondifficult" classifications by combining scores from several scales. Temperament questionnaires also vary in length; however, most questionnaires provide some context in which parents are asked to recall and rate the intensity and frequency of their infants' behavior.

The popularity of parent-report questionnaires is largely due to their low cost and ease of administration. Temperament questionnaires usually require about 30 minutes to complete and can be completed at the parents' convenience (Rothbart & Goldsmith, 1985; Rothbart & Mauro, 1990). Another advantage of questionnaires is that they utilize parents' experiences with their child. Researchers have suggested that parents are optimal reporters of difficult temperament due to the extensive time spent interacting with their infants across numerous different contexts. Evidence suggests that both parents usually agree about infant temperament traits (Bates et al., 1979; Lyon & Plomin, 1981; Rothbart & Derryberry, 1981).

Although parental report of infant difficult temperament through the questionnaire format has many advantages, the use of questionnaires is not without criticism. As Rothbart and Goldsmith (1985) noted, potential variations in temperament questionnaires emerge as a result of rater characteristics, the interaction between infant and rater, and factors stemming from the questionnaire itself. Of these sources of variation, parental rating bias has captured most of the empirical attention (Vaughn, Bradley, Joffe, Seifer, & Barglow, 1987). Research has shown that socioeconomic status (Sameroff, Seifer, & Elias, 1982), depression (Hart, Field, & Roitfarb, 1999), and elevated levels of anxiety (Sameroff et al., 1982; Vaughn, Taraldson, Crichton, & Egeland, 1981) are related to parental reports of infant difficult temperament. In fact, a body of research has suggested that parental characteristics (aggression, suspicion, and impulsivity) and parents' working models of their infant measured prenatally are related to postbirth reports of infant difficultness and temperament in general (Wolk, Zeanah, Garcia Coll, & Carr, 1992; Zeanah & Anders, 1987; Zeanah, Keener, Stewart, & Anders, 1985). More recently, Pedersen, Huffman, Del Carmen, and Bryan (1996) reported that mothers who prenatally rated cry recordings as more adverse described their 3-month-old infants as being more fussy or difficult. In another study, maternal characteristics accounted for more variance in ITQ scores than observations of infant behavior (Sameroff et al., 1982). Additionally, empirical evidence demonstrates that when mothers and trained observers use the ITQR, ICQ, IBQ, and the EAS temperament survey to assess the same infant behavior at home, there is low agreement (Seifer, Sameroff, Barrett, & Krafchulk, 1994). Collectively, these studies indicate that parental reports of infant temperament and difficultness may be influenced by factors that have little association with infant emotionality and behaviors.

Because of the subjective component of parental report measures, researchers have turned to more objective methods of assessing infant temperament: home and laboratory observations (Garcia Coll, Kagan, & Resnick, 1984; Goldsmith & Rothbart, 1991; Kagan, Resnick, & Gibbons, 1989; Riese, 1987a, 1987b; Rothbart, 1986). Both of these techniques utilize a behavioral assessment approach and are therefore thought to minimize subjectivity in evaluating the infant's disposition. Home observations may be semistructured or standardized assessments. During the semistructured home observation, the infant and the caregiver (usually the mother) interact for approximately 1 hour while a trained observer codes the occurrence and intensity of infant behaviors. The trained observer tries to minimize interference so that a more natural representation of the infant's temperament may be assessed. Standardized home observations resemble the characteristics of laboratory assessments and are distinct from semistructured home observations as they use standard tasks designed to elicit infant emotional and behavioral responses. Established behavioral assessment batteries include the Behavioral Assessment of Infant Temperament (Garcia Coll, Halpern, Vohr, Seifer, & Oh, 1992) and the Laboratory Temperament Assessment Battery (LAB-TAB) (prelocomotor and locomotor version; Goldsmith & Rothbart, 1991). During these standardized tasks, infants interact with a variety of individuals (i.e., caregiver, experimenter, strangers) and engage in numerous challenging procedures (i.e., toy removal, gentle arm restraint, and engaging with novel stimuli), in order to assess individual differences in emotion and regulation.

Whereas home or lab observations reduce subjective perception, these methods also have several drawbacks. Some common complaints are that observational methods require more time and financial commitment than parental reports. Unlike questionnaires, where the greater number of items asked results in higher reliability, numerous home observations and laboratory procedures are required to obtain a reliable approximation of infant temperament. Specifically, it has been demonstrated that aggregating 6 to 8 separate home observations provides a reliable estimate of infant temperament (Seifer et al., 1994). Additionally, despite the great time investment, observational methods may restrict the opportunity to witness a range of infant emotions and intensity. Moreover, the presence of a stranger in the home may alter the normal behavior of the parent and the infant. Finally, low-intensity behaviors in the laboratory may be related to sampling bias, since parents of infants with difficult temperament might be less prone to participate in laboratory studies.

In response to the potential biases that each method of difficult temperament assessment brings, researchers have often chosen to utilize multiple assessment methods simultaneously to address unrelated sources of variation (Goldsmith, Lemery, Buss, & Campos, 1999; Seifer et al., 1994). As mentioned previously, repeating the same method to measure infant behavior raises reliability (Hubert, Wachs, Peters-Martin, & Gandour, 1982; Matheny, Wilson, & Nuss, 1984). It cannot, however, control for method bias. In fact, using this technique compounds method error. A multiple measure, multi-informant, multiprocedural approach does address and reduce method bias (Goldsmith et al., 1999; Seifer et al., 1994). In 1985, Rothbart and Goldsmith used parent report, home observation, and laboratory assessment in conjunction to gain a more comprehensive understanding of infant reactivity and regulation. Using a multimethod technique is beneficial because it utilizes the strengths of the individual method while controlling for measurement error and bias. This approach allows parents to report infant responses based on their extensive experience, while allowing observers to report on temperamental differences seen in the home context and in a more standardized environment on multiple occasions. This approach, importantly, appreciates the fact that an infant's behavior may vary across context (home, laboratory) and interaction with individuals (mother, father, strangers/ experimenters).

Developmental Outcomes of Difficult Temperament

Research on the developmental outcomes of infants with difficult temperament has been conducted. However, difficult temperament in infancy influences more than the infant. In this section, the effect of difficult temperament on parenting, the parent-child relationship, and later infant behavior is discussed.

As might be expected when interacting with a fussy, inconsolable child, observational research has shown that mothers of irritable infants are less responsive to their infants and exhibit lower levels of positive maternal behavior (Lowinger, 1999; Owens, Shaw, & Vondra, 1998; Schuler, Black, & Starr, 1995). Moreover, these mother-infant dyads experienced trouble establishing affective synchrony, an important factor in later infant emotion regulation skills (Keefe, Kotzen, Froese-Fritz, & Curtain, 1996). Although there are many studies that report that mothers of difficult infants behave in insensitive ways toward their infants, the majority of these studies were conducted with highly stressed samples (i.e., depressed and/or low socioeconomic status [SES]). Thus, the relation between difficult temperament and maternal behaviors could not be isolated from the effect of low SES or depressive symptoms. However, van den Boom and Hoeksma (1994) isolated the influence of difficult temperament in low-income mothers by examining the parenting behavior of mothers with their irritable and nonirritable infants. This study reported that low-income mothers of irritable infants demonstrated less visual contact, effective stimulation, physical contact, and soothing behaviors than low-income mothers of nonirritable infants. Thus, difficult temperament contributed to the expression of poor parenting behavior in low-income samples.

Difficult temperament in infancy also appears to influence mothers' perceptions of their parenting abilities (Gross, Conrad, Fogg, & Wothke, 1994; Teti & Gelfand, 1991). Specifically, infant difficult temperament was related to the mothers' belief that they were ineffective in regulating their infant's affective states. Consequently, mothers with low self-efficacy exhibited more negative psychological functioning and maternal behavior (Gross et al., 1994). Self-efficacy, on the other hand, was found to buffer the effect of difficult temperament on maternal parenting behavior, such that mothers who believed that they were effective emotion regulation agents were less likely to act insensitively to their infants (Teti & Gelfand, 1991; Teti, Gelfand, & Pompa, 1990).

Most studies support the notion that difficult temperament alone or in combination with other variables (parental depression, martial satisfaction, and economic stress) places infants at an increased risk for future adjustment problems (Sanson, Smart, Prior, & Oberklaid, 1993). For example, a positive relation between infant difficult temperament and later insecure attachment has been shown (Susman-Stillman, Kalkoske, Egeland, & Waldman, 1996). Although maternal

sensitivity exhibited during infancy acts as a mediator for this relationship, the development of an insecure attachment is not trivial. Indeed, empirical evidence has demonstrated that children with insecure attachments are at a higher risk for interpersonal difficulties, early preschool and later academic problems, and behavior problems (Londerville & Main, 1981; Shaw & Vondra, 1995). The direct link between difficultness and cognitive and academic performance has also been studied (Field et al., 1978; Guerin, Gottfried, & Thomas, 1997; Maziade, Cote, Boutin, Bernier, & Thivierge, 1989; Roth, Eisenberg, & Sell, 1984); however, collectively the findings are inconsistent.

Even though difficult temperament places infants at increased risk for interpersonal, cognitive, and academic impairment, most studies have concentrated on the link between difficult temperament and later behavioral problems (Bates, Maslin, & Frankel, 1985; Cameron, 1978; Lee & Bates, 1985; Shaw & Vondra, 1995; Thomas et al., 1968). Wolkind and Desalis (1982) reported that maternal perceived difficultness predicted behavioral problems at 42 months. Research has also shown that difficultness measured in infancy predicts adolescent behavior problems (Guerin, Gottfried, & Thomas, 1997). In this longitudinal study, temperamental difficultness measured at 18 months was related to parental reports of behavioral problems from 39 months to 12 years. Specifically, fussy, hard-to-soothe infants were found to be at increased risk for aggressive behaviors, attention difficulties, and thought problems in the clinical range according to parental and/or teacher report. Although difficult infants were 6 to 10 times more likely to meet clinical criteria for aggression measured by parental report, it is important to note that not every difficult infant expressed behavioral problems later in life.

Whereas the effect of difficult temperament on low-risk mothers is not well understood, collectively, the previous studies highlight how difficult temperament in infancy may interact with present environmental and psychological stress to produce lower perceptions of parenting ability, less than optimal parenting behavior, and negative child outcome. In fact, the goodness-of-fit model (Mangelsdorf, Gunnar, Kestenbaum, Lang, & Andreas, 1991; Super & Harkness, 1994) would suggest that difficult temperament in infancy would only result in negative outcomes when the environment that sustains the infant is deficient (parental stress, insensitivity, psychological impairment, etc.). This goodness-of-fit perception is partially supported by the empirical evidence which shows that parental efficacy and sensitivity mediate the relation between difficult temperament and later academic, socioemotional, and interpersonal behavior.

Summary of the Research on Difficult Temperament

Presently, there is a lack of consensus concerning the underlying elements that make up difficult temperament. This absence of agreement undoubtedly reflects the ongoing debate about temperament in general. Nevertheless, most researchers concur that difficult temperament in infancy is characterized by frequent fussing and a hard-to-soothe disposition. Unlike infant colic, empirical efforts have demonstrated that difficult temperament is moderately stable and is associated with negative outcomes for parents and infants alike. Although some studies report that difficult temperament directly places infants at increased risk for psychological, relational, and behavioral problems, most research suggests that difficult temperament indirectly impacts infant adjustment by combining with other parental stressors. This notion is further supported by findings indicating that interventions which successfully alter parental sensitivity, attitudes, expectations, and/or behaviors have proven to buffer the negative effects of difficult temperament (Cohen et al., 1999; van den Boom, 1994). Future research on difficult temperament should focus on assessment. In particular, researchers should aim to reduce rater and method bias by employing a multiple informant and multiple assessment approach. This technique is critical for comprehending the nature of difficult temperament and investigating developmental outcomes.

COMPLIANCE

Toward the end of the second year of life, changes in children's abilities result in an increase in expectations by parents (Maccoby, 1980). The ability to self-locomote means that toddlers now can obtain the objects they desire, while advances in cognitive and language ability make it easier for parents to communicate rules and standards. Coincident to this growth is the toddler's emerging sense of self, particularly self-evaluation and an understanding of wrongdoing (Stipek, Gralinski, & Kopp, 1990). Thus, rather than swoop in to prevent their infant from handling a delicate object, parents of toddlers can verbally transmit the prohibition with the expectation that their child will inhibit his or her behavior. However, the toddler, with newfound abilities, a renewed interest in the environment, and an emerging sense of autonomy, may not always heed the demands of the parent, leading to conflict and negativism. Indeed, conflicts between mothers and children in early childhood peak around 30 months of age (Klimes-Dougan & Kopp, 1999) and discipline encounters can occur as frequently as once every 9 minutes (Power & Chapieski, 1986). It is no surprise, then, that this period of development is called the terrible twos. If conflict between the parent and toddler persists, the outcome can be poor for the child, often leading to referral to a professional or, in the extreme case, abuse on the part of the parent. Thus, understanding the development of the ability to control behavior in response to external demands, or compliance, is an important task for parents and the professionals that work with them. In this section, we review the developmental course of compliance, taking into consideration the various types of both compliance and noncompliance. Recent findings regarding the outcome of compliance and its counterpart, noncompliance, are then reviewed, followed by suggestions for future research. Finally, the assessment of compliance/noncompliance is discussed.

Development

The ability of the child to respond appropriately to external demands, or compliance, is considered an important developmental task and, as mentioned above, several processes contribute to its emergence. In her developmental framework for self-regulation, Kopp (1982) includes compliance, which she considers a form of control, the developmental level that precedes self-control and self-regulation. According to Kopp, control emerges around 12 to 18 months of age and requires such cognitive processes as intentionality, goal-directed behavior, and memory. In support of this hypothesized developmental process are studies which have empirically demonstrated that increases in compliance parallel increases in comprehension (Kaler & Kopp, 1990), self-concept (Stipek et al., 1990), and overall developmental level (Vaughn, Kopp, & Krakow, 1984). Other processes have also been linked to the development of compliance in toddlers. Individual differences in focused attention, spontaneous restraint, and mother-oriented motivation were found to be related to increases in compliance (Kochanska, Tjebkes, & Forman, 1998). Alternatively, the inability to regulate emotional reactivity in infancy was found to predict later toddler noncompliance (Stifter, Spinrad, & Braungart-Rieker, 1999).

Because children's reactions to requests by parents can vary qualitatively as well as quantitatively, several researchers have proposed that the dichotomous category of compliance/noncompliance be further differentiated (Crockenberg & Litman, 1990; Kuczynski, Kochanska, Radke-Yarrow, & Girnius-Brown, 1987; Vaughn et al., 1984). Noncompliance has been delineated into self-assertion (refusing without negative affect), defiance (refusing to follow a directive with negative affect), and passive noncompliance (ignoring parental request). Whereas defiance and passive noncompliance are considered unskillful methods of refusal (Kuczynski & Kochanska, 1990) and are associated with emotion dysregulation (Stifter et al., 1999), self-assertion is believed to be a more competent reflection of the child's growing autonomy that elicits more positive responses from the environment (Crockenberg & Litman, 1990). Indeed, self-assertive children are more likely to engage in negotiation with their mothers (Kuczynski et al., 1987) and to be more developmentally advanced (Vaughn et al., 1984).

More recently, Kochanska and Askan (1995) further differentiated compliance into that which is done wholeheartedly and enthusiastically (committed compliance) and that which, although not oppositional, requires sustained input from the parent (situational compliance). Each of these compliance types is proposed to have a distinct motivational basis. This contention is supported by studies that reveal different antecedents, consequences, and developmental pathways. First, as expected, committed compliance increases with age, whereas situational compliance decreases with age (Kochanska & Askan, 1995). Longitudinally, spontaneous restraint in infancy was predictive of committed but not situational compliance (Kochanska et al., 1998). Likewise, mother-child mutually positive affect and maternal gentle control were associated with committed but not situational compliance (Kochanska & Askan, 1995), while direct control was found to be associated with situational compliance and negatively related to committed compliance (Braungart-Rieker, Garwood, & Stifter, 1997). Finally, committed compliance but not situational compliance was shown to predict later internalization (Kochanska, Askan, & Koenig, 1995).

Coincident or possibly consequential to the development of newfound abilities in toddlers is an increase in parental expectations for behavior. In addition, parents are changing the way they interact with their children in discipline situations. Using an open-ended questionnaire, Gralinski and Kopp (1993) found that mothers' expectations increased and changed with child age. Everyday rules were expected from infants as early as 13 months of age and consisted of rules related to the safety of the child. Parents not only increased the number and types of everyday rules for child behavior during the second year, but by 30 months parental expectations expanded to include other domains such as family routines and self-care. Finally, the compliance rates of the children as reported by mothers increased alongside the increase in parental demand. Thus, it appears that parents are using observed developmental advances to inform them about what they can expect from infants and toddlers. The same might be said for what parents do in situations that require toddler compliance. Mothers observed interacting with their children in a demand situation were shown to make equal amounts of "do" and "don't" demands (Kuczynski & Kochanska, 1995). "Do" commands consisted of requests to carry out an action such as putting toys away, whereas "don't" commands required prohibitions such as resisting touching a tempting toy. "Do's" were found to be most often associated with pro-social action and behaviors that benefitted the child or others and less often associated with demands for appropriate behavior, which was related more to "don'ts." Interestingly, "do's" were found to be more difficult for infants and toddlers to comply with than "don'ts" (Kochanska & Askan, 1995), suggesting that such demands from mothers promote social competence. Indeed, when mothers made more "do" demands, their children were less likely to have behavior problems as preschoolers (Kuczynski & Kochanska, 1995).

Assessing Compliance/Noncompliance

In most studies of compliance and noncompliance in toddlers, this behavior is measured through observations during specifically designed tasks. The most common task is the cleanup task, which usually occurs after a free play session (Braungart-Rieker et al., 1997; Crockenberg & Litman, 1990; Kochanska & Askan, 1995). During this task, either the parent or the experimenter asks the child to put the toys away. In other laboratory situations, compliance is assessed either in response to maternal directives spontaneously emitted during a series of tasks (Kuczynski & Kochanska, 1990; Londerville & Main, 1981) or in response to maternal requests during a teaching task (Kaler & Kopp, 1990; Rocissano, Slade, & Lynch, 1987). Observed child compliance has also been measured in response to maternal demands in the home (Williams & Forehand, 1984) and experimenter demands in the laboratory (Stifter et al., 1999).

As mentioned above, there are several types of compliance and noncompliance; thus, behaviors exhibited in response to parental or experimental requests are coded and categorized accordingly. Compliance to a demand can be further differentiated into committed compliance and situational compliance. Committed compliance is coded if the child willingly cooperates with a request, whereas situational compliance requires constant external reminders (Kochanska & Askan, 1995). So, in response to a request to clean up, a child who exhibits committed compliance would begin to put toys away after only one or two requests

from the parent, whereas the child who exhibits situational compliance would require repeated requests or directives to complete the task.

There are also different types of noncompliance: passive noncompliance, defiance, and self-assertion. A child who uses passive noncompliance generally ignores the request. Using the cleanup example, when the parent requests that the child put the toys away, the child would continue to play with the toys, disregarding the request. Defiance is characterized by refusal accompanied by negative affect and aggression. Thus, a child who defies his mother when asked to cleanup might say "no" with an angry tone, have a temper tantrum, and/or throw the toys. Self-assertion, on the other hand, is typically coded as a verbal refusal to comply but without negative affect, as illustrated in the statement, "I'll clean this up later, okay?" Codes are usually applied to either segments (e.g., every 30 seconds) of a cleanup task, which are then tallied, or to the entire cleanup period.

Paper-and-pencil measures have also be used to assess compliance/noncompliance, although less often than observational assessments. Gralinksi and Kopp (1993), in a study examining the development of everyday rules of conduct, asked parents to report the degree of compliance to certain maternal requests such as not spilling drinks and washing up when requested. Noncompliance can also be assessed using the Child Behavior Checklist (CBCL) 2–3 Years (Achenbach, Edelbrock, & Howell, 1987). The CBCL is a 100-item measure that asks parents to rate on a 3-point scale the degree to which the expression of a behavior is true (not true, somewhat true, very true) for their child. Behaviors such as defiance, inability to wait, and uncooperativeness could be used to assess parental or teachers' perceptions of the child's compliance. Moreover, a cluster of items representing oppositional/defiant behaviors, which includes such behavior as stubbornness, whining, and temper tantrums, has been identified. The interpretation of the CBCL for toddlers, however, should be used with caution, as high levels of noncompliant behaviors may represent either developmental delays or, as mentioned above, the child's assertion of independence. Taking into consideration the developmental rather than chronological age of the child is important when interpreting these data.

The Socialization of Compliance

Whereas important developmental milestones in infancy need to be met before a toddler can effectively comply with parental requests, the research on compliance/noncompliance has been dominated by the role of parents in socializing rules and standards for conduct. Most of the studies were conducted using a free play/cleanup laboratory design or home observations of naturalistic conflicts. Taken together, the findings suggest that mothers who used clear, short, firm reprimands were more likely to elicit compliance (Pfiffner & O'Leary, 1989; Williams & Forehand, 1984), whereas physical enforcement was likely to perpetuate noncompliance (Kuczynski & Kochanska, 1990; Power & Chapieski, 1986). Other studies have examined the contingency of maternal responses to child demands, and the consensus appears to be that parents whose responses are contingent and synchronous (Parpal & Maccoby, 1985; Rocissano, Slade, & Lynch, 1987; Schaffer & Crook, 1980) have children who are more compliant. These findings are supported by a study of infant attachment and compliance, which revealed that secure infants were more compliant and that mothers of secure infants used more gentle discipline than mothers of insecure infants (Londerville & Main, 1981). In summary, these data suggest that when parental expectations are communicated in a firm, clear, and responsive manner, children are more likely to respond appropriately.

Perhaps more relevant to mental health professionals are studies which have demonstrated that maternal mood, specifically depression, may influence parental control strategies and subsequently child compliance. In a series of studies examining depressed mothers, daughters of depressed mothers were more noncompliant than daughters of nondepressed mothers (Kuczynski et al., 1987), and children of depressed mothers exhibited more passive noncompliance (Kuczynski & Kochanska, 1990). This may be due to the mothers' style of control, which was characterized as lower in demands and reprimands at age 2

years (Kochanska, Kuczynski, & Maguire, 1989). These findings demonstrate that maternal mood may disrupt the ability to socialize standards of conduct, which may result in more problem behavior later on (Leadbeater, Bishop, & Raver, 1996).

Developmental Outcomes

Although historically, research on child compliance/noncompliance has focused more on parenting behavior and control techniques than on child characteristics, several models and findings indicate that noncompliance, particularly that which persists beyond the toddler period, is the result of the interaction between the noncompliant child and the frustrated, demanding, authoritarian parent. This pattern of behavior is reflected in the coercion model (Chamberlain & Patterson, 1995), which proposes that escalation of negative behavior on the part of the child and ineffective discipline strategies on the part of the parent can result in problem behavior. This dynamic is supported by data from several studies. Shaw, Keenan, and Vondra (1994) examined infant precursors of 3-year externalizing behavior in low-income families. For boys, noncompliance and maternal responsiveness was predictive of 2-year aggression, which in turn was predictive of externalizing behavior (for girls, only noncompliance was predictive of externalizing behaviors). In another study, for preschool-aged boys who were rated by their parents as "hard to manage" (Campbell, 1997), negative maternal control and early problem behavior (including noncompliance) together predicted the maintenance of the problem behavior and teacher ratings of externalizing problems using the CBCL (Achenbach & Edelbrock, 1983). Thus, persistent noncompliance in combination with harsh, negative parenting or lack of responsiveness appears to be a significant risk factor for later difficulties. Indeed, direct noncompliance with parental requests in childhood is believed to be an early form of antisocial behavior (Dishion, French, & Patterson, 1995).

A second developmental outcome related to early compliance/noncompliance is the development of conscience or the internalization of rules and standards of conduct. According to Kochanska (1993), "emerging compliance to parental demands is often considered the first step on the road to internalization of the standards of conduct" (p. 335). When children begin to comply with parental requests, it is usually done within the confines of parental supervision. Eventually, children adopt these standards as their own and regulate their behavior without parental monitoring. Kochanska (1991; Kochanska & Askan, 1995; Kochanska et al., 1995) has conducted several studies that demonstrate that compliance, particularly committed compliance, is related to conscience development. Consistent with the socialization literature, Kochanska has also shown that compliance and subsequent internalization depend upon maternal behavior. Specifically, mother-child mutually positive orientations were positively related to committed compliance, negatively related to noncompliance (Kochanska & Askan, 1995), and related to both contemporaneous and longitudinal observations of internalization (Kochanska, 1997; Kochanska et al., 1995). The development of conscience also depends upon the child's ability to feel affective discomfort when not adhering to parental demands (Hoffman, 1983). Using individual differences in fear arousal, Kochanska demonstrated that highly fearful children developed internalization earlier when their mothers de-emphasized power assertion (Kochanska, 1991) and used gentle discipline. On the other hand, fearless children did not benefit from any particular style of maternal control; rather, mutually positive orientation (Kochanska, 1997) and secure attachment (Kochanska, 1995) interacted with fearlessness to predict later internalization.

The research thus far on early compliance suggests that compliance, particularly committed compliance, is related to more positive outcomes such as internalization and fewer behavior problems. The outcomes for noncompliance, on the other hand, depend upon the type of noncompliance and the style of maternal discipline. Self-assertion has more positive outcomes, while defiance, particularly if it is persistent and combined with harsh, power-assertive parental control techniques, increases the risk for later problem behavior.

Summary of the Research on Compliance

To date, much is known about the development of compliance and the social antecedents and concomitants of this important developmental task. The ability to respond appropriately to parental requests emerges around 18 months of age and appears to be related to responsive, mutually positive, firm parenting. However, the relationship between parenting behaviors and compliance/noncompliance in young children has focused exclusively on maternal behavior. This is understandable, as mothers are more likely to be the primary caregiver during these formative years when the processes related to compliance begin. However, the lack of information about the father's role in the socialization of rules and standards is remarkable given that fathers are often the family disciplinarians. Much of the research comparing parental styles of discipline suggests that a father's communicative and discipline style leads to children's expectation and acceptance of his use of power assertion when requesting obedience (Grusec & Goodnow, 1994). If this is true, then it would be important to examine whether fathers introduce such approaches when children are just learning parental expectations.

Child characteristics such as temperament have also been implicated in the emergence of compliance (Kochanska, 1993). Specifically, fearfulness was found to moderate parental style to predict the child's internalization of parents' rules and standards. Temperament, however, is a multidimensional construct. Other dimensions of temperament may also contribute to this outcome. For example, Stifter (Stifter et al., 1999) found that infants who were more anger reactive but could not regulate their anger were more likely to be defiant, whereas those who were anger reactive and successfully regulated their affect showed the least defiance. It may be that different dimensions of temperament have different consequences for compliance/noncompliance.

The majority of studies on compliance have been done with American White, middle-class samples. In light of the important cultural influences on expectations for behavior, this gap in the literature is striking. Studies have demonstrated significant cultural differences in expectations for the display of emotional behavior (Mesquita & Frijda, 1992). Thus one might assume differences in the expectation of compliance, and, in turn, the developmental course of this behavior. Similarly, societies that emphasize the self may be more accepting of certain forms of noncompliance such as self-assertion, while societies that emphasize the interdependence of individuals might not. Future research is needed to assess whether cultural differences affect the emergence and developmental course of compliance.

Finally, several studies have demonstrated the role of compliance, or lack thereof, in social competence. Whereas compliance was found to provide the foundation for internalization, noncompliance is considered to be an early marker for conduct disorders. Few studies have examined the development of self-assertion, a form of noncompliance that is considered appropriate for the toddler age. It would be interesting to examine the developmental trajectory of toddlers who use self-assertion rather than defiance when refusing to follow parental demands. Do these children continue to be self-assertive, or do they learn that in some situations they can challenge the parent's demand but in others they accept the parent's request willingly? Are these children more socially competent and popular than who exhibit committed compliance? Research on self-assertion may show that this form of noncompliance has more positive than negative outcomes when exhibited in toddlerhood.

CONCLUSION

Aside from clear and diagnosable medical conditions, parents' primary complaint to clinicians during the infancy period relates to excessive crying, generally crying that cannot be soothed or tolerated. There are, however, important distinctions to be made about crying in infancy. First, crying in early infancy increases over the first two months of life and then decreases thereafter. Thus, excessive crying may be misattributed if the developmental course of crying is not understood. Second, crying in excess of the normative rate during the first three months of life is categorized as colic. Colic is a transient condition that is currently conceptualized as a "regulatory" problem. Importantly, colic ends around the third to fourth month of an infant's life and appears to have few consequences for the child. Third, crying excessively is also a characteristic of difficult temperament but can be distinguished from colic in several ways. Colic occurs only in early infancy and thus is not a stable phenomenon. Difficult temperament, on the other hand, can be observed both during and well after early infancy and is a relatively stable condition. Also, whereas colic manifests itself as intense crying bouts of long duration, difficult temperament is usually defined as frequent bouts of fussiness. Finally, because of the persistence of difficult temperament, more negative outcomes are likely. It appears that difficult temperament taxes the parental environment, leading to stressful interactions and negative perceptions. Clinicians receiving complaints of excessive crying should be aware of these distinctions and use appropriate measures to validate parental assessments.

As infants enter their second year, with more cognitive and motor skills, they begin to confront demands to control their behavior. Coincidental to these increased skills in toddlers is a sense of autonomy and independence from needing parents to assist them. Unfortunately, for parents and toddlers alike, the two developmental tasks are often at odds with one another. The result is toddler noncompliance, which can be demonstrated in a variety of ways. Temper tantrums are the most excessive, negative form of noncompliance, whereas passive noncompliance, or disregarding a parental demand, is the least negative but not necessarily the least problematic. Persistent noncompliance can lead to the development of behavior problems, but this will most likely occur in the context of a parenting environment that is low in warmth and gentle discipline. It is important for clinicians who work with parents complaining of noncompliance in their toddlers to inform them about the developmental needs of their child. A child who refuses a request without expressing negative affect may be asserting independence, an important developmental task for toddlers. With parental understanding and acceptance, the risk for negative child outcomes can be diminished.

References

Achenbach, T., & Edelbrock, C. (1983). *Manual for the Child Behavior Checklist and Revised Child Behavior Profile*. Burlington, VT: Department of Psychiatry, University of Vermont.

Achenbach, T., Edelbrock, C., & Howell, C. (1987). Empirically based assessment of the behavioral/emotional problems of 2- and 3-year-old children. *Journal of Abnormal Child Psychology, 15*, 629–650.

Barr, R. (1990). The normal crying curve: What do we really know? *Developmental Medicine and Child Neurology, 32*, 356–362.

Barr, R. G. & Desilets, J. (n.d.). *The normal crying curve: Hoops and hurdles*. Unpublished manuscript.

Barr, R. G., & Gunnar, M. (2000). Colic: The "transient responsivity" hypothesis. In R. G. Barr, B. Hopkins, & J. Green (Eds.), *Crying as a sign, symptom and a signal: Clinical, emotional and developmental aspects of infant and toddler crying* (pp. 41–66). Cambridge: Cambridge University Press.

Barr, R. G., Korner, M., Bakeman, R., & Adamson, L. (1991) Crying in !Kung San infants: A test of the cultural specificity hypothesis. *Developmental Medicine and Child Neurology, 33*, 601–610.

Barr, R., Kramer, M., Boisjoly, C., McVey-White, L., & Pless, B. (1988). Parental diary of infant cry and fuss behavior. *Archives of Diseases in Childhood, 63*, 380–387.

Barr, R. G., Rotman, A.,Yaremko, J., Leduc, D., & Francoeur,T. (1992). The crying of infants with colic: A controlled empirical description. *Pediatrics, 90*(1), 14–21.

Barr, R. G., St James-Roberts, I., & Keefe, M. (2001). *New evidence on unexplained early infant crying*. Calverton, NY: Johnson & Johnson Pediatric Institute.

Bates, J. E. (1983). Issues in the assessment of difficult temperament: A reply to Thomas, Chess, and Korn. *Merrill-Palmer Quarterly, 29*, 89–97.

Bates, J. E. (1986). The measurement of temperament. In R. Plomin & J. Dunn (Eds.), *The study of temperament changes, continuities and challenges* (pp. 1–11). Hillsdale, NJ: Lawrence Erlbaum.

Bates, J. E., Freeland, C. A., & Lounsbury, M. L. (1979). Measurement of infant difficultness. *Child Development, 50*, 950–959.

Bates, J. E., Maslin, C. A., & Frankel, K. A. (1985). Attachment security, mother-infant interaction, and temperament as predictors of behav-ior-problems ratings at age three years. *Monographs of the Society for Research in Child Development, 50*, 167–193.

Bates, J. E, Wachs, T. D., & VandenBos, G. R. (1995). Trends in research on temperament. *Psychiatric Services, 46*, 661–663.

Bell, S., & Ainsworth, M. (1972). Infant crying and maternal responsiveness. *Child Development, 43*, 1171–1190.

Bowlby, J. (1982). *Attachment and loss: Vol. 1. Attachment*. New York: Basic Books.

Braungart-Rieker, J., Garwood, M. M., & Stifter, C. A. (1997). Compliance and noncompliance: The roles of maternal control and child temperament. *Journal of Applied Developmental Psychology, 18*, 411–428.

Brazelton, T. (1962). Crying in infancy. *Pediatrics, 29*, 579–588.

Buss, A. H., & Plomin, R. (1975). *A temperament theory of personality development*. New York: Wiley.

Buss, A. H., & Plomin, R. (1984). *Temperament: Early developing personality traits*. Hillsdale, NJ: Lawrence Erlbaum.

Campbell, S. B. (1997). Behavior problems in preschool children: Developmental and family issues. In T. H. Ollendick & R. J. Prinz (Eds.), *Advances in clinical child psychology* (pp. 1–26). New York: Plenum Press.

Cameron, J. R. (1978). Parental treatment, children's temperament, and the risk of childhood behavioral problems. I. Relationships between parental characteristics and changes in children's temperament over time. *Annual Progress in Child Psychiatry and Child Development*, 233–244.

Canivet, C., Hagander, B., Jakobsson, I., & Lanke, J. (1996). Infant colic—less common than estimated? *Acta Paediatrica, 85*, 454–458.

Carey, W. (1968). Maternal anxiety and infantile colic: Is there a relationship? *Clinical Pediatrics, 7*, 590–595.

Carey, W. (1970). A simplified method for measuring infant temperament. *Journal of Pediatrics, 77*, 188–194.

Carey, W. B. (1984). "Colic"—Primary excessive crying as an infant-environment interaction. *Pediatric Clinics of North America, 31*, 993–1005.

Carey, W. B., & McDevitt, S. C. (1978). Revision of the infant temperament questionnaire. *Pediatrics, 61*, 735–739.

Chamberlain, P., & Patterson, G. R. (1995). Discipline and child compliance in parenting. In M. Bornstein (Ed.), *Handbook of parenting. Vol. 4:*

Applied and practical parenting (pp. 205–225). Mahwah, NJ: Lawrence Erlbaum.

Clarke-Stewart, A. K., Fitzpatrick, M. J., Allhusen, V. D., & Goldberg, W. A. (2000). Measuring difficult temperament the easy way. *Journal of Developmental and Behavioral Pediatrics, 21,* 207–220.

Cohen, N. J., Muir, E., Parker, C. J., Brown, M., Lojkasek, M., Muir, R., & Barwick, M. (1999). Watch, wait, and wonder: Testing the effectiveness of a new approach to mother-infant psychotherapy. *Infant Mental Health Journal, 20*(4), 429–451.

Crockenberg, S., & Litman, C. (1990). Autonomy as competence in 2-year-olds: Maternal correlates of child defiance, compliance, and self-assertion. *Developmental Psychology, 26*(6), 961–971.

Crowcroft, N. S., & Strachan, D. P. (1997). The social origins of infantile colic: Questionnaire study covering 76 747 infants. *British Medical Journal, 314,* 1325–1328.

DiPietro, J. A., & Porges, S. W. (1988). Reactivity of preterms to gavages feeding. *Infant Behavior and Development, 11*(Special ICIS Issue), 73.

Dishion, T., French, D., & Patterson, G. (1995). The development and etiology of antisocial behavior. In D. Cicchetti & D. Cohen (Eds.), *Developmental psychopathology* (Vol. 2, pp. 421–471). New York: Wiley.

Field, T., Hallock, N., Ting, G., Dempsey, J., Dabiri, C., & Shuman, H. H. (1978). A first-year follow-up of high-risk infants: Formulating a cumulative risk index. *Child Development, 49,* 119–131.

Garcia Coll, C. T., Halpern, L. F., Vohr, B. R., Seifer, R., & Oh, W. (1992). Stability and correlates of change of early temperament in preterm and full-term infants. *Infant Behavior and Development, 15,* 137–153.

Garcia Coll, C. T., Kagan, J., & Resnick, J. S. (1984). Behavioral inhibition in young children. *Child Development, 55,* 1005–1019.

Goldsmith, H. H., Buss, K. A., & Lemery, K. S. (1997). Toddler and childhood temperament: Expanded content, stronger genetic evidence, new evidence for the importance of environment. *Developmental Psychology, 33,* 891–905.

Goldsmith, H. H., Buss, K. A., Plomin, R., Rothbart, M. K., Thomas, A., Chess, S., Hinde, R. A., & McCall, R. B. (1987). Roundtable: What is temperament: Four approaches. *Child Development, 58,* 505–529.

Goldsmith, H. H., & Campos, J. J. (1982) Toward a theory of infant temperament. In R. N. Emde & R. J. Harmon (Eds.), *The development of attachment and affiliative systems* (pp. 161–193). New York: Plenum Press.

Goldsmith, H. H., Lemery, K. S., Buss, K. A., & Campos, J. J. (1999). Genetic analyses of focal aspects of infant temperament. *Developmental Psychology, 35,* 972–985.

Goldsmith, H. H., & Rothbart, M. K. (1991). Contemporary instruments for assessing early temperament by questionnaires and in the laboratory. In J. Strelau & A. Angleitner (Eds.), *Explorations in temperament* (pp. 249–272). New York: Plenum Press.

Gormally, S., & Barr, R. (1998). Of clinical pies and clinical cues: Proposed pie as a clinical approach to complaints of early crying and colic. *Ambulatory Child Health, 3,* 137–153.

Gralinski, J. H., & Kopp, C. B. (1993). Everyday rules for behavior: Mother's requests to young children. *Developmental Psychology, 29*(3), 573–584.

Gross, D., Conrad, B., Fogg, L., & Wothke, W. (1994). A longitudinal model of maternal self-efficacy, depression, and difficult temperament during toddlerhood. *Research in Nursing and Health, 17,* 207–215.

Grusec, J. E., & Goodnow, J. J. (1994). Impact of parental discipline methods on the child's internalization of values: A reconceptualization of current points of view. *Developmental Psychology, 30*(1), 4–19.

Guerin, D. W., Gottfried, A. W., & Thomas, C. W. (1997). Difficult temperament and behaviour problems: A longitudinal study from 1.5 to 12 years. *International Journal of Behavioral Development, 21,* 71–90.

Hart, S., Field, T., & Roitfarb, M. (1999). Depressed mothers' assessments of their neonates' behavior. *Infant Mental Health Journal, 20,* 200–210.

Hide, D. & Guyer, B. (1982). Prevalence of infant colic. *Archives of Disease in Childhood, 57,* 559–560.

Hofacker, N. V., & Papousek, M. (1998). Disorders of excessive crying, feeding, and sleeping. *Infant Mental Health Journal, 19,* 180–201.

Hoffman, M. (1983). Affective and cognitive processes in moral internalization. In E. Higgins, D. Ruble, & W. Hartup (Eds.), *Social cognition and social development: A sociocultural perspective* (pp. 236–274). New York: Cambridge University Press.

Hubert, N. C., Wachs, T. D., Peters-Martin, P., &

Gandour, M. J. (1982). The study of early temperament: Measurement and conceptual issues. *Child Development, 53,* 571–600.

Humphry, R. A., & Hock, E. (1989). Infants with colic: A study of maternal stress and anxiety. *Infant Mental Health Journal, 10,* 263–272.

Kaler, S. R., & Kopp, C. B. (1990). Compliance and comprehension in very young toddlers. *Child Development, 61,* 1997–2003.

Kagan, J. (1982). The construct of difficult temperament: A reply to Thomas, Chess, and Korn. *Merrill-Palmer Quarterly, 28,* 21–24.

Kagan, J., Resnick, J. S., & Gibbons, J. (1989). Inhibited and uninhibited types of children. *Child Development, 60,* 838–845.

Keefe, M., Kotzen, A. M., Froese-Fritz, A., & Curtain, M. (1996). A longitudinal comparison of irritable and nonirritable infants. *Nursing Research, 45,* 4–9.

Klimes-Dougan, B. & Kopp, C. B. (1999). Children's conflicts tactics with mothers: A longitudinal investigation of the toddler and preschool years. *Merrill-Palmer Quarterly, 45*(2), 226–241.

Kochanska, G. (1991). Socialization and temperament in the development of guilt and conscience. *Child Development, 62,* 1379–1392.

Kochanska, G. (1993). Toward a synthesis of parental socialization and child temperament in early development. *Child Development, 64,* 325–347.

Kochanska, G. (1995). Children's temperament, mothers' discipline, and security of attachment: Multiple pathways to emerging internalization. *Child Development, 66,* 597–615.

Kochanska, G. (1997). Mutually responsive orientation between mothers and their young children: Implications for early socialization. *Child Development, 68,* 94–112.

Kochanska, G., & Askan, N. (1995). Mother-child mutually positive affect, the quality of child compliance to requests, prohibitions, and maternal control as correlates of early internalization. *Child Development, 66,* 236–254.

Kochanska, G., Askan, N., & Koenig, A. (1995). A longitudinal study of the roots of preschoolers' conscience: Committed compliance and emerging internalization. *Child Development, 66,* 1752–1769.

Kochanska, G., Kuczynski, L., & Maguire, M. (1989) Impact of diagnosed depression and self-reported mood on mothers' control strategies. *Journal of Abnormal Child Psychology, 17,* 493–511.

Kochanska, G., Tjebkes, T. L., & Forman, D. R. (1998). Children's emerging regulation of conduct: Restraint, compliance, and internalization from infancy to the second year. *Child Development, 69*(5), 1378–1389.

Kopp, C. B. (1982). Antecedents of self regulation: A developmental perspective. *Developmental Psychology, 18,* 199–214.

Kuczynski, L., & Kochanska, G. (1990). Development of children's noncompliance strategies from toddlerhood to age 5. *Developmental Psychology, 26*(3), 398–408.

Kuczynski, L., & Kochanska, G. (1995). Function and content of maternal demands: Developmental significance of early demands for competent action. *Child Development, 66,* 616–628.

Kuczynski, L., Kochanska, G., Radke-Yarrow, M., & Girnius-Brown, O. (1987). A developmental interpretation of young children's noncompliance. *Developmental Psychology, 23,* 799–806.

Leadbeater, B. J., Bishop, S. J., & Raver, C. C. (1996). Quality of mother-toddler interactions, maternal depressive symptoms, and behavior problems in preschoolers of adolescent mothers. *Developmental Psychology, 32*(2), 280–288.

Lee, C. L., & Bates, J. E. (1985). Mother-child interaction at age two years and perceived difficult temperament. *Child Development, 56,* 1314–1325.

Lehtonen, L., Korhonen, T., & Korvenranta, H. (1994). Temperament and sleeping patterns in colicky infants during the first year of life. *Developmental and Behavioral Pediatrics, 15*(6), 416–420.

Lehtonen, L., & Korvenranta, H. (1995). Infantile colic: Seasonal incidence and crying profile. *Archives of Pediatric Adolescent Medicine, 149,* 533–536.

Lemery, K. S., Goldsmith, H. H., Klinnert, M. D., & Mrazek, D. A. (1999). Developmental models of infant and childhood temperament. *Developmental Psychology, 35,* 189–204.

Lester, B., Boukydis, C., Garcia-Coll, C., & Hole, W. (1990). Colic for the developmentalist. *Infant Mental Health Journal, 11*(4), 321–333.

Londerville, S., & Main, M. (1981). Security of attachment, compliance, and maternal training methods in the second year of life. *Developmental Psychology, 17*(3), 289–299.

Lowinger, S. (1999). Infant irritability and early mother-infant reciprocity patterns. *Infant & Child Development, 8,* 71–84.

Lyon, M. E., & Plomin, R. (1981). The measurement of temperament using parental ratings. *Journal of Child Psychology and Psychiatry and Applied Disciplines, 22,* 47–53.

Maccoby, E. (1980). *Social development: Psychological growth and the parent-child relationship.* New York: Harcourt Brace Jovanovich.

Mangelsdorf, S., Gunnar, M., Kestenbaum, R., Lang, S., & Andreas, D. (1991). Infant proneness-to-distress temperament, maternal personality, and mother-infant attachment: Associations and goodness-of-fit. *Child Development, 61,* 820–831.

Matheny, A. P., Wilson, R. S., & Nuss, S. M. (1984). Toddler temperament: Stability across settings and over ages. *Child Development, 55,* 1200–1211.

Maziade, M., Cote, R., Boutin, P., Bernier, H., & Thivierge, J. (1989). Temperament and intellectual development: A longitudinal study from infancy to four years. In S. Chess & A. Thomas (Eds.), *Annual progress in child psychiatry and child development* (pp. 335–349). New York: Brunner/Mazel.

Medoff-Cooper, B., Carey, W. B., & McDevitt, S. C. (1993). The Early Infancy Temperament Questionnaire. *Journal of Development and Behavioral Pediatrics,* 14, 230–235.

Mesquita, B., & Frijda, N. (1992). Cultural variations in emotions: A review. *Psychological Bulletin, 112,* 179–204.

Miller, A. R., Barr, R. G., & Eaton, W. O. (1993). Crying and motor behavior of six-week-old infants and postpartum maternal mood. *Pediatrics, 92*(4), 551–558.

Owens, E. B., Shaw, D. S., & Vondra, J. I. (1998). Relations between infant irritability and maternal responsiveness in low-income families. *Infant Behavior and Development, 21,* 761–777.

Paradise, J. L. (1966). Maternal and other factors in the etiology of the infantile colic. *JAMA, 197,* 123–131.

Parpal, M., & Maccoby, E. E. (1985). Maternal responsiveness and subsequent child compliance. *Child Development, 56,* 1326–1334.

Pedersen, F. A., Huffman, L. C., del Carmen, R., & Bryan, Y. E. (1996) Prenatal maternal reactivity to infant cries predicts postnatal perceptions of infant temperament and marriage appraisal. *Child Development, 67,* 2541–2552.

Pettit, G. S., & Bates, J. E. (1984). Continuity of individual differences in the mother-infant relationship from six to thirteen months. *Child Development, 55,* 729–739.

Pfiffner, L. J., & O'Leary, S. G. (1989). Effects of maternal discipline and nurturance in toddler's behavior and affect. *Journal of Abnormal Child Psychology, 17,* 527–540.

Pineyard, B. J. (1992). Infant colic and maternal mental health: Nursing research and practice concerns. *Issues in Comprehensive Pediatric Nursing, 15,* 155–167.

Porter, F. L., Porges, S. W., & Marshall, R. E. (1988). Newborn pain cries and vagal tone: Parallel changes in response to circumcision. *Child Development, 59,* 495–505.

Power, T. G., & Chapieski, M. L. (1986). Child-rearing and impulse control in toddlers: A naturalistic investigation. *Developmental Psychology, 22,* 271–275.

Prudhomme White, B., Gunnar, M., Larson, M., Donzella, B., & Barr, R. (2000). Behavioral and physiological responsivity, sleep, and patterns of daily cortisol production in infants with and without colic. *Child Development, 71,* 862–877.

Rautava, P., Helenius, H., & Lehtonen, L. (1993). Psychosocial predisposing factors for infantile colic. *British Medical Journal, 307,* 600–604.

Rautava, P., Lehtonen, L., Helenius, H., & Sillanpa, M. (1995). Infantile colic: Child and family three years later. *Pediatrics, 96*(1), 43–47.

Riese, M. L. (1987). Temperament stability between the neonatal period and 24 months. *Developmental Psychology, 23,* 216–222.

Rocissano, L., Slade, A., & Lynch, V. (1987). Dyadic synchrony and toddler compliance. *Developmental Psychology, 23,* 698–704.

Roth, K., Eisenberg, N., & Sell, E. R. (1984). The relation of pre-term and full term infants' temperament to test-taking behaviors and developmental status. *Infant Behavior and Development,* 7, 495–505.

Rothbart, M. K. (1981). Measurement of temperament in infancy. *Child Development, 52,* 569–578.

Rothbart, M. K. (1982). The concept of difficult temperament: A critical analysis of Thomas, Chess, and Korn. *Merrill-Palmer Quarterly, 28,* 35–40.

Rothbart, M. K. (1986). Longitudinal observation of infant temperament. *Developmental Psychology, 22,* 356–366.

Rothbart, M. K., & Derryberry, P. (1981). Development of individual differences in temperament. In M. E. Lamb & A. L. Brown (Eds.),

Advances in developmental psychology (Vol. 1, pp. 37–86). Hillsdale, NJ: Lawrence Erlbaum.

Rothbart, M. K., & Goldsmith, H. H. (1985). Three approaches to the study of infant temperament. *Developmental Review, 5,* 237–260.

Rothbart, M. K., & Mauro, J. A. (1990). Questionnaire approaches to the study of infant temperament. In J. Colombo & J. Fagan (Eds.), *Individual difference in infancy: Reliability, stability, prediction* (pp. 411–429). Hillsdale, NJ: Lawrence Erlbaum.

Rowe, D. C., & Plomin, H. G. (1977). Temperament in early childhood. *Journal of Personality Assessment, 41,* 150–156.

Rubin, S. & Pendergast, M. (1984). Infantile colic: Incidence and treatment in a Norfolk community. *Child: Care, Health and Development, 10,* 219–226.

Sanson, A., Smart, D., Prior, M., & Oberklaid, F. (1993). Precursors of hyperactivity and aggression. *Journal of the American Academy of Child and Adolescent Psychiatry, 32,* 1207–1216.

Sameroff, A. J., Seifer, R., & Elias, P. K. (1982). Early development of children at risk for emotional disorder. *Monographs of the Society for Research in Child Development, 47*(7, Serial No. 199).

Schaffer, H. R., & Crook, C. K. (1980). Child compliance and maternal control techniques. *Developmental Psychology, 16,* 54–61.

Schuler, M. E., Black, M. M., & Starr, R. H. (1995). Determinants of mother-infant interaction: Effects of prenatal drug exposure, social support, and infant temperament. *Journal of Clinical Child Psychology, 24,* 397–405.

Seifer, R., Sameroff, A. J., Barrett, L. C., & Krafchulk, E. (1994). Infant temperament measured by multiple observations and mother report. *Child Development, 65,* 1478–1490.

Shaw, D., Keenan, K., & Vondra, J. (1994). Developmental precursors of externalizing behavior: Ages 1 to 3. *Developmental Psychology, 30,* 355–364.

Shaw, D. S., & Vondra, J. I. (1995). Infant attachment security and maternal predictors of early behavior problems: A longitudinal study of low-income families. *Journal of Abnormal Child Psychology, 23,* 335–357.

Slabach, E. H., Morrow, J., & Wachs, T. (1991). Questionnaire measurement of infant and child temperament: Current status and future directions. In J. Strelau & A. Angleitner (Eds.), *Explorations in temperament: International perspectives on theory and measurement. Perspec-*

tives on individual differences (pp. 205–234). New York: Plenum Press.

Sloman, J., Bellinger, D., & Krentzel, C. (1990). Infantile colic and transient developmental lag in the first year of life. *Child Psychiatry and Human Development, 21*(1), 25–36.

Stifter, C. A. (2001). Life after unexplained crying: Child and parent outcomes. In R. Barr, I. St James-Roberts, & M. Keefe (Eds.), *New evidence on unexplained early crying: Its origins, nature and management* (pp. 273–288). Calverton, NY: Johnson & Johnson Pediatric Institute.

Stifter, C. A., & Bono, M. (1998). The effect of infant colic on maternal self-perception and mother-infant attachment. *Child: Care, Health and Development, 24,* 339–351.

Stifter, C. A, Bono, M., & Spinrad, T. (in press). Parent characteristics and conceptualizations associated with the emergence of infant colic. *Journal of Reproductive and Infant Psychology.*

Stifter, C. A., & Braungart, J. (1992). Infant colic: A transient condition with no apparent effects. *Journal of Applied Developmental Psychology, 13,* 447–462.

Stifter, C. A., Spinrad, T., & Braungart-Rieker, J. (1999). Toward a developmental model of child compliance: The role of emotion regulation in infancy. *Child Development, 70,* 21–32.

Stipek, D. J., Gralinski, J. H., & Kopp, C. B. (1990). Self-concept development in the toddler years. *Developmental Psychology, 26*(6), 972–977.

St James-Roberts, I., Bowyer, J., Varghese, S., & Sawdon, J. (1994). Infant crying patterns in Manali and London. *Child: Care, Health, and Development, 20,* 323–337.

St James-Roberts, I., Conroy, S., & Wilsher, K. (1995). Clinical, developmental and social aspects of infant crying and colic. *Early Development and Parenting, 4,* 177–189.

St James-Roberts, I., Conroy, S., & Wilsher, K. (1996). Bases for maternal perceptions of infant crying and colic behaviour. *Archives of Disease in Childhood, 75,* 375–384.

St James-Roberts, I., Conroy, S., & Wilsher, K. (1998a). Links between maternal care and persistent infant crying in the early months. *Child: Care, Health and Development, 24*(5), 353–376.

St James-Roberts, I., Conroy, S., & Wilsher, K. (1998b). Stability and outcome of persistent infant crying. *Infant Behavior and Development, 21*(3), 411–435.

St James-Roberts, I., & Haili, T. (1991). Infant crying patterns in the first year: Normal community and clinical findings. *Journal of Child Psychology and Psychiatry, 32*(6), 951–968.

St James-Roberts, I., & Plewis, I. (1996). Individual differences, daily fluctuations, and developmental changes in amounts of infant waking, fussing, crying, feeding, and sleeping. *Child Development, 67,* 2527–2540.

Super, C., & Harkness, S. (1994). Temperament and the developmental niche. In W. Carey & S. McDevitt (Eds.), *Prevention and early intervention: Individual differences as risk factors for the mental health of children: A festschrift for Stella Chess and Alexander Thomas* (pp. 115–125). Philadelphia: Blackwell.

Susman-Stillman, A., Kalkoske, M., Egeland, B., & Waldman, I. (1996). Infant temperament and maternal sensitivity as predictors of attachment security. *Infant Behavior and Development, 19,* 33–47.

Taubman, B. (1984). Clinical trial of the treatment of colic by modification of parent-infant interaction. *Pediatrics, 74,* 998–1003.

Teti, D. M., & Gelfand, D. M. (1991). Behavioral competence among mothers of infants in the first year: The mediational role of maternal self-efficacy. *Child Development, 62,* 918–929.

Teti, D. M., Gelfand, D. M., & Pompa, J. (1990). Depressed mothers' behavioral competence with their infants: Demographic and psychosocial correlates. *Development and Psychopathology, 2,* 259–270.

Thomas, A., & Chess, S. (1977). *Temperament and development.* New York: Brunner-Mazel.

Thomas, A., & Chess, S. (1982). Temperament and follow-up to adulthood. In R. Porter & G. M. Collins (Eds.), *Temperamental differences in infants and young children* (CIBA Foundation Symposium 89) (pp. 168–175). London: Pitman.

Thomas, A., Chess, S., & Birch, H. G. (1968). *Temperament and behavior disorders in children.* New York: New York University Press.

Thomas, A., Chess, S., & Korn, S. J. (1982). The reality of difficult temperament. *Merrill-Palmer Quarterly, 28,* 1–20.

Treem, W. R. (1994). Infant colic: A pediatric gastroenterologist's perspective. *Pediatric Clinics of North America, 41,* 1121–1138.

van den Boom, D. C. (1994). The influence of temperament and mothering on attachment and exploration: An experimental manipulation of sensitive responsiveness among lower-class mothers with irritable infants. *Child Development, 65,* 1457–1477.

van den Boom, D. C., & Hoeksma, J. B. (1994). The effect of infant irritability on mother-infant interaction: A growth-curve analysis. *Developmental Psychology, 30,* 581–590.

Vaughn, B. E., Bradley, C. F., Joffe, L. S., Seifer, R., & Barglow, P. (1987). Maternal characteristics measured prenatally are predictive of ratings of temperamental "difficulty" on the Carey infant temperament questionnaire. *Developmental Psychology, 23,* 152–161.

Vaughn, B. E, Kopp, C. B., & Krakow, J. B. (1984). The emergence and consolidation of self-control from eighteen to thirty months of age: Normative trends and individual differences. *Child Development, 55,* 990–1004.

Vaughan, B. E., Taraldson, B. J., Crichton, L., & Egeland, B. (1981). The assessment of infant temperament: A critique of the Carey Infant Temperament Questionnaire. *Infant Behavioral Development, 4*(1), 1–17.

Wachs, T. D. (1994). Commenting on Plomin (1994) genetics, nurture, and social development: An alternative viewpoint. *Social Development, 3,* 66–70.

Wachs, T. D. (1999). The what, why, and how of temperament: A piece of the action. In L. Balter & C. S. Tamis-LeMonda (Eds.), *Child psychology: A handbook of contemporary issues* (pp. 23–44). Philadelphia: Psychology Press.

Wessel, M. A., Cobb, J. C., Jackson, E. B., Harris, G. S., & Detwiler, A. C. (1954). Paroxysmal fussing in infancy, sometimes called "colic." *Pediatrics, 14,* 421–434.

Williams, C. A., & Forehand, R. (1984). An examination of predictor variables for child compliance and noncompliance. *Journal of Abnormal Child Psychology, 12*(3), 491–504.

Wolff, P. (1987). *The development of behavioral states and the expression of emotions in early infancy.* Chicago: University of Chicago Press.

Wolk, S., Zeanah, C. H., Garcia Coll, C. T., & Carr, S. (1992). Factors affecting parents' perceptions of temperament in early infancy. *American Journal of Orthopsychiatry, 62*(1), 71–82.

Wolkind, S. N., & Desalis, W. (1982). Infant temperament, maternal mental states and child behavior problems. In R. Porter & G. M. Collins (Eds.), *Temperamental differences in infants and young children* (pp. 221–239) (CIBA Foundation Symposium 89). London: Pitman.

Worobey, J., & Blajda, V. M. (1989). Temperament ratings at 2 weeks, 2 months, and 1 year: Differential stability of activity and emotionality. *Developmental Psychology*, 25(2), 257–263.

Zeanah, C. H., & Anders, T. F. (1987). Subjectivity in parent-infant relationships: A discussion of internal working models. *Infant Mental Health Journal*, 8(3), 237–250.

Zeanah, C. H., Keener, M. A., Stewart, L., & Anders, T. F. (1985). Prenatal perception of infant personality: A preliminary investigation. *Journal of the American Academy of Child Psychiatry*, 24(2), 204–210.

6

The Role of Sensory Reactivity in Understanding Infant Temperament

Nathan A. Fox
Cindy P. Polak

A number of models of adult personality and infant temperament include individual differences in reactivity to sensory stimuli as a central factor in understanding behavioral style of the individual. Sensory reactivity has primarily been evaluated via questionnaires and caregiver report. Behavioral or physiological measurement of sensory reactivity has only assessed differences *within* a specific sensory modality and has not looked at reactivity *across* the different senses. It therefore remains unclear whether individual differences in sensory reactivity are due to a general physiological arousal that underlies all the senses or whether sensitivity to stimulation is modality specific. From a clinical perspective, determining the nature of sensory reactivity may be useful because it can provide information from which to develop a sensory battery that can be administered during the initial assessment of an infant or toddler. The purpose of this chapter is to (1) provide a brief historical review of the role of sensory reactivity in models of adult personality and infant temperament, (2) present an overview of the measurement of each sensory domain, and (3) discuss the assessment of sensory reactivity within

clinical settings and the implications of such assessment for understanding individual differences in infant and toddler behavior.

Alexander Thomas and Stella Chess first introduced the concept of temperament in developmental psychology in the late 1960s. These child psychiatrists were interested in understanding the ways in which infants differed from each other with regard to their reactions and responsivity to the environment. Since Thomas and Chess's early work, other models of temperament have been put forth (e.g., Buss & Plomin, 1975, 1984; Rothbart, 1981). Common to each of these models (as well as to Thomas and Chess) is the notion that temperament, in part, reflects the manner in which the individual reacts to sensory stimulation. This notion of individual differences in sensory reactivity has a long history in the adult personality literature. Eysenck (1967a), in developing his model of introversion and extroversion, argued that one of the characteristic differences among individuals is the degree to which they are reactive to sensory stimuli and the degree to which they seek sensory stimulation. Introverts, he postulated, are highly sensitive to sensory stimuli and seek to reduce their exposures, while extroverts are insensitive (with high thresholds) and thus seek out exposure.

Sensory stimuli vary in many dimensions, including their intensity, complexity, frequency, and hedonic valence. Individual responses to these stimuli may be characterized by (1) the intensity of one's response, (2) the degree to which stimulation elicits approach or avoidance, and (3) the affective tone of the response. Reactivity or responsivity to sensory stimulation is thought to be an innate characteristic that displays stability over time and influences social interactions (Goldsmith, 1983). Thus, individuals are thought to maintain their characteristic response to sensory stimulation across development. Temperament is thought to have a strong biological basis, in part because these individual differences are identifiable early in the first year of life. Although temperament is thought to reflect an innate, stable, biological characteristic, there is evidence that the environment affects an individual's behavioral style. Researchers have examined the manner in which certain styles of parenting interact with specific temperaments in the development of adaptive social behavior (Clarke, Kochanska, & Ready, 2000; Kochanska, 1997). Thus, an understanding of temperament must reflect individual differences in behavioral style as well as the manner in which such styles are modified by environmental input.

Although differences in sensory reactivity have been documented in both infants and adults, whether this trait is modality specific (e.g., infants show the same degree of reactivity to auditory but not visual stimulation) or whether it is due to general threshold differences that are modality nonspecific has yet to be determined. Such a distinction may be both useful and important in conceptualizing early temperament, assessing individual differences in temperament, and ultimately in developing interventions or providing information to parents about infant temperament. For example, assume that an infant is highly reactive to sounds of different intensities but does not show this same individual difference with regard to the visual modality. Such a temperamental pattern would have implications for caregiving and ultimately for the development of social behavior. We have found, for example,

that infants who subsequently display socially withdrawn behavior are more likely to show heightened reactivity to auditory but not visual stimuli (Himmelfarb, Marshall, Bar-Haim, & Fox, 2000). Heightened reactivity of the infant and young child to auditory stimuli may in fact contribute to socially withdrawal behavior. Some infants and young children may find loud noises and multiple auditory input aversive, preferring to withdraw from such environments to contexts with less intense auditory input. In a recent study, Bar-Haim, Marshall, Fox, Schorr, and Gordon-Salant (submitted) found that 7- to 10-year-old socially withdrawn children displayed abberant patterns of basic sensory processing compared to controls. Specifically, the socially withdrawn children showed faster auditory brainstem responses and decreased amplitude of the mismatch negativity, an evoked response generated by standard and deviant auditory sounds.

Unfortunately, the study of individual differences in infant sensory reactivity has relied primarily on questionnaire data, although more direct methods of assessment are available. In this chapter we (1) review research that has examined the role of sensory reactivity in adult personality development and models of infant temperament, (2) survey methods developed to assess infant reactivity in each sensory domain, and (3) discuss current research on methods for assessing sensory reactivity and sensory integration.

THE ROLE OF INDIVIDUAL DIFFERENCES IN SENSORY REACTIVITY IN THE STUDY OF ADULT PERSONALITY AND INFANT TEMPERAMENT

Hans Eysenck (1967b) was the first to raise the notion that individual differences in sensory reactivity are associated with adult personality. Eysenck (1967b, 1981) argued that such differences were a function of the arousal system of the central nervous system. This notion had its origins in the observations of Pavlov (1936) that there were individual differences in the time it took an animal to condition. Pavlov attributed these differences in the animals he studied to the strength or excitability of the animal's nervous system. Eysenck adapted this argument while developing his model of personality types (introverts and extroverts). In his model, individuals characterized by low arousal would seek stimulation (extroverts), while individuals whose nervous systems were characterized by high arousal would seek to limit their exposure to stimuli (introverts). Differences in strength of the nervous system were related to the speed at which individuals would condition. Those with strong nervous systems (extroverts) were less easily conditioned. Those with weak nervous systems (introverts) were more easily conditioned and hence more susceptible to both reward and punishment. A series of studies by Eysenck and his students empirically verified the model of these two different personality types. These studies examined differences in sensory reactivity and conditioning among introverts and extroverts (Eysenck, 1967b, 1979; McLaughlin & Eysenck, 1967). In general, these studies confirmed the general relation between sensory reactivity and introversion/extroversion, although the broad foundation of CNS arousal does not appear to adequately describe the neural correlates of these personality types.

For example, data collected with adult introverts and extroverts show that introverts are more sensitive to low-auditory frequencies (Stelmack & Campbell 1974; Stelmack & Michaud-Achorn, 1985), to pain (Barnes, 1975; Haier, Robinson, Braden, & Williams, 1984; Schalling, 1971), to olfactory stimulation (Herbener, Kagan, & Cohen, 1989), and to visual thresholds (Siddle, Morish, White, & Mangan, 1969). Questionnaire data collected have found relations between sensory reactivity and personality. Aron and Aron (1997) found high intercorrelations between heterogeneous self-reported sensitivities to caffeine, hunger, pain, overstimulation, and strong sensory input. In addition, sensitive adults also self-reported being easily overaroused, startling easily, and being highly conscientious (Aron & Aron, 1997).

A second theory that focuses on the role of sensory reactivity in moderating personality development is Strelau's (1983, 1998) regulative theory of temperament. Sensory reactivity in this model is defined as sensory threshold (e.g., intensity level of sensory stimulation that is necessary to evoke a discernible response). Individuals are thought to regulate their exposure to stimulation by approaching or avoiding a stimulus in order to obtain or maintain an optimal level of arousal that is experienced as a positive mood. Strelau argued that an individual's proneness to experience positive and negative emotions is determined in part by differences in ease of excitation of specific structures of the limbic system.

Thomas and Chess (1977), considered to be the founders of modern work on infant temperament, utilized observational data from the New York Longitudinal Study (NYLS) to derive nine temperamental dimensions. Among these dimensions was one they termed threshold of responsiveness, which was defined as the minimum amount of stimulation needed to elicit a noticeable response or change across one or all sensory modalities (Thomas & Chess, 1984). According to Thomas and Chess, infants differ in their threshold to respond to stimulation, with some infants responding to intense stimulation while others react to lower levels of stimulus intensity.

It is unclear whether Thomas and Chess viewed threshold of responsiveness as modality specific or modality general. What is critical is the notion that infant behavioral style may be influenced by the degree to which an infant will react to the level of stimulation in the environment. In addition, such reactions will influence the manner in which caregivers perceive the infant. Researchers interested in assessing infants along the nine Thomas and Chess dimensions have relied upon questionnaires developed by Carey and McDevitt and others (e.g., Carey & McDevitt, 1978; Fullard, McDevitt, & Carey, 1984; Medoff-Cooper, Carey, & McDevitt, 1993). In particular, Carey and McDevitt (1978) developed the Revised Infant Temperament Questionnaire (RITQ). This measure consists of 95 items that can be endorsed by caregivers to assess infant temperament. Caregivers use a 6-point Likert scale ranging from 1 (almost never) to 6 (almost always) to describe the frequency with which a particular statement is true for their infant. The items are randomized as to the category and content area, and some items have high-low reversals. Questions on the RITQ ask caregivers to report about specific behaviors of the infant in certain situations (for example, the infant's reactions to new food or to strangers). Caregiver responses are then scored in the nine categories of temperament defined by Thomas and Chess (1977).

Another conceptualization of infant temperament by Rothbart places individual differences in reactivity in a central role. According to her model (Rothbart & Derryberry, 1981), infant temperament is characterized by the manner in which infants respond to sensory stimulation, including the latency and intensity of their response and ultimately the way in which they are able to modulate that response. Rothbart does not assume that individual differences in reactivity in one modality will generalize to other modalities. Rather, she is concerned with the pattern of individual reactivity in each modality across context. Rothbart developed a questionnaire to assess infant reactivity (Infant Behavior Questionnaire; Rothbart, 1981). This questionnaire taps infant response across a wide range of contexts (e.g., during feeding, during bathing and dressing, after sleeping, and during play) in which infants might show reactive responses to a wide range of stimulus modalities (auditory, visual, tactile). Questions are answered on a 7-point Likert scale (there are 94 items), and the factor structure defines six dimensions including activity level, soothability, distress to novelty, distress to limitations, smiling and laughter, and duration of orienting. Examples of items include questions about how often the infant cried or showed distress when tickled or seemed distressed while waiting for food.

Among the more recent research on infant temperament is work that has directly assessed individual differences in infant behavioral reactive responses to auditory and visual stimuli. This work has been completed by Kagan (Garcia-Coll, Kagan, & Resnick, 1984; Kagan, Reznick, Clark, Snidman, & Garcia-Coll, 1984) and Fox (Calkins, Fox, & Marshall, 1996; Fox, Henderson, Rubin, Calkins, & Schmidt, 2001) within the context of their work on the origins of behavioral inhibition and social withdrawal in children.

Kagan and his colleagues (Garcia-Coll, Kagan, & Resnick, 1984; Kagan et al., 1984) assessed sensory reactivity in 4-month-old infants in three modalities: visual, auditory, and olfactory. Infants watched colorful moving mobiles for 20 seconds, heard an audiotape of people saying sentences, heard a female speaking different syllables, heard a balloon pop behind their heads, and had a cotton swab dipped in dilute alcohol placed under their nostrils. Observers coded infant motor and emotional reactivity. Four different profiles of reactivity (high reactive, aroused, distressed, and low reactive), were derived from these trials by coding for the total number of movements/extensions of the limbs and arching back, and the amount of crying, fretting and fussing, vocalizations, and smiling across the sessions (Kagan, 1994). Kagan predicted that highly reactive infants would be more likely to display behavioral inhibition as toddlers compared to less reactive controls. Data from his longitudinal studies have confirmed these predictions. For example, Kagan and Snidman (1991) found that infants who became highly motoric and fretful in response to the sensory battery at 4 months showed more fearful behavior at 9 months. Interestingly, Kagan and Snidman (1991) also found that individual differences in fear scores were preserved from 9 to 14 months and that at 4.5 years of age, children who showed high motoric activity and fretting at 4 months of age talked less and smiled less frequently with an unfamiliar female experimenter (Kagan et al., 1984).

Fox and colleagues (Calkins et al., 1996; Fox et al., 2001) utilized the identical screening methods developed by Kagan to examine differences in reactivity at 4 months of age. They identified three groups of infants (those displaying high motor reactivity, high negative affect, and low positive affect; those displaying high motor reactivity, low negative affect, and high positive affect; and those displaying low motor, negative, and positive affect reactions) in terms of their response to the auditory and visual stimuli. Fox and colleagues report that infants in the high motor, high negative category were more likely to display behavioral inhibition at 14 months of age (Calkins et al., 1996), while infants in the high motor, low negative, and high positive affect group were more likely to display exuberant positive social behaviors as preschool children (Fox et al., 2001).

Other than these few studies of individual differences in sensory reactivity, much of the developmental data have focused on the abilities of young infants to detect and process different qualities of sensory stimuli. In general, two types of behavioral responses have been used to study sensory reactivity in infants: those spontaneously emitted (unconditioned) and those that are conditioned (Aslin, 1987). Examples of spontaneously emitted responses used in vision research include elicited motor responses (blinking, pupillometry, accommodation, eye movements, reaching, and locomotion), brain wave responses (ABR and ERP), and visual fixation responses (preferential looking and habituation). Spontaneously emitted response utilized in auditory research also include elicited motor responses (startle activity, blinking, eye blink inhibition, head orientation), psychophysiological responses (heart rate, respiration, skin potential, and cortical and brainstem evoked responses), and habituation of visual fixation; examples of conditioned responses often used in vision research include high-amplitude sucking and operant conditioning (head turning and foot kicking), while conditioned responses used in auditory research include sucking responses (high-amplitude and two-interval), operant head turning, and contingent orienting (visual fixation and head turning).

It is important to note that much of the work on sensory reactivity with infants has looked at the developmental course of sensory processing rather than individual differences in reactivity. These developmental data can be used to determine what types of stimuli (i.e., which sensory modality, stimulus characteristics) infants and toddlers are able to process, and to develop measures that assess individual differences in sensory reactivity between infants. In the following section, we briefly review some of the data collected by both behavioral and electorphysiological techniques to assess sensory processing in infants and toddlers.

ASSESSMENT OF INFANT SENSORY REACTIVITY

Although there is some evidence for individual differences in reactivity to sensory stimuli in infants and young children, much of these data examine stimulus-specific reactivity (e.g., infants who display differential thresholds for auditory or visual or tactile stimuli) but do not investigate whether differences in threshold exist across all sensory modalities. Some evidence suggests that stimulus reactivity may generalize across sensory modalities during the first year of life. Arguments have been made for the perception of stimulus equivalence, particularly with regard to intensity early in infancy. For example, Lewkowicz (2000) reviews evidence that neonates exhibit nonspecific patterns of responsiveness that generalize across sensory modalities and that neonatal responsiveness appears to be controlled by the infant's general state of arousal and the overall amount of stimulation. Moreover, Lewkowicz and Turkewitz (1980) showed that young infants are able to equate auditory and visual stimulation on the basis of intensity and that they do so spontaneously, without any training. If that is the case, then it would be reasonable to predict that a young infant's response to stimulation, regardless of its modality of origin, might be the same as long as the effective intensity of stimulation is equated. Importantly, such unimodal stimulus processing appears to change over the first year of life, and infants are less likely to detect intensity differences across modalities in similar ways later in development. In the following sections, we review the methods for assessment of sensory reactivity by domain.

Auditory Reactivity

Differences in auditory reactivity have been demonstrated prenatally (Kisilevsky, Fearon, & Muir, 1998; Sohmer, Geal-Dor, & Weinstein, 1994). In the auditory modality, reactivity can be assessed peripherally or centrally. Auditory reactivity is usually assessed via threshold for intensity, frequency, and temporal resolution of the stimulus (Werner & Marean, 1996). Multiple methods have been employed in these assessments. Table 6.1 presents a review of studies examining these issues. The ability to discriminate large changes in the temporal or intensive characteristics of auditory stimuli appears to be present at birth. These abilities improve over the first months of life so that by 3 months of age, infant responses to small changes in auditory threshold for tem-

Table 6.1 Assessment of Auditory Reactivity in Infants and Toddlers

Auditory Domain	Methods	Youngest Population Tested	Selected Studies
Temporal resolution	Gap detection with conditioned head turn procedure	3 months	Werner et al. (1992)
	Gap detection	6 months	Morrongiello & Trehub (1987)
	Temporal order discrimination and auditory evoked responses	Neonate	Simos & Molfese (1997)
Frequency resolution	Behavioral	3 months	Olsho (1985) Schneider et al. (1990) Spetner & Olsho (1990) Hall & Grose (1991)
	Auditory brain response (ABR)	3 months	Folsom (1985) Folsom & Wynne (1986) Klein (1984) Sininger & Abdala (1996) Sininger et al. (1997)
Intensity resolution	Cardiac acceleration/deceleration	Neonate	Bartoshuck (1962, 1964) Turkewitz et al. (1971) Moffit (1973)
	Head-turning procedure	Neonate	Sinnott & Aslin (1985) Tarquinio et al. (1990) Schneider et al. (1988)
	ABR amplitude	8 months	Durieux-Smith et al. (1985) Cornacchia et al. (1983)
Fetal motor reactivity	Vibroacoustic stimulation	Prenatally	Kisilevsky et al. (1998) Sohmer et al. (1994)

poral, frequency, and intensity resolution are present.

Visual Reactivity

Two types of visual stimulus features, constancy and complexity, are the most useful for looking at visual threshold reactivity in infants. Although a larger number of techniques have been employed to test these features, the majority of this work has been completed via two techniques: the forced-choice preferential looking procedure (FPL) and the visual evoked response (VEP). The FPL (Teller, 1979) depends on the fact that infants choose to look at novel or interesting items more than less interesting ones. An infant's looking behavior in response to two simultaneously presented (usually adjacent) stimulus fields is observed. One field contains a physically measurable stimulus embedded in a surround and the

other field includes a blank or neutral component with a matched surround. Preferential fixation of the embedded stimulus is interpreted as the ability to detect that stimulus. Threshold values for detection of stimuli can be estimated from the number of positive responses made by the infant.

The second method of estimating visual thresholds in infants and toddlers involves the recording of a visual evoked response. The VEP is an electrical potential recorded from the scalp over the visual cortex that occurs within the first 250 ms of stimulus presentation and is used as an index of processing in the visual cortex (Hartmann, 1995). For this type of testing an infant's attention is not necessary, although they do have to fixate and accommodate on the stimulus. Regan (1977) developed a modification of the VEP procedure, the Sweep VEP, in which stimuli are presented in rapid succession so that recording time is decreased, thereby reducing variability across subjects. Table 6.2 briefly reviews some of the studies that utilize FLP and VEP in the testing of stimulus constancy and stimulus complexity in infants and toddlers. On the whole, data from studies that examine visual thresholds in infants suggest that the choice of visual stimuli is important, since the detection of certain types of stimulus features comes on-line at different times. At birth they can do one thing and at 3 months they can do another. For this reason, it is important to choose stimulus features that are developmentally appropriate to ensure that the infant is able to see them.

Olfactory Reactivity

There has been little systematic study of olfaction in infants. Most studies of infant olfactory threshold reactivity involve the presentation of an odor stimulus via the nose, usually on some type of pad or cotton swab, and then coding the infant's facial expressions or behavioral responses (Burdach, Koster, & Kroeze, 1985; Cernoch & Porter, 1985; Soussignan, Schall, & Marlier, 1999). This type of testing procedure has a number of prob-

lems. It is difficult to ensure that the same concentration of odor has been administered to each infant, given differences in infant respiration and method of presentation. Studies of olfaction often utilize standardized presentations using masks and ask adult participants to inhale at specified time points, both procedures utilized to ensure standardized presentation. In general, studies of infant olfaction have found that this sense is fully developed at birth and that infants are able to discriminate among a variety of odorants as neonates. Table 6.3 provides an overview of the behavioral and physiological assessments of infants and toddlers.

Taste Reactivity

Taste reactivity testing has been conducted, examining infant response to sweet, salty, sour, and bitter stimuli (Cowart, Young, Feldman, & Lowry, 1997). Stimuli used for these studies include liquids of sucrose, sodium chloride, citric or hydrochloric acid, and quinine (sulfate or hydrochloride) or caffeine differing in concentration. The most common measure used to assess

Table 6.2 Assessment of Visual Reactivity in Infants and Toddlers

Visual Domain	Method	Youngest Population Tested	Selected Studies
Stimulus Constancies			
Brightness	Forced-choice preferential looking	7-week-olds	Dannemiller & Banks (1983) Dannemiller (1985)
Contrast	Forced-choice preferential looking	3-month-olds	Stephens & Banks (1985) Banks et al. (1985) Slater et al. (1985)
	Visual evoked response	6-week-olds	Fiorentini et al. (1983) Kelly et al. (1997)
Size	Behavioral	4-month-olds	Granrund (1986) Slater et al. (1990)
Stimulus Complexity			
Amount of stimulus information	Habituation	Newborn	Greenberg & O'Donnell (1972)
Contour density	Visual Evoked Response	6-week-olds	Karmel et al. (1974)
Size	Preference	Newborn	Fantz & Fagan (1975) Miranda & Fantz (1971)
Number of stimulus elements	Preference	Newborn	Fantz & Fagan (1975) Miranda & Fantz (1971)

Table 6.3 Assessment of Olfactory Reactivity in Infants and Toddlers

Olfactory Domain	Methods Employed to Study Reactivity	Youngest Population Tested	Selected Studies
Presentation of odor stimulus via the nose	Facial expression or behavioral responses	Newborn	Burdach et al. (1985) Cernoch & Porter (1985) MacFarlane (1975) Lipsitt et al. (1963) Soussignan et al. (1999) Steiner (1979)
	Electroencephalogram	3 months	Kendal-Reed & VonToller (1992)

taste reactivity is facial expression or nonnutritive sucking. More often than not, taste stimuli are presented on the tongue, and there are problems with standardization of presentation. Therefore, although infant taste reactivity may be well developed at birth, the assessment of this sense's thresholds has not been investigated in a standardized or systematic manner, thereby making it difficult to draw any precise conclusions about the nature of infant taste thresholds. Table 6.4 lists several studies that have investigated behavioral and physiological responses to taste in infants and toddlers.

Tactile Reactivity

A variety of techniques have been employed in the study of taction in adults, including vibration stimuli applied at different angles to the skin by pins or probes, and items moved across the skin at periodic and aperiodic intervals including air puffs, embossed letters, and household items such as sandpaper, cloth, and steel wool (Greenspan & Bolanowski, 1996). In adults the three ba-

sic dimensions of taction—intensity, temporality, and spatial perception—have been studied most intensively.

Although a wide array of techniques has been used to attempt to examine infants' and toddlers' reactivity to tactile stimuli, no systematic methods have been employed (table 6.5). Such lack of methodical evaluation of tactile reactivity in this group is problematic for a number of reasons. First, data suggest that different parts of the body vary considerably as to their capacity for affective and discriminative sensibility (Parent, 1996). For example, skin can be classified into three types: glabrous or hairless skin (e.g., skin of the palm); hairy skin (skin that has hair); and mucocutaneous skin (skin that borders the entrances to the body's interior). In fact, not only does each skin type have different properties (e.g., elasticity, resilience, thickness, attachment to subcutaneous tissue, etc.), sensitivity within these three skin types can also vary substantially as a function of body region, age, gender, and species (Agache, Monneur, Lévêque, & DeRegal, 1980; Escoffier et al., 1989; Grahame, 1970). For this reason, it

Table 6.4 Assessment of Taste Reactivity in Infants and Toddlers

Taste Domain	Methods Employed to Study Reactivity	Youngest Population Tested	Selected Studies
Presentation of taste stimulus via the tongue	Facial expression or behavioral responses	Newborn	Graillion et al. (1997) Rosenstien & Oster (1998) Steiner (1979)
Taste substance embedded in gelatin-based nipple	Sucking		Maone et al. (1990)

Table 6.5 The Assessment of Tactile Reactivity in Infants and Toddlers

Tactile Domain	Methods Employed to Study Reactivity	Youngest Population Tested	Selected Studies
Arm restraint	Behavioral reactivity	5-month-olds	Fox (1989)
Inoculation	Behavioral reactivity	Neonates	Worobey & Lewis (1989)
Heel-stick	Behavioral reactivity	Neonates	Lewis et al. (1989)
Cold pressor	Behavioral reactivity	Neonates	Riese (19787)

is important to understand the particular properties of the body region under study when assessing reactivity. Second, the temperature of skin has been shown to significantly affect vibratory sensitivity (Bolanowski & Verrillo, 1982). Thus, skin temperature should be assessed and controlled for in examining tactile reactivity in infants and young children.

THE CLINICAL ASSESSMENT OF SENSORY REACTIVITY IN INFANTS AND TODDLERS

Several attempts have been made to develop standardized methods to assess a child's sensory functioning. These methods have utilized both behavioral observations of the child and parental report of the child's sensory responsivity and adaptability. The most systematic attempt at developing a parent reporting measure of child sensory reactivity is that of Dunn and Brown (1997). They developed an instrument that assesses children's responses to sensory events in their daily activities. This measure utilizes a 5-point Likert scale and assesses the amount of time the child engages in 125 different behaviors. Items require parents to rate their child's sensory responses to a series of behavioral statements that fall into eight categories (auditory, visual, taste/smell, movement, position, touch, activity level, and emotional/social). For example, items relating to sensation-seeking behavior ask caregivers if children enjoy strange noises or if they are always touching other people or objects.

Dunn and Brown (1997) factor analyzed data from 1,115 parents of children between the ages of 3 and 10 years. This analysis yielded nine factors including sensory seeking, emotionally reactive, low endurance/tone, oral sensory sensitivity, inattention/distractibility, poor registration, sensory sensitivity, sedentary, and fine motor/perceptual. Interestingly, the factor loadings did not reflect different sensory systems but rather the variety of child reactions to sensory experiences. Also, the authors found that reactivity to a specific modality was not as good a predictor of general sensory reactivity as global response across sensory modality. While the Sensory Profile (Dunn & Brown, 1997) is used as an assessment of sensory irregularities in children, this scale lacks reliability and validity data. Moreover, the factor structure remains unclear, as some questionnaire items load on unrelated factors, while other items load on more than one scale (Barton & Robins, 2000).

Another parent report measure developed to assess sensory reactivity in children is the Sensory Rating Scale (SRS; Provost & Oetter, 1993). The SRS, usually completed by the primary caregiver, is used to evaluate sensory responsiveness in infants 9 to 36 months of age. The scale is intended by its authors to tap sensory defensive behaviors and examines sensitivity to stimuli in various modalities and avoidance behaviors. The scale yields five subscales that measure response to touch, movement, hearing, vision, and temperament. It provides a 5-point Likert scale to rate the frequency with which an infant displays specific behaviors, with higher scores indicating more sensory defensive behaviors. For example, the SRS asks caregivers if children react negatively to loud noises or if they like to be held only when they choose.

One of the earliest attempts to examine sensory reactivity via behavioral responsivity in children was made by Kootz and his colleagues (Kootz, Marinelli, & Cohen, 1981) in a study comparing response times in autistic children and normal controls. Kootz et al. (1981) presented three types of stimuli to these two groups of children, representing three modalities: (1) auditory (1,000-Hz tone at a 74-dB sound pressure level); (2) visual (light produced by a bare 25-W bulb placed 1.2 m from the child); and (3) tactile (a small electromagnetic vibrator attached by a small band to the child's nondominant hand). Each child was asked to press a key as soon as he or she perceived the presence of the stimulus. While Kootz et al. (1981) found that autistic children's responses were significantly slower than those of the control group children, both groups showed a similar hierarchy of sensitivity to the three sensory modalities (auditory, visual, and tactile), responding fastest to auditory stimuli and slowest to tactile stimulation.

A number of published tests have been used to behaviorally assess infant and toddler sensory reactivity. These instruments allow practitioners to assess a child's ability to regulate sensory input and to respond to different stimuli in a series of structured activities. The most widely used behavioral assessment of sensory function in infants is the Test of Sensory Function in Infants (TSFI; DeGangi & Greenspan, 1989). The TSFI, often used by occupational therapists to identify sensory processing deficits in infants, is a 24-item measure that assesses the sensory integration of five areas of sensory function, including (1) reactivity to tactile deep pressure, (2) visual-tactile integration, (3) adaptive motor responses, (4) ocular-motor control, and (5) reactivity to vestibular stimulation (DeGangi & Greenspan, 1989). DeGangi and Greenspan designed this measure to focus on the integration of the senses with the tactile and vestibular domains, based on the belief that these two domains are essential to the development of fine and gross motor skills and to motor planning abilities. The authors hypothesize that dysfunction in the integration of tactile and vestibular sensory input underlies disturbances in daily function (e.g., sleep, feeding, state control, mood regulation) as well as in hyper- or hyposensitivity to auditory, tactile, visual, and vestibular function.

Caregivers, parents, teachers, and health care providers will often attest to the fact that children respond differentially to similar life experiences and that such differences are present early in life. Several studies have demonstrated that infant temperament can greatly affect the way in which caregivers interact with an infant as well as how caregivers feel about themselves. For example, a study by Breitmayer and Ricciuti (1988) showed that alert infants received more social contact than active ones and that irritable infants were soothed most often. In addition, a study by Klein (1984) suggested that temperamentally easy infants receive more sensory and social stimulation, at both 6 and 12 months of age.

At present, there is a growing body of knowledge about how to manage difficult behavior in young children (Greenspan, 1992; Zero to Three, 1994). Greenspan (1992; Greenspan & Weider, 1993) suggests that children who present with behavioral difficulties that are associated with sensory processing and motor planning functions may be at risk for developing regulatory disorders. Greenspan and colleagues propose that for children from birth to age 3 there exist three subtypes of regulatory disorders (hypersensitive, underreactive, and motorically disorganized/impulsive types), which are characterized by one predominant pattern of behavior and sensory functioning. For example, the hypersensitive subtype is highly reactive to sensory input, although their level of sensitivity may vary across sensory modalities and they tend to display either fearful or defiant behavior (Zero to Three, 1994). Greenspan (1992) suggests that children meeting criteria for regulatory disorder in accordance with the *Diagnostic Classification of Mental Health and Developmental Disorders of Infancy and Early Childhood* (DC:0–3) may be at risk for variety of disorders relating to self-regulation including attention deficits, oppositional behavior, tantrums, and some forms of social isolation.

It is possible, however, that variation in infant behavior could be a result of temperamental differences rather than due to a pathological condition. As has been noted, individual differences in sensory threshold and reactivity are considered to be a major component of most models of infant temperament. Rather than viewing infants with high or low levels of sensory reactivity as presenting with some clinically significant symptomatology in need of therapeutic intervention, it may be possible to make adjustments to these children's living environments to match their temperamental constitutions to promote more optimal functioning. For example, health care professionals might offer parents specific suggestions about how best to respond to their child or how to alter the child's environment to reduce his or her distress. Clinicians may also encourage parents to change their responses to children's difficult behavior by suggesting they help their child identify a series of steps that permit him or her to help master stressful situations. In addition, caregivers can increase their child's exposure to different types of sensory experiences that they can easily process in order to facilitate their engagement with the external environment (Greenspan & Weider, 1993).

CONCLUSION AND FUTURE DIRECTIONS

While sensory reactivity holds a central role in many theories of infant temperament, it is still generally evaluated via questionnaires to parents or caregivers. Little systematic work has assessed reactivity across different modalities, although, as seen in the above review, the research methods are available for such evaluations within specific modalities. There is an obvious need for the development of standardized behavioral measures of sensory reactivity, and such measures must include concern for reliability of assessment and validity of outcome. Such approaches should include both behavioral assessment and standard questionnaire methods that assess reactivity across multiple everyday contexts of caregiving.

From an assessment perspective, understanding variations in infant sensory reactivity may play a critical role in reformulating the manner in which infant and toddler behavior is perceived by caregivers and health care professionals. More emphasis should be placed on ways that the environment can be altered to provide a goodness of fit with the child's sensory processing responses. Parents form perceptions of their infant's temperament and personality as a function of the infant's response to everyday social interactions and caregiving experiences. Knowledge of individual variation in sensory reactivity and parental reinterpretation of the meaning and significance of an infant's behavioral repertoire may have important consequences for the manner in which parents interact with and respond to their child.

References

Agache, P. G., Monner, C., Lévêque, J.–L., & Dermal, J. (1980). Mechanical properties and Young's modulus of human skin in vivo. *Archives of Dermatological Research, 269,* 221–232.

Aron, N. E., & Aron, A. (1997). Sensory-processing sensitivity and its relation to introversion and emotionality. *Journal of Personality and Social Psychology, 73,* 345–368.

Aslin, R. N. (1987). Visual and auditory development in infancy. In J. D. Osofsky (Ed.), *Handbook of infant development* (pp. 5–97). New York: John Wiley.

Banks, M. S., Stephens, B. R., & Hartman, E. E. (1985). The development of basic mechanisms of pattern vision: Spatial frequency channels. *Journal of Experimental Child Psychology, 40*(3), 501–527.

Bar-Haim, Y., Marshall, P. J., Fox, N. A., Schorr, E., & Gordon-Salant, S. *Auditory sensory processing in socially withdrawn children.* Manuscript submitted for publication.

Barnes, G. (1975). Extraversion and pain. *British Journal of Social and Clinical Psychology, 14,* 303–308.

Barton, M. L., & Robins, D. (2000). Regulatory disorders. In C. H. Zeanah, Jr. (Ed.), *Handbook of infant mental health* (2nd ed., pp. 311–325). New York: Guilford Press.

Bartoshuk, A. K. (1962). Human neonatal cardiac acceleration to sound: Habituation and dishabituation. *Perceptual and Motor Skills, 15,* 15–27.

Bartoshuk, A. K. (1964). Human neonatal cardiac responses to sound: A power function. *Psychonomic Science, 1,* 151–152.

Bolanowski, S. J., Jr., & Verrillo, R. T. (1982). Temperature and criterion effects in a somatosensory subsystem: A neurophysiological and psych-physical study. *Journal of Neurophysiology, 48,* 836–855.

Breitmayer, B. J., & Ricciuti, H. N. (1988). The effect of neonatal temperament on caregiver behavior in the newborn nursery. *Infant Mental Health Journal, 9,* 158–172.

Burdach, K. J., Koster, E. P., & Kroeze, H. A. (1985). Interindividual differences in acuity for odor and aroma. *Perceptual and Motor Skills, 60,* 723–730.

Buss, A. H., & Plomin, R. (1975). *A temperament theory of personality development*. New York: Wiley-Interscience.

Buss, A. H., & Plomin, R. (1984). *Temperament: Early developing personality traits*. Hillsdale, NJ: Lawrence Erlbaum.

Calkins, S. D., Fox, N. A., & Marshall, T. (1996). Behavioral and physiological antecedents of inhibited and uninhibited behavior. *Child Development, 67*, 523–540.

Carey, W. B., & McDevitt, S. C. (1978). Revision of the infant temperament questionnaire. *Pediatrics, 61*, 735–739.

Cernoch, J. M., & Porter, R. H. (1985). Recognition of maternal axillary odors by infants. *Child Development, 56*, 1593–1598.

Clarke, L. A., Kochanska, G., & Ready, R. (2000). Mothers' personality and its interaction with child temperament as predictors of parenting behavior. *Journal of Personality and Social Psychology, 79*, 274–285.

Cornacchia, L., Martini, A., & Morra, B. (1983). Air and bone conduction brainstem responses in adults and infants. *Audiology, 22*, 430–437.

Cowart, B. J., Young, I. M., Feldman, R. S., & Lowry, L. D. (1997). Clinical disorders of smell and taste. In G. K. Beauchamp & L. Bartoshuk (Eds.), *Tasting and smelling: Handbook of perception and cognition* (2nd ed., pp. 175–198). San Diego, CA: Academic Press.

Dannimiller, J. L. (1985). The early phase of dark adaptation in human infants. *Vision Research, 25*, 207–212.

Dannimiller, J. L., & Banks, M. S. (1983). The development of light adaptation in human infants. *Vision Research, 23*, 599–609.

DeGangi, G. A., & Greenspan, S. I. (1989). The development of sensory function in infants. *Physical and Occupational Therapy in Pediatrics, 8*, 21–33.

Dunn, W., & Brown, C. (1997). Factor analysis on the sensory profile from a national sample of children without disabilities. *American Journal of Occupational Therapy, 51*, 490–499.

Durieux-Smith, A., Edwards, C. G., Picton, T. W., & McMurray, B. (1985). Auditory brainstem responses to clicks in neonates. *Journal of Otolaryngology, 14*, 12–18.

Escoffier, C., De Rigal, J., Rochefort, A., Vasselet, R., Leveque, J.-L., & Agache, P. G. (1989). Age-related mechanical properties of human skin: An in vivo study. *Journal of Investigative Dermatology, 93*, 353–357.

Eysenck, H. J. (1967a). *The biological basis of personality*. Springfield, IL: Thomas.

Eysenck, H. J. (1967b). Personality and extra-sensory perception. *Journal of the Society for Psychical Research, 44*, 55–71.

Eysenck, H. J. (1979). The conditioning model of neurosis. *Behavioral and Brain Sciences, 2*, 155–199.

Eysenck, H. J. (1981). *A model for personality*. New York: Springer-Verlag.

Fantz, R. L., & Fagan, J. F. (1975). Visual attention to size and number of pattern details by term and preterm infants during the first six months. *Child Development, 16*, 3–18.

Fiorentini, A., Pirchio, M., & Spinelli, D. (1983). Development of retinal and cortical responses to pattern reversal in infants: A selective review. *Behavior and Brain Research, 10*(1), 99–106.

Folsom, R. C. (1985). Auditory brain stem responses from human infants: Pure tone masking profiles for clicks and filtered clicks. *Journal of the Acoustical Society of America, 78*, 555–562.

Folsom, R. C., & Wynne, M. K. (1986). Auditory brainstem responses from human adults and infants: Restriction of frequency contribution by notched-noise masking. *Journal of the Acoustical Society of America, 80*, 1057–1064.

Fox, N. (1989). Psychophysiological correlates of emotional reactivity during the first year of life. *Developmental Psychology, 25*, 364–372.

Fox, N. A., Henderson, H. A., Rubin, K. H., Calkins, S. D., & Schmidt, L. A. (2001). Continuity and discontinuity of behavioral inhibition and exuberance: Psychophysiological and behavioral influences across the first four years of life. *Child Development, 72*, 1–21.

Fullard, W., McDevitt, S. C., & Carey, W. B. (1984). Assessing temperament in one- to three-year-old children. *Journal of Pediatric Psychology, 9*, 205–217.

Garcia-Coll, C., Kagan, J., & Reznick, J. S. (1984). Behavioral inhibition in young children. *Child Development, 55*, 1005–1019.

Goldsmith, H. H. (1983). Genetic influences on personality from infancy to adulthood. *Child Development, 54*, 331–355.

Grahame, R. (1970). A method for measuring human skin elasticity in vivo with obsservations on the effects of age, sex, and pregnancy. *Clinical Science, 39*, 223–238.

Graillon, A., Barr, R. G., Young, S. N., Wright, J.

H., & Hendricks, L. A. (1997). Differential response to intraoral sucrose, quinine and corn oil in crying human newborns. *Physiology and Behavior, 62*(2), 317–325.

Granrund, C. E. (1986). Binocular vision and spatial perception on 4- and 5-month-old infants. *Journal of Experimental Psychology: Human Perception and Performance, 12*(1), 36–49.

Greenberg, D. J., & O'Donnell, W. J. (1972). Infancy and the optimal level of stimulation. *Child Development, 43*, 639–645.

Greenspan, S. (1992). *Regulatory disorders. Infancy and early childhood: The practice of clinical assessment and intervention with emotional and developmental challenges.* Madison, CT: International Universities Press.

Greenspan, J. D., & Bolanowski, S. J. (1996). The psychophysics of tactile perception and its peripheral physiological basis. In L. Kruger (Ed.), *Pain and touch* (pp. 25–103). San Diego: Academic Press.

Greenspan, S., & Weider, S. (1993). Regulatory disorders. In C. H. Zeanah, Jr. (Ed.), *Handbook of infant mental health* (pp. 280–290). New York: Guilford Press.

Haier, R. J., Robinson, D. L., Braden, W., & Williams, D. (1984). Evoked potential augmenting-reducing and personality differences. *Personality and Individual Differences, 5*(3), 293–301.

Hall, J. W., III, & Grose, J. H. (1991). Notched-noise measures of frequency selectivity in adults and children using fixed-masker-level and fixed-signal-level presentation. *Journal of Speech and Hearing Research, 34*, 651–660.

Hartmann, E. E. (1995). Infant visual development: An overview of studies using visual evoked potential measures from Harter to the present. *International Journal of Neuroscience, 80(Special Issue)*, 203–235.

Herbener, E. S., Kagan, J., & Cohen, M. (1989). Shyness and olfactory thresholds. *Personality and Individual Differences, 10*(11), 1159–1163.

Himmelfarb, D., Marshall, P. J., Bar-Haim, Y., & Fox, N. A. (2000). *Relations of early negative reactivity to later social behavior, internalizing problems, and cardiac patterns: Effects of stimulus modality.* Poster presented at the 12th Biennial International Conference on Infant Studies, Brighton, England.

Kagan, J. (1994). *Galen's Prophecy: Temperament in human nature.* New York: Basic Books.

Kagan, J., Reznick, S. J., Clarke, C., Snidman, N., & Garcia-Coll, C. (1984). Behavioral inhibition to the unfamiliar. *Child Development, 55*, 2212–2225.

Kagan, J., & Snidman, N. (1991). Infant predictors of inhibited and uninhibited profiles. *Psychological Science, 2*, 40–44.

Karmel, B. Z., Hoffman, R. F., & Fegy, M. J. (1974). Processing of contour information by human infants evidenced by pattern-dependent potentials. *Child Development, 45*, 39–48.

Kelly, J. P., Borchert, K., & Teller, D. Y. (1997). The development of chromatic and achromatic contrast sensitivity in infancy as tested with the sweep VEP. *Vision Research, 37*, 2057–2072.

Kendal-Reed, M., & Van Toller, S. (1992). Brain electrical activity mapping: An exploratory study of infant responses to odours. *Chemical Senses, 17*(6), 765–777.

Kisilevsky, B., Fearon, I., & Muir, D. W. (1998). Fetuses differentiate vibroacoustic stimuli. *Infant Behavior and Development, 21*(1), 25–45.

Klein, P. S. (1984). Behavior of Israeli mothers toward infants in relation to infants' perceived temperament. *Child Development, 55*, 1212–1218.

Kochanska, G. (1997). Mutually responsive orientation between mothers and their young children: Implications for early socialization. *Child Development, 68*, 94–112.

Kootz, J. P., Marinelli, B., & Cohen, D. J. (1981). Sensory receptor sensitivity in autistic children: Response times to proximal and distal stimuli. *Archives of General Psychiatry, 38*, 271–273.

Lewis, M., Worobey, J., & Thomas, D. (1989). Behavioral features of early reactivity: Antecedents and consequences. *New Directions for Child Development, 45*, 33–46.

Lewkowicz, D. J. (2000). The development of intersensory temporal perception: An epigenetic systems/limitations view. *Psychological Bulletin, 126*, 281–308.

Lewkowicz, D. J., & Turkewitz, G. (1980). Crossmodal equivalences in early infancy: Auditory-visual intensity matching. *Developmental Psychology, 16*, 597–607.

Lipsitt, L. P., Engen, T., & Kaye, H. (1963). Developmental changes in the olfactory threshold of the neonate. *Child Development, 34*(2), 371–376.

Maone, T. R., Mattes, R. D., Bernbaum, J. C., &

Beauchamp, G. K. (1990). A new method for delivering a taste without fluids to preterm and term infants. *Developmental Psychobiology, 23*(2), 179–191.

Medoff-Cooper, B., Carey, W. B., & McDevitt, S. C. (1993). The Early Infancy Temperament Questionnaire. *Journal of Developmental & Behavior Pediatrics, 14*, 230–235.

McLaughlin, R. J., & Eysenck, H. J. (1967). Extraversion, neurotocism and paired-associates learning. *Journal of Experimental Research in Personality, 2*, 128–132.

Miranda, S. B., & Fantz, R. L. (1971). *Distribution of visual attention of newborn infants among patterns varying in size and number of detail.* Proceedings. Washington, DC: American Psychological Association.

Moffit, A. R. (1973). Intensity discrimination and cardiac reaction in young infants. *Developmental Psychology, 8*(3), 357–359.

Morrongiello, B. A., & Trehub, S. E. (1987). Age-related changes in auditory temporal Perception. *Journal of Experimental Child Psycholology, 44*(3), 413–426.

Olsho, L. (1985). Infant auditory perception: Tonal masking. *Infant Behavior and Development, 7*, 27–35.

Parent, A. (1996). *Carpenter's Human Neuroanatomy* (9th ed.). Baltimore: Williams and Wilkins.

Pavlov, I. (1936). *Lectures on conditioned reflexes.* New York: Liveright.

Provost, B., & Oetter, P. (1993). The sensory rating scale for infants and young children: Development and reliability. *Physical and Occupational Therapy in Pediatrics, 13*, 15–35.

Regan, D. (1977). Speedy assessment of visual acuity in amblyopia by the evoked potential method. *Ophthalmologica, 175*(3), 159–164.

Riese, M. L. (1987). Temperament stability between the neonatal period and 24 months. *Developmental Psychology, 23*, 216–222.

Rosenstein, D., & Oster, H. (1988). Differential facial responses to four basic tastes in newborns. *Child Development, 59*, 1555–1568.

Rothbart, M. K. (1981). Measurement of temperament in infancy. *Child Development, 52*, 569–578.

Rothbart, M. K., & Derryberry, P. (1981). Development of individual differences in temperament. In M. E. Lamb & A. L. Brown (Eds.), *Advances in developmental psychology* (Vol. 1, pp. 37–86). Hillside, NJ: Lawrence Erlbaum.

Schalling, D. (1971). Tolerance for experimentally induced pain as related to personality. *Scandinavian Journal of Psychology, 12*, 271–281.

Schneider, B. A., Bull, D., & Trehub, S. E. (1988). Biaural unmasking in infants. *Journal of the Acoustical Society of America, 83*, 1124–1132.

Schneider, B. A., Morrongiello, B. A., & Trehub, S. E. (1990). The size of the critical band in infants, child, and adults. *Journal of Experimental Psychology: Human Perception and Performance, 16*, 642–652.

Siddle, D. A., Morrish, R. B., White, K. D., & Mangan, G. L. (1969). Relation of visual sensitivity to extraversion. *Journal of Experimental Research in Personality, 3*(4), 264–267.

Simos, P. G., & Molfese, D. L. (1997). Electrophysiological responses from a temporal order continuum in the newborn infant. *Neuropsychologia, 35*, 89–98.

Sininger, Y. S., & Abdala, C. (1996). Hearing threshold as measured by auditory brainstem responses in human neonates. *Ear and Hearing, 17*, 395–401.

Sininger, Y. S., Abdala, C., & Cone-Wesson, B. (1997). Auditory threshold sensitivity of the human neonate as measured by the auditory brainstem response. *Hearing Research, 104*, 27–38.

Sinnott J. M., & Aslin, R. N. (1985). Frequency and intensity discrimination in human infants and adults. *Journal of the Acoustical Society of America, 78*(6), 1986–1992.

Slater, A., Earle, D. C., Morison, V., & Rose, D. (1985). Pattern preferences at birth and their interaction with habituation-induced novelty preferences. *Journal of Experimental Child Psychology, 39*, 37–54.

Slater, A., Mattock, A., & Brown, E. (1990). Size constancy at birth: Newborn infants' responses to retinal and real size. *Journal of Experimental Child Psychology, 49*, 314–322.

Sohmer, H., Geal-Dor, M., & Weinstein, D. (1994). Human fetal auditory threshold improvement during maternal oxygen respiration. *Hearing Research, 75*, 145–150.

Soussignan, R., Schaal, B., & Marlier, L. (1999). Olfactory alliesthesia in human neonates: Prandial state and stimulus familiarity modulate facial and autonomic responses to milk odors. *Developmental Psychobiology, 35*, 3–14.

Spetner, N. B., & Olsho, L. W. (1990). Auditory frequency resolution in human infancy. *Child Development, 61*, 632–652.

Steiner, J. E. (1979). Human facial expression in response to taste and smell stimulation. *Advances in *Child Development and Behavior, 13,* 257–295.

Stelmack, R. M., & Campbell, K. B. (1974). Extraversion and auditory sensitivity to high and low frequency. *Perceptual and Motor Skills, 38,* 875–879.

Stelmack, R. M., & Michaud-Achorn, A. (1985). Extraversion, attention, and auditory evoked response. *Journal of Research in Personality, 19,* 416–428.

Stephens, B. R., & Banks, M. S. (1985). The development of basic mechanisms of pattern vision: Spatial frequency channels. *Journal of Experimental Child Psychology, 40,* 501–27.

Strelau, J. (1983). *Temperament, personality, activity.* London: Academic.

Strelau, J. (1998). *Temperament: A psychological perspective.* New York: Plenum Press.

Tarquinio, N., Zelazo, P. R., & Weiss, M. J. (1990). Recovery of neonatal head turning to decrease sound pressure level. *Developmental Psychology, 26,* 752–758.

Teller, D. Y. (1979). The forced-choice looking procedure: A psychophysiological technique for use with human infants. *Infant Behavior and Development, 2,* 135–153.

Thomas, A., & Chess, S. (1984). Genesis and evolution of behavioural disorders: From infancy to early adult life. *American Journal of Psychiatry, 141,* 1–9.

Thomas, A., & Chess, S. (1977). *Temperament and development.* New York: Brunner/Mazel.

Turkewitz, G., Moreau, T., & Birch, H. G. (1971). Relationships among responses in the human newborn: The non-association and non-equivalence among different indicators of responsiveness. *Psychophysiology, 7,* 233–247.

Werner, L. A., & Marean, G. C. (1996). *Human auditory development.* Boulder, CO: Westview Press.

Werner, L. A., Marean, G. C., Halpin, C. F., Spetner, N. B., & Gillenwater, J. M. (1992). Infant auditory temporal acuity: Gap detection. *Child Development, 63,* 260–272.

Worobey, J., & Lewis, M. (1989). Individual differences in the reactivity of young infants. *Developmental Psychology, 25,* 663–667.

Zero to Three, National Center for Clinical Infant Programs (1994). *Diagnostic classification of mental health and developmental disorders of infancy and early childhood.* Washington, DC: Author.

III

DIAGNOSTIC ISSUES RELATING TO CLASSIFICATION AND TAXONOMY

Growing parental and policy interest in early behavioral intervention as well as increasing numbers of prescriptions for psychotropic medication to treat early attention, affective, and behavioral disturbances in early childhood have highlighted the need for valid diagnostic assessment in the earliest years. Yet, the diagnostic assessment of psychopathology in young children is severely limited at this time by the current status of diagnostic classification for infants, toddlers, and preschool-aged children. This section provides an overview of diagnostic issues relating to taxonomy and classification for infants and young children. Currently, there is some controversy over whether the young child assessment field can utilize or modify existing diagnostic systems of classification despite limitations in this population or if a newly developed system designed for infants and young children is more appropriate. Authors of chapters in this section review the background and make recommendations for advancing an appropriate diagnostic classification system for young children.

Adrian Angold and Helen Link Egger summarize the current status of the nosology of psychi-

atric disorders in preschool children. First, they address any lingering concerns over whether categorical diagnostic approaches are appropriate for the classification of preschool emotional and behavioral disorders. Next, they review four major diagnostic systems for preschoolers. Finally, they identify gaps in the research that need to be addressed to advance a developmentally based approach toward the understanding and classification of preschool disorders.

Recognizing the need for a classification system to address problems relevant to very young children whose assessment needs are not well met by the *DSM* systems, the National Center for Clinical Infant Programs spent 8 years developing the *Diagnostic Classification of Mental Health and Developmental Disorders of Infancy and Early Childhood* (DC:0–3) multiaxial system for classifying problems in infants and toddlers. It is derived from developmental theory and clinical work with infants and young children. In addition, it utilizes diagnostic terminology specific to this age group but also complementary to that of the *DSM* system.

Alicia Lieberman, Kathryn Barnard, and Serena Wieder describe the DC:0–3 diagnostic classification system. They discuss diagnostic issues generally as they relate to clinical assessment in infancy and early childhood, make recommendations for conducting assessments using the DC: 0–3, and provide a comparison of the DC:0–3 and the *DSM* systems. In addition, they also describe how DC:0–3 was developed, review existing validity and reliability research, and provide clinical vignettes illustrating three diagnostic categories.

Thomas Achenbach and Leslie Rescorla present an empirically based paradigm for the assessment of young children. They argue that assessment methods for young children should be standardized, flexible, applicable under diverse conditions for diverse purposes, and cost effective. The implications for improving nosologies of early childhood disorders are addressed in terms of the need for identifying actual patterns of problems manifested by young children, obtaining normative data from different sources, and integrating data from multiple sources for both clinical and research purposes.

The authors in this section provide an overview of the strengths and limitations of current systems of nosology for young children. They are in agreement in suggesting that more research from multiple sources of data is needed to establish the psychometric properties of established diagnostic categories for young children. At the same time, there is some disagreement among the authors in this section regarding the importance of observation as part of routine diagnostic evaluation. The authors also emphasize the role of functional impairment in improving the validity of diagnostic classification.

7

Psychiatric Diagnosis in Preschool Children

Adrian Angold

Helen Link Egger

WHAT IS A DIAGNOSIS?

DelCarmen-Wiggins and Carter have provided a nice summary of the key problems for preschool nosology: "The researcher or clinician interested in understanding and evaluating clinically significant mental health problems in infants and toddlers is challenged by rapid developmental change in the first few years of life, the immediate relevance of a dynamic caregiving environment, and the problem of distinguishing normal, temperamental variations from signs of pathology" (DelCarmen-Wiggins & Carter, 2001, p. 8). In considering the current status of preschool nosology, we will need to keep these challenges firmly in mind.

In its simplest form, a diagnosis is a statement about the presence of a *health condition*. According to the World Health Organization (WHO, 1999, p. 191), "a health condition is an alteration or attribute of the health status of an individual that may lead to distress, interference with daily activities, or contact with health services; it may be a disease (acute or chronic), disorder, injury or trauma, or reflect other health-related states such

as pregnancy, aging, stress, congenital anomaly, or genetic predisposition." It is generally accepted that many behavioral and emotional problems fall within the ambit of this definition; hence the existence of official nosologies of psychiatric disorders like the *DSM-IV* (American Psychiatric Association, 1994) and ICD-10 Classification of Mental and Behavioural Disorders (WHO, 1992). These classifications are typically descriptive rather than etiological, grouping individuals according to patterns of presenting symptoms and signs, rather than their putative causes. The reason for this is that we usually do not know enough about the causes of the major mental disorders to produce an etiological classification (though hopefully one day we will). However, it has proved useful from many perspectives to have even such limited nosologies. For instance, we are accustomed to the use of diagnoses for service planning, targeting treatment, selecting phenomenologically similar individuals for clinical trials, and other forms of research in other branches of psychiatry. Note that there is no implication here that a disorder is a chthonic product of the individual, only that the individual displays an identifiable perturbation of health status. In other words, health conditions may well be caused (wholly or in part) by agencies external to the individual (as with all infectious diseases and many other disorders like lung cancer [smoking], mesothelioma [asbestos], or allergies).

In practice, it is also important to be aware that a diagnosis is a *probabilistic* statement about the presence of a health condition. This is most apparent in the early stages of the diagnostic process, when a differential diagnosis is entertained until a clear front-runner emerges. However, it is often the case that the borders between diagnoses are fuzzy (as with the distinction between systemic lupus erythematosus and scleroderma), and mixed presentations are relatively common. In such situations a single final diagnosis may never be reached, though the class of disorder may have been identified. However, for many purposes it is necessary or convenient to reduce what is often a complex relative probability statement to a simple yes/no decision. This is particularly true when treatment is to be given, or cases and controls are to be selected for research purposes. The reason that such simplification is useful is that treatment is not a linear function of symptom level. Severe hypertension should be treated with antihypertensive medications in adequate doses, but it does not follow that the correct treatment for normal blood pressure is a very low dose of an antihypertensive. At some (arbitrary, but sensible) point, the decision to treat or not to treat has to be made, and that decision is inherently dichotomous. The key message here is that uncertainty and the use of imperfect diagnostic rules are common in medicine as a whole, and are not the sole preserve of psychiatry.

As the previous examples illustrate, such a nosology does not imply that a clearly bounded class of individuals with a particular disease exists. In some cases, such classes can be relatively easily identified; in others it is clear that "normality" and "disease" shade into one another (late-onset Alzheimer's disease or depression, for example). Neither should different diagnoses necessarily be expected to be sharply delineated from one another (especially in the early stages of their identification). The existence of widespread comorbidity among psychiatric disorders in older children, adolescents, and adults raises a host of questions about each individual diagnosis (Angold, Costello, & Erkanli, 1999) but does not invalidate the whole diagnostic process. We would hardly claim that having separate diagnoses for carcinoma of the bronchus and chronic bronchitis is invalidated by the fact that they often occur together.

It is also worth pointing out that the hoary old debate about the relative merits of "categorical" and "continuous" approaches to diagnosis has by now mostly subsided into recognition that both have their place (Achenbach, 1990) and that the two approaches are by no means antithetical. For example, when a cutoff point is imposed on a continuously distributed scale measure of psychopathology (like the Child Behavior Checklist) to define "clinical" and "nonclinical" groups, a diagnosis is being made. A momentary glance at most *DSM-IV* categories indicates that even this haven of categorical diagnosis typically depends upon adding up the count of relevant symptoms and seeing whether that count falls above a predetermined cutoff point.

What Constitutes a *Valid* Diagnosis?

A nosology always represents our current "best guess" at how to usefully divide up the universe of health conditions. Hence nosologies change as we learn more about diseases. At any point in time, there will be categories associated with very different levels of belief about their appropriateness. Some will be long established and subject to little change, like Down syndrome; others, like attention-deficit hyperactivity disorder (ADHD), will be well-established in some ways, but needing extension in others (what should the diagnostic criteria be in adults, for instance?). Still others will be new categories, which could turn out to be significant improvements on older approaches, or could later be dropped. The *DSM* criteria for overanxious disorder are a case in point here. This disorder was introduced in *DSM-III*, revised substantially in *DSM-III-R*, and eliminated altogether in *DSM-IV*.

A variety of procedures have been suggested for the validation of psychiatric diagnostic categories (e.g., Robins & Guze, 1970); all, however, involve attempts to demonstrate that a distinctive pattern of symptoms, signs, and test results ("syndrome") is associated with specific differences in external associated features. Such features include patterns of disability resulting from the syndrome, its psychological and psychosocial correlates, patterns of genetic risk, anatomical and physiological associations, natural history, and treatment response. Diagnostic validity is, therefore, the end product of a long research process along multiple dimensions and not a single true/false statement. That validating research process can be seen as one of construct validation. When Cronbach and Meehl (1955) presented their description of that concept, it was in relation to the validation of measures of psychological constructs. However, the notion can be applied more generally to the validity of constructs themselves (see, e.g., Waldman, Lilienfeld, & Lahey, 1995 for a helpful discussion and illustration of this approach in relation to the disruptive behavior disorders).

It is better to think of particular diagnoses being more or less well-supported by the available data, rather than trying to determine whether they are "valid" in some unitary sense. At present, so few research data are available in relation to preschool psychopathology that most diagnoses are unsupported by *any* convincing research data. The absence of evidence, however, should not be seen as invalidating any nosology. To invalidate a diagnostic category one needs evidence that the category has failed in the construct validation process. The hypothesis, say, that the *DSM-IV* system provides a good method of parsing psychopathology in preschoolers is, therefore, tenable but, for the most part, unsupported by any but the weakest of evidence. As we shall see below, the same is true of the available alternatives to *DSM-IV*. This initially depressing conclusion needs to be set in the light of the broader recent history of diagnostic research in children, and we now turn our attention to that topic.

DOUBTS ABOUT THE APPROPRIATENESS OF CATEGORICAL DIAGNOSIS FOR PRESCHOOLERS

Though many see the development of categorical diagnosis for preschoolers as a natural outgrowth of three decades of work that have led even strong supporters of dimensional approaches to agree that categorical diagnosis has an important place in psychiatric research with older children (see e.g., Achenbach, 1995), there remains, in the infant and preschool field, a resistance to it. There are several principal objections (reviewed in Emde, Bingham, & Harmon, 1993):

1. *Because (a) the boundaries between types of preschool emotions and behaviors are not as sharply demarcated as for older children or adults and (b) symptoms and syndromes are unstable and transient, it is not possible to identify discrete diagnostic categories of disorders.* These are empirical issues. There is no evidence that preschool symptoms and syndromes are any less well demarcated or stable than those of older individuals. Indeed, several studies have indicated that preschool externalizing and internalizing problems are (a) predictors of negative outcomes years later and (b) often quite stable (e.g., Campbell, Breaux, Ewing, & Szumowski, 1986; Campbell & Ewing, 1990; Campbell, Ewing, Breaux, & Szumowski, 1986; Fischer, Rolf, Hasazi, & Cummings, 1984; Ialongo, Edelsohn, Werthamer-Larsson, Crockett, & Kellam, 1993, 1995, 1996; Keenan, Shaw, Walsh, Delliquadri, & Giovannelli, 1997; Keenan & Wakschlag, 2000; Kellam, Ling, Merisca, Brown, & Lalongo, 1998; Lavigne et al., 1998b, 1998c; McGee, Partridge, Williams, & Silva, 1991; Richman, Stevenson, & Graham, 1982).

2. *Current diagnostic systems take little account of the fact that early childhood is a period of rapid development.* This is true, but the more important question is, "Given that we need a classification of some sort, where should we start?" If we are to create a decently developmental scheme that recognizes underlying psychopathological consistencies across varying developmental manifestations, surely it makes sense to start with what we know about older children rather than giving up on the task. The *DSM* system has been justly criticized for giving only the faintest nods to developmental issues, but that has often been because insufficient data were available to support modification of adult-based diagnostic criteria. Where such modifications have been introduced, it has often been because it was shown that the adult criteria were inadequate to capture the relevant pathology in children (as with the anxiety disor-

ders). On the other hand, the application of adult criteria has sometimes led to the surprising conclusion that they worked much better than expected. The obvious example here concerns childhood depression, which was typically held not to exist until the application of unmodified adult criteria showed that it certainly did (Angold, 1988). As a result, we now have clinical trials that have supported the use of both psychosocial treatments and medications for unipolar depression in children. Investigating the properties of a nondevelopmental set of criteria is a good strategy for identifying ways in which those criteria need to be modified to take account of developmental phenomena.

3. *The categorical approach to diagnosis will locate the pathology "in the child" rather than "in the child's relationships," and thus will ignore the importance of the relational contexts of a young child's behaviors.* For many reasons it has proved useful to regard certain phenomena as being characteristics of individuals, but that does not deny the importance of social context as causes, mediators, and moderators of those phenomena. Furthermore, we already know that some forms of childhood psychopathology (e.g., autism) are better regarded as being characteristics of the child, and old formulations of them in terms of caregiver interaction style have been abandoned. There is also plenty of evidence that (1) certain relatively stable behavioral and physiological reaction patterns are associated with current and future psychopathology (see e.g., the many studies of infant temperament and its interactions with physiological measures and social contextual factors, e.g., Bates, Maslin, & Frankel, 1985; Calkins & Fox, 1992; Carey, Fox, & McDevitt, 1977; Earls & Jung, 1987; Emde et al., 1992; Gersten, 1986; Gunnar, Mangelsdorf, & Larson, 1989; Gunnar, Porter, Wolf, Rigatuso, & Larson, 1995; Gunnar, Tout, de Haan, Pierce, & Stansbury, 1997; Hay & O'Brien, 1984; Jansen, Fitzgerald, Ham, & Zucker, 1995; Kagan, 1994; Maziade, Caron, Côté, Boutin, & Thivierge, 1990; Maziade, Côté, Bernier, Boutin, & Thivierge, 1989; Maziade, Cote, Boutin, Bernier, & Thivierge, 1987; Maziade, Côté, Thivierge, Boutin, & Bernier, 1989; Rothbart & Mauro, 1990; Tubman & Windle, 1995; Wertlieb, Weigel, Springer, & Feldstein,

1987), and (2) genetic components are involved in preschool psychopathology (Kagan, 1994; van den Oord, Koot, Boomsma, Verhulst, & Orlebeke, 1995; van den Oord, Verhulst, & Boomsma, 1996). The issue is not whether psychopathology "resides in" the child or the child's social context, but how the characteristics of the child and of the social context work to produce psychopathology (Bronfenbrenner, 1974).

4. *It is not clinically appropriate or desirable to assign psychiatric diagnoses to young children because it raises the risk of labeling the child who might be defined or stigmatized in a way that will adversely affect his or her future development* (Campbell, 1990). As with the preceding objections, this argument was long ago raised against the use of psychiatric diagnosis for children and adolescents in general. It has largely fallen by the wayside as the utility of specific treatments for specific diagnoses has been established (as with stimulants in the treatment of ADHD; Goldman, Genel, Bezman, & Slanetz, 1998). We believe that it will suffer the same fate as we learn more about preschool psychopathology. There are also many circumstances in which a diagnosis must be made. For instance, the decision to provide treatment services must be based upon a categorical (yes/no) decision about whether there is "something wrong" with the child. "Something wrong" is a crude form of diagnosis. Even when continuous measures derived from questionnaires are used to measure psychopathology, cutoff points are still applied to define "clinical ranges." Being "in the clinical range" or "above a certain t-score on a subscale" are both forms of diagnosis. The descriptive, prescriptive nosologies embodied in the *DSM-IV* and *Diagnostic Classification of Mental Health and Developmental Disorders of Infancy and Early Childhood* (DC:0–3; Zero to Three, 1994) are in many ways no different from these examples, except that they rely upon specific categories derived from clinical experience. We should also be aware that *DSM-IV* diagnoses are mandated for the receipt of federal block grant funds to states for the provision of services for seriously emotionally disturbed children (58 Fed. Reg., 1993), and that typical current third-party health care reimbursements are diagnosis dependent.

PSYCHIATRIC RESEARCH IN PRESCHOOLERS IS ABOUT 30 YEARS BEHIND RESEARCH WITH OLDER CHILDREN AND ADOLESCENTS

Preschool psychiatric research is now in a position similar to that of older children's psychiatry circa 1970. Clinical syndromes such as school phobia, separation anxiety, ADHD, autism, and conduct disorder had all been described, but the official nosologies (*DSM-II* in the United States and ICD-9 elsewhere) contained only very generic categories, without any specific rules for determining when diagnostic criteria were met. By 1970 a number of older general population studies (Cullen & Boundy, 1966; Cummings, 1944; Griffiths, 1952; Haggerty, 1925; Lapouse, 1966; Lapouse & Monk, 1958, 1964a, 1964b; Long, 1941; McFie, 1934; Olson, 1930; Wickman, 1928; Young-Masten, 1938; Yourman, 1932) had reported prevalences of individual problem behaviors from parents and teachers of older children and adolescents. A number of factor analytic studies also existed, beginning in the 1940s, that had begun to form the basis of what later emerged as a fairly consistent set of factors resulting from parent report questionnaires (see Achenbach & Edelbrock, 1978, for a scholarly summary of the earlier work). There was just a single diagnostic general population study—the first Isle of Wight study—that employed a multistage high-risk sampling procedure with final clinician-based diagnoses based on parent reports of symptoms and observations of the children's behavior during the interview (Graham & Rutter, 1968; Rutter & Graham, 1966, 1968).

Whereas great strides have been made in our understanding of the psychopathology of older children and adolescents since 1970, far less progress has been made with preschool psychopathology. We can, however, take heart from the fact that since 1970 we have learned a tremendous amount about psychopathology through the codevelopment of interview (and other measures of psychopathology) and nosology. The time has come to begin a similar process for preschoolers.

DIAGNOSTIC SYSTEMS FOR PRESCHOOLERS

Four diagnostic systems are currently available for use with preschoolers: (1) the *DSM-IV* of the American Psychiatric Association; (2) the World Health Organization's ICD-10; (3) the Diagnostic Classification: 0–3, produced by the diagnostic classification task force of Zero to Three and the National Center for Clinical Infant Programs; and (4) classification schemes based on factor analyses of scales. *DSM-IV* and ICD-10 have converged very substantially compared with *DSM-III* and ICD-9, and share the same basic approach to the definition of disorders. They can, therefore, conveniently be dealt with together, especially since there appears to be no empirical literature on preschoolers that has formally used ICD-10.

DSM-IV and ICD-10

Since these two systems are widely known and used, we do not describe them here.

A few clinical studies have made *DSM* diagnoses for preschoolers using parent interviews designed for older children, chart reviews, or unstructured clinical interviews (Cantwell & Baker, 1989; Hooks, Mayes, & Volkmar, 1988; Keenan & Wakschlag, 2000; Shaw, Keenan, Vondra, Delliquadri, & Giovannelli, 1997; Wakschlag & Keenan, submitted). For example, Keenan and colleagues (1997) reported that 26.4% of 104 low-income 5-year-olds had a *DSM-III-R* diagnosis (14.9% with an externalizing disorder and 14.9% with an internalizing disorder). While the sample was too small to assess individual diagnostic comorbidity, they did not find statistically significant comorbidity between externalizing and internalizing disorders. In another study, Keenan and Wakschlag (2000) reported that 80% of 79 low-income preschoolers referred to their preschool behavior problems clinic met criteria for a disruptive behavior disorder (DBD). The DBDs were highly comorbid with each other, but emotional symptoms and disorders were not assessed. Both studies used the Kiddie Schedule for Affective Disorders and Schizophrenia (K-SADS) (combined with clinical consensus in the second interview), for which no reliability or validity data are available for very young children. Two clinical studies by Kashani and his colleagues indicated that depressive disorders conforming to *DSM* criteria can be detected in preschool children (Kashani, Allan, Beck, Bledsoe, & Reid, 1997; Kashani, Ray, & Carlson, 1984). In a sample of 100 preschoolers seen in a psychiatric clinic, 4% met criteria for a *DSM-III* diagnosis of depression based on an unstructured clinical interview. In a second study of 300 preschoolers (ages 2–6 years), 2.7% (*n* = 8) met *DSM-IV* criteria for dysthymic disorder. All of these children had concurrent aggressive behavior and all had a comorbid diagnosis (developmental disorder, *n* = 3; major depression, *n* = 2; oppositional defiant disorder [ODD], *n* = 2; ADHD, *n* = 1; and an anxiety disorder, *n* = 1) (Kashani et al., 1997).

A small number of community studies have attempted to assess preschool psychiatric diagnoses using one version of the *DSM* or another. Earls' 1982 study of all 100 3-year-olds on Martha's Vineyard identified 14 children with a *DSM-III* disorder (5 with separation anxiety disorder, 4 with ODD, 2 with ADHD, 2 with pica, 2 with avoidant disorder, and 2 with adjustment disorder with mixed emotional features). Conduct disorder symptoms were not assessed, and comorbidity between Axis I disorders was not reported. The clinical consensus diagnoses were based on a parent questionnaire and a child play session. Kashani, Holcomb, and Orvaschel's (1986) study of 109 preschoolers enrolled in two nursery schools in the Midwest found only one child with *DSM-III* major depression, but 9 of 109 (8.3%) had significant depressive symptoms. Anger, irritability, lack of cooperation, and apathy were found more often in children with depressive symptoms. Shaw, Owens, Giovannelli, and Winslow (2001) reported rates of DBDs in 5-year-old boys recruited from low-income families using the Allegheny County's Women, Infants, and Children Program when they were 6 to 17 months old. By mother report on the KSADS-E, 3.5% had ADHD only, 5.2% had ODD only, 3% had conduct disorder (CD) only, and 4.3% had ADHD comorbid with either ODD or CD. In total, therefore, 16% had a mother-reported DBD.

The first (and only) reasonably large-scale epidemiological diagnostic investigation of preschoolers has been reported in a series of articles beginning in 1993 by Lavigne and his colleagues (Arend, Lavigne, Rosenbaum, Binns, & Christoffel, 1996; Dietz, Lavigne, Arend, & Rosenbaum, 1997; Lavigne et al., 1993, 1994, 1996, 1998a, 1998b, 1998c, 1999; Lavigne, Binns, et al., 1998; Lavigne, Schulein, & Hahn, 1986) but its findings are sadly undermined by an overall response rate of only 44.6%. They examined the presentation of psychopathology in a nonreferred sample of 3,860 preschool children (ages 2–5 years) identified through a pediatric clinic. The Child Behavior Checklist (CBCL) was administered to all of the children. Next, 191 children who scored at 90% or above on the CBCL and 319 matched "low scorers" (total *N* = 510) were reassessed with the CBCL and a number of other measures, including the Rochester Adaptive Behavior Inventory and play observation of the child. Two psychologists independently reviewed the protocol (but did not conduct a clinical interview) and used their "best estimate" to make *DSM-III-R* diagnoses. The interrater reliability was mediocre (overall weighted mean kappa of .61), except in the case of CD, even though the two raters used exactly the same information. Where there were disagreements, consensus diagnoses were made. The prevalence of any Axis I disorder was 21.4%; 9.1% were defined as "severe" by a CGAS score below 60. The prevalences of specific Axis I disorders were: 16.8% for ODD; 2.0% for ADHD; and 4.6% for parent-child relationship problems. The rates for specific emotional disorders ranged from 0.3 to 0.7% with 0.3% meeting criteria for depression not otherwise specified (*n* = 7). Also, 5.4% of the children had comorbid disorders, defined as "a disruptive disorder comorbid with an emotional disorder or other disorder." The rate of "pure" ODD was twice as high for boys, but the rates of "comorbid ODD" were similar in boys and girls. The prevalence of ODD was highest in 3-year-olds (22.5%) and lowest in 5-year-olds (15%) (Lavigne et al., 1996). The very low rates of emotional disorders found here may reflect the difficulty of measuring internalizing symptoms and identifying anxiety and depressive disorders in young children. Since no structured diagnostic assessment was used, it is impossible to know what rules the clinicians adopted in making their diagnostic judgments. On the other hand, perhaps parents of depressed and anxious children were concentrated in the very large group that refused to participate in the study.

If nothing else, these studies have indicated that instruments and nosologies designed and tested for use with older children appear to be applicable to younger children, and yield overall estimates of the prevalence of any diagnosis rather similar to those seen in older children and adolescents in comparable populations. However, there is also great variation in the apparent rates of specific diagnoses from study to study, and little evidence about what patterns of comorbidity really pertain (though it does appear that some forms of comorbidity can already be seen in the preschool years). Despite this, there is also evidence of continuity between preschool psychopathology and later psychopathology (Campbell & Ewing, 1990; Campbell, Ewing, et al., 1986; Earls, 1980; Fischer et al., 1984; McGee et al., 1991; Richman et al., 1982). Again we see a situation very much like that pertaining to diagnosis in older children and adolescents before the general adoption of structured interviews designed for those age groups (Gould, Wunsch-Hitzig, & Dohrenwend, 1981).

DC:0–3 Diagnostic System

Dissatisfaction with many aspects of the *DSM* diagnostic system among infant psychiatrists led to the development of the "Zero to Three" classification scheme (DC:0–3) (Zero to Three, 1994). It is based on systematic case reporting from various centers and expert consensus. The system is multiaxial, and its axes involve substantial divergence from those familiar from the *DSM-IV*. Axis I is the "primary diagnosis," equivalent to the "clinical disorders" of *DSM-IV*'s Axis I. Five major diagnostic groupings are defined: (1) disorders of social development and communication (autism and pervasive developmental disorders); (2) psychic trauma disorders (acute and chronic); (3) regulatory disorders; (4) disorders of affect (anxiety disorders, mood disorders, mixed disorder of emotional expressiveness, and deprivation syndrome); and (5) adjustment reaction disorders. The inclusion of regulatory disorders ("disturbances in sensory, sensorimotor, or organizational processing") represents an attempt to classify "constitutional or maturational" difficulties that

are not considered in the *DSM* or ICD taxonomies at all. This section constitutes the most innovative portion of DC:0–3's first axis. DC:0–3 does not attempt an exhaustive classification; rather, it focuses on areas of the *DSM* system regarded as being in particular need of addition or modification.

Axis II is a relationship disorder classification. Six basic relationship disorders are recognized: overinvolved, underinvolved, anxious/tense, angry/hostile, mixed relationship disorder, and abusive (subdivided into verbally, physically, and sexually abusive). The criteria for each Axis II disorder are subdivided into three groups addressing (1) the behavioral quality of the interaction, (2) its affective tone, and (3) the character of the psychological involvement of the parent in the interaction. An appendix provides a Parent-Infant Relationship Global Assessment Scale (PIR-GAS) that provides a 0–90 rating scale of the level of relationship functioning, with nine anchoring range descriptions.

Axis III covers medical and developmental disorders and conditions, and therefore resembles *DSM-IV*'s Axis III. However, an interesting twist is added in that *DSM-IV* or ICD-10 diagnoses should also be recorded here. Thus the DC:0–3 commendably invites comparison with its "competitors." Axis IV covers psychosocial stressors, like *DSM-IV*. Axis V at first sight appears to be similar to *DSM-IV*'s Global Assessment of Functioning, being labeled "Functional Emotional Developmental Level." However, it is quite different, since it presents a set of age-specified developmental achievements and a description of how to rate and code the child's performance in relation to these achievement levels.

So far, rather few studies have employed the DC:0–3 in a research protocol, but the work that has been done indicates that it would be unwise to ignore the warnings about the potential probable inadequacies of the *DSM/ICD* systems contained in its pages. In Reams's clinical study, 144 children aged 1 to 4 years in legal custody were assessed by a clinician (Reams, 1999). Over half met criteria for a DC:0–3 diagnosis. Thomas and Clark (1998) evaluated 64 1- to 4-year-olds referred to an infant psychiatry clinic for disruptive behavior. They compared the *DSM-IV* and DC:0–3 classifications of the children's problems using an unstructured clinical assessment, and concluded that the DC:0–3 is useful in guiding relational intervention strategies. Michael Scheeringa, Charles Zeanah, and colleagues investigated the utility of *DSM-IV* versus DC:0–3 alternative criteria for the diagnosis of PTSD and reactive attachment disorder, in a series of small clinical studies, and concluded that the alternative criteria provide a better description of these disorders in preschoolers (Boris, Zeanah, Larrieu, Scheeringa, & Heller, 1998; Scheeringa, Peebles, Cook, & Zeanah, 2001; Scheeringa & Zeanah, 1995; Scheeringa, Zeanah, Drell, & Larrieu, 1995).

Dunitz and her colleagues (Dunitz, Scheer, Kvas, & Macari, 1996) used a 6-hour multidisciplinary assessment to generate *DSM-IV* and DC:0–3 diagnoses on 82 infants aged 1 to 24 months. They found quite good agreement between the classifications when similar categories were provided by both, that the regulatory disorders of DC:0–3 provided categories for some infants unclassifiable by the *DSM-IV*, and that *DSM-IV* sleep disorder, oppositional defiant disorder, reactive attachment disorder, adjustment disorder, posttraumatic stress disorder, and separation anxiety disorder categories were all identifiable, discriminable, and useful in their sample. They concluded that sometimes one system provided a better descriptively fitting diagnosis for a child, while in other cases the other had a better-fitting category. This original study provides one useful model for how further examinations of the relative utility of different diagnostic systems might be conducted, even when only cross-sectional data are available.

Along rather similar lines, Thomas and Guskin (2001) applied clinical diagnostic procedures to 82 18- to 47-month-olds attending an early childhood psychiatry clinic who received DC:0–3 diagnoses of traumatic stress disorder, disorder of affect, or regulatory disorder. Where similar categories were available in the *DSM* system, the majority of children received diagnoses similar to those generated by use of DC:0–3. The majority of children with DC:0–3 regulatory disorder diagnoses received a *DSM* disruptive disorder diagnosis, although nearly a third received a *DSM* emotional or adjustment disorder diagnosis. One problem with this approach to studying diagnostic questions is that only a single *DSM* diagnosis

was given to each child, but we have already seen that comorbidity between emotional and disruptive symptomatology is probably common in preschoolers. It may be that focusing on a "primary" diagnosis increases apparent disagreement between systems by ignoring "secondary" diagnoses that might have corresponded more closely with one or more diagnoses generated by the other system. However, both these studies suggest that, while the DC:0–3 system incorporates phenomenology not considered in the *DSM-IV* or ICD-10, the latter systems contain categories that provide diagnostic havens for preschool children whom the DC:0–3 labels as suffering from regulatory disorders.

This suggests an important track for further investigation. First, it may be that what DC:0–3 calls regulatory disorders are early forms of various types of *DSM*/ICD disruptive (and sometimes emotional) disorders. If this is the case, then it will not help to have a separate set of diagnostic categories for regulatory disorders. Rather, we should adjust the *DSM*/ICD diagnostic rules (or rubrics) to direct attention to patterns of symptoms of the relevant *DSM*/ICD disorders that are particularly manifested in younger children. On the other hand, it may be that the DC:0–3 regulatory disorders are indicative of the presence of a group of disorders that are later associated with symptoms that overlap with the familiar *DSM*/ICD disorders (like ODD), but that are not fully encompassed by those disorders. In that case, it would be preferable to carve out the regulatory disorders into categories separate from the current *DSM*/ICD disorders. Only longitudinal studies of the relationships of symptoms within individuals over time will tell us which option it would be best to adopt. As a final note here, we should also beware of starting any crude competition between DC:0–3 and *DSM*/ICD over which nosology is right. We can be quite sure that *all are wrong* in significant ways. The important question is, "How can we do better than we do now?"

Questionnaire Studies of Behavioral Symptoms and Generic Behavioral Domains in Preschoolers

Studies from the 1940s and 1950s (e.g., Cummings, 1944; Griffiths, 1952; Macfarlane, Allen,

& Honzik, 1954), demonstrated that individual symptoms of what we would now call ADHD, ODD, and aggression were very common in preschool children, that such problems were more common in boys than girls, and that these symptoms were associated with lax parenting. They also illustrated a point that seems often to have been forgotten—that some conduct problems now associated with *DSM-IV* conduct disorder, like lying and some forms of aggression, actually have their peak prevalences before age five, rather than during adolescence (Loeber & Stouthamer-Loeber, 1997; Tremblay et al., 1999). While less attention was paid to the internalizing disorders, a variety of fears and worries and social anxiety and withdrawal were also found to be common.

A few more recent questionnaire studies have focused on broad domains of behavior and have estimated the overall prevalence of any type of preschool psychopathology at somewhere between 7% and 25% (Briggs-Gowan, Carter, Moye Skuban, & McCue Horwitz, 2001; Earls, 1980; Earls et al., 1982; Earls & Richman, 1980a, 1980b; Jenkins, Bax, & Hart, 1980; Koot & Verhulst, 1991; Richman, 1977; Richman et al., 1974, 1982; Stevenson, Richman, & Graham, 1985; Thomas, Byrne, Offord, & Boyle, 1991).

Factor Analytic Studies of Questionnaire Measures of Preschoolers

Despite the use of checklists of widely varying length and content, with different informants (parents, preschool teachers), the broad distinction between emotional (internalizing) and behavioral (externalizing) syndromes has consistently emerged from factor analytic studies of preschoolers (Achenbach, Edelbrock, & Howell, 1987; Achenbach & Rescorla, 2000; Behar & Stringfield, 1974; Crowther, Bond, & Rolf, 1981; Koot, van den Oord, Verhulst, & Boomsma, 1997; Koot & Verhulst, 1991; McGuire & Richman, 1986; Richman et al., 1982; van den Oord et al., 1995). However, attempts to extract more than two factors have had less consistent results. Other syndromes identified by factor analysis have included sleep problems (Achenbach et al., 1987; Achenbach & Rescorla, 2000; Koot et al., 1997), somatic symptoms (Achenbach et al.,

Achenbach & Rescorla, 2000; Koot et al., 1997), autistic/bizarre behavior (Rescorla, 1986), anxious/depressed behavior (Achenbach et al., 1987; Achenbach & Rescorla, 2000; Rescorla, 1986), immature habits (toilet training items) (Rescorla, 1986), autoerotic behavior (thumbsucking and masturbation) (Rescorla, 1986), overactivity/attention problems (Achenbach & Rescorla, 2000; Behar & Stringfield, 1974; Koot et al., 1997; Rescorla, 1986), fearful/dependent behavior (Rescorla, 1986), anxiety (Koot et al., 1997), oppositional behavior (Koot et al., 1997), aggressive behavior (Achenbach et al., 1987; Achenbach & Rescorla, 2000; Koot et al., 1997; Rescorla, 1986), destructive behavior (Achenbach et al., 1987), depressed behavior (Rescorla, 1986), perfectionism/obsessionality (Achenbach et al., 1987; Rescorla, 1986), social withdrawal/depression (Achenbach et al., 1987; Koot et al., 1997; Rescorla, 1986), and withdrawal (Achenbach & Rescorla, 2000). Most of these factors have been found to account for very little variance (often less than 5%), though they typically have high short-term test-retest reliability.

The most recently developed of the Achenbach family of multi-informant scales, the CBCL 1½–5 and the Caregivers-Teachers Report Form (C-TRF), also generate five "*DSM*-oriented scales," reflecting affective, anxiety, pervasive developmental, ADHD, and oppositional defiant problems. Hopefully this is a sign that old battles over whether the empiricism embodied in factor analysis is better than the empiricism of the *DSM* or ICD processes (or vice versa) may once and for all be replaced by collaboration.

At this point, there are too few studies using too few scales for us to be at all sure that the cross-scale stability of factors seen with older children is apparent with preschoolers. However, it is undoubted that the psychometric properties of instruments like the CBCL 1½–5 are very encouraging. First, the fact that an instrument like the CBCL identifies stable syndromes in this age range gives the lie to the idea that rapid developmental change makes it impossible to identify such syndromes. Second, the syndromes identified by the CBCL 1½–5 are very similar to those derived from older samples, suggesting that attempts to examine *DSM*-like disorders in younger children will not be futile. However, as is the case with older children, a major limitation of the scale-score approach is its exclusion of rare symptoms that are often associated with the most severe conditions. No single system can be expected to provide an assessment panacea.

THE WAY FORWARD

A first beginning has been made in defining meaningful psychiatric syndromes in preschoolers and infants. A start has also been made on the development of appropriate structured approaches to measuring their symptomatology. The latter is clearly a prerequisite for the former, so we begin by indicating what we regard as being critical needs for research in this area:

Determining the Key Informants About Preschool Symptomatology

Adult psychiatric research typically depends upon self-reports of symptomatology, often accompanied by structured clinical observation. This approach was long ago discarded as being inadequate for child and adolescent psychiatry. We now accept that multiple informants are required for the adequate assessment of children. However, it is worth remembering that only 20 or 30 years ago, the discovery of a great deal of disagreement between the results of parent and child interviews was interpreted as being an index of the lack of validity of child interviews (Herjanic, Herjanic, Brown, & Wheatt, 1975; Rutter & Graham, 1968). Since then, researchers have come to regard parents, children, and teachers as providing information from different points of view (and bases of knowledge). Hence the development of the "or rule" for diagnosis: If any key informant reports the presence of a symptom, it is typically regarded as being present, regardless of whether any other informant reports it. We no longer expect to have child self-reports validated by similar reports from another informant. As a starting point, this seems a reasonable approach to take with preschoolers as well. However, it raises four big problems: (1) Who should be the key informants? (2) Diagnostic instrumentation is currently available for only one of the likely key informants (the parent). (3) It is not

clear how to combine information from preschooler self-reports because preschoolers simply cannot complete adult-style diagnostic interviews. (4) The role of observation of interactions has yet to be worked out as far as structured diagnosis is concerned.

Who Should Be Key Informants

It is currently standard practice in child psychiatric research to collect diagnostic information using standardized diagnostic interviews with both the index child and one parent. Family studies often add an interview with a second parent. Some studies also add a diagnostic interview with a teacher. Structured interviews that are tied to the *DSM* system are available for use with all these informants. It is, therefore, possible to apply the "or rule" for counting symptoms in a fairly straightforward way, because all these informants can be asked to describe the same set of phenomena in pretty much the same way.

It is immediately apparent that this is not the case for preschoolers. Parent interviews present no theoretical problem here (but see below for other problems), since preschoolers have parents in just the same way as older children do. However, they do not all have teachers in the way that most older children do. There is no "standard" setting equivalent to the school for preschoolers. Rather, children of this age find themselves in all sorts of different daytime settings. Some spend the days at home with their parents, some are with nannies, some are in kindergarten, some are in day care, and many spend different days of the week in different settings. It is not, therefore, apparent exactly what equivalent to the teacher of older children ought to be adopted as an informant, or what such potential informants can typically be expected to know about the children in their care. These are things that we need to find out.

There are a priori reasons for wanting to collect information from children themselves. For instance, children may be the only available voluntary sources about such matters as physical and sexual abuse. It also seems likely that, as with older children, parents and others may be unaware of even high levels of depressive or anxious symptomatology. However, we do not know whether this is really the case, or to what degree preschool children can provide information that is directly relevant to the diagnostic process. We do know that children's self-reports of such things as depressive and anxiety symptoms at age 5 are predictive of maladjustment years later (Ialongo et al., 1993, 1995; Martini, Strayhorn, & Puig-Antich, 1990), and so there is reason to collect such information. However, it is also clear that preschoolers cannot provide all the information necessary for making DSM- or ICD-based diagnoses. In particular, they are quite unable to date the onsets and durations of their symptoms as required by these nosologies. There is also good reason to doubt that children this young are capable of conceptualizing (much less reporting) many of the phenomena described in those systems. Research on younger children's memory has shown that in free-recall situations they volunteer much less information than older children, but that what is volunteered is as accurate as that volunteered by older children. However, in forced-choice recall, younger children respond with both an increased amount of accurate information and an increased amount of *inaccurate* information (Bruck, Ceci, & Hembrooke, 1998; Ornstein, Gordon, & Larus, 1992). This suggests that, as an initial strategy, it makes sense to make the best one can of information freely provided when working with younger children. Indeed, promising efforts to develop assessments of psychopathology for younger children have wisely focused on the free responses of children to story stems and puppet interactions (Measelle, Ablow, Cowan, & Cowan, 1998; Warren, Emde, & Sroufe, 2000; Warren, Oppenheim, & Emde, 1996) and simple picture-based questionnaire responses (Ialongo et al., 1993, 1995; Martini et al., 1990).

Lack of Validated Diagnostic Instrumentation for Key Informants

As we have already seen, the DSM-IV, ICD-10, and DC:0–3 all provide descriptions of symptomatology that needs to be considered in younger children. However, at this writing no adequately validated instrument is available for use with any informant that implements the requirements of these systems. Such studies have been conducted

for parent and teacher questionnaires, but these do not cover all the relevant symptoms by any means. This sorry situation demands rapid rectification.

Difficulty of Combining Information From Preschooler Self-Reports

Responses in preschool self-response situations do not map directly onto the requirements of any nosology, so the simple "or rule" breaks down. Little is known about the construct validity of preschool child self-reports in relation to psychopathology, but what we do know indicates that it would be unwise to ignore this source of information. However, researchers must develop more sophisticated algorithms for incorporating such information into the diagnostic process than have been necessary with older children.

The Role of Observations of Interactions Has Yet to Be Worked Out As Far As Structured Diagnosis Is Concerned

We argue above that the fact that many preschool problems occurred in the context of problematic patterns of family interaction was not a bar to the use of psychiatric diagnosis. However, that does not mean that familial and other interaction patterns should be ignored in the diagnostic process. Nothing could be further from the truth. We have argued elsewhere (Angold, Costello, Farmer, Burns, & Erkanli, 1999) that insufficient attention has been paid to relationship-based diagnoses in older children, and there is every reason to avoid selective inattention to such problems in preschoolers. The observation of interactions in experimental and unstructured environments has long been a part of the research armamentarium of developmentalists interested in the cognitive and social development of infants and young children, and it would seem willfully shortsighted to ignore this aspect of the assessment of psychosocial functioning in younger children. Once again, however, we have no agreed guidelines as to how such assessments should be incorporated into the diagnostic process. Here again, we need research to determine which components of which assessments are required for which diagnoses.

CONCLUSION

It may seem at this point that the message of this chapter is essentially negative. We have identified numerous missing pieces in the puzzle of preschool psychopathology. But that is not our conclusion. Rather, we return to the analogy between our understanding of psychopathology and its treatment in older children and adolescents 30 years ago and the state of knowledge in preschool psychopathology today. The last three decades have seen the transformation of child and adolescent psychiatry, and we predict that the next 20 years will similarly transform preschool psychiatry. Much that we have learned about older children can be used to guide the preschool research agenda, with the result that we can expect progress to be more rapid than it was with older children. It is hard to think of an area of psychopathology more ready for an explosive growth of understanding, or one that holds more promise for the future.

References

Achenbach, T. M. (1990). "Comorbidity" in child and adolescent psychiatry: Categorical and quantitative perspectives. *Journal of Child and Adolescent Psychopharmacology, 1,* 271–278.

Achenbach, T. M. (1995). Diagnosis, assessment, and comorbidity in psychosocial treatment research. *Journal of Abnormal Child Psychology, 23,* 45–65.

Achenbach, T. M., & Edelbrock, C. S. (1978). The classification of child psychopathology: A review and analysis of empirical efforts. *Psychological Review, 85,* 1275–1301.

Achenbach, T. M., Edelbrock, C., & Howell, C. T. (1987). Empirically based assessment of the behavioral/emotional problems of 2- and 3-year-old children. *Journal of Abnormal Child Psychology, 15,* 629–650.

Achenbach, T. M., & Rescorla, L. A. (2000). *Manual for the ASEBA preschool forms and profiles: An integrated system of multi-informant assessment.* Burlington, VT: University of Vermont Department of Psychiatry.

American Psychiatric Association (1994). *Diagnostic and statistical manual of mental disorders* (4th ed.). Washington, DC: Author.

Angold, A. (1988). Childhood and adolescent depression. II. Research in clinical populations. *British Journal of Psychiatry, 153,* 476–492.

Angold, A., Costello, E. J., & Erkanli, A. (1999). Comorbidity. *Journal of Child Psychology and Psychiatry, 40,* 57–87.

Angold, A., Costello, E. J., Farmer, E. M. Z., Burns, B. J., & Erkanli, A. (1999). Impaired but undiagnosed. *Journal of the American Academy of Child and Adolescent Psychiatry, 38,* 129–137.

Arend, R., Lavigne, J. V., Rosenbaum, D., Binns, H. J., & Christoffel, K. K. (1996). Relation between taxonomic and quantitative diagnostic systems in preschool children: Emphasis on disruptive disorders. *Journal of Clinical Child Psychology, 25,* 388–387.

Bates, J. E., Maslin, C. A., & Frankel, K. A. (1985). Attachment security, mother-child interaction, and temperament as predictors of behavior-problem ratings at age three years. *Monographs of the Society for Research in Child Development, 50,* 167–193.

Behar, L., & Stringfield, S. (1974). A behavior rating scale for the preschool child. *Developmental Psychology, 10,* 601–610.

Boris, N. W., Zeanah, C. H., Larrieu, J. A., Scheeringa, M. S., & Heller, S. S. (1998). Attachment disorders in infancy and early childhood: A preliminary investigation of diagnostic criteria. *American Journal of Psychiatry, 155,* 295–297.

Briggs-Gowan, M. J., Carter, A. S., Moye Skuban, E., & McCue Horwitz (2001). Prevalence of social-emotional and behavioral problems in a community sample of 1- and 2-year-old children. *Journal of the American Academy of Child and Adolescent Psychiatry, 40,* 811–819.

Bronfenbrenner, U. (1974). Ecology of childhood. *Child Development, 45,* 1–5.

Bruck, M., Ceci, S. J., & Hembrooke, H. (1998). Reliability and credibility of young children's reports: From research to policy and practice. *American Psychologist, 53,* 136–151.

Calkins, S. D., & Fox, N. A. (1992). The relations among infant temperament, security of attachment, and behavioral inhibitions at twenty-four months. *Child Development, 63,* 1456–1472.

Campbell, S. B. (1990). *Behavior problems in preschool children: Developmental and clinical issues.* New York: Guilford Press.

Campbell, S. B., Breaux, A. M., Ewing, L. J., & Szumowski, E. K. (1986). Correlates and predictors of hyperactivity and aggression: A longitudinal study of parent-referred problem preschoolers. *Journal of Abnormal Child Psychology, 14,* 217–234.

Campbell, S. B., & Ewing, L. J. (1990). Follow-up of hard-to-manage preschoolers: Adjustment at age 9 and predictors of continuing symptoms. *Journal of Child Psychology and Psychiatry, 6*, 871–889.

Campbell, S. B., Ewing, L. J., Breaux, A. M., & Szumowski, E. K. (1986). Parent-referred problem three-year-olds: Follow-up at school entry. *Journal of Child Psychology and Psychiatry, 27*, 473–488.

Cantwell, D. P., & Baker, L. (1989). Stability and natural history of DSM-III childhood diagnoses. *Journal of the American Academy of Child and Adolescent Psychiatry, 28*, 691–700.

Carey, W. B., Fox, M., & McDevitt, S. C. (1977). Temperament as a factor in early school adjustment. *Pediatrics, 60*, 621–624.

Cronbach, L. J., & Meehl, P. E. (1955). Construct validity in psychological tests. *Psychological Bulletin, 52*, 281–302.

Crowther, J. H., Bond, L. A., & Rolf, J. E. (1981). The incidence, prevalence, and severity of behavior disorders among preschool-age children in day care. *Journal of Abnormal Child Psychology, 9*, 23–42.

Cullen, K. J., & Boundy, C. A. P. (1966). The prevalence of behavior disorders in the children of 1000 Western Australian families. *Medical Journal of Australia, 2*, 805–808.

Cummings, J. D. (1944). The incidence of emotional symptoms in school children. *British Journal of Educational Psychology, 14*, 151–161.

DelCarmen-Wiggins, R., & Carter, A. (2001). Introduction—Special Section: Assessment of infant and toddler mental health: Advances and challenges. *Journal of the American Academy of Child and Adolescent Psychiatry, 40*, 8–10.

Dietz, K. R., Lavigne, J. V., Arend, R., & Rosenbaum, D. (1997). Relation between intelligence and psychopathology among preschoolers. *Journal of Clinical Child Psychology, 26*, 99–107.

Dunitz, M., Scheer, P. J., Kvas, E., & Macari, S. (1996). Psychiatric diagnoses in infancy: A comparison. *Infant Mental Health Journal, 17*, 12–23.

Earls, F. (1980). Prevalence of behavior problems in 3-year-old children: A cross-national replication. *Archives of General Psychiatry, 37*, 1153–1157.

Earls, F. (1982). Application of DSM-III in an epidemiological study of preschool children. *American Journal of Psychiatry, 139*, 242–243.

Earls, F., Jacobs, G., Goldfein, D., Silbert, A., Beardslee, W. R., & Rivinus, T. (1982). Concurrent validation of behavior problems scale to use with 3-year-olds. *Journal of the American Academy of Child Psychiatry, 21*, 47–57.

Earls, F., & Jung, K. G. (1987). Temperament and home environment characteristics as casual factors in the early development of childhood psychopathology. *Journal of the American Academy of Child and Adolescent Psychiatry, 26*, 491–498.

Earls, F., & Richman, N. (1980a). Behavior problems in pre-school children of West Indian-born parents: A re-examination of family and social factors. *Journal of Child Psychology and Psychiatry, 21*, 107–117.

Earls, F., & Richman, N. (1980b). The prevalence of behavior problems in three-year-old children of West Indian-born parents. *Journal of Child Psychology and Psychiatry, 21*, 99–106.

Emde, R. N., Bingham, R. D., & Harmon, R. J. (1993). Classification and the diagnostic process in infancy. In C. H. Zeanah, Jr. (Ed.), *Handbook of infant mental health* (pp. 225–235). New York: Guilford Press.

Emde, R. N., Plomin, R., Robinson, J., Corley, R., DeFries, J., Fulker, D. W., Reznick, J. S., Campos, J., Kagan, J., & Zahn-Waxler, C. (1992). Temperament, emotion, and cognition at fourteen months: The MacArthur longitudinal twin study. *Child Development, 63*, 1437–1455.

58 Fed. Reg. 29425 (1993).

Fischer, M., Rolf, J. E., Hasazi, J. E., & Cummings, L. (1984). Follow-up of a preschool epidemiological sample: Cross-age continuities and predictions of later adjustment with internalizing and externalizing dimensions of behavior. *Child Development, 55*, 137–150.

Gersten, M. (1986). *The contribution of temperament to behavior in natural contexts.* Unpublished doctoral dissertation, Harvard University Graduate School of Education, Cambridge, MA.

Goldman, L. S., Genel, M., Bezman, R. J., & Slanetz, P. J. (1998). Diagnosis and treatment of attention-deficit/hyperactivity disorder in children and adolescents. *Journal of the American Medical Association, 279*, 1100–1107.

Gould, M. S., Wunsch-Hitzig, R., & Dohrenwend, B. (1981). Estimating the prevalence of child psychopathology. *Journal of the American Academy of Child Psychiatry, 20*, 462–476.

Graham, P., & Rutter, M. (1968). The reliability and validity of the psychiatric assessment of the child. II. Interview with the parent. *British Journal of Psychiatry, 114,* 581–592.

Griffiths, W. (1952). *Behavior difficulties of children as perceived and judged by parents, teachers, and children themselves.* Minneapolis: University of Minnesota Press.

Gunnar, M. R., Mangelsdorf, S., & Larson, M. (1989). Attachment, temperament, and adrenocortical activity in infancy: A study of psychoendocrine regulation. *Developmental Psychology, 25,* 355–363.

Gunnar, M. R., Porter, F. L., Wolf, C. M., Rigatuso, J., & Larson, M. C. (1995). Neonatal stress reactivity: Predictions to later emotional temperament. *Child Development, 66,* 1–13.

Gunnar, M. R., Tout, K., de Haan, M., Pierce, S., & Stansbury, K. (1997). Temperament, social competence, and adrenocortical activity in preschoolers. *Developmental Psychobiology, 31,* 65–85.

Haggerty, M. E. (1925). The incidence of undesirable behavior in public school children. *Journal of Educational Research, 12,* 102–122.

Hay, D. A., & O'Brien, P. J. (1984). The role of parental attitudes in the development of temperament in twins at home, school, and in test situations. *Geneticae Medicae et Germellologiae, 36,* 239–248.

Herjanic, B., Herjanic, M., Brown, F., & Wheatt, T. (1975). Are children reliable reporters? *Journal of Abnormal Child Psychology, 3,* 41–48.

Hooks, M. Y., Mayes, L. C., & Volkmar, F. R. (1988). Psychiatric disorders among preschool children. *Journal of the American Academy of Child and Adolescent Psychiatry, 27,* 623–627.

Ialongo, N., Edelsohn, G., Werthamer-Larsson, L., Crockett, L., & Kellam, S. (1993). Are self-reported depressive symptoms in first-grade children developmentally transient phenomena? A further look. *Development and Psychopathology, 5,* 433–457.

Ialongo, N., Edelsohn, G., Werthamer-Larsson, L., Crockett, L., & Kellam, S. (1995). The significance of self-reported anxious symptoms in first grade children: Prediction to anxious symptoms and adaptive functioning in fifth grade. *Journal of Child Psychology and Psychiatry, 36,* 427–437.

Ialongo, N., Edelsohn, G., Werthamer-Larsson, L., Crockett, L., & Kellam, S. (1996). The course of aggression in first-grade children with and without comorbid anxious symptoms. *Journal of Abnormal Child Psychology, 24,* 445–456.

Jansen, R. E., Fitzgerald, H. E., Ham, H. P., & Zucker, R. A. (1995). Pathways into risk: Temperament and behavior problems in three- to five-year-old sons of alcoholics. *Alcoholism: Clinical and Experimental Research, 19,* 501–509.

Jenkins, S., Bax, M., & Hart, H. (1980). Behaviour problems in pre-school children. *Journal of Child Psychology and Psychiatry, 21,* 5–17.

Kagan, J. (1994). *Galen's prophecy: Temperament in human nature.* New York: Basic Books.

Kashani, J. H., Allan, W. D., Beck, N. C. J., Bledsoe, Y., & Reid, J. C. (1997). Dysthymic disorder in clinically referred preschool children. *Journal of the American Academy of Child and Adolescent Psychiatry, 36,* 1426–1433.

Kashani, J. H., Holcomb, W. R., & Orvaschel, H. (1986). Depression and depressive symptoms in preschool children from the general population. *American Journal of Psychiatry, 143,* 1138–1143.

Kashani, J. H., Ray, J. S., & Carlson, G. A. (1984). Depression and depressive-like states in preschool-age children in a child development unit. *American Journal of Psychiatry, 141,* 1397–1402.

Keenan, K., Shaw, D. S., Walsh, B., Delliquadri, E., & Giovannelli, J. (1997). DSM-III-R disorders in preschool children from low-income families. *Journal of the American Academy of Child and Adolescent Psychiatry, 36,* 620–627.

Keenan, K., & Wakschlag, L. S. (2000). More than the terrible twos: The nature and severity of behavior problems in clinic-referred preschool children. *Journal of Abnormal Child Psychology, 28,* 33–46.

Kellam, S., Ling, X., Merisca, R., Brown, C., & Lalongo, N. (1998). The effect of the level of aggression in the first grade classroom on the course and malleability of aggressive behavior into middle school. *Development and Psychopathology, 10,* 165–185.

Koot, H. M., van den Oord, E. J. C. G., Verhulst, F. C., & Boomsma, D. I. (1997). Behavioral and emotional problems in young preschoolers: Cross-cultural testing of the validity of the child behavior checklist/2–3. *Journal of Abnormal Child Psychology, 25,* 183–196.

Koot, H. M., & Verhulst, F. C. (1991). Prevalence of problem behavior in Dutch children aged 2–3. *Acta Psychiatrica Scandinavica, 83,* 1–37.

Lapouse, R. (1966). The epidemiology of behavior

disorders in children. *American Journal of Disfunctional Children, 111,* 594–599.

Lapouse, R., & Monk, M. A. (1964a). Behavior deviations in a representative sample of children: Variation by sex, age, race, social class and family size. *American Journal of Orthopsychiatry, 34,* 436–446.

Lapouse, R. L., & Monk, M. A. (1958). An epidemiologic study of behavior characteristics in children. *American Journal of Public Health, 48,* 1134–1144.

Lapouse, R. L., & Monk, M. A. (1964b). Behavior deviations in a representative sample of children. *American Journal of Orthopsychiatry, 34,* 436–447.

Lavigne, J. V., Arend, R., Rosenbaum, D., Binns, H. J., Christoffel, K. K., Burns, A., & Smith, A. (1998a). Mental health service use among young children receiving pediatric primary care. *Journal of the American Academy of Child and Adolescent Psychiatry, 37,* 1175–1183.

Lavigne, J. V., Arend, R., Rosenbaum, D., Binns, H. J., Christoffel, K. K., & Gibbons, R. D. (1998b). Psychiatric disorders with onset in the preschool years. I. Stability of diagnoses. *Journal of the American Academy of Child and Adolescent Psychiatry, 37,* 1246–1254.

Lavigne, J. V., Arend, R., Rosenbaum, D., Binns, H. J., Christoffel, K. K., & Gibbons, R. D. (1998c). Psychiatric disorders with onset in the preschool years. II. Correlates and predictors of stable case status. *Journal of the American Academy of Child and Adolescent Psychiatry, 37,* 1255–1261.

Lavigne, J. V., Arend, R., Rosenbaum, D., Sinacore, J., Cicchetti, C., Binns, H. J., Christoffel, K. K., Hayford, J. R., & McGuire, P. (1994). Interrater reliability of the DSM-III-R with preschool children. *Journal of Abnormal Child Psychology, 22,* 679–690.

Lavigne, J. V., Arend, R., Rosenbaum, D., Smith, A., Weissbluth, M., Binns, H. J., & Christoffel, K. K. (1999). Sleep and behavior problems among preschoolers. *Developmental and Behavioral Pediatrics, 20,* 164–169.

Lavigne, J. V., Binns, H. J., Arend, R., Rosenbaum, D., Christoffel, K. K., Hayford, J. R., & Gibbons, R. D. (1998). Psychopathology and health care use among preschool children: A retrospective analysis. *Journal of the American Academy of Child and Adolescent Psychiatry, 37,* 262–270.

Lavigne, J. V., Binns, H. J., Christoffel, K. K., Rosenbaum, D., Arend, R., Smith, K., Hayford,

J. R., McGuire, P. A., & Pediatric Practice Research Group (1993). Behavioral and emotional problems among preschool children in pediatric primary care: Prevalence and pediatricians' recognition. *Pediatrics, 91,* 649–655.

Lavigne, J. V., Gibbons, R. D., Christoffel, K. K., Arend, R., Rosenbaum, D., Binns, H., Dawson, N., Sobel, H., & Issacs, C. (1996). Prevalence rates and correlates of psychiatric disorders among preschool children. *Journal of the American Academy of Child and Adolescent Psychiatry, 35,* 204–214.

Lavigne, J. V., Schulein, M. J., & Hahn, Y. S. (1986). Psychological aspects of painful medical conditions in children. II. Personality factors, family characteristics and treatment. *Pain, 27,* 147–169.

Loeber, R., & Stouthamer-Loeber, M. (1997). The development of juvenile aggression and violence: Some common misconceptions and controversies. *American Psychologist, 53,* 242–259.

Long, A. (1941). Parents' reports of undesirable behavior in children. *Child Development, 12,* 43–62.

Macfarlane, J. W., Allen, L., & Honzik, M. P. (1954). *University of California publications in child development.* Berkeley: University of California Press.

Martini, D. R., Strayhorn, J. M., & Puig-Antich, J. (1990). A symptom self-report measure for preschool children. *Journal of the American Academy of Child and Adolescent Psychiatry, 29,* 594–600.

Maziade, M., Caron, C., Côté, R., Boutin, P., & Thivierge, J. (1990). Extreme temperament and diagnosis. *Archives of General Psychiatry, 47,* 477–484.

Maziade, M., Côté, R., Bernier, H., Boutin, P., & Thivierge, J. (1989). Significance of extreme temperament in infancy for clinical status in preschool years. I. Value of extreme temperament at 4–8 months for predicting diagnosis at 4.7 years. *British Journal of Psychiatry, 154,* 533–543.

Maziade, M., Cote, R., Boutin, P., Bernier, H., & Thivierge, J. (1987). Temperament and intellectual development: A longitudinal study from infancy to four years. *American Journal of Psychiatry, 144,* 144–150.

Maziade, M., Côté, R., Thivierge, J., Boutin, P., & Bernier, H. (1989). Significance of extreme temperament in infancy for clinical status in preschool years. II. Patterns of temperament change and implications for the appearance of disorders. *British Journal of Psychiatry, 154,* 544–551.

McFie, B. S. (1934). Behavior and personality difficulties in school children. *British Journal of Educational Psychology, 4,* 34.

McGee, R., Partridge, F., Williams, S., & Silva, P. A. (1991). A twelve-year follow-up of preschool hyperactive children. *Journal of the American Academy of Child and Adolescent Psychiatry, 30,* 224–232.

McGuire, J., & Richman, N. (1986). The prevalence of behavioral problems in three types of preschool group. *Journal of Child Psychology and Psychiatry and Allied Disciplines, 27,* 455–472.

Measelle, J. R., Ablow, J. C., Cowan, P. A., & Cowan, C. P. (1998). Assessing young children's views of their academic, social, and emotional lives: An evaluation of the self-perception scales of the Berkeley Puppet Interview. *Child Development, 69,* 1556–1576.

Olson, W. C. (1930). *Problem tendencies in children.* Minneapolis: University of Minnesota Press.

Ornstein, P. A., Gordon, B. N., & Larus, D. M. (1992). Children's memory for a personally experienced event: Implications for testimony. *Applied Cognitive Psychology, 6,* 49–60.

Reams, R. (1999). Children birth to three entering the state's custody. *Infant Mental Health Journal, 20,* 166–174.

Rescorla, L. A. (1986). Preschool psychiatric disorders: Diagnostic classification and symptom patterns. *Journal of the American Academy of Child Psychiatry, 25,* 162–169.

Richman, N. (1977). Behaviour problems in preschool children: Family and social factors. *British Journal of Psychiatry, 131,* 523–527.

Richman, N., Stevenson, J., & Graham, P. (1982). *Preschool to school: A behavioural study.* London: Academic Press.

Richman, N., Stevenson, J. E., Graham, P. J., Ridgely, M. S., Goldman, H. H., & Talbott, J. A. C. (1974). Prevalence of behaviour problems in 3-year-old children: An epidemiological study in a London borough. *Journal of Child Psychology and Psychiatry, 16,* 277–287.

Robins, E., & Guze, S. B. (1970). Establishment of diagnostic validity in psychiatric illness: Its application to schizophrenia. *American Journal of Psychiatry, 126,* 107–111.

Rothbart, M. K., & Mauro, J. A. (1990). Temperament, behavioral inhibition, and shyness in childhood. In H. Leitenberg (Ed.), *Handbook of social and evaluation anxiety* (pp. 139–160). New York: Plenum Press.

Rutter, M., & Graham, P. (1966). Psychiatric disorder in 10- and 11-year-old children. *Proceedings of the Royal Society of Medicine, 69,* 382–387.

Rutter, M., & Graham, P. (1968). The reliability and validity of the psychiatric assessment of the child. I. Interview with the child. *British Journal of Psychiatry, 114,* 563–579.

Scheeringa, M. S., Peebles, C. D., Cook, C. A., & Zeanah, C. H. (2001). Toward establishing procedural, criterion, and discriminant validity for PTSD in early childhood. *Journal of the American Academy of Child and Adolescent Psychiatry, 40,* 52–60.

Scheeringa, M. S., & Zeanah, C. H. (1995). Symptom expression and trauma variables in children under 48 months of age. *Infant Mental Health Journal, 16,* 259–270.

Scheeringa, M. S., Zeanah, C. H., Drell, M. J., & Larrieu, J. A. (1995). Two approaches to the diagnosis of posttraumatic stress disorder in infancy and early childhood. *Journal of the American Academy of Child and Adolescent Psychiatry, 34,* 191–200.

Shaw, D. S., Keenan, K., Vondra, J. I., Delliquadri, E., & Giovannelli, J. (1997). Antecedents of preschool children's internalizing problems: A longitudinal study of low-income families. *Journal of the American Academy of Child and Adolescent Psychiatry, 36,* 1760–1767.

Shaw, D. S., Owens, E. B., Giovannelli, J., & Winslow, E. B. (2001). Infant and toddler pathways leading to early externalizing disorders. *Journal of the American Academy of Child and Adolescent Psychiatry, 40,* 44–51.

Stevenson, J., Richman, N., & Graham, P. (1985). Behaviour problems and language abilities at three years and behavioural deviance at eight years. *Journal of Child Psychology and Psychiatry, 26,* 215–230.

Thomas, B. H., Byrne, C., Offord, D. R., & Boyle, M. H. (1991). Prevalence of behavioral symptoms and the relationship of child, parent, and family variables in 4- and 5-year-olds: Results from the Ontario Child Health Study. *Journal of Developmental and Behavioral Pediatrics, 12,* 177–184.

Thomas, J. M., & Clark, R. (1998). Disruptive behavior in the very young child: Diagnostic classification: 0–3 guides identification of risk factors and relational interventions. *Infant Mental Health Journal, 19,* 229–244.

Thomas, J. M., & Guskin, K. A. (2001). Disruptive behavior in young children: What does it mean? *Journal of the American Academy of Child and Adolescent Psychiatry, 40,* 44–51.

Tremblay, R. E., Japel, C., Perusse, D., Boivin, M., Zoccolillo, M., Montplaisir, J., & McDuff, P. (1999). The search for the age of "onset" of physical aggression: Rousseau and Bandura revisited. *Criminal Behavior and Mental Health, 9,* 24–39.

Tubman, J. G., & Windle, M. (1995). Continuity of difficult temperament in adolescence: Relations with depression, life events, family support, and substance use across a one-year period. *Journal of Youth and Adolescence, 24,* 133–153.

van den Oord, E. J. C. G., Koot, H. M., Boomsma, D. I., Verhulst, F. C., & Orlebeke, J. F. (1995). A twin-singleton comparison of problem behaviour in 2–3-year-olds. *Journal of Child Psychology and Psychiatry, 36,* 449–458.

van den Oord, E. J. C. G., Verhulst, F. C., & Boomsma, D. I. (1996). A genetic study of maternal and paternal ratings of problem behaviors in 3-year-old twins. *Journal of Abnormal Psychology, 105,* 349–357.

Wakschlag, L. S., & Keenan, K. (submitted). Further validation of early disruptive behavior disorders: Factors distinguishing high-risk preschoolers with and without ODD/CD.

Waldman, I. D., Lilienfeld, S. O., & Lahey, B. B. (1995). Toward construct validity in the childhood disruptive behavior disorders: Classification and diagnosis in *DSM-IV* and beyond. In T. H. Ollendick & R. J. Prinz (Eds.), *Advances in clinical child psychology* (pp. 323–363). New York: Plenum Press.

Warren, S. L., Emde, R. N., & Sroufe, A. (2000). Internal representations: Predicting anxiety from children's play narratives. *Journal of the American Academy of Child and Adolescent Psychiatry, 39,* 100–107.

Warren, S. L., Oppenheim, D., & Emde, R. N. (1996). Can emotions and themes in children's play predict behavior problems? *Journal of the American Academy of Child and Adolescent Psychiatry, 35,* 1331–1337.

Wertlieb, D., Weigel, C., Springer, T., & Feldstein, M. (1987). Temperament as a moderator of children's stressful experiences. *American Journal of Orthopsychiatry, 57,* 234–245.

Wickman, E. K. (1928). *Children's behavior and teachers' attitudes.* New York: Commonwealth Fund.

World Health Organization (1992). *ICD-10: The ICD-10 classification of mental and behavioural disorders: Clinical descriptions and diagnostic guidelines.* Geneva: Author.

World Health Organization (2001). *Iinternational classification of functioning, disability and health: ICF.* Geneva: Author.

Young-Masten, I. (1938). Behavior problems of elementary school children: A descriptive and comparative study. *Genetic Psychology Monographs, 20,* 123–180.

Yourman, J. (1932). Children identified by their teachers as problems. *Journal of Educational Sociology, 5,* 334–343.

Zero to Three, National Center for Clinical Infant Programs (1994). *Diagnostic classification of mental health and developmental disorders of infancy and early childhood.* Arlington, VA: Author.

8

Diagnosing Infants, Toddlers, and Preschoolers: The Zero to Three Diagnostic Classification of Early Mental Health Disorders

Alicia F. Lieberman
Kathryn E. Barnard
Serena Wieder

This chapter describes the diagnostic classification system developed by Zero to Three: National Center for Infants, Toddlers and Families to promote knowledge and professional communication about the mental health and developmental disorders of infancy and early childhood. This clinical instrument, named *Diagnostic Classification of Mental Health and Developmental Disorders of Infancy and Early Childhood* (DC:0–3; Zero to Three, 1994), is based on the premise that comprehensive assessment and accurate diagnosis are necessary foundations for timely intervention in the first years of life. The short-term goal is to alleviate the child's current psychological distress through early identification and immediate intervention. The long-term goal is to prevent the consolidation of early mental health disorders into chronically maladaptive patterns of functioning.

DC:0–3 reflects the primary features of the field of infant mental health because it advocates an approach to diagnosis that is multidisciplinary, preventive, developmentally oriented, and relationship based. Its development was guided by three primary principles. The first principle is that the psychological functioning of infants, toddlers, and preschoolers unfolds in the context of their close emotional relationships and moment-to-moment interactions with parents and caregivers. The second principle is that constitutional characteristics, including temperamental predispositions, play a major role in how children register and process real-life events and emotional experiences. At the same time, because of the central importance of emotional relationships, the caregiver's supportive response to the child can modulate and even transform constitutional vulnerabilities so that they do not derail the child's developmental course. The third principle is that the family's cultural values and child-rearing mores form an indispensable matrix for understanding the child's behavior and developmental course (Lieberman, Wieder, & Fenichel, 1997).

The chapter includes a discussion of diagnostic issues in the first years of life, recommendations about the format and content of the assessment process, an overview of DC:0–3 and a comparison between this diagnostic system and the *Diagnostic and Statistical Manual of Mental Disorders*, Fourth Edition (*DSM-IV*; American Psychiatric

Association, 1994), a description of how DC:0–3 was developed, a review of existing validity and reliability research, and presentations of clinical vignettes illustrating some diagnosytic categories. For the sake of conciseness, the term *parent* is used throughout the chapter, unless otherwise indicated, to refer to the child's biological parents or primary caregivers, regardless of the person's biological relation to the child.

THE NEED FOR A DIAGNOSTIC CLASSIFICATION OF EARLY MENTAL HEALTH DISORDERS

Diagnosing infants and very young children presents daunting challenges, which range from issues of scientific feasibility to questions of ethical propriety. The rapid pace of development in infancy and early childhood makes early diagnosis resemble a moving target because the child's symptoms might change in the course of the assessment in response to neurodevelopmental maturation, the acquisition of new competencies, and changes in environmental circumstances. The question raised by these rapid developmental fluctuations is: Can the mental health disorders of infancy and early childhood be accurately diagnosed?

The answer provided by DC:0–3 is that accurate diagnosis is possible when the diagnostic process is responsive to the developmental pace of the first years of life by framing children's psychological functioning as the outcome of transactional exchanges between children and their environment, particularly the parents or primary caregivers (Sameroff & Emde, 1989). In arriving at a diagnosis, it is more important to identify the factors that must be addressed to improve prognosis than it is to detect continuities of disorder over time (Emde, Bingham, & Harmon, 1993). In other words, the diagnostic process in infancy must be approached not as a search for the diagnostic category that best fits the child, but rather as an opportunity for therapeutic input that allows for an evaluation of how the intervention changes the clinical situation. When initial interventions are made in the context of the assessment, the diagnostic process can shed light on the interplay between the child's individual charac-

teristics and the familial, social, and cultural context interacting with these characteristics.

From this perspective, an optimally conducted diagnostic process is designed to fulfill three functions. First, the clinician must gather comprehensive information about the infant and the environmental circumstances influencing the child. Second, a solid working relationship with the child's parents needs to be established because parental collaboration improves the quality of reporting and lays the foundation for effective treatment. Third, the process must constitute an educational and therapeutic experience in its own right by expanding the parents' understanding of the child's emotional, social, and cognitive strengths and vulnerabilities and by providing the child with developmentally appropriate opportunities for interaction.

It follows that clinical interventions are best offered during the diagnostic process whenever risk factors are identified, even if the assessment protocol has not yet been completed. For example, developmental guidance might be given to parents when maladaptive or pathogenic caregiving practices are uncovered. When parents modify harmful responses to their child, the diagnostic picture of the infant might change in response to the improved child-rearing conditions. It is essential to assess the parental willingness to make use of the clinician's suggestions and to evaluate the success or failure of these trial interventions as integral components of the diagnostic process.

From a scientific perspective, there is much debate about the relative merits of categorical versus dimensional approaches to the understanding of child functioning (Rutter & Tuma, 1988; Achenbach, 1988). Traditional medical models conceptualize disorders as categorical, viewing them as discrete entities that are either present or absent and do not overlap with each other. In this view, disorder is qualitatively different from normative functioning. One difficulty raised by the categorical approach is that different mental health disorders often occur in the same person, a phenomenon known as comorbidity. The etiological reasons for comorbidity are poorly understood. The prevalence of comorbid conditions has been used to argue that diagnostic classifications should be used to categorize disorders rather than to categorize individuals and to emphasize that diagnosis must be the outcome of a comprehensive assessment encompassing multiple domains of individual functioning and environmental circumstances (Rutter & Gould, 1985). These recommendations are incorporated in DC:0–3.

From an ethical perspective, there is concern that diagnosing young children is equivalent to giving them negative labels that can color how they are perceived and treated by their parents, teachers, peers, and the widening social circle in which they function. This concern is rooted in the regrettable fact that diagnostic categories often acquire pejorative meanings because of the popular fear associated with adult mental illness and its treatment. It is natural to fear that a similar pejorative use will be attached to the diagnosis of mental health disorders of infancy and early childhood. However, stigma is likely to decrease when diagnosis incorporates sensitivity to contextual factors and when it becomes the foundation for implementing effective treatment.

Based on these considerations, the answer to the question of whether it is feasible to make accurate diagnoses of mental health disorders of infancy and early childhood is: yes, provided that diagnosis is the result of a developmentally guided assessment process where the child's psychological functioning is understood as open to modification in the context of maturational and environmental changes. The importance of a diagnostic classification system is elucidated below.

FUNCTIONS OF A DIAGNOSTIC CLASSIFICATION SYSTEM

A diagnostic classification system fulfills several functions. It guides clinical observation and systematizes the way these observations are organized by providing detailed descriptions of patterns of affect regulation, self-care, role performance, thinking, interpersonal behavior, and social adjustment. It creates a shared vocabulary that facilitates communication among professionals regarding age-appropriate normative behavior and its deviations. It guides research about the etiology and course of mental health disorders. It provides a conceptual framework for making clinical

hypotheses, ruling out the possibility of certain disorders, and orchestrating treatment decisions. At the practical level, it increases service availability by providing an instrument that enables clinicians to be reimbursed for professional services.

DC:0–3 represents an effort to address the challenge of early diagnosis through the collaborative efforts of a multidisciplinary team of infant mental health practitioners who met regularly between 1987 and 1993 to formulate a classification system based on expert consensus. The different components of the instrument are considered provisional because they are open to change as knowledge about the manifestations, etiology, and developmental course of early mental health disorders continues to accumulate through observation, clinical practice, and empirical research. The system will be revised and updated periodically on the basis of continuing discussion of clinical cases and research findings.

THE ASSESSMENT PROCESS

A comprehensive assessment usually lasts between three and five sessions and involves at least weekly 1-hour sessions. Although substantial preliminary conclusions can often be made earlier in some cases, other cases call for more extensive evaluation, particularly when specialized assessments are needed (e.g., visual, auditory, or sensorimotor evaluations) or when there is contradictory information from a variety of sources. Some clinical settings have the flexibility to offer intensive diagnostic evaluations where sessions can take place daily or every other day; in other settings, the sessions are sometimes spaced over the course of several weeks. The timetable and length of time over which the diagnostic process unfolds usually varies with the urgency and complexity of the diagnostic questions, the needs and circumstances of the family, the availability of the different clinicians involved, and the regulations of the clinical setting.

An important assessment decision is choosing whom to include in the evaluation. The baby and his or her primary caregiver are indispensable participants in the process. Depending on the circumstances, the assessor may choose to include one or both parents, a noncustodial parent, baby-sitters or other childcare providers, and/or siblings. When the child is in foster care, it is important to weigh the clinical implications of involving both the biological and foster parents, although the quality of the assessment information will be enhanced by including all the people most saliently involved in the child's care.

Different clinical settings have different approaches to the use of structured, semistructured, or unstructured assessment protocols. In general, each approach has advantages and disadvantages. The use of a structured format and standardized instruments can yield systematic information about a variety of domains, but the clinician might not be able to ascertain the emotional meaning of this information unless parents are given the opportunity to elaborate on their answers and discuss their feelings about the events reported.

Conversely, an unstructured clinical format can elicit clinically meaningful links, but important areas may be overlooked if they are not emotionally salient for the parent or the child or if the assessor does not think to focus on them.

A comprehensive assessment is informed by a variety of disciplines. Regardless of their particular area of specialization, clinicians must be sufficiently familiar with other fields to make use of the knowledge these disciplines can contribute to the diagnostic process. For example, the evaluation of prenatal and perinatal factors needs to be informed by findings from the field of obstetrics. Pediatrics helps to frame questions about the child's growth and health. Developmental psychology is needed to assess the achievement of age-expected milestones in emotional, social, cognitive, and sensorimotor functioning. Clinical psychology and psychiatry inform the assessor's understanding of the parent's and the child's psychiatric history and current functioning, family psychodynamics, and the intergenerational transmission of relationship patterns and trauma. Occupational therapy sheds light on questions of sensorimotor integration (see chapter 13). Social work frames the assessor's understanding of institutional influences on family functioning. Sociology and anthropology inform the understanding of how cultural values and mores, socioeconomic circumstances, and sociopolitical processes such as poverty, racism, war, and migration affect psychological functioning (see chapter 2).

Clearly, no assessor can be an expert in all of these disciplines, let alone the subspecialties that are often called for to assess the child's functioning. However, this partial listing illustrates the importance of a multidisciplinary perspective in assessing infants and young children. The assessor needs to cultivate a willingness to consult with experts from other disciplines and to make referrals when appropriate.

A comprehensive assessment leading to an accurate diagnostic picture needs to yield clinically rich information in these areas:

- Child presenting symptoms
- Current constitutional characteristics, temperamental propensities, and developmental functioning in the domains of language, cognition, sensorimotor integration, affect regulation, and interpersonal relatedness
- Developmental history, including prenatal and perinatal influences and timetable of developmental milestone achievements in the above domains
- Parental psychological functioning and parenting competence
- Family functioning, including marital stresses and cultural background
- Quality of the parent-child relationship and interactive patterns, including parental perception of the child and positive and negative attributions to the child
- Daily routines and caregiving practices
- Family circumstances, including psychosocial history and current stressors

In the process of making a diagnosis, these areas need to be considered in conjunction with each other, weighing their mutual influences and making judgments about the relative role of different factors in contributing to the child's areas of dysfunction and competence.

OVERVIEW OF THE DC:0–3 CLASSIFICATION SYSTEM

Multiaxial Framework

DC:0–3 is organized in five axes. This framework resembles the organization of *DSM-IV*, but it is not identical because DC:0–3 has a built-in focus on developmental issues of the first years of life that is largely absent from *DSM-IV*. In both diagnostic classification systems, Axis I provides primary diagnostic categories that describe the individual's functioning. However, a major difference in the two systems emerges in the conceptualization of Axis II, which in DC:0–3 consists of the classification of relationship disorders because this is a major component of many mental health disorders of infancy and early childhood. In contrast, the *DSM-IV* Axis II addresses the classification of personality disorders, which are considered chronic rather than acute and are not compatible with the rapid developmental pace of the first years of life. Both systems use Axis III to document medical conditions, but DC:0–3 also includes developmental disorders in this axis. Both systems use Axis IV to document psychosocial and environmental problems, which in DC:0–3 consist of situations that are stressful for young children, while *DSM-IV* lists adult-oriented stresses. Axis V is conceptualized developmentally in DC:0–3, providing guidelines for the assessment of the functional emotional developmental level of young children. In *DSM-IV*, this axis also focuses on the assessment of functioning, but the anchor behaviors are not developmentally based. Finally, DC:0–3 has a relationship-based counterpart to the *DSM-IV* Global Assessment of Functioning (GAF) scale. It is called the Parent-Infant Relationship Global Assessment Scale (PIR-GAS), and it provides a range from "well adapted" to "grossly impaired." An overview of DC:0–3 is provided below, with additional comparisons to *DSM-IV* when relevant.

Axis I: Primary Diagnosis

Axis I comprises the following main categories:

100. Traumatic Stress Disorder
200. Disorders of Affect (Anxiety; Mood Disorder: Prolonged Bereavement/Grief Reaction; Mood Disorder: Depression; Mixed Disorder of Emotional Expressiveness; Gender Identity Disorder; and Reactive Attachment Deprivation/Maltreatment Disorder of Infancy)
300. Adjustment Disorder
400. Regulatory Disorders (Hypersensitive, Underreactive, Motorically Disorganized/Impulsive, and Other)
500. Sleep Behavior Disorder
600. Eating Behavior Disorder
700. Disorders of Relating and Communicating (Patterns A, B, and C)

DC:0–3 provides a systematic decision tree that guides the assessor in selecting the appropriate diagnosis when the child's symptom constellation can be classified under more than one category. This is a common occurrence in infancy and early childhood because of the child's limited behavioral repertoire.

The decision tree reflects DC:0–3's emphasis on environmental factors as contributing to the child's functioning. The first decision to be made is to determine the occurrence of traumatic stress as an etiological factor in the child's disordered functioning. Traumatic stresses consist of the child's direct experience or witnessing of an event or series of events, sudden or chronic, that involve actual or threatened death or serious injury to the child or others (e.g., natural disaster, assault, domestic violence, physical abuse). The category of Traumatic Stress Disorder receives priority if the child encountered at least one of these events, on the assumption that the symptom picture would not occur in the absence of the traumatic stressor.

If the environmental events experienced by the child are not sufficiently severe to constitute trauma but represent a stressful disruption of the child's routine and daily experience, then the diagnosis of Adjustment Disorder should be considered. Adjustment Disorder is diagnosed when the child shows symptoms for no longer than four months in response to a clear disruption of established routines such as entry into group care, change of substitute caregiver, family move, or illness. The time-limited definition of this diagnostic category means that Adjustment Disorder is necessarily a working diagnosis that is confirmed retroactively if the child's difficulties subside within the 4-month time boundary.

The infant's and young child's constitutional or maturational characteristics constitute the second set of criteria to be considered in making a primary diagnosis. The diagnosis of Regulatory Disorder is made when the child shows marked difficulties in regulating and integrating physiological, sensory, motor, attentional, or emotional processes to achieve a quiet alert state or a positive affective state (Greenspan, 1992; Greenspan & Wieder, 1993). This disorder is diagnosed when children's sensory or information-processing difficulties are significant enough to interfere with daily routines and with the formation and quality of interpersonal relationships. Examples of regulatory problems are over- or underreactivity to sensory input (sound, light, tactile stimulation, temperature); oral-motor coordination problems or hypersensitivity; deficits in visual-spatial perception, auditory processing, or motor planning; and the capacity to attend and focus. In making the diagnosis, the caregiver's perceptions and capacity to tolerate the child's idiosyncrasies need to be evaluated. Some caregivers experience a fussy, unpredictable baby as challenging but normal, whereas others might find the same behaviors as indicators that something is wrong with the child (Barton & Robins, 2000). For this reason, the diagnosis of Regulatory Disorder is optimally made on the basis of independent observations of the child in a variety of settings and with a variety of caregivers.

The categories included under Disorders of Affect are considered when no traumatic stress or significant change has occurred and when no constitutional or maturational anomalies have been identified. These categories describe a variety of symptom constellations that need to be evaluated in the context of the child's environmental conditions. Two categories are clearly linked to characteristics of the caregiving environment. Prolonged Bereavement/Grief Reaction denotes the negative impact of loss of the parent or a primary caregiver on the child's psychological functioning. Reactive Attachment Deprivation/Maltreatment Disorder of infancy describes responses to persistent parental neglect or abuse, frequent changes of primary caregiver, or inconsistent availability of the primary caregiver. It should be reserved for inadequate basic physical and emotional care. The other categories of affective disorder have less clearly delineated etiological factors. They include Anxiety, Depression, Mixed Disorder of Emotional Expressiveness, and Gender Identity Disorder, all of which are described in terms of the affective and behavioral

difficulties shown by the child in a variety of environmental contexts.

Infants and young children sometimes show eating and sleeping problems in the absence of other symptoms. Two primary diagnostic categories, Sleeping Behavior Disorder and Eating Behavior Disorder, should be considered when the diagnostic process has ruled out the presence of environmental disruptions that may lead to traumatic stress or adjustment problems, maturational/constitutional problems underlying possible regulatory disorders, or one of the categories of Affect Disorders.

Disorders of Relating and Communicating consist of severe difficulties in relating and communicating, combined with difficulties in the regulation of physiological, sensory, attentional, motor, cognitive, somatic, and affective processes. Within this overarching rubric, a diagnosis of Multisystem Development Disorder (MSDD) is indicated when there is significant impairment in, but not complete lack of, the ability to engage in an emotional and social relationship with the primary caregiver; significant impairment in communication; significant dysfunction in auditory processing; and significant dysfunction in other sensory processes.

The primary diagnoses described in DC:0–3 are intended to complement existing diagnostic categories that are applicable to infants and young children in the *DSM-IV* classification system. For example, diagnoses of Pica and Rumination are specific feeding disorders of infancy and early childhood that are well described in *DSM-IV*. Similarly, the *DSM-IV* diagnoses of Autism, Pervasive Developmental Disorder not otherwise specified, and other disorders of relating and communicating should be used whenever appropriate. The primary diagnostic categories offered in DC:0–3 have the purpose of providing diagnostic alternatives specifically tailored to the developmental characteristics of infants, toddlers, and preschoolers and are written to reflect the specific symptoms shown by children who experience mental health disorders in the first four years of life.

Axis II: Relationship Disorder Classification

A unique feature of DC:0–3 is that it provides a classification of relationship disorders. Axis II reflects a basic premise in the field of infant mental health that young children develop in the context of their primary emotional relationships, and that the affective quality of these relationships has a profound influence in shaping the child's developmental course toward mental health or disorder. The adaptive function of emotional ties for the child's physical survival and emotional well-being has been well documented in the literature (Emde, 1989). Two extensive and complementary bodies of research have used different terms to refer to the parent-child relationship. The term *attachment* refers to the child's specific affective bond with the mother, father, and other primary caregivers that impels the child to turn preferentially to these figures for safety and protection in situations of uncertainty, danger, and fear (Bowlby, 1969, 1973, 1980). The term *bonding* refers to the parental side of the parent-child relationship, and describes the parent's loving commitment to the child as an emotional priority in the parent's life (Klaus & Kennell, 1982).

From an ethological perspective, attachment and bonding are complementary processes that promote infant survival and well-being. In individual circumstances, these two processes may be disconnected. A child may be passionately attached to a parent who is emotionally detached, abusive, or otherwise unable to provide the child with developmentally appropriate caregiving experiences. Conversely, a parent may have a powerful emotional commitment to a child that seems incapable of reciprocating these feelings of love due to constitutional problems or a history of trauma or neglect. Although a review of the literature on child abuse, neglect, maltreatment, and constitutional problems in relatedness and communication is beyond the scope of this chapter, comprehensive textbooks exist that provide overviews of these topics (Cicchetti & Cohen, 1995; Osofsky & Fitzgerald, 2000; Zeanah, 2000). The unanimous conclusion of decades of research on these topics is that relationship disorders have a deleterious effect on early personality development and can become a powerful etiological factor in the ontogenesis of psychopathology.

In DC:0–3, Axis II is intended to diagnose the presence of a clinical problem in the child's relationship with the primary caregiver, usually the parent. A disorder in this axis needs to be specific to the relationship assessed, meaning that the child's behavioral disturbances while interacting with the parent are not observed in the child's relationships with other caregivers. If the relationship disorder does not affect the child's functioning in other domains, only an Axis II diagnosis is given. For example, a mother's negative mental representations of her 12-month-old as a replica of his authoritarian father may lead her to constrict his exploration and punish him inappropriately for noncompliance in an effort to raise a well-behaved child. The child may respond by becoming increasingly avoidant of interaction with her. However, he may have loving and pleasurable relationships with his father, grandparents, child care providers, and peers that provide protective influences in his development. In such a case, the mother and child may have a disordered relationship that has not led to the development of individual problems in the child.

Conversely, a child may have a primary diagnosis on Axis I without having a relationship disorder on Axis II. This may be the case when the etiology of the child's mental health disorder is linked to maturational or constitutional characteristics or environmental events that do not affect the quality of the parent-child relationship. For example, an 8-month-old baby may avoid eye contact with his mother and squirm on physical contact with her due to constitutional characteristics that make her hyperresponsive to visual and tactile stimulation, but the mother may respond by modulating her behavior in ways that are responsive to the child's needs. Similarly, a 2-year-old child may develop multiple fears as the result of having been bitten by a dog, but he may consistently turn to his parents for reassurance and protection, and they may consistently respond to him in empathetic and supportive ways. In these two examples, the child's individual difficulties do not set the stage for a relationship disorder due to the parents' sensitive behavior and developmentally appropriate interventions.

To assess a relationship disorder, it is necessary to elicit the parent's subjective experience of the child and to conduct direct observations of the child-parent interaction. Three aspects of the relationship are assessed: the *behavioral interaction* between parent and child, including the developmental appropriateness of parental behaviors, contingency of mutual response, flexibility in responding to each other's agendas, and cooperativeness in resolving conflict; *affective tone*, involving predominantly positive or negative emotions; and *parental psychological involvement*, consisting of the types of perceptions and attitudes that the parent experiences toward the child. The relationship disorder categories include Overinvolved, Underinvolved, Anxious/Tense, Angry/Hostile, Mixed, and Abusive.

The categorical classification approach of Axis II is supplemented by the use of a scale, the PIR-GAS, that assesses the global quality of the child-parent relationship along a continuum of adaptation, from well adapted (90) to severely impaired (10). The middle range, "distressed," (50) denotes relationships that are more than transiently affected by internal or external stressors but still retain some flexibility and resilience. Parents may or may not be concerned about the disturbed patterns of relationships, but the level of disturbance is moderate enough that the child is unlikely to develop overt clinical symptoms as the result of the relationship difficulty.

Axis III: Medical and Developmental Disorders and Conditions

Axis III is used to note physical (including medical and neurological) health, mental health, and/or developmental diagnoses made using other diagnostic classification systems, including the *DSM-IV*, ICD-10, and specific classifications used by speech/language, occupational, and physical therapists and special educators.

Axis IV: Psychosocial Stressors

Psychosocial stressors can contribute to the severity and specific manifestations of mental health disorders in infants and young children. They may do so by affecting the child directly (for example, a childhood illness) or indirectly (for example, through a parent's illness that affects the quality of caregiving available to the child). The stressors may be acute or enduring and may have a single source or involve multiple, cumulative events. Three factors are used in Axis IV to assess the impact of a stressful event on the child's functioning: the severity of the stressor,

the developmental level of the child, and the availability of caregivers able to buffer the impact of the event on the child. Axis IV provides a list of stressors that are marked as acute or enduring by the clinician. It also includes a 7-point scale to assess the overall impact of the stress, ranging from 1 (no obvious effects) to 7 (significant derailment in developmentally appropriate levels of functioning).

Axis V: Functional Emotional Developmental Level

Axis V has the purpose of identifying the developmental level at which the child organizes affective, interactive, communicative, sensory, and motor experience. It directs the clinician to assess the child's capacity to perform at age-appropriate levels in the following essential domains of functioning: mutual attention, mutual engagement, interactive intentionality and reciprocity, representational/affective communication, representational elaboration, and representational differentiation. The description of Axis V includes the age range at which these competencies are expected to appear and guidelines for assessing the specific level achieved by the child. The assessment of the child's competencies should be based on observations of the child in interaction with each parent and other significant caregivers. As the child becomes increasingly comfortable with the clinician through the course of the evaluation, the levels achieved by the child in interaction with the clinician should also be noted. Axis V provides a 5-point scale that summarizes the child's overall functional emotional developmental level, from 1 (has fully reached expected levels) to 5 (has not mastered any prior expected levels).

Case Illustrations

The DC:0–3 manual includes a section of case vignettes submitted by clinicians participating in the Zero to Three Diagnostic Classification Task Force. These clinicians worked in a variety of settings, including infant mental health programs, child psychiatry clinics, early intervention programs, and private practice. The vignettes provide brief descriptions of the clinical picture, the rationale for selecting the primary diagnosis, highlights of the intervention provided, and a diagnostic summary of the five axes.

In addition, *The DC:0–3 Casebook* is available as a guide to use the diagnostic classification system in assessment and treatment planning (Lieberman et al., 1997). The casebook has the purpose of illustrating how the diagnostic categories are used clinically to organize the information that emerges in the course of the assessment, how to develop working hypotheses about etiology and prognosis, and how to link the diagnostic picture to decisions about treatment. The importance of the parents' active participation in the assessment and genuine collaboration in the treatment is illustrated through the description of specific intervention modalities addressing the parents' experience of themselves, their child, and their circumstances. The influence of cultural factors, including ethnicity, immigrant status, and socioeconomic conditions, in shaping parental perceptions of the child, the clinician, and the assessment and treatment process is highlighted through clinical illustrations. The casebook material stresses that a culturally informed perspective enriches the assessor's repertoire in developing and implementing the treatment plan in active collaboration with the parents.

A Retrospective Look at the Creation of DC:0–3

When the Zero to Three Diagnostic Classification Task Force began working on the issue of diagnostic assessment in 1987, its purpose was to develop a classification system that would promote interdisciplinary communication about the phenomena clinicians were observing in the infants they were assessing and treating. A related goal was to create a diagnostic system that could be used to document the need for mental health services for infants. A premise of the task force was that if disturbances were recognized early, before they became consolidated, preventive guidance with the parents would minimize the further development of aberrant behaviors both in the infant and in the parent-child relationship.

At the beginning of its deliberations, members of the task force grappled with the question of whether a diagnosis could be made in a child under the age of three. Two opinions were voiced.

One opinion held that it was neither possible nor desirable to make a diagnosis about an infant as an individual because during the earliest years clinical problems could exist in the parent-infant relationship but not in the infant alone. The second opinion held that babies could have diagnosable constitutional problems that predated interactional stresses and could be the earliest manifestation of a predisposition to a mental health disorder.

One of the goals of the task force was to gather empirical evidence to inform this debate. Task force members collected systematic clinical case information from their own clinics, yielding a sample of 224 cases. A clinical record was devised for collecting uniform information. The database included referral information, reported signs and symptoms, history, assessment of the child and family, and a record of the diagnosis and treatment plan.

Findings showed that the average child age at referral was 25.7 months; 60% of the children referred were boys. The majority of the parents were married, had completed college, and were European American. The most frequent behavioral complaints by the parents involved sleeping problems, feeding/eating difficulties, tantrums, aggressive behavior, oppositional behavior, and language delays. Clinicians' primary areas of concern involved the child's quality of relatedness and reciprocal interaction, level of social/emotional adaptation, mood, and developmental delays. The most common medical problems were failure to thrive, congenital anomalies, chronic health problems, neurological disorders, and respiratory problems. The evaluation of sensorimotor functioning revealed visual, auditory, tactile, vestibular, kinesthetic, motor planning, and motor tone symptoms in approximately 10 to 15% of the cases. The most frequent of these difficulties were auditory, tactile, motor planning, and tone symptoms.

Assessment of the parents revealed that the clinicians' primary areas of concern involved parenting competence, including the parents' ability to provide basic emotional care, and marital and family stress.

The data were analyzed using *DSM-IV* and preliminary DC:0–3 diagnostic categories. Using DC:0–3, the most frequent diagnostic categories were regulatory disorder and anxiety. Only 16 cases out of 224 did not meet criteria for a disorder using this instrument. When *DSM-IV* was used, fewer cases were classified as meeting criteria for disorder. The most frequent *DSM-IV* categories were Reactive Attachment Disorder, Adjustment Disorder, Pervasive Development Disorder, and Posttraumatic Stress.

In assessing the child's context, the environment was labeled as problematic in 62% of the cases using both diagnostic systems. There were acute stressors in 40% of the cases and enduring stress in 58%. The mother-child relationship was judged to be disordered in 17% of the cases, versus 5% for fathers and 3% for other caregivers. These findings indicated that, while there was a high level of environmental stress including the parent-child relationship, many children had a diagnosable mental health problem in the absence of clinical problems in the parent-child relationship. These findings provided preliminary empirical documentation for the feasibility and desirability of a diagnostic classification system and provided the foundation for the further refinement of the DC:0–3 categories.

During 1999–2001, a study of the reliability and validity of the DC:0–3 classification system was undertaken (Barnard et al., 2002). Clinicians with experience in using the DC:0–3 and *DSM-IV* systems saw eight cases. The average child age was 25 months; 5 of the children were males. One primary clinician using a commonly agreed protocol for assessment saw each case. The common protocol included an interview guide that focused on developmental and behavioral history and specific concerns, family history, family circumstances, traumatic exposures, the child's social-emotional history, the child's daily routines, and parenting experiences. Observations were structured to evaluate the child during the parent interview, family snack, unstructured free play, structured dyadic interaction, guided parent play, and diagnostic play. Standardized assessments were used to examine concurrent validity issues. These instruments included the Child Behavior Checklist (CBCL; Achenbach, 1992), the Infant-Toddler Social Emotional Assessment (ITSEA; Carter, Little, Briggs-Gowan, & Kogan, 1999; the Infant-Toddler Symptom Checklist (ITSC; De-Gangi, 2000), the Sensory Profile or Infant-Tod-

dler Sensory Profile (Dunn, 1999a, 1999b), the Temperament and Atypical Behavior Scales (Bagnato, Neisworth, Salvia, & Hunt, 1999), Parenting Stress Index (PSI; Abidin, 1990), the Center for Epidemiological Studies Depression Scale (CES-D; Radloff, 1977), and the Caregiver/Teacher Rating Form (Achenbach & Rescorla, 2000, 2001).

Raw data from each case (interviews, observations, test forms) were reviewed by one to three of the other team members, and a consensus was reached for all axes of DC:0–3 and for the *DSM-IV* diagnosis. Table 8.1 gives the DC:0–3 Axis I and II and *DSM-IV* diagnosis for the eight cases. The rating clinicians concluded that the DC:0–3 primary diagnosis was a better fit for the symptoms and behaviors reported and observed in the child than the *DSM-IV* classification. Five of the eight cases were diagnosed as having a Regulatory Disorder. These problems in sensory and emotional regulation, attention, and sensorimotor functioning are most likely to be identified by parents who are cognizant of the symptoms. Unfortunately, most primary care providers are not aware of these regulatory issues and consider that fussiness in infants is a developmental stage that will resolve spontaneously. An important finding was that the DC:0–3 diagnosis was always validated by the reported history, the symptom screening tests, and the observations made of child-parent interaction during play, structured task, guided play, family snack, and diagnostic play.

Fifty percent of the cases (*n* = 4) had diagnosed Parent-Child Relationship Problems (Axis II). In many ways, this small sample mirrored the early data from the late 1980s, including the prevalence of referrals during toddlerhood, the predominance of males, the high frequency of regulatory problems, and the existence of child diagnoses with and without accompanying parent-child relationship issues. More research is needed to evaluate the reliability and validity of the DC:0–3 classification system. This pilot study provided a common structure for such studies to be conducted. Other researchers have conducted studies aimed at establishing procedural, criterion, and discriminant validity for one specific diagnostic category, traumatic stress disorder (Scheeringa & Zeanah, 1995; Scheeringa, Zea-

Table 8.1 Diagnosis of Eight Cases on Zero to Three Axis I and II and *DSM-IV*

DC:0–3 Axis I Primary Diagnosis	*DSM-IV* Primary Diagnosis	DC:0–3 Axis II Parent-Child Relationship Diagnosis
201 Anxiety	309.21 Anxiety	Child caregiver but not with parents
403 Regulatory Type III	309.00-90 Adjustment	Mother, anxious/tense
401 Regulatory Type I	Attention Deficit and Hyperactivity	No disorder
404 Regulatory Type IV, other	Developmental Disorder Coordination Disorder Feeding Disorder Language Disorder	No disorder
403 Regulatory Type II	Expressive Language 315.31	Mother, disturbance, no disorder
204 Mixed Disturbance of Emotional Expressiveness	Expressive Language 315.31, Feeding Disorder Resolved 307.53	Grandmother, mixed, underinvolved, anxious/tense
MSDD, Pattern B	MR 317-319 Pervasive Developmental Disorder; Autistic 299.0	No disorder
4-1 Regulatory Type I	Expressive Language Disorder 315.15 Mixed Receptive/Expressive Language Disorder 315.15 Parent-Child Problem	Mother, angry/hostile

nah, Drell, & Larrieu, 1995). The model used in these studies can be applied to the investigation of other specific diagnostic categories as well.

CASE EXAMPLES
UTILIZING DC:0–3

Regulatory Disorder

This example of a regulatory problem in a very young infant, 5 months of age, demonstrates how early recognition of the sensorimotor problems and appropriate treatment can reduce the symptoms and prevent the development of a parent-child relationship problem during the early months of life. This case represents issues that are currently routinely ignored in primary health care and that need to be brought to the attention of primary health providers to enhance quality of care (Barnard, 1999).

The Assessment Process

The assessment process consisted of four sessions: an initial home visit, a joint visit to the pediatri-

cian, a physical therapy evaluation, and a feedback session to plan the intervention. Each of these sessions lasted approximately one hour.

Charles, 5 months old, was first seen at the request of a home visitor who was providing services through an Early Head Start Program to Charles's older sister and mother. The presenting complaints were Charles's colicky behavior and the difficulty his mother was having consoling him. The home visitor reported that "everything had been tried," with little success.

Home Visit

The assessor conducted a home visit in the presence of the home visitor. Mother and baby were alone in the house. As the assessor interviewed the mother and the home visitor and observed the child, important information emerged. Charles had had forceful reflux since birth, and this condition was being treated with only partial success by controlling his posture after feedings. His weight gain was adequate. He had a head tilt to the left from birth and there was an asymmetry to the neck and upper shoulder musculature. He had never played with his legs or feet and showed resistance when pushing his legs into extension. He was unable to roll to his back or tummy but was otherwise active and socially engaging. He could maintain a sitting position for a short period, as expected for his age. However, when his protective balance reflexes were tested while seated, he showed no spontaneous use of his arms for balancing.

The assessor's first impression of Charles's mood was that he was very alert but appeared tired at the same time. He was interested in a multicolored rattle with a face design when the assessor offered it to him at a distance, and he made repeated attempts to reach the rattle until he succeeded. He was less interested in a green block and made several unsuccessful attempts to reach it. He was very dependent on his mother's holding and rocking him to maintain a content alert state, and he frequently had minor fussy periods which the mother managed to control by increasing stimulation. The assessor asked the home visitor to hold Charles, to see how he managed with someone other than his mother. He stayed alert without fussing for 20 minutes while held by the home visitor, who used body contact and visual stimulation to keep him alert. The mother reported that he was happiest when undressed and on his changing table. The assessor found he was in the best alert state when placed on a regular table with no tactile contact from others.

Charles's mother reported spending the majority of the day keeping Charles entertained and said that without her attention he cried inconsolably. She also reported that Charles became irritable and fussy when his father tried to care for him. The mother interpreted this reaction as an indication that Charles sensed her own tension with her husband, with whom she was having marital difficulties.

The assessor asked for the mother's permission to try to get Charles upset in order to observe the child's strategies for self-soothing. With the mother's agreement, the assessor played with Charles, did some pull to sits, and asked his mother to leave the room briefly. Within 5 minutes of her departure, Charles was crying hard. He showed none of the developmentally expected self-consoling behaviors (fingers to mouth, rocking), and in fact it took considerable work,

first on the assessor's part and then by mother, to get him to quiet down. He finally settled when she held him against her body and gave him a bottle of formula. He soon fell asleep, and after 15 to 20 minutes of sleep he had almost no body movement and no rapid eye movement.

The mother reported that he slept 7 to 8 hours at night without waking. When doing a 24-hour recall of his sleep, feedings, and fussiness, she reported that he had 7 feedings a day, 9.5 hours of sleep, and almost continuous bouts of fussing during the day. The amount of sleep reported is about 4 hours per day less than expected at this age.

The home visit led the assessor to conclude that Charles used environmental stimulation in the environment to control his state. For example, he used a parent's holding and jiggling, but did so only with two of the family members. He had an intensity about visual intake and also seemed to like a lot of kinesthetic and vestibular stimulation, but his response to tactile stimuli was variable. Although there were marital stresses, these did not seem severe enough to explain Charles's irritability. The mother-child relationship seemed reasonably well adapted, with the mother responsive to Charles's signals and Charles showing strongly preferential behavior toward his mother.

These observations led the assessor to conclude that a diagnosis of Regulatory Disorder needed to be ruled out. For this purpose, the assessor suggested a neurodevelopmental workup, and offered to go with the mother to a visit with the pediatrician to request a referral for this service.

Pediatrician Visit

Charles was a "happy camper" during the visit, displaying no fussiness! This is typical of the variable behavior of infants, who may not display their most troubled behavior precisely when the assessor needs to document earlier observations. The pediatrician listened to the story about Charles's irritability and reduced amount of sleep, observed the contrast between this history and Charles's happy state, and stated that he did not think Charles had a problem. He also pointed out that his son had the same pattern of crying.

However, he agreed, albeit reluctantly, to a referral to the Children's Therapy Center for a physical therapy evaluation.

Physical Therapy Evaluation

When Charles was 6 months old, the physical therapist performed a sensory motor assessment, which included an examination of his motor development and processing of sensory stimulation. Charles had normal muscle tone, with increased extensor posturing in the pelvis and legs in supine and supported standing. The left lateral head tilt became more pronounced with any postural challenge. He did not like being on his tummy. When laid on his back, he did not conform his head and upper body to the surface immediately. Instead he forcefully flexed his head and upper body 1 inch or more off the surface.

With encouragement, as the physical therapist placed her hands on his shoulders, he was able to lie prone and reach for and play with toys with both hands. He was not able to do any bridging (pushing bottom into the air with feet on the surface), although this is very typical for an infant between 5 and 6 months. There was moderate resistance to passive hip and lower trunk flexion. Invited to play with his legs and feet, the resistance softened and he actively began to hold his legs and feet in flexion and abduction.

Charles looked easily to both sides, but his reaching to either side was different. When he looked and reached to the right, he reached across his body with the left hand for the toy. His neck tilted more forcefully to the left and his trunk rotated to the right. When enticed to look and reach to the left, he extended his neck and back to do so and did not reach across his body to the left with the right arm. He could roll to the left side, but was unable to roll to the right. He had been able to maintain sitting during the past month.

Charles's behavior, though atypical for his age, is commonly seen in infants with torticollis, a condition characterized by tight muscles in the neck on one side of the body that make the child appear off balance. Head position and sensory experience dominated by lateral head control in one direction can have a strong impact on righting and balancing responses in the rest of the body.

The sensorimotor findings were consistent with an early partially resolved torticollis, the asymmetrical muscle mass on the back of his neck. Because of positioning practices associated with the reflux problem and feeding, he had had little opportunity to spend time on his stomach and to develop strength and balance in that area.

On the basis of these findings, Charles received three weeks of regular therapy sessions. The mother was given advice about how to hold and handle Charles to normalize sensory input and promote more centered alignment and neck strength.

The mother followed through with the physical therapy and the recommendations. Within two weeks, the child's irritability and crying were greatly reduced. Charles was no longer fussing, although he still had occasional reflux. The mother was much happier with the baby. She began working on her own issues—losing weight, treatment for her own depression, and working on improving her relationship with her husband. When the assessor saw Charles and his mother four months later for a follow-up visit, Charles was an alert and happy 10-month-old baby, crawling and practicing standing and walking with no remaining asymmetry.

The following diagnostic decisions were made:

Axis I. Regulatory Disorder, Type I: Hypersensitive

Axis II. No diagnosis

Axis III. Feeding reflux; resolving torticollis

Axis IV. No psychosocial stressors

Axis V. Functional emotional developmental level 2: age-appropriate level but vulnerable to stress

PIR-GAS. Perturbed (70). Relationships in this range are functioning less than optimally in some way. The disturbance is limited to one domain of functioning and overall the relationship functions reasonably well. The disturbance lasts from a few days to a few weeks.

Traumatic Stress Disorder

Lorraine, aged 11 months, was referred to a child mental health clinic two months after falling down the steep stairs leading from the family's second-floor apartment to the ground floor. Her mother, who was five months pregnant at the time, was struggling with the baby carriage and with the child when Lorraine lurched forward and lost her balance, going all the way down the stairs, smashing her forehead on the ground floor below. She received a cut just above her right eyebrow that bled profusely and necessitated two stitches to close. Lorraine's mother screamed in panic when she saw her child falling down, and later reported that she had a brief image of Lorraine lying dead at the bottom of the stairs. Her screams brought out a neighbor, who kindly took mother and child to the nearest emergency room for treatment. Lorraine had to be held forcibly by her terrified mother as the doctor examined her and sewed the wound.

This frightening episode became the focus of recurrent nightmares for mother and child. Both of them began to wake up abruptly during the night. The mother kept dreaming that the event was happening again and again; the child screamed at the top of her lungs and refused to go back to sleep by herself. The mother and the father were exhausted from lack of sleep, and the child fell asleep at odd hours during the day, disrupting her nighttime sleep cycle and contributing to her awakenings during the night.

Lorraine also showed other symptoms of reexperiencing the fall. She cried in anguish whenever the family had to use the stairs, which were the only way to get in and out of the apartment, and alternately clung to her mother and hit her when they were negotiating the stairs. This fear of the stairs represented both distress at reminders of the trauma and an avoidance of these reminders. The mother became frightened of going out with Lorraine when her husband was not with them for fear that another fall would ensue as she and the child struggled with each other on the stairs.

Within a month of the event, Lorraine began to throw herself on the floor for no apparent reason, and would get up without saying a word only to throw herself on the floor again. This motoric reenactment of the fall seemed also to be an effort to gain mastery of the frightening event by controlling its occurrence and predicting when it would happen.

Simultaneously, Lorraine began to resist walking autonomously and often insisted on being carried in her father's arms. She often resisted being held and carried by her mother, who was now seven months pregnant and increasingly stressed by the physical demands of her pregnancy and by the sequelae of the traumatic event she and Lorraine had gone through. In addition, Lorraine became aggressive and defiant with her mother, often hitting her and refusing to comply with her mother's requests. She became very clingy with her father and cried inconsolably when her father went to work in the mornings. During dinner, she insisted on being fed by her father and refused to feed herself, although she had done this with pleasure before falling down the stairs.

Family Evaluation

An evaluation of the family circumstances indicated a reasonably well-adjusted family before the accident. The mother and the father had a basically good marriage and were looking forward to their new baby's birth, although both admitted that the second pregnancy had not been planned and both wished there were more spacing between the two children. The mother, in particular, felt guilty before the accident about what she described as "imposing a new baby on Lorraine and depriving her of her babyhood." After the accident, she expressed increased remorse about the pregnancy and harbored the belief that Lorraine would not have fallen if the mother had not been encumbered in her movements by the pregnancy. The father was quite supportive of both the mother and the child, and tried to reassure the mother that the accident had not been her fault. However, he occasionally lost his temper and became brusque and withdrawn when he was excessively tired by long hours at work and the extended lack of sleep. The couple were able to negotiate these marital squabbles nicely by talking about what triggered them and showing understanding of each other's experience.

The Process of Assessment

The assessment lasted three weeks and included three sessions. The first session lasted 1.5 hours, included only both parents and the assessor, and involved developmental and family history and interview-based assessment of the child's functioning, the mother's and father's individual functioning and marital relationship, and family circumstances and daily caregiving routines. The second session lasted 1 hour and consisted of a naturalistic free play session with Lorraine and her mother and father, with the clinician taking the role of a participant observer. The third session again included only the mother and the father, meeting with the clinician for a feedback session.

For the second session, which included direct observation of the child and the parent-child interaction, the toys were selected with Lorraine's age in mind and consisted of a baby doll, a baby bottle, a stuffed teddy bear, building blocks, and cooking and kitchen utensils. Lorraine and her parents were encouraged to play spontaneously during the first part of the session and, after Lorraine warmed up to the assessor, the assessor set up a symbolic reenactment of the fall down the stairs by encouraging Lorraine to build a tower with building blocks and observing her reaction when it fell down. Lorraine's response showed the enduring impact of the event. She burst into tears when the tower fell down, went to her mother and clung to her, and within 30 seconds started alternating between hitting her mother and straining toward her father. She only calmed down when her father held her while whispering words of reassurance. He was then encouraged by the assessor to build a very short tower with Lorraine, which did not fall down.

The feedback session consisted of a description of Lorraine's enduring emotional reactivity to the traumatic stress of falling down the stairs, which affected her relationship with her mother and father and was also beginning to constrict her freedom to explore. The assessor pointed out that Lorraine's reactions were possibly amplified by the mother's guilt about her perceived role in the accident, including her pregnancy and the diminished physical nimbleness and emotional availability to Lorraine. The assessor recommended infant-parent psychotherapy with Lorraine and her mother (Fraiberg, 1980; Lieberman, Silverman, & Pawl, 2000), which was conducted for six months, spanning the new baby's birth and Lorraine's adjustment to the new situation. The treatment included occasional developmental guidance with the father to encourage an active role in helping Lorraine during the stresses of the

new baby's birth and changed family routines. At the end of treatment, Lorraine had shown a marked reduction in her emotional lability and anger at her mother, was able to show tenderness to her baby sister, and had regained her original zest to explore, although she was still more reactive to stress and more cautious about physical exploration than she had been before the accident. The diagnostic picture was as follows:

Axis I. Traumatic Stress Disorder.

Axis II. Relationship Disorder with Mother: Anxious/Tense; No Relationship Disorder with Father.

Axis III. No chronic medical conditions; facial cut due to accidental fall.

Axis IV. Psychosocial stressors: sudden injury; birth of sibling.

Axis V. Functional emotional developmental level: 2; age-appropriate level but vulnerable to stress and with constricted range of affects.

PIR-GAS. With mother: 40 (disturbed). The dyad is at significant risk for dysfunction. The relationship's adaptive qualities are beginning to be overshadowed by problematic features that adversely affect the subjective experience of one or both partners.

Anxiety Disorder

Dara was referred for assessment at age 3 years because her parents felt bewildered by the child's angry responses to her new sister, difficulty separating from her mother, mood swings, and difficulty adjusting to new situations.

The Process of Assessment

The assessment comprised four sessions lasting 1 hour each. The first two sessions involved interviews with the mother and the father to gather information about the reasons for the consultation, Dara's developmental history, and family circumstances, including the impact of Dara's behavior on the parents' marriage and on family life. The third session consisted of a play session with Dara and her parents. The final session involved feedback on the evaluation, outlining the plans for a time-limited intervention, and the continuation of a process of self-reflection for the parents about their subjective experience of themselves, each other, and their child.

During the initial interview, the parents described Dara as a lovely but needy baby from the start. They reported that she was welcomed after a joyful pregnancy and uneventful delivery. However, they found that she always wanted to be held and soothed and that her "3-month colic" went on for 6 months. By then the mother had decided to stay at home instead of returning to work and the parents enjoyed Dara's development, as she learned to sit, stand, wave, and clap. She walked at an early age but never ran off freely, always staying close to her mother or father. She seemed wary of others and would only stay with Grandma, who often came to visit. In addition, Dara did not like change. The parents reported that she hated going to new places and seemed to be afraid of anything unfamiliar. The only time Dara appeared to enjoy herself was with her friends on play dates at home or when alone with one of her parents, craving their undivided attention.

When Dara was in her second year, two events turned her world upside down. Her sister Sarah was born when she was 28 months old, and the first few months were quiet enough. However, her father soon began commuting to another state, coming home only for weekends, and then the family moved to join him at his new job 6 months later, just before Dara turned 3. At this time, Dara had to adapt to a new house, new preschool, new friends, and a baby sister who was just beginning to crawl.

The hardest time of the day was when Sarah, the new baby, was being put to bed. Dara insisted that Sarah go to bed first, knowing that she would then get her mother to herself, but watching Sarah nurse and be rocked by her mother often catapulted her into a frenzy of kicking, throwing toys, and uncontrolled yelling and crying. The parents reported that they had tried "everything" to help Dara during these times, including treats, extra time reading and playing alone with her, time-outs, and locking her in her room, but that nothing worked. Even watching her favorite video could not keep her from coming into Sarah's room at bedtime. They also tried letting her cuddle next to her mother while the mother nursed or rocked Sarah, but this also worked only occasionally.

The mother became very tense at bedtime because she feared that Dara might lash out at her or the baby. Only when the father was home at bedtime, and the children could be divided between the parents, did the evening sometimes go quietly. Even on such nights, however, Dara insisted that her mother stay with her until she fell asleep, and she would often waken in the middle of the night yelling and calling out for her parents. However, she did not run to their room.

The parents drew a vivid contrast between Dara and her easygoing little sister, who persisted in reaching out to her and whose "fuse" was as long as Dara's was short. The mother described herself as falling asleep overwhelmed by feelings of love, anger, and fear toward this child who, in her words, made her feel incompetent and helpless. She asked herself whether Dara's refusal to let others help her as she called out "Only Mommy" might mean that Dara still needed her and loved her and would give her another chance at being a good mother.

The situation had strong negative repercussions for the parents' marriage. Dara's mother and father argued about how to discipline her and how to reassure her. They blamed each other for the situation, asking such questions as why did they have another child, why did the father work such long hours, why did they move, and who was the more incompetent parent. They gave up going out alone and no longer enjoyed the intimacy they had shared before the focus of their attention turned to Dara. During the assessment, the parents alternated between blaming themselves and each other for not being strict enough, being inconsistent, being too loving, and many other perceived faults as they tried to find a reason for Dara's behavior.

During the following session, the parents reported that the separations had become increasingly difficult, especially at night. Dara had begun to insist that the lights stay on, but did not answer when her parents asked her if she was afraid. In fact, while able to express her desires and her objections, Dara did not talk about her feelings or answer many "why" questions. She played alone with toys and liked to build, but baby dolls and animals got scant attention.

She seemed to prefer to play alone, though not happily, as long as her mother or father were nearby. The assessment period overlapped with Halloween, and the parents reported that on Halloween Dara hid behind her mother and would not go up to anyone's house for trick or treat. Instead, she waited by her mother and accepted happily the candy that some older children shared with her. Prior to going out that evening, she had refused to wear the pretty Snow White costume that her grandmother had sent as a present. That night, after returning home, she asked where the ghosts and witches lived and her voice trembled as she looked about her room. She did not seem reassured when her parents told her that ghosts and witches are not real.

As part of the evaluation, Dara's parents were asked to play and interact with her in the office playroom. Dara did not explore the room and sat on the couch glued to her mother. She did not respond to questions asking her what she wanted to play with. Even when her mother offered her a baby doll, she turned away, her eyes glaring at the basket of dinosaurs and jungle animals. When her father picked up a tiger and moved it toward her in a stalking manner, saying, "Hey, Dara, look at this!," she yelled, "Stop!" The father quickly put it away. He asked her whether she would play ball with him and tossed a soft ball to her before she could say no. Dara kicked it away. The father persisted, relying on a simple game she usually enjoyed to help her get more comfortable, and she started to move to catch the ball. When the mother asked to join them, the father turned to Dara to decide who would get the ball next and she slowly began to relax, able to control the next turn in a predictable game, even smiling as her father started clowning around in an attempt to lower her anxiety in this new situation. Soon everyone was on his or her feet moving in the small space, and Dara's defensiveness appeared to decrease.

A few minutes later, the mother noticed baskets with figures, including Snow White. She exclaimed, "Look, Dara, here is Snow White and the seven dwarfs! She's wearing the same dress Grandma bought you for Halloween!" Dara paused and quietly asked, "Is the queen there?" This time her eyes did not leave the basket as her mother turned it over, and out came the dwarfs, the prince, the queen, and the witch. Dara began to scream and cry, "Put it away, put it away!" and curled up on the couch. Her mother ran over to comfort her, asking, "What's wrong?" but Dara's head was buried in her lap and she did not look up.

The father began to gather the toys when the clinician urged him to tell the witch that he would not allow her to hurt Dara. The father seemed surprised but complied quickly. He then threw the witch doll in the box and said in a booming voice, "You will not get out of here." Turning to Dara, he told her that she did not need to worry any more. Dara asked in an urgent tone of voice, "Where is the queen, where is the queen?" and breathed a sigh of relief as her father told her that the queen had gone to jail and would never be a queen anymore. He then put the witch and the queen in a box and asked Dara to help him seal the box with tape to make sure they could not come out. Dara hesitated but helped him with the tape, and nodded quietly when her mother asked her if she felt better. The father reassured her that she was safe now. Dara pointed to the top shelf of the bookcase and the father put the box up high. Everybody smiled.

Dara then accepted her mother's invitation to explore the room, and they walked around as Mom offered her various things. Dara finally picked up a baby doll and bottle and fed her. She stayed clear of the jungle animals and the other boxes of figures, but laughed a bit when her mother pretended to cry for the baby. As the session ended, attempts to get Dara to express her feelings or opinions were unfruitful. But she looked up at the shelf before leaving the room.

In the following session with the parents the mother reported, "We never do this. We never play this way." She recalled that Dara ran out of the room while watching the movie Snow White but did not realize that Dara was scared. She reported that she herself had loved the movie as a child, but reflected that maybe she was a bit older when she first watched it. The clinician explained that symbolic solutions helped their bright little girl feel safer because she was still too young to know what was real and what was not, in spite of her well-developed cognitive skills.

The clinician and the parents discussed the challenges and stress Dara had experienced in the previous months, and how her symptoms related to specific sources of anxiety, some of which were developmentally appropriate while others were in reaction to environmental changes. While she was clearly a sensitive child, an examination of her sensory profile indicated she did not present significant regulatory difficulties and could be communicative and interactive, but was currently flooded by anxiety, which resulted in her clingy, fearful, and distressed behaviors and her emotional constriction.

As the assessment proceeded, the clinician asked the parents more information about themselves, their marriage, their childhoods, and what Dara's difficulties meant to them. As they examined their conflicts and confusion, they began a process of reflection, which would help them understand themselves and their daughter better.

They arrived at a plan in which the parents would learn floor time play with Dara for about six sessions and would each do floor time for at least an hour daily at home. They would also meet weekly without Dara to discuss the floor time sessions and how to help her at home. The goals would be to broaden Dara's emotional zone of safety, to tolerate a wider range of emotions, to become increasingly capable of using language and symbolic play, to encourage more talking and thinking, to relate to her sister, and to handle the day-to-day challenges that had brought them in for help. In addition, they would address their feelings and concerns. At the end of this period they would reevaluate Dara's and their own needs.

According to DC:0–3, the diagnostic profile can be summarized as follows:

> Axis I. Anxiety Disorder (201).
> Axis II. Tendency toward anxious/tense relationship (903).
> Axis III. None.
> Axis IV. Psychosocial stress: severe effects.
> Axis V. Functional emotional developmental level: 4. Has the capacity of age-expected forms but vulnerable to stress and does not function and is constricted within full range of expected affects, that is, closeness but not assertion, anger, fear, and anxiety.
> PIR-GAS. Distressed (50).

CONCLUSION

DC:0–3 is based on considerable clinical evidence and preliminary empirical evidence demonstrating the feasibility and usefulness of a diagnostic classification manual to classify mental health and developmental disorders of infancy and early childhood.

DC:0–3 is based on an approach to diagnostic evaluation that stresses the importance of viewing the child in a developmental, relational, and cultural context, and integrating knowledge derived from a variety of disciplines that shed light on the child's functioning from a biological, psychological, and sociological perspective. Such an approach calls for a multifaceted assessment process that incorporates sustained attention to the child's relationship with primary caregivers, the caregivers' areas of strength and vulnerability as these are manifested in relation to the child and in the family's emotional climate, the stresses impinging on the family system, and the culturally determined values guiding the caregivers' child-rearing practices.

The usefulness of this approach has been demonstrated through several studies showing that DC:0–3 is more sensitive to the identification of early mental health disorders than the widely used *DSM-IV*, which is primarily appropriate for older children, adolescents, and adults. Further research is needed to establish the psychometric properties of the diagnostic categories, but the instrument represents an important first step in legitimizing a diagnostic approach to the mental health problems of infancy and early childhood.

References

Abidin, R. R. (1990). *Parenting stress index* (3rd ed.). Charlottesville, VA: Pediatric Psychology Press.

Achenbach, T. M. (1988). Integrating assessment and taxonomy. In M. Rutter, A. H. Tuma, & I. S. Lann (Eds.), *Assessment and diagnosis in child psychopathology* (pp. 300–343). New York: Guilford Press.

Achenbach, T. M. (1992). *Manual for the Child Behavior Checklist/2–3 and 1992 profile.* Burlington, VT: University of Vermont, Department of Psychiatry.

Achenbach, T. M., & Rescorla, L. A. (2000). *Manual for ASEBA preschool forms and profiles.* Burlington, VT: University of Vermont, Research Center for Children, Youth and Families.

Achenbach, T. M., & Rescorla, L. A. (2001). *Manual for ASEBA school-age forms and profiles.*

Burlington, VT: University of Vermont, Research Center for Children, Youth and Families.

American Psychiatric Association (1994). *Diagnostic and statistical manual of mental disorders* (4th ed.). Washington, DC: Author.

Bagnato, S. J., Neisworth, J. T., Salvia, J., & Hunt, F. M. (1999). *Temperament and Atypical Behavior Scales (TABS): Early childhood indicators of developmental dysfunction (TABS assessment tool and TABS screener)*. Baltimore, MD: Paul H. Brooks.

Barnard, K. E. (1999). Unpublished case report, University of Washington, Seattle, WA.

Barnard, K., Wieder, S., Carter, A., Clark, R., Thomas, J., Weston, D., & Fenichel, E. (2002). *The DC:0–3 assessment protocol project: Final report to the Commonwealth Fund*. Unpublished manuscript, Zero to Three, Washington, DC.

Barton, M. L., & Robins, D. (2000). Regulatory disorders. In C. H. Zeanah, Jr. (Ed.), *Handbook of infant mental health* (2nd ed., pp. 311–325). New York: Guilford Press.

Bowlby, J. (1969/1982). *Attachment and loss: Attachment*. New York: Basic Books.

Bowlby, J. (1973). *Attachment and loss: Separation*. New York: Basic Books.

Bowlby, J. (1980). *Attachment and loss: Loss*. New York: Basic Books.

Carter, A. S., Littler, C., Briggs-Gowan, M. J., & Kogan, N. (1999). The Infant-Toddler Social and Emotional Assessment (ITSEA): Comparing parent ratings to laboratory observations of task mastery, emotion regulation, coping behaviors, and attachment status. *Infant Mental Health Journal, 20*(4), 375–392.

Cicchetti, D., & Cohen, D. J. (Eds.). (1995). *Developmental psychopathology*. New York: Wiley & Sons.

DeGangi, G. A. (2000). *Pediatric disorders of regulation in affect and behavior: A therapist's guide to assessment and treatment*. San Diego, CA: Academic Press.

Dunn, W. (1999a). *Sensory profile: User's manual*. San Antonio, TX: Psychological Corporation.

Dunn, W. (1999b). *Infant-toddler sensory profile: User's manual*. San Antonio, TX: Psychological Corporation.

Emde, R. N. (1989). Toward a psychoanalytic theory of affect: I. The organizational model and its propositions. In S. Greenspan & G. H. Pollock (Eds.), *The course of life, Vol. 1: Infancy* (pp. 165–191). Madison, CT: International Universities Press.

Emde, R. N., Bingham, R. D., & Harmon, R. J. (1993). Classification and the diagnostic process in infancy. In C. H. Zeanah, Jr. (Ed.), *Handbook of infant mental health* (pp. 225–236). New York: Guilford Press.

Fraiberg, S. (1980). *Clinical studies in infant mental health*. New York: Basic Books.

Greenspan, S. I. (1992). *Infancy and early childhood: The practice of clinical assessment and intervention with emotional and developmental challenges*. Madison, CT: International Universities Press.

Greenspan, S. I., & Wieder, S. (1993). Regulatory disorders. In C. H. Zeanah, Jr. (Ed.), *Handbook of infant mental health* (pp. 280–290). New York: Guilford Press.

Klaus, M. H., & Kennell, J. H. (1982). *Parent-infant bonding* (2nd ed.). St. Louis, MO: Mosby.

Lieberman, A. F., Silverman, R., & Pawl, J. H. (2000). Infant-parent psychotherapy: Core concepts and current approaches. In C. H. Zeanah (Ed.), *Handbook of infant mental health* (2nd ed., pp. 472–484). New York: Guilford Press.

Lieberman, A. F., Wieder, S., & Fenichel, E. (Eds.). (1997). *The DC:0–3 casebook: A guide to the use of 0 to 3's diagnostic classification of mental health and developmental disorders of infancy and early childhood in assessment and treatment planning*. Washington, DC: Zero to Three, National Center for Infants, Toddlers and Families.

Osofsky, J. D., & Fitzgerald, H. E. (Eds.). (2000). *WAIMH handbook of infant mental health*. New York: Wiley & Sons.

Radloff, L. S. (1977). The CES-D scale: A self-report depression scale for research in the general population. *Applied Psychological Measurement, 9*, 385–401.

Rutter, M., & Gould, M. (1985). Classification. In M. Rutter, A. H. Tuma, & I. S. Lann (Eds.), *Assessment and diagnosis in child psychopathology* (pp. 437–452). New York: Guilford Press.

Rutter, M., & Tuma, A. (1988). Assessment and diagnosis in child psychopathology. In M. Rutter, A. Tuma, & M. Hussein (Eds.), *Assessment and diagnosis in child psychopathology* (pp. 437–452). New York: Guilford Press.

Sameroff, A. J., & Emde, R. N. (Eds.). (1989). *Relationship disturbances in early childhood: A developmental approach*. New York: Basic Books.

Scheeringa, M. S., & Zeanah, C. H. (1995). Symptom differences in traumatized infants and young children. *Infant Mental Health Journal, 16*, 259–270.

Scheeringa, M., Zeanah, C. H., Drell, M. J., & Larrieu, J. A. (1995). Two approaches to the diagnosis of posttraumatic stress disorder in infancy and early childhood. *Journal of the
American Academy of Child and Adolescent
Psychiatry, 34*(5), 694.

Wieder, S., & Greenspan, S. (1992). An integration
of developmental-structuralist and mediated
learning experience (MLE) approaches to
learning. *International Journal of Cognitive Education and Mediated Learning, 2*(3), 210–223.

Zeanah, C. H., Jr. (Ed.). (2000). *Handbook of infant
mental health* (2nd ed., pp. 548–558). New
York: Guilford Press.

Zero to Three, National Center for Clinical Infant
Programs (1994). *Diagnostic classification of mental health and developmental disorders of infancy
and early childhood.* Arlington, VA: Author.

9

Empirically Based Assessment and Taxonomy: Applications to Infants and Toddlers

Thomas M. Achenbach
Leslie A. Rescorla

This chapter describes applications of empirically based assessment to young children. It explains and illustrates a paradigm that has been applied to assessment of adaptive and maladaptive functioning in many developmental periods. Certain principles of the paradigm are similar across developmental periods, but the specific assessment procedures, aspects of functioning, sources of data, and applications vary with the developmental period. We first outline some developmental issues in assessment. We then discuss the historical context that has engendered the empirically based assessment paradigm. Thereafter, we present challenges for assessing young children, how the empirically based paradigm meets these challenges, and how this paradigm relates to assessment according to diagnostic categories. We also outline clinical applications, future extensions, and limitations of the paradigm.

DEVELOPMENTAL ISSUES

To advance research and practice, mental health assessment must take account of developmental differences in adaptive functioning, as well as developmental sequences for transitions from one level of functioning to another. Young children are highly variable in their functioning across time, situational context, and interaction partners. Because they have less self-control and self-awareness than older children, young children are more reactive both to their environments and to their bodily states. This means that their behavior in one context at one point in time, such as during a clinical examination, may be less representative of their typical functioning than is true for older children or adults.

Although young children can communicate via gestures, words, body language, and play, they cannot contribute to the assessment process in the same ways as older children. It is therefore essential to obtain the perspectives of adults who observe the children over extended periods at home and in other contexts.

Early childhood is marked by dramatic developmental changes in language, motor skills, control of physical functions, play, emotional regulation, and interpersonal interactions. However, children differ greatly in their developmental progress. Instruments for assessing young children therefore need to be multidimensional in order to capture diverse aspects of functioning. In addition, assessment instruments need to be standardized, quantified, and normed, so that a child can be compared to representative samples of children of the same age and gender across various domains of functioning. However, assessment also needs to be flexible to take account of variations in children's functioning, readiness to interact, and adaptation to particular contexts.

HISTORICAL PERSPECTIVES ON EMPIRICALLY BASED ASSESSMENT

Mental health assessment has long been linked to psychiatric diagnosis. In the version of the psychiatric diagnostic model embodied in the American Psychiatric Association's (1994) *Diagnostic and Statistical Manual of Mental Disorders*, Fourth Edition (*DSM-IV*), a key function of assessment is to assign cases to categories that are defined by diagnostic criteria.

Concepts of childhood disorders have often been shaped by adult diagnostic categories, many of which originated in the 19th century (Kraepelin, 1883). Examples of categories that originated in the 19th century include major depression, schizophrenia, bipolar disorders, and obsessive-compulsive disorders. As attention to particular kinds of child psychopathology has increased, adult diagnostic categories have provided models for conceptualizing many childhood disorders. For example, when childhood depressive disorders became accepted in the 1970s, they tended to be viewed in terms of criteria for adult depressive disorders, without much allowance for developmental differences (Carlson & Cantwell, 1982; Schulterbrandt & Raskin, 1977).

One of the first diagnostic categories specific to very young children was early infantile autism (Kanner, 1943). Recognition of the many variations and degrees of autistic phenomena has now spawned increasing use of autistic-spectrum diagnoses such as Asperger's disorder and pervasive developmental disorder not otherwise specified (PDD-NOS; American Psychiatric Association, 1994). In addition to PDD, *DSM-IV* categorizes early psychopathology in terms of Rett's disorder,

feeding disorders, and reactive attachment disorder. A more differentiated diagnostic classification for disorders of infants and young children has been published by Zero to Three (1994).

Because third-party payers typically require diagnoses to justify services, *DSM* diagnoses designed for older children and adults are often applied to young children whose problems do not match early childhood diagnostic categories such as PDD. Examples include attention-deficit/hyperactivity disorder (ADHD), oppositional defiant disorder (ODD), generalized anxiety disorder (GAD), and even bipolar disorders. Although such disorders may in fact occur in young children, the relevance, validity, and reliability of *DSM* criteria for these disorders need to be tested and compared with alternative ways of understanding young children's problems. For example, systematic research is needed on the prevalence, patterning, and discriminative power of the symptoms that the *DSM* uses to define early childhood disorders.

NEED FOR BETTER ASSESSMENT OF YOUNG CHILDREN

Assessment of young children's mental health is still in an early stage of development. Major challenges include: standardizing assessment procedures, delineating syndromes, identifying adaptive competencies, validating diagnostic criteria, determining prevalence rates, and testing clinical cutoff points. Improved assessment is urgently needed for the following reasons:

1. To evaluate children who are exposed to various risks, such as prenatal exposure to substances, loss of parents, parental psychopathology, neglect, abuse, and poor nutrition.
2. To provide early screening and services for conditions that may interfere with development and learning.
3. To understand apparent surges in the prevalence of PDD phenomena.
4. To evaluate the use of psychoactive medications with children below the ages for which the effects of such medications have been adequately studied.

To help young children, we need assessment methods that can be applied in standardized ways to diverse children evaluated in diverse contexts for diverse purposes. The methods need to be usable by professionals having different kinds of training and playing different roles with respect to the children. Assessment must be able to take account of possible variations related to ethnicity, family constellations, socioeconomic status (SES), languages spoken in the home, risk factors, and reasons for needing evaluation. The contexts may include hospitals, pediatric practices, early education, and child and family service. They may also include children's biological and adoptive families, foster homes, day care, programs for immigrants and refugees, forensic situations involving abuse, neglect, or custody issues, and mental health services. The purposes may include assessment for planning therapeutic and educational interventions, deciding on placements, and preventing maladaptive development. Other purposes include resolution of legal and custody issues, and research on etiologies, correlates, interventions, and outcomes. The professionals may include nurses, educators, child development specialists, pediatricians, child and family service workers, social workers, psychiatrists, and psychologists.

In addition to challenges presented by the diversity of children, contexts, purposes, and professionals, there are formidable challenges in specifying (a) what should be assessed, (b) what is feasible to assess in practical and cost-effective ways, (c) how to assess it, and (d) how to communicate findings. Young children's behavior may change from one context and interaction partner to another. It also changes rapidly with development. Problems that may be evident in one context at one point in time may appear to be quite different in other contexts at other points in time. Furthermore, young children cannot be expected to report on their own functioning. Direct observations of the children's behavior and reports by parents, caregivers, and preschool teachers are thus essential for assessment.

Various specialized assessment procedures may be needed for particular conditions. For example, assessment of autism may require different procedures than assessment of ODD. Specialized procedures may also be needed when investigating possible sexual abuse. However, in addition to specialized procedures, broadly applicable standardized procedures are needed to help diverse professionals communicate about diverse children assessed under diverse conditions. This is especially important in the screening phase of assessment, when we need to cast a wide net to detect possible problems. Alternatives to the current *DSM* diagnostic categories are needed to capture actual patterns of maladaptive functioning manifested by young children. The following sections present the empirically based paradigm for meeting these needs.

THE EMPIRICALLY BASED PARADIGM

Two primary objectives of the empirically based paradigm are: (a) to provide reliable and valid procedures for assessing behavioral and emotional problems, and (b) to identify patterns of co-occurring problems that can provide a basis for taxonomic constructs.

The empirically based paradigm employs large pools of descriptive items rated by people who see the subjects under everyday conditions, such as parents and teachers (Achenbach & McConaughy, 1997). For young children, ratings can be obtained from parents, day care providers, home-based caregivers, Head Start teachers, foster parents, and nursery school teachers. The empirically based paradigm also provides instruments for assessing adults, which can be especially useful for comprehensive family assessment that includes the parents of young children (Achenbach & Rescorla, 2003). Assessment of parents can help to identify strengths and problems in the family that may affect the child and may be important to consider in designing interventions. Because interventions usually involve parents, it is also important to evaluate outcomes by reassessing parents, as well as their children.

Constructing Assessment Instruments

In the first stage of constructing empirically based instruments, candidate items are selected by reviewing the literature on problems and adaptive functioning relevant to the developmental period to be assessed. Candidate items are also generated by consulting mental health professionals and the kinds of informants for whom the items are intended, such as parents and teachers. Rating instruments comprising the candidate items are then pilot tested by having them completed for samples of subjects who are considered to be functioning within the normal range and also for various clinical samples. Revisions are made on the basis of psychometric findings and rater comments. Further pilot editions are then tested and iteratively refined.

After successive pilot editions culminate in a satisfactory instrument, the instrument is used to assess large samples that are representative of relevant populations. The instrument is also used to assess large clinical samples. The item scores obtained by subjects in these samples are then analyzed to construct scales that reflect actual patterns of co-occurring problems, as described next.

The Bottom-Up Approach to Deriving Syndromes

The empirically based paradigm can be thought of as working from the bottom up. As illustrated in figure 9.1, the bottom-up approach starts with scores for specific problem items (or symptoms) obtained for large samples of individuals who have numerous problems or have been referred for clinical services. In our applications of the empirically based paradigm, items rated by infor-

mants such as parents and teachers are typically scored as 0 = not true, 1 = somewhat or sometimes true, and 2 = very true or often true. Multivariate statistical analyses, such as factor analysis, are then applied to the quantitative associations among problem items in order to identify groups of problems that tend to occur together. The groups of problem items are called syndromes in the sense of "things that go together." (The original Greek meaning of *syndrome* was "the act of running together.") In the bottom-up approach, syndromes are thus sets of problems (or symptoms) that are empirically found to co-occur.

Some syndromes may be caused primarily by experiential factors. Others may be caused primarily by genetic and other physical factors. And still others may reflect combinations of experiential and physical factors. Whatever their causes, the empirically based syndromes reveal patterns of problems that provide starting places for describing children's functioning, for identifying areas in which children have few or many problems, and for evaluating outcomes. The syndromes also provide foci for research on etiology, developmental course, and responsiveness to particular interventions.

A child's score on a syndrome is obtained by summing the ratings for the items that make up the syndrome. To provide a basis for judging the degree of deviance indicated by a particular syndrome score, the rating form is used to assess a

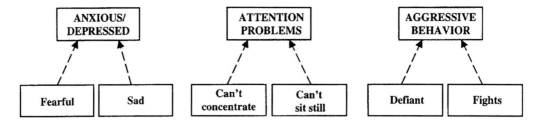

Derives syndromes from statistical associations among problems

Starts with data on problems

Figure 9.1 The bottom-up approach to assessment and taxonomy.

large representative sample of children. The distributions of scores in this normative sample are then used to provide a basis for judging how a particular child's scores on each syndrome compare with the scores of typical peers. To make it easy for users to view all of a child's scale scores and item scores, the scores are displayed on profiles. Table 9.1 summarizes the main features of the empirically based paradigm.

The empirically based approach emphasizes the importance of cross-informant comparisons. Scores derived from different informants are systematically compared in order to reveal consistencies and discrepancies in children's functioning across settings. Profiles describing children's functioning in relation to normative samples can also guide treatment efforts, because they highlight which problems deviate most from norms for children of the same age and gender.

The Top-Down Approach

The bottom-up approach contrasts with the top-down approach that has been used to construct diagnostic categories for *DSM-III*, *DSM-III-R*, and *DSM-IV* (American Psychiatric Association, 1980, 1987, 1994). In the top-down approach, committees of experts negotiate diagnostic categories and then select criteria that determine which individuals qualify for each diagnosis. Although field trials have been conducted for some diagnostic categories, the categories have not been derived empirically from data on relevant samples of subjects. Furthermore, other than IQ tests for diagnosing mental retardation, the *DSM* does not specify assessment operations for determining whether a particular child meets criteria for particular diagnoses (Widiger & Clark, 2000). Especially problematic for assessing children, the *DSM* does not specify how to aggregate data from different informants, such as when a father says his child is too fearful, the mother says the child is no different than other 3-year-olds, the Head Start teacher says the child is very disturbed by changes in routine, and the day care provider says the child worries a lot.

Although the *DSM*'s categories are constructed from the top down, many of the child categories published since 1980 have resembled empirically based syndromes in being defined in terms of specific problems, without imputing particular etiologies (American Psychiatric Association, 1980, 1987, 1994). Furthermore, numerous studies have shown statistically significant associations between some *DSM* diagnoses and certain empirically based syndromes. Some of these studies have reported associations for particular classes of disorders, such as depression (Rey & Morris-Yates, 1992) and disruptive disorders (Arend, Lavigne, Rosenbaum, Binns, & Christoffel, 1996). Other studies have reported associations for broader arrays of disorders (Edelbrock & Costello, 1988; Gould, Bird, & Jaramillo, 1993; Kasius, Ferdinand, van den Berg, & Verhulst, 1997; Weinstein, Noam, Grimes, Stone, & Schwab-Stone, 1990). Despite convergence between some *DSM* categories and empirically based syndromes, however, further progress hinges on using data more systematically to derive diagnostic constructs rather than using data primarily for post hoc ratification of official diagnostic criteria.

Table 9.1 Main Features of the Empirically Based Paradigm

1. Starts with pools of candidate items.
2. Rating instruments comprising the items are iteratively pilot tested and refined.
3. Instruments are used to assess large samples of individuals.
4. The item scores are analyzed to derive syndrome scales that reflect patterns of co-occurring problems.
5. The syndrome scales are displayed on profiles in relation to normative distributions of scores.

APPLICATIONS OF THE EMPIRICALLY BASED PARADIGM TO YOUNG CHILDREN

The empirically based paradigm was first applied to young children when the Child Behavior Checklist (CBCL) for Ages 2–3 was constructed in 1981 for assessment of low birthweight children (see Achenbach, Edelbrock, & Howell, 1987). This was followed by the Caregiver-Teacher Report Form for Ages 2–5 (C-TRF; Achenbach, 1997).

In 2000, we published revisions of these instruments (Achenbach & Rescorla, 2000) that improved on the previous versions in the following ways: (a) the age range of both the CBCL and the C-TRF were extended so that both forms now span ages 1½–5; (b) normative data were collected for both forms as part of the 1999 National Survey of Children, Youths, and Adults; (c) the Language Development Survey (LDS; Rescorla, 1989), a parent-report screening tool for language delay, was added to the CBCL/ 1½–5; (d) new empirically based scales were developed for the CBCL/1½–5 and C-TRF; (e) new *DSM*-oriented scales were constructed for both instruments; and (f) new computerized scoring programs were developed to provide cross-informant comparisons for up to eight forms per child. The Achenbach System of Empirically Based Assessment (ASEBA) preschool instruments have been used in over 200 published studies (listed by Bérubé & Achenbach, 2004). In the following sections, we describe the development of the instruments and summarize how they can be used to assess young children.

The Child Behavior Checklist for Ages 1½–5 and the Caregiver-Teacher Report Form

The CBCL/1½–5 is completed by parents, parent surrogates, and others who see children in homelike contexts. Two items from the CBCL/ 2–3 (Achenbach, 1992) were replaced by new items for the CBCL/1½–5. The C-TRF is completed by day care providers and preschool teachers (Achenbach & Rescorla, 2000). No items were changed from the C-TRF/2–5 (Achenbach, 1997). The CBCL/1½–5 and the C-TRF have 82 similar problem items, plus 17 items that are specific to home versus day care and preschool contexts, and an open-ended item for adding other problems that are not listed on the forms. Both forms request respondents to rate each item as 0 = not true, 1 = somewhat or sometimes true, or 2 = very true or often true of the child now or within the past 2 months.

Both forms also request descriptions of behavior, illnesses, disabilities, what concerns the respondent most about the child, and the best things about the child. The forms thus obtain not only quantitative scores for each problem item, but also descriptions of the child's functioning in the respondent's own words. Each form requires only fifth-grade reading skills and can be completed independently by most respondents in about 10 minutes. If there are questions about a respondent's ability to complete a form independently, the following procedure is recommended: An interviewer hands the respondent the form while retaining a second copy. The interviewer then says, "I'll read you the questions on this form and I'll write down your answers." Respondents with adequate reading skills will often start answering without waiting for the questions to be read. However, for respondents who cannot read well, this procedure avoids embarrassment while maintaining the standardization of the assessment process.

The Language Development Survey

Because language is so important for young children's adaptive development, the CBCL/1½–5 includes the LDS (Rescorla, 1989). The LDS requests respondents to provide information about possible risk factors for language delays, to report five of the child's best word combinations if the child is combining words, and to circle on a 310-word vocabulary list the words used by the child. The average length of children's word combinations and the number of vocabulary words reported by parents are scored in relation to national norms for children within particular age ranges (Achenbach & Rescorla, 2000).

Multiple studies have demonstrated the ability of the LDS to identify language delays that have been corroborated by other assessment procedures (e.g., Klee et al., 1998; Rescorla & Alley, 2001). Inclusion of the LDS with the CBCL/ 1½–5 makes it easy to simultaneously determine whether children who are suspected of having language delays are indeed delayed and whether they are also reported to have more behavioral/ emotional problems than normative samples of peers. Conversely, when assessing behavioral/ emotional problems, practitioners can obtain data on language delays simultaneously with data on behavioral/emotional problems.

Figure 9.2 displays the scores obtained from the LDS completed for 2-year-old Jamie by his mother. Jamie's mother reported word combina-

CBCL/1.5-5 Language Development Survey for Boys

ID: P76543-001
Name: Jamie S. Barnes
Clinician: Dr. Ames

Gender: Male
Age: 25 months

Date Filled: 12/06/00
Birth Date: 11/05/98
Agency: CMCH
Verified: Yes

Informant: Samantha Barnes
Relationship: Mother

I.	Born early?	No
II.	Birth weight?	8 lb 0 oz
III.	Ear infections?	0-2

IV.	Other language spoken?	No
V.	Delayed speech in family?	No
VI.	Worried about development?	Yes
VII.	Says words spontaneously?	Yes
VIII.	Combines words?	Yes

Average Length Of Phrases	2.5

Vocabulary Score	74

Vocabulary Score

Vocabulary Score displayed only for ages 18-23 months, 24-29 months, and 30-35 months.

	18-23 months	24-29 months	30-35 months
Total Words		74	
Percentile		25	

Scores <= 15th percentile suggest delayed vocabulary development.

Average Length Of Phrases

Average Length of Phrases displayed only for ages 24-29 months and 30-35 months.

	24-29 months	30-35 months
Avg. Length	2.50	
Percentile	30	

Scores <= 20th percentile suggest delayed phrase development.

Figure 9.2 Language Development Survey (LDS) scores for 2-year-old Jamie.

tions that averaged 2.50 words. This score was at the 30th percentile for children of Jamie's age. Jamie's mother also reported 74 vocabulary words, which scored at the 25th percentile. Compared to norms for his age, Jamie's scores for word combinations and vocabulary were thus somewhat low but in the normal range.

Empirically Based Syndromes for Young Children

The procedures outlined in table 9.1 were used to identify syndromes of co-occurring problems via factor analyses of the CBCL/1½–5 and C-TRF (Achenbach & Rescorla, 2000). To identify syndromes, it is necessary to analyze forms on which substantial numbers of problems are endorsed. We therefore included all children from the 1999 National Survey sample scoring above the median for total problems, whether or not they had been referred for mental health services. We also included many other children from clinical and nonclinical settings whose total problems scores were at or above the National Survey median (total N for factor analyses of the CBCL/1½–5 = 1,728; for the C-TRF = 1,113). Analyses conducted for each gender separately on each instrument identified the following six syndromes for both genders scored on both instruments: aggressive behavior, anxious/depressed, attention problems, emotionally reactive, somatic complaints, and withdrawn. In addition, analyses of the CBCL/1½–5 identified a syndrome designated as sleep problems, which consists of sleep-related items that are not assessed by the C-TRF.

Profiles of Syndromes

A child's score for each item of each syndrome and the total score for each syndrome are displayed on a profile, as shown for 2-year-old Jamie in figure 9.3. The profile displays Jamie's scores in relation to scores for a national normative sample of children. The normative sample for the CBCL/1½–5 consisted of 700 children from the 1999 National Survey who had not been referred for mental health or special education services in the preceding 12 months. The broken lines printed across the profile indicate a normal range, a borderline clinical range, and a clinical range. Scores above the top broken line are in the clinical range, that is, above the 97th percentile of scores obtained by children in the national normative sample. Scores below the bottom broken line are in the normal range, that is, below the 93rd percentile of scores obtained by children in the national normative sample. Scores between the broken lines are in the borderline clinical range, that is, the 93rd through 97th percentiles.

By looking at the profile in figure 9.3, you can see that Jamie's mother's ratings yielded scores in the clinical range (above the top broken line) on the emotionally reactive, sleep problems, and attention problems syndromes. Her ratings yielded a score in the borderline clinical range (between the broken lines) on the anxious/depressed syndrome. And her ratings yielded scores in the normal range (below the bottom broken line) on the somatic complaints, withdrawn, and aggressive behavior syndromes.

Although the profile in figure 9.3 documents Jamie's mother's views of his problems in relation to national norms, comprehensive assessment requires data from multiple sources, as addressed in the following section.

CROSS-INFORMANT COMPARISONS

Children often behave differently in different settings and with different interaction partners. Furthermore, two people seeing the same behavior may report it differently. Meta-analyses of correlations between scores obtained from informants' reports of problems for 1½- to 19-year-olds found an average correlation of .60 between pairs of informants who play similar roles with respect to children, such as pairs of parents and pairs of teachers (Achenbach, McConaughy, & Howell, 1987). Between informants who play different roles with respect to children, such as parents versus teachers and teachers versus mental health workers, the correlations averaged .28.

For the recent revisions of the empirically based preschool instruments, we found mean correlations across all scales of .61 between pairs of parents completing the CBCL/1½–5, .65 between pairs of caregivers and teachers completing the C-TRF, and .40 between parents completing

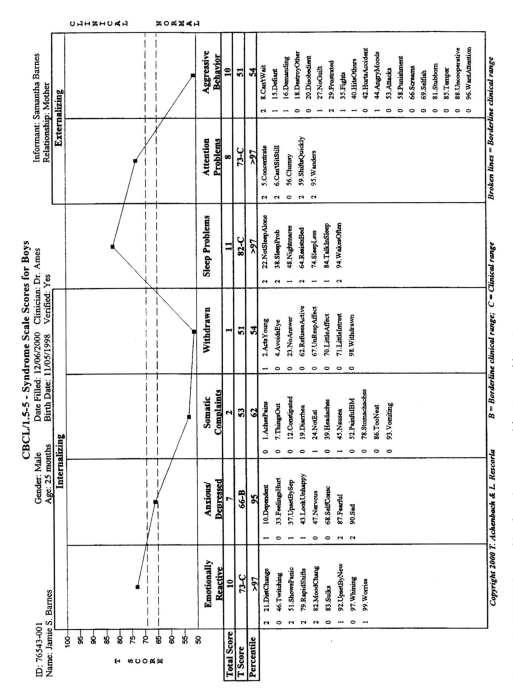

Figure 9.3 CBCL/1½–5 profile of syndromes scored for 2-year-old Jamie.

the CBCL/1½–5 and caregivers or teachers completing the C-TRF. For total problems scores, the mean cross-informant correlations were .65, .72, and .50, respectively (Achenbach & Rescorla, 2000).

The Importance of Cross-Informant Comparisons

Even though reports by each kind of informant may be reliable and valid in their own right, the modest agreement among informants indicates that no single informant can substitute for all others. Because children's behavior varies from one context and interaction partner to another, and because informants differ in what they notice, remember, and report, comprehensive assessment requires data from multiple informants.

The CBCL/1½–5 and C-TRF forms enable users to obtain data in parallel ways from each parent, other adults who live with the child, day care providers, and preschool teachers. To help users quickly and efficiently compare multiple reports for each child, software for scoring the forms prints profiles from up to eight CBCL/1½–5 and C-TRF forms per child. Users can look at the profiles to identify important similarities and differences in their patterns and elevations of scale scores. In addition, the software prints correlations between ratings by each pair of informants and compares these correlations with correlations obtained for large reference samples of similar pairs of informants. This enables users to evaluate how well particular informants agree with one another in rating a particular child. The software also prints side-by-side comparisons of the scores obtained from each informant on each item and each scale. Users can thus see at a glance the items and scales on which there are consistencies versus inconsistencies among the informants.

Illustration of Side-By-Side Comparisons of Syndrome Scores

As an example, figure 9.4 illustrates cross-informant comparisons of syndrome scale scores obtained from CBCL/1½–5 forms completed by Jamie's mother, father, and grandmother, plus C-TRF forms completed by his day care provider and preschool teacher. By looking at figure 9.4, you can see that all five informants scored Jamie

in the clinical range on the attention problems syndrome. All three informants who live with Jamie also scored him in the clinical or borderline clinical range on the CBCL/1½–5 sleep problems syndrome, which is not scored on the C-TRF. On the emotionally reactive syndrome, Jamie's mother scored him in the clinical range, but the other four informants scored him in the high normal or borderline clinical range. On the anxious/depressed syndrome, all informants scored Jamie in the high normal or borderline clinical range, whereas they all scored him in the normal range on the somatic complaints, withdrawn, and aggressive behavior syndromes.

The bar graphs in figure 9.4 indicate that adults who play different roles and see Jamie in different contexts all reported more problems from the attention problems syndrome than were reported for most boys in the national normative samples for the CBCL/1½–5 and C-TRF. In addition, the three adults who live with Jamie all reported more sleep problems than were reported for most boys in the CBCL/1½–5 national normative sample. There is thus consistent evidence that Jamie has high enough levels of attention problems and sleep problems to warrant professional help. On the other hand, no informant's ratings placed Jamie above the normal range on the somatic complaints, withdrawn, or aggressive behavior syndromes. There is thus consistent evidence that Jamie does not need special help in these areas.

The cross-informant comparisons in figure 9.4 reveal a more mixed picture with respect to the emotionally reactive and anxious/depressed syndromes. Jamie's mother rated him in the clinical range on the emotionally reactive syndrome, whereas the other informants rated him in the borderline or high normal ranges. By looking at another page of the printout of the cross-informant comparisons (not shown), we can view side-by-side comparisons of all informants' ratings of each item on each scale. There we would see that Jamie's mother's ratings of items of the emotionally reactive syndrome included scores of 2 (very true or often true) for items 21 (Disturbed by any change in routine), 51 (Shows panic for no good reason), 79 (Rapid shifts between sadness and excitement), and 82 (Sudden changes in mood or feelings). Her ratings also included scores of 1

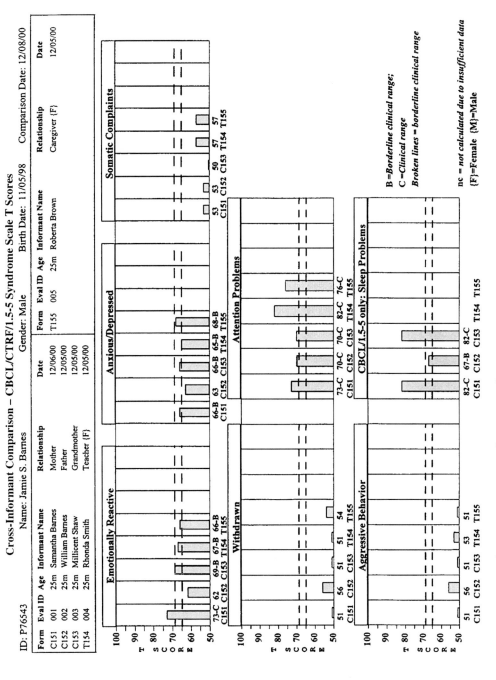

Figure 9.4 Cross-informant comparisons of Jamie's syndrome scores.

(somewhat or sometimes true) for items 92 (Upset by new people or situations) and 99 (Worries).

Although the other raters scored most of the same items as present, they rated fewer items 2 than Jamie's mother did, resulting in scores that were in the high normal or borderline ranges. This suggests that Jamie's interactions with his mother may be more intense (or that she may perceive them as being more intense) than his interactions with other people. However, combined with the high normal and borderline clinical range scores obtained from all five informants on the anxious/depressed syndrome, the findings suggest that possible affective problems should be considered in planning interventions for Jamie.

DSM-ORIENTED SCALES

Because practitioners and researchers are often expected to evaluate children's problems in terms of diagnostic categories, there is a need to link empirically based assessment with such categories. As outlined earlier, the empirically based paradigm takes a bottom-up approach whereby syndromes are derived statistically to reflect patterns of problems (many of which correspond to DSM "symptoms") that are found to co-occur in large samples of individuals rated by various kinds of informants. The DSM, by contrast, takes a top-down approach whereby experts formulate diagnostic categories and then select symptoms and other criteria for defining each category. Although numerous studies have shown statistically significant associations between DSM diagnoses and empirically based syndromes, the obtained associations vary greatly according to the basis for making DSM diagnoses, the sources of data, the particular diagnostic categories, and the analytic methods (e.g., Arend et al., 1996; Edelbrock & Costello, 1988; Gould et al., 1993; Kasius et al., 1997; Rey & Morris-Yates, 1992; Weinstein et al., 1990).

Construction of DSM-Oriented Scales

To help practitioners and researchers view the problem items of the CBCL/1½–5 and C-TRF in relation to DSM diagnostic categories as well as empirically based syndromes, we constructed DSM-oriented scales as follows (Achenbach, Dumenci, & Rescorla, 2000):

1. We asked 16 experienced child psychiatrists and psychologists from 10 cultures to rate each of the CBCL/1½–5 and C-TRF problem items as not consistent with each of nine DSM diagnostic categories; somewhat consistent; or very consistent. All the raters had published research on children's behavioral/emotional problems.
2. Raters were given the DSM criteria for guidance, but one-to-one matching of the problem items to DSM criteria was not required to justify ratings of very consistent. Problem items could thus be judged very consistent with the raters' concepts of particular DSM categories even if the DSM criteria did not include precise counterparts of the items.
3. Items that were rated as very consistent with a DSM category by at least 10 of the 16 raters (63%) were deemed to be sufficiently consistent with DSM categories to be included in the DSM-oriented scales.
4. Because of major overlaps in DSM diagnostic criteria, as well as in the obtained ratings of the problem items, the nine DSM categories were collapsed into the following five scales: Affective Problems (including major depressive disorder and dysthymic disorder); Anxiety Problems (including generalized anxiety disorder, separation anxiety disorder, and specific phobia); Attention Deficit/Hyperactivity Problems (including hyperactive-impulsive and inattentive types); Pervasive Developmental Problems (including Asperger's disorder and autistic disorder); and Oppositional Defiant Problems.
5. Separately for the CBCL/1½–5 and C-TRF, we constructed profiles for scoring the five DSM-oriented scales, which comprise the items of each form that were judged to be very consistent with the DSM categories. Because 17 items differ on the CBCL/1½–5 versus C-TRF, there are some differences between the items of the CBCL/1½–5 and C-TRF versions of the DSM-oriented scales. For example, the C-TRF version of the Attention Deficit/Hyperactivity Problems Scale has more items than the CBCL/1½–5 version, because more atten-

tion problems items are appropriate for rating by day care providers and teachers than by parents and parent surrogates.

Profiles of *DSM*-Oriented Scales

The profiles of *DSM*-oriented scales are analogous to the profiles of empirically based syndromes, as illustrated by the profile of *DSM*-oriented scales shown for 2-year-old Jamie in figure 9.5. Like the scales for the empirically based syndromes, the score for each *DSM*-oriented scale is computed by summing the 0-1-2 ratings of the items that comprise the scale. The profiles of *DSM*-oriented scales display children's scores in relation to the same national normative samples as for the empirically based scales, with percentiles, *T* scores, and normal, borderline, and clinical ranges displayed in the same way as for the empirically based scales. Users can thus view a child's functioning in terms of *DSM*-oriented scales as well as empirically based syndromes in relation to the same national norms. The profile in figure 9.5 reflects C-TRF ratings of Jamie by his day care provider.

As you can see in figure 9.5, Jamie's score on the Attention Deficit-Hyperactivity Problems Scale is in the clinical range on the *DSM*-oriented profile scored from ratings by Jamie's day care provider. This suggests that Jamie might meet criteria for a *DSM* diagnosis of ADHD, although the *DSM* ADHD criteria are really geared to older children and may not discriminate very well between 2-year-olds who do or do not have attention deficits. Figure 9.5 also shows that the day care provider's ratings placed Jamie in the borderline clinical range on the Affective Problems and Anxiety Problems scales but in the normal range on the Pervasive Developmental Problems and Oppositional Defiant Problems scales. The moderate elevations on the Affective and Anxiety Problems scales suggest that the practitioner should check the *DSM* criteria to see whether Jamie would qualify for any affective or anxiety disorder diagnoses. However, the scores in the normal range on the Pervasive Developmental and Oppositional Defiant Problems scales suggest that he would not quality for *DSM* diagnoses in these areas.

Users should keep in mind that a particular score on a *DSM*-oriented scale is not directly equivalent to a *DSM* diagnosis, because the items of the *DSM*-oriented scales do not correspond precisely to *DSM* criteria. For example, some *DSM* diagnoses have criteria for impairment, age of onset, and duration. In addition, on our *DSM*-oriented scales, both the specific items and the scale scores are quantified, whereas in the *DSM* itself, each criterion and diagnosis is based on yes-or-no judgments. Furthermore, the *DSM* criteria are the same for both genders, all ages, and all sources of data. Our *DSM*-oriented scales, by contrast, are scored in relation to norms based on children's gender, age, and on whether the data come from parent figures or from caregivers and teachers. The normed *DSM*-oriented scales illustrate ways in which future editions of the *DSM* could take account of age, gender, and informant variations.

APPLICATIONS IN SERVICE SETTINGS

The CBCL/1½–5 and C-TRF are appropriate for use in a wide variety of service settings. The standardized rating forms can be completed by people such as parents, parent surrogates, day care providers, and preschool teachers when children are evaluated in various contexts. In medical practices, for example, pediatricians, family practitioners, and nurse practitioners can have parents routinely complete the CBCL/1½–5 at home or in waiting rooms when children are brought for checkups and immunizations. Using hand scoring or computer scoring, staff members such as receptionists, clerical workers, and physician assistants can quickly generate profiles like the one displayed in figure 9.3 for 2-year-old Jamie. The profiles and completed CBCL/1½–5 forms can then be given to the practitioner who will see the child and parents.

By looking at the profile and the LDS scoring form, the practitioner can quickly see whether the child is in the normal range with respect to problem scores and language development. If the child is not in the normal range, the practitioner can use the profile and the descriptive comments written on the CBCL/1½–5 as a basis for asking the parent about the child's functioning. In cases

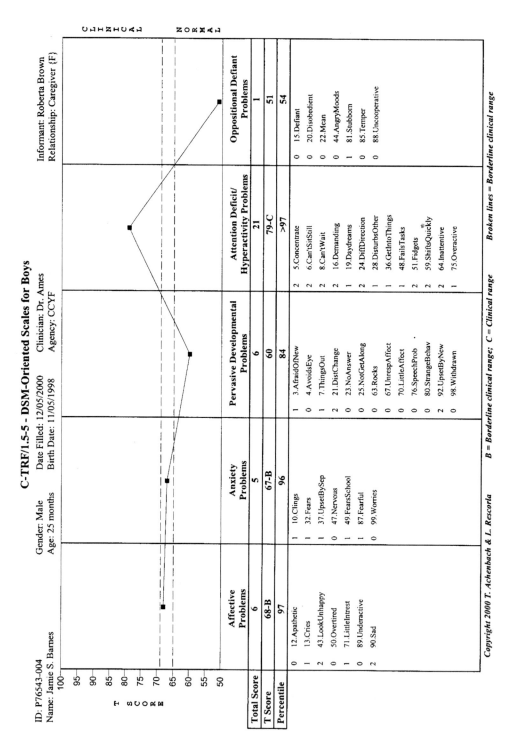

Figure 9.5 C-TRF profile of DSM-oriented scales scored for 2-year-old Jamie by his day care provider.

where parents themselves raise questions about their child's functioning, the practitioner can use the completed CBCL/1½–5 and profile as a basis for answering questions and deciding whether further evaluation is needed.

As an example, if a parent is concerned about a child's sleep problems or attention problems, the practitioner can quickly see whether the child's score on the sleep problems or attention problems syndrome is in the normal, borderline, or clinical range. The practitioner can then decide whether reassurance and advice concerning the particular problems are appropriate or whether further evaluation is warranted. Further evaluation may include having another family member complete the CBCL/1½–5 or having day care providers and preschool teachers complete the C-TRF. If syndrome scores are very elevated or if there is evidence for deviance in multiple areas, the practitioner may elect to refer the family to a specialist. With parents' consent, the completed CBCL/1½–5, LDS, and profile forms can be sent to the specialist to provide intake information.

Other applications include use of the empirically based assessment instruments as part of the intake and evaluation process in special education, child development, and mental health settings. Whether referrals arise from concerns about language development, cognitive functioning, stressful experiences such as abuse or neglect, or behavior problems, it is always helpful to have a standardized picture of the child's behavioral and emotional problems and language development, as seen by people who live with the child. Such a picture is also essential for evaluations related to adoption and foster placement. The options for scoring DSM-oriented scales from the same forms as the empirically based syndromes additionally provide practitioners with a basis for evaluating children in terms of DSM diagnoses.

READMINISTRATION OF FORMS

In addition to providing initial assessment data, the CBCL/1½–5, LDS, and C-TRF can be readministered during and after interventions to evaluate changes and outcomes, as exemplified in studies of interventions for low-birthweight children from low-SES families (Brooks-Gunn et al.,

1994) and for children at-risk because of psychosocial adversities (Kitzman et al., 1997). These studies have demonstrated the sensitivity of empirically based scales to the effects of interventions. At each administration of the forms, users can evaluate children's functioning in terms of the LDS, each of the 99 specific problem items, each syndrome and DSM-oriented scale, broadband internalizing and externalizing groupings of syndromes, and total problems scores. Any and all of these levels can be used to target interventions and to evaluate changes. For example, the profiles scored from the forms completed for 2-year-old Jamie indicated needs for help with attention problems and sleep problems. However, the evidence for affective problems also suggested that these should not be ignored. If interventions focus only on Jamie's attention problems and/or sleep problems, treatments for these problems may unwittingly neglect or even exacerbate Jamie's possible affective problems. Similarly, if reassessments during and after the interventions focus only on attention and/or sleep problems, lack of improvement or even worsening in other areas might not be detected.

RESEARCH APPLICATIONS

To advance knowledge and services related to assessment of mental disorders in young children, many kinds of research are needed. Research requires reliable and valid assessment procedures for determining what problems each child has relative to norms for the child's age and gender and for comparing reports by different informants with each other. Informants' reports can also be compared to information obtained via clinical examinations and behavioral observations. Because the significance of early problems depends partly on how they relate to later development and to long-term outcomes, it is important for assessment of early functioning to be readily analyzable in relation to assessment of later functioning.

School-Age Counterparts of the Preschool Instruments

The CBCL/1½–5 and C-TRF have counterpart instruments for assessing school-age children and adolescents. The Child Behavior Checklist for Ages 6–18 (CBCL/6–18; Achenbach & Rescorla, 2001) is completed by parents and surrogates to report their children's competencies and problems, many of which have counterparts on the CBCL/1½–5. Similarly, the Teacher's Report Form for Ages 6–18 (TRF; Achenbach & Rescorla, 2001) is completed by teachers to report students' adaptive functioning and problems, many of which have counterparts on the C-TRF. The CBCL/6–18 and TRF are scored on profiles that display empirically based syndromes derived from factor analyses of large samples of school-age children. *DSM*-oriented scales analogous to those for the preschool instruments are also scored on profiles for the school-age instruments. The profiles for both the syndromes and the *DSM*-oriented scales display scores in relation to national norms for the child's age and gender, according to CBCL ratings by parents and TRF ratings by teachers.

Longitudinal Analyses of Empirically Based Syndromes

Because empirically based syndromes are scored quantitatively from items that are tailored to particular developmental periods, the empirically based instruments can be used to test predictive relations to long-term developmental patterns and outcomes. This can be done by performing longitudinal analyses of relations between early and later scores on the empirically based syndromes.

As an example of longitudinal analyses of this sort, the preschool CBCL was used in a study of children who had participated in an experimental intervention designed to facilitate the development of low-birthweight infants (Achenbach, Howell, Aoki, & Rauh, 1993). The intervention was implemented by a pediatric nurse who worked with the infants and their mothers during seven sessions before the infants left the hospital, followed by home visits at 3, 14, 30, and 90 days after discharge from the hospital. The subjects included low-birthweight infants who had been randomly assigned to either the intervention or to a control condition, plus a normal-birthweight comparison group.

As part of a long-term outcome evaluation, the children were assessed at ages 2 and 3 years by having parents complete the preschool CBCL. At later ages up to 9 years, the children were assessed by having parents complete the CBCL/6–18. The longitudinal correlations between scores for the aggressive behavior syndrome at age 2 and later ages were substantial, ranging from .65 between ages 2 and 4 to .50 between ages 2 and 9 (Achenbach & Rescorla, 2001). There is considerable evidence from other sources that the empirically based aggressive behavior syndrome reflects a traitlike pattern that is stable over long periods of development from childhood to adulthood, even though some of the specific behaviors change (Achenbach, Howell, McConaughy, & Stanger, 1995; Stanger, Achenbach, & Verhulst, 1997). Multiple studies have reported significant biochemical correlates and high heritability for the CBCL aggressive behavior syndrome (Birmaher et al., 1990; Edelbrock et al., 1995; Gabel et al., 1993; Hanna, Yuwiler, & Coates, 1995; Scerbo & Kolko, 1994; Schmitz, Fulker, & Mrazek, 1995; Stoff, Pollock, Vitiello, Behar, & Bridger, 1987; van den Oord, Boomsma, & Verhulst, 1994).

Another finding from the study of low-birthweight children is shown in figure 9.6, which depicts scores on the TRF attention problems syndrome for the three groups of children at ages 7 and 9 years. As figure 9.6 shows, there was a divergence between attention problems scores for the low-birthweight children who received the experimental intervention versus the low-birthweight control children. This divergence reflects the fact that TRF attention problem scores declined from age 7 to 9 for the intervention children. For the control children, by contrast, attention problems scores increased from age 7 to 9. By age 9, the intervention children's attention problems scores were significantly ($p = .002$) lower than the control children's scores.

It may seem surprising that a divergence between attention problems scores could become significant at age 9 following an intervention that occurred in the first postnatal months. However, the divergence between attention problems scores mirrored a divergence in Kaufman Achievement Test scores that occurred from ages 7 to 9, with the achievement scores becoming significantly ($p = .02$) higher for the intervention than the control children at age 9.

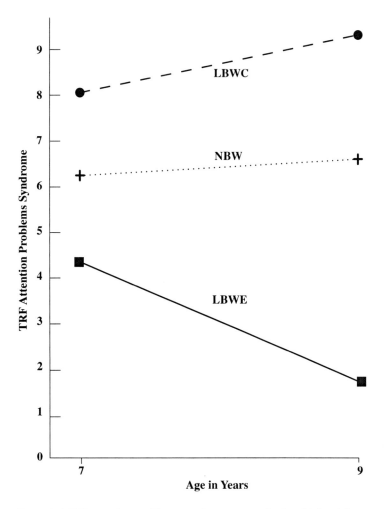

Figure 9.6 TRF attention problems syndrome scores for low birthweight experimental (LBWE), low birthweight control (LBWC), and normal birthweight (NBW) children.

Measures of cognitive ability, including the McCarthy (1972) Scales and the Kaufman Assessment Battery (Kaufman & Kaufman, 1983), also showed significant divergence between the intervention and control children through age 9, although the divergence started much earlier. The important point is that the empirically derived attention problems syndrome rated by teachers was sensitive to long-term effects of an infant intervention program in ways that were analogous to individually administered achievement and ability tests.

POTENTIAL APPLICATIONS TO INFANTS

Although the empirically based approach has not yet been applied to children below 18 months of age, it could potentially be extended to infants and young toddlers. Like older children, infants show important individual differences in their functioning. These individual differences are often explained in terms of infant temperament. For example, some infants are "easy" to handle, while others are deemed "difficult," "colicky," "poorly regulated," or "slow to warm up." As with older children, the same behavior may be perceived and experienced quite differently by different observers. For example, the same infant might be perceived as calm, serene, and self-contained by one parent and as underactive, passive, and insufficiently responsive by another parent. Furthermore, as is the case with older children, these variations in infants' behavioral and emotional characteristics affect their caregivers. For example, more difficult or more sensitive babies may be harder to parent and may increase parental stress. In addition, differences in caregivers' behavior can also affect infants' behavior, such as vocalization, crying, smiling, and physical exploration.

Most people who work with infants and toddlers recognize that early behavioral characteristics can be transient. That is, a child who is more cranky, fearful, or resistant than most other 12-month-olds may look quite normal by age 3, just as a hyperactive, noncompliant 3-year-old or inhibited, anxious 4-year-old may not show these problems by age 6. On the other hand, developmental research on psychopathology demonstrates that characteristics identified on the empirically based instruments as early as ages 2 and 3 predict *DSM-IV* diagnoses many years later (e.g., Mesman & Koot, 2001).

To apply the empirically based paradigm to infants, we could construct pools of items that sample various infant characteristics that can be judged by relevant informants. Candidate items that are appropriate for infants can be selected from existing instruments for toddlers, as well as from surveys of parents, health care providers, mental health workers, and day care providers. Many such items already exist on various instruments. The CBCL/1½–5 has about 40 items that may be appropriate for assessing infants. The items should be pilot tested with parents and parent surrogates as informants, because they observe infants under the greatest variety of conditions. To take account of infants' rapid development and their reactivity to environmental changes, relatively short rating periods would be needed, perhaps 2, 3, or 4 weeks.

Informants other than parents would also be needed for infant assessment. Primary health care providers would probably be the most widely available nonparental informants. However, because health care providers cannot be expected to observe infants over such diverse occasions as parents, the items rated by health care providers should be keyed to the office conditions under which they typically see children.

A pool of items intermediate between those designed for parents and those designed for office use could be created for home visitors and for day care providers. Although these kinds of informants would not be as universally available as parents and office-based providers, they would be useful additional sources of data when they are available.

Empirically based assessment is intended to supplement rather than to substitute for other kinds of assessment, such as the Brazelton and Nugent (1995) Scales, Bayley (1993) Scales, measures of temperament (Kagan, 1998; Rothbart & Bates, 1998), medical assessment, and interactions with clinicians who are thoroughly trained to assess infants. However, at very low cost, empirically based assessment can obtain data on a wide range of problems from diverse informants. Multivariate analyses of these data can be used to derive taxonomic constructs that can then be tested for consistency across the different types of informants and also for developmental stability and change during infancy.

For both the clinical and research assessment of individual infants, data from multiple informants can be systematically compared to identify consistencies and inconsistencies. By first using the infant versions of empirically based assessment instruments and then assessing the same children with the toddler versions of the instruments, we can determine which taxonomic constructs are appropriate for only the early periods or only the later periods, and which ones span these developmental periods. Table 9.2 summarizes the main steps involved in applying the empirically based approach to infants.

LIMITATIONS AND CHALLENGES

The empirically based paradigm embodies a bottom-up approach to assessing and aggregating behavioral and emotional problems. It is designed to advance integration of data from multiple

Table 9.2 Application of the Empirically Based Approach to Assessment of Infants

1. Identify candidate items in toddler instruments.
2. Obtain candidate items from parents, clinicians, day care providers.
3. Pilot test instruments completed by parents, clinicians, home visitors, day care providers.
4. Iteratively refine instruments on the basis of item prevalence, psychometrics, respondent comments.
5. Apply polished instruments to normative and clinical samples.
6. Derive syndromes via multivariate analyses.
7. Norm syndromes.
8. Test discriminative and predictive power.

sources, conceptualization of maladaptive functioning, and research. It is also designed to improve clinical assessment and services. However, it is intended to be integrated with rather than to substitute for cognitive assessment, physical examinations, observations, and developmental histories. Each of these is essential for comprehensive assessment and understanding of young children. Detailed knowledge of family functioning and relationships is also needed to understand both the liabilities and strengths that characterize families.

Evaluation of cognitive, physical, and family functioning requires considerable time and effort by skilled clinicians. At low cost, empirically based assessment adds much useful data without requiring clinicians' time. However, clinicians must ultimately integrate empirically based assessment data with other data. A major challenge is to help clinicians weigh and integrate various kinds of data in order to make the best decisions for each child. To meet this challenge, we need continual study and evaluation of ways to optimize clinicians' organization and utilization of information.

An additional challenge is to determine how effectively the empirically based approach can be applied to children younger than 18 months. With relatively little investment, items can be assembled and pilot tested with parents, day care providers, and others who have extended contacts with very young children. The items can then be tested for reliability, cross-informant agreement, and validity with respect to discriminating between important criterion groups of

children. Items can also be developed and tested for health professionals and home visitors to complete on the basis of their more limited contacts with children.

If enough items prove to be effective, data for large samples of children can be factor analyzed to derive empirically based scales. Scales oriented toward *DSM* and Zero to Three diagnostic categories can also be constructed by having experts rate the consistency of each item with each diagnostic category. If more substantial investments are made, national norms can be obtained for the various kinds of scales. As demonstrated by existing instruments and profiles for ages 1½ to 5, this approach may yield economical and practical assessment instruments that can be completed for very young children by diverse informants under diverse conditions. The result would be an assessment system that could be used to obtain extensive data on which to base taxonomic and diagnostic constructs appropriate for very young children. These constructs, in turn, could guide development of a formal nosology and normed scales for early childhood disorders.

SUMMARY AND CONCLUSION

We have outlined the empirically based paradigm for assessment and taxonomy of behavioral and emotional problems. This paradigm has produced standardized assessment instruments, empirically based syndrome scales, *DSM*-oriented scales, and profiles for multiple developmental periods starting at 18 months of age. Translated into 68 languages, the empirically based instruments are widely used for clinical and research purposes throughout the world (Bérubé & Achenbach, 2004).

Because there is no single gold standard for assessing behavioral and emotional problems, the empirically based approach employs parallel assessment forms to obtain data from multiple informants who see children in different contexts and from different perspectives. Available software for scoring the assessment instruments systematically compares item and scale scores obtained from up to eight informants per child. The software also computes correlations between ratings by different informants and compares these correlations with correlations obtained for large reference samples of informants. The CBCL/1½–5 includes the LDS for assessing language development and delays at ages 18 to 35 months.

Because *DSM*-oriented scales are scored from the same rating forms and are normed on the same national samples as the empirically based syndromes, users can directly compare reports of children's problems grouped according to *DSM* categories and grouped according to empirically based syndromes. Categorical cutoff points on all the scales enable users to categorize children as being in the normal, borderline clinical, or clinical range according to *DSM*-oriented and empirically based scales.

Clinical applications of empirically based instruments include routine use in health care settings to identify children with deviant problem scores and to advise parents, day care providers, and teachers who are concerned about a child's problems. Other clinical applications include use of the empirically based instruments to evaluate children seen in special education, child development, and mental health settings; to evaluate changes during interventions, as well as outcomes following interventions; and to evaluate children involved in adoption and foster placement.

Research applications include identifying correlates of different kinds of problems, tracking the developmental course of problems, testing the efficacy of pharmacotherapy and other interventions, identifying etiological factors, and evaluating prevention programs. Because the CBCL/1½–5 and C-TRF have counterpart forms for assessing school-age children and adolescents, it is easy to test predictive relations between scores obtained on the forms for ages 1½ to 5 and the forms for ages up to 18.

Procedures have been outlined for extending the empirically based approach to children younger than 18 months of age. At low cost, the empirically based approach can be used to assess large clinical and normative samples of children. The data can then be used to derive taxonomic and diagnostic constructs which, in turn, can guide development of a formal nosology of early childhood disorders. For comprehensive assessment, such procedures should be used with other infant assessment procedures, such as the Brazelton and Nugent (1995) scales, Bayley (1993)

scales, measures of temperament, medical assessment, and interactive assessment by clinicians.

To improve nosologies of early childhood disorders, it is important to document actual patterns of problems manifested by young children, to employ normative data from different sources, and to integrate data from multiple sources for both clinical and research purposes.

References

Achenbach, T. M. (1992). *Manual for the Child Behavior Checklist/2–3 and 1992 profile.* Burlington, VT: University of Vermont, Department of Psychiatry.

Achenbach, T. M. (1997). *Guide for the Caregiver-Teacher Report Form for ages 2–5.* Burlington, VT: University of Vermont, Department of Psychiatry.

Achenbach, T. M., Dumenci, L., & Rescorla, L. A. (2000). *Ratings of relations between DSM-IV diagnostic categories and items of the CBCL/1½–5 and C-TRF.* Burlington, VT: University of Vermont, Department of Psychiatry. Available at: www.ASEBA.org.

Achenbach, T. M., Edelbrock, C., & Howell, C. T. (1987). Empirically based assessment of the behavioral/emotional problems of 2–3-year-old children. *Journal of Abnormal Child Psychology, 15,* 629–650.

Achenbach, T. M., Howell, C.T., Aoki, M., & Rauh, V. (1993). Nine-year outcome of the Vermont Intervention Program for Low Birthweight Infants. *Pediatrics, 91,* 45–55.

Achenbach, T. M., Howell, C. T., McConaughy, S. H., & Stanger, C. (1995). Six-year predictors of problems in a national sample. III. Transitions to young adult syndromes. *Journal of the American Academy of Child and Adolescent Psychiatry, 34,* 658–669.

Achenbach, T. M., & McConaughy, S. H. (1997). *Empirically based assessment of child and adolescent psychopathology: Practical applications* (2nd ed.). Thousand Oaks, CA: Sage.

Achenbach, T. M., McConaughy, S. H., & Howell, C. T. (1987). Child/adolescent behavioral and emotional problems: Implications of cross-informant correlations for situational specificity. *Psychological Bulletin, 101,* 213–232.

Achenbach, T. M., & Rescorla, L. A. (2000). *Manual for ASEBA preschool forms and profiles.* Burlington, VT: University of Vermont, Research Center for Children, Youth, and Families.

Achenbach, T. M., & Rescorla, L. A. (2001). *Manual for the ASEBA school-age forms and profiles*. Burlington, VT: University of Vermont, Research Center for Children, Youth, and Families.

Achenbach, T. M., & Rescorla, L. A. (2003). *Manual for the ASEBA adult forms and profiles*. Burlington, VT: University of Vermont, Research Center for Children, Youth, and Families.

American Psychiatric Association (1980). *Diagnostic and statistical manual of mental disorders* (3rd ed.). Washington, DC: Author.

American Psychiatric Association (1987). *Diagnostic and statistical manual of mental disorders* (3rd ed. rev.). Washington, DC: Author.

American Psychiatric Association (1994). *Diagnostic and statistical manual of mental disorders* (4th ed.). Washington, DC: Author.

Arend, R., Lavigne, J. V., Rosenbaum, D., Binns, H. J., & Christoffel, K. K. (1996). Relation between taxonomic and quantitative diagnostic systems in preschool children: Emphasis on disruptive disorders. *Journal of Clinical Child Psychology, 25*, 388–397.

Bayley, N. (1993). *Bayley scales of infant development* (2nd ed.). New York: Psychological Corporation.

Bérubé, R. L., & Achenbach, T. M. (2004). *Bibliography of published studies using ASEBA instruments: 2004 edition*. Burlington, VT: University of Vermont, Research Center for Children, Youth, and Families.

Birmaher, B., Stanley, M., Greenhill, L., Twomey, J., Gavrilescu, A., & Rabinovich, H. (1990). Platelet imipramine binding in children and adolescents with impulsive behavior. *Journal of the American Academy of Child and Adolescent Psychiatry, 29*, 914–918.

Brazelton, T. B., & Nugent, J. K. (1995). *Neonatal behavioural assessment scale* (3rd ed.). London: MacKeith Press.

Brooks-Gunn, J., McCarton, C. M., Casey, P. H., McCormick, M. C., Bauer, C. R., Bernbaum, J. C., Tyson, J., Swanson, M., Bennett, F. C., Scott, D. T., Tonascia, J., & Meinert, C. L. (1994). Early intervention in low-birth-weight premature infants. *Journal of the American Medical Association, 272*, 1257–1262.

Carlson, G. A., & Cantwell, D. P. (1982). Diagnosis of childhood depression: A comparison of the Weinberg and DSM-III criteria. *Journal of the American Academy of Child Psychiatry, 21*, 247–250.

Edelbrock, C., & Costello, A. J. (1988). Convergence between statistically derived behavior problem syndromes and child psychiatric diagnoses. *Journal of Abnormal Child Psychology, 16*, 219–231.

Edelbrock, C., Rende, R., Plomin, R., & Thompson, L. A. (1995). A twin study of competence and problem behavior in childhood and early adolescence. *Journal of Child Psychology and Psychiatry, 36*, 775–785.

Gabel, S., Stadler, J., Bjorn, J., Shindledecker, R., & Bowden, C. (1993). Dopamine-beta-hydroxylase in behaviorally disturbed youth. Relationship between teacher and parent ratings. *Biological Psychiatry, 34*, 434–442.

Gould, M. S., Bird, H., & Jaramillo, B. S. (1993). Correspondence between statistically derived behavior problem syndromes and child psychiatric diagnoses in a community sample. *Journal of Abnormal Child Psychology, 21*, 287–313.

Hanna, G. L., Yuwiler, A., & Coates, J. K. (1995). Whole blood serotonin and disruptive behaviors in juvenile obsessive-compulsive disorder. *Journal of the American Academy of Child and Adolescent Psychiatry, 34*, 28–35.

Kagan, J. (1998). Biology and the child. In W. Damon (Ed.), *Handbook of child psychology* (5th ed., pp. 177–236). New York: Wiley.

Kanner, L. (1943). Autistic disturbances of affective contact. *Nervous Child, 2*, 217–250.

Kasius, M. C., Ferdinand, R. F., van den Berg, H., & Verhulst, F. C. (1997). Associations between different diagnostic approaches for child and adolescent psychopathology. *Journal of Child Psychology and Psychiatry, 38*, 625–632.

Kaufman, A. S., & Kaufman, N. L. (1983). *Kaufman assessment battery for children*. Circle Pines, MN: American Guidance Service.

Kitzman, H., Olds, D., Henderson, C., Hanks, C., Cole, R., Tatelbaum, R., McConnochie, K., Sidora, K., Luckey, D., Shaver, D., Engelhardt, K., James, D., & Barnard, K. (1997). Effect of prenatal and infancy home visitation by nurses on pregnancy outcomes, childhood injuries, and repeated childbearing. *Journal of the American Medical Association, 278*, 644–652.

Klee, T., Carson, D. K., Gavin, W. J., Hall, L., Kent, A., & Reece, S. (1998). Concurrent and predictive validity of an early language screening program. *Journal of Speech, Language, and Hearing Research, 41*, 627–641.

Kraepelin, E. (1883). *Compendium der psychiatrie.* Leipzig: Abel.

McCarthy, D. (1972). *McCarthy scales of children's abilities.* New York: Psychological Corporation.

Mesman, J., & Koot, H. M. (2001). Early preschool predictors of preadolescent internalizing and externalizing DSM-IV diagnoses. *Journal of the American Academy of Child and Adolescent Psychiatry, 40,* 1029–1036.

Rescorla, L. (1989). The Language Development Survey: A screening tool for delayed language in toddlers. *Journal of Speech and Hearing Disorders, 54,* 587–599.

Rescorla, L., & Alley, A. (2001). Validation of the Language Development Survey: A parent report tool for identifying language delay in toddlers. *Journal of Speech, Language, and Hearing Research, 44,* 434–445.

Rey, J. M., & Morris-Yates, A. (1992). Diagnostic accuracy in adolescents of several depression rating scales extracted from a general purpose behavior checklist. *Journal of Affective Disorders, 26,* 7–16.

Rothbart, M. K., & Bates, J. E. (1998). Temperament. In W. Damon (Ed.), *Handbook of child psychology* (5th ed., pp. 105–176). New York: Wiley.

Scerbo, A. S., & Kolko, D. (1994). Salivary testosterone and cortisol in disruptive children: Relationship to aggressive, hyperactive, and internalizing behaviors. *Journal of the American Academy of Child and Adolescent Psychiatry, 33,* 1174–1184.

Schmitz, S., Fulker, D. W., & Mrazek, D. A. (1995). Problem behavior in early and middle childhood: An initial behavior genetic analysis. *Journal of Child Psychology and Psychiatry, 36,* 1443–1458.

Schulterbrandt, J. G., & Raskin, A. (Eds.). (1977). *Depression in childhood: Diagnosis, treatment, and conceptual models.* New York: Raven.

Stanger, C., Achenbach, T. M., & Verhulst, F. C. (1997). Accelerated longitudinal comparison of aggressive versus delinquent syndromes. *Development and Psychopathology, 9,* 43–58.

Stoff, D. M., Pollock, L., Vitiello, B., Behar, D., & Bridger, W. H. (1987). Reduction of 3-H-imipramine binding sites on platelets of conduct disordered children. *Neuropsychopharmacology, 1,* 55–62.

van den Oord, E. J. C. G., Boomsma, D. I., & Verhulst, F. C. (1994). A study of problem behaviors in 10- to 15-year-old biologically related and unrelated international adoptees. *Behavior Genetics, 24,* 193–205.

Weinstein, S. R., Noam, G. G., Grimes, K., Stone, K., & Schwab-Stone, M. (1990). Convergence of DSM-III diagnoses and self-reported symptoms in child and adolescent inpatients. *Journal of the American Academy of Child and Adolescent Psychiatry, 29,* 627–634.

Widiger, T. A., & Clark, L. A. (2000). Toward *DSM-V* and the classification of psychopathology. *Psychological Bulletin, 126,* 946–963.

Zero to Three, National Center for Infants, Toddlers, and Families (1994). *Diagnostic classification of mental health and developmental disorders of infancy and early childhood.* Washington, DC: Author.

IV

MEASUREMENT ISSUES

Sound instrumentation is the cornerstone of valid and meaningful assessment. To ensure validity and maintain scientific integrity, there is a need to employ a multidomain, multimethod, multi-informant approach. In particular, methods to systematically integrate multiple informant dimensional measures and observational approaches that inform diagnostic formulations and assessment work with young children are needed. Further, it is crucial to understand the child's social-emotional and behavioral functioning within the context of his or her overall developmental or cognitive functioning.

The chapters in this section address these important concerns regarding the development of reliable, valid, and clinically informative tools for the assessment of infant and preschool mental health. Walter Gilliam and Linda Mayes present a review of clinical and psychometric approaches integrating developmental assessment and infant mental health evaluation. They note that conducting a developmental evaluation can provide not only straightforward information concerning developmental level but also an opportunity to observe and reflect on what the infant is doing. It

also offers clinicians glimpses into the expectations and abilities of parents or other caregivers with respect to how they are able to provide structure, reassurance and acceptance to the infant. They suggest that developmental assessment offers the astute clinician a lens through which the world may be viewed from the perspective of the infant and caregiver. They note that rather than focus solely on standard scores, the goal of developmental assessment is to understand how the infant interacts with and responds to the parental or caregiving environment. They review the various models of infant/toddler developmental testing (describing important distinctions, for example, between the Bayley and the Mullen scales) and the key components of a developmental assessment. They conclude with a discussion of what to expect in a developmental assessment that is sensitively and skillfully conducted.

Another essential assessment method for understanding the mental health status of infants, toddlers, and preschoolers, who are just beginning to communicate their feelings and thoughts, is observation. Marina Zelenko reviews the behavioral observational methods available to the clinician. She presents the major domains of child, parental, and dyadic functioning that may be targeted for observation. She discusses different types of observation including naturalistic, semi-structured, and structured approaches and presents the advantages and disadvantages of each approach. Given the importance of setting for the young child, three main observational settings are reviewed including the clinic, home, and day care/preschool setting. (For more on measurement across settings, see part VII.)

Given the importance of obtaining adequate domain coverage with respect to psychiatric symptoms and impairment, Helen Link Egger and Adrian Angold present their work on the development of a comprehensive structured interview for parents to diagnose psychiatric disorders in young children. They review the assessment tools for preschool psychopathology and the background research on the development of a struc-

tured interview for parents in this age group. While not yet providing utility in clinic settings, the structured interview for parents of preschoolers is used mostly as a research tool at this time. The authors are hopeful, however, that the field will progress to refine the interview and computerize its components, which will increase its clinical utility significantly.

Taken together, the measurement approaches described in this section offer complementary approaches based on varying sources of information. The authors emphasize the importance of considering the developmental level of the child, his or her cognitive and emotional resources, and the familial or parenting context. While the authors of the first two chapters highlight the critical role of careful observation, the final chapter by Egger and Angold offers the promise of a standard and reliable interview method for assessing psychiatric disorders in young children.

10

Integrating Clinical and Psychometric Approaches: Developmental Assessment and the Infant Mental Health Evaluation

Walter S. Gilliam
Linda C. Mayes

Developmental assessment with infants and toddlers can provide a wealth of information useful to mental health clinicians. Beyond simple information about the level of developmental skills acquisition, developmental assessment can provide a vantage point for considering the infant's approach to dealing with novel objects and people, level of motivation and curiosity, methods of coping with frustration, and adeptness at navigating social challenges. Conducting a developmental evaluation can provide an opportunity for parents to observe and reflect on what the infant is doing. It also offers clinicians glimpses into the expectations and abilities of parents or other caregivers with respect to how they are able to offer structure, reassurance, and acceptance to the infant. Essentially, developmental assessments can provide the astute clinician a lens through which the world may be viewed from the perspective of the infant and caregivers. Indeed, the word *assidere*, (the Greek origin of *assessment*) literally means "to sit beside," and hence to get to know someone (Bagnato & Neisworth, 1999). Although too often the focus is on quantitative scores in isolation, the goal of developmental assessment is to achieve a better understanding of the development of the infant within the context of how the infant and caregivers interact with each other and with the clinician.

Although the utility of developmental assessment is the focus of this chapter, it is perhaps easier to state definitively what infant assessments cannot provide. Developmental assessments do not provide a measure of fixed or immutable intelligence. Similar to other aspects of mental assessment, developmental results are descriptive, with only limited application for etiological understanding or detailed prognosticating. Developmental assessments, however complete and skillfully done, cannot provide sure predictions of long-term outcome or parcel out the complex contributions of endowment, experience, and maturational forces. Despite these caveats, assessment of infant development can be highly useful, and in many cases is essential to proper clinical treatment. Skillfully done, developmental assessments can help create a more complete picture of the child's current developmental level and environmental context that can be invaluable to sound clinical decision making and treatment planning.

WHAT IS A DEVELOPMENTAL ASSESSMENT, AND WHEN IS IT WARRANTED?

Generally, developmental assessments provide a description of the infant's functional capacities, the relationships among the various domains of development such as language and socialization, the child's ability to adapt, and the range of coping strategies in the child's repertoire. For the very young infant, developmental assessments describe neurodevelopmental functioning and individual regulatory capacities. For caregivers, the evaluation provides information about both their child and the potential therapeutic value of the alliance established with the clinician. Indeed, the developmental assessment process itself can be an effective intervention tool for increasing the maternal involvement and responsiveness of low socioeconomic status and adolescent mothers (Worobey & Brazelton, 1990). For the referring clinician, the assessment may provide a more integrated view of the infant's psychological, as well as physical, status.

Concerns regarding possible developmental delay generally fall into five broad categories: personal identity and social competence, communication and language (including receptive language, expressive language, and speech articulation), motor (including fine motor control and eye-hand coordination and gross motor control and locomotion), cognitive problem solving, and adaptive self-help and independence skills. Apart from concerns regarding development in these five domains, there are several other areas of concern for which developmental assessment may provide essential information. One such area of clinical concern is *disturbances in self-regulatory capacities*, such as sleep or eating disturbances, including food refusal, night terrors, repeated waking, low frustration tolerance, or problems in impulse control and aggressivity. Self-stimulatory behaviors, such as rocking or head banging, may indicate the presence of a variety of problems including regulatory difficulties, environmental stressors, or sensory processing problems. *Social and environmental disturbances* are another potential area of clinical concern. These may include serious disturbances in predominant mood and environmental conditions such as repeated or prolonged separations from primary attachment figures, neglect, abuse, and exposure to violence, all of which place infants at risk for social and affective disturbances (Kaufman & Henrich, 2000). *Neurodevelopmental disorders*, such as autism and other pervasive developmental disorder spectrum conditions and genetic and metabolic forms of mental retardation, are a third category of clinical concern. *Psychophysiological disturbances* are a fourth category that may include failure to thrive, recurrent vomiting, wheezing, or chronic skin rashes, and other conditions that may impede development. Clearly, any one of these problems may have physical causes, but clinicians should be alert to the close connection between physiological and psychodevelopmental adjustment in young children.

Developmental assessments may help provide information that can complement other clinical data to obtain a better picture of how infants cope with developmental tasks, handle frustration, and make use of their caregivers as sources of comfort, reassurance, and joy. In each of these conditions, a developmental assessment provides a profile of the child's relative strengths and weaknesses in specific developmental domains (e.g., motor skills; cognitive abilities; communication and language; and adaptive behaviors in areas such as socialization, independence, and coping) that in turn may guide plans for interventions. Consideration of the infant's social development within the context of caregiver-infant interaction traditionally has not always received equal attention relative to development in other areas. Relative to assessment of infant cognitive, language, and motor development, which trace their history back nearly a century, the assessment of social and behavioral development in infancy is a relatively recent endeavor.

For young children, issues of development are central to appropriate diagnosis, particularly in cases where the key concerns include potential developmental delays, communication and language disorders, or social disabilities (i.e., the pervasive developmental disorder spectrum). Indeed, mental health clinicians are frequently consulted about developmental concerns, and in these cases the developmental assessment may be a centerpiece of the overall assessment. These issues can include both suspected developmental delays and various physiological and environmental conditions that may place infants at increased risk for developmental delays. Prematurity and other serious medical conditions, which may result in hospitalization or other restriction of appropriate stimulation early in a child's life, may lead to altered parent-child interaction and adversely affect development (Minde, 2000). Various genetic and metabolic disorders (including Down syndrome, fragile X, and Prader-Willi syndrome; certain sex chromosome anomalies, such as Klinefelter's syndrome; and poorly managed phenylketonuria [PKU]) have known neurodevelopmental implications (Madrid & Marachi, 1999). Although specific developmental and behavioral sequelae are associated with each of these conditions, the extent varies, and developmental assessment can be useful to document the level of impairment and better target developmental interventions. Exposure to environmental toxins, such as in fetal alcohol syndrome and lead poisoning, has been associated with both developmental delays and behavioral dysregulation. Also, central nervous system damage (e.g., traumatic brain injuries and intraventricular hemorrhages) can, of course, lead to developmental sequelae, and follow-up with a developmentalist can be invaluable in understanding the level of functional impairment and tracking recovery. Of course, the specific disturbances and conditions listed above are usually inextricably mediated by the social context of the child (Zeanah, Boris, & Larrieu, 1997). Although developmental assessments may be highly useful in clinical formulation and treatment planning, they are not able to determine the proportion of the overall impairment attributable to these various potential causal factors.

SOME BASIC CONSIDERATIONS WHEN CHOOSING A FORMAL DEVELOPMENTAL ASSESSMENT TOOL

A large array of formal developmental assessment tools for infants and toddlers exists. In this section, we discuss the various types of developmental assessment tools, considering both issues of their clinical utility and their psychometric validity. Below are some basic guidelines for choosing an infant developmental test that best meets the clinician's specific needs. These guidelines also help provide a framework for evaluating the usefulness of some of the various tests currently in use. Four areas of consideration are presented: purpose, sources of data, types of quantifiable data provided, and standardization and psychometric properties.

Purpose

A developmental test may be useful for one or more of several different purposes: diagnosis, screening, and early intervention planning. Not all tests are designed equally well for these three purposes, and selecting the correct tests to match the stated purpose is essential. Diagnostic tests are used to provide information necessary for either clinical or eligibility-oriented diagnoses. Screening tests are used when it is desirable to use a relatively brief instrument to identify infants who may be at risk for delayed development and would benefit from further diagnostic testing. Usually screening tests are used when relatively many children need to be assessed and a full diagnostic assessment for all children would be too costly or cumbersome. Intervention-planning tests are used to plan an individualized early intervention program once children have been diagnosed. These instruments help identify important programmatic goals and objectives or track an infant's achievement of these goals over time in order to document the effects of the intervention.

Sources of Data

Developmental assessment instruments, like all assessment procedures, are methods of collecting and organizing data. Developmental tests for infants use one or more of at least three different types of data: direct assessment, incidental observation, and caregiver report. It is important to acknowledge the strengths and limitations of each data source. Direct assessment during the administration of a developmental test has the strength of a standardized observational context so that an infant's performance may be directly compared to other infants with the assumption that the material was presented in a consistent manner. The limitation of direct assessment, however, is that it represents only a small sample of the infant's developmental repertoire that will be influenced greatly by current issues regarding the infant's motivation, mood, comfort, and responsiveness to the examiner and the evaluative process. Clinical observation of the infant and caregiver-infant interactions can provide essential information. However, since the situational contexts are seldom standardized, the clinician must rely on his or her own internalized set of norms and developmental expectations. Caregiver report surveys are a useful addition to formal assessment, in particular to document behaviors that occur too infrequently to be observed in a clinical evaluation, or to assess the caregivers' individual perspectives of the infant. However, caregiver reports should not be the sole measure of the infant's development, since they are highly subject to rater bias (Meisels & Wasik, 1990). Given the strengths and limitations of each of these sources of data, a comprehensive assessment should utilize multiple sources of data across multiple contexts.

Types of Quantifiable Data Provided

Besides the vast amount of qualitative data obtained by careful observation during testing, most developmental assessment procedures provide several methods of quantifying results. Of the several different types of scores available, standard scores and age equivalents are the most commonly used. *Standard scores* are the most robust scores obtainable and represent the infant's performance in relationship to other infants of about the same chronological age. Common forms of standard scores include z scores, deviation scores, and T scores, the latter two being linear transformations of the former. Most tests provide some guidance on how to describe an infant's standard score by placing the scores in descriptive bands (e.g., average, below average, mildly delayed, etc.).

Age equivalent scores represent an estimate of the chronological age (typically expressed in months) at which the typically developing infant would demonstrate the skills observed in the infant being assessed. This type of score is often appealing to many caregivers and others with little or no training in psychometric tests, since the interpretation is seemingly straightforward. However, age equivalent scores on developmental tests are notoriously easy to misinterpret and may lead to erroneous conclusions (Gilliam & Mayes, 2002). First, age equivalent scores tend to be highly unstable, with the infant's performance on only one or two items having a potentially large effect on the age equivalent. Second, age equivalent scores may imply too much about an infant's development, especially when the child's skills are highly scattered. When an infant's performance on a developmental scale shows considerable scatter, age equivalents are best expressed as a range, if expressed at all. Third, developmental delay expressed in age equivalents does not adequately address the frequency or severity of the delays at any given age. Finally, the type of data used to compute age equivalents is too weak statistically to support the calculation of confidence intervals that are useful in placing the score within the context of appropriate bands of error. This lack of confidence intervals further exacerbates the preceding limitations. Of course, there are times when age equivalents may be the best or only option available for expressing an infant's performance (e.g., when the extent of developmental delay is so great that standard scores cannot be easily calculated and percentile ranks below the first percentile are obtained).

Standardization and Psychometric Properties

To yield reliable results, developmental tests should be standardized and normed on a sample of infants that are reasonably representative of the population to which the infant belongs and for which the clinician wishes to use as a contextual framework. Also, normative data should be no more than about a decade old in order to keep pace with intergenerational escalation in test performance. Grossly outdated norms often yield inflated standard scores (Flynn, 1984) that may lead to erroneously disqualifying infants for needed services.

The soundness of a psychometric test is judged based on its reliability (the ability to produce similar results under differing conditions) and validity (the collection of evidence that suggests that the test measures what it is supposed to measure). Test-retest coefficients, a measure of a test's stability over time, are often lower for infant tests than for tests designed for older children, due in part to the rapidity of early development. Besides their use in evaluating the psychometric soundness of a test, reliability coefficients also serve a clinically relevant purpose by providing bands of error around obtained scores, acknowledging the measurement error inherent in all tests. Validity represents an accumulation of evidence that together builds a case for the accuracy of that test. Specifically, infant developmental tests are expected to correlate significantly with other similar tests, to reflect developmental changes that result from expected maturation, and to be sensitive to the presence of diagnosable disorders with clear developmental manifestations.

In addition to standard issues of reliability and validity, psychometric properties that are more individually relevant are also important. For example, it is important that developmental tests have adequate floors and ceilings. In other words, there should be enough lower-level items that significant developmental delays can be detected in even the youngest infants for which the test is to be used (floor). Likewise, there should be enough upper-level items that significant developmental precocity can be detected in the oldest children for whom the test is to be used (ceiling). Since standard scores are obtained by comparing an infant's performance to that of similar-age peers, the degree to which the normative data approximates the infant's age also is important. The current standard in infant developmental tests is normative bands of 1 month for infants up to 12 or 18 months old, and 1- to 2-month bands for infants up to 36 months old. In other words, infant tests typically compare an infant's performance to other infants no more than 1 month older or younger, whereas a toddler's performance might be compared to other toddlers 1 to 2 months older or younger. Of course, normative bands that are narrow are preferable to those that are wider. (For a more complete discussion of standardization and psychometric considerations with infant developmental tests, see Gilliam and Mayes, 2000, 2002.)

A REVIEW OF SELECTED DEVELOPMENTAL TESTS

Basically, developmental tests fall into the three basic headings of screening tests, neonatal neuro-behavioral tests, and infant/toddler developmental tests. Screening tests are brief assessments of a child's current level of functioning, used to determine which children may be developmentally at risk, requiring further diagnostic assessment. They are intended to be used routinely when a comprehensive assessment for all children would be either too costly or unwarranted. These instruments usually are not as reliable or valid as comprehensive assessment tools, due largely to their brevity. Developmental screening tests, though serving an important role in detection and surveillance, are largely outside of the scope of this chapter. (For discussions of developmental screening tests, see Meisels, 1989; Gilliam and Mayes, 2000. For a review of developmental screening instruments in primary care settings, see chapter 23.) A few of the most widely used neonatal and infant developmental tests are discussed below and presented in table 10.1.

Neonatal Assessment Tests: The Brazelton Neonatal Behavioral Assessment Scale

Several specific procedures exist for assessing infants during the neonatal period (birth to 4 weeks). Although clinicians assessing infants often are not asked to evaluate neonates, the conceptual point inherent in these instruments—combining an assessment of innate capacities with attention to individual variability and responsivity—is relevant to all assessments of infants and young children. Although the predecessor scale to the Graham/Rosenblith Behavioral Test for Neonates (Rosenblith, 1979) was the first neonatal development test, the Brazelton Neonatal Behavioral Assessment Scale (NBAS), currently in its second edition (NBAS-2; Brazelton, 1984), dominates the field today.

The NBAS-2 is intended to assess the neonate's current level of neurobehavioral organization, capacity to respond to the stress of labor and delivery, and adjustment to the ex utero environment. It is designed for use with neonates 37 to 44 weeks gestational age who do not currently need mechanical supports or oxygen, but has also been used extensively with premature and otherwise medically fragile newborns. It takes about 20 to 30 minutes to administer, followed by about 15 minutes to record and score the neonate's per-

Table 10.1 Selected Formal Tests of Neonatal and Infant/Toddler Development

	Age	Domains	Norm Sample	Reliability/Validity	Comments
Neonatal Assessment Tests					
Brazelton Neonatal Behavioral Assessment Scale-2 (Brazelton, 1984)	37–44 weeks Gestational age	NI, B, PS	Not applicable	High interrater reliability, weak test-retest, poor predictor beyond first year	Most widely used neonatal test
Infant/Toddler Development Tests					
Bayley Scales of Infant Development-II (Bayley, 1993)	1–42 months	Mental, M, B	Large, representative	Excellent for mental, adequate for psychomotor, varied for behavior	Most widely used and validated infant test
Mullen Scales of Early Learning (Mullen, 1995)	0–68 months	GM, FM, VR, RC, EC	Large, representative	Adequate to exceptional	Most useful for toddlers and pre-schoolers
Battelle Developmental Inventory (Newborg et al., 1984)	0–95 months	PS, Ad; GM; FM; EC; RC; Cg (and subdomains)	Small, representative	Numerous psychometric concerns cast significant doubts (see text)	Used considerably, despite many test flaws

Note: Ad = adaptive or self-help skills; B = behavior; Cg = cognitive or problem solving; EC = expressive communication/language; FM = fine motor; GM = gross motor; M = motor or physical; NI = neurological intactness; PS = personal-social; RC = receptive communication/language; VR = visual reception.

formance. Items assess the neonate's neurological intactness, behavioral organization (e.g., state regulation and autonomic reactivity), and interactiveness and responsiveness with both animate and inanimate stimuli on the basis of 27 behavioral items and 20 reflexes, scored along a 7- to 9-point continuum. Although with considerable training interrater reliability for the NBAS-2 has been shown to be adequate, studies of the test-retest reliability of the original NBAS suggest poor temporal stability for most items (Lancione, Horowitz, & Sullivan, 1980; Sameroff, 1978). The validity of the NBAS is supported by research that has demonstrated its ability to correctly identify neonates who are underweight or who have experienced in utero drug and alcohol exposure, maternal malnutrition, and gestational diabetes. Furthermore, the NBAS has been shown to predict infant-parent attachment and subsequent infant development. Unfortunately, research has not consistently shown the NBAS to be a good predictor of infant development much beyond the first year of life (Horowitz & Linn, 1982; Vaughn et al., 1980). Of the dimensions assessed by the NBAS, state control appears the most stable and predictive (Als, Tronick, Lester, & Brazelton, 1979), possibly speaking to the fundamental importance of early state regulatory capacities for other more complex functions, such as attention and social interactiveness, that emerge in the first year.

Infant/Toddler Development Tests

Of the various models of infant developmental tests, the norm-referenced multidomain model is arguably the most enduring (Gilliam & Mayes, 2000). Based on the work of Gesell and Bayley, development is assessed in multiple distinct yet interrelated domains. The most notable and widely used examples of these tests (each described below) are the Bayley Scales of Infant Development, currently in its second edition (BSID-II; Bayley, 1993), the Mullen Scales of Early Learning (MSEL; Mullen, 1995), and the Battelle Developmental Inventory (BDI; Newborg, Stock, Wnek, Guidubaldi, & Svinicki, 1984). Additionally, criterion-referenced instruments are also popular among professionals who wish to compare an infant's development to expectations based either on a particular model of development (e.g., Piaget's model of infant cognitive development) or expected programmatic outcomes. Though not typically useful for diagnostic or screening purposes, criterion-referenced tests may be quite useful when planning intervention programs. (For a more complete discussion of Piagetian and other multidomain and criterion-referenced tests, see Gilliam and Mayes, 2000, 2002.)

Before discussing the BSID and the MSEL, some words of caution are offered regarding the BDI. Although the BDI is an exceedingly popular test that is used extensively throughout America, especially among professionals working in publicly funded early intervention and special education programs, several serious problems exist in its norming and validation (Boyd, 1989; McLinden, 1989). First, there are no data to support the internal reliability of the scales, and a general lack of procedural details in the manual makes it difficult to evaluate the reported test-restest and interrater reliability coefficients (McLinden, 1989). Second, the concurrent validity of the various domains is based on findings from exceptionally small studies, ranging from only 10 to 37 subjects, and concurrent validity coefficients for the cognitive domain of the BDI are very weak (ranging from $r = .44$ to $r = .50$; Newborg et al., 1984). Third, the normative bands used to derive standard scores are far too wide, resulting in gravely erroneous scores for children who are on either the young or old end of each of the norm groups (Boyd, 1989). Due to these normative discontinuities, a child can score solidly in the average range just before he or she turns ½, 1, 1½, 2, 2½, 3, 4, 5, 6, or 7 years old, and a day or so later, with the exact same performance, obtain a standard score in the range suggestive of serious developmental delay or mental retardation (Boyd, 1989). Additionally, the BDI takes a relatively long time to administer (ranging from 1 to 2 hours for a typically developing child, depending on the child's age), and since many of the items on each of the scales can be scored on the basis of either direct assessment, naturalistic observation, or caregiver report, it is impossible to partial out differences in formal test behavior versus informant report (Gilliam & Mayes, 2000). These limitations greatly reduce the diagnostic utility of the BDI and may even lead to grossly distorted assessment results that could result in either underidentifying children with serious developmental delays or unduly alarming caregivers. For these reasons, diagnostic use of the BDI for infants and toddlers in general is not recommended, and BDI results administered by others should be interpreted very cautiously.

Bayley Scales of Infant Development–II

The BSID-II (Bayley, 1993) is clearly the most widely used measure of the development of infants and toddlers in both clinical and research settings, and its extensive history of test development and validation makes it the most psychometrically sophisticated infant test on the market. The BSID-II is applicable to children from 1 through 42 months of age, and administration time is about 25 to 35 minutes for infants under 15 months old and up to 60 minutes for children over 15 months. There are two main components of the BSID-II: the Mental Development Index (MDI) and the Psychomotor Development Index (PDI). The MDI provides information about the child's language development and problem-solving skills, while the PDI assesses the child's gross and fine motor development. Additionally, the BSID-II includes a Behavior Rating Scale (BRS) that assesses attentional capacities, social engagement, affect and emotion, and the quality of the child's movement and motor control. The BSID-II provides a method for obtaining age equivalence scores for four facets of development: cognitive, language, social, and motor. Unfortunately, serious problems of item density and a lack of empirical evidence to support the reliability and validity of these facet scores greatly diminishes their utility (Gilliam & Mayes, 2002).

The standardization sample is exceedingly large (by infant assessment standards) and nationally representative. For the MDI, reliability and concurrent validity coefficients are adequate to very high, whereas these coefficients for the PDI are marginal at best (Gilliam & Mayes, 2000, 2002; Salvia & Ysseldyke, 1991). In general, the BSID-II appears to have some ability to predict which infants will score very poorly on intelligence tests in their preschool years. Although modest predictive correlations between infant

scores and IQ scores during the later preschool years have been reported for both the original BSID and the BSID-II (Bayley, 1993; McCall, 1979; Ramey, Campbell, & Nicholson, 1973; Siegel, 1979), the BSID-II shows only limited ability to accurately predict specific IQ scores, especially in typically developing infants, and should not be thought of as an IQ test (Gibbs, 1990; Whatley, 1987).

Mullen Scales of Early Learning

A relatively recent addition is the MSEL (Mullen, 1995). This revision of the original Mullen scales combined earlier versions of the test designed for infants and preschoolers into one test with continuous norms from birth through 68 months. The MSEL takes about 15 to 60 minutes to administer, depending on the age of the child (15 minutes at 1 year old, 30 minutes at 3 years, and 60 minutes at 5 years). The MSEL assesses child development in five separate domains: gross motor, visual reception (primarily visual discrimination and memory), fine motor, receptive language, and expressive language. The gross motor scale is only applicable to children from birth through 33 months old and does not contribute to the overall early learning composite score.

Normative data for the MSEL is based on a sample of 1,849 children from across America, somewhat overrepresentative of children from the Northeast. Internal reliability ranges from .75 to .83 for MSEL subtests and is .91 for the overall developmental score. Median 1- to 2-week test-retest reliability coefficients range from .78 to .96 across subtests, and interrater reliability coefficients range from .94 to .98. The MSEL receptive and expressive language scales show acceptable correlation with similar scales from the Preschool Language Assessment Scale, .85 and .80, respectively. The gross motor scale correlates with the BSID-II PDI at .76, and the fine motor scale correlates with the Peabody Fine Motor Scale at .70. These correlations for the motor scales also are acceptable. Overall, these validation studies are quite promising. Additional studies, however, of the MSEL's concurrent and predictive validity, particularly with specific subpopulations, are warranted.

Comparing the BSID-II and MSEL

There are several meaningful differences between the BSID-II and MSEL that impact the utility of these instruments for both clinical and research purposes. No single tool is useful for all purposes, and an examination of the differences between these two assessment instruments is informative when selecting the most appropriate tool for any given assessment need.

First, the most obvious difference between the BSID-II and the MSEL is that the latter provides assessment in five distinct areas of infant development, whereas the former only provides two global scores, measuring mental and motor abilities. Where the BSID-II provides only a single measure of mental development, combining items that measure a variety of cognitive and communicative skills, the MSEL breaks these into three distinct scales that measure visual processing and problem solving, receptive communication, and expressive communication. Also, where the BSID-II provides only a global measure of motor functioning, the MSEL breaks motor functioning into two scales, measuring fine motor and gross motor skills. Infants may present with developmental concerns in specific areas, such as communication and language development, and in these cases it is almost always desirable to obtain clinical and psychometric data that assess the area of greatest concern while obtaining measures of functioning in other domains of development that might not be delayed. For example, when assessing an infant with suspected communication delays, one might document with the MSEL that the delays are limited to expressive language development and that receptive language development and visual processing-oriented problem-solving skills are age appropriate. Further assessment could then focus more specifically on the areas of concern. Such detailed assessment with BSID-II would be complicated, and the clinician would have to rely largely on clinical observation alone. However, this level of finer differentiation with the MSEL comes at a cost. Since the total number of items is divided over a larger number of scales, each scale of the MSEL has less item density, and this results in reduced reliability for the MSEL scales relative to the BSID-II scales.

Second, items within each of the MSEL scales are arranged and administered in serial order, whereas items on the BSID-II are clustered into various item sets that are appropriate for different ages of infants. The purpose of these item sets is to provide specific item clusters so that examiners who work with infants of specific ages would only need to know how to administer the specific items that correspond to the infants' chronological ages. Unfortunately, the advent of the item sets with the BSID-II has created some confusion among infant examiners, in terms of which item set to use for infants born prematurely (Ross & Lawson, 1997). Indeed, the choice of which item set to use as a starting point can significantly impact the infant's final score (Gauthier, Bauer, Messinger, & Closius, 1999). For testers that use the corrected age procedure, the test developers recommend using the same item set that corresponds to the normative group used for determining that child's standard score (Matula, Gyurke, & Aylward, 1997).

Third, all items on the BSID-II account for an equal number of points (0 versus 1), whereas on the MSEL some items are worth only 1 point while others are worth as many as 5. Therefore, difficulties or strengths on a single item may have a relatively large impact on a child's obtained standard score. Finally, norm group sizes for infants and toddlers are different between these two tests. On the BSID-II, an infant or toddler's performance up to 36 months old is normed against other children within 1 month of the child's chronological age. On the MSEL, however, this is only true for infants under 15 months old. For 15- to 30-month-old infants, the MSEL has 2-month-wide norm groups, and after 30 months the norm groups increase to 3 months wide. Clearly, as has been demonstrated earlier in the chapter with regard to the BDI, the width of the norm groups to which the infant's performance will be contrasted can have a massive influence on the reliability of the obtained data, likely due to the incredible rapidity with which infants develop. In an examination of this issue with the BSID-II, using both the normative data from which the BSID-II was standardized ($N = 1,600$) and a clinical data set of high-risk infants ($N = 264$), it was found that the 1-month normative bands may be too wide for infants 18 months and younger, suggesting that infant performance on developmental tests should be referenced against infants that are much closer to their age (Gilliam, Mayes, & Hazen, 2001). Further research with the MSEL might indicate that the 2- and 3-month-wide bands for older infants and toddlers might also introduce unacceptable levels of error.

KEY COMPONENTS OF A DEVELOPMENTAL ASSESSMENT

As part of the overall mental health assessment, the developmental assessment consists of at least three fundamental skill areas: (a) caregiver interviewing; (b) observation of the infant, caregiver, and the dyadic and family system (both as a part of the formal developmental testing and as a part of clinical observation); and (c) synthesis of the information, from both within and outside of the developmental assessment. While interviewing, observing, and synthesizing are skills involved in all mental health assessment, each has unique aspects in the process of assessing development in infants.

Interviewing

It is axiomatic that skillful interviewing is central to a complete developmental assessment since much of the data about infants' daily functioning and their relationships with others come from interviews with the caregivers. Skillful interviewing techniques include letting caregivers begin their story wherever they choose; using directed, information-gathering questions in such a way as to clarify but not disrupt the parents' account; and listening for affect as much as content. Importantly, nearly every step of the assessment process requires an alliance between clinician and caregiver, since infants usually perform better when they are in the company of familiar adults, and the initial interview between clinician and family is crucial in setting the tone for such an alliance. Moreover, establishing an alliance is central to evaluating infants' interactions with the adults in their world. Indeed, infant assessments may be compromised when no familiar adults are avail-

able to meet with the clinician and be with the infant. Unfortunately, it is often in cases involving the most severe environmental disturbance (e.g., abuse and neglect) that clinicians do not have access to caregivers that are able to describe the infant's developmental history and home functioning.

Addressing Caregiver Fears and Fantasies Regarding the Mental Health Assessment

When parents, foster parents, or other caregivers are available, skillful interviewing is also critical in helping parents follow through with the assessment process. Coming for a developmental evaluation or participating in one while their infant is hospitalized is enormously stressful and often frightening for caregivers. Clinicians working with infants and their families need to understand that, regardless of what caregivers have been told about the assessment, caregivers' fears and fantasies about the process are often as potent as the facts of the presenting problem. Some caregivers may have begun to see their infant as damaged or defective in some way and may feel afraid or guilty about the effect of their own behavior on the infant (e.g., alcohol or illegal substance use during pregnancy). Their fears of what the infant's problems signify may be expressed in many ways. It is possible that they may anticipate that their infant has a serious developmental disability, such as autism or mental retardation, or that the infant will have serious emotional difficulties in school, or that they themselves will be, or already are, inadequate caregivers. It is always a vulnerable time for caregivers, and clinicians should keep in mind that what may seem to them inconsequential moments and statements during the assessment may be memorable and powerful for many caregivers. Furthermore, the stress of coming for an assessment may affect the caregivers' abilities to report about the infant's development. Often, the "facts" start to change as the alliance between caregivers and clinician develops.

Active Listening

When first interviewed, caregivers may be reluctant to be candid or may not themselves be fully aware of their own perceptions and beliefs about the infant. Open-ended questions, allowing caregivers to begin their story wherever they feel most comfortable and conveying a nonjudgmental attitude are crucial beginning points in establishing the working alliance (Hirshberg, 1996). Also, at the risk of stating the obvious, such interviews involve considerably more listening than active questioning. Indeed, the type of active listening involved in this type of interview requires the clinician to do much more than just passively collect and record requested information. Rather, it involves forming numerous connections between "factual" information, observational information (the reactions of the caregivers and their affective responses), and an appreciation of the context of the relationships between the infant, caregivers, and the clinician.

The Content of the Interview

The central purpose of interviews with caregivers is to gather information about the infant and the caregivers. The important areas to cover in terms of the infant's development are the medical history and major developmental milestones; the history of the mother's pregnancy, delivery, and immediate perinatal period; the number, ages, and health of family members; and how the infant fits in the family's daily life (Cox, 1999). The meaning of the individual child for all caregivers is an important window on the infant's place in the family. Many infants and toddlers attend child care or early intervention programs, and the perception of those teachers, as well as their relationship with the infant's primary caregivers at home, also is important.

More specifically, the interviewer should try to get a picture of the caregivers' perceptions of the infant's level of functioning in several areas (Seligman, 2000). These include motor development and activity level, speech and communication, problem-solving and play, self-regulation (ease of comforting, need for routines), relationships with others, and level of social responsiveness. Questions about whether or not the pregnancy was planned or came at a good time for the family and what expectations the parents had for the infant provide important information about perceptions, disappointments, and stresses. Similarly, asking the caregivers of whom the infant re-

minds them or what traits in their infant they like best and least may be useful avenues for learning about how the parents view both the infant and his or her place within their family.

Severe abuse, abandonment, multiple placements, or seriously ill parents are examples of situations in which the clinician will not have available certain critical sources of information. In these instances, certain hypotheses suggested by the child's presentation and status may be left unconfirmed. As in situations where the time for evaluation is brief, it is most important for clinicians to acknowledge which aspects of their diagnostic formulation are relatively certain, which are not, and what information would likely be clarifying, were it available (for more information, see Gilliam and Mayes, 2002).

Techniques of Organizing Information

Provence (1977) has suggested that a productive method of gathering developmental and family data is to ask the caregivers to describe a day in the life of their child. Provence outlined how this question can be the framework for learning about daily activities, how the infant and caregivers interact throughout the day, and about interactions around mealtime, bedtime, or times of distress. When all major caregivers are present for the interview, this question provides a time for each of them to present descriptions of his or her time with, and perceptions of, the child. The Infant-Toddler Developmental Assessment (IDA; Provence, Erikson, Vater, & Palmeri, 1995), appropriate for infants from birth to 36 months, is particularly useful in providing a schema for organizing important information from caregiver interviews, medical/developmental records, and behavioral observations (Erikson, 1996). Additionally, clinicians may use semi-structured interviews, such as the Vineland Adaptive Behavior Scales (Sparrow, Balla, & Chicchetti, 1984), which is currently under revision, both to collect quantitative developmental data and to provide an opportunity to open new areas of clinical discussion. Additionally, well-validated parent and child care-provider report instruments that assess infant social-emotional development, such as the Infant-Toddler Social and Emotional Assessment (Carter & Briggs-Gowan, 2001), can provide invaluable information about an infant's externalizing, internalizing, regulatory, and competency behaviors.

Observing

Clinical observation begins from the very first contact with the caregivers and infant, including the caregiver interview addressed above. Many important observations of the infant and infant-caregiver and familial interactions can be obtained during the course of formal developmental assessment. Benham (2000) has provided an elaborated framework for structuring observations of infants and toddlers that may be useful during clinical assessment. In many cases, however, the formal developmental evaluation alone may not provide sufficient opportunity to observe all of the important behaviors of the infant and caregiver. Infants may behave differently with different caregivers and in varying contexts. For this reason, both naturalistic and structured analogue procedures can often be used to gather additional observational data that can be useful for both clinical and research purposes (Zeanah et al., 1997). Also, play-based developmental assessment may allow the clinician the opportunity to observe the infant and caregivers in a less structured format than provided by the formal developmental assessment. Play observations can be very useful in gaining additional information about the infant's cognitive, symbolic/linguistic, social, and motor development, as well as assessing internal emotional states and conflicts and the infant's internal dynamic representations of the world (Close, 1999, 2002). For a more extensive review of observation in infant and young child assessment, see chapter 11.

Observation is the fundamental skill needed for measuring infants' development. After all, most diagnostic evaluations are based on observation of physical signs and behavioral responses. However, what distinguishes the observational skill necessary for developmental assessment is that it occurs on many levels simultaneously and is perhaps the area in which the developmentalist's dual role as both generalist and specialist is most evident. The observational skills inherent in assessments of infants require a blend of free-floating attention bounded by a structure. In other words, while the clinician must be comfortable enough in the setting to attend to whatever occurs, he or she also must have a mental framework by which to organize the observations collected during the session. Such a framework entails at least four broad areas: (a) predominant affective tone of the infant and caregivers, (b) the infant's involvement in the situation (curiosity and interest), (c) the infant's use of others (child's use of the caregivers or examiner), and (d) the infant's reactions to transitions (initial meetings, end of sessions, changes in amount of structure). In addition to providing valuable clinical data of diagnostic utility, observing the infant's behaviors in each of these areas can provide information essential to the appropriate administration and pacing of assessment stimuli in a manner that will optimize the infant's performance and provide for a more pleasant assessment experience.

Predominant Affective Tone of the Infant and Caregivers

During the first 2 to 3 months of life, infants' emotional states are defined primarily in terms of contentment versus distress. By about 2 to 3 months of age, however, infants have undergone dramatic changes in their cognitive and emotional organization. The emotion of contentment differentiates into both contentment and joy, while states of distress are further definable in terms of sadness and anger (Lewis, 1993). However, regulation of emotional states is something that infants develop over time and is related to skills infants learn through interaction with their caregivers (Kopp, 1989). The formal developmental assessment provides an opportunity for clinical observation of how the infant and caregiver modulate emotional states associated with dealing with the examiner as a stranger, interest in novel objects, frustration when unable to master a task or when denied a desired object, and joy during interaction with the adults or testing materials. The emotional reactivity of the infant can be observed in terms of the onset, duration, and intensity of his or her emotional reactions during the assessment sessions. Similarly, the degree to which the caregiver is attuned to the infant's emotional states and is able to help modulate the infant's emotional reactivity can often be observed during the formal developmental assessment (Tronick, Cohn, & Shea, 1986). This caregiver sensitivity has been linked both to infants' ability to regulate their own emotional states and to their level of behaviors designed to elicit continued social interactions from the caregiver (Kogan & Carter, 1996; van den Boom, 1994). Of course, caregiver psychopathology can have a tremendous negative impact on the infant's development of emotional self-regulation, and maternal depression has been found consistently to be related to negative emotional states and poorly developed emotional regulation in infants (Field et al., 1988).

The Infant's Involvement in the Situation

The developmental assessment provides many opportunities to observe how the infant reacts to novel stimuli. Although many of the objects used in traditional developmental tests may be somewhat familiar to the infant (e.g., blocks, dolls, etc.), many other objects (e.g., bells, pegboards, etc.) are likely to be novel, and the assessment process itself is atypical. Infants' preferences for novel stimuli are present from birth. Under ideal assessment conditions when an infant is not too sleepy or distressed, the clinical evaluator should expect to observe a significant amount of curiosity and interest from the infant. By the first month of life, infants typically will follow visually moving objects, prefer novelty, and show habituation to stimuli. In fact, the degree of attention and stimulus habituation shown by infants has been found to be significantly predictive of later cognitive development (Bornstein & Sigman, 1986; McCall & Carriger, 1993). Of course, observable curiosity and interest is related to the degree of attachment between the infant and the caregiver, such that securely attached infants are more able to monitor their environment because they devote less energy to monitoring the availability of the caregiver (Crockenberg & Leerkes, 2000). Furthermore, secure attachment during infancy is associated with more compliant behavior during toddlerhood (Londerville & Main, 1981), and this may manifest as observable social motivation to comply with the expectations of the caregiver and clinician during the developmental assessment tasks.

Secure caregiver attachment and the infant's ability to regulate his or her emotion and modulate feelings of frustration help lay the groundwork for effectance or mastery motivation (Crockenberg & Leerkes, 2000). Effectance motivation is observed during the developmental assessment as the infant's seemingly intrinsic desire to master a given task or to achieve a planned goal. Of course, effectance also depends on the infant's developing understanding of cause and effect, which is first observable by about the fifth or sixth month of life and later gives rise to means-end reasoning and increased goal-directed behavior (Gilliam & Mayes, 2002). For example, by about 6 months most infants are able to obtain an attractive ring by adaptively pulling on an attached string. By about 12 months of age, trial-and-error problem solving begins to replace the conditioned response learning observable in the first year, and from about 18 to 24 months internal problem solving begins to be more observable, as the infant's mental ability to hold and manipulate internal representations increases. Appreciation of this development in problem-solving abilities is a matter of clinical observation, since most formal developmental assessment tools only measure whether the infant *can* master the tasks, not *how*.

The Infant's Use of Others

At about 7 to 9 months of age, infants develop a clearer grasp of intersubjectivity, the knowledge that others can understand their thoughts, feelings, gestures, and sounds. This developing sense of intersubjectivity leads a host of prelinguistic communicative behaviors aimed at communicating material wants, a desire for social interaction or comfort, and joint attention, where the infant expresses his or her desire to share an experience with the caregiver (Prizant, Wetherby, & Roberts, 2000). During the developmental assessment, this is most commonly observable as social referencing, where the infant visually looks to the caregiver or another trusted person for reassurance or emotional regulation. Beginning at about 8 months, infants typically start to show increasing stranger anxiety (in this case, the examiner). Through social referencing, the infant looks to his or her caregiver for cues that the stranger is safe and is to be trusted. Similarly, infants may look to their caregivers to resolve uncertainty regarding how to approach the developmental tasks presented during the assessment. When an infant's social referencing is met with positive affect from the caregiver, the infant is most likely to respond with approach behaviors, whereas the opposite is true if the infant's referencing is met with either negative or neutral caregiver affect (Walden & Ogan, 1988).

Infants also may use social referencing and joint attention to share joy or obtain acceptance when they have mastered a developmental assessment task. Astute clinical observation at the point in time when an infant masters a developmental task may reveal the degree to which the infant is motivated primarily through effectance (i.e., a desire to master the task) or through the social reinforcement the child expects to receive from the caregiver or the examiner. In the former case, the infant may show joyful affect at succeeding at the task and then may quickly wish to share that affect with his or her caregiver (or the examiner) through establishing joint attention to the success. In the latter case, the infant may first socially reference the caregiver to obtain social reinforcement before showing positive affect himself or herself. Overall, the developmental assessment provides many opportunities to observe spontaneous linguistic and prelinguistic social communication between the infant and caregivers.

The Infant's Reactions to Transitions and Social Exposure Over Time

The developmental assessment also affords many rich opportunities to observe how the infant and the infant-caregiver dyad negotiate the many transitions that take place during the course of the assessment and how the infant's reaction to the evaluator and the testing situation changes over the course of time. Initial meetings provide a context for observing how the infant approaches strangers in a novel context. Do the infant's reactions to the examiner display a developmentally normal level of stranger anxiety or is the anxiety poorly modulated, such that the infant becomes distressed and difficult to console, or is there an absence of stranger anxiety, such that the infant seems socially indiscriminant? If the infant is de-

veloping a secure attachment to the caregiver, some level of stranger anxiety or wariness by 8 months of age is expected, and utilization of caregiver social referencing should be observed as a way for the infant to modulate his or her emotional reaction. A responsive caregiver will appreciate this and provide the infant reassurance. Is the infant able to relinquish test items throughout the session, and is the caregiver able to help the infant negotiate relinquishments by providing comfort or well-planned distractions? Is the infant able to relinquish the testing setting at the end of sessions and is the caregiver helpful to the infant by providing anticipatory cues to buffer the abruptness of transitions? By nature, some test tasks are more structured or passive (e.g., puzzles, books, etc.) while others are less structured or more active (e.g., gross motor tasks). How adept is the infant at negotiating these changes? Also, over the course of time, does the infant warm up to the examiner and engage in increasingly reciprocal interactions?

The Three Levels of Observation

Within the four broad areas of observation described above, the clinician makes observations continuously on at least three levels. Perhaps the most obvious level is the observation of how the child responds to the structured assessment items administered during formal testing. As stated above, observations during formal testing should not be confined solely to whether the child passes or fails a given item, but should include how the child approaches the task. The second level of observation during an infant assessment is how the child reacts to the situation apart from the formal testing structure. Does the child approach toys, initiate interactions, and reference the examiner or the caregivers? How does the child react in the beginning of the evaluation versus later when the situation and the examiner are more familiar?

The third observational level is a specific focus on the interactions between caregivers and infant. The clinician makes these observations throughout the evaluation process and revises his or her hypotheses as both caregivers and infant become familiar with the process. How to interpret the behaviors one observes between caregivers and child in terms of their ongoing relationship is learned partially by experience and requires time to gather many observational points. However, several general areas may provide important descriptive clues. Does the child refer to the caregivers for both help and reassurance? Similarly, does the child show his successes to the caregivers, and do the caregivers respond? Another important observation for toddlers is whether or not the child leaves the caregivers' immediate company to work with items or explore. For infants, how caregivers hold, feed, and comfort their baby may be windows into the emerging dyadic and familial relationships. A caregiver participates with his or her child during such sessions in varying ways, and the clinician continuously will be assessing qualitative aspects of that participation—how intrusively involved, withdrawn, or comfortably facilitative the caregiver is. One of the most important lessons when learning how to observe interactions between infants and caregivers is that clinical observations, even when based in a naturalistic setting, may or may not be an adequate reflection of what is typical for that particular family. Adults may appear very different as individuals in their own right, compared to when they are interacting with their children. Also, the assessment context where one's child (and by implication, oneself as a person and as a caregiver) is observed by another is anxiety provoking in varying degrees for all caregivers, and may profoundly alter their caregiving style.

Formal quantitative developmental evaluation is only part of the overall clinical assessment of infants. Indeed, in some ways, formal testing is the least critical of the clinical assessment tasks and serves more as a frame for clinicians to guide their observations (Gilliam, 1999). It is not sufficient in assessing infants simply to say that the infant is either developmentally delayed or age adequate. For very young children, assessing development involves elaborating a more complex view of the child and his or her environment, and at this age, every developmental evaluation must include descriptions of behavior and the qualitative aspects of the child's behavior in the structured setting. For example, *when* the infant first turned to a voice or successfully retrieved a toy in an age-appropriate manner may be less important than *how* he or she responded to these tasks (e.g., with excitement, positive affect, and energy versus slowly, deliberately, and with little affective response). Such qualitative observations are often the best descriptors of those capacities for which we have few standardized assessment techniques but that are absolutely fundamental for fueling the development of motor, language, and problem-solving skills. Through observing how infants do what they do, the clinician gains information about how infants cope with frustration and how they engage the adult world, as well as about their emotional expressiveness, their capacity for persistence and sustained attention, and the level of investment and psychological energy given to their activities.

Synthesizing the Information

The process of synthesizing all the data gathered from the different sources during an assessment is a technique and skill unto itself. Moreover, how this synthesis, with its attendant recommendations, is conveyed to caregivers and other professionals is another essential step in the assessment process, and the assessment is not complete until the therapeutic alliance among all stakeholders is brought to fruition in a collaborative formulation. Infant assessments often involve referring pediatricians and other clinicians, all of whom need to be included individually in the clinician's data-gathering interviews and in the final synthesis.

The synthesis of information from an infant assessment differs from the synthesis involved in other medical diagnostic processes in that there are very few specific diagnostic categories that encapsulate all the findings of an infant assessment. The synthesis involved in an infant assessment requires a bringing together of all the data gathered from interviews, observations, and testing into a qualitative description of that infant's capacities in different functional areas (motor, problem-solving, language and communication, and social) and of the infant's current strengths and weaknesses. It also involves integrating the assessment information in the context of the infant's individual environment. For example, an infant who has experienced multiple foster placements may be socially delayed, but such a finding may assume a different significance for an infant who has had a stable home environment.

Synthesizing the large amount of data obtained from a comprehensive clinical infant assessment can be quite daunting. As stated previously, in performing the infant assessment the clinician must be both generalist and specialist. The clinician must draw upon and synthesize knowledge from child psychiatry, pediatrics, neurology, developmental psychology, speech/language therapy, physical and occupational therapy, and often genetics and endocrinology (Mayes & Gilliam, 1999). Increasingly, clinicians evaluating young children also need to know about early childhood education programs and early intervention, as well as laws regarding child abuse, neglect, and domestic violence. Knowledge from these diverse fields allows a clinician to place the results of a developmental assessment in a meaningful context for the individual child and leads to a better conceptualization of treatment options. For example, understanding the physiological effects of prolonged malnutrition and episodic starvation in infancy (Dickerson, 1981; Shonkoff & Marshall, 1990) helps the clinician evaluate the relatively greater gross motor delays of a child with failure to thrive who has no other neurological signs. Similarly, understanding the effects of a parent's affective disorder on a child's responsiveness to the external world (Seifer & Dickstein, 2000) adds another dimension to understanding the infant's muted or absent social interactiveness, babbling, and smiling.

Finally, it is often during the synthesis process that the therapeutic effect for caregivers participating in the assessment is most evident. At the very least, caregivers often change their perceptions of their infant's capacities. They may see strengths in their infant they had not previously recognized or become deeply and painfully aware of weaknesses and vulnerabilities that they may or may not have acknowledged before the assessment. Any of these changes in perceptions may affect the caregivers' view of themselves and of their role as caregivers. Also, infants often change during the assessment process, as their caregivers become more involved in the alliance with the clinician, and they experience, at least temporarily, another adult's concern and interest in their family. Emphasizing the potentially therapeutic value of an assessment underscores that the synthesis process is not simply wrapping up the assessment and conveying information, but is also a time to explore with the caregivers the meaning of the process for them and their infant.

CONCLUSION

The assessment of infant mental health is multicontextual. It is not possible to understand the mental health needs of an infant without also striving to understand the dyadic, familial, community, and cultural contexts in which the infant is developing. Indeed, understanding an infant's developing capacities and relationships within these contexts is at the very heart of infant mental health assessment. Just as it is necessary to understand an infant within these contexts, it is also essential to attend to the ways in which the infant's unique level of multifaceted development shapes, and is shaped by, these important relationships (Shonkoff & Phillips, 2000).

Assessment of an infant's development can provide far more than a sense of the baby's developing competencies across a variety of interrelated domains. Skillfully performed and astutely observed, developmental assessment also provides an opportunity to appreciate more directly the caregivers' expectations, fantasies, and fears regarding the infant's developing competence and to better understand how the quality of the caregiver-infant relationship might influence the infant's social motivation to please his or her caregivers and develop a more autonomous sense of self-efficacy. Although achieving a better understanding of the infant's development is the explicit focus of these assessments, the assessment process also provides many opportunities to acquire insight into how the infant's social context supports his or her development, and how the infant's developing sense of competence and autonomy, in turn, supports the caregivers' developing sense of their own role as a nurturer.

ACKNOWLEDGMENTS   The authors wish to express gratitude to the many families and infants who have sought consultation at the Yale University Child Study Center and have, in turn, taught us so much about our work.

References

Als, H., Tronick, E., Lester, B. M., & Brazelton, T. B. (1979). Specific neonatal measures: The Brazelton Neonatal Behavior Assessment Scale. In J. Osofsky (Ed.), *Handbook of infant development* (pp. 185–215). New York: Wiley.

Bagnato, S. J., & Neisworth, J. T. (1999). Collaboration and teamwork in assessment for early intervention. *Child and Adolescent Psychiatric Clinics of North America, 8,* 347–363.

Bayley, N. (1993). *Bayley scales of infant development* (2nd ed.). San Antonio, TX: Psychological Corporation.

Benham, A. L. (2000). The observation and assessment of young children including use of the Infant-Toddler Mental Status Exam. In C. H. Zeanah, Jr. (Ed.), *Handbook of infant mental health* (2nd ed., pp. 249–265). New York: Guilford Press.

Bornstein, M. H., & Sigman, M. D. (1986). Continuity in mental development from infancy. *Child Development, 57,* 251–274.

Boyd, R. D. (1989). What a difference a day makes: Age-related discontinuities and the Battelle Developmental Inventory. *Journal of Early Intervention, 13,* 114–119.

Brazelton, T. B. (1984). *Neonatal behavioral assessment scale* (2nd ed.). Clinics in Developmental Medicine (No. 88). Philadelphia: J. B. Lippincott.

Carter, A. S., & Briggs-Gowan, M. J. (2001). *Infant toddler social and emotional assessment (ITSEA): Manual* (v 1.1). Unpublished manuscript.

Close, N. (1999). Diagnostic play interview: Its role in comprehensive psychiatric evaluation. *Child and Adolescent Psychiatric Clinics of North America, 8,* 239–255.

Close, N. (2002). *Listening to children: Talking with children about difficult issues.* Boston: Allyn and Bacon.

Cox, C. E. (1999). Obtaining and formulating a developmental history. *Child and Adolescent Psychiatric Clinics of North America, 8,* 271–279.

Crockenberg, S., & Leerkes, E. (2000). Infant social and emotional development in family context. In C. H. Zeanah, Jr. (Ed.), *Handbook of infant mental health* (2nd ed., pp. 60–90). New York: Guilford Press.

Dickerson, J. W. T. (1981). Nutrition, brain growth and development. In K. J. Connolly & H. R. Prechtl (Eds.), *Maturation and development: Biological and psychological perspectives* (pp. 110–130). Clinics in Developmental Medicine (No. 77/78). Philadelphia: J. B. Lippincott.

Erikson, J. (1996). The Infant-Todder Developmental Assessment (IDA): A family-centered transdisciplinary assessment process. In S. J. Meisels & E. Fenichel (Eds.), *New visions for the developmental assessment of infants and young children* (pp. 147–167). Washington, DC: Zero to Three, National Center for Infants, Toddlers, and Families.

Field, T., Healy, B., Goldstein, S. Perry, S., Bendell, D., Schanberg, S., Zimmerman, E. A., & Kuhn, C. (1988). Infants of depressed mothers show "depressed" behaviors even with nondepressed adults. *Child Development, 59,* 1569–1579.

Flynn, J. R. (1984). The mean IQ of Americans: Massive gains 1932 to 1978. *Psychological Bulletin, 95,* 29–51.

Gauthier, S. M., Bauer, C. R., Messinger, D. S., & Closius, J. M. (1999). The Bayley Scales of Infant Development-II: Where to start? *Journal of Developmental and Behavioral Pediatrics, 20*(2), 75–79.

Gibbs, E. D. (1990). Assessment of infant mental ability: Conventional tests and issues of prediction. In E. D. Gibbs & D. Teti (Eds.), *Interdisciplinary assessment of infants: A guide for early intervention professionals* (pp. 77–90). Baltimore, MD: Brookes.

Gilliam, W. S. (1999). Developmental assessment: Its role in comprehensive psychiatric assessment of young children. *Child and Adolescent Psychiatric Clinics of North America, 8,* 225–238.

Gilliam, W. S., & Mayes, L. C. (2000). Developmental assessment of infants and toddlers. In C. H. Zeanah, Jr. (Ed.), *Handbook of infant mental health* (2nd ed., pp. 236–248). New York: Guilford Press.

Gilliam, W. S., & Mayes, L. C. (2002. Clinical assessment of infants and toddlers. In M. Lewis (Ed.), *Child and adolescent psychiatry: A comprehensive textbook* (3rd ed., pp. 507–525). Baltimore, MD: Lippincott, Williams and Wilkins.

Gilliam, W. S., Mayes, L. C., & Hazen, E. P. (2001, April). *Age-related normative discontinuities and the Bayley-II: A meaningful source of psychometric error in research and clinical use.* Paper presented at the biennial meeting of the Society for Research in Child Development, Minneapolis, MN.

Hirshberg, L. M. (1996). History-making, not history-taking: Clinical interviews with infants and their families. In S. J. Meisels & E. Fenichel (Eds.), *New visions for the developmental assessment of infants and young children* (pp. 85–124). Washington, DC: Zero to Three, National Center for Infants, Toddlers, and Families.

Horowitz, F. D., & Linn, L. P. (1982). The neonatal behavioral assessment scale. In M. Wolraich & D. K. Routh (Eds.), *Advances in developmental pediatrics, 3* (pp. 223–256). Greenwich, CT: JAI.

Kaufman, J., & Henrich, C. (2000). Exposure to violence and early childhood trauma. In C. H. Zeanah, Jr. (Ed.), *Handbook of infant mental health* (2nd ed., pp. 195–207). New York: Guilford Press.

Kogan, N., & Carter, A. S. (1996). Mother-infant reengagement following the still-face: The role of maternal emotional availability in infant affect regulation. *Infant Behavior and Development, 19,* 359–370.

Kopp, C. B. (1989). Regulation of distress and negative emotions: A developmental view. *Developmental Psychology, 25,* 343–354.

Lancione, E., Horowitz, F. D., & Sullivan, J. W. (1980). The NBAS-K 1: A study of its stability and structure over the first month of life. *Infant Behavior and Development, 3,* 341–359.

Lewis, M. (1993). The emergence of human emotions. In M. Lewis & J. M. Haviland (Eds.), *Handbook of emotions* (pp. 223–235). New York: Guilford Press.

Londerville, S., & Main, M. (1981). Security of attachment, compliance, and maternal training methods in the second year of life. *Developmental Psychology, 17,* 289–299.

Madrid, A., & Marachi, J. P. (1999). Medical assessment: Its role in comprehensive psychiatric evaluation. *Child and Adolescent Psychiatric Clinics of North America, 8,* 257–270.

Matula, K., Gyurke, J. S., & Aylward, G. P. (1997). Response to commentary. Bayley Scales-II. *Developmental and Behavioral Pediatrics, 18,* 112–113.

Mayes, L. C., & Gilliam, W. S. (Guest Eds.). (1999). Comprehensive psychiatric assessment of young children [Special issue]. *Child and Adolescent Psychiatric Clinics of North America 8*(2).

McCall, R. B. (1979). The development of intellectual functioning in infancy and the prediction of later IQ. In J. Osofsky (Ed.), *Handbook of infant development* (pp. 707–741). New York: Wiley.

McCall, R. B., & Carriger, M. S. (1993). A meta-analysis of infant habituation and recognition memory performance as predictors of later IQ. *Child Development, 64,* 57–79.

McLinden, S. E. (1989). An evaluation of the Battelle Developmental Inventory for determining special education eligibility. *Journal of Psychoeducational Assessment, 7,* 66–73.

Meisels, S. J. (1989). Can developmental screening tests identify children who are developmentally at risk? *Pediatrics, 83,* 578–585.

Meisels, S. J., & Wasik, B. A. (1990). Who should be served? Identifying children in need of early intervention. In S. J. Meisels & J. P. Shonkoff (Eds.), *Handbook of early childhood intervention* (pp. 605–632). New York: Cambridge University Press.

Minde, K. (2000). Prematurity and serious medical conditions in infancy: Implications for development, behavior, and intervention. In C. H. Zeanah, Jr. (Ed.), *Handbook of infant mental health* (2nd ed., pp. 176–194). New York: Guilford Press.

Mullen, E. M. (1995). *Mullen scales of early learning: AGS edition.* Circle Pines, MN: American Guidance Service.

Newborg, J., Stock, J., Wnek, L., Guidubaldi, J., & Svinicki, J. S. (1984). *Battelle developmental inventory (BDI).* Allen, TX: DLM/Teaching Resources.

Prizant, B. M., Wetherby, A. M., & Roberts, J. E. (2000). Communication problems. In C. H. Zeanah, Jr. (Ed.), *Handbook of infant mental health* (2nd ed., pp. 282- 297). New York: Guilford Press.

Provence, S. (1977). Developmental assessment. In M. Green & R. Haggarty (Eds.), *Ambulatory pediatrics* (pp. 374–383). Philadelphia: Saunders.

Provence, S., Erikson, J., Vater, S., & Palmeri, S. (1995). *Infant-toddler developmental assessment.* Chicago: Riverside Publishing.

Ramey, C. T., Campbell, F. A., & Nicholson, J. E. (1973). The predictive power of the Bayley Scales of Infant Development and the Stanford-Binet Intelligence Test in a relatively constant environment. *Child Development, 44,* 790–795.

Rosenblith, J. F. (1979). The Graham/Rosenblith behavioral examination for newborns: Prognostic value and procedural issues. In J. Osofsky (Ed.), *Handbook of infant development* (pp. 216–249). New York: Wiley.

Ross, G., & Lawson, K. (1997). Commentary. Using the Bayley-II: Unresolved issues in assessing the development of prematurely born children. *Developmental and Behavioral Pediatrics, 18,* 109–111.

Salvia, J., & Ysseldyke, J. E. (1991). *Assessment* (5th ed.). Boston: Houghton Mifflin.

Sameroff, A. J. (Ed.). (1978). Organization and stability of newborn behavior: A commentary on the Brazelton Neonatal Behavioral Assessment Scale. *Monographs of the Society for Research in Child Development, 43.*

Seifer, R., & Dickstein, S. (2000). Parental mental illness and infant development. In C. H. Zeanah, Jr. (Ed.), *Handbook of infant mental health* (2nd ed., pp. 145–160). New York: Guilford Press.

Seligman, S. (2000). Clinical interviews with families of infants. In C. H. Zeanah, Jr. (Ed.), *Handbook of infant mental health* (2nd ed., pp. 211–221). New York: Guilford Press.

Shonkoff, J. P., & Marshall, P. C. (1990). Biological bases of developmental dysfunction. In S. J. Meisels & J. P. Shonkoff (Eds.), *Handbook of early childhood intervention* (pp. 35–52). New York: Cambridge University Press.

Shonkoff, J. P., & Phillips, D. A. (Eds.) (2000). *From neurons to neighborhoods: The science of early childhood development.* Washington, DC: National Academy Press.

Siegel, L. S. (1979). Infant perceptual, cognitive, and motor behaviors as predictors of subsequent cognitive and language development. *Canadian Journal of Psychology, 33,* 382–394.

Sparrow, S. S., Balla, D. A., & Chicchetti, D. V. (1984). *Vineland adaptive behavior scales.* Circle Pines, MN: American Guidance Service.

Tronick, E. Z., Cohn, J., & Shea, E. (1986). The transfer of affect between mothers and infants. In T. B. Brazelton & M. W. Yogman (Eds.), *Affective development in infancy* (pp. 11–25). Norwood, NJ: Ablex.

van den Boom, D. C. (1994). The influence of temperament and mothering on attachment and exploration: An experimental manipulation of sensitive responsiveness among lower-class mothers with irritable infants. *Child Development, 65,* 1457–1477.

Vaughn, B. E., Taraldson, B., Crichton, L., & Egeland, B. (1980). Relationships between neonatal behavioral organization and infant behavior during the first year of life. *Infant Behavior and Development, 3,* 47–66.

Walden, T. A., & Ogan, T. A. (1988). The development of social referencing. *Child Development, 59,* 1230–1240.

Whatley, J. (1987). Bayley Scales of Infant Development. In D. Keyser & R. Sweetland (Eds.), *Test critiques* (Vol. 6, pp. 38–47). Kansas City, MO: Westport.

Worobey, J., & Brazelton, T. B. (1990). Newborn assessment and support for parenting. In E. D. Gibbs & D. M. Teti (Eds.), *Interdisciplinary assessment of infants: A guide for early intervention professionals* (pp. 137–154). Baltimore, MD: Brookes.

Zeanah, C. H., Boris, N. W., Heller, S. S., Hinshaw-Fuselier, S., Larrieu, J., Lewis, M., Palomino, R., Rovaris, M., & Valliere, J. (1997). Relationship assessment in infant mental health. *Infant Mental Health Journal, 18,* 182–197.

Zeanah, C. H., Boris, N. W., & Larrieu, J. A. (1997). Infant development and developmental risk: A review of the past 10 years. *Journal of the American Academy of Child and Adolescent Psychiatry, 36,* 165–178.

11

Observation in Infant-Toddler Mental Health Assessment

Marina Zelenko

In 1931, H. Winkler wrote: "In order to penetrate into child's essential character, a comprehensive observation of the individual child is necessary over a long period. A child's behavior at later ages can be understood only in the light of the observations made in the kindergarten; early studies are often of great value in vocational guidance, the care of adolescents, and the work of the juvenile court" (p. 1). The author highlighted the importance of systematic observation and documentation of the child's "bodily development; home and kindergarten environment; relationships to teacher and companions; activities; intelligence, emotional life; and will; moral development; and undesirable behavior" (Winkler, 1931, pp. 1–15). This early work emphasizes the role of behavioral observations in understanding the child's character and in predicting later functioning. It also defines important observational guidelines that clinicians and researchers follow today: we observe multiple domains of the child's development and evaluate the child's behavior and relationships in a consistent fashion, over a period of time, and in different environments.

Observation as a clinical assessment method is indebted to behavioral science. Behavioral specialists have made a unique contribution to the field by developing detailed observation techniques and scoring systems to quantify the observations of natural behaviors (Wenar, 1990). Our understanding of observational findings was advanced further by integration of the behavioral approach with a normative-developmental perspective, which highlights the importance of accounting for the developmental processes and emphasizes the use of appropriate reference groups in assessment (Edelbrock, 1984; Ollendick & King, 1991). Another powerful perspective that has been directing advancements in child assessment is the bioecological approach, which implies that human development takes place through progressively more complex reciprocal interactions between an active, evolving biopsychosocial human organism and its immediate external environment (Bronfenbrenner, 1999). This perspective suggests the importance of including in observation the child's characteristics, the child's environment, and interactions between the child and the environment over time.

The evolution of behavioral observational methods, enriched with developmental and bioecological perspectives, has brought us to the level of scientific and clinical sophistication that allows for development and clinical implementation of standardized and valid observational techniques. There have been some advances in this direction, for example, protocols for observation of child-parent interactions (Forehand et al., 1979; Jones, Reid, & Patterson, 1975) that have been validated and adopted in a clinical setting. Still, observational methods are often used without due regard for their psychometric characteristics, including their reliability, validity, and clinical utility (Ollendick & King, 1991). Systematic implementation of standardized observational protocols in research and clinical practice is necessary to enhance our understanding and management of childhood mental health problems; it will enable us to describe objectively and measure diverse children's behaviors, to compare observational findings, and to design standardized interventions and evaluate their outcome.

To plan observation, one defines several parameters: the purposes and the focus of the observation, what setting and type of observation will be used, who is going to perform the observation and record the findings and how that will be done, and how the findings will be interpreted and assessed. The choice of these parameters depends on the nature of the particular assessment question. The objective of this chapter is to discuss these general parameters of observation in mental health work with young children. Across various assessment settings, there is always much variability in ways observation is set up and conducted, and the data are assessed and interpreted. My goal is to provide the reader with a framework to facilitate planning observation in a systematic fashion—a first step in obtaining valid observational data.

FOCUS OF OBSERVATION

Depending on a particular assessment question, observation may involve one or several domains of the child's functioning, such as different areas of development or the child's behavioral or emotional responses. More focused observation may be undertaken to understand a particular, already identified problem. For example, in the case of a feeding difficulty, observation may be focused on the feeding process. Because of the importance of child-parent relationships in the mental health and development of young children, assessment also includes observation of child-parent interactions. It is helpful to observe the child in separate sessions with all caregivers as well as in family sessions with multiple family members, including siblings.

This section discusses the process of selecting and defining the target behavior. I then present a list of clinically relevant domains of child, parent, and dyadic functioning that may be a focus of observation.

Selecting and Defining Target Behavior

To select what behaviors need to be observed, an evaluator initially gathers information from several sources, such as parents' and other caregivers' interviews and behavioral checklists. The discussion about the behavior in question should be focused and detailed. For instance, if a mother reports that her 3-year-old son is "aggressive," it is necessary to ask her to describe the behavior in concrete terms and give as many specific examples of the child's aggressive behaviors as possible. It is also important to know where and when the behavior occurs (e.g., in the preschool and on a playground) and with whom (e.g., peers and teachers). It is always useful to include in observation antecedents and consequences of the behavior—the approach used widely by behavioral clinicians (Wenar, 1990): What were the interactions between the boy and his playmate before the pushing? What were the playmate's and the teacher's responses?

In selecting and defining the target behaviors, clinicians must make multiple decisions. Should we include in our definition of the boy's aggression pushing only or angrily throwing toys as well? If throwing toys were included, would it be throwing toys at people only or just random angry throwing of toys? Should we also include angry verbalizations and threats of harm? Should we consider all these behaviors together to derive an ultimate aggression score or would it be more beneficial to consider, observe, and measure these behaviors separately? If we want to derive a single index of aggressiveness, how should we weight different behaviors?

Barton and Ascione (1984) suggest that the selected observed behavior should bear an obvious relation to the referral problem, for example, physical fights for aggression; number of bites of food for food refusal. Behaviors may also be selected by noting the difference in behavior between the client and the peer group (does the 3-year-old boy push his playmates more often than other children in his day care?) or between the client and existing local or general developmental norms (does the pushing happen more often than we would expect in a 3-year-old boy?).

By answering these questions, we are developing an objective, or operational, definition of the behavior. This process is critical to the validity of the data. The objective definition provides the observer with a comprehensive set of decision rules for detecting the target behavior and distinguishing it from other responses. Without objective definitions, we might get lost in ambiguous and idiosyncratic meanings that often are inherent in colloquial or general terms, such as "hard to manage" or "out of control." Children's behaviors are so variable, equivocal, and inferential that even experts may disagree as to whether the young child is "aggressive" or merely "assertive," and often they need to define different levels of "aggression." A reader interested in the process of development of objective definitions is referred to an excellent review by Barton and Ascione (1984).

Domains of Observation

In the following sections, I present major domains of child, parent, and dyadic functioning that may be targeted domains for observation. The lists reflect accumulated collective experience of clinicians working with young children and reported in the literature (American Academy of Child and Adolescent Psychiatry, 1997; Benham, 2000; Wenar, 1990). Although not exhaustive, the lists are meant to be a starting point for the reader. The experienced clinician might add other observable dimensions.

Child Domain

Observation of the child includes: (a) general appearance, including size, level of nourishment, maturity according to age, dysmorphic features

and notable medical problems, dress, hygiene, and body language; (b) reaction to situations, including initial reaction and subsequent adjustment to the setting, exploratory behaviors, and reaction to transitions; (c) self-regulation, including state and sensory regulation, activity level, attention span, and frustration tolerance; (d) modes, ranges, intensity, and duration of affective expressions, including tone of voice, posture, and facial expression; (e) behaviors suggestive of fears, dissociative states, or hallucinations; (f) aggressive behaviors; (g) structure and content of play; (h) motor, cognitive, and speech and language development.

Parent Domain

Clinically relevant dimensions of parental behavior may include: (a) the level of affection toward the child and the willingness to engage the child both verbally and nonverbally; (b) the level of attunement to the child's cues, protectiveness, and emotional responses; (c) the use of limits and the manner in which the parent allows or facilitates autonomous play; (d) the ability to regulate the child's emotional state, affect, behavior, and attention; (e) thematic content of the child-parent play and the role played by the parent.

Dyadic Interaction and Relatedness Domain

Observation of dyadic interactions and relatedness may include: (a) the child's capacity and desire for affective involvement with the parent; (b) amount and extent of physical and eye contact and the quality and quantity of verbal exchange in the child-parent dyad; (c) shared interests, simple imitation, and attuned exchanges during dyadic interactions; (d) the level of dyadic pleasure and harmony and mutual engagement during play; (e) attachment behaviors; (f) the child's capacity for and interest in interpersonal relatedness and the manner and extent to which the child engages in or initiates play with other persons. The last item may include the child's capacity for relatedness and the quality of interactions with siblings and other members of the family, teachers, peers, and the evaluator.

TYPES OF OBSERVATION

Observation may be naturalistic, structured, unstructured, or participant observation, depending on the amount of instruction and the role of the observer. In this section, I consider different types of observation and discuss advantages and challenges of their application in practice.

Naturalistic Observation

Naturalistic observation is observation of the child's behavior in natural environments, without instructions or interference from the observer. Naturalistic observation provides a record of the child's behaviors that occur spontaneously. Naturalistic observations of children may be conducted in home, school or day care, and playground settings (Harrison, 1973; Odehnal & Severova, 1975; Patterson, 1977; Stoolmiller, Eddy, & Reid, 2000). Naturalistic observation is the gold standard and the cornerstone of the behavioral and developmental sciences. It has provided scientists with a great many insights into child behavior and development and has served as a foundation in designing clinical and laboratory assessment procedures (e.g., Ainsworth, 1963; Ainsworth, Blenar, Waters, & Wall, 1978).

Although it is an invaluable source of information, naturalistic observation may be quite time and resource consuming and not always practical in today's busy clinical practice. The observers may not have enough time during field observations to wait until the behaviors of interest occur spontaneously. Further, natural conditions may vary considerably, which may make comparisons between children's behaviors challenging.

Structured and Unstructured Observation and Participant Observation

Structured procedures have been designed to elicit a behavior of interest under standardized conditions that are consistently and reliably defined by the observer for all participants. Structured protocols usually involve several consecutive tasks that the participants are asked to perform. Work by Forehand and his colleagues (1979) offers an example of earlier structured protocols focused on child management behaviors, such as child compliance and parent discipline methods. Among more recent examples of structured tasks is a system developed by Crowell and Fleschmann (1993). This protocol includes assessment of a toddler's compliance: following an evaluator's instructions, the mother asks the toddler, who is engaged in play, to stop playing and put the toys away. Yet another example of a structured task is assessment of the child's reaction to separation from and reunion with the parent (Boris, Fueyo, & Zeanah, 1997; Clark, 1985). Structured tasks may be performed in any setting; most often they are done in the clinic.

Structured tasks often are combined with unstructured observation of the child and parent behavior. In unstructured or free play, the parent is instructed to play with the child for 15 to 20 minutes "just as they would at home" while the observer is in the room or observes through a one-way mirror. Free play is a useful starting point in the assessment; it helps both the child and the parent to adjust and feel more comfortable in the room (Segal & Webber, 1996). This type of observation is not entirely naturalistic because it involves an artificial setting, some instructions to the parents, and possible interference of other environment-related factors. The combination of structured and unstructured observation is often referred to as semistructured observation. Semistructured assessments are widely used in mental health assessments of young children (Luby & Morgan, 1997; Thomas, Guskin, & Klass, 1997; Zeanah et al., 1997).

To elicit particular reactions or to redirect the assessment, the clinician may actively engage in the child's play, for example, trying to stimulate the child's fantasy play, to evoke the child's highest level of functioning, or to expand on themes presented by the child or raised as concerns by the parents (Benham, 2000). This type of observation, when an evaluator assumes an active role in interactions with the child, is called participant observation.

Although many structured and semistructured assessments are used in research and clinical practice, only rarely do behaviors elicited artificially correspond with naturalistic observations (Gardner, 2000). For example, Webster-Stratton (1985) studied structured and unstructured activities in the clinic setting and found low consistency of the children's behaviors. Likewise, the examination of child-parent interactions during different tasks at home showed little consistency between structured tasks and more natural interactions (Dunn, Stocker, & Plomin, 1990; Pett, Wampold, Vaugan-Cole, & East, 1992). Overall, a few studies exploring behaviors in structured versus unstructured conditions in the same setting suggest that behaviors during unstructured tasks are more reflective of the naturally occurring behaviors and may have more predictive value (Gardner, Burton, Wilson, & Ward, 2000; Gardner, Sonuga-Barke, & Sayal, 1999).

If the use of natural observation is not feasible, I suggest considering protocols that have been validated by naturalistic observation. Semistructured protocols that include unstructured behaviors and interactions are preferable, as they have been shown to be more true to life than strictly structured protocols.

OBSERVATIONAL SETTINGS

This section discusses three main observational settings: clinic, home, and day care or preschool. First I describe the practical aspects of observation in the clinical setting and suggest some basic guidelines that might help standardize assessment conditions across different clinics. Then I discuss observation in natural settings including home and day care or preschool and review advantages and limitations of different observational settings.

Observation in the Clinical Setting

A great majority of mental health assessments of young children are performed in the clinical setting, which usually includes a clinician's office and a playroom. Initial observations of the family are obtained during the initial interview in the clinician's office. This office should have within close reach a handful of toys for children of different age groups and should be spacious enough for a child and several adults, in case the interview includes several family members. Many clinicians prefer to meet with adults only during the first meeting, to avoid unnecessary exposure of the child to perhaps sensitive information.

Further assessment of the child and the family is performed in a playroom. It is advisable to set up different playrooms for children of different ages in order to have an optimal room size, furniture, and toys. I suggest that the playroom for a young child be relatively small so the child does not "get lost" in it and is able to explore, develop a sense of control of the space, and reach for toys. At the same time, the playroom should be spacious enough for the child and at least two adults to feel comfortable. An ideal playroom has minimum furniture and a carpeted floor. A one-way mirror and an observation room are helpful to allow videotaping and observation by the clinicians, parents, and trainees.

Accessible toys (not too many) should be chosen to elicit the highest range of the child's functioning. Manipulative toys are helpful to assess the child's concentration, fine motor coordination, and frustration tolerance and to observe parent-child interaction around challenging activity. Toys for pretend play are used to stimulate the child to create make-believe stories that give important clues about children's emotional life and experiences (Benham, 2000).

The advantage of the clinical setting is that observation at the clinic is usually more time efficient than at home or day care. Evaluations in clinic setting also allow assessment of all children in the same standardized conditions (i.e., in the same room, with the same toys). At the same time, in working with high-risk families that might have difficulties with transportation or commitments, there is a higher chance of missed appointments in the clinic setting than in home or day care. The major drawback of the clinical setting is that it is unknown to what extent behaviors observed at the clinic are representative of home behaviors. In fact, studies comparing behaviors in the clinical and home settings during the same tasks have shown poor consistency of behaviors and have demonstrated that the frequency of the same behaviors at home and in the clinic may be quite different (Belsky, 1980; Kniskern, Robinson, & Mitchell, 1983; Webster-Stratton, 1985).

A few studies comparing behaviors during structured tasks in the clinic with naturalistic observations at home also showed low rates of consistency of the behaviors, suggesting that structured clinic observations may not be helpful in discriminating which children are more difficult at home compared to their peers (Webster-Stratton, 1985). For this reason, and because of state-related changes in children's behavior (e.g., due to illness or fatigue), it is advisable to observe children during multiple sessions and always ask parents after assessments whether the child's behavior was different from what normally happens at home.

Observation at Home and Day Care or Preschool

Observation at home and day care or preschool includes two major components: observation of the child and the family and observation of the environments themselves. In this chapter, the focus is on observation of the child and the family. A reader interested in the assessment of young children's environment is referred to an excellent book, *Human Environments Across the Life Span*, particularly chapters by Bradley (1999) and Friedman and Amadeo (1999).

Observation at home and day care or preschool allows naturalistic observation of the child's behavior and interactions. Day care or preschool observations are useful when a young child presents with problematic behaviors in these settings, especially if the child attends the setting regularly and spends significant amounts of time there. The problematic behavior may reflect characteristics of the child or be related to the setting conditions or result from the mismatch between the child and the setting (Benham, 2000). As with other naturalistic observations, observation at day care is quite time consuming.

If the presenting problem manifests mostly at home, home observation provides an opportunity to clarify the nature of the difficulty. In addition to observing the child's behavior and interactions with the family, the home observer has an opportunity to observe the child's daily home activities, such as play, feeding, bathing, or going to bed.

Home visitation has a long history, extending back to Elizabethan times in England and existing in the United States since at least the 1880s (Charity Organization Society of the City of New York, 1883). Home observation has many challenges. The family may perceive the presence of an unfamiliar observer as intrusive or judgmental—this is particularly true about home visitations to impoverished families with known psychosocial difficulties (Cowan, Powell, & Cowan, 1996). Sometimes, multiple visits are required to develop rapport with the family and to be able to observe the child and the family in a variety of different everyday tasks. Difference in education, social and economic status, and cultural differences between the observer and the family may be important factors in home observation. To be an unobtrusive observer in a stranger's house calls for sensitivity and skill that require training and practice.

When it is not possible for the clinician to conduct observations in the child's natural settings (e.g., home, preschool, day care), observations in clinical settings may be supplemented with behavior ratings from providers in the child's natural settings (e.g., teachers, day care providers, parents) (Bates, 1994).

RECORDING OBSERVATIONS

When the observational focus, type, and setting are identified, the next task is to define how the observation data will be gathered and recorded. This section discusses methods of recording and techniques of quantifying observations.

Although videotaping is now used with increasing frequency to record observations, hand-written observations are still common in both research and clinical practice (e.g., Stoolmiller, Eddy, & Reid, 2000). A well-designed observation sheet that includes basic information (e.g., date, time, participants' and observer's names, etc.) helps to facilitate hand recording. Contemporary technology allows using computers for recording observational findings. Using portable computers, the information can be entered directly into the scoring computer program.

Videotaping

Videotaping has been used widely in mental health practice as an essential part of structured and semistructured interactional protocols (Clark, Paulson, & Conlin, 1993). Videotaping of children's behaviors and reviewing the videotape with parents has been used as part of developmental assessments (Pawl & Lieberman, 1997) and as a therapeutic intervention (McDonough, 1995; Zelenko & Benham, 2000). Videotaping may be used in different settings, including the clinic, home, or day care. It offers a less time-consuming and more cost-effective way to observe, especially if behaviors of interest happen regularly at the same location. For example, to observe the child's sleep pattern, a camera may be placed at home above the child's bed (Anders, Goodlin-Jones, & Zelenko, 1998).

In the clinic or research laboratory, videotaping may be performed with stationary cameras or with a camera on a tripod in the playroom. It also can be performed from the observational room through a one-way mirror. If stationary video cameras are placed in the playroom and controlled from the observation room, it is advisable to have at least two video cameras placed across the room from each other to make sure that all space in the room is observed by the cameras. The best results usually are achieved when a trained assistant whose sole task is to manage the cameras performs videotaping.

Videotaping young children has its challenges. An assistant performing videotaping should be ready to follow the child's unpredictable movements in the room and adjust the focus of the camera according to the quickly changing situation. In choosing a videotaping focus, one has to consider the importance of recording minute details (e.g., eye expressions) versus the importance of being able to observe all physical space. Video cameras that are used for recording without an observer usually record behaviors occurring in a limited space and with a fixed focus. New developments in technology offer advanced options in the use of videotaping in naturalistic observations, such as videotaping by hidden cameras controlled remotely through the Internet or by cameras with telephoto lenses (Pepler & Craig, 1995). Interpretation of the videotapes may be complicated by inadequate quality of the tapes and requires extensive training and practice. Even good-quality videotapes often lack the ability to capture affective complexity and register all the facets of the interaction (e.g., facial expressions of all participants at the same time).

Quantifying Techniques

To choose a quantifying technique, it is helpful to first estimate the natural occurrence of the target behavior. Parents' and teachers' reports are often useful; a pilot observation may provide a more precise estimation. The pilot observation allows the clinician to choose an optimal time, length, and quantifying method of observation. For example, if the child develops tantrums mostly during feeding, observation may be limited to mealtimes. Depending on the estimated natural occurrence of the target behavior, the length of observation may vary: frequent behaviors may require shorter observations, while infrequent behaviors may need relatively lengthy observations.

This subsection reviews a number of methods for quantifying behavioral observations. For more detailed information regarding these methods, including computation of the observer agreement, the reader is referred to Wenar (1990) and Barton and Ascione (1984).

Frequency Recording

Frequency recording is recording the number of times the behavior occurs within a specific period. This approach is best suited when the behaviors are discrete, that is, the beginning and the end are clearly determined, so it is easy to separate each experience. The method provides meaningful data when each behavior takes approximately the same amount of time. If some of the behaviors (say, temper tantrums) last a minute and some an hour, the frequency method would not be appropriate due to the lack of sensitivity to this difference.

Duration Recording

Duration is a direct measure of the amount of time a child engages in a particular behavior. This is a measure of the interval of time between the onset and termination of the behavior. As with the frequency method, the behavior should be discrete. It should also last for an appreciable time; for example, it would be hard to measure the duration of blinking.

Interval Rating

Interval rating is recording the occurrence or non-occurrence of a behavior in a series of equal time intervals (e.g., 10 seconds). The number of intervals in which the behavior occurs is then calculated. This method is best suited for recording relatively frequent behaviors, when more than one response is being recorded, more than one individual is observed, or for behaviors that cannot be recorded using the frequency or duration methods.

There are multiple variations of this method. When the behavior is scored if it occurs at any part of the observation interval or the entire interval, the method is referred to as *partial interval recording*. For instance, if a child were throwing toys for 5 seconds out of a 10-second observation interval, the behavior would be scored. In *whole interval recording*, a behavior is scored only if it lasted throughout the entire observation interval. In this method, throwing toys would be scored only if the child were throwing toys for the entire 10 seconds of observation. Another variation of the interval method is *time-sampling*, when an observer observes the behavior for a period of time and then spends the next period recording behaviors that occurred during the previous interval. This sequence is repeated for the duration of the entire observational episode. *Momentary time sampling* means that the behavior is scored as occurring only if it occurs at a signal. For instance, upon hearing the signal "observe," an observer makes immediate determination as to whether the behavior is occurring.

Sequential Data Recording

Sequential data recording refers to a class of methods that estimate the temporal relation between behaviors and interactions. The approach has been suggested by behavioral scientists for analysis of antecedent behavior-consequence relations (Wenar, 1990). It is very useful for recording parent-child interactions. For example, this method would allow assessing the probability of the child's compliance in response to the parent's instruction during a 2-minute period after the instruction was given.

Qualitative Recording

Qualitative analyses of behavior, in addition to qualitative measurements of behavior, are crucial to our understanding of the child's behavior. It is important not only how many times or for how long the behavior occurred but also to know the *quality* of the behavior. Intensity, for instance, is an important dimension of the child's behavior that is not reflected by measures of frequency or duration. One method to quantify the quality of the behavior is to create a hierarchy of the responses, for example, a hierarchy of the child's tantrum behaviors from "mild" to "severe." This method requires that each step is operationally defined and given a rank on a scoring scale. For instance, mild tantrum behavior is defined as loud negative vocalizations in the presence of angry mood and given a score of 1, while severe is defined as loud screaming and kicking and given a score of 5.

Combined Recording Techniques

To obtain more sensitive measurements that can capture the complexity of human behavior, it is helpful to combine techniques measuring different aspects of behavior. For example, combined assessment of frequency, duration, *and* intensity of aggressive outbursts allows more comprehensive measurement than assessment only of frequency, duration, *or* intensity of the aggressive outbursts. Further, in addition to quantitative and qualitative characteristics of separate behavioral episodes, it is important to consider global impressions about the behavior over the entire observation period.

One of the best examples of a valid and reliable measure that does just that is the attachment behavior scales developed by Ainsworth and colleagues (1978). The scales provide global ratings as well as concrete examples of the behaviors, which are defined in terms of frequency, duration, and intensity. For example, "maintaining contact with the mother" is rated on a scale of 7 to 1, from "very active and persistent effort to maintain contact" to "no physical contact or no effort to maintain it." Each global rating is illustrated by three or four examples of the contact-maintaining behavior. The examples include the frequency and length of the contact as well as the quality of the infant's effort to maintain the contact; for example, "the contact lasts between 1 minute and 2 minutes" or "the infant initiates contact at least two times."

In work with infants aged 12 to 18 months, my colleagues and I are applying Ainsworth's approach to assessment of infant emotional negativity and aggressive behaviors. We use a combination of the interval rating approach with quantitative, qualitative, and global assessments. The entire assessment time is broken into 10-second intervals, and each interval is assigned a rating. Each rating is operationally defined in terms of frequency, duration, and intensity of the behaviors. The interval ratings over the entire observation period then are averaged to derive a mean score. This approach has shown good test-retest reliability and relative ease in obtaining observer agreement (Zelenko et al., in press). This and similar techniques allow precise measurement of the behaviors in a research laboratory.

In clinical practice, due to time and staff limitations, evaluators may prefer to make global assessments of infant behavior over the entire observation period rather than conducting meticulous microanalyses of brief intervals. Perhaps the development of practical global rating scales that are validated by microanalysis of the behavior is a solution for this dilemma. Encouragingly, preliminary data (Gschwendt, 2001) have shown that global ratings of observed infant behavior correspond well with computer-scored duration of the behavior as well as with behavior ratings on the Bayley Infant Development Scales (Bayley, 1969).

THE ROLE OF THE OBSERVER

This section discusses ethical considerations, the role of the observer in clinical and research observation, and issues of observer training, reliability, and reactivity.

Ethical Considerations

In conducting observations, attention to ethical issues must take precedence over all other consid-

erations, even at the expense of developing a less optimal observational system. Prior to observation, the evaluator should explain to the child's guardians the purpose of the observation and the observational procedures, discuss the methods to ensure confidentiality, and, if relevant, obtain consent for videotaping. No one can be given access to the information without the parent's permission; the child or the guardians have a right to stop the observation at any point and have access to the information that the observer has on file. Users of direct observation should be careful not to extend their comments about the child beyond the limits of the objective data.

Observer's Role

The role of the observer is different in research than in a clinical context. In research practice, observation is often performed by trained research assistants whose interaction with the family otherwise is limited. Research observation is focused on the studied behaviors, and the observer is expected to follow the research protocol closely and reliably.

In clinical practice, the goal of an assessment is usually to gather comprehensive information about the child and the family. The clinician often has to attend to multiple areas simultaneously. These may include the child's cognitive, motor, and language development, affect, quality of play, quality of interactions with parents, and frustration tolerance, to name just a few. The clinician's role in observation may be active and include spontaneous new directions to the child and the parent, for example, if the clinician wishes to address a particular domain that has not been assessed yet. The assessment in clinical practice is often a starting point of the intervention and, therefore, along with the development of the diagnostic formulation, the clinician's primary task during the assessment is to develop a rapport with the child and the family. Thus, clinical observation may require the clinician to improvise and change or postpone the preplanned protocol.

Training

The main quality of an observer is the ability to recognize and register the behavior in question.

The often tedious and laborious work of observation requires intense, focused, sustained attention and the ability to make quick decisions. The skill of observation is critical in work with young children and should necessarily be part of the training of mental health professionals (Coll, 2000). In research, training the observers is essential in obtaining reliable observation data (Barton & Ascione, 1984). This training involves obtaining thorough knowledge of the operational definitions and the recording system and practicing viewing prerecorded videotapes (see Barton & Ascione, 1984, for more details about observer training). Because both inter- and intraobserver agreements tend to decrease over time, frequent monitoring and repeated training procedures are highly desirable (Achenbach & Edelbrock, 1978; Wenar, 1990).

In clinical practice, evaluators often have to rely on other observers, such as parents and teachers. Parents and teachers may be asked to record, in some objective and systematic way, the frequency and duration of specific child behaviors as well as the contextual situation and consequences. These reports may provide valuable information to supplement other assessment data (Bates, 1994).

Reliability

Reliability refers to the extent to which observers' recordings of behaviors correspond with actual behavioral events, that is, whether the behaviors were accurately recorded. Reliability of behavioral observations has been found to be affected by complexity and clarity of the objective definitions, the number of behaviors coded simultaneously, and characteristics of the observers, their expectations, and prior training and experience (La Greca, 1983; Wenar, 1990). For example, untrained observers (parents, teachers) are more influenced by their own expectations than trained observers (Johnson & Bolstad, 1973). Even in trained observers, expectations for change or improvement have significant effect on global or subjective ratings of behavior; moreover, the feedback may influence observers into giving biased behavioral ratings (Kent & Foster, 1977). These findings further emphasize the importance of training in observation and suggest that it is

useful to provide at least some training to parents and teachers participating in observation.

Observer Reactivity

One of the concerns in the use of observation in research has been observer reactivity, that is, the potential influence of the observer's presence on the participants' behavior. Research on this issue, however, has shown that the presence of the observer does not necessarily affect the nature of the behaviors (Jacob, Tennenbaum, Selhamer, & Bargiel, 1994; Johnson & Bolstad, 1973; Kier, 1996). The extent of observer reactivity may differ from one participant to another (Lewis et al., 1996); for example, parents who are more anxious or uneasy with the evaluation, as in cases of court-ordered or custody evaluations, may be affected by the process of observation to a higher degree.

Minimizing the obtrusiveness of the assessment by observing behind a one-way mirror or using concealed video equipment instead of in vivo observers might help to reduce observer reactivity (Gardner, 2000; Johnson, Christensen, & Bellamy, 1976; Pepler & Craig, 1995; Pett et al., 1992). Allowing some time for the child and family to warm up in the beginning of the observation and familiarizing the families with the recording procedures might also help to reduce observer effects (Gardner, 1987; Kier, 1996). While some suggest that observation by a familiar person makes the interactions more natural (Gardner, 1987), others argue that previous familiarity with the observer may itself influence the behavior (Kazdin, 1982). Further research is needed to clarify the effectiveness of these strategies in reducing reactivity and their potential effects on the validity of observation in different populations.

Clinically, observer reactivity may be a positive phenomenon (La Greca, 1983). The awareness of being observed may promote self-monitoring, which can be clinically helpful. For instance, a mother who monitors her own critical behaviors toward her child may find that she is less critical and more supportive of the child as a result of self-monitoring. When assessment is the goal, it is desirable to decrease observer reactivity; when intervention is the goal, observer reactivity can be maximized to enhance the effectiveness of the procedure (La Greca, 1983, p. 125).

OBSERVATIONAL INSTRUMENTS

In both clinical and research practice, an observer needs some framework to systematize observation, organize the findings, and convey the findings to other professionals. This could be achieved by using validated assessment protocols. This section presents some examples of observational instruments that are used in research and clinical practice (see table 11.1). While more detailed description of observational instruments is beyond the scope of this chapter, the instruments used for assessments of the young child's functioning in particular domains may also be found in other chapters (e.g., chapter 3). Not all instruments that are used in infant mental health are validated and standardized at this time. Validation and standardization of the instruments and procedures and their implementation in clinical practice is one of the major tasks in the field of infant mental health.

INTERPRETATION OF OBSERVATIONAL FINDINGS

After observational findings are recorded and systematized, they are examined and interpreted. In a young child, the same observed behaviors might have different meanings. For example, clinging to a caregiver may be a reaction to a new setting in a shy child, a sign of temporary regression as a result of illness or trauma, a sign of delayed socioemotional development, or behavior that is culturally acceptable or even encouraged and reinforced by the parent. To understand and interpret the observational findings correctly and to create a comprehensive picture of the child's functioning, one has to consider numerous factors. They may include possible impact of the observational format and setting; the relationship with a person the child is observed with; the larger psychosocial contexts, such as family and culture; the child's physical and cognitive development; and state-related factors such as illness, hunger, or fatigue. Interpreting observations, evaluators also should be aware that their perceptions of the child and the family might be affected by their own personal experience; thus, it is often helpful to obtain feedback from a supervisor or colleague.

This section discusses sources of information that complement and clarify observational findings in young child mental health assessment. These sources include parents' and other caregivers' reports, the child's and caregiver's individual histories, and family history.

Parental Reports

Most of the initial information about the child's functioning is conveyed to an evaluator through a parental report that represents the parent's perception of the child. This perception reflects a variety of environmental and individual parent and child factors intertwined in the context of the child-parent relationship. Thus, parental reports are based on definitions that are likely to be specific to the parent and, therefore, are likely to be affected by systematic personal biases such as the parent's expectations, mood, or attributions about the child (Briggs-Gowan, Carter, & Schwab-Stone, 1996; Eddy, Dishio, & Stoolmiller, 1998; Fergusson, Lynskey, & Horwood, 1993; Prescott et al., 2000). On the other hand, some studies suggest that parental reports may be quite reliable (Carter, Little, Briggs-Gowan, & Kogan, 1999) and have long-term predictive validity (Olson, Bates, Sandy, & Lanthier, 2000).

Overall, the literature regarding relationships between observational measures and parental reports suggests that the two sources may measure different dimensions of the child's behavior, and, thus, offer unique information (Huffman et al., 1998; Webster-Stratton, 1998). While parental reports on a child's behavior provide invaluable information to complement and clarify the observational findings, direct observation helps to reveal parental biases and achieve more objective understanding of the child' behavior.

Other Caregivers' Reports

It is not unusual to have two different caregivers (for example, a mother and a grandmother) present conflicting reports regarding behaviors of the same young child. Examination of these reports along with direct observation of the child's behavior with the caregivers separately helps clarify to what extent the child's behavior is consistent across the relationships and whether the reported

Table 11.1 Observational Instruments for Infant and Toddler Assessment

Instrument	Age	Assessment Domains	Utility, Purpose, and Method	Psychometric Properties
Bayley Scales of Infant Development (BSID; Bayley, 1993)	1–42 months	Assesses mental, motor, and behavior development, including perceptual, memory, problem-solving, communicative, and verbal skills, motor skills, and affective and behavioral responses to the examiner and the testing.	Is used to examine infants' developmental strengths and weaknesses for clinical and research purposes. The test is a structured play session that involves a succession of tasks presented by an examiner.	Reliability and validity established. Standardization includes race, gender, parent education, urban/rural residence.
Infant Mullen Scales of Early Learning (MSEL; Mullen, 1991)	0–3 years	Assesses gross motor, visual, and receptive and expressive language organization.	Is used to identify strengths and weaknesses in specific domains and helps to make specific recommendations.	Reliability established. Standardization includes race, gender, parental occupation, residence.
Transdisciplinary Play-Based Assessment (TPBA; Linder, 1990)	6 months–6 years	Assesses socioemotional, cognitive, language, communication, and sensorimotor development.	Is used for clinical assessment and intervention to elicit the child's highest level of functioning. Includes structured and unstructured tasks in a creative play environment.	Not standardized. No validity data available.
The Infant and Toddler Mental Status Exam (ITMSE; Benham, 2000)	0–5 years	Reflects traditional domains of the mental status exam modified for use in young children. Includes child's individual and interactional behaviors and sensory and state regulation.	Is used in clinical practice to organize and convey clinical observations. May be used to organize observational data derived from different sources; does not require an observational protocol.	Not standardized. No validity data available.
Parent-Child Early Relational Assessment (PCERA; Clark, 1985)	0–5 years	Assesses affective and behavioral quality of child-parent interactions, identifies strengths and concerns regarding parent-child relationships.	Is used in clinical and research practice. Includes semistructured child-parent interactions that are videotaped, rated, and reviewed with parents.	Interrater reliability and discriminant validity have been established. Normative data exist.

discrepancy reflects the reporter's bias. The child's behavior, however, may indeed be different with different caregivers. Behaviors in early childhood are often relationship specific (Zeanah, Boris, & Scheeringa, 1997), a phenomenon that perhaps represents an existence of multiple working models of the relationships in early childhood (Bowlby, 1982). These multiple models later consolidate or evolve into a primary relationship model that becomes the most influential in the development of the child's personality. Thus, exploration of all important child-caregiver relationships through the caregivers' reports and direct observation is warranted.

Caregiver History

The caregiver's individual history and the family context are very important in interpreting the caregiver's perceptions of the child's behavior and in understanding the caregiver's interactions with the child. In some cases, parental perception of the child and attitudes toward the child may be greatly distorted by the caregiver's own past experience and earlier unresolved feelings (Fraiberg, 1980). For example, a caregiver who often starved as a young child may perceive the child's hungry crying as an expression of greediness. At the same time, the caregiver's attributions based on his or her own early history may have a potential to influence the child's behavior and the development of the child's personality (Silverman & Lieberman, 1999). For example, maternal expectations that the child will be aggressive may possibly reinforce aggressive tendencies in the child. It is necessary to be aware of these psychodynamic processes while interpreting observed behaviors with a particular caregiver.

Family Cultural Background

People with different cultural backgrounds may perceive the same behaviors differently and attach different meanings to them. To interpret observational findings and caregivers' reports accurately, the evaluator should have an understanding of the family's sociocultural background (Barrera, 1994). It may be even more important to be aware of the evaluator's limits of knowledge about the family culture and of possible differences between the

family's and the evaluator's own cultures. Respectful and empathic inquiry about culturally acceptable views and approaches helps to develop rapport with the family and obtain better understanding of the child's behaviors and the family's interactions.

Child's Medical, Genetic, and Developmental History

Medical, genetic, and developmental information about the child is another essential part of mental health evaluation of a young child. This includes information about prenatal, perinatal, and neonatal periods; data on the child's motor, cognitive, and language development; toilet training; sleeping, eating, and physical growth; as well as medical illnesses, injuries, surgeries, and medications. Particular attention should be paid to apparent changes or discontinuities in the child's developmental progress or level of functioning (American Academy of Child and Adolescent Psychiatry, 1997). A history of psychological traumas and stressors affecting the child and the family should be gathered, including child maltreatment (Lieberman & Zeanah, 1995; Roberts et al., 1995), medical illness (Mayes, 1995), death in the family, birth of a sibling, significant parental absence, moving, and so on.

Presenting symptoms in infants and toddlers are limited in range and often seem to be physical in nature, such as problematic sleep, feeding problems, or irritability. Close collaboration of mental health professionals with pediatricians is important to make sure that physical aspects of the behavioral problem are addressed, but also for better understanding of the observed behavior. The child may display aberrant movements or behaviors due to physical discomfort, pain, or a chronic physical or genetic condition. It is important to keep in mind that the presence of a physical condition does not exclude the presence of a psychological disturbance. Physical and psychological conditions frequently coexist because physical conditions, especially chronic, may affect the child's mental health and development as well as the caregiver's well-being and the family dynamics. Comprehensive multidisciplinary evaluation helps to disentangle physical and psychological aspects of the presentation.

CONCLUSION AND
FUTURE DIRECTIONS

This chapter is devoted to the use of observation in young child mental health assessment. Multiple practical aspects of observation and advantages and limitations of the current approaches have been reviewed. The topics discussed include focus, settings, and types of observation; recording methods and quantifying techniques; issues of systematization and interpretation of observational findings; and the role of the observer, including ethical considerations and matters of training, reliability, and observer reactivity.

Founded on meticulous work of behavioral scientists and enriched with a normative-developmental approach and bioecological perspectives, the science and art of observation has become increasingly sophisticated, progressing from relatively unstructured global observations to methodical observational techniques and valid scoring systems. The major direction in the field's evolution at this time is the development of psychometrically sound, true to life, and practical observational procedures that can be systematically implemented in clinical practice.

References

Achenbach, T. M., & Edelbrock, C. S. (1978). The classification of child psychopathology: A review and analysis of empirical efforts. *Psychological Bulletin, 85,* 1275–1301.

Ainsworth, M. D. S. (1963). The development of infant-mother interaction among the Ganda. In B. M. Foss (Ed.), *Determinants of infant behavior* (pp. 67–104). New York: Wiley.

Ainsworth, M. D. S., Blenar, M. C., Waters, E., & Wall, S. (1978). *Patterns of attachment.* Hillsdale, NJ: Lawrence Erlbaum.

American Academy of Child and Adolescent Psychiatry (1997). Practice parameters for the psychiatric assessment of infants and toddlers (0–36 months). *Journal of the American Academy of Child and Adolescent Psychiatry, 36,* 215–365.

Anders, T. F., Goodlin-Jones, B. L., & Zelenko, M. (1998). Infant regulation and sleep-wake state development. *Zero to Three, Bulletin of the National Center for Clinical Infant Programs, 19*(2), 5–8.

Barrera, I. (1994). Thoughts on the assessment of young children whose sociocultural background is unfamiliar to the assessor. *Zero to Three, Bulletin of the National Center for Clinical Infant Programs, 14,* 9–13.

Barton, E. J., & Ascione, F. R. (1984). Direct observation. In T. Ollendick & M. Herson (Eds.), *Child behavioral assessment* (pp. 166–194). New York: Pergamon Press.

Bates, J. E. (1994). Parents as scientific observers of their children's development. In S. L. Friedman & H. C. Haywood (Eds.). *Developmental follow-up: Concepts, domains, and methods* (pp. 197–216). San Diego: Academic Press.

Bayley, N. (1969). *Bayley scales of infant development.* New York: Psychological Corporation.

Belsky, J. (1980). Mother-infant interactions at home and in the laboratory: A comparative study. *Journal of Genetic Psychology, 137,* 37–47.

Benham, A. L. (2000). The observation and assessment of young children including use of the Infant-Toddler Mental Status Exam. In C. H. Zeanah, Jr. (Ed.), *Handbook of infant mental health* (2nd ed., pp. 249–265). New York: Guilford Press.

Boris, N. W., Fueyo, M., & Zeanah, C. H. (1997). The clinical assessment of attachment in children under five. *Journal of the American Academy of Child and Adolescent Psychiatry, 36,* 291–293.

Bowlby, J. (1982). *Attachment* (Vol. I, 2nd ed.). New York: Basic Books.

Bradley, R. H. (1999). The home environment. In S. L. Friedman & T. D. Wachs (Eds.), *Measuring the environment across the life span* (pp. 31–56). Washington, DC: American Psychological Association.

Briggs-Gowan, M., Carter, A., & Schwab-Stone, M. (1996). Discrepancies among mother, child, and teacher reports: Examining the contribution of maternal depression and anxiety. *Journal of Abnormal Psychology, 24,* 749–765.

Bronfenbrenner, U. (1999). Environments in developmental perspective: Theoretical and operational models. In S. L. Friedman & T. D. Wachs (Eds.), *Measuring the environment across the life span* (pp. 3–28). Washington, DC: American Psychological Association.

Carter, A. S., Little, C., Briggs-Gowan, M. J., & Kogan, N. (1999). The Infant-Toddler Socio-Emotional Assessment (ITSEA): Comparing parent ratings to laboratory observations of task mastery, emotion regulation, coping behaviors, and attachment status. *Infant Mental Health Journal, 20,* 375–392.

Charity Organization Society of the City of New York. (1883). *Hand-book for friendly visitors among the poor* (pp. 1–18). New York: G.P. Putnam's Sons.

Clark, R. (1983). *Interactions of psychiatrically ill and well mothers and their young children: Quality of maternal care and child competence.* Unpublished doctoral dissertation, Northwestern University, Evanston, IL.

Clark, R. (1985). *The parent-child early relational assessment.* Madison: Department of Psychiatry, University of Wisconsin Medical School.

Clark, R., Paulson, A., & Conlin, S. (1993). Assessment of developmental status and parent-infant relationships: The therapeutic process of evaluation. In C. H. Zeanah (Ed.), *Handbook of infant mental health* (pp. 191–209). New York: Guilford Press.

Coll, X. (2000). Who needs to observe infants? Infant observation in the training of child and adolescent mental health workers. *Child Psychology and Psychiatry Review, 5,* 25–29.

Cowan, P. A., Powell, D., & Cowan, C. P. (1996). Parenting interventions: A family systems perspective. In I. E. Sigel & K. A. Renninger (Eds.), *Handbook of childpsychology. Vol. 4: Child psychology in practice* (5th ed., pp. 3–72). New York: John Wiley.

Crowell, J. A., & Fleschmann, M. A. (1993). In C. H. Zeanah (Ed.), *Handbook of infant mental health* (pp. 210–221). New York: Guilford Press.

Dunn, J., Stocker, C., & Plomin, R. (1990). Assessing the relationships between young siblings: A research note. *Journal of Child Psychology and Psychiatry, 31,* 983–991.

Eddy, J. M., Dishio, T., & Stoolmiller, M. (1998). The analysis of intervention change in children and families: Methodological and conceptual issues embedded in intervention studies. *Journal of Abnormal Child Psychology, 26,* 53–71.

Edelbrock, C. S. (1984). Developmental considerations. In T. H. Ollendick & M. Hersen (Eds.), *Child behavioral assessment: Principles and procedures* (pp. 46–65). Elmsford, NY: Pergamon Press.

Fergusson, D., Lynskey, M., & Horwood, L. (1993). The effects of maternal depression on maternal ratings of child behavior. *Journal of Abnormal Child Psychology, 21,* 245–271.

Forehand, R., Sturgis, E. T., McMahon, R. J., Aguar, D., Green, K., Wells, K. C., & Breiner, J. (1979). Parent behavioral training to modify child non-compliance: Treatment generalization across time and from home to school. *Behavior Modification, 3,* 3–25.

Fraiberg, S. (1980). *Clinical studies in infant mental health.* New York: Basic Books.

Friedman, S. L., & Amadeo, J.-A. (1999). The child-care environment: Conceptualizations, assessments, and issues. In S. L. Friedman & T. D. Wachs (Eds.), *Measuring the environment across the life span* (pp. 127–165). Washington, DC: American Psychological Association.

Gardner, F. (1987). Positive interaction between mothers and children with conduct problems: Is there training for harmony as well as fighting? *Journal of Abnormal Child Psychology, 17,* 223–233.

Gardner, F. (2000). Methodological issues in the direct observation of parent-child interaction: Do observational findings reflect the natural behaviors of participants? *Clinical Child and Family Psychology Review, 3*(3), 185–198.

Gardner, F., Burton, J., Wilson, C., & Ward, S. (2000). Parent-child interaction and preschool conduct problems: How consistent is behavior observed in different settings in the home? Unpublished manuscript.

Gardner, F., Sonuga-Barke, E., & Sayal, K. (1999). Parents anticipating misbehavior: An observational study of strategies parents use to prevent conflict with behavior problem children. *Journal of Child Psychology and Psychiatry, 40,* 1185–1196.

Gschwendt, M. (2001). *Early manifestations of infant aggression.* Unpublished doctoral dissertation, Stanford University, Stanford, CA.

Harrison, P. R. (1973). A naturalistic investigation of the behavior of preschool children. *Dissertation Abstracts International, 33*(8-B), 3918.

Huffman, L. C., Bryan, Y. E., del Carmen, R., Pedersen, F. A., Doussard-Roosvelt, J. A., & Porges, S. W. (1998). Infant temperament and cardiac vagal tone: Assessments at twelve weeks of age. *Child Development, 69,* 624–635.

Jacob, T., Tennenbaum, D., Selhamer, R. A., & Bargiel, K. (1994). Reactivity effects during naturalistic observation of distressed and nondistressed families. *Journal of Family Psychology, 8,* 354–363.

Johnson, S. M., & Bolstad, O. D. (1973). Methodological issues in naturalistic observations: Some problems and solutions for field research. In L. A. Hamerlynck, L. C. Handy, &

E. J. Mash (Eds.), *Behavior change: Methodology, concepts, and practice* (pp. 7–67). Champaign, IL: Research Press.

Johnson, S. M., Christensen, A., & Bellamy, G. T. (1976). Evaluation of family intervention through unobtrusive audio recordings: Experiences in "bugging" children. *Journal of Applied Behavior Analysis, 9,* 213–219.

Jones, R. R., Reid, J. B., & Patterson, G. R. (1975). Naturalistic observations in clinical assessment. In P. McReynolds (Ed.), *Advances in psychological assessment* (Vol. 3, pp. 123–148). San Francisco: Jossey-Bass.

Kazdin, A. E. (1982). Observer effects: Reactivity of direct observation. In D. P. Hartmann (Ed.), *Using observers to study behavior* (pp. 5–19). San Francisco: Jossey Bass.

Kent, R. N., & Foster, S. L. (1977). Direct observation procedures: Methodological issues in naturalistic settings. In A. R. Ciminero, K. S. Calhoun, & H. E. Adams (Eds.), *Handbook of behavioral assessment* (pp. 89–117). New York: Wiley-Interscience.

Kier, C. (1996). How natural is "naturalistic home observation"? Observer reactivity in infant-sibling interaction. *Proceedings of the British Psychological Society, 4,* 79.

Kniskern, J. R., Robinson, E. A., & Mitchell, S. K. (1983). Mother-child interaction at home and laboratory settings. *Child Study Journal, 13,* 23–39.

La Greca, A. M. (1983). Interviewing and behavioral observations. In E. Walker & M. Roberts (Eds.), *Handbook of clinical child psychology* (pp. 109–131). New York: Wiley.

Lewis, C., Kier, C., Hyder, C., Prenderville, N., Pullen, J., & Stephens, A. (1996). Observer influences on fathers and mothers: An experimental manipulation of the structure and function of parent-infant conversation. *Early Development and Parenting, 5,* 57–68.

Lieberman, A. F., & Zeanah, C. H. (1995). Disorders of attachment in infancy. *Child and Adolescent Psychiatry Clinics of North America, 4,* 571–587.

Linder, T. (1990). *Transdisciplinary play-based assessment: A functional approach to working with young children.* Baltimore: Paul H. Brookes.

Luby, J. L., & Morgan, K. (1997). Characteristics of an infant/preschool psychiatric clinic sample: Implications for clinical assessment and nosology. *Infant Mental Health Journal, 18*(2), 209–220.

Mayes, L. C. (1995). The assessment and treatment of the psychiatric needs of medically compromised infants: Consultation with preterm infants and their families. *Child and Adolescent Psychiatry Clinics of North America, 4,* 555–570.

McDonough, S. (1995). Promoting positive early parent-infant relationships through interaction guidance. *Child and Adolescent Psychiatric Clinics of North America, 4,* 661–673.

Mullen, E. N. (1991). *The infant Mullen scales of early learning: Instrument descriptions.* Cranston, RI: T.O.T.A.L. Child.

Odehnal, J., & Severova, M. (1975). A method of observing child behavior under natural conditions and possibilities of its application in developmental psychology. *Psychologia a Patopsychologia Dietata, 10,* 407–416.

Ollendick, T., & King, N. (1991). Developmental factors in child behavioral assessment. In P. R. Martin (Ed.), *Handbook of behavior therapy and psychological science: An integrative approach* (pp. 57–72). New York: Pergamon Press.

Olson, S. L., Bates, J. E., Sandy, J. M., & Lanthier, R. (2000). Early developmental precursors of externalizing behavior in middle childhood and adolescence. *Journal of Abnormal Psychology, 28*(2), 119–133.

Patterson, G. R. (1977). Naturalistic observation in clinical assessment. *Journal of Abnormal Child Psychology, 5,* 309–322.

Pawl, J. H., & Lieberman, A. E. (1997). Infant-parent psychotherapy. In J. D. Noshpitz (Ed.), *Handbook of child and adolescent psychiatry. Vol. 1: Infants and preschoolers: Development and syndromes* (pp. 339–351). New York: Wiley.

Pepler, D. J., & Craig, W. M. (1995). A peek behind the fence: Naturalistic observation of aggressive children with remote audio-visual recording. *Developmental Psychology, 31,* 548–553.

Pett, M. A., Wampold, B. E., Vaugan-Cole, B., & East, T. D. (1992). Consistency of behaviors within a naturalistic setting: An examination of the impact of context and repeated observations on mother-child interactions. *Behavioral Assessment, 14,* 367–385.

Prescott, A., Bank, L., Reid, J., Knutson, J., Burraston, B., & Eddy, J. M. (2000). The veridicality of punitive childhood experiences reported by adolescents and young adults. *Child Abuse and Neglect, 24,* 411–423.

Roberts, J. E., Burchinal, M. R., Zeisel, S. A., Neebe, E. C., Hooper, S. R., Roush, J., Scheeringa, M. S., & Zeanah, C. H. (1995).

Symptom expression and trauma variables in children under 48 months of age. *Infant Mental Health Journal, 16,* 250–270.

Segal, M., & Webber, N. T. (1996). Non-structured play observations: Guidelines, benefits, and caveats. In S. J. Meisels & E. Fenichel (Eds.), *New visions for the developmental assessment of infants and young children.* Washington, DC: Zero to Three, National Center for Infants, Toddlers, and Families.

Silverman, R. C., & Lieberman, A. F. (1999). Negative maternal attributions, projective identification, and the intergenerational transmission of violent relational patterns. *Psychoanalytic Dialogues, 9,* 161–186.

Stoolmiller, M., Eddy, J. M., & Reid, J. B. (2000). Detecting and describing preventive intervention effects in a universal school-based randomized trial targeting delinquent and violent behavior. *Journal of Consulting and Clinical Psychology, 68*(2), 296–306.

Thomas, J. M., Guskin, K. A., & Klass, C. S. (1997). Early development program: Collaborative structures and processes. *Infant Mental Health Journal, 18*(2), 198–208.

Webster-Stratton, C. (1985). Comparisons of behavioral transactions between conduct-disordered children and their mothers in the clinic and at home. *Journal of Abnormal Child Psychology, 13,* 169–184.

Webster-Stratton, C. (1998). Preventing conduct problems in head start children: Strengthening parental competencies. *Journal of Consulting and Clinical Psychology, 66*(5), 715–730.

Wenar, C. (1990). *Developmental psychopathology.* New York: McGraw-Hill Publishers.

Winkler, H. (1931). *Principles for the observation and judgment of three- to six-year-olds in the kindergarten.* Munich: Reinhardt.

Zeanah, C. H., Boris, N. W., Heller, S. S., Hinshaw-Fuselier, S., Larrieu, J. A., Lewis, M., Palomino, R., Rovaris, M., & Valliere J. (1997). Relationship assessment in infant mental health. *Infant Mental Health Journal, 18*(2), 182–197.

Zeanah, C. H., Boris, N. W., & Scheeringa, M. S. (1997). Psychopathology in infancy. *Journal of Child Psychology and Psychiatry, 38,* 81–99.

Zelenko, M., & Benham, A. (2000). Videotaping as a therapeutic tool in psychodynamic infant-parent therapy. *Infant Mental Health Journal, 21*(3), 192–203.

Zelenko, M., Kraemer, H. C., Huffman, L., Gschwendt, M., Pageler, N., & Steiner, H. (in press). Heart rate correlates of attachment behavior in young mothers and their infants. *Journal of the American Academy of Child and Adolescent Psychiatry.*

12

The Preschool Age Psychiatric Assessment (PAPA): A Structured Parent Interview for Diagnosing Psychiatric Disorders in Preschool Children

Helen Link Egger
Adrian Angold

In this chapter we describe the Preschool Age Psychiatric Assessment (PAPA), a parent interview for diagnosing psychiatric symptoms and disorders in preschool children aged 2 through 5 years (Egger, Ascher, & Angold, 1999). The PAPA is one of a suite of interviews that employs a consistent approach to the assessment of psychopathology in childhood, adolescence, and young adulthood. The first of these interviews to be developed was the Child and Adolescent Psychiatric Assessment (CAPA), which collects information from children and adolescents aged 9 through 18 years and their parents (Angold et al., 1995). The first edition of the CAPA was developed at the Institute of Psychiatry in London. It has been updated and modified repeatedly since 1986 by the Developmental Epidemiology Program at Duke University Medical Center. The CAPA has been used to assess psychiatric disorders and disability in thousands of children in multiple research studies and has been demonstrated to be a reliable and valid measure of childhood psychopathology in children 9 through 18 years old (Angold & Costello, 1995).

In October 1998, members of the National Head Start Mental Health Consortium contacted us and requested that we develop an interview for parents of preschoolers based on the CAPA. We had been considering the development of such a measure for some time, and this request provided the needed stimulus, including a small amount of money, for us to begin. The PAPA is derived from the CAPA, but represents a significant revision of the interview content and structure to make it relevant for the assessment of very young children. The PAPA includes all *DSM-IV* criteria (American Psychiatric Association, 1994) insofar as they are relevant to younger children, items in the Diagnostic Classification: 0–3 (DC: 0–3; Zero to Three, 1994), an alternative psychiatric diagnostic classification for young children, and the Research Diagnostic Criteria–Preschool Age (RDC-PA) (Task Force on Research Diagnostic Critera, in press), as well as potentially relevant behaviors and symptoms experienced by preschoolers and their families that do not currently appear in any of these diagnostic systems. The interview also assesses disability resulting from symptoms, family environment and relationships, family psychosocial problems, and life events. Work on the PAPA was begun in the fall of 1998, and the first edition was finalized during the summer of 1999. As of September 2003, we have completed the 1.4 version of the PAPA.

While there is considerable evidence that young children experience emotional and behavioral symptoms that impede their development and interfere with their capacity to function as expected, there is no consensus that these symptoms should be considered within a diagnostic framework. Data from the dimensional assessment of preschool emotional and behavioral disorders and our experience in developing psychiatric nosology for older children both point to the feasibility of identifying clinically meaningful psychiatric disorders in young children (see chapter 7 for a full discussion of these issues). We believe that the questions of whether it is clinically relevant or appropriate to identify psychiatric disorders in young children are empirical questions that must be addressed in a systematic way.

To begin this task, the field must have adequate diagnostic tools. The PAPA grew out of the recognition that currently there is no standardized or reliable method for assessing psychiatric disorders in preschool children. Checklist measures such as the Child Behavior Checklist (CBCL; Achenbach & Edelbrock, 1983; Achenbach & Rescorla, 2000), which identify constellations of behaviors and symptoms and measure their frequency using Likert scales, have been used for a number of years to identify behaviors that lie outside the norm for same-age peers. While information from such measures has been essential in establishing that we can identify aberrant behaviors in young children, these data do not provide information about the severity, duration, onset, or context of behaviors. Thus, the information gathered through checklists is not specific enough to enable researchers or clinicians to make diagnoses based on either the *DSM* or DC:0–3 system.

The lack of diagnostic measures for preschool psychopathology has resulted partly from the absence of consensus on how disorders present at different ages during the preschool years. There are currently five diagnostic systems that can be applied to preschool children: The first and second are *DSM-IV* (American Psychiatric Association, 1994) and ICD-10 (World Health Organization, 1992), which are essentially consistent with each other. While *DSM* and ICD are the most widely known diagnostic systems, they have never attempted to encompass the range of preschool psychopathology or offered modifications of diagnoses for this age group and are relatively unreflective of the developmental differences in the presentation of psychiatric symptoms in children. The third system is the RDC-PA, a collaborative effort sponsored by the American Academy of Child and Adolescent Psychiatry to modify *DSM-IV* criteria to make them developmentally appropriate for young children (Task Force on Research Diagnostic Criteria, in press). Based on reviews of current data and the clinical/ expert consensus of the researchers involved in the development of the RDC-PA, the RDC-PA is meant to be a working document, to facilitate research on preschool psychopathology. The fourth system is the DC:0–3, an alternative diagnostic classification system developed by a task force of infant psychiatrists, psychologists, pediatricians, and social workers affiliated with the organization Zero to Three (1994) that was developed to address the deficiencies of the *DSM*/ICD approach for the classification of psychopathology in infants and young children. The DC:0–3, published in 1994, includes alternative diagnoses (e.g., for anxiety and depressive disorders), new diagnostic categories (e.g., regulatory disorders), and a reframing of the *DSM* multiaxial system. DC:0–3 attempts to fill in gaps left by the *DSM* approach, but the reliability and validity of its diagnostic approach have yet to be convincingly demonstrated. The fifth and last potential diagnostic system for identifying psychopathology in young children is the use of "clinically significant" cutoff points on symptom counts defined by checklists. The CBCL cutoff points, as well as the recently added "*DSM*-like scales" for the CBCL 1½–5, have been shown to be clinically useful and, perhaps, useful as screening measures, but do not include enough specificity on frequency, duration, and onset to be able to generate specific psychiatric diagnoses. Neither, for that matter, do they come anywhere near covering all the relevant symptoms.

Thus, one of the great challenges in developing a structured assessment of psychopathology in young children is that the development of the measures must go hand in hand with the development of a coherent and clinically meaningful psychiatric nosology for preschool children. The measure must be inclusive of the range of possible presentations of symptoms in preschool children, so that it will be possible to test empirically the usefulness and meaningfulness of various diagnoses and the various diagnostic systems across this period of rapid developmental change.

A REVIEW OF STUDIES APPLYING DIAGNOSTIC CRITERIA TO PRESCHOOLERS

A few studies have assessed the applicability of *DSM-IV* psychiatric diagnoses in young children (a review of the results of these studies can be found in chapter 7). These studies either have used sections of interviews created for use with older children that have been somewhat modified to be developmentally appropriate for younger children or have based diagnoses on clinical consensus based on multiple sources including observational assessments and checklist measures. For example, Keenan and Wakschlag have used a portion of the Schedule for Affective Disorders and Schizophrenia for School-Age Children (K-SADS) to measure *DSM-IV* oppositional defiant disorder (ODD) and conduct disorder (CD) symptoms and diagnoses in 2- through 5-year-olds (Keenan & Shaw, 1994; Keenan, Shaw, Walsh, Delliquadri, & Giovannelli, 1997; Keenan & Wakschlag, 2000; Wakschlag & Keenan, 2001). They are currently working on modifications of that instrument, but, at this writing, no version is available for use by others. The K-SADS has also been used by other researchers for assessing disruptive disorders in 5- and 6-year-olds (Lahey et al., 1998; Shaw, Owens, Giovannelli, & Winslow, 2001; Shaw, Owens, Vondra, Keenan, & Winslow, 1996). Speltz and colleagues used an unmodified version of the Diagnostic Interview Schedule for Children (DISC) to diagnose *DSM-III-R* ODD in 4- and 5-year-olds (Speltz, DeKlyen, Greenberg, & Dryden, 1995; Speltz, McClellan, DeKlyen, & Jones, 1999). Joan Luby has used a modified DISC depression section in her research on preschool depression (Luby, 2000).

The alternative approach has been to base diagnostic decisions on clinical consensus. In the only population-based study of preschool *DSM* psychiatric disorder, Lavigne and colleagues used a combination of the CBCL, observational assessments, and measures of adaptive behaviors to make clinical consensus diagnoses of the preschoolers they studied (Arend, Lavigne, Rosenbaum, Binns, & Christoffel, 1996; Dietz, Lavigne, Arend, & Rosenbaum, 1997; Lavigne et al., 1993, 1994, 1996, 1998a, 1998b, 1998c, 1999; ; Lavigne, Binns, et al., 1998; Lavigne, Schulein, & Hahn, 1986). Similarly, the multisite study of the psychopharmacological treatment of preschool attention-deficit/hyperactivity disorder (ADHD) uses a clinical consensus model for diagnosing ADHD and other disorders in preschool-aged subjects (personal communication, Lawrence Greenhill, 2001).

Most of the studies examining DC:0–3 diagnoses have used unstructured clinical interviews to make diagnoses (Boris, Zeanah, Larrieu, Scheeringa, & Heller, 1998; Dunitz, Scheer, Kvas, & Macari, 1996; Reams, 1999; Scheeringa, Peebles, Cook, & Zeanah, 2001; Scheeringa & Zeanah, 1995; Scheeringa, Zeanah, Drell, & Larrieu, 1995; Thomas & Clark, 1998; Thomas & Guskin, 2001). Michael Scheeringa and Charles Zeanah have developed a semistructured interview for clinicians to use to assess key parent-reported symptoms of DC:0–3 disorders, including relationship disorders (Scheeringa & Zeanah, 1994). However, this instrument lacks a glossary or definitions of the items being measured.

No published psychometric data is available on any of the preschool measures described above. Another problem is that most of these studies have targeted a specific diagnosis or group of diagnoses rather than the range of possible disorders, limiting exploration of the effects of comorbidity in this age group. Even Lavigne's study, which assessed a range of psychiatric disorders, lumps specific diagnostic categories into broad categories (e.g., "disruptive disorders" instead of discrete categories of ADHD, ODD, or CD).

Development of a preschool measure of psychopathology faces another challenge that arises from the focus of the infant/preschool psychiatry field on prevention as much as intervention. From a developmental perspective, researchers are interested not only in the presentation of fully developed disorders, but also in describing the emergence of disorders. Therefore, a developmentally appropriate preschool measure must encompass not only the symptoms found in current diagnostic schema, but also early manifestations of disorders. Description of how disorders emerge over time may enable researchers and clinicians to plan interventions that prevent or ameliorate the development of problems as the child grows older.

As our brief review of the status of assessment tools for preschool psychopathology suggests, there is a need for new assessment tools for diagnosing psychiatric symptoms of disorders in preschool children. The next question is what kind of assessment should be developed.

WHY IS A STRUCTURED INTERVIEW A GOOD PLACE TO BEGIN?

While the clinical interview has always had a preeminent place in the diagnosis of psychiatric disorders, the development of structured psychiatric interviews is fairly recent. Structured interviews aim to incorporate the approaches used by clinicians to gather information on symptoms and experiences from patients, while at the same time standardizing the process of obtaining the information so as to improve its consistency and reliability. The need for a structured approach arose from the recognition that different clinicians using unstructured approaches to assess the same patient would often disagree about the individual's diagnosis (Cantwell & Baker, 1988; Gould, Shaffer, Rutter, & Sturge, 1988; Remschmidt, 1988).

The medical decision-making literature has demonstrated that clinicians are affected by information collection biases that shape the reliability of diagnostic decisions (Angold & Fisher, 1999). These include the tendency to come to diagnostic determinations before they have collected all the relevant information by either selectively collecting information that confirms the diagnosis or ignoring data that disconfirms the posited diagnosis (see Achenbach, 1985, for a helpful introduction to the basics of the medical decision-making literature).

As Angold laid out in 1999, the problems with unstructured clinical interviews delineate the tasks that must be accomplished by a structured interview to address these problems. Angold writes, "A structured interview must fulfill these four goals:

1. Structure information coverage, so that all interviewers will have collected all relevant information from all subjects.
2. Define the ways in which relevant information is to be collected.
3. Make a diagnosis only after all relevant confirmatory and disconfirmatory information has been collected.
4. Structure the process by which relevant confirmatory and disconfirmatory information is combined to produce a final diagnosis" (Angold & Fisher, 1999, p. 35).

INTERVIEWER-BASED VERSUS RESPONDENT-BASED INTERVIEWS

There are two different approaches to structuring the collection of information in a structured interview: interviewer based (or sometimes called investigator based) and respondent based (Angold et al., 1995). Angold describes the distinction between the two approaches as a difference in what is structured: in an interviewer-based interview, the mind of the interviewer is structured, while in a respondent-based interview, it is the questions put to the subject that are structured.

The PAPA is an interviewer-based interview, which means that the interview schedule serves as a road map to guide the interviewer in determining whether symptoms are present on the basis of information provided by the person being interviewed. Clear definitions of symptoms are provided in a detailed glossary, and the interviewer is expected to question until he or she can decide whether the symptoms described meet these definitions. It is the job of the interviewer to make the decision whether a symptom (as defined in the glossary) is present. In a respondent-based interview, the interviewer makes no decisions about the presence of symptoms. Prescribed questions are asked verbatim in a preset order, and the interviewee's responses are recorded with a minimum of interpretation or clarification by the interviewer. The DISC (Costello, Edelbrock, Dulcan, Kalas, & Klaric, 1984; Edelbrock & Costello, 1990) is an example of a respondent-based interview. While the respondent-based approach decreases variability in content due to differing interviewing styles, the rigid format limits the interviewer's ability to rephrase questions when respondents do not understand their intent or meaning. Areas that pose particular hazards are atypical disorders such as obsessive-compulsive disorder and psychosis. For example, the question "do you wash your hands often?," which might be asked to identify compulsive behavior, could be answered *yes* by a respondent who considers washing his or her hands after each use of the toilet as "often."

We call interviews with detailed definitions of symptom concepts *glossary based* (Angold & Fisher, 1999). The PAPA provides detailed definitional glossaries at the symptom level, which means that the task of the interviewer is most clearly specified at the level of the definition of symptoms. Both lay and clinical interviewers can be trained to use such interviews, because clinical knowledge is built into the item definitions. The task of the interviewer is to apply these definitions to the material collected during the interview to determine whether symptoms, as defined in the glossary, are present and, if so, to what degree. Symptom definitions are provided both in the glossary and on the interview schedule, and rules are specified to allow nonclinicians to code the intensity, frequency, duration, and date of onset of symptoms separately. For instance, rules for coding the intensity of "depressed mood" specify the degree of intrusiveness of the symptom into other activities, the degree of uncontrollability, and the range of activities that must be affected for depressed mood to be regarded as being symptomatic. The glossary also contains guidance on how to deal with situations involving complex combinations of symptoms and how to determine exactly which symptoms should be coded as being present. This approach has been shown to allow nonclinicians to make reliable judgments of symptom severity while using a highly flexible questioning format with heavy emphasis on getting descriptions and examples of possible pathological emotions and behaviors to ensure that

codings are not based on the informant's misunderstanding of what was being asked about (Angold & Costello, 1995; Angold et al., 1995; Costello, Angold, March, & Fairbank, 1998).

The interviewer-based approach is very well suited to preschool assessment at this point in its history. To produce an adequate respondent-based interview (such as the DISC), one needs a great deal of information about exactly what questions to ask, in what order, if the relevant information is to be collected. The ability to produce such an interview, therefore, depends on having solid information about the usual presentations of problems. Such a knowledge base is lacking for preschoolers. The interviewer flexibility demanded by the PAPA is a great help in such a situation. In essence, each interview can be seen as a structured mini focus group that can provide information about relevance, appropriateness, cultural sensitivity, and calibration of glossary definitions, coding rules, and questions on the schedule. We have made a great deal of use of interviewer feedback in modifying the CAPA over the years, and we expect that such feedback will be even more important for the PAPA because we start from a weaker knowledge base regarding preschoolers.

Initially, we thought that "down-aging" the CAPA would be a straightforward, even easy task. We would remove the items or sections that were obviously irrelevant to young children (e.g., stealing cars, substance abuse), reword other items, and add a few discrete items (e.g., assess functioning at day care as well as school). While these changes were necessary, they were far from sufficient. We soon understood that the task of developing a comprehensive and clinically useful interview to assess preschoolers was much more difficult and complicated than we had initially thought. From the pared-down CAPA, we began to build the PAPA.

THE CONTENT OF THE PAPA

The current version of the PAPA includes sections on the following topics: a brief developmental assessment; family structure and function; play and peer and sibling relationships; day care/ school experiences and behaviors; food-related behaviors; sleep behaviors; elimination problems; somatization; accidents; conduct problems; ADHD; separation anxiety; anxious affect; worries; rituals and repetitions; regulation/habits; tics; sterotypies; reactive attachment; depression; mania; dysregulation; life events; posttraumatic stress disorder (PTSD); disabilities; parental psychopathology; marital satisfaction; and socioeconomic status. Table 12.1 lists the steps we took to construct a preschool version of the CAPA. A detailed description of these changes follows.

Developmentally Informed Modification of *DSM-IV* and ICD-10 Criteria

We changed the *DSM-IV* and ICD-10 criteria so that they were relevant and measurable for young children. In some instances, we removed clearly irrelevant items (e.g., rape or truancy from the CD section). In others we recast items to make them more relevant to preschoolers (e.g., items on inappropriate sexual talk or play as a substitute for CAPA information about sexual history or sexual aggression). However, although we included functional equivalents for symptoms, we cannot assume that the substituted symptom or

---

Table 12.1 The Development of the PAPA: Steps in Revision

1. Developmentally informed modification of *DSM-IV* and ICD-10 criteria
2. Addition of DC:0–3 symptoms and diagnoses
3. Inclusion of relevant checklist symptoms
4. Inclusion of developmentally relevant symptoms and behaviors not included in reviewed measures, e.g., sleep, eating and feeding, and play symptoms and behaviors
5. Inclusion of a brief developmental assessment
6. Inclusion of regulatory functions
7. Modification of the assessment of the settings where preschoolers spend their day
8. Modification of the life events section
9. Expanded assessment of the content and context of behaviors and emotions
10. Inclusion of the assessment of the relationship context of behaviors
11. Minimization of predetermined cutoff points
12. Modification of the assessment of disabilities due to the child's symptoms and behaviors
13. Review by a panel of infant and preschool mental health experts leading to further revision

---

behavior will work in the same way as the symptom used for older children. Rather, we need to test their usefulness in our diagnostic algorithms.

Addition of DC:0–3 Symptoms and Diagnoses

We added symptoms and diagnoses included in the DC:0–3. For a diagnosis such as reactive attachment disorder, this meant including symptoms found only in the DC:0–3 definition of the disorder, as well the symptoms in the *DSM-IV* criteria, so that we could compare the utility of each diagnosis. For diagnoses such as regulatory disorders that are unique to DC:0–3, we had to add all of the items necessary to make the diagnosis. Operationalization of many of the symptoms described in DC:0–3 proved to be a challenge.

After the completion of the RDC-PA, we also completed a version of the PAPA that enabled us to develop separate *DSM-IV*, DC:0–3, and RDC-PA algorithms so as to compare the relative reliability, validity, and prevalence of these different diagnostic formulations.

Inclusion of Relevant Checklist Symptoms

We added relevant items from the CBCL, as well as items from a review of the other measures assessing preschool behavior such as the Preschool Behavior Questionnaire (Behar, 1977) and the Infant-Toddler Social and Emotional Assessment (ITSEA; Briggs-Gowan, 1996, 1998; Briggs-Gowan, Carter, Moye Skuban, & McCue Horwitz, 2001; Carter, Little, Briggs-Gowan, & Kogan, 1999) that are not covered in the CAPA.

Inclusion of Developmentally Relevant Symptoms and Behaviors Not Included in Reviewed Measures

We also reviewed the literature on preschool psychopathology and included symptoms and behaviors described in this literature that were not included in the measures we reviewed. Examples included the incorporation of alternative criteria for posttraumatic stress disorder and reactive attachment disorder in very young children as proposed by Zeanah, Boris, and Scheeringa (Boris et al., 1998; Scheeringa et al., 1995, 2001; Scheeringa & Zeanah, 1995) that differ from the *DSM-IV*, ICD-10, and DC:0–3 criteria, as well as the inclusion of items for disruptive disorders described by Wakschlag and Keenan (2001). Whenever possible, we drew on the work of other researchers to support our modifications. Thus, for example, Keenan and Wakschlag's work on the presentation of ODD and CD in young children (Keenan & Wakschlag, 2000), Scheeringa and Zeanah's work (Scheeringa et al., 1995, 2001; Scheeringa & Zeanah, 1995) and Harmon's work on PTSD (Bingham & Harmon, 1996), Boris and Zeanah's work on reactive attachment disorder (Boris et al., 1998), Luby's work on depression (Luby, 2000), Anders's work on sleep disorders (Anders & Eiben, 1997, 2000; Gaylor, Goodlin-Jones, & Anders, 2001; Keener, Zeanah, & Anders, 1990), Chatoor's work on eating disorders (Chatoor, Ganiban, Colin, Plummer, & Harmon, 1998; Chatoor, Ganiban, Harrison, & Hirsch, 2001; Chatoor, Ganiban, Hirsch, Borman-Spurrell, & Mrazek, 2000; Chatoor, Getson, Menvielle, & Brasseaux, 1997; Chatoor, Hirsch, Ganiban, Persinger, & Hamburger, 1998), and Warren's work on anxiety disorders (Warren, Emde, & Sroufe, 2000; Warren, Huston, Egeland, & Sroufe, 1997; Warren, Schmitz, & Emde, 1999) each informed our revision of the relevant sections of the PAPA.

Inclusion of a Brief Developmental Assessment

We decided not to "reinvent the wheel" by including diagnostic measures of constructs that already have well-validated measures. Examples include developmental delays and autism or other pervasive developmental disorders (PDDs). However, a brief developmental assessment introduces the PAPA, primarily to orient the interviewer to the developmental level of the child being discussed. Standardized developmental assessments such as the Vineland Adaptive Behavior Scales (Sparrow & Cicchetti, 1989) or the Battelle Developmental Inventory (Newborg, Stock, Wnek, Guidubaldi, & Svinicki, 1984), and/or a cognitive assessment such as the Stanford-Binet Intelligence Scale (Thorndike, Hagen, & Sattler, 1986) to determine mental age, or the Differential Ability Scale (DAS; Elliot, 1990), used in conjunction

with the PAPA, can provide a complete developmental assessment. For PDDs, screening items are included to signal the potential need for a more extensive assessment with a measure such as the Autism Diagnostic Observation Schedule (ADOS; Lord et al., 1989; Lord, Rutter, & LeCouteur, 1994) and the Autism Diagnostic Interview (ADI; Holdgrafer & McLennan, 1988; Lord et al., 1994).

Inclusion of Regulatory Functions

Since population-based norms for many preschool behaviors and symptoms do not yet exist, we realized that it is important to include assessments of areas not explicitly included in current diagnostic criteria. Thus, we developed comprehensive sections on sleep behaviors (e.g., bedtime rituals, place of sleep initiation, behaviors interfering with sleep initiation, nap history, etc.); feeding history and eating behaviors; toileting history and elimination patterns; play and peer relationships; and day care and school settings and experiences (see below for further elaboration). These sections include both developmentally appropriate and potentially pathological behaviors. Completion of these sections will provide not only an indication of problem areas but also a portrait of the child's routines and the quality and content of daily interactions with family members, other adults, and peers. With these data we will be able to begin to describe how the child's experiences at home, in the community, and in relationship with others affect the development of psychopathology.

Modification of the Assessment of the Settings Where Preschoolers Spend Their Day

In the CAPA, we had found it appropriate to divide the settings in which each child operated into "home," "school," and "elsewhere." Such a division simply does not work for preschoolers. Some children may be in preschool; others might be in an out-of-home day care center. Others remain home with a parent, another relative, or a nonrelative caregiver. Many young children experience life in multiple settings during the week. The caregiving section of the PAPA assesses the variety of settings and variety of providers who care for the child throughout a typical week. We also assess the ratio of adult caregivers to children in each setting.

Modification of the Life Events Section

We also changed the sections that assess events occurring in the life and environment of the child to reflect the stressors affecting young children. As in the CAPA, we look at two kinds of stressful events. Life events that have occurred in the primary period (previous 3 months) are termed group A events. Onset for group A events are generally within the 3-month period except for the items "lives/attends day care or school in a chronically unsafe environment" and "reduction in standard of living," which may predate but extend into the primary period. Group B events are those that have occurred at any time during the child's life and include events such as physical and sexual abuse, death of a parent, and natural disasters. Examples of our addition to the life events section include a detailed history of accidents including vehicular accidents, falls, ingestion of poisons, near drowning, and burns, as well as items such as hospitalization of the child, separation of the child from significant attachment figures for more than 24 hours, or becoming homeless. For each of the life events, we also gather detailed information on whether the parent can link the occurrence of the life event with 22 possible changes in the child's behaviors, emotions, or relationships. Examples of problems that might be attributed to the occurrence of the life event include new or increased fears or anxieties, increased crying, regression of toileting skills or language, increased aggression, or changes in the quality of the child's relationships with parents, other adults, siblings, or peers. These "attributed problems" trigger the interviewer to complete the PTSD section of the PAPA.

Expanded Assessment of the Content and Context of Behaviors and Emotions

Because we have not yet explicitly identified the parameters of "disordered" behavior at different ages during the preschool years, we developed detailed assessment of the content and context of

many behaviors. For example, in the conduct section we developed a detailed assessment of tantrums. Consider the criterion for ODD: child "often loses temper." In the CBCL/1½–5, there is an item called "temper tantrums or hot temper." The parent must decide whether this item is not true, somewhat or sometimes true, or very true for the child (Achenbach & Rescorla, 2000). There is a presumption that the interviewer and the interviewee, or the clinician and the patient, agree upon what constitutes a temper tantrum and what frequency "often" refers to. In considering the range of behaviors for 2-year-olds compared with 5-year-olds, common knowledge suggests that the average 2-year-old will have tantrums significantly more often than 5-year-olds, but this higher frequency might be "normal" for 2-year-olds, while the relatively lower frequency might be "abnormal" for 5-year-olds. By providing a clear definition of temper tantrums in our glossary and by separating the presence of the symptom from the frequency and duration of the symptom, we will be able empirically to define what constitutes "often" having temper tantrums at different ages. But even when we can determine whether the child has, in the last 3 months, had at least one "discrete episode of excessive temper, frustration or upset, manifested by shouting, crying or stamping, and/or involving violence or attempts at damage directed against oneself, other people, or property," we still need more information to delineate the specific content and context of tantrums. Thus we also assess the content of the tantrums (e.g., the constellation of symptoms that constitute a tantrum, such as hitting, biting, and breaking toys), the triggers of tantrums (e.g., fatigue versus "out of the blue"), and finally the relationship context of the tantrum (e.g., with whom and how often the child has tantrums with central adult figures in his or her life).

Inclusion of the Assessment of the Relationship Context of Behaviors

The assessment of the relationship context of preschool behavior is one of the most important modifications of the PAPA. Young children, much more than older children and adolescents, are dependent on their adult caregivers who, for the most part, make decisions about the child's activities and interactions. For most symptoms and behaviors, we assess the presence of symptoms and behaviors within key relationships to determine whether the specific symptom or behavior occurs in one or two specific relationships or is generalized across all relationships. Thus, using PAPA data, we have the opportunity to explore one of the key tenets of infant psychiatry: the idea that clinical disturbances in infants and young children are not simply behavioral problems but relationship disturbances (Zeanah, 2000, p. 222).

Minimization of Predetermined Cutoff Points

Another key feature of the PAPA lies in its attempt to collect as much descriptive information as possible using as few arbitrary cutoff points for symptoms and screens for sections of the PAPA as possible. Sometimes cutoff points or screens have to be imposed in order to make information collection feasible, but we have tried to keep them to a minimum.

An example is depressed mood. To meet *DSM-IV* criteria, depressed mood must occur "most of the day, nearly every day . . . [during a] two week period" (American Psychiatric Association, 1994, p. 327). Yet we know so little about the presentation of symptoms in preschool children that cutoff points set by *DSM* diagnostic criteria or even common sense run the risk of excluding manifestations of the behavior that are in fact pathological. Since we collect separately coded information about the frequency and duration of each positive item, we can set these cutoff points empirically after the data are collected. As our understanding of the presentations of psychopathology in this age group develops, we will be able to revise the PAPA or develop new assessment measures that derive their cutoff points and screens from a solid foundation of knowledge.

Modification of the Assessment of Disability

We revised the assessment of disability resulting from the presence of symptoms. Like the CAPA, the PAPA separately assesses the presence of the symptoms and the presence of disabilities due to the presence of the symptom. Here we use the World Health Organization's International Classification of Functioning, Disability and Health (ICIDH-2) definition of disabilities as negative functional outcomes *resulting* from health conditions, involving significant deviation from or loss of normal or expected function (Angold & Costello, 2000; World Health Organization, 2001). We measure disability in two areas of functioning: (1) the performance of a task or action by an individual, which is called *activity* and (2) an individual's involvement in life situations, which is called *participation*. Activity limitations are difficulties an individual may have in the performance of activities. Participation restrictions are problems an individual may have in the manner or extent of involvement in life situations, including social relationships. The disability rating has three functions: to determine the overall effect of behaviors and feelings on broad areas of functioning in specific settings and in specific relationships, to determine the level of that impairment, and to determine if the child has received treatment for these behaviors. By separately assessing the effect of symptoms on functioning and on the quality of the child's relationships with significant others, we can distinguish between functional impairment and distress caused by the symptoms.

In the CAPA, disability is assessed at the end of the interview for each category of symptom found to be present. In the PAPA, we maintain this structure but change the manifestations of disability. First, we assess the impact of the behaviors in three different settings (home, nonparental caregiving settings such as day care or school, and other settings such as church). For example, do the child's oppositional behaviors interfere with family routines such as bath time or bedtime? Does the child receive special services at school or day care? Has the child been asked to leave a school or day care setting because of these behaviors? Do the child's behaviors prevent the family from going to a restaurant or on other family outings? Second, we assess how the behaviors affect the child's relationships with parents, siblings, other adults, and other children. Do the behaviors create discord in or withdrawal from relationships with these various people? Finally, we assess whether the child has received any treatment including psychosocial interventions or medications for these problems ever and in the previous 3 months. This approach permits the respondent to attribute disability in a given area (e.g., emotional discord in relationship to the primary caregiver) to one or more symptom areas (e.g., both anxiety and conduct disorder), and conversely to attribute disabilities in multiple areas to the same symptom (e.g., expulsion from preschool and discord in child's relationships with parents due to oppositional behavior).

Review and Revision by a Panel of Infant and Preschool Mental Health Experts

Last, we recruited a panel of reviewers with expertise in infant and young child mental health to review and critique serial drafts of the PAPA. The panel included Charles Zeanah and his group (Tulane University), Robert Emde (University of Colorado at Denver), Alice Carter (Boston University), Margaret Briggs-Gowan (Yale University), Harry Wright (University of South Carolina), Ron Dahl (University of Pittsburgh), Dale Hay (University of Cardiff, Wales), and Roseanne Clark, Donna Weston, Jean Thomas, and other members of the DC:0–3 work group.

THE STRUCTURE OF THE PAPA

Figure 12.1 shows a typical page of the PAPA interview schedule. The item shown is from the separation anxiety section of the interview. In the top left-hand column (1) are the name and a brief description of the symptom as a reminder to the interviewer. Fuller definitions are given in the glossary. This definition is followed by two types of questions: mandatory probes (2, emphasized in bold and with an asterisk) and discretionary probes (3). Mandatory and discretionary probes are defined below. The middle column contains coding rules and directions (4). Number 5 points out an example of the coding of the relationship context of the symptom. Code boxes completed by the interviewer are found in the far right column (6).

Judgments about the presence of symptoms are made by the interviewer on the basis of whether the statements of the subject conform to the definitions of symptoms and the rules for coding them contained in the glossary. These deci-

sions are objective because the task of the interviewer is to implement the rules contained in the glossary, not to make subjective judgments.

To implement the definitions and rules laid out in the glossary, the interviewer collects information using a structured questioning sequence provided by the interview schedule. The interview schedule provides two types of questions for the interviewer to ask the subject: *mandatory* and *discretionary* probes.

Mandatory probes must be asked, verbatim, of all interviewees unless the information they seek is already known to the interviewer (e.g., the parent has already mentioned that the particular symptom is present in response to some other probe). Mandatory probes are included to increase the uniformity of questioning among interviewers and ensure coverage of all items. We allow interviewers to skip mandatory probes if they already know the information so as to maintain the rapport between the interviewer and the interviewee, since interviewees often feel that the interviewer is not listening to them if they are asked a question for which they have already provided an answer.

Discretionary probes are suggested follow-up questions if the mandatory probes do not provide sufficient information for the interviewer to code the item. The discretionary probes lead the interviewer through the different aspects of the symptom that need to be coded (e.g., duration, frequency, or onset of the symptom). Interviewers are also trained to ask whatever additional follow-up questions they feel are necessary to enable them to fully code the item. In particular, they may find that information given at a particular point seems to contradict some previous statement. They are then required to sort out the apparent conflict and make the appropriate adjustments to previous codings, if necessary.

The PAPA is printed with the interview schedule appearing on the left-hand page. The facing page on the right is left blank so that the interviewer can take notes and record descriptions and examples of any emotions or behaviors that are present. Clinicians are well aware of the importance of collecting descriptions and examples of a child's behavior. Asking for descriptions of the child's actual behavior goes a long way toward preventing misinterpretations of the mean-

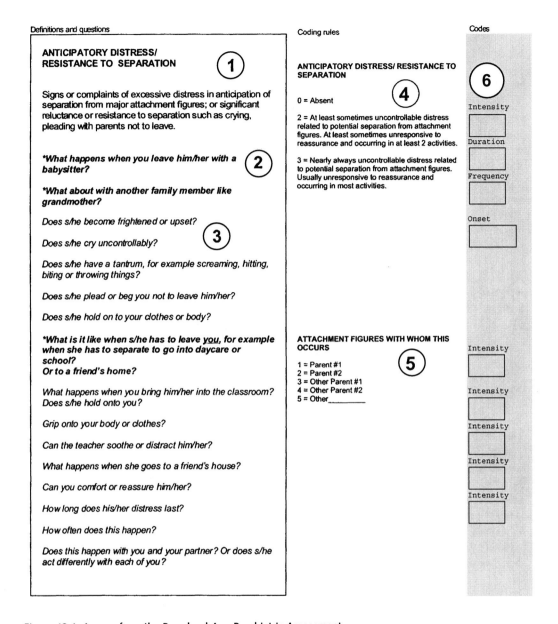

Figure 12.1 A page from the Preschool Age Psychiatric Assessment.

ing of the questions being asked. We have also found that parents appreciate the opportunity to describe their child's experiences. This approach to gathering information conveys a sense of the interviewer's real interest in the child and any problems the interviewee may be having with her or him. PAPA interviewers are trained to make use of these descriptions in determining their final codings. Our data checkers also match the de-

scriptions and examples to the codings chosen by the interviewers to ensure quality control.

The Primary Period

The PAPA focuses on the 3 months immediately preceding the interview. This is called the primary period. Lifetime occurrence is also collected for some symptoms, such as fire setting, suicide attempts, and certain potentially traumatic life events. The 3-month primary period was chosen because of concern about the reliability of memory for periods longer than this. This concern has been reinforced by our finding that the reliability of recall for dates of onset of symptoms falls off very rapidly after 3 to 5 months in both parents and children (Angold, Erkanli, Costello, & Rutter, 1996), although the relative order of onset dates was quite reliably recalled (intraclass correlation = .68 for both parents and children). Others have also described children's particular difficulties with questions concerning dates and timing with the DISC (Breton et al., 1995), and it seems likely that the numerous dating requirements incorporated into current official diagnostic criteria add to the unreliability of diagnostic measures by demanding feats of memory for dates of which most humans (both adults and children) are incapable.

Length of the PAPA

In the test-retest study of the PAPA completed in May 2003, the mean length of the PAPA interview was 1 hour and 47 minutes. The mean length for children with a *DSM-IV* disorder was 2 hours and 12 minutes. The length of the interview is clearly affected by the degree of psychopathology present and, to some extent, the interactional style of the parent. As we continue to refine the PAPA based on our own use of it in our studies, we expect to be able to streamline the interview. We are well aware that the interview should not cause undue burden on the parents.

Making a Diagnosis from a PAPA Interview

The interviewer codes the PAPA after the interview is completed. Coding takes about an hour. After the coding is completed, data are entered into a customized computer database that can be modified to suit the requirements of a particular study or clinical setting. Computerized algorithms, written in SAS, generate diagnoses for *DSM-IV*, ICD-10, DC:0–3, RDC-PA, and a variety of symptom, impairment, life events, and family functioning scale scores. As we have emphasized, the flexibility of the PAPA data will enable us empirically to investigate the reliability

and validity of these discrete diagnostic systems for young children and to examine whether clustering of symptoms suggests alternative diagnostic approaches not encompassed in the current criteria.

Data from the PAPA will make diagnoses, but that does not mean that any user of the PAPA is constrained to use those diagnoses. The symptom coding system has been designed to allow maximum flexibility for the construction of all sorts of scales and categories. We believe that such flexibility is absolutely necessary in a situation in which so little empirical data is available to support the constructs.

Modularization

The PAPA is modularized, so that particular sections can be used separately from the rest of the interview. To reduce repetitive questioning, where similar phenomena are involved in multiple diagnoses (as with sleep problems), those phenomena are usually grouped together, rather than being split up in relation to each diagnosis. However, it is an easy task to select the sections that are needed to cover a particular diagnosis.

Interviewer Selection and Training

The principle requirement for PAPA interviewers is that they can follow the structure provided by the interview, while showing sensitivity and intelligence in getting descriptions of behavior. CAPA trainees have included psychiatrists, psychologists, social workers, nurses, and graduate and bachelor's-level personnel with little or no previous clinical experience. PAPA training requires 1 to 2 weeks of classroom work and 1 to 2 weeks of practice. Didactic training on the glossary and interview methods is interspersed with role-playing, taped and live interviews, and feedback. Certification by a qualified PAPA trainer is required before using the PAPA in the field. Information about the PAPA and training is found on our Web site (http://devepi.duhs.duke.edu).

FUTURE DIRECTIONS

Test-Retest Study

In May 2003, we completed data collection on a National Institutes of Mental Health (NIMH)-

funded test-retest reliability study of the PAPA. Full description of the study design and results are presented in a paper submitted for publication (Egger & Angold, 2003). Here we provide an overview of the study and the results.

The study consisted of two parts: a screening phase and a test-retest phase. After obtaining informed consent, we screened 1,080 parents of children ages 2 through 5 years who were attending a large primary care practice at Duke University Medical Center over 18 consecutive months for both well-child and sick-child visits. Our screening measure was the CBCL/1½–5 (Achenbach & Rescorla, 2000). Children who obtained a *T* score at or above 40 on the total symptom score of the CBCL (top 30% based on CBCL/1½–5 norms) were considered "screen high" (highs). Stratifying by age, gender, and race (equal numbers of African American and non–African American [largely White]), we selected 193 screen highs and randomly (using a random number generator) selected 114 parents whose children had a *T* score less than 40 ("screen lows") to take part in the interview phase of the study. The total number of parent participants was 307.

The design of our study enabled us to weight the data from these 307 subjects back to the screening population, thereby providing data on the reliability and prevalence of psychiatric disorders and symptoms in this primary care pediatric practice. Since rates of psychiatric disorders in randomly selected pediatric primary care samples of school-age children and adolescents have been found to be similar to general population prevalence rates (e.g., Costello et al., 1988), these figures also serve as estimates of the reliability of measuring mental health problems in preschool children in the community.

The PAPA was administered twice within a 1-week period, so that by the end of the data collection our interviewers had conducted 614 PAPA interviews. While 20.7% of eligible families declined to participate in the test-retest study, only 2.2% (*n* = 7) of those who completed a first interview refused to complete a second PAPA interview, suggesting that participants did not find the first PAPA interview overly burdensome.

We used Cohen's kappa (Cohen, 1960) to assess agreement on categorical variables, and the intraclass correlation coefficient (ICC) to assess the agreement between syndrome scale scores. Here we report weighted reliability statistics that reflect unbiased estimates of reliability for this pediatric primary care sample. A kappa of 0.6 to 0.8 is considered substantial, from 0.4 to 0.6 moderate, and from 0.2 to 0.4 fair (Landis & Koch, 1977).

The diagnostic reliability of diagnoses ranged from 0.43 to 0.79. The kappas for some of the anxiety disorders (e.g., simple phobia, kappa = 0.43) were somewhat lower than for depression (kappa = 0.57), externalizing disorders (ODD, kappa = 0.67; ADHD, kappa = 0.74), and other anxiety disorders including social phobia (kappa = 0.57) and PTSD (kappa = 0.67). The kappa for having any *DSM-IV* Axis I disorder was 0.61.

Scale scores representing counts of *DSM-IV* symptoms were constructed for the individual diagnostic categories, as well as for the composite categories (e.g., scales for any anxiety disorder symptom). The reliability of scale scores ranged from ICCs of 0.60 to 0.87. Comparison with the kappas and ICCs reported from community studies of the reliability of the Parent DISC (Shaffer, Lucas, & Richters, 1999) and the Structured Clinical Interview for *DSM-III-R* (SCID; Williams et al., 1992), a widely used structured adult psychiatric interview, shows that the reliability of the PAPA diagnoses and scale scores are comparable to the results for these interviews used with parents of older children and adults. For example, the kappa for a PAPA depression diagnosis was 0.57 with an ICC of 0.67 for the depression symptom scale. In the community study of the Parent DISC the kappa was 0.55 and the ICC 0.51, while in the test-retest study of the SCID the kappa was 0.47 and the ICC 0.52. The kappa for a PAPA diagnosis of ADHD was, as noted above, 0.74 with an ICC of 0.80. In the DISC test-retest study, the kappa was 0.60 and the ICC 0.61. The SCID study did report ADHD results. The PAPA clearly performs as reliably, if not more reliably in some areas, than these commonly used structured interviews.

While low reliability in the test-retest paradigm clearly identifies a degree of measurement error, it also reflects a systematic reduction in reliability called the *attenuation effect*, where subjects in a test-retest paradigm tend to report fewer symptoms in the second test administration. Attenuation, so familiar from studies of the Diagnostic Interview for Children and Adolescents (DICA), DISC, and symptom scales (Angold, Erkanli, Loeber, et al., 1996; Angold, Erkanli, Silberg, Eaves, & Costello, 2002; Costello et al., 1984; Jensen et al., 1992, 1995; Lauritsen, 1998; Lucas, 1992; Lucas et al., 1999; Piacentini et al., 1999), was also found with the PAPA. We found significant diagnostic attenuation for generalized anxiety disorder (GAD), any anxiety disorder, and any emotional disorder. Attenuation was, not surprisingly, easier to detect in the symptom scale scores and was significant for depressive symptoms, GAD symptoms, any anxiety symptoms, and any behavioral symptoms.

We stratified the sample so that we could test for differences in reliability resulting from age, gender, and race. However, we found no significant differences in reliability (either kappas or ICCs) in respect to any of these factors. We were particularly pleased (a) that the PAPA proved just as reliable when used with the parents of 2-year-olds as it did when referring to older preschoolers, and (b) that it worked as well with African American parents as with White parents.

These results suggest that the PAPA is a reliable measure for assessing mental health symptoms in preschool children. Of course, reliability does not tell us anything about the validity of diagnoses. Questions about validity can now be addressed using this, and other, reliable measurement tools.

Spanish Version of the PAPA

The same group that translated the CAPA into Spanish is currently translating the PAPA, so that we can expect a Spanish version soon.

Computerization of the PAPA

We are also pursuing computerization of the PAPA. While paper-and-pencil administration of the PAPA has many advantages, including the ability to maintain eye contact and rapport with the subject while unobtrusively taking notes, ease of movement from one part of the interview schedule to another, and the opportunity to record examples in shorthand, there are also critical disadvantages. The major difficulty is the data entry step. Currently the interviewer codes the interview schedule; it is checked to ensure that the notes taken during the interview are consistent with the selected codings; and then these data are double-entered into the database. While these multiple steps contribute to the accuracy and integrity of the data, they also are time consuming and potentially limit the use of the interview to those with the capacity to develop and maintain such a data entry system. This is probably not that difficult for a research program but potentially challenging for a clinician who would be interested in using the measure. A computerized version of the interview would enable us to embed the data storage and analysis within the program. Researchers or clinicians would be able to input the data and receive an immediate report on the results of the interview.

During the summer of 2003, we began work on the computerized version of the PAPA, which we call the ePAPA. The ePAPA is being designed to run on a tablet personal computer (tablet PC). The tablet PC enables an interviewer to write with a stylus on the computer screen. This advance (and the fact that the technology is reliable and affordable) will make the ePAPA a viable alternative to the paper-and-pencil version of the PAPA. We had been concerned that a conventional laptop with an upright screen and keyboard would interfere with both ease of administration and the interviewer's rapport with the interviewee. The computer screen might be experienced as a wall by the interviewee, distancing him or her from the interviewer. Or the interviewer might have less eye contact with the interviewee if he or she was not a confident typist who often had to look at the keyboard. We also felt that it would be more difficult to type, rather than write, detailed examples from parents on all positive symptoms or behaviors. Since both the rapport and recording of clinical examples are so critical to the coding and checking of the PAPA, we were very excited when the tablet PC's writing function proved to be effective. Another advantage of the tablet PC is that it sits flat like a writing tablet. It can be placed on a table or the interviewer's lap.

We are developing two tools that will make up the ePAPA: the ePAPA interview and the ePAPA coding tool. The interview will be similar to the current PAPA interview schedule, except it will be on the tablet PC, not printed on paper. The interviewer will conduct the interview, gathering data to be coded after the interview. The interviewer will then code the interview using the ePAPA coding tool. Developing two separate tools has a number of advantages. First, it preserves our approach of coding the PAPA after the entire interview is completed, which gives the interviewer an opportunity to reflect on whether the child meets the symptoms and behaviors as defined in the glossary. Second, the coding tool will serve as a freestanding data entry tool for those researchers or clinicians who would like to continue to use the paper-and-pencil version of the PAPA. Embedded in the coding tool will be multiple checks on the validity of the data (e.g., a frequency for a symptom cannot be entered if the interviewer did not code the symptom as present, or an inconsistent or nonsensical date cannot be entered, such as an onset of a symptom that would be earlier than the child's birth). While there will be costs associated with licensing the ePAPA and the purchase of a tablet PC, there will be considerable savings in printing costs and double data entry costs. We plan to release a 1.0 version of the ePAPA in spring 2004. We will also work toward the development of a Web-enabled clinical version of the ePAPA.

A further step in computerization would be to develop online training so that interviewers could be appropriately and adequately trained in use of the PAPA without having to travel to Durham, North Carolina (and without our trainer traveling to the site). Development of an online training course and remote access certification of training in the PAPA will follow computerization of the measure.

CONCLUSION

The PAPA Is Necessary but Not Sufficient

The PAPA is a necessary but not sufficient measure of psychopathology in young children. The PAPA collects symptom and impairment information from a parent (or guardian). It is, therefore, but one component in the overall assessment of the preschooler. Our research program is focused on the development of a structured parent interview as a first step in the development of a comprehensive set of measures for assessing preschool psychopathology. Multiple informants, including both parents, other caregivers (teachers, day care providers, baby-sitters, other relatives), and the child are critical for developing an adequate representation of the child's behaviors and experiences. While data suggest that parents of preschoolers are perhaps better informants about their children than parents of older children, it is also clearly established that parents are only fair to good reporters of their child's emotions and behaviors (Achenbach, McConaughy, & Howell, 1987; Angold & Costello, 1996; Bird, Gould, & Staghezza, 1992; Edelbrock, Costello, Dulcan, Conover, & Kalas, 1986; Jensen et al., 1999). Numerous studies have shown that, in particular, parents report significantly fewer anxiety or depression symptoms than their children themselves report (e.g., Angold et al., 1987; Renouf & Kovacs, 1994). Direct observations of the child alone and interacting with the primary caregiver are also important for assessment of young children. Ideally, these observations occur in the child's home or day care or school setting and are conducted at more than one point in time to develop a comprehensive and accurate portrait of the child's behaviors, emotions, and experiences. Direct interviews with the young child about his or her feelings and experiences are also an essential component of a comprehensive assessment, particularly for emotional disorders. Current methods such as the Berkeley Puppet Interview (Ablow et al., 1999; Measelle, Ablow, Cowan, & Cowan, 1998), which has been shown to be reliable with children 4 to 8 years old, and the MacArthur Story-Stem Battery (Macfie et al., 1999; Oppenheim, Emde, & Wamboldt, 1996; Oppenheim, Emde, & Warren, 1997; Oppenheim, Nir, Warren, & Emde, 1997; Petrill et al., 1998; Toth, Cicchetti, Macfie, & Emde, 1997; Warren et al., 1999, 2000; Warren, Oppenheim, & Emde, 1996), which has been used with children as young as 3 years, are promising but do not encompass the full preschool age range. A critical question we will address in our research program is how best to combine the information from different informants and different assessment methods to make diagnostic decisions.

Clinical Implications

It is probably fair to say that clinicians do not enjoy doing respondent-based interviews very much because the questions they can ask are so highly constrained. They may not be convinced that the parent understood the question, but if they add their own questions then the advantages of using a respondent-based interview are lost, because an unstructured component has been added. On the other hand, training on an interviewer-based interview such as the PAPA is usually of interest to clinicians because it raises a number of issues about interviewing style and strategy that few have had time or encouragement to think through during their training. Thus, interviewer-based interviews may be particularly suitable for use in clinical assessments. The CAPA has been used in several clinical and treatment studies.

At this point in the development of the PAPA and our understanding of the presentation of psychopathology in preschool children, the PAPA will be primarily used as a research diagnostic tool. As of fall 2003, the PAPA is being used in more than 6 NIMH-funded studies. While our understanding of how to identify and treat mental health disorders in young children is at an early stage, we are hopeful that the field will make progress in the next few years in understanding how to define and assess psychopathology in preschool children. As we demonstrate the reliability of the PAPA, refine the interview, and move forward on computerization, we will, we believe, be able to offer an instrument with potential clinical utility. Since the PAPA can be modularized, clinicians will be able to choose which sections of the PAPA to use so that they can focus on the disorders they are particularly interested in identifying. The goal of the PAPA and our research program in preschool psychopathology is to contribute to an empirically grounded picture of preschool psychiatric symptoms and disorders that can be translated into effective diagnostic, screening, and treatment approaches to help young children and their families. We know, as clinicians, researchers, and parents, that young children and their families are suffering because of behavioral and emotional problems. We hope that the PAPA will contribute to increasing our understanding of how to ameliorate and alleviate their pain.

References

Ablow, J. C., Measelle, J. R., Kraemer, H. C., Harrington, R., Luby, J., Smider, N., Dierker, L., Clark, V., Dubicka, B., Heffelfinger, A., Essex, M. J., & Kupfer, D. J. (1999). The MacArthur Three-City Outcome Study: Evaluating multi-informant measures of young children's symptomatology. *Journal of the American Academy of Child and Adolescent Psychiatry, 38,* 1580–1590.

Achenbach, T. M. (1985). *Assessment and taxonomy of child and adolescent psychopathology.* Beverly Hills, CA: Sage.

Achenbach, T. M., & Edelbrock, C. (1983). *Manual for the child behavior checklist and child behavior profile.* Burlington, VT: University of Vermont.

Achenbach, T. M., McConaughy, S. H., & Howell, C. T. (1987). Child/adolescent behavioral and emotional problems: Implications of cross-informant correlations for situational specificity. *Psychological Bulletin, 101,* 213–232.

Achenbach, T. M., & Rescorla, L. A. (2000). *Manual for the ASEBA preschool forms and profiles: An integrated system of multi-informant assessment.* Burlington, VT: University of Vermont Department of Psychiatry.

American Psychiatric Association (1994). *Diagnostic and statistical manual of mental disorders* (4th ed.). Washington, DC: Author.

Anders, T., & Eiben, L. (2000). Sleep disorders. In C. Zeanah (Ed.), *Handbook of infant mental health* (2nd ed., pp. 326–338). New York: Guilford Press.

Anders, T. F., & Eiben, L. A. (1997). Pediatric sleep disorders: A review of the past 10 years. *Journal of the American Academy of Child and Adolescent Psychiatry, 36,* 9–20.

Angold, A., & Costello, E. J. (1995). A test-retest reliability study of child-reported psychiatric symptoms and diagnoses using the Child and Adolescent Psychiatric Assessment (CAPA-C). *Psychological Medicine, 25,* 755–762.

Angold, A., & Costello, E. J. (1996). The relative diagnostic utility of child and parent reports of oppositional defiant disorders. *International Journal of Methods in Psychiatric Research, 6,* 253–259.

Angold, A., & Costello, E. (2000). *A review of the issues relevant to the creation of a measure of disability in children based on the World Health Organization's International Classification of Functioning and Disability (ICIDH-2).* World Health Organization.

Angold, A., Erkanli, A., Costello, E. J., & Rutter, M. (1996). Precision, reliability and accuracy in the dating of symptom onsets in child and adolescent psychopathology. *Journal of Child Psychology and Psychiatry, 37,* 657–664.

Angold, A., Erkanli, A., Loeber, R., Costello, E. J., Van Kammen, W., & Stouthamer-Loeber, M. (1996). Disappearing depression in a population sample of boys. *Journal of Emotional and Behavioral Disorders, 4,* 95–104.

Angold, A., Erkanli, A., Silberg, J., Eaves, L., & Costello, E. (2002). Depression scale scores in 8–17-year-olds: Effects of age and gender. *Journal of Child Psychology and Psychiatry, 43,* 1052–1063.

Angold, A., & Fisher, P. W. (1999). Interviewer-based interviews. In D. Shaffer, C. Lucas, & J. Richters (Eds.), *Diagnostic assessment in child and adolescent psychopathology* (pp. 34–64). New York: Guilford Press.

Angold, A., Prendergast, M., Cox, A., Harrington, R., Simonoff, E., & Rutter, M. (1995). The Child and Adolescent Psychiatric Assessment (CAPA). *Psychological Medicine, 25,* 739–753.

Angold, A., Weissman, M. M., John, K., Merikangas, K. R., Prusoff, B. A., Wickramaratne, P., Gammon, G. D., & Warner, V. (1987). Parent and child reports of depressive symptoms in children at low and high risk of depression. *Journal of Child Psychology and Psychiatry, 28,* 901–915.

Arend, R., Lavigne, J. V., Rosenbaum, D., Binns, H. J., & Christoffel, K. K. (1996). Relation between taxonomic and quantitative diagnostic systems in preschool children: Emphasis on disruptive disorders. *Journal of Clinical Child Psychology, 25,* 388–387.

Behar, L. (1977). The Preschool Behavior Questionnaire. *Journal of Abnormal Child Psychology, 5,* 265–275.

Bingham, R., & Harmon, R. (1996). Traumatic stress in infancy and early childhood: Expression of distress and development issues. In C. R. Pfeffer (Ed.), *Severe stress and mental disturbance in children* (pp. 499–532). Washington, DC: American Psychiatric Press.

Bird, H. R., Gould, M. S., & Staghezza, B. (1992). Aggregating data from multiple informants in child psychiatry epidemiological research. *Journal of the American Academy of Child and Adolescent Psychiatry, 31,* 78–85.

Boris, N. W., Zeanah, C. H., Larrieu, J. A., Scheeringa, M. S., & Heller, S. S. (1998). Attachment disorders in infancy and early childhood: A preliminary investigation of diagnostic criteria. *American Journal of Psychiatry, 155,* 295–297.

Breton, J.-J., Bergeron, L., Valla, J.-P., Lepine, S., Houde, L., & Gaudet, N. (1995). Do children aged 9 to 11 years understand the DISC version 2.25 questions? *Journal of the American Academy of Child and Adolescent Psychiatry, 34,* 946–956.

Briggs-Gowan, M. J. (1996). A parent assessment of social-emotional and behavior problems and competence for infants and toddlers: Reliability, validity, and associations with maternal symptoms and parenting stress. *Dissertation Abstracts International: Section B: The Sciences and Engineering, 57*(6-B), 4051.

Briggs-Gowan, M. J. (1998). Preliminary acceptability and psychometrics of the infant-toddler social and emotional assessment (ITSEA): A new adult-report questionnaire. *Infant Mental Health Journal, 19*(4), 422–445.

Briggs-Gowan, M. J., Carter, A. S., Moye Skuban, E., & McCue Horwitz (2001). Prevalence of social-emotional and behavioral problems in a community sample of 1- and 2-year-old children. *Journal of the American Academy of Child and Adolescent Psychiatry, 40,* 811–819.

Cantwell, D. P., & Baker, L. (1988). Issues in the classification of child and adolescent psychopathology. *Journal of the American Academy of Child and Adolescent Psychiatry, 27,* 521–533.

Carter, A., Little, C., Briggs-Gowan, M., & Kogan, N. (1999). The Infant-Toddler Social and Emotional Assessment (ITSEA): Comparing parent ratings to laboratory observations of task mastery, emotion regulation, coping behaviors and attatchment status. *Infant Mental Health Journal, 20,* 375–392.

Chatoor, I., Ganiban, J., Colin, V., Plummer, N., & Harmon, R. (1998). Attachment and feeding problems: A reexamination of nonorganic failure to thrive and attachment insecurity. *Journal of the American Academy of Child and Adolescent Psychiatry, 37,* 1217–1224.

Chatoor, I., Ganiban, J., Harrison, J., & Hirsch, R. (2001). Observation of feeding in the diagnosis of posttraumatic feeding disorder of infancy. *Journal of the American Academy of Child and Adolescent Psychiatry, 40,* 595–602.

Chatoor, I., Ganiban, J., Hirsch, R., Borman-Spurrell, E., & Mrazek, D. A. (2000). Maternal characteristics and toddler temperament in infantile anorexia. *Journal of the American Academy of Child and Adolescent Psychiatry, 39,* 743–751.

Chatoor, I., Getson, P., Menvielle, E., & Brasseaux, C. (1997). A feeding scale for research and clinical practice to assess mother-infant interaction in the first three years of life. *Infant Mental Health Journal, 18,* 76–91.

Chatoor, I., Hirsch, R., Ganiban, J., Persinger, M., & Hamburger, E. (1998). Diagnosing infantile anorexia: The observation of mother-infant interactions. *Journal of the American Academy of Child and Adolescent Psychiatry, 37,* 959–967.

Costello, A. J., Edelbrock, C. S., Dulcan, M. K., Kalas, R., & Klaric, S. H. (1984). *Development and testing of the NIMH diagnostic interview schedule for children in a clinic population: Final report (contract no. RFP-DB-81-0027).* Rockville, MD: NIMH Center for Epidemiologic Studies.

Costello, E. J., Angold, A., March, J., & Fairbank, J. (1998). Life events and post-traumatic stress: The development of a new measure for children and adolescents. *Psychological Medicine, 28,* 1275–1288.

Costello, E. J., Costello, A. J., Edelbrock, C., Burns, B. J., Dulcan, M. K., Brent, D., et al. (1988). Psychiatric disorders in pediatric primary care: Prevalence and risk factors. *Archives of General Psychiatry, 45,* 1107–1116.

Dietz, K. R., Lavigne, J. V., Arend, R., & Rosenbaum, D. (1997). Relation between intelligence and psychopathology among preschoolers. *Journal of Clinical Child Psychology, 26,* 99–107.

Dunitz, M., Scheer, P. J., Kvas, E., & Macari, S. (1996). Psychiatric diagnoses in infancy: A comparison. *Infant Mental Health Journal, 17,* 12–23.

Edelbrock, C., & Costello, A. J. (1990). Structured psychiatric interviews for children and adolescents. In G. Goldstein & M. Hersen (Eds.), *Handbook of psychological assessment* (pp. 276–290). New York: Pergamon Press.

Edelbrock, C., Costello, A. J., Dulcan, M. K., Conover, M. C., & Kalas, R. (1986). Parent-child agreement on child psychiatric symptoms assessed via structured interview. *Journal of Child Psychology and Psychiatry, 27,* 181–190.

Egger, H. L., & Angold, A. (2003). *The Preschool Age Psychiatric Assessment: Results from a test-retest reliability study.* Manuscript submitted for publication.

Egger, H. L., Ascher, B. H., & Angold, A. (1999). *The preschool age psychiatric assessment: Version 1.1.* Unpublished interview schedule. Durham, NC: Center for Developmental Epidemiology, Department of Psychiatry and Behavioral Sciences, Duke University Medical Center.

Elliot, C. (1990). *Differential ability scales: Administration manual.* San Antonio, TX: Psychological Corporation.

Gaylor, E. E., Goodlin-Jones, B. L., & Anders, T. F. (2001). Classification of young children's sleep problems: A pilot study. *Journal of the American Academy of Child and Adolescent Psychiatry, 40,* 61–67.

Gould, M. S., Shaffer, D., Rutter, M., & Sturge, C. (1988). UK/WHO study of ICD-9. In M. Rutter, A. H. Tuma, & I. S. Lann (Eds.), *Assessment and diagnosis in child psychopathology* (pp. 37–65). New York: Guilford Press.

Holdgrafer, M., & McLennan, J. (1988). Autism Diagnostic Interview: A standardized investigator-based instrument. *Journal of Autism and Developmental Disorders, 19*(3), 363–387.

Jensen, P., Roper, M., Fisher, P. W., Piacentini, J., Canino, G., Richters, J., et al. (1995). Test-retest reliability of the Diagnostic Interview Schedule for Children (DISC 2.1): Parent, child, and combined algorithms. *Archives of General Psychiatry, 52,* 61–71.

Jensen, P. S., Rubio-Stipec, M. A., Canino, G., Bird, H. R., Dulcan, M. K., Schwab-Stone, M. E., & Lahey, B. B. (1999). Parent and child contributions to diagnosis of mental disorder: Are both informants always necessary? *Journal of the American Academy of Child and Adolescent Psychiatry, 38,* 1569–1579.

Jensen, P. S., Shaffer, D., Rae, D., Canino, G., Bird, H. R., Dulcan, M. K., et al. (1992, October). *Attenuation of the Diagnostic Interview Schedule for Children (DISC 2.1): Sex, age, and IQ relationships.* Paper presented at the 39th annual meeting of the AACAP, Washington, DC.

Keenan, K., & Shaw, D. S. (1994). The development of aggression in toddlers: A study of low-income families. *Journal of Abnormal Child Psychology, 22,* 53–77.

Keenan, K., Shaw, D. S., Walsh, B., Delliquadri, E., & Giovannelli, J. (1997). DSM-III-R disorders in preschool children from low-income families. *Journal of the American Academy of Child and Adolescent Psychiatry, 36,* 620–627.

Keenan, K., & Wakschlag, L. S. (2000). More than the terrible twos: The nature and severity of behavior problems in clinic-referred preschool children. *Journal of Abnormal Child Psychology, 28,* 33–46.

Keener, M., Zeanah, C., & Anders, T. (1990). Infant temperment, sleep organization, and nighttime parental interventions. In S. Chess & M. Hertzig (Eds.), *Annual progress in child psychiatry and child development* (pp. 257–274). Philadelphia: Brunner/Mazel.

Lahey, B. B., Pelham, W. E., Stein, M. A., Loney, J., Trapani, C., Nugent, K., Kipp, H., Schmidt, E., Lee, S., Cale, M., Gold, E., Hartung, C. M., Willcutt, E., & Baumann, B. (1998). Validity of DSM-IV attention-deficit/hyperactivity disorder for younger children. *Journal of the American Academy of Child and Adolescent Psychiatry, 37,* 695–702.

Landis, J. R., & Koch, G. (1977). The measurement of observer agreement for categorical data. *Biometrics, 33,* 159–174.

Lauritsen, J. L. (1998). The age-crime debate: Assessing the limits of longitudinal self-report data. *Social Forces, 77*(1), 127–154.

Lavigne, J. V., Arend, R., Rosenbaum, D., Binns, H. J., Christoffel, K. K., Burns, A., & Smith, A. (1998a). Mental health service use among young children receiving pediatric primary care. *Journal of the American Academy of Child and Adolescent Psychiatry, 37,* 1175–1183.

Lavigne, J. V., Arend, R., Rosenbaum, D., Binns, H. J., Christoffel, K. K., & Gibbons, R. D. (1998b). Psychiatric disorders with onset in the preschool years. I. Stability of diagnoses. *Journal of the American Academy of Child and Adolescent Psychiatry, 37,* 1246–1254.

Lavigne, J. V., Arend, R., Rosenbaum, D., Binns, H. J., Christoffel, K. K., & Gibbons, R. D. (1998c). Psychiatric disorders with onset in the preschool years. II. Correlates and predictors of stable case status. *Journal of the American Academy of Child and Adolescent Psychiatry, 37,* 1255–1261.

Lavigne, J. V., Arend, R., Rosenbaum, D., Sinacore, J., Cicchetti, C., Binns, H. J., Christoffel, K. K., Hayford, J. R., & McGuire, P. (1994).

Interrater reliability of the DSM-III-R with preschool children. *Journal of Abnormal Child Psychology, 22,* 679–690.

Lavigne, J. V., Arend, R., Rosenbaum, D., Smith, A., Weissbluth, M., Binns, H. J., & Christoffel, K. K. (1999). Sleep and behavior problems among preschoolers. *Developmental and Behavioral Pediatrics, 20,* 164–169.

Lavigne, J. V., Binns, H. J., Arend, R., Rosenbaum, D., Christoffel, K. K., Hayford, J. R., & Gibbons, R. D. (1998). Psychopathology and health care use among preschool children: A retrospective analysis. *Journal of the American Academy of Child and Adolescent Psychiatry, 37,* 262–270.

Lavigne, J. V., Binns, H. J., Christoffel, K. K., Rosenbaum, D., Arend, R., Smith, K., Hayford, J. R., McGuire, P. A., & Pediatric Practice Research Group (1993). Behavioral and emotional problems among preschool children in pediatric primary care: Prevalence and pediatricians' recognition. *Pediatrics, 91,* 649–655.

Lavigne, J. V., Gibbons, R. D., Christoffel, K. K., Arend, R., Rosenbaum, D., Binns, H., Dawson, N., Sobel, H., & Issacs, C. (1996). Prevalence rates and correlates of psychiatric disorders among preschool children. *Journal of the American Academy of Child and Adolescent Psychiatry, 35,* 204–214.

Lavigne, J. V., Schulein, M. J., & Hahn, Y. S. (1986). Psychological aspects of painful medical conditions in children. II. Personality factors, family characteristics and treatment. *Pain, 27,* 147–169.

Lord, C., Rutter, M., Goode, S., Heemsbergen, J., Jordan, H., Mawhood, L., & Schopler, E. (1989). Autism diagnostic observation schedule: A standardized observation of communicative and social behavior. *Journal of Autism and Developmental Disorders, 19,* 185–212.

Lord, C., Rutter, M., & LeCouteur, A. (1994). Autism Diagnostic Interview-Revised: A revised version of a diagnostic interview for caregivers of individuals with possible pervasive developmental disorders. *Journal of Autism and Developmental Disorders, 24,* 659–685.

Luby, J. (2000). Depression. In C. Zeanah (Ed.), *Handbook of infant mental health* (pp. 382–396). New York: Guilford Press.

Lucas, C. P. (1992). The order effect: Reflections on the validity of multiple test presentations. *Psychological Medicine, 22,* 197–202.

Lucas, C. P., Fisher, P., Piacentini, J., Zhang, H., Jensen, P. S., Shaffer, D., et al. (1999). Features of interview questions associated with attenuation of symptom reports. *Journal of Abnormal Child Psychology, 27,* 417–428.

Macfie, J., Toth, S. L., Rogosch, F. A., Robinson, J., Emde, R. N., & Cicchetti, D. (1999). Effect of maltreatment on preschoolers' narrative representations of responses to relieve distress and of role reversal. *Developmental Psychology, 35,* 460–465.

Measelle, J. R., Ablow, J. C., Cowan, P. A., & Cowan, C. P. (1998). Assessing young children's views of their academic, social, and emotional lives: An evaluation of the self-perception scales of the Berkeley Puppet Interview. *Child Development, 69,* 1556–1576.

Newborg, J., Stock, J. R., Wnek, L., Guidubaldi, J., & Svinicki, J. (1984). *Battelle developmental inventory (BDI).* Allen, TX: DLM Teaching Resources.

Oppenheim, D., Emde, R. N., & Wamboldt, F. S. (1996). Associations between 3-year-olds' narrative co-constructions with mothers and fathers and their story completions about affective themes. *Early Development and Parenting, 5,* 149–160.

Oppenheim, D., Emde, R. N., & Warren, S. (1997). Children's narrative representations of mothers: Their development and associations with child and mother adaptation. *Child Development, 68,* 127–138.

Oppenheim, D., Nir, A., Warren, S., & Emde, R. N. (1997). Emotion regulation in mother-child narrative co-construction: Associations with children's narratives and adaptation. *Developmental Psychology, 33,* 284–294.

Petrill, S. A., Saudino, K., Cherny, S. S., Emde, R. N., Fulker, D. W., Hewitt, J. K., & Plomin, R. (1998). Exploring the genetic and environmental etiology of high general cognitive ability in fourteen- to thirty-six-month-old twins. *Child Development, 69,* 68–74.

Piacentini, J., Roper, M., Jensen, P., Lucas, C., Fisher, P., Bird, H., et al. (1999). Informant-based determinants of symptom attenuation in structured child psychiatric interviews. *Journal of Abnormal Child Psychology, 27,* 417–428.

Reams, R. (1999). Children birth to three entering the state's custody. *Infant Mental Health Journal, 20,* 166–174.

Remschmidt, H. (1988). German study of ICD-9. In M. Rutter, A. H. Tumain, & I. S. Lann (Eds.), *Assessment and diagnosis in child psychopathology* (pp. 66–83). London: Guilford Press.

Renouf, A. G., & Kovacs, M. (1994). Concordance between mothers' report and children's self-reports of depressive symptoms: A longitudinal study. *Journal of the American Academy of Child and Adolescent Psychiatry, 33,* 208–216.

Scheeringa, M. S., Peebles, C. D., Cook, C. A., & Zeanah, C. H. (2001). Toward establishing procedural, criterion, and discriminant validity for PTSD in early childhood. *Journal of the American Academy of Child and Adolescent Psychiatry, 40,* 52–60.

Scheeringa, M. S., & Zeanah, C. H. (1994). *Posttraumatic stress disorder semi-structured interview and observational record for infants and young children.* Unpublished manuscript. Tulane University.

Scheeringa, M. S., & Zeanah, C. H. (1995). Symptom expression and trauma variables in children under 48 months of age. *Infant Mental Health Journal, 16,* 259–270.

Scheeringa, M. S., Zeanah, C. H., Drell, M. J., & Larrieu, J. A. (1995). Two approaches to the diagnosis of posttraumatic stress disorder in infancy and early childhood. *Journal of the American Academy of Child and Adolescent Psychiatry, 34,* 191–200.

Shaffer, D., Lucas, C. P., & Richters, J. E. (1999). *Diagnostic assessment: Child and adolescent psychopathology.* New York: Guilford Press.

Shaw, D. S., Owens, E. B., Giovannelli, J., & Winslow, E. B. (2001). Infant and toddler pathways leading to early externalizing disorders. *Journal of the American Academy of Child and Adolescent Psychiatry, 40,* 44–51.

Shaw, D. S., Owens, E. B., Vondra, J. I., Keenan, K., & Winslow, E. B. (1996). Early risk factors and pathways in the development of early disruptive behavior problems. *Development and Psychopathology, 8,* 679–699.

Sparrow, S. S., & Cicchetti, D. V. (1989). The Vineland Adaptive Behavior Scales. In C. S. Newmark (Eds.), *Major psychological assessment instruments* (pp. 199–231). Needham Heights, MA: Allyn and Bacon.

Speltz, M., DeKlyen, M., Greenberg, M., & Dryden, M. (1995). Clinic referral for oppositional defiant disorder: Relative significance of attatchment and behavioral variables. *Journal of Abnormal Child Psychology, 23,* 487–507.

Speltz, M., McClellan, J., DeKlyen, M., & Jones, K. (1999). Preschool boys with oppositional defiant disorder: Clinical presentation and diagnostic change. *Journal of the American Academy of Child and Adolescent Psychiatry, 38,* 838–845.

Task Force on Research Diagnostic Criteria: Infancy and Preschool. (in press). Research diagnostic criteria for infants and preschool children: The process and empirical support. *Journal of the American Academy of Child and Adolescent Psychiatry.*

Thomas, J. M., & Clark, R. (1998). Disruptive behavior in the very young child: Diagnostic classification: 0–3 guides identification of risk factors and relational interventions. *Infant Mental Health Journal, 19,* 229–244.

Thomas, J. M., & Guskin, K. A. (2001). Disruptive behavior in young children: What does it mean? *Journal of the American Academy of Child and Adolescent Psychiatry, 40,* 44–51.

Thorndike, R. L., Hagen, E. P., & Sattler, J. M. (1986). *Stanford-Binet intelligence scale* (4th ed.). Chicago: Riverside.

Toth, S. L., Cicchetti, D., Macfie, J., & Emde, R. N. (1997). Representations of self and other in the narratives of neglected, physically abused, and sexually abused preschoolers. *Development and Psychopathology, 9,* 781–796.

Wakschlag, L., & Keenan, K. (2001). Clinical significance and correlates of disruptive behavior in environmentally at-risk preschoolers. *Journal of Clinical Child Psychology, 30,* 262–275.

Warren, S. L., Emde, R. N., & Sroufe, A. (2000). Internal representations: Predicting anxiety from children's play narratives. *Journal of the American Academy of Child and Adolescent Psychiatry, 39,* 100–107.

Warren, S. L., Huston, L., Egeland, B., & Sroufe, L. A. (1997). Child and adolescent anxiety disorders and early attachment. *Journal of the American Academy of Child and Adolescent Psychiatry, 36,* 637–644.

Warren, S. L., Oppenheim, D., & Emde, R. N. (1996). Can emotions and themes in children's play predict behavior problems? *Journal of the American Academy of Child and Adolescent Psychiatry, 35,* 1331–1337.

Warren, S. L., Schmitz, S., & Emde, R. N. (1999). Behavioral genetic analyses of self-reported anxiety at 7 years of age. *Journal of the American Academy of Child and Adolescent Psychiatry, 38,* 1403–1408.

Williams, J. B., Gibbon, M., First, M. B., Spitzer, R. L., Davies, M., Borus, J., et al. (1992). The Structured Clinical Interview for *DSM-III-R* (SCID). II. Multisite test-retest reliability. *Archives of General Pychiatry, 49*(8), 630–636.

World Health Organization (1992). *ICD-10: The ICD-10 classification of mental and behavioral disorders: Clinical descriptions and diagnostic guidelines.* Geneva: Author.

World Health Organization (2001). *ICIDH-2: International classification of functioning, disability and health.* Geneva: Author.

Zeanah, C. H., Jr. (Ed.). (2000). *Handbook of infant mental health* (2nd ed.). New York: Guilford Press.

Zero to Three, National Center for Clinical Infant Programs (1994). *Diagnostic classification of mental health and developmental disorders of infancy and early childhood.* Arlington, VA: Author.

V

PROBLEMS IN EARLY DEVELOPMENT AND STATE REGULATION: ASSESSING DISORDERS WITH AN ONSET IN INFANCY OR TODDLERHOOD

Individual differences in temperament, sensory reactivity, and regulatory functioning, including state regulation, influence both typical and atypical developmental trajectories (see chapters 5 and 6). This part is devoted to understanding those problems associated with sensory processing and regulation functioning. When these problems become severe enough to interfere with or impair the child's developmental progress or family functioning, a diagnosis related to early state regulation might be in order.

In this part, disorders related to early development and state regulation that first present in infancy are discussed. While parents have brought concerns related to variations in early patterns of eating, sleeping, playing, and emotional expression to mental health experts as well as to a variety of other specialists including pediatricians and occupational therapists for years, within the mental health field there is limited consensus and indeed a fair amount of controversy concerning nomenclature. We are fortunate to have contributions for this part by three leading scholars who are attempting to develop diagnostic nosologies based on dysregulation in infancy and early

toddlerhood. Although there is consensus among infant mental health researchers on the importance of regulation and dysregulation more generally for psychopathology in the earliest years (see part II), the specifics of how the conceptualization of regulation translates to notions of disorder remain highly controvertial (see also chapter 8). Although relatively new and still under development, we present discussion of state-related disorders in the next three chapters as a beginning to unravel the puzzle as to how state-related, constitutionally based elements of early functioning evolve into disorders.

Although the DC:0–3 uses the rubric "regulatory disorders" to describe such difficulties (see chapter 8), Lucy Miller, JoAnn Robinson, and Debra Moulton are investigating a related construct known as sensory modulation dysfunction in the occupational therapy literature. They compare and contrast their conceptual model of this disorder to the evolving classification of regulatory disorders in the DC:0–3 in hopes of reaching a broader understanding of and assessment protocol for sensory-related difficulties in early childhood. They also describe related internal and external factors that may lead to anticipation (and prevention) of a mismatch between innate dispositions and reactions to external dimensions. They present preliminary data concerning the interrelationship of sensation, emotion, and attention. They report that sensory problems are associated with abnormal attention and emotion responses, suggesting that sensory-related disorder may place children at risk for attention and affective disorders in later childhood. They conclude that evaluating sensory processing difficulties can be an important contribution to the overall assessment of mental health in infants and young children.

Beth Goodlin-Jones and Thomas Anders present a transactional model of sleep-wake state development, which they assert supports their belief that sleep problems in infancy may be more appropriately understood as relationship problems. A multiaxial assessment scheme and detailed nosology are presented that classify sleep within a developmental framework. They recommend that future research relate nighttime sleep patterns to daytime functioning.

The regulatory disorders that present in infancy included in this part highlight their relation to parental interaction. Though many questions remain unanswered, the investigators in this section present pioneering work in conceptualizing disorders related to regulatory functioning. Future studies need to address both the validity of the proposed criteria and the relation of the disorders to relationship functioning.

Irene Chatoor and Jody Ganiban describe their work investigating feeding disorders in infancy and toddlerhood. In their work, which is based on extensive clinical case studies as well as research, they have been developing a comprehensive classification scheme of feeding disorders

in infancy. They suggest that the basis for internally regulated eating is established during the first years of life and that the key to internal regulation is the development of an infant-parent communication system that allows the infant to signal hunger and satiety states and the parents to respond to these cues accordingly. They note that parents help their infants to regulate eating and prepare them to move from mutual regulation to internally self-regulated eating. They also suggest that this development parallels the emergence of self-regulation in other domains, including self-regulation of emotions, and is part of the major developmental transition to autonomy during the toddler years. They present diagnostic criteria for six individual feeding disorders, describing interactional issues as well as existing clinical and empirical studies. They recommend that more research be conducted to validate the disorders as well as elucidate the relation of feeding disorders in infancy to eating disorders in later childhood, adolescence, and adulthood.

The authors of the chapters in this section all emphasize the importance of adopting a goodness-of-fit model. Specifically, all recognize the significance of the match between state-related characteristics and cues of the child and the responsivity of the early caregiving environment to those cues in transitioning from a developmentally appropriate mutually regulated transaction system to autonomy and self-regulation. The authors suggest that the processes involved in achieving regulation may be fluid and dynamic. Thus, unlike subsequent stages of development when problems become more entrenched and possibly treatment resistant, early state regulation may hold the promise for the most effective intervention approaches.

13

Sensory Modulation Dysfunction: Identification in Early Childhood

Lucy Jane Miller
JoAnn Robinson
Debra Moulton

For decades, large numbers of infants and toddlers have been identified by occupational therapy clinicians as having sensory-related disorders (Bundy, Lane, & Murray, 2002; Roley, Blanche, & Schaaf, 2001). These disturbances have been termed *sensory integration dysfunction* (Ayres, 1972a; Cermak, Koomar, & Szklut, 1999; Kranowitz, 1998; Parham & Mailloux, 2001). Among psychologists and other mental health experts, there has been widespread recognition of a problem for infants and toddlers that has similar sensory components and is termed *regulatory disorder* (Greenspan & Wieder, 1993; Greenspan, Wieder, & Simons, 1998). It is important to illuminate the similarities and differences between these two diagnostic categories in order to advance toward a broader, more comprehensive understanding of sensory disorders in early childhood, to increase the clinical utility of terms, and to increase effective communication for more focused prevention and intervention.

The overall objective of the chapter is to familiarize mental health professionals with the existence of these sensory problems and to highlight the importance of evaluating sensory processing difficulties when determining a diagnostic formulation in young children referred for a variety of behavioral difficulties. First, we provide a brief discussion of definitional issues and compare and contrast mental health and occupational therapy perspectives of sensory-related disorders. Second, we provide an overview of the developmental issues relevant to the understanding of sensory-related disorders. Third, we provide a discussion of sensory modulation dysfunction (SMD), including a brief description of related empirical evidence. Finally, we review the clinical implications for assessment of sensory-related disorders and conclude by highlighting the questions that remain to be addressed in future research.

DEFINITIONAL ISSUES

This section clarifies the definition of various terms used in the area of sensory-related disorders within the field of occupational therapy (OT) and by the National Center for Clinical Infant Programs (NCCIP). Within OT, this classification scheme was developed in relation to a condition termed sensory integration dysfunction (DSI; Fisher & Murray, 1991). Within NCCIP, descriptions of sensory and motor processes are found under a condition termed regulatory disorders (Zero to Three, 1994). The development of classification schemes for DSI and for regulatory disorders developed in parallel; they continue to evolve independently. Though conceptually related, the DC:0–3 scheme and the DSI patterns of dysfunction have not previously been compared in the literature.

Sensory Integration Dysfunction

Ayres (1972a), an occupational therapist and educational psychologist, first proposed use of the term *sensory integration dysfunction*. This pattern of disturbance has also been called dysfunction in sensory integration, and a recent consensus paper recommended use of the abbreviation DSI to avoid confusion with SIDS, sudden infant death syndrome (Miller & Lane, 2000). Ayres proposed that DSI is a multifaceted problem including the following discrete patterns of dysfunction differentiated by Lane, Miller, and Hanft (2000):

1. *Sensory detection dysfunction*, difficulty with awareness or registration of incoming sensory signals. Difficulties with sensory detection are observed in children who seek an unusual amount of sensation (for example, smelling everyday objects such as doorknobs) or who do not appear to feel even highly salient sensation (for example, they touch a hot surface and do not feel pain).

2. *Sensory modulation dysfunction*, difficulty modulating and regulating the degree, intensity, and nature of responses to sensory input in a graded and adaptive manner, so that an optimal range of performance and adaptation to life challenges is maintained (for example, overresponding to an unexpected tap on the shoulder with aggressive lashing out or by withdrawing).

3. *Sensory discrimination dysfunction*, difficulty perceiving the particular characteristics of objects without seeing them (for example, stereognosis is the ability to know what you are touching or feeling without vision, such as knowing you are handling keys in your pocket).

4. *Postural dysfunction*, difficulty maintaining functional body patterns (for example, normal muscle tone, awareness of body position, and movement through space (Lane et al., 2000).

5. *Dyspraxia*, difficulty with the conceptualization, organization, and execution of nonhabitual motor tasks. Praxis is engaged when the demands of the action are novel or challenging (nonautomatic) and require ideation, planning, modification, or self-monitoring for their adaptive execution. This problem is believed to have a sensory component in some children observed, as problems executing fine motor, gross motor, or visual motor tasks combine with inadequate perception of the underlying sensory demands of the tasks.

The second pattern above, SMD, is one of the primary patterns of DSI found in infants and young children and therefore is highlighted in this chapter (Ayres, 1966, 1972a, 1979, 1989; Fisher, Murray, & Bundy, 1991; Lane, 2002; Parham & Mailloux, 2001). While everyone experiences difficulty modulating their response to sensory input at some moments in life, to be considered SMD, these difficulties in regulating responses to sensation must be so severe that normal daily routines are impaired. People with SMD may also have other patterns of DSI.

While theoretical descriptions of SMD in children ages birth to 3 years appear in the literature (Schaaf, 2001; Williamson & Anzalone, 2001), there are only a few empirical references validating the disorder, all with children ages 4 years and older (McIntosh, Miller, Shyu, & Hagerman, 1999; Miller et al., 1999; Miller, Reisman, McIntosh, & Simon, 2001). In infants and toddlers, the sensory processing difficulties associated with SMD often present as sleep disorders, eating disorders, problems with organized play, and emotional outbursts after sensory input (Williamson & Anzalone, 2001). More research is needed to differentiate normal developmental variations in early patterns of sleeping, eating, playing, and emotion regulation from behavioral patterns of SMD.

Regulatory Disorders in the DC:0–3

The National Center for Clinical Infant Programs, Zero to Three has developed a taxonomy for infant and toddler diagnostic classification of developmental disorders, the *Diagnostic Classification of Mental Health and Developmental Disorders of Infancy and Early Childhood* (DC:0–3; Zero to Three, 1994). This classification, which is becoming widely used by clinicians, was developed through systematic observation and theoretical consolidation by expert clinicians (see chapter 8).

According to the DC:0–3, regulatory disorders present in infancy and toddlerhood as an inability to regulate behaviors and responses in the domains of physiology, sensation, attention, motor, and affective processes (DeGangi, 2000). Children show difficulties in modulating and integrating physiological, sensory, motor, attentional, or emotional processes to achieve an organized, calm, and alert state (Greenspan & Wieder, 1993). These difficulties, which are thought to represent constitutional and maturational characteristics, can interfere with both cognitive (learning) and social (relationship) domains.

The DC:0–3 scheme identifies four types of regulatory disorders:

1. *Type I: Hypersensitive.* These children are overresponsive to a variety of stimuli. Two behavioral patterns are described: (a) fearful/cautious and (b) negative/defiant. The former category includes compromised visual-spatial processing abilities, whereas the latter category does not. Children in both categories have sensorimotor patterns that are overresponsive to tactile, auditory, and visual stimuli.

2. *Type II: Underreactive.* These children are underresponsive to a variety of stimuli. The two behavioral patterns are (a) withdrawn/difficult to engage and (b) self-absorbed. The former category co-occurs with apathy, depression, limited responsivity to sensation, and impoverished motor exploration. Dyspraxia and auditory/verbal processing problems may occur, but visual-spatial skills are intact. The second category, self-absorbed, includes inattentive, distractible, and preoccupied behaviors with a preponderance of solitary play that may be rich in fantasy. These children have decreased auditory and verbal skills, particularly receptive language, and may or may not have other sensorimotor problems.

3. *Type III: Motorically disorganized, impulsive.* These children crave sensory input and have poorly controlled behavior. The two behavioral patterns are (a) aggressive/fearless and (b) impulsive/disorganized. These children have extremely high activity levels, seeking extraordinary touch contact and deep pressure stimulation. The child may intrude on others' space and materials. They exhibit poor motor planning and organization that may be interpreted as aggression. Sensory underresponsivity is hypothesized to relate to craving input and to poor motor modulation and planning.

4. *Type IV: Other.* The category is for children who meet criteria for regulatory disorder but are not described by types I, II, or III.

Overlap Between DC:0–3 and SMD Classification Taxonomies

The sensory and motor processes described under the rubric of regulatory disorder parallel the behavioral descriptions of DSI (Roley et al., 2001). The behavioral manifestations of these patterns of dysfunction are similar. In addition, there appears to be much overlap with respect to subtypes. The overlap between the subtypes of SMD and regulatory disorders is reflected in table 13.1.

DEVELOPMENTAL ISSUES

A young child's emotional and behavioral distress, particularly if it is persistent, is potentially quite challenging for parents and clinicians. In infancy and early childhood, the source of the distress may relate to sensory, emotional, and attentional dysregulation. At present, however, there is very little empirical data that can guide a clear demarcation between these three related domains of functioning. Nonetheless, a careful screening of sensory, emotional, and attentional systems may be clinically useful in understanding sensitivity to sensory stimuli in relation to emotional reactivity.

Emotion Regulation and Sensory Processing

To understand the developmental perspective of emotion regulation as it relates to sensory processing, it is necessary to briefly summarize theo-

Table 13.1 Overlap Between Regulatory Disorder and SMD Categorizations

Regulatory Disorder Categorization		SMD Categorization
401: Type I	Hyperreactive	Oversensitive/active
402: Type II	Underreactive	Undersensitive/passive
403: Type III	Motorically disorganized, impulsive	Undersensitive/active (SMD) and/or dyspraxia (DSI)

ries of emotion and the relation between emotion and behavioral adaptation. This brief review provides a framework for the later discussion of emotion regulation and dysregulation as it relates to SMD.

Theories of Emotion Regulation

Various disciplines refer to emotions as configurations of feelings, intentions, and actions; some theories focus only on one or another of these components, while others consider the entire emotion process. Cognitive theories of emotion (Lazarus, 1991; Scherer, 1984) are particularly relevant because they provide an understanding of the role of sensory processing in the emotion generation process. While not specifically developmental, core principles of the cognitive perspective can be adapted to the emotional experience of infants, toddlers, and young children.

Different emotional states correspond to distinct mental and bodily experiences. For most individuals, the experiences of joy and fear are easily discriminated, but for some, the experiences of fear, anger, or sadness are not so clearly different. For infants and toddlers, who have not yet had the opportunity to fully develop a differentiated emotional repertoire, this may be especially true. Distress may be experienced as a blend of fear and anger, creating confusing behavioral signals for caregivers. With development comes an emerging emotional competence that includes the child's ability to verbally differentiate and label emotional experiences (Saarni, 1990).

An emotional state is also fundamentally a state of *action readiness* (Frijda, Kuipers, & ter Schure, 1989). When people like something, the emotion of joy readies them to approach. When they are frustrated, they are similarly ready to approach, but also to attack and remove the frustra-

tion. When they are afraid, they prepare to leave. This description suggests a primitive, automatic process that fits what is observed in young children when they like, dislike, or fear what is happening in their environment. They often act quickly, without pause, on the emotional impulses that arise from contact with particular sensations. Throughout early childhood, adults socialize children to slow down this impulse to act and to adapt to culturally accepted modes of expressing their joy, frustration, and fear (Saarni, 1990).

Emotions arise only when we appraise something in the environment as important to our goals (Lazarus, 1991). If something is not important, an emotion will not arise. For example, a 4-month-old infant typically does not react with distress when a stranger approaches because he or she has not yet developed the pattern of responses that signal the crystallization of specific attachments, whereas a 10-month-old who has developed attachments and a concomitant stranger anxiety will react with distress. This appraisal process is thought to be highly automatic, especially in relation to sensory stimuli, and is evident in the infant's reactions to the smell of its mother's breast milk within several days after birth (Scherer, 1984). Kandel and Schwartz (1991) call this appraisal a "valuation" that filters information, allowing some information in and excluding other information.

Sensory nerves feed the amygdala, one of the central areas in the brain where the emotion appraisal process arises, through subcortical as well as neocortical pathways (LeDoux, 1993). Nerve signals from the amygdala are directly linked to the autonomic nervous system, the part of the nervous system responsible for heart and respiration rates and the release of various hormones that prepare the body for action. Autonomic responses associated with emotion are evident in infancy as early as the newborn period (Fox, 1989; Fox & Davidson, 1986).

Hence, bodily sensations may be the first conscious signal that something is awry or feels good. An emotionally distressed child commonly reports a stomachache or other physical ailments. Adults often socialize the young child's experience, interpreting for the child the cause of these internal bodily sensations and feelings. For children and adults whose bodily sensations are well regulated, socialization of emotion happens smoothly. For example, the exhilaration of happiness in reuniting with someone will be expressed through smiling, positive vocalizations, and embracing. However, for a child who is hypersensitive to touch, embracing may be uncomfortable. While this child might initially appear happy by smiling and vocalizing during reunion, when the embrace occurs, the child may withdraw from contact or even cry. This confusing set of behaviors may lead parents to feel hurt or confused, possibly initiating a complex maladaptive interaction process.

Emotion Regulation and Behavioral Adaptation

The child's signaling of his or her experience of an event is the beginning of the adaptation process. To the extent that sensory experiences are commonly shared in a culture (e.g., strong odors are disliked; hugging creates pleasure), adults will accurately interpret a child's responses. However, when an individual's sensory experiences are unusual, either in terms of their source (e.g., aversion to being held) or in terms of the threshold of perception as noxious, adults may misinterpret the child's response. For example, avoidance of sensory stimulation may be interpreted as fear, and the child may be allowed to avoid many situations to reduce his or her distress. Seeking of sensory stimulation may be misread as out-of-control behavior, and the child may be punished. Thus, children with SMD may detect sensory information at too high or low a level, thus triggering emotional process that are not appropriate to the context of specific tasks, environments, or cultures. Most individuals do not react emotionally to sensory stimuli experienced in the low to middle range. However, individuals who experi-

ence lights as too bright, sounds as too loud, or wind as too powerful may try to avoid these experiences or may experience strong emotional reactions or distress in these situations.

A child's adaptive functioning is supported when sensory stimuli are not overwhelming and when emotions are well regulated. Cole, Michel, and Teti (1994) define emotion regulation as "the ability to respond to the on-going demands of experience with a range of emotions in a manner that is socially tolerable and sufficiently flexible to permit spontaneous reactions as well as the ability to delay spontaneous reactions as needed" (p. 76). Emotions are considered dysregulated if interference with other functions (e.g., sustained attention, activating memory, or interacting with others) occurs. For example, children with attention deficit disorder have poor peer relations in part because of their poorly timed and excessive expression of positive affect (Cole et al., 1994). Thus, both regulated and dysregulated emotions are attempts to control behavior and communicate intentions to others.

Achieving consistent emotion regulation is a major developmental task, largely accomplished by school age, but unreliable in early childhood. Cole et al. (1994) describe two major types of emotion dysregulation: underregulation and overregulation. Underregulated behaviors tend to be overly expressive or extreme and require others to assist the child to maintain control, by soothing or limiting the child's exposure to events that give rise to strong emotions. Overregulated emotions are held in tightly, as in the freezing response, and the child may need assistance from others to express what they experience. Both underregulated and overregulated emotions lead to compromises in the child's ability to respond flexibly in certain contexts and may place the child at risk for psychopathology. When difficulties in emotion regulation become pervasive, across multiple contexts and long periods of time, treatment for an emotional disorder may be considered.

We now turn our focus specifically to the characteristics of SMD. We describe the following: (a) behavioral description of SMD subtypes, (b) a conceptual model of SMD, and (c) recent research that examines the empirical evidence of the existence of SMD as a syndrome, including a parent rating scale to detect SMD and a psycho-physiological laboratory procedure to confirm the behavioral diagnosis.

RESEARCH ON SENSORY MODULATION DISORDER

A recent initiative developed a consensus of terminology related to children with DSI (Hanft, Miller, & Lane, 2000; Lane et al., 2000; Miller & Lane, 2000). Clarifying terminology was perceived as a starting point for clear communication within the field, as well as across other related disciplines. Particular emphasis was placed on differentiating between the normal processes of sensory functioning, and the abnormal processes and behaviors associated with DSI, with SMD representing only one of several patterns of DSI.

Individuals respond to sensations along a spectrum, and for an individual to have SMD, not only must abnormal emotional and behavioral responses to sensation be observed, but adaptive functioning must also be impaired. Typically, children with SMD have responses that are so impaired that significant daily life challenges occur. For example, a mother in our study commented, "My family is in jail. We can't go anywhere together because we never know when Johnny will fall apart. We have stopped going to church, and we never go to a movie or shopping together, since one of us has to stay home with him." More research is needed to document not only emotional and behavioral responses characteristic of SMD but also levels of impaired functioning that co-occur.

SMD has been described in a variety of chapters and newsletter manuscripts, but in only a few peer-reviewed publications (see, for example, Ayres, 1972a; Bundy et al., 2002; Fisher et al., 1991; Kimball, 1993; Kinnealey & Miller, 1993; Parham & Mailloux, 2001; Roley et al., 2001). As research generally has grown in this area, the concept of sensory modulation dysfunction has evolved. It began with definitions based strictly on behavioral descriptions of children by clinicians (Ayres, 1972a) and with factor analytic studies (Ayres, 1969, 1972c, 1977) of standardized neuropsychological scales, such as the South-ern California Sensory Integration Test (Ayres, 1972b) and the Sensory Integration and Praxis Scale (Ayres, 1989). More recently, conceptions of SMD have broadened to include physiological constructs related to functioning, emphasizing the role of the autonomic nervous system in regulating underlying processes responsible for sensory responsivity (McIntosh, Miller, Shyu, & Hagerman, 1999; Miller et al., 1999; Parush, 1993; Parush et al., 1997; Schaaf, 2001; Schaaf, Miller, Sewell, & O'Keefe, 2003).

Subtypes of SMD

Two primary types of SMD have emerged in the OT literature based on different types of behaviors presented by children. They developed as an outgrowth of clinical observations, similar to the way that the DC:0–3 schemes developed. The types are oversensitive and undersensitive to sensory stimulation (Dunn, 1999; Koomar & Bundy, 2002; Lane, 2002). Behaviors of children who are oversensitive include fight, fright, and freeze responses. Behaviors of children who are undersensitive include sensation seeking and lack of awareness of sensation. Table 13.2 details behaviors (and sensory-related examples) associated with the two behaviorally derived primary subtypes of SMD.

Our research team has organized these responses in a 2 × 2 conceptual framework, in a clarification of the model proposed by Dunn (1997). This new conceptualization highlights both passive and active categories in the oversensitive and undersensitive behavioral responses to sensory stimulation. The framework is presented in table 13.3.

While table 13.3 highlights two subtypes of SMD, some children have *fluctuating SMD*, with responses that are at times oversensitive and, at other times, undersensitive. These fluctuations may occur in response to external circumstances or may be related to different responses in various sensory systems. For example, a child may demonstrate sensory seeking in one domain (e.g., movement) while exhibiting sensory avoiding in another domain (e.g., tactile). To guide both empirical and clinical work, a conceptual model is needed that can address the complex, internal

Table 13.2 Behaviors Associated with Two Primary Types of SMD

Oversensitive to Sensation	Undersensitive to Sensation
Flight—may withdraw from sensation (e.g., may run and hide under a table with ears covered when they hear a vacuum or a fire engine)	*Overfocused*—children perseverate on tasks; shifting attention between tasks or environments is difficult (e.g., take physical prompt to move from one task to another; may watch a video over and over and become overfocused on it so that you have to touch them to get their attention)
Fight—children become highly aroused with sensation and may become aggressive (e.g., when standing in line with other children and jostled, may hit person behind them in line)	*Unaware*—May respond lethargically when presented with normal levels of stimuli, needing intense stimulus over a long period to notice stimulus (e.g., may not notice pain when they fall down; may seem withdrawn or in their own world unless stimulus is intense)
Freeze—Distressed by sensation; may over-respond to low levels of stimulation (e.g., may freeze in seat and show severe distress when they hear fire bell in fire drill at school)	*Seeks*—May need an atypically large or long duration of sensation to feel the stimulus (e.g., can spin or swing "forever" without really seeming to feel it; jump, run, crash into walls or jump on mattresses for long periods of time)

processes involved in SMD as well as the external stimulation.

A Conceptual Model of SMD

Miller, Reisman, McIntosh, and Simon (2001) developed a conceptual model of SMD to depict the internal and external factors affecting children with SMD (see figure 13.1).

The model embodies ideas from a long tradition of developmental literature on the importance of context as it influences children's development (Bronfenbrenner, 1979; Cole, 1985; Vygotsky, 1962). The external dimensions of this conceptual model reflect the contextual elements that affect the way in which SMD manifests at a particular moment. SMD occurs when a mismatch exists between what is expected of a child and what he or she can do (Bates & Wachs, 1994; Chess & Thomas, 1995; DeGangi, 2000). Table 13.4 reflects the limitations in functional participation that can result from SMD (e.g., problems at home, at school, and in the community).

The conceptual model also incorporates internal dimensions of SMD. The dimensions, represented by the three circular levels in figure 13.1, represent sensation, attention, and emotion, each divided into quadrants: oversensitive, normal sen-

Table 13.3 Active and Passive Behavioral Response Characteristics for Two SMD Subtypes

	Oversensitive Behaviors	Undersensitive Behaviors
Active behavioral response	*Defensive*: moves away or strikes out with stimulation	*Seeks stimulation*: constantly pursues sensory input
Passive behavioral response	*Anxious*: becomes quiet, worried, or withdraws from sensory stimulation	*Unaware*: lethargic; uninterested unless stimulation is intense

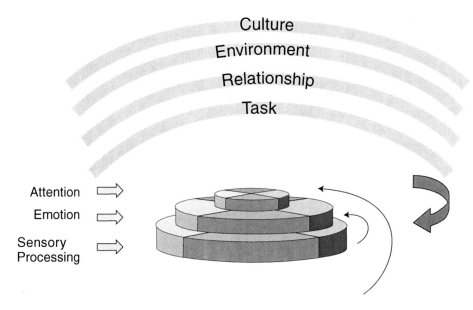

Figure 13.1 Ecological model of sensory modulation.

sitivity, undersensitive, and fluctuating sensitivity. The internal dimensions describe individual differences among persons in the following areas:

1. *Sensation*—the ability to receive and manage sensory information resulting in appropriate responses
2. *Emotion*—the ability to accurately perceive emotional cues and regulate affective and behavioral responses
3. *Attention*—the ability to sustain performance and inhibit impulsivity for task completion and effective interpersonal relationships

This model draws on the classic formulation of temperament by Chess and Thomas (1984), who relied on variations in sensation, emotion, and attention to describe the typical styles of responding in early childhood. Findings from the MacArthur Longitudinal Twin Study (Emde, Plomin, & Hewitt, 2001) suggest that there are genetic influences on emotion expression and attention in infancy and early childhood. However, little is known about the constitutional basis of sensation.

Table 13.5 reflects the individual impairments that can occur from limitations in the three internal dimensions. These impairments may occur in isolation but are frequently combined (e.g., a difficulty in sensation may co-occur with an attention or emotion problem).

By considering both internal and external dimensions of SMD, one may predict certain mismatches between children's innate disposition and how they react to the external dimensions of their world. In the temperament literature, such mismatches are associated with poor functioning of the parent-child dyad; however, little empirical research has been conducted on the consequence of temperamental mismatches or the relation of temperament and sensory responsivity; thus, at present the concept primarily has clinical utility.

The Need for More Research on
Regulatory Disorders and SMD

Behavioral descriptions of regulatory disorder are similar to those of SMD. Yet, little empirical evidence differentiates the two classifications. Given the strong similarity in subtypes noted in table 13.1, children in the 0 to 3 age group with dysfunction might be given either or both diagnoses. The empirical evidence comparing validity and

Table 13.4 Functional Participation Limitations Related to Mismatch Between Child's Capacities and External Dimensions

External Dimensions	Behaviors Observed in Child
Relationship expectations	Child with SMD cannot tolerate expected closeness in relationships; is unable to make and keep friends; fights with siblings and peers; poor participation in family routines and outings.
Task expectations	Child with SMD needs specified conditions to complete tasks (e.g., structuring the task to have small steps to reduce its complexity).
Environmental expectations	Child with SMD requires specific environment to maintain appropriate arousal level (e.g., creating a quiet, nondistracting space in which to work). May have severe difficulties at school because environment causes inattention and/or aggression.
Cultural expectations	Child with SMD responds negatively to demands of the general culture (i.e., cannot comfortably attend birthday parties, go to community celebrations such as parades, participate in team sports, go to church, libraries, parks, etc.).

clinical utility of both categories, regulatory disorder and SMD, is lacking.

Although DC:0–3 appears to be a reasonable clinical taxonomy, little data exist related to the validity of the separate groupings in the taxonomy. The DC:0–3 classification scheme discusses the relative importance of physiology, sensation, attention, and motor processes to dysregulated behavior but does not demonstrate these abnormalities empirically. Thus, the constitutional and neurodevelopmental bases of regulatory disorders

Table 13.5 Functional Limitations in SMD Related to Internal Dimensions

Internal Dimension	Impairment Observed in Behavior
Sensory symptoms	Severe over- or undersensitivity to tactile, movement, taste, smell, auditory, or visual stimuli
Emotional symptoms	Aggression, anger, dysregulation, tearfulness, withdrawal, anxiety, depression
Attentional symptoms	Poor sustained attention, poor impulse control, hyperactivity; overfocused and unable to transition

have not yet been validated. The DC:0–3 case summary book focuses on affective and psychosocial aspects of the disorder, and the presumed underlying, neurodevelopmental processes are not addressed (Lieberman, Wieder, & Fenichel, 1997). The DC:0–3 developers discuss the need to refine the diagnostic system (Zero to Three, 1994); however, this has not been accomplished to date. Given the relative novelty of Axis I (400) regulatory disorders, empirical research in this domain is particularly required. Elements of syndrome validation such as the contributions of etiology (i.e., genetics, environment, brain mechanisms), developmental trajectory, and treatment effects (Pennington, 1991) are not specified in DC:0–3 or the DC:0–3 case summary book. Future empirical work should specify these aspects of regulatory disorder so that the convergent and discriminant validity of the syndrome can be evaluated.

Empirical evidence related to SMD is also lacking, although a spurt in research has begun to correct this deficiency (Ahn, Miller, Milberger, & McIntosh, in press; Miller et al., 1999, 2001; Mangeot et al., 2001; Ognibene, McIntosh, Miller, & Raad, 2003; Schaaf et al., 2003). More research is needed to better characterize SMD in relation to emotional and behavioral patterns of dysregulation in the early years. Neither researchers using the DC:0–3 categorization nor those using the SMD classification taxonomy have provided research or theoretical information describing the relation between regulatory disorders and SMD, perhaps because the two diagnostic classifications began at about the same time in different professional milieus, and each was unaware of the other until publication. Research bridging the gap between these two distinct but related conceptualizations would be useful to elucidate whether or not the terms are referring to the same processes and behaviors.

PRELIMINARY STUDIES OF SMD

We currently are studying SMD at the Sensory Treatment And Research (STAR) Processing Center at The Children's Hospital and the University of Colorado Health Sciences Center in Denver, Colorado. We have collected pilot data on sensory, emotional, and attentional functioning of children with SMD compared to typically developing children on (a) psychometric indicators of sensory functioning and (b) psychophysiological indicators of sensory functioning. To implement the work, we needed to develop appropriate measures of sensory responsivity.

Measures

Parent Report Measure
for Sensory Responsivity

We have developed a parent-report screening measure of functional sensory behaviors that discriminates between children who are developing normally and children with SMD. We started our scale development using 125 items from the Sensory Profile (SP; Dunn, 1999). Since emotional and fine motor domains were included in the original SP and 51% of the SP items did not load on factors, we conducted content analysis, item analysis, and factor analysis to create a shorter tool (38 items) that focused only on the construct of sensory responsivity, called the Short Sensory Profile (SSP; McIntosh, Miller, Shyu, & Dunn,

1999). Sample items for each of the seven subtests of SSP are provided in table 13.6. The SSP has a stable factor structure, reflecting the various sensory constructs hypothesized by the literature to be affected in SMD. Four subtests measure aspects of active oversensitivity: Tactile Sensitivity, Movement Sensitivity, Auditory/Visual Sensitivity, and Taste/Smell Sensitivity. One subtest, Auditory Filtering, relates to filtering sensory information. One subtest, Underresponsive/Seeks Sensation, is related to active sensory seeking. One subtest, Low Energy/Weak, relates to passive undersensitivity. Two subtests, Auditory Filtering and Underresponsive/Seeks Sensation, correlate highly with items on *DSM-IV* behavioral descriptions for ADHD (Ognibene, 2002). Figure 13.2 demonstrates the difference in performance between children with and without SMD on all seven subtests of the SSP ($p < .01$) (McIntosh, Miller, Shyu, & Dunn, 1999). We are currently developing more comprehensive assessments (parent, teacher, and clinician) of SMD behaviors with more items representing each quadrant, depicted in table 13.3 (Miller & Schoen, 2003; Moulton, 2002).

Physiological Laboratory Paradigm
to Measure SMD

We also developed a psychophysiological laboratory paradigm, the Sensory Challenge Protocol, to measure sensory reactivity, and tested its reliability and validity (Mangeot et al., 2001; McIntosh, Miller, Shyu, & Hagerman, 1999; Miller et al., 1999, 2001). In this laboratory paradigm, a child between 3 and 8 years of age enters a room decorated like a "pretend space ship." The child watches a short segment from the film *Apollo 13* while we attach electrodes. We measure physiological reactivity in three conditions: (a) a baseline condition of physiological reactivity for 2 minutes when no stimulus is presented, (b) a sensory challenge condition where the experimenter presents a series of 50 sensory stimuli in a controlled manner (i.e., ten 3-second sensory stimuli are presented in each of five sensory domains: olfactory, auditory, visual, tactile, and vestibular), and (c) a 2-minute recovery condition of physiological reactivity while the child watches a simple cartoon.

Table 13.6 Short Sensory Profile Subtests and Example Items

Domain	Sample Items
1. Tactile sensitivity	1. Reacts emotionally or aggressively to touch 2. Has difficulty standing in line or close to other people
2. Taste/smell sensitivity	1. Picky eater, especially regarding food textures 2. Limits self to particular food textures/temperatures
3. Movement sensitivity	1. Fears falling or heights 2. Becomes anxious or distressed when feet leave the ground
4. Underresponsive/ seeks sensation	1. Becomes overly excitable during movement activity 2. Jumps from one activity to another so that it interferes with play
5. Auditory filtering	1. Has difficulty paying attention 2. Is distracted or has trouble functioning if there is a lot of noise around
6. Low energy/weak	1. Poor endurance/tires easily 2. Has a weak grasp
7. Visual/auditory sensitivity	1. Responds negatively to unexpected or loud noises 2. Covers eyes or squints to protect eyes from light

Two physiological measures are collected continuously through the baseline, challenge, and recovery conditions that provide data related to the degree to which the child responds to the sensory stimuli. The measures are called (1) *electrodermal reactivity* (EDR), a marker of sympathetic nervous system activity, and (2) *vagal tone* (VT), a marker of parasympathetic nervous system functioning.

Using the Sensory Challenge Protocol, we compared EDR and VT for typically developing children and children clinically diagnosed with

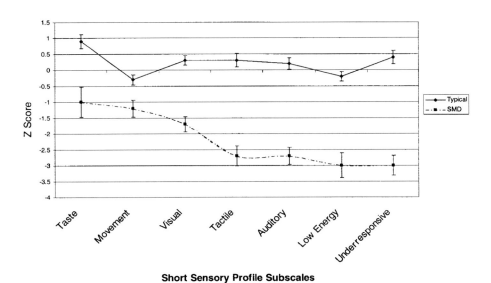

Figure 13.2 Typically developing children compared to children with SMD on the short sensory profile.

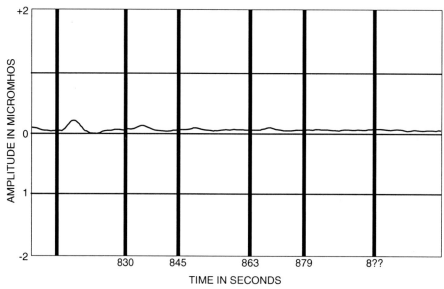

Figure 13.3 EDR for typically developing child.

SMD ($n = 38$). Figures 13.3 and 13.4 display a short segment of the EDR profiles of two children. In both figures, the bold vertical lines represent the sensory stimulus administered for 3 seconds. Time is represented along the horizontal axis at the bottom of the illustration. The curving line in the figure represents the child's electrodermal response to the stimuli. In figure 13.3, the response of a typically developing child is displayed. The child is seen to orient to the first stimulus (curved line goes up in amplitude after the first vertical line) and notices the second stimulus (curved line slopes upward after the second vertical line, although not as high as after stimulus 1), and then the responses are seen to diminish or habituate.

A segment from the profile of a child with SMD is seen in figure 13.4. The child's response is quite different from the response of the typically developing child. This child experiences a stronger reaction (higher amplitude), more continuous reactions (multiple peaks), and poor cessation of reaction over time (does not habituate after multiple trials of identical stimuli).

Differences between typically developing children ($n = 19$) and children referred with SMD ($n = 19$) were significant ($p < .01$), with large ef-

fect sizes (>.80; Cohen, 1992) on the three EDR variables, amplitude, frequency, and habituation (McIntosh, Miler, Shyu, & Hagerman, 1999). Figure 13.5 depicts group differences between children with SMD and typically developing children on EDR.

In a preliminary study, the vagal tone patterns of 49 children with SMD were examined (Schaaf, 2001; Schaaf et al., 2003). Two atypical subgroups of children with SMD appeared; one with extremely low VT and one with extremely high VT (some children with SMD had normal VT in response to sensory stimulation across time). Cross-validation of this data with a larger sample is currently under way.

Association of Sensation, Emotion, and Attention in SMD

In this section, we present preliminary findings on the relation of symptoms within the internal domains specified in the model presented above: sensation, emotion, and attention. We have collected pilot data on associations among sensation, attention, and emotion in children with and without SMD. Our findings suggest that the three domains are interconnected.

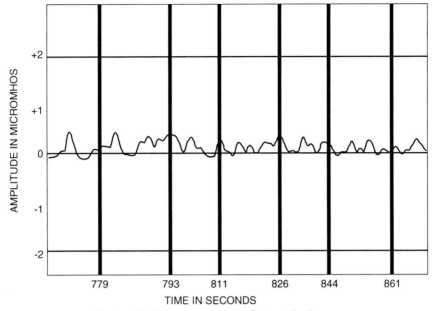

Each vertical line represents an olfactory stimulus.

Figure 13.4 EDR for child with SMD.

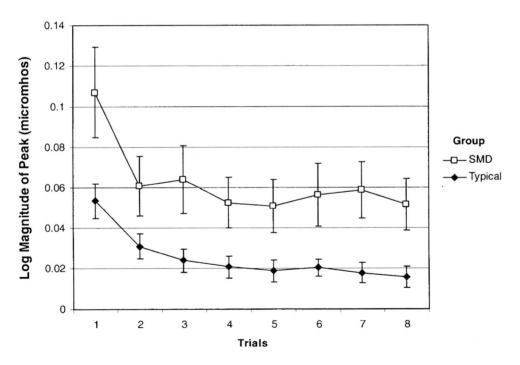

Figure 13.5 EDR amplitude differences between children with SMD and typically developing children. Each trial represents the mean value of that order of stimuli for all sensory domains summed (e.g., trial 1 = olfactory stimulus 1 plus auditory stimulus 1 plus visual stimulus 1 plus tactile stimulus 1 plus vestibular stimulus 1 divided by 5).

In a set of pilot studies, we assessed sensation, attention, and emotion in a group of 16 typically developing children and 33 children with SMD ages 3 to 7 years. Controls were typically developing children who were screened by parent report and were reported to have no birth trauma, have positive educational experiences, were not receiving special therapeutic services, and have age-appropriate relationships. Children with SMD met three criteria: scores greater than −3 standard deviations below the mean on the Short Sensory Profile, hyperreactive EDR, and clinician recommendation after a comprehensive evaluation as detailed in Miller et al. (2001) and McIntosh, Miller, Shyu, and Hagerman (1999). All children had normal intelligence quotients and no *DSM-IV* diagnoses. This inclusion criterion ruled out children with co-occurring comorbid diagnosis such as autistic disorder and/or fragile X syndrome; however, children in the sample may have comorbid attentional and anxiety disorders. We administered the psychophysiological laboratory tests described earlier (McIntosh, Miller, Shyu, & Hagerman, 1999; Miller et al., 1999, 2001). In addition, parent report measures of emotional responses, attentional abilities, and sensory processing were administered.

For this study, we used information from three standardized parent rating scales:

- The Short Sensory Profile (McIntosh, Miller, Shyu, & Dunn, 1999), all subtests: (1) Tactile, (2) Taste/Smell, (3) Visual/Auditory, (4) Movement Sensitivity, (5) Under-Responsive/Seeks Sensation, (6) Auditory Filtering, and (7) Low Energy/Weak
- The Leiter International Performance Scale–Revised (Roid & Miller, 1997), parent rating on three subtests: (1) Attention, (2) Impulsivity, and (3) Activity Level
- The Child Behavior Checklist (Achenbach, 1991), all subtests: (1) Withdrawn, (2) Somatic Complaints, (3) Anxious/Depressed, (4) Social Problems, (5) Thought Problems, (6) Attention Problems, (7) Sex Problems, (8) Delinquent Problems, and (9) Aggressive Behavior

Canonical correlation was used to predict a combination of several criterion variables from several predictor variables. We selected this technique because we were undertaking exploration of relationships among a large number of measures to assess our three domains (Gall, Borg, & Gall, 1996). Three sets of analyses were conducted to evaluate the associations among all three domains (sensation, attention, and emotion). The first set of analyses evaluated sensation and attention; the second set evaluated emotion and attention; and the third set evaluated sensation and emotion. In these analyses, each of the three domains was consistently correlated with each of the other two domains.

Sensation and Attention

The first set of analyses assessed the relation of sensation to attention. All sensory and attention subscales were correlated to the first root ($r = .44$), indicating that poor performance on all sensory subtests is associated with poor attention, impulsivity, and hyperactivity. Interpretation of root 2 ($r = .63$) indicates that the sensory subtests Low Energy/Weak, Movement Sensitivity, and Tactile Sensitivity were positively associated with only the inattention variable, and were negatively correlated with the hyperactivity variable. This preliminary data suggests that children with low scores in all sensory domains are likely to have problems with attention in general and may be at risk for ADHD. The second root indicates that those children with only low energy and movement/tactile sensitivity may be at risk for ADHD inattentive subtype. Caution must be used in interpreting results, as sample size is limited. While these data are exploratory, our findings suggest that sensation-related functioning may be linked to risk for attention-related disorders.

Emotion and Attention

The second set of analyses used canonical correlation to examine the relation between emotion and attention subtests. Only one root was found in this young age group, demonstrating that a general relation between all emotion and attention subtests exists. Not surprisingly, children with attention difficulties are likely to have socioemotional difficulties as well. This finding is consistent with other studies linking attention problems with socioemotional difficulties (for a discussion of socioemotional difficulties associated with attentional disturbances, see chapter 20).

Sensation and Emotion

The third set of analyses evaluated the relation between sensory and emotion variables. One significant root was found, indicating a relation between all sensory and emotion subscales. Thus, children with sensory problems in all areas were likely to have emotional problems in all areas. As with studies 1 and 2, interpretation is limited by the exploratory nature of the investigation and the small sample size.

Preliminary data suggest that some children with sensory processing difficulties in the early years may be at risk for the development of attention and emotion-related disorders. They also highlight the importance of examining sensory processing problems in children when attention and emotion-related problems are present.

CLINICAL IMPLICATIONS AND DIRECTIONS FOR FUTURE RESEARCH

As increasing numbers of children are referred for attentional and emotional difficulties at increasingly young ages, the importance of identifying early precursors or risk factors associated with these disturbances takes on some urgency. Though our work suggests that sensory problems co-occur with problems in attention and emotion, only rarely is sensory functioning considered in the evaluation and treatment of children in child psychology clinics.

Our findings and conceptual model suggest that sensory-related problems may be critically important in understanding, conceptualizing, and diagnosing early emotional and behavioral disorders in young children. Though many clinically related questions remain in differentiating SMD from emotion regulation and attention problems, and specifically differentiating SMD and regulatory disorder classifications of disabilities in infants and toddlers, clinicians can begin to explore this area on a case-by-case basis by including measures of sensory responsivity in their evaluations of children referred with regulatory disor-

ders, emotion regulation disorders, and attention disorders (see tables 13.7 and 13.8 for a list of evaluations that assess or screen sensory processing in young children).

Our research focuses on children with sensory modulation dysfunction. Our work and the preliminary findings reviewed here raise several questions for future research. First, can normal developmental variations in early patterns of sleep, eating, play, emotion, and attention regulation be differentiated from behavioral patterns in SMD? Second, can sensory responsivity profiles be used to identify risk for and diagnosis of attentional (and attentional subtypes) and affective disorders in young children? Third, can a reliable method to differentiate the sensory, emotion, and attentional aspects of dysregulated behavior in young children be established? Fourth, can we develop ways to assess the compatibility or incompatibility (i.e., mismatch) between the child's internal sensory-related characteristics and the external/contextual factors that influence the child's development? In addition, future empirical research is needed to validate and differentiate SMD and regulatory disorder.

SUMMARY AND CONCLUSION

In this chapter, we have discussed the overlap between two diagnostic classification systems that describe children who have atypical responses to sensory stimulation: regulatory disorders and sensory modulation dysfunction. We have detailed the definitions of these two syndromes and compared and contrasted behaviors described by each. Our overall objective was to familiarize mental health professionals with sensory modulation dysfunction and to highlight the importance of evaluating sensory processing disorders in a comprehensive assessment of problems in infants and young children referred for a variety of behavioral difficulties.

This chapter also provides a conceptual model for the association among sensation, attention, and emotion, and preliminary empirical evidence evaluating the relations among the three dimensions. It is hoped that the conceptual model and preliminary empirical findings presented here on sensory-related problems will generate hypothe-

Table 13.7 Assessments That Directly Evaluate Sensory Integration Functioning

Name	Age and Population Characteristics	Components Measured	Format and Subtests	Source
Brazelton Neonatal Behavioral Rating Scale (Second Edition)	0–1 month	Personal and social skills; gross and fine motor reflexes; tactile and vestibular senses	Informal/structured, quantified observation	Brazelton, T. B. (1984). *Brazelton Neonatal Behavioral Rating Scale* (2nd ed.). Philadelphia: J.B. Lippincott.
Clinical observations of sensory integration dysfunction*				Dunn, W. (1981). *Clinical observations of sensory integration dysfunction.* Bethesda, MD: American Occupational Therapy Association.
DeGangi-Berk Test of Sensory Integration	3–5 years	Vestibular-based sensory integrative functions of postural control, bilateral motor integration, and reflex integration	Criterion-referenced, quantified observations, limited validity data provided	Berk, R. A., & DeGangi, G. A. (1983). *DeGangi-Berk Test of Sensory Integration.* Los Angeles: Western Psychological Services.
Developmental Test of Visual-Motor Integration	3–7; preschool to adult	Visual-motor integration (e.g., copying geometric forms and shapes)	Norm referenced. One version of the test for ages 3 to 7; second version for preschool children through adults. Subtests include VMI Visual Perception and VMI Motor Coordination	Beery, K., & Buktenica, N. (1997). *Developmental Test of Visual-Motor Integration.* Cleveland, OH: Modern Curriculum Press.
Early Coping Inventory: A measure of adaptive behavior	4–36 months	Sensorimotor organization, reactivity, self-initiation during situational coping	48-item observation instrument	Zeitlin, S., Williamson, G. G., & Szczepanski, M. A. (1988). *Early Coping Inventory: A measure of adaptive behavior.* Bensonville, IN: Scholastic Testing Service.
Infant/Toddler Sensory Profile	Birth to 36 months	Measure sensory processing abilities and profile the effect of sensory processing on functional performance in the daily life of a child	Parent questionnaire Birth to 6 months: 36 items 7 to 36 months: 48 items	Dunn, W. (2002). *Infant/Toddler Sensory Profile.* San Antonio, TX: Psychological Corporation.
Infant-Toddler Symptom Checklist	7–30 months	Regulatory disorders and sensory processing during functional activities	Parent questionnaire; five age-range checklists	DeGangi, G. A., & Poisson, S. (1995). *Infant-Toddler Symptom Checklist.* San Antonio, TX: Therapy Skill Builders.

Name	Age Range	Area	Description	Reference
Miller Assessment for Preschoolers (MAP)	2 years, 9 months–5 years, 8 months	Difficulties in praxis	Developmental screening test	Miller, L. J. (1988). *Miller Assessment for Preschoolers (MAP)*. San Antonio, TX: Psychological Corporation.
Sensorimotor History Questionnaire for Preschoolers	3–4 year olds	Sensory integration and self-regulation	51-item questionnaire with five subscales that prescreen problems in self-regulation, sensory processing of touch and movement, motor planning, emotional maturity, and behavioral control	DeGangi, G. A., & Balzer-Martin, L. (1999). The Sensorimotor History Questionnaire for Preschoolers. *Journal of Developmental and Learning Disorders, 3*(1), 59–83.
Sensory Integration and Praxis Test	4.6–8.11 years School-aged children who are relatively high functioning	Sensory and perceptual function	17 subtests; sensory and perceptual function in visual perceptual, visual, vestibular and postural, and somatosensory domains	Ayres, A. J. (1989). *Sensory integration and praxis tests*. Los Angeles: Western Psychological Services.
Sensory Profile	5–10 years (supplementary information on 3- and 5-year-olds)	Sensory processing, modulation, behavioral, and emotional responses	Parent questionnaire with 125 items; divides into 9 factor groupings and/or 14 subtests by domain	Dunn, W. (1999). *The Sensory Profile*. San Antonio, TX: Psychological Corporation.
Short Sensory Profile	3–10 years	Functional aspects of sensory dysfunction	38-item questionnaire with 7 subtests that screen sensory dysfunction	McIntosh, D. N., Miller, L. J., Shyu, V., & Dunn, W. (1999). Overview of the Short Sensory Profile. In W. Dunn (Ed.), *The Sensory Profile: Examiner's Manual* (pp. 59–73). San Antonio, TX: Psychological Corporation.
Test of Attention in Infants	7–30 months	Sustained attentional behaviors	5 age-specific versions; 4 subtests measure sustained attention to visual, auditory, tactile, and multisensory inputs	DeGangi, G. A. *Test of Attention in Infants*. Rockville, MD: Reginald S. Lourie Center for Infants and Young Children.
Test of Sensory Functions in Infants	4–18 months	Regulatory disorders, developmental delay, risk for learning disorders	Diagnostic, criterion referenced. Subtests include reactivity to tactile deep pressure and vestibular stimulation, adaptive motor functions, visual-tactile integration, ocular-motor control	DeGangi, G. A., & Greenspan, S. I. (1989). *Test of Sensory Functions in Infants*. Los Angeles: Western Psychological Corporation.

(continued)

Table 13.7 Continued

Name	Age and Population Characteristics	Components Measured	Format and Subtests	Source
Toddler and Infant Motor Evaluation (T.I.M.E.)	4–42 months	Quality of movement; links motor abilities to functional abilities, life roles, and occupations	Examiner-guided parent-child play in a natural environment. Five primary subtests measure mobility, stability, motor organization, social and emotional abilities, and functional performance. Three clinical subtests: quality rating, component analysis, and atypical positions	Miller, L. J., & Roid, G. H. (1993). *Toddler-Infant Motor Evaluation (T.I.M.E.)*. San Antonio, TX: Psychological Corporation
Touch Inventory for Elementary School-Aged Children	Elementary school-aged children	Screens for tactile defensiveness	26-question screening tool (individual self-report)	Royeen, C. B., & Fortune, J. C. (1990). Touch Inventory for Elementary School-Aged Children. *American Journal of Occupational Therapy, 44,* 165–170.
Touch Inventory for Preschoolers	Preschool-age children	Screening tool for tactile defensiveness	46 questions to be completed by teachers or guardians of the subject	Royeen, C. B. (1987). Touch Inventory for Preschoolers. *Physical and Occupational Therapy in Pediatrics, 7*(1), 29–40.
Evaluation of Sensory Processing Version 4		.		Parham, D. (2002). Evaluation of Sensory Processing. In A. C. Bundy, E. A. Murray, & S. J. Lane (Eds.), *Sensory Integration: Theory & Practice* (2nd ed., pp. 193–196). Philadelphia: F. A. Davis.

*Many versions of sets of checklists summarizing "clinical observations" (e.g., soft neurological signs of sensory disorders) exist. The most commonly used observational checklist is taught during the sensory integration and praxis (SIPT) intensive training courses sponsored by the SIPT publisher, Western Psychological Services. The compendium by Dunn is noted here as it is published, whereas the WPS clinical observation checklist is not published.

Table 13.8 Other Assessments Typically Administered While Sensory Integration Functions Are Observed Throughout the Evaluation

Name	Age and Population Characteristics	Components Measured	Format and Subtests	Source
Bayley Scales of Infant Development (second edition)	2 mos.–2.5 years	Infant visual recognition memory, habituation of attention to visual stimuli, visual preference and acuity, quality of movement, sensory integration, perceptual-motor integration, fine motor reflexes	Norm-referenced for 14 age groups; administration involves having child respond to a series of stimuli	Bayley, N. (1993, 1984, 1969). *Bayley Scales of Infant Development* (2nd ed.). San Antonio, TX: Psychological Corporation.
Brigance Diagnostic Inventory of Early Development	0–7 years	Communication, cognition, self-help, gross motor, fine motor	Criterion referenced, 200-item test, 11 sections. Questions answered by oral or written responses, or by pointing to a picture.	Brigance, A. H. (1978). *Brigance Diagnostic Inventory of Early Development.* North Billerica, MA: Curriculum Associates.
Bruininks-Oseretsky Test of Motor Proficiency	4.5–14 years	Gross motor, praxis, fine motor, visual-motor integration	Norm referenced; 8 subtests assess gross and fine motor development. 46-item complete battery or 14-item short form	Bruininks, R. H. (1978). *Bruininks-Oseretsky Test of Motor Proficiency.* Circle Pines, MN: American Guidance Service.
Developmental programming for infants and young children	0–6 years	Personal and social skills, communication, cognition, self-help, gross motor, fine motor, visual-motor integration	Criterion referenced, made up of 6 scales, which assess developmental norms in perception/fine motor, self-care, language, etc.	Rogers, S. J., & D'Eugenio, D. B. (1977). *Developmental programming for infants and young children.* University of Michigan.
Erhardt Developmental Prehension Assessment	0–6 years	Praxis, reflexes, fine motor, visual motor integration	Criterion referenced, informally structured, quantified observations	Erhardt, R. P. (1989, 1982). *Erhardt Developmental Prehension Assessment.* San Antonio, TX: Therapy Skill Builders.
FirstSTEP (screening test for evaluating preschoolers)	2 years, 9 months–6 years, 2 months	Identifies presence of developmental risk by assessing cognition, communication and language, motor, social-emotional, and adaptive functioning	Norm referenced for ages 2 to 9; domains include cognition, language, and motor; checklists include adaptive, social-emotional, and parent/teacher scales	Miller, L. J. (1993). *The FirstSTEP (screening test for evaluating preschoolers).* San Antonio, TX: Psychological Corporation.

(continued)

Table 13.8 Continued

Name	Age and Population Characteristics	Components Measured	Format and Subtests	Source
Gesell Preschool Test	2.5–6 years	Personal social skills, communication, gross motor, fine motor	Norm referenced. Contains a variety of tasks and activities, including oral, paper and pencil, and building block sections.	Ames, L. B, Gillespie, C., Haines, J., & Ilg, F. L. (1986). *Gesell Preschool Test*. Rosemon, NH: Programs for Education.
Hawaii Early Learning Profile	0–36 months	Personal social skills, communication, cognition, self-help, gross motor, fine motor, visual-motor integration	Criterion referenced: curriculum-based, not standardized. Includes 7 developmental domains, most of which are further divided into sequential subareas of development.	Furuno, S., O'Reilly, L., Hosaka, C. M, Inatsuka, T. T., Allman, T. L., & Zeisloft, B. (1985, 1979). *Hawaii Early Learning Profile*. Palo Alto, CA: VORT Corporation.
Learning Accomplishment Profile–Revised	36–72 months	Personal social skills, communication, cognition, self-help, gross motor, fine motor	Criterion referenced	Sanford, A. R., & Zelman, J. G. (1981). *Learning Accomplishment Profile–Revised*. Winston-Salem, NC: Kaplan Press.
Motor-Free Visual Perceptual Test	4–11 years	Visual-motor integration	Norm referenced; individually administered, multiple-choice test. Five aspects of visual perception covered: spatial relationships, visual discrimination, figure-ground discrimination, visual closure, and visual memory.	Colaruso, R. P., & Hammill, D. D. (1996). *Motor-Free Visual Perceptual Test*. San Rafael, CA: Academic Therapy Publications.

Movement Assessment of Infants	0–12 months	Gross motor and reflexes	Informal/structured, quantified observations	Chandler, L. S., Andrews, M. S., & Swanson, M. W. (1980). *Movement assessment of infants.* Rolling Bay, WA: Movement Assessment of Infants.
Peabody Developmental Motor Scales (second edition)	7 years	Gross motor, praxis, fine motor, visual-motor integration	Norm and criterion referenced. Two components: Gross Motor Scale and Fine Motor Scale	Folio, M. R., & Fewell, R. R. (2000, 1983). *Peabody Developmental Motor Scales* (2nd ed.). Austin, TX: PRO-ED.
Test of Visual Motor Skills	2–13 years	Visual-motor integration and functioning	Norm referenced; assesses design copying skill	Gardner, M. F. (1986). *Test of Visual Motor Skills.* San Francisco, CA: Children's Hospital of San Francisco.
Test of Visual Perceptual Skills	4–12 years	Visual perception	Norm referenced. Subtests include visual discrimination, visual closure, visual memory, and visual-spatial relations. Items in subtests increase in difficulty.	Gardner, M. F. (1992). *Test of Visual-Perceptual Skills.* Burlingame, CA: Psychological and Educational Publications.

ses for future work in this area. While a plethora of research questions about evaluation tools remain, the inclusion of sensory processing as one aspect of a comprehensive diagnostic assessment of young children is imperative. Regardless of the diagnostic label (e.g., SMD or regulatory disorder), early identification of sensory-related problems, evaluation of related environmental and contextual domains, and appropriate sensory-based intervention can have dramatic and global effects on young children and aid their families in understanding and coping with behaviors that result from sensory dysfunction.

ACKNOWLEDGMENTS   We are grateful to the parents and children who participated in this study. We thank the Wallace Research Foundation, which provided primary support for this research. Support was also obtained from NIH 1K01 HD01183–01 and 1R21 HD/AR41614–01; The Children's Hospital Research Scholar Award, Denver, CO; HealthOne Alliance; and grant number 5 M01 RR00069, General Clinical Research Centers Program, National Center for Research Resources, NIH. We thank Dr. D. Matthews and other staff and faculty at The Children's Hospital, Department of Rehabilitation.

References

Achenbach, T. M. (1991). *Manual for the Child Behavior Checklist/4–18 and 1991 profile.* Burlington, VT: University of Vermont, Department of Psychiatry.

Ahn, R. R., Miller, L. J., Milberger, S., & McIntosh, D. N. (in press). Prevalence of parents' perceptions of sensory processing disorders among kindergarten children. *American Journal of Occupational Therapy.*

Ayres, A. J. (1966). Interrelation of perception, function, and treatment. *Journal of the American Physical Therapy Association, 46*(7), 741–744.

Ayres, A. J. (1969). Deficits in sensory integration in educationally handicapped children. *Journal of Learning Disabilities, 2,* 160–168.

Ayres, A. J. (1972a). *Sensory integration and learning disorders.* Los Angeles: Western Psychological Services.

Ayres, A. J. (1972b). *Southern California sensory integration tests.* Los Angeles, CA: Western Psychological Services.

Ayres, A. J. (1972c). Types of sensory integrative dysfunction among disabled learners. *American Journal of Occupational Therapy, 26*(1), 13–18.

Ayres, A. J. (1977). Cluster analyses of measures of sensory integration. *American Journal of Occupational Therapy, 31*(6), 362–366.

Ayres, A. J. (1979). *Sensory integration and the child.* Los Angeles: Western Psychological Services.

Ayres, A. J. (1989). *Sensory integration and praxis tests.* Los Angeles: Western Psychological Services.

Bates, J. E., & Wachs, T. D. (1994). *Temperament: Individual differences at the interface of biology and behavior.* Washington, DC: American Psychological Association.

Bronfenbrenner, U. (1979). *The ecology of human development.* Cambridge, MA: Harvard University Press.

Bundy, A. C., Lane, S. J., & Murray, E. A. (Eds.). (2002). *Sensory integration: Theory and practice* (2nd ed.). Philadelphia: F.A. Davis.

Cermak, S. A., Koomar, J. A., & Szklut, S. (1999). Making sense of sensory integration. Retrieved September 19, 2002 from http://www.SInet work.org/articles/makingsensescript4.pdf.

Chess, S., & Thomas, A. (1984). *Origins and evolution of behavior disorders.* New York: Brunner/Mazel.

Chess, S., & Thomas, A. (1995). *Temperament in clinical practice.* New York: Guilford Press.

Cohen, J. (1992). Quantitative methods in psychology: A power primer. *Psychological Bulletin, 112*(1), 155–159.

Cole, P. M. (1985). The zone of proximal development: Where culture and cognition create each other. In J. V. Wertsch (Ed.), *Culture, communication, and cognition: Vygotskian perspectives* (pp. 146–161). Cambridge, England: Cambridge University Press.

Cole, P. M., Michel, M. K., & Teti, M. O. (1994). The development of emotion regulation and dysregulation: A clinical perspective. In N. Fox (Ed.), *The development of emotion regulation: Biological and behavioral considerations. Monographs of the Society for Research in Child Development* (Vol. 59, Serial No. 240, pp. 73–100).

DeGangi, G. A. (2000). *Pediatric disorders of regulation in affect and behavior: A therapist's guide to assessment and treatment.* San Diego, CA: Academic Press.

Dunn, W. (1997). The impact of sensory processing abilities on the daily lives of young children and their families: A conceptual model. *Infants and Young Children, 9*(4), 23–35.

Dunn, W. (1999). *The Sensory Profile: Examiner's manual.* San Antonio, TX: Psychological Corporation.

Emde, R. N., Plomin, R., & Hewitt, J. K. (2001). *The transition from infancy to early childhood.* Oxford: Oxford University Press.

Fisher, A. G., & Murray, E. A. (1991). Introduction to sensory integration theory. In A. G. Fisher, E. A. Murray, & A. C. Bundy (Eds.), *Sensory integration: Theory and practice* (pp. 3–26). Philadelphia: F.A. Davis.

Fisher, A. G., Murray, E. A., & Bundy, A. C. (1991). *Sensory integration: Theory and practice.* Philadelphia: F.A. Davis.

Fox, N. A. (1989). Psychophysiological correlates of emotional reactivity during the first year of life. *Developmental Psychology, 25*(3), 364–372.

Fox, N. A., & Davidson, R. J. (1986). Taste-elicited changes in facial signs of emotion and the asymmetry of brain electrical activity in human newborns. *Neuropsychologia, 24,* 417–422.

Frijda, N. H., Kuipers, P., & ter Schure, E. (1989). Relations among emotion, appraisal, and emotional action readiness. *Journal of Personality and Social Psychology, 57,* 212–228.

Gall, M. D., Borg, W. R., & Gall, J. P. (Eds.). (1996). *Educational research: An introduction* (6th ed.). White Plains, NY: Longman.

Greenspan, S. I., & Wieder, S. (1993). Regulatory disorders. In C. H. Zeanah (Ed.), *Handbook of infant mental health* (pp. 280–290). New York: Guilford Press.

Greenspan, S. I., Wieder, S., & Simons, R. (1998). *The child with special needs.* Reading, MA: Addison Wesley.

Hanft, B. E., Miller, L. J., & Lane, S. J. (2000). Toward a consensus in terminology in sensory integration theory and practice. Part 3: Observable behaviors: Sensory integration dysfunction. *Sensory Integration Special Section Quarterly, 23*(3), 1–4.

Kandel, E. R., & Schwartz, J. H. (1991). Directly gated transmission at central synapses. In E. R. Kandel, J. H. Schwartz, & T. M. Jessell (Eds.), *Principles of neural science* (pp. 153–172). East Norwalk, CT: Appleton and Lange.

Kimball, J. G. (1993). Sensory integrative frame of reference. In P. Kramer & J. Hinojosa (Eds.), *Frames of reference for pediatric occupational therapy* (pp. 87–167). Baltimore, MD: Williams and Wilkins.

Kinnealey, M., & Miller, L. J. (1993). Sensory integration/learning disabilities. In H. L. Hopkins & H. D. Smith (Eds.), *Willard and Spackman's occupational therapy* (8th ed., pp. 474–489). Philadelphia: J.B. Lippincott.

Koomar, J. A., & Bundy, A. C. (2002). Creating direct intervention from theory. In A. C. Bundy, S. J. Lane, & E. A. Murray (Eds.), *Sensory integration: Theory and practice* (pp. 261–306). Philadelphia: F.A. Davis.

Kranowitz, C. S. (1998). *The out-of-sync child: Recognizing and coping with sensory integration dysfunction.* New York: Berkley.

Lane, S. J. (2002). Sensory modulation. In A. C. Bundy, S. J. Lane, & E. A. Murray (Eds.), *Sensory integration: Theory and practice* (2nd ed., pp. 101–122). Philadelphia: F.A. Davis.

Lane, S. J., Miller, L. J., & Hanft, B. E. (2000). Toward a consensus in terminology in sensory integration theory and practice. Part 2: Sensory integration patterns of function and dysfunction. *Sensory Integration Special Interest Section Quarterly, 23*(2), 1–3.

Lazarus, R. S. (1991). *Emotion and adaptation.* New York: Oxford University Press.

LeDoux, J. E. (1993). Emotional networks in the brain. In M. Lewis & J. Haviland (Eds.), *Handbook of emotions* (pp. 109–118). New York: Guilford Press.

Lieberman, A., Wieder, S., & Fenichel, E. (Eds.). (1997). *DC: 0–3 casebook.* Washington, DC: Zero to Three, National Center for Infants, Toddlers, and Families.

Mangeot, S. D., Miller, L. J., McIntosh, D. N., McGrath-Clarke, J., Simon, J., Hagerman, R. J., & Goldson, E. (2001). Sensory modulation dysfunction in children with attention deficit hyperactivity disorder. *Developmental Medicine and Child Neurology, 43,* 399–406.

McIntosh, D. N., Miller, L. J., Shyu, V., & Dunn, W. (1999). Overview of the Short Sensory Profile (SSP). In W. Dunn (Ed.), *The sensory profile: Examiner's manual* (pp. 59–73). San Antonio, TX: Psychological Corporation.

McIntosh, D. N., Miller, L. J., Shyu, V., & Hagerman, R. (1999). Sensory-modulation disruption, electrodermal responses, and functional behaviors. *Developmental Medicine and Child Neurology, 41,* 608–615.

Miller, L. J., & Lane, S. J. (2000). Toward a consensus in terminology in sensory integration theory and practice. Part 1: Taxonomy of neurophysiological processes. *Sensory Integration Special Interest Section Quarterly, 23*(1), 1–4.

Miller, L. J., McIntosh, D. N., McGrath, J., Shyu, V., Lampe, M., Taylor, A. K., Tassone, F., Neitzel, K., Stackhouse, T., & Hagerman, R. (1999). Electrodermal responses to sensory stimuli in individuals with fragile X syndrome: A preliminary report. *American Journal of Medical Genetics, 83*(4), 268–279.

Miller, L. J., Reisman, J. E., McIntosh, D. N., & Simon, J. (2001). An ecological model of sensory modulation: Performance of children with fragile X syndrome, autism, attention-deficit/ hyperactivity disorder, and sensory modulation dysfunction. In S. S. Roley, E. I. Blanche, & R. C. Schaaf (Eds.), *Understanding the nature of sensory integration with diverse populations* (pp. 57–88). San Antonio, TX: Therapy Skill Builders.

Miller, L. J., & Schoen, S. (2003). *The Sensory Responsivity Scale.* Manuscript in preparation.

Moulton, D. S. (2002). *Development and beginning validation of a teacher test of sensory modulation disruption.* Unpublished doctoral dissertation, University of Denver, Denver, CO.

Ognibene, T. C. (2002). *Distinguishing sensory modulation dysfunction from attention-deficit/ hyperactivity disorder: Sensory habituation and response inhibition processes.* Unpublished doctoral dissertation, University of Denver, Denver, CO.

Ognibene, T. C., McIntosh, D. N., Miller, L. J., & Raad, J. M. (2003). *Sensory habituation and response inhibition in children with attention deficit/hyperactivity disorder.* Manuscript submitted for publication.

Parham, L. D., & Mailloux, Z. (2001). Sensory integration. In J. Case-Smith (Ed.), *Occupational therapy for children* (4th ed., pp. 329–381). St. Louis, MO: Mosby.

Parush, S. (1993). *Behavioral and electrophysiological correlates of attention deficit hyperactivity disorder with and without tactile defensiveness.* Unpublished doctoral dissertation, Hebrew University, Israel.

Parush, S., Sohmer, H., et al. (1997). Somatosensory functioning in children with attention deficit hyperactivity disorder. *Developmental Medicine and Child Neurology, 39,* 464–468.

Pennington, B. F. (1991). Issues in syndrome validation. In B. F. Pennington (Ed.), *Diagnosing learning disorders: A neuropsychological framework* (pp. 23–31). New York: Guilford Press.

Roid, G. H., & Miller, L. J. (1997). *Leiter international performance scale–Revised.* Wood Dale, IL: Stoelting.

Roley, S., Blanche, E. I., & Schaaf, R. C. (Eds.). (2001). *Understanding the nature of sensory integration with diverse populations.* San Antonio, TX: Therapy Skill Builders.

Saarni, C. (1990). Emotional competence: How emotions and relationships become integrated. In R. Thompson (Ed.), *Nebraska symposium on motivation: 36. Socioemotional development* (pp. 115–182). Lincoln, NE: University of Nebraska Press.

Schaaf, R. C. (2001). *Parasympathetic nervous system functions in children with sensory modulation dysfunction.* Unpublished doctoral dissertation, Bryn Mawr College, Bryn Mawr, PA.

Schaaf, R. C., Miller, L. J., Sewell, D., & O'Keefe, S. (2003). Children with disturbances in sensory processing: A pilot study examining the role of the parasympathetic nervous system. *American Journal of Occupational Therapy, 57*(4), 442–449.

Scherer, K. R. (1984). On the nature and function of emotion: A component process approach. In K. R. Scherer & P. Ekman (Eds.), *Approaches to emotion* (pp. 293–317). Hillsdale, NJ: Lawrence Erlbaum.

Vygotsky, L. S. (1962). *Thought and language.* Cambridge, MA: MIT Press.

Williamson, G. G., & Anzalone, M. E. (2001). *Sensory integration and self-regulation in infants and toddlers: Helping very young children interact with their environment.* Washington, DC: Zero to Three, National Center for Clinical Infant Programs.

Zero to Three, National Center for Clinical Infant Programs (1994). *Diagnostic classification of mental health and developmental disorders of infancy and early childhood.* Arlington, VA: Author.

14

Sleep Disorders

Beth L. Goodlin-Jones
Thomas F. Anders

One of the most common problems experienced by infants, toddlers, and preschoolers is sleep problems, particularly settling difficulties at bedtime and frequent night wakings (Anders, 1994; Ferber & Kryger, 1995; Schaefer, 1995). Difficulties in sleep affect both the individual child and the child's family. Sleep problems are typically identified by parental complaint, since young children do not complain about their sleep. Often, a child who wakens frequently at night is quite content to be awake as long as a parent interacts with him or her in the middle of the night. Not only does the sleep problem affect the amount of rest in the night for the entire family, it also potentially alters the parent-child interaction due to the level of disruption and fatigue experienced by both parent and child. Further, sleep difficulties may lead to cognitive problems and emotional distress, and higher rates of sleep problems are associated later in childhood with behavioral and learning difficulties (e.g., Stores, 1999). It is estimated that approximately 20% of young children between the ages of 1 and 3 years experience sleep problems (Zuckerman, Stevenson, & Baily, 1987). Sleep problems in young children are also fairly persistent (Kataria, Swanson, & Trevathan, 1987) and may be related to earlier sleep patterns (Gaylor, Goodlin-Jones, & Anders, 2001). Further, sleep problems are one of the concerns most frequently mentioned by parents to pediatricians (Mindell, Moline, Zendell, Brown, & Fry, 1994).

RELATIONSHIP CONTEXT

In the past, sleep was thought of as a characteristic of the individual. However, the young child's sleep-wake system is regulated by parent-child interaction and is affected by the child's cognitive, emotional, and social experiences (Anders, 1994; Goodlin-Jones, Burnham, & Anders, 2000). The social regulation provided by the external environment, namely the primary caregiver and family, is responsible for facilitating the developing self-regulation of sleep and other behaviors during infancy and toddlerhood. Numerous transitions occur each day between sleep and waking, and each one offers an opportunity for homeostatic regulation (e.g., hunger, temperature, separation, reunion, comfort) (Anders, Goodlin-Jones, & Sadeh, 2000). Contingent responsiveness during these transitions facilitates the development of self-regulation and is concordant with a secure attachment relationship (Ainsworth, Blehar, Waters, & Wall, 1978; Sroufe, Duggal, Weinfield, & Carlson, 2000). Failure to respond consistently and predictably to aid the child during these transitions leads to poor regulation or dysregulation. We acknowledge our bias, therefore, as viewing sleep and waking state organization as dependent largely upon the psychosocial context of the young child during the first years of life (Anders 1994; Goodlin-Jones et al., 2000). Thus, within this perspective, assessment of sleep problems in the young child necessarily involves assessment of the emerging parent-child relationship and the psychosocial factors that influence the child's process of self-regulation.

There is widespread consensus among developmental researchers and child clinicians that the infant or toddler must be evaluated and treated within the context of the family or caregiving unit (Zeanah, Boris, & Larrieu, 1997). Indeed, to make this happen, a diagnostic approach involving assessment of the relationships involving the child remain critical for an accurate understanding of the child's sleep problem. Of course, it is important to rule out other causes for sleep problems. For example, medical concerns such as middle ear infections, congestion, pain, or allergies must be excluded. If any of these medical concerns are present, appropriate intervention and treatment must begin. Sometimes, however, after successful medical treatment, the sleep problem may continue due to the establishment of parent-child interaction patterns in the middle of the night that serve to maintain the sleep problem (Spasaro & Schaefer, 1995). Thus, while sleep problems may originally have one set of causes, different factors may maintain the problems once they are established.

The publication of *Diagnostic Classification of Mental Health and Developmental Disorders of Infancy and Early Childhood* (DC:0–3; Zero to Three, 1994) highlighted the importance of the relational assessment for mental health and developmental disorders during the first years of life, including sleep problems. This chapter reviews a transactional model of sleep-wake state develop-

ment of sleep problems in infants and toddlers and examines the hypothesis that sleep problems and sleep disorders are often related to disturbances in the parent-child relationship. Hence, in contrast to medical approaches to sleep disorders, the relational assessment is a critical feature of sleep problem assessment. The chapter briefly reviews the normative development of sleep and waking in infants and toddlers. We then discuss the most common sleep problems, settling difficulties and night waking, and different methods of assessment. Last, we briefly review a transactional model to provide a framework for assessment and a newly proposed classification scheme to classify sleep problems in infants and toddlers, which provides clinicians and researchers with an objective and quantifiable framework.

SLEEP BEHAVIOR

Normative Patterns

As sleep problems are generally identified on the basis of parent report, it is critical to place such concerns in the context of what is known about normative patterns of sleep regulation. Sleep occupies a majority of an infant's or toddler's life. In terms of sleep-wake state development, sustained wakeful periods are exhibited in normal infants by 6 weeks of age (Ferber & Kryger, 1995). During the first months of life, sleep behavior slowly begins to reflect circadian or day-night organization as well as additional maturational changes. Sleep is not a single behavior but consists of two distinct states—rapid eye movement (REM) sleep and non–rapid eye movement (NREM) sleep. REM sleep is an "activated" brain state in terms of neurophysiological activity. It is called active sleep because the child's eyes move rapidly in bursts under closed lids, heart rate and breathing patterns are rapid, and many small body jerks, facial grimaces, and finger twitches are observable. In contrast, NREM sleep, also called quiet sleep, is metabolically slowed and more highly regulated. The child appears restful and does not exhibit the signs of heightened activity characteristic of REM sleep. Heart rate and respiratory pattern are slow and regular. These differences between REM and NREM sleep are apparent at birth. Newborns typically begin a bout of sleep in REM. However, by 3 months of age, sleep onsets more often occur in NREM sleep, which is typical for older children and adults. During the first 3 months of life, full-term infants spend 50% of their sleeping time in REM sleep and 50% of their sleeping time in NREM sleep. After 6 months of age, REM sleep proportionally decreases and NREM sleep increases. By adolescence, REM sleep accounts for only 20% of sleep time, and four distinct stages of NREM sleep account for the remaining 80%. Further, two interrelated biological clocks organize these two states. The *diurnal clock* organizes a circadian, or daily, cycle of sleep and waking, while an *ultradian clock* organizes the shorter (60- to 90-minute) REM-NREM sleep cycle. These timing changes and a lengthening of the sleep bout lead to sleep-wake consolidation, also known as sleeping through the night.

Diurnal Organization:
The Sleep-Wake Cycle

Typically developing full-term newborns have a total sleep time of 16 to 17 hours each day, and this time decreases to 14 to 15 hours by 1 year of age (Sheldon, 1996). Short periods of wakefulness interrupt sleep every 3 to 4 hours in the newborn infant. Within the first month following birth, sleep and waking patterns begin to adapt to the light-dark cycle and to parent schedules. By 6 months of age, the 4-hour sleep period of the newborn lengthens to 6 hours, and several of these longer periods, under control of the diurnal clock, are shifted to the nighttime. A 6-hour bout of sleep from 11 p.m. to 5 a.m. without waking is considered sleeping through the night (Cohen, 1999). The infant's nighttime awakenings become fewer in number and shorter in duration. At the same time, wakeful periods during the day become longer, and are interrupted only by brief periods of napping sleep.

In Westernized societies, 1-year-olds typically have one or two long bouts of sleep at night and two naps, of approximately 1 to 2 hours each, during the day. Like the newborn, the 1-year-old may still sleep 16 hours, on average, in the 24-hour period, but diurnal organization of sleep and waking is clearly evident. In the second year, one of the daytime naps disappears and sleep becomes restricted to two clock times—one long episode during the night and one brief nap during the afternoon (Weissbluth, 1995). The change from a crib to a bed typically happens after the second birthday. There is a gradual reduction in total sleep time to about 11 hours by 5 years of age. In the preschool years, many children give up the remaining daytime nap and sleep becomes truly monophasic, although a tendency for afternoon naps remains throughout adulthood. The typical bedtime for children ages 2 to 5 years is between 7 and 9 p.m. and the typical rise time is between 6:30 and 8 a.m. (Weissbluth, 1987). A recent report with 1-year-olds living in northern Israel also observed a similar average bedtime (8:38 p.m.) (Scher et al., 1995). Of course, bedtimes and rise times may differ in other cultural contexts.

Ultradian Organization:
The REM-NREM Cycle

During sleep, active and quiet sleep periods alternate one with the other in what is called the REM-NREM sleep cycle. When a young infant falls asleep after a period of waking, the initial sleep episode is typically a REM period. In early infancy, REM and NREM sleep periods then alternate with each other in 50- to 60-minute sleep cycles. After 3 months of age, REM periods continue to recur every 50 to 60 minutes; however, the amount of REM sleep in each cycle begins to shift. REM sleep predominates in the later sleep cycles of the night and NREM sleep predominates in the earlier cycles, especially during the deep stages of NREM sleep that occur primarily in the first third of the sleep period. By 3 years of age, ultradian organization resembles that of adult sleep, except for the length of a single sleep cycle. The 90-minute adult sleep cycle length develops by adolescence.

SLEEP PROBLEMS

The identification of a sleep problem in a young child depends on many factors. The most common problems identified in young children are difficulty settling at the beginning of the night and the frequency of waking during the night

(Ferber & Kryger, 1995; Gaylor et al., 2001). From a developmental perspective, the earliest parental concerns appear to be night waking problems followed by problems of falling asleep (Lozoff, Wolf, & Davis, 1985). Then, at a later age, settling at the beginning of the night for toddlers and preschoolers is often the problem that a parent will report.

There are no empirically derived, quantitative metrics for young children from birth to 3 years that aid in the identification of sleep problems. Researchers have employed several different criteria to identify problem behaviors. For example, Lozoff and colleagues (1985) defined sleep problems as struggles in settling at bedtime or the occurrence of night waking on three or more nights per week. In contrast, Richman (1981) described more detailed criteria that defined a generic infant sleep disorder. Her criteria include: night waking three or more times per night, cosleeping with a parent, 20 minutes of awake time during the night, or requiring parental presence to fall asleep or refusing to go to bed for more than 30 minutes. Symptoms must be present 5 to 7 nights per week and for a 3-month duration. It is possible to derive a composite score that distinguishes among severe, moderate, or mild sleep problems (Richman, 1981, 1985). Although these criteria have been used in several studies, they have not been developed into a classification scheme for clinicians and sleep professionals. Other professionals have suggested that since sleep difficulties are so common, they should be considered an annoying part of normal development rather than a problem or disorder (Ferber, 1987).

The rates of these common sleep problems vary according to which definition or criteria are used. An early community survey that included several questions about sleep reported that approximately 20% of 1- to 2-year-olds have a night waking problem (five times or more per week) (Richman, 1981). A more recent study employing Richman's criteria observed a sleep problem rate of 17.3% in 14-month-olds, but the rate increased to 35.5% when the criteria were based on maternal ratings rather than Richman's research criteria (Morrell, 1999). Other studies in normal 2-year-old children report similar rates of waking problems (Bernal, 1973; Richman, 1987). Another study with 3-year-olds found the rate of sleep problems to be as high as 29% (Zuckerman et al., 1987).

In general, regardless of the definition, more recent prevalence rates of these problems seem similar across industrialized societies, with rates in Australia, Israel, and the United States averaging 25 to 33% (Armstrong, Quinn, & Dadds, 1994; Johnson, 1991; Mindell, 1993; Scher et al., 1995). It also appears that once sleep problems are present, they may persist during early childhood, with rates varying from 25 to over 80% over 3 years (Jenkins, Owens, Bax, & Hart, 1984; Kataria et al., 1987; Van Tassel, 1985; Zuckerman et al., 1987). However, other studies have reported far less persistence, with rates lower than 20%, for children followed from infancy through 56 months of age (Wolke, Meyer, Ohrt, & Riegel, 1995).

Oftentimes, prevalence estimates of sleep problems may be considered underestimates if the researcher relied solely on parental report. Parents vary widely in their tolerance and what they consider problematic sleep behavior (Richman, 1987). For example, one questionnaire study found 21% of toddlers had a night waking problem, but only 12% of the parents reported it as a sleep problem (Crowell, Keener, Ginsburg, & Anders, 1987). Similarly, during a telephone interview in another study, only one (10%) family endorsed their child's sleep behavior as a problem out of 10 families who had a child that met criteria for a sleep problem (Gaylor et al., 2001). A long delay in settling for the night might be viewed as enjoyable by some parents who like the repeated bids for interaction (Jaffa, Scott, Hendriks, & Shapiro, 1993). Further, cultural variations in the time of going to bed and the amount of time asleep at night are important to consider (Richman, 1987). Clearly, one of the unresolved dilemmas in the extant literature is whether parental distress about a child's sleep problem should be a major criterion for diagnosis. Differentiating between actual sleep patterns and sleep patterns that are problematic for parents due to their expectations is essential for understanding prevalence rates and the development of sleep problems. Several assessments including questionnaires and sleep logs are reviewed in a later section of this chapter.

Time-lapse video recordings in the home of

healthy infants have been used to observe sleep onset and night waking behavior in an objective manner (Anders, Halpern, & Hua, 1992; Goodlin-Jones, Eiben, & Anders, 1997). These studies have demonstrated that night awakenings per se are not problematic. Typically, infants average one to three awakenings each night throughout the first year of life. By 12 months of age, 70% of infants are able to return to sleep on their own without alerting their parents. However, approximately 30% of the infants signal or cry out for their parents and appear to need their assistance to return to sleep in the middle of the night. These infants have been called *signalers*. Other babies are much better able to soothe themselves to sleep following the awakening. These infants are called *self-soothers*. Even among toddlers, very few children really sleep the whole night through. As infants mature, however, most of them gradually switch from signaling to self-soothing (Anders et al., 1992; Richman, 1987). The adult sleeper also typically has one to three brief arousals and returns to sleep without awareness of the arousal, hence exhibiting effective self-soothing. Other objective measures of sleep in young children, using actigraphic recording or recording of motility patterns, also report nighttime wakings that may be undetected by the parents if they are not signaled (Sadeh, Lavie, Scher, Tirosh, & Epstein, 1991; Thoman & Acebo, 1995). Hence, it is the signaling behavior rather than the awakening that concerns the parents (Minde et al., 1993).

CLASSIFICATION OF SLEEP PROBLEMS

Both researchers and clinicians have used the extant classification schemes of sleep problems in the *Diagnostic and Statistical Manual of Mental Disorders*, Fourth Edition (*DSM-IV*; American Psychiatric Association, 1994) and the *International Classification of Sleep Disorders: Diagnostic and Coding Manual* (ICSD-DCM; American Sleep Disorders Association, 1990). However, both schemes fit poorly for young children. For example, the *DSM-IV* defines dysomnias as a group of disorders characterized by difficulty in initiating or maintaining sleep. However, infants

and toddlers rarely meet the impairment and/or severity criteria necessary to make a definitive diagnosis in the *DSM-IV* categorical system. The ICSD-DCM subclassifies "extrinsic" sleep disorders into categories using terms such as inadequate sleep hygiene, adjustment sleep disorder, insufficient sleep syndrome, or sleep-onset association disorder. For each of these syndromes there are duration and acuity criteria; however, the criteria are neither empirically nor developmentally determined.

The DC:0–3 (Zero to Three, 1994) is a multi-axial diagnostic scheme, developed by infant mental health specialists, that focuses on young children from birth to 3 years. Sleep problems may be classified as a primary disorder or as a symptom of another primary disorder, such as traumatic stress disorder. However, there are no empirically derived criteria in the DC:0–3 to aid in classification of sleep problems. Hence, an age-appropriate and culturally sensitive classification scheme for infant and toddler sleep disorders is needed that can be used reliably by researchers and clinicians alike.

Anders and his colleagues have proposed a classification scheme that modifies *DSM-IV* criteria for dysomnia for younger children (ages 12 to 36 months and older; see tables 14.1 and 14.2) (Anders et al., 2000; Gaylor et al., 2001). Because young children rarely meet strict *DSM-IV* criteria for diagnosis, the term *protodysomnias* was used to suggest a potential precursor of a later full-blown dysomnia. By using a *DSM-IV* prototype, it is hoped that this new scheme receives the widest dissemination and acceptance possible. It is presented after we describe the assessment of sleep problems in infant and toddlers. To date, our classification scheme has not been integrated with the ICD-9 classification system.

A TRANSACTIONAL MODEL OF SLEEP-WAKE REGULATION

Sleep-wake states develop within a psychosocial context that influences sleep patterns and bedtime routines. A transactional model (Fiese & Sameroff, 1989) has been adopted to examine the numerous factors involved in the development of sleep-wake patterns and self-regulation

Table 14.1 Classification of Sleep Onset Problems in Young Children

Classification	Age	Settling to Sleep and Reunions* (Must Meet Any 2 of the 3 Criteria)
Perturbation (1 episode/week for at least 1 month)	12–24 months of age	(1) >30 minutes to fall asleep, (2) parent remains in room for sleep onset, (3) more than three reunions
	>24 months of age	(1) >20 minutes to fall asleep, (2) parent remains in room for sleep onset, (3) more than two reunions
Disturbance (2–4 episodes/week for at least 1 month)	12–24 months of age	(1) >30 minutes to fall asleep, (2) parent remains in room for sleep onset, (3) more than three reunions
	>24 months of age	(1) >20 minutes to fall asleep, (2) parent remains in room for sleep onset, (3) more than two reunions
Disorder (5–7 episodes/week for at least 1 month)	12–24 months of age	(1) >30 minutes to fall asleep, (2) parent remains in room for sleep onset, (3) more than three reunions
	>24 months of age	(1) >20 minutes to fall asleep, (2) parent remains in room for sleep onset, (3) more than two reunions

*Reunions reflect resistances going to bed (e.g., repeated bids, protests, struggles).

(Anders 1994; Anders, Goodlin-Jones, & Zalenko, 1998; Goodlin-Jones et al., 2000). As is true for other behavioral realms, sleep patterns develop largely through transactions between the child's characteristics and the caregiving environment. Since relationships develop and change over time, the psychosocial context that influences the child's sleep pattern is dynamic and changing. Hence, to understand how sleep patterns develop, it is important to consider all of the components of the transactional model, including the child's behavior and characteristics, parent-child interactions, and also the parent's expecta-

tions, cultural values, and psychological well-being (Goodlin-Jones et al., 2000). In this section, we briefly review the factors as they are outlined in the model.

The transactional model assumes that regulation of sleep-wake states is mediated most readily by proximal influences such as parent-child interactions during transitions between sleep and waking. Other proximal influences include the primary caregiver's current state of physical and psychological well-being, the primary caregiver's own childhood representations and social support networks, the family's economic condition, and

Table 14.2 Classification of Night Waking in Toddlers

Classification	Age	Frequency and Duration of Nighttime Awakenings*
Perturbation (1 episode/week for longer than 1 month	12–24 months of age	>3 awakenings/night totaling >30 minutes
	24–36 months of age	≥2 awakening/night totaling >20 minutes
	>36 months of age	≥2 awakening/night totaling >10 minutes
Disturbance (2–4 episodes/week for longer than 1 month)	12–24 months of age	>3 awakenings/night totaling >30 minutes
	24–36 months of age	≥2 awakening/night totaling >20 minutes
	>36 months of age	≥2 awakening/night totaling >10 minutes
Disorder (5–7 episodes/week for longer than 1 month)	12–24 months of age	>3 awakenings/night totaling >30 minutes
	24–36 months of age	≥2 awakening/night totaling >20 minutes
	>36 months of age	≥2 awakening/night totaling >10 minutes

Note: Occurs after child has been asleep for >10 minutes.
*Awakenings are associated with signaling (i.e., crying or calling).

the infant's temperament and physical health. More distal factors in the transactional model include the broader cultural context of the family and indirect environmental influences. According to this model, proximal stressors such as infant physical illness or maternal depression affect parent-child interaction surrounding regulation of sleep, and these altered interactions affect the family context. Family well-being may be influenced by particular cultural practices, in terms of seeking advice from a professional, which then alters parent-child interaction around sleep-wake transitions. Thus, the dynamic interplay of proximal and more distal factors continuously influences the consolidation of sleep-wake states. An example of some of the influences outlined by the transactional model follows. A more thorough discussion of these influential factors is published elsewhere (Goodlin-Jones et al., 2000).

Parental Characteristics

The role that parental characteristics play in the development of sleep problems has received a great deal of attention. In particular, maternal psychopathology, particularly mood disorders, has been identified as a significant factor in mother-child relationship difficulties. Higher levels of depression in mothers during the infant's first year are associated with less than optimal mother-infant interactive behaviors, and infants of depressed mothers exhibit less persistence in their interactions (Field, Healy, Goldstein, Perry, & Bendell, 1988; Martinez et al., 1996). Maternal depression has often been found to be associated with children's night waking problems (Adair, Bauchner, Phillip, Leverson, & Zuckerman, 1991; Bernal, 1973; Paret, 1983; Van Tassel, 1985). For example, Zuckerman and colleagues (1987) reported that maternal depression was more common for 8-month to 3-year-old children with sleep problems than for children without sleep problems. Higher levels of maternal depressive feelings were correlated with fewer bouts of self-soothing during the middle of the night in infants under 1 year of age (Goodlin-Jones et al., 1997). Further, a study with a middle-class sample in Australia reported that maternal report of a sleep problem in infants between 6 and 12 months of age was a significant predictor of a higher depression score on the Edinburgh Postnatal Depression Scale (Hiscock & Wake, 2001). In addition to an association with depressive symptomatology, high levels of maternal separation anxiety in mothers of 1-year-olds were significantly related to night waking (Scher & Blumberg, 1999).

As these studies have all been correlational in nature, it is possible that disturbed maternal mood may be due to the sleep problem itself. Yet one study reported that even after resolution of postpartum depression, infant sleep problems remained elevated (Murray, 1991). Also, maternal mood may influence the parenting behavior that helps establish a child's sleep-wake organization. For example, a study reported that mothers who disclosed more difficulty in their *expectations* on setting limits and ability to handle sleep problems in toddlers had more sleep difficulties in their own toddlers (Morrell, 1999). It is possible that mothers with depressed mood would also have lowered expectations about managing sleep problems and might influence their child's sleep-wake organization in a less than optimal manner.

Maternal internal working models of relationships, as theorized by attachment researchers, may be influential contributors to infant and toddler behavior problems, including sleep and feeding problems (Benoit, Zeanah, Parker, Nicholson, & Coolbear, 1997). In a recent article by Ward, Lee, and Lipper (2000), insecure infant-mother attachments (at 17.4 months), as measured by Strange Situation testing, were concordant in 66% of the cases with mothers' Adult Attachment Interview (AAI) ratings of their own attachment history. Also, insecure infant attachment classification was strongly associated with nonorganic failure-to-thrive disorder (66% insecure). Insecure adult attachment classifications in mothers have also been significantly associated with maternal reports of toddler sleep problems (Benoit, Zeanah, Parker, & Minde, 1992). These results suggest that the mothers' own relationship history, as measured by the AAI, may reflect a difficulty in separating from the child and difficulty in supporting the child's developing self-regulation. However, a study among a group of 94 nonrisk infants and their mothers found only marginal associations between night waking behavior and the quality of the attachment relationship (Scher, 2001). Maternal reports of more fussiness in 1-year-olds were related to more night waking. Others have also suggested that a mother who overresponds to her infant's waking may be responding from her own experience of personal trauma (Minde, 1988). Rather than view these maternal characteristics as mother blaming, Zeanah and Larrieu (2000) recommend them as potential targets for assessment and clinical intervention with the mothers. Moreover, more research needs to be aimed at understanding the role of fathers, both with respect to the father-child relationship and the father's role in supporting or regulating the mother-child relationship.

Infant Characteristics

Numerous infant characteristics may contribute to the development of sleep problems, including gender, temperament, physical status, feeding style, and birth order. An occasional study has reported significant gender differences in sleep problems. For example, male infants have been found to exhibit higher frequencies of night waking and lower levels of self-soothing (Anders et al., 1992; Goodlin-Jones, Burnham, Gaylor, & Anders, 2001; Scher et al., 1995). There are numerous reports on the role of infant temperament, in terms of easy versus difficult infants, contributing to sleep difficulties. For example, significant associations have been observed between night-waking problems, short sleep duration, and difficult or demanding temperaments (Atkinson, Vetere, & Grayson, 1995; Keefe, Kotzer, Froese-Fretz, & Curtin, 1996; Novosad, Freudigman, & Thoman, 1999; Sadeh, Lavie & Scher, 1994; Schaefer, 1990; Weissbluth & Liu, 1983). Difficulties in state regulation and self-soothing in the night may account for the temperamental differences (Minde, 1988). In contrast, other researchers have not found significant relationships between temperamental differences and sleep problems (Messer, 1993; Scher et al., 1998; St. James-Roberts & Plewis, 1996). Many studies have described how temperamental differences are associated with different interaction patterns with parents (Seifer, 2000). Hence, it is possible for differing parent-child interaction pat-

terns to then indirectly impact sleep-wake behavior.

Individual behavioral differences in early infancy have been related to the infant colic syndrome, whose cardinal symptom is excessive crying (Barr, 2000). Several studies have examined the hypothesis that infants with colic syndrome have more difficult temperaments (Minde et al., 1993; White, Gunnar, Larson, Donzella, & Barr, 2000). Interestingly, infants with colic syndrome have been rated by parents as poor sleepers and sleep an average of 2 hours less per 24-hour period than control infants (Minde et al., 1993; White et al., 2000). Clearly, individual differences observed in the colic syndrome and shortened sleep may reflect alterations in the coordination of circadian rhythms. Assessment of individual differences in sleep-wake organization must consider early maturational differences, as evident in the colic syndrome, as well as other variables.

In addition to behavioral differences, other individual characteristics of the infant must be considered during an assessment process. Significant associations have been reported for birth order, with firstborn infants exhibiting greater difficulties in settling and night waking (Scher et al., 1995; Walters, 1993). More frequent night waking has been reported in infants that are nursing compared to bottle-fed infants (Elias, Nicolson, Bora, & Johnston, 1986). However, other studies have not concurred with this difference (Messer, 1993). Interestingly, some studies have described brief nursing modifications, such as providing a larger feeding prior to mother's bedtime, to alter the night waking patterns (e.g., Pinilla & Birch, 1993). Also, sleep difficulties have been reported as more common in young children with physical ailments and developmental disabilities, including in utero substance exposure, neurodevelopmental disorders, and mental retardation (Regalado, Schechtman, Del Angel, & Bean, 1995; Piazza, Fisher, & Kahng, 1996). A more thorough discussion of infant characteristics and sleep problems may be found elsewhere (Ferber & Kryger, 1995; Goodlin-Jones et al., 2000).

Parent-Infant Interaction

The impact of parent-child interaction as a critical regulator of sleep-wake transitions and the process of consolidation is clear. It is one of the most consistent findings for factors influencing sleep problems in early childhood (Anders, 1994; Ferber & Kryger, 1995; Goodlin-Jones et al., 2000; Ware & Orr, 1992). The manner in which the parent conducts the bedtime routine influences how the child settles at the beginning of the night and the child's behavior after a nighttime awakening. A typical pattern of rubbing or rocking an infant to sleep may be associated with sleep onset, which is then expected again in the middle of the night if the child wakens again (Adair et al., 1991; Anders et al., 1992). Mothers who were rated as inconsistent in their handling of the infant at bedtime and who fluctuated between different styles of interaction had infants who exhibited delays in falling asleep (Scher & Blumberg, 1999). According to the American Academy of Pediatrics, it is best to place the child drowsy but awake in its own bed at the beginning of the night (Cohen, 1999). Young children supposedly develop a "positive sleep association" when they make the mental association between lying quietly in their bed by themselves and falling asleep. Parental presence at the beginning of the night may discourage the use of a sleep aid by the child (for example, rather than holding a soft blanket, the child may lie against or be held by a parent) (Wolf & Lozoff, 1989). Infants 3 months old and 8 months old who used a sleep aid were more likely to be placed in their bed awake and to use the sleep aid to self-soothe in the middle of the night (Anders et al., 1992). Last, the absence of a regular bedtime routine is associated with sleep problems (Cohen, 1999; Quine, 1992).

Family

Characteristics of a child's family are proximal factors that may influence sleep problems; however, few studies have reported on this topic. Consistent with findings of a regular bedtime schedule facilitating sleep regulation, particularly chaotic families with erratic schedules directly influence bedtime routines negatively (e.g., Shonkoff & Brazelton, 1993). Changes associated with financial stress that alter family and marital interactions may be contributors to infant sleep problems (Guedeney & Kreisler, 1987). Future re-search on the role family characteristics play in the development of sleep-wake organization is clearly needed.

Culture

In terms of more distal factors impacting sleep problems, cultures vary greatly both in the identification of what constitutes a sleep problem and in child-rearing practices related to sleep. For example, ethnic and cultural practices may determine family sleeping arrangements and the presence of cosleeping, which will affect sleep-wake regulation (McKenna et al., 1993). Cosleeping during the first few months of life may increase the number of brief, spontaneous arousals from sleep, thus lessening the risk for the occurrence of sudden infant death syndrome (Mosko, Richard, & McKenna, 1997). In children older than 6 months, cosleeping in the parent's bed is viewed as more problematic in Caucasian families than in African American families (Lozoff, 1995).

Where an infant should sleep, either in a crib or in the parents' bed, continues to be discussed by practitioners of westernized medicine (e.g., Nakamura, Wind, & Danello, 1999). While many health professionals recommend solitary sleeping arrangements for young children, nearly half (46%) of the mothers in a survey conducted in pediatric offices in a large city indicated that they were cosleeping with their infants who were 6 months or younger (Gibson, Dembofsky, Rubin, & Greenspan, 2000). Similarly, in a longitudinal survey completed in the United Kingdom, where the mainstream ideology also supports solitary sleeping, 70% of new parents were cosleeping with their infants, although all had planned to practice solitary sleeping when questioned prior to the infants' birth (Ball, Hooker, & Kelly, 1999). All mothers indicated ease of caregiving when cosleeping and increased feelings of comfort for the infant in their decision to cosleep. Interestingly, a new study with 101 normal, full-term infants contrasted the sleep patterns of long-term cosleepers (for 6 months) with short-term cosleepers and noncosleepers (Hunsley & Thoman, 2002). The long-term cosleepers exhibited a pattern of markedly lower arousal levels in their sleep, which is a pattern that has been associated with stress. With future studies, more may be learned about the implications over the long term for cosleeping practices.

Of course, changes in mainstream recommendations and professional beliefs may influence parenting practices and cultural values. An example is the dramatic shift to a nonprone sleeping position now adhered to by a majority of new parents receiving pediatric care for their infants. Two years after the American Academy of Pediatrics recommended that all healthy infants be positioned on their backs or sides for sleeping, a survey found that 72% of new parents were using the recommendations with their infants (Gibson et al., 2000). Clearly, obtaining an accurate history of the sleeping arrangements and the cultural and personal reasons for those arrangements and whether those arrangements have changed over time is part of the assessment. The clinician must clarify where and when the baby sleeps, with whom, and whether it is for the entire night. It is also important to assess both the mother's and father's like or dislike of these arrangements.

Environmental Regulators

The contribution of environmental factors to infant sleep patterns may be considered direct regulators, such as light-dark cycles, or indirect factors, such as socioeconomic status. There is little systematic information on most environmental variables. The diurnal activity of a family may support a child's sleeping pattern if all family members maintain an active daytime pattern and follow it with a quiet nighttime period. This might differ greatly for an infant whose family has a prolonged period of noise and activity in the household due to alternating work and sleep schedules by family members. Also, an infant who lives in a one-room dwelling with all other members on different schedules will experience variable activity levels throughout the day compared to an infant that has its sleeping area in a separate room. One study reported socioeconomic differences in parent-child interaction during bedtime routines (Scott & Richards, 1990). Other studies have examined the impact of maternal employment on sleep problems and found that maternal employment is associated with greater settling and night waking difficulties (Scher et al., 1995; Van Tassel, 1985).

ASSESSMENT OF SLEEP PROBLEMS

Researchers have developed several different ways of measuring sleep in young children. The most common approach has been to interview parents regarding their child's sleep behavior during the previous night or during the past typical week. Several different questionnaires or daily diaries are available for use. For example, Seifer and colleagues have developed a sleep habits questionnaire for use with parents of toddlers and preschool children that yields a summary score (Seifer, Dickstein, Spirito, & Owens-Stively, 1996). The 63 questions cover such topics as sleepiness during the day, naps, bedtime routines, and night waking behavior. The Children's Sleep Habit Questionnaire (CSHQ) is a similar questionnaire that has been validated and standardized for children ages 4 to 10 years (Owens, Spirito, & McGuinn, 2000). The CSHQ contains 46 items that are summed into eight subscales and a total score. Another sleep questionnaire, called the Albany Sleep Problem Scale, covers similar questions and may also be summarized into a single score (Durand, 1998). Daily diaries or behavior logs that require monitoring of sleep onsets, waking bouts, and rise times by a 24-hour clock are also widely available (e.g., Durand, 1998; Minde et al., 1993). An example of a sleep diary is shown in figure 14.1. Using these methods, most parents report that, by 6 months of age, their infants slept through the night. However, as mentioned earlier, it is the signaled wakings that are most reliably recorded by caregivers (Anders et al., 1992).

Another traditional method, polysomnography, requires a sleep laboratory and the physiological monitoring of several body systems simultaneously. Polygraphic methods use electrodes taped to the face, scalp, limbs, chest, and just in front of the nasal airway to record the patterns of brain waves (EEG), muscle tone (EMG), eye movements (EOG), heart rate (ECG), and respiration characteristic of REM and NREM sleep states (Sheldon, 1996). Not surprisingly, bringing a toddler or young child to a sleep laboratory and having multiple electrodes applied over the child's body for one or more nights is not popular with parents or their children. Nor is the sleep laboratory a naturalistic research environment. Last, the cost for a sleep laboratory assessment is

Child's Name : _____

Sleep Diary
Remember, please fill in blocks regarding the previous night's sleep

	Sat	Sun	Mon	Tues	Weds	Thurs	Fri
Date							
Time went to bed in evening							
Time went to sleep in evening							
Time(s) woke during the night							
Time(s) went to sleep again							
Time woke in the morning							
Time of nap(s)							
Time you went to bed							

NOTES (Unusual or atypical events)

_____
_____
_____
_____
_____
_____
_____
_____
_____

Figure 14.1 Example of a sleep diary for parent or caregiver to complete each morning.

high and may be a major limitation (Thoman & Acebo, 1995). However, if a clinician is concerned about any of the sleep apnea syndromes, it is useful to bring the child to a certified sleep center for a complete multichannel, polygraphic evaluation.

Several other reliable, nonpolygraphic methods have been developed that provide objective assessments of sleep behavior and can be used in the infant's own home. These include time-lapse videosomnography, actigraphy, and direct bedside behavioral observation (Thoman & Acebo,

1995). Anders and his colleagues have pioneered the use of time-lapse video recording of sleep and waking (Anders & Keener, 1985; Anders & Sostek, 1976). A small camcorder on a tripod is placed next to the infant's crib or bassinet to film a baby's movement patterns (active and quiet) throughout the night. Because the camera's low-level lens, sensitive to infrared light, allows recording in the dark, the family's natural environment is not disturbed. The time-lapse feature mimics slow motion recording, so that 24 hours of continuous sleep and waking can be filmed on a single 1-hour cassette tape. When the videotape is replayed in the laboratory, the baby's active and quiet behavioral patterns of sleep are coded reliably. The baby's waking behaviors at the beginning of the night, in the middle of the night, and in the morning are scored. The ability of the baby to soothe itself back to sleep after an awakening, or whether the baby begins to fuss and cry (signal) to get help in getting back to sleep, is also scored. During the first few months of life, 95% of infants cry (signal) after an awakening and require a parental response before returning to sleep. By 8 months of age, however, 60 to 70% of infants are able to self-soothe after a nighttime awakening. It has also been noted that both the frequency and length of awakenings at night tend to decrease with age (Anders et al., 1992).

Time-lapse video recording has its limitations as a research method. The video recorder can only record what happens in the infant's crib, and usually only for a 24-hour period without a cassette change. When the baby is out of the crib, the camera films an empty bed. In order to record anywhere the baby goes, an actigraph must be used. An actigraph is a computer chip, encased in a lightweight, wristwatch-sized container that is strapped around the baby's ankle or wrist to continuously record activity (motility) levels and patterns. These are clearly different during REM sleep, NREM sleep, and waking. Although it is not waterproof, the actigraph is otherwise pretty rugged and can record continuously for up to 7 days. In general, actigraphs are better than time-lapse video recordings for longer-term studies that record sleep for several days and nights. Actigraph reports have been shown to accurately record information on a child's sleep behaviors when compared to a sleep diary (Lockley, Skene, & Arendt, 1999). Unfortunately, an actigraph does not allow observation of the baby, nor of parent-infant interactions during the night. Time-lapse video recordings capture interactions as they occur around bedtime and when the baby awakens in the middle of the night. Of course, some investigators use both methods simultaneously.

ASSESSMENT TOOLS

It is helpful to use the framework provided by the transactional model in the assessment of infant sleep problems. There are four areas to focus on in the assessment, including (1) the nature of the sleep behavior and whether a problem exists, (2) infant characteristics, (3) parent-child interaction patterns, and (4) contextual factors including proximal factors of parental characteristics and family context and more distal factors including cultural and environmental factors (Anders et al., 2000). The following questions must be addressed: Does an infant's sleep schedule fit well with the family's schedule in a socially appropriate way, and is the infant's need for sleep met by the current schedule? What is a typical day like in terms of rise time, naps, and bedtime? What type of interaction is typical at bedtime and naptime? How regular are the sleep patterns? How long does it take the child to fall asleep once in the sleeping place? Does the child fall asleep alone or with others? Does the child waken during the night and cry out for someone? How many times during the night, and how many nights during the week? Who usually responds? How long does it take the child to return to sleep? What soothing techniques are required? What sleep aids does the child use? What are interactions like in the middle of the night?

If sleeping difficulties are present, a sleep diary (such as the one provided in figure 14.1) should be completed for 1 to 2 weeks. A sleep diary would require approximately 1 minute each morning after the child's rise time for the parent to complete. It is best that the parent complete this diary each morning immediately after the child has risen. The sleep diary gives a clearer picture of a child's sleep-wake behavior over the course of a typical week than can be described by a parent in a brief interview. Also, a sleep questionnaire about a recent typical week that provides a quantifiable score, such as that developed by Seifer and colleagues (1996), Owens and colleagues (2000), or Durand (1998) is helpful.

An interview with the primary caregiver should be conducted to assess composition of the family, sleeping arrangements, family history of sleep problems, family's general economic well-being, and employment outside of the home. If time permits, a structured interview to assess the adult's past childhood relationships, for example with the AAI, is recommended (George, Kaplan, & Main, 1996). Also, a structured interview with the mother on her perceptions and subjective experience of her infant may be extremely useful (Working Model of the Child Interview; Benoit et al., 1997). The interview also needs to explore the cultural values of the family in terms of child-rearing and sleep practices and the extent to which extended family members and social supports are available. Completion of standardized questionnaires on the current psychological well-being of both parents should also be completed. It is important to directly observe parent-child interaction on a fairly standardized task or game to assess the quality of the relationship. Numerous reports provide standardized techniques for semistructured play situations (e.g., for review see Wyly, 1997; chapter 3). For children between approximately 12 and 24 months of age, the current state of the parent-child relationship may also be assessed in an experimental paradigm known as the Strange Situation (Ainsworth et al., 1978). The goal in these observations is to classify the relationship rather than an individual. Thus, a child may exhibit a relationship with a secure or balanced classification with one parent but be classified in the other caregiving relationship as insecure. Last, if time permits, multiple observations of different situations, such as feeding or play, for assessment of the relationship quality are preferable to a single assessment.

ALTERNATIVE CLASSIFICATION SCHEME

A brief review of a newly proposed scheme for sleep problems is presented in this section. The goals of this scheme are to recognize the developmental changes in sleep-wake behavior and to quantify sleep problems in young children in a manner useful to researchers and clinicians. Three assumptions underlie this classification. First, no sleep problems are classified prior to 12 months of age due to the changeable nature of sleep during the first year of life. Second, this classification is used with solitary-sleeping infants only, not infants who are cosleeping as a planned arrangement. Reactive cosleeping patterns as a temporary solution to a sleeping problem may be appropriately classified with this scheme. Third, measurement of symptoms should be as objective as possible and should not rely solely on parental report.

In the new scheme, a multilevel perturbation/disturbance/disorder classification is applied to sleep onset and night-waking protodysomnias, each graded on objective data and categorized by age. The details of the classification scheme are available in tables 14.1 and 14.2 and may also be reviewed in Anders, Goodlin-Jones, and Sadeh (2000). Briefly, perturbations are part of normal development and describe behaviors that last less than 1 month. Disturbances and disorders classify behaviors that are more frequent and have persisted for at least 1 month. For example, sleep-onset protodysomnias are problems with settling at the beginning of the night. There are criteria for ages 12 to 24 months and older than 24 months, graded for three levels of severity based on duration and frequency of the behaviors. The criteria are outlined in table 14.1. A 12- to 24-month-old child has a perturbation if, on one night per week for more than 1 month, it takes longer than 30 minutes to fall asleep or a parent remains in the room while the child falls asleep, or the child has more than three reunions with the parent for one more hug or, in some manner, physically resists the bed. Two of the three criteria must be met. This child would be rated as having a disturbance in sleep-onset protodysomnia if this behavior happened two to four nights each week for a month or longer. A disorder would be classified if this 12- to 24-month-old child had this behavior on five to seven nights per week for a month or longer. Similarly, a classification for sleep-onset protodysomnia is made for children older than 24 months in the same manner but reduces the length of time for sleep onset to 20 minutes and the number of reunions to two.

In terms of night-waking protodysomnia, a similar classification scheme has been developed that grades severity by the frequency with which night waking occurs and has separate criteria for 12- to 24-month olds, 24- to 36-month-olds, and older than 36 months. For the 12- to 24-month-old child, a perturbation in this category would be defined by three signaled night wakings each night or remaining awake in the middle of the night for 30 minutes one night each week. A disturbance would be classified for the same child if there were at least three signaled awakenings for two to four nights per week or being awake for at least 30 minutes in the middle of the night two to four nights per week. A disorder would be appropriate as the classification for this child if there were at least three signaled awakenings or the child remained awake in the middle of the night for at least 30 minutes for five to seven nights per week for at least a month's duration.

Perturbations occur frequently with all normal young children and are short-term disruptions in behavior. Parental reassurance and education should be sufficient to regain the normal sleep pattern. However, both disturbances and disorders require more focused intervention, guided by the transactional framework for assessment and treatment. The intervention may range from brief coaching and guidance on bedtime routines and sleep hygiene to multiple sessions of parent-child relationship-focused therapy with collateral individual psychotherapy sessions for the primary caregiver. This upper range of intervention possibilities would be appropriate if parental psychological distress is significantly impacting the parent-child relationship and altering regular and predictable caregiving routines. Which particular blend or mixture of interventions is most appropriate depends on the outcome of the assessment, including the factors outlined in the transactional model. The framework may be used throughout the assessment to collect information about each domain or factor once organic etiologies have been ruled out. It is helpful to explain this framework to parents during the assessment so they may be encouraged to gain an understanding of both the assessment and intervention process.

SUMMARY AND CONCLUSION

This chapter briefly reviews the current literature related to the maturation of sleep and waking patterns during early development, and the assessment and diagnosis of sleep problems. A proposed developmental nosology of sleep disorders is reviewed that is based on quantitative indices of sleep onset and night-waking behaviors graded by severity and age. It is important to note that, despite almost a half century of intensive research into the neurophysiological organization of sleep across all mammalian species, little has been discovered that explains the purpose and functions of sleep. How much sleep is needed throughout the life cycle? How is disordered sleep defined? In early childhood, the parents define the occurrence of common sleep problems. Two children of the same age may awaken the same number of times during the night for the same length of time, and both may require parental intervention to return to sleep. One family may define the intrusion on their sleep as a major problem, and the other may not.

In general, it is important that appropriate, objective developmental measures of sleep and waking behavior be established (Anders et al., 2000). It is equally important to assess the infant's daytime functioning to ascertain whether sleep fragmentation per se is associated with disturbances in attention, memory, learning, social interaction, mood regulation, and/or physical development. Significant sleep deprivation in children has been associated with failure to thrive, hyperactivity, depression, and short attention span (e.g., Gruber, Sadeh, & Raviv, 2000; Lavigne et al., 1999). Thus, future sleep research will need to objectively assess nighttime sleep and wakefulness as well as daytime well-being in both children who are brought to the professional for evaluation of a sleep problem and in children of similar ages whose parents are not seeking assistance.

References

Adair, R., Bouchner, H., Phillip, B., Levenson, S., & Zuckerman, B. (1991). Night waking during infancy: Role of parental presence at bedtime. *Pediatrics, 87,* 500–504.

Ainsworth, M. D. S., Blehar, M. C., Waters, E., & Wall, S. (1978). *Patterns of attachment: A psychological study of the strange situation*. Hillsdale, NJ: Lawrence Erlbaum.

American Psychiatric Association (1994) *Diagnostic and statistical manual of mental disorders* (4th ed.). Washington, DC: Author.

American Sleep Disorders Association (1990). *The international classification of sleep disorders: Diagnosis and coding manual* (2nd ed.). Lawrence, KS: Allen Press.

Anders, T. F. (1994). Infant sleep, nighttime relationships and attachment. *Psychiatry, 57*, 11–21.

Anders, T. F., Goodlin-Jones, B., & Sadeh, A. (2000) Sleep disorders. In C. H. Zeanah (Ed.), *Handbook of infant mental health* (2nd ed., pp. 326–338). New York: Guilford Press.

Anders, T. F., Goodlin-Jones, B. L., & Zalenko, M. (1998). Infant regulation and sleep-wake state development. *Bulletin of Zero to Three, 19*, 5–8.

Anders, T. F., Halpern, L. F., & Hua, J. (1992). Sleeping through the night: A developmental perspective. *Pediatrics, 90*, 554–560.

Anders, T. F., & Keener, M. A. (1985). Developmental course of nighttime sleep-wake patterns in full-term and premature infants during the first year of life. *Sleep, 8*, 173–192.

Anders, T. F., & Sostek, A. M. (1976). The use of time-lapse video recording of sleep-wake behavior in human infants. *Psychophysiology, 13*, 155–158.

Armstrong, K. L., Quinn, R. A., & Dadds, M. R. (1994). The sleep patterns of normal children. *Medical Journal of Australia, 161*, 202–206.

Atkinson, E., Vetere, A., & Grayson, K. (1995). Sleep disruption in young children: The influence of temperament on the sleep patterns of pre-school children. *Child: Care, Health, and Development, 21*, 233–246.

Ball, H. L., Hooker, E., & Kelly, P. J. (1999). Where will the baby sleep? Attitudes and practices of new and experienced parents regarding cosleeping with their newborn infants. *American Anthropologist, 101*, 143–151.

Barr, R. G. (2000). Excessive crying. In A. J. Sameroff, M. Lewis, & S. M. Miller (Eds.), *Handbook of developmental psychopathology* (2nd ed., pp. 327–350). New York: Plenum Press.

Benoit, D., Zeanah, C. H., Boucher, C., & Minde, K. K. (1992). Sleep disorders in early childhood: Association with insecure maternal attachment. *Journal of the American Academy of Child and Adolescent Psychiatry, 31*, 86–93.

Benoit, D., Zeanah, C. H., Parker, K. C., Nicholson, E., & Coolbear, J. (1997) "Working model of the child interview": Infant clinical status related to maternal perceptions. *Infant Mental Health Journal, 18*, 107–121.

Bernal, J. (1973). Night waking in infants during the first 14 months. *Developmental Medicine and Child Neurology, 14*, 362–372.

Cohen, G. J. (1999). *American Academy of Pediatrics guide to your child's sleep*. New York: Random House.

Crowell, J., Keener, M., Ginsburg, N., & Anders, T. (1987). Sleep habits in toddlers 18 to 36 months old. *Journal of the American Academy of Child and Adolescent Psychiatry, 26*, 510–515.

Durand, V. M. (1998). *Sleep better!* Baltimore: Paul H. Brookes.

Elias, M. F., Nicolson, N. A., Bora, C., & Johnston, J. (1986). Sleep/wake patterns of breast-fed infants in the first 2 years of life. *Pediatrics, 77*(3): 322–329.

Ferber, R. (1987). The sleepless child. In C. Guilleminault (Ed.), *Sleep and its disorders in children* (pp. 141–163). New York: Raven Press.

Ferber, R., & Kryger, M. (Eds.). (1995). *Principles and practice of sleep medicine in the child*. Philadelphia: Saunders.

Field, T., Healy, B., Goldstein, S., Perry, S., & Bendell, D. (1988). Infants of depressed mothers show "depressed" behavior even with nondepressed adults. *Child Development, 59*, 1569–1579.

Fiese, B. H., & Sameroff, A. J. (1989). Family context in pediatric psychology: A transactional perspective. *Journal of Pediatric Psychology, 14*, 293–314.

Gaylor, E. E., Goodlin-Jones, B. L., & Anders, T. F. (2001). Classification of young children's sleep problems: A pilot study. *Journal of the American Academy of Child and Adolescent Psychiatry, 40*, 61–67.

George, C., Kaplan, N., & Main, M. (1996). *Adult attachment interview protocol* (3rd ed.). Unpublished manuscript, University of California, Berkeley.

Gibson, E., Dembofsky, C., Rubin, S., & Greenspan, J. (2000). Infant sleep position practices 2 years into the "Back to Sleep" campaign. *Clinical Pediatrics, 39*, 285–289.

Goodlin-Jones, B. L., Burnham, M. M., & Anders,

T. F. (2000). Sleep and sleep disturbances. In A. J. Sameroff, M. Lewis, & S. M. Miller (Eds.), *Handbook of developmental psychopathology* (2nd ed., pp. 309–325). New York: Plenum Press.

Goodlin-Jones, B. L., Burnham, M. M., Gaylor, E. E., & Anders, T. F. (2001). Night waking, sleep-wake organization, and self-soothing in the first year of life. *Journal of Developmental and Behavioral Pediatrics, 22,* 226–233.

Goodlin-Jones, B. L., Eiben, L. A., & Anders, T. F. (1997). Maternal well-being and sleep-wake behaviors in infants: An intervention using maternal odor. *Infant Mental Health Journal, 18,* 378–393.

Gruber, R., Sadeh, A., & Raviv, A. (2000). Instability of sleep patterns in children with attention-deficit/hyperactivity disorder. *Journal of the American Academy of Child and Adolescent Psychiatry, 39,* 495–501.

Guedeney, A., & Kriesler, L. (1987). Sleep disorders in the first 18 months of life: Hypothesis on the role of mother-child emotional exchanges. *Infant Mental Health Journal, 8,* 307–318.

Hiscock, H., & Wake, M. (2001). Infant sleep problems and postnatal depression: A community-based study. *Pediatrics, 107*(6), 1–9.

Hunsley, M., & Thoman, E. B. (2002). The sleep of co-sleeping infants when they are not co-sleeping: Evidence that co-sleeping is stressful. *Developmental Psychobiology, 40,* 14–22.

Jaffa, T., Scott, S., Hendriks, J., & Shapiro, C. (1993). Sleep disorders in children. *British Medical Journal, 306,* 640–643.

Jenkins, S., Owens, C., Bax, M., & Hart, H. (1984). Continuities of common behavioral problems in preschool children. *Journal of Developmental and Behavioral Pediatrics, 12,* 108–114.

Johnson, C. M. (1991). Infant and toddler sleep: A telephone survey of parents in one community. *Journal of Developmental and Behavioral Pediatrics, 12,* 108–114.

Kataria, S., Swanson, M. S., & Trevathan, G. E. (1987). Persistence of sleep disturbances in preschool children. *Journal of Pediatrics, 110,* 642–646.

Keefe, M. R., Kotzer, A. M., Froese-Fretz, A., & Curtin, M. (1996). A longitudinal comparison of irritable and nonirritable infants. *Nursing Research, 45,* 4–9.

Lavigne, J. V., Arend, R., Rosenbaum, D., Smith, A., Weissbluth, M., Binns, H. J., & Christoffel, K. (1999). Sleep and behavior problems among preschoolers. *Journal of Developmental and Behavioral Pediatrics, 20,* 164–169.

Lockley, S., Skene, D., & Arendt, J. (1999). Comparison between subjective and actigraphic measurement of sleep and sleep rhythms. *Journal of Sleep Research, 8,* 175–183.

Lozoff, B. (1995). Culture and family: Influences on childhood sleep practices and problems. In R. Ferber & M. Kryger (Eds), *Principles and practice of sleep medicine in the child* (pp. 69–73). Philadelphia: Saunders.

Lozoff, B., Wolf, A., & Davis, N. (1985). Sleep problems seen in pediatric practice. *Pediatrics, 75,* 477–483.

Martinez, A., Malphurs, J., Field, T., Pickens, J., Yando, R., Bendell, D., Valle, C., & Messinger, D. (1996). Depressed mothers' and their infants' interactions with nondepressed partners. *Infant Mental Health Journal, 17,* 74–80.

McKenna, J. J., Thoman, E. B., Anders, T. F., Sadeh, A., Schechtman, V. L., & Glotzbach, S. F. (1993). Infant-parent co-sleeping in an evolutionary perspective: Implications for understanding infant sleep development and sudden infant death syndrome. *Sleep, 16,* 263–282.

Messer, D. (1993). The treatment of sleeping difficulties. In I. St. James-Roberts, G. Harris, & D. Messer (Eds.), *Infant crying, feeding, and sleeping* (pp. 194–210). New York: Harvester Wheatsheaf.

Minde, K. (1988). Behavioral abnormalities commonly seen in infancy. *Canadian Journal of Psychiatry, 33,* 741–747.

Minde, K., Popiel, K., Leos, N., Falkner, S., Parker, K., & Handley-Derry, M. (1993). The evaluation and treatment of sleep disturbances in young children. *Journal of Child Psychology and Psychiatry, 34,* 521–533.

Mindell, J. A. (1993). Sleep disorders in children. *Health Psychology, 12,* 151–162.

Mindell, J. A., Moline, M. L., Zendell, S. M., Brown, L. B., & Fry, J. M. (1994). Pediatricians and sleep disorders: Training and practice. *Pediatrics, 94,* 194–200.

Morrell, J. M. B. (1999). The role of maternal cognitions in infant sleep problems as assessed by a new instrument, the maternal cognitions about infant sleep questionnaire. *Journal of Child Psychology and Psychiatry, 40,* 247–258.

Mosko, S., Richard, C., & McKenna, J. (1997). Maternal sleep and arousals during bed sharing with infants. *Sleep, 20,* 142–150.

Murray, L. (1991). Intersubjectivity, object relations theory, and empirical evidence from mother-infant interactions. *Infant Mental Health Journal, 12*, 219–232.

Nakamura, S., Wind, M., & Danello, M. (1999). Review of hazards associated with children placed in adult beds. *Archives of Pediatrics and Adolescent Medicine, 153*, 1019–1023.

Novosad, C., Freudigman, K., & Thoman, E. B. (1999). Sleep patterns in newborns and temperament at eight months: A preliminary study. *Journal of Developmental and Behavioral Pediatrics, 20*, 99–105.

Owens, J., Spirito, A., & McGuinn, M. (2000). The Children's Sleep Habit Questionnaire (CSHQ): Psychometric properties of a survey instrument for school-aged children. *Sleep, 23*, 1043–1051.

Paret, I. (1983). Night waking and its relationship to mother-infant interaction in nine-month-old infants. In J. Call, E. Galenson, & R. Tyson (Eds.), *Frontiers of infant psychiatry* (pp. 171–177). New York: Basic Books.

Piazza, C. C., Fisher, W. W., & Kahng, S. W. (1996). Sleep patterns in children and young adults with mental retardation and severe behavioral disorders. *Developmental Medicine and Child Neurology, 38*, 335–344.

Pinilla, T., & Birch, L. (1993). Help me make it through the night: Behavioral entrainment of breast-fed infants' sleep patterns. *Pediatrics, 91*, 436–444.

Quine, L. (1992). Severity of sleep problems in children with severe learning difficulties: Description and correlates. *Journal of Community and Applied Social Psychology, 2*, 247–268.

Regalado, M. G., Schechtman, V. L., Del Angel, A. P., & Bean, X. D. (1995). Sleep disorganization in cocaine-exposed neonates. *Infant Behavior and Development, 18*, 319–327.

Richman, N. (1981). A community survey of characteristics of one to two year olds with sleep disruptions. *Journal of the American Academy of Child Psychiatry, 20*, 281–291.

Richman, N. (1985). A double-blind trial of treatment in young children with waking problems. *Journal of Child Psychology and Psychiatry, 26*, 591–598.

Richman, N. (1987). Surveys of sleep disorders in children in a general population. In C. Guilleminault (Ed.), *Sleep and its disorders in children* (pp. 115–140). New York: Raven Books.

Sadeh, A., Lavie, P., & Scher, A. (1994). Sleep and temperament: Maternal perceptions of temperament of sleep-disturbed toddlers. *Early Human Development, 44*, 311–322.

Sadeh, A., Lavie, P., Scher, A., Tirosh, E., & Epstein, R. (1991). Actigraphic home monitoring of sleep-disturbed and control infants and young children: A new method for pediatric assessment of sleep-wake patterns. *Pediatrics, 87*, 494–499.

Schaefer, C. E. (1990). Night waking and temperament in early childhood. *Psychological Report, 67*, 192–194.

Schaefer, C. E. (Ed.) (1995). *Clinical handbook of sleep disorders in children*. Northvale, NJ: Jason Aronson.

Scher, A. (2001). Attachment and sleep: A study of night waking in 12-month-old infants. *Developmental Psychobiology, 38*, 274–285.

Scher, A., & Blumberg, O. (1999). Night waking among 1-year-olds: A study of maternal separation anxiety. *Child: Care, Health and Development, 25*, 323–334.

Scher, A., Tirosh, E., Jaffe, M., Rubin, L., Sadeh, A., & Lavie, P. (1995). Sleep patterns of infants and young children in Israel. *International Journal of Behavioral Development, 18*, 701–711.

Scher, A., Tirosh, E., & Lavie, P. (1998). The relationship between sleep and temperament revisited: Evidence for 12-month-olds: A research note. *Journal of Child Psychology and Psychiatry, 39*, 785–788.

Scott, G., & Richards, M. (1990). Night waking in 1-year-old children in England. *Child: Care, Health and Development, 16*, 283–302.

Seifer, R. (2000). Temperament and goodness of fit. In A. J. Sameroff, M. Lewis, & S. M. Miller (Eds.), *Handbook of developmental psychopathology* (2nd ed., pp. 257–276). New York: Kluwer Academic.

Seifer, R., Dickstein, S., Spirito, A., & Owens-Stively (1996). Parent reports about sleep habits of infants and toddlers. Symposium, Infant Sleep: Descriptions and Interventions, conducted at the International Conference on Infant Studies, Providence, RI.

Sheldon, S. H. (1996). *Evaluating sleep in infants and children*. New York: Lippincott-Raven.

Shonkoff, J., & Brazelton, T. (1993). Paradise lost: Delayed parenthood in the carefully planned life. In E. Fenichel & S. Provence (Eds.), *Development in jeopardy* (pp. 177–202). Madison, CT: International Universities Press.

Spasaro, S. A., & Schaefer, C. E. (1995). Infant night waking. In C. E. Schaefer (Ed.), *Clinical handbook of sleep disorders in children* (pp. 49–68). Northvale, NJ: Jason Aronson.

Sroufe, L. A., Duggal, S., Weinfield, N., & Carlson, E. (2001). Relationships, development, and psychopathology. In A. J. Sameroff, M. Lewis, & S. M. Miller (Eds.), *Handbook of developmental psychopathology* (2nd ed., pp. 75–92). New York: Plenum Press.

St. James-Roberts, I., & Plewis, I. (1996). Individual differences, daily fluctuations, and developmental changes in amounts of infant waking, crying, fussing, and sleeping. *Child Development, 67,* 2527–2540.

Stores, G. (1999). Children's sleep disorders: Modern approaches, developmental effects, and children at special risk. *Developmental Medicine and Child Neurology, 41,* 568–573.

Thoman, E., & Acebo, C. (1995). Monitoring of sleep in neonates and young children. In R. Ferber & M. Kryger (Eds.), *Principles and practice of sleep medicine in the child* (pp. 55–68). Philadelphia: Saunders.

Van Tassel, E. B. (1985). The relative influence of child and environmental characteristics on sleep disturbances in the first and second years of life. *Developmental and Behavioral Pediatrics, 15,* 174–178.

Walters, J. (1993). Sleep management: The hidden agenda. *Child: Care, Health, and Development, 19,* 197–208.

Ward, M. J., Lee, S. S., Lipper, E. G. (2000). Failure-to-thrive is associated with disorganized infant-mother attachment and unresolved maternal attachment. *Infant Mental Health Journal, 21,* 428–442.

Ware, J., & Orr, W. (1992). Evaluation and treatment of sleep disorders in children. In C. E. Walker & M. Roberts (Eds.), *Handbook of clinical child psychology* (2nd ed., pp. 261–282). New York: Wiley.

Weissbluth, M. (1987). *Sleep well: Peaceful nights for your child and you.* London: Unwin Hyman.

Weissbluth, M. (1995). Naps in children: 6 months–7 years. *Sleep, 18,* 82–87.

Weissbluth, M., & Liu, K. (1983). Sleep patterns, attention span, and infant temperament. *Journal of Developmental and Behavioral Pediatrics, 4,* 34–36.

White, B. P., Gunnar, M. R., Larson, M. C., Donzella, B., & Barr, R. G. (2000). Behavioral and physiological responsivity, sleep, and patterns of daily cortisol production in infants with and without colic. *Child Development, 71,* 862–877.

Wolf, A., & Lozoff, B. (1989). Object attachment, thumbsucking, and the passage to sleep. *Journal of the American Academy of Child and Adolescent Psychiatry, 28,* 287–292.

Wolke, D., Meyer, R., Ohrt, B., & Riegel, K. (1995). The incidence of sleep problems in preterm and fullterm infants discharged from neonatal special care units: An epidemiological investigation. *Journal of Child Psychology and Psychiatry, 36,* 203–223.

Wyly, M. V. (1997). *Infant assessment.* Boulder, CO: Westview.

Zeanah, C. H., Boris, N. W., & Larrieu, J. A. (1997). Infant development and developmental risk: A review of the past 10 years. *Journal of the American Academy of Child and Adolescent Psychiatry, 36,* 165–178.

Zeanah, C. H., & Larrieu, J. A. (2000). Mother-blaming, relationship psychopathology, and infant mental health: A commentary on Ward, Lee, & Lipper (2000). *Infant Mental Health Journal, 21,* 443–447.

Zero to Three, National Center for Clinical Infant Programs (1994). *Diagnostic classification of mental health and developmental disorders of infancy and early childhood.* Arlington, VA: Author.

Zuckerman, B., Stevenson, J., & Baily, V. (1987). Sleep problems in early childhood: Continuities, predictive factors, and behavioral correlates. *Pediatrics, 80,* 664–671.

15

The Diagnostic Assessment
and Classification
of Feeding Disorders

Irene Chatoor

Jody Ganiban

One of the most common pediatric problems is feeding difficulties. It is estimated that 25% of otherwise normally developing infants and up to 80% of those with developmental handicaps have feeding problems (Lindberg, Bohlin, & Hagekull, 1991; Reilly, Skuse, Wolke, & Stevenson, 1999). Feeding disorders can disrupt the infant's early development and are linked to later deficits in cognitive development (Reif, Beler, Villa, & Spirer, 1995), behavioral problems (Galler, Ramsey, Solimano, Lowell, & Mason, 1988), and eating disorders (Marchi & Cohen, 1990). Longitudinal research also suggests that feeding problems are stable over time (Dahl, Rydell, & Sundelin, 1994; Stice, Agras, & Hammer, 1998). Consequently, it is extremely important to identify, understand, and treat early feeding problems. However, research on early feeding problems has been hampered by the lack of a standard classification system. As Emde, Bingham, and Harmon (1993) have pointed out, classification schemes are crucial tools for determining the etiology of a specific disorder, the course of the disorder, and the efficacy of treatment.

The objective of this chapter is to describe the development of self-regulated feeding and to propose a comprehensive classification scheme for feeding disorders that present during infancy and early childhood. We describe specific feeding disorders that can arise when the feeding process is chronically disrupted and present diagnostic criteria for each disorder. This chapter concludes with a discussion of how the proposed diagnostic criteria should be validated, along with recommendations regarding the clinical assessment of feeding disorders.

Specifically, this chapter presents (a) previous attempts to classify disorders of feeding; (b) the developmental progression of feeding during infancy and childhood, and a discussion of child and parent characteristics that can disrupt feeding; (c) a proposed diagnostic classification of feeding disorders in infants and young children, including diagnostic criteria, a clinical description, and existing data for each proposed subtype; (d) clinical recommendations regarding the assessment of feeding disorders, including empirically based strategies for clinical practice;

(e) future directions for research; and (f) a summary.

PAST ATTEMPTS TO DEFINE DISORDERS OF FEEDING

Historically, the term failure to thrive (FTT) was used as a catchall diagnosis for all feeding disorders. Clinicians initially distinguished between two forms of FTT: organic FTT and nonorganic FTT (Wittenberg, 1990). Organic FTT represents growth failure that can be traced to a medical cause. Nonorganic FTT is thought to reflect maternal deprivation or parental psychopathology (Duniz et al., 1996; Kedesdy & Budd, 1998; Patton & Gardner, 1963). A third category was later added to describe growth failure that is related to a mixture of organic and environmental factors (Homer & Ludwig, 1981). In recent years, the use of FTT as a diagnostic category for feeding disorders has been sharply criticized. A primary concern is that not all infants with feeding disorders demonstrate FTT (Benoit, 1993). Goldbloom (1987) has also pointed out that FTT is a purely descriptive term for growth failure, rather than a diagnosis. Consistent with this view, some researchers have argued that FTT represents a symptom, rather than a diagnostic category (Benoit, 1993; Chatoor, 1997; Kessler, 1999).

To address the need for diagnostic criteria for feeding disorders, *DSM-IV* (American Psychiatric Association, 1994) adopted a descriptive approach and introduced "feeding disorder of infancy and early childhood" as a diagnostic category. The diagnostic criteria for this disorder emphasize the child's weight status over the child's specific feeding behaviors. The specific criteria include persistent failure to eat adequately with significant failure to gain weight or significant loss of weight over at least 1 month; the disturbance is not due to an associated gastrointestinal or other medical condition; the disturbance is not accounted for by another mental disorder or by lack of available food; the onset is before the age of 6 years. These criteria exclude whole groups of children who have feeding disorders without weight problems and feeding disorders associated with medical conditions. In addition, these criteria do not capture the different subtypes of feeding difficulties

that have been described with a variety of labels by various authors (see table 15.1).

To address this problem, some authors have suggested subclassification systems of feeding disorders according to various organic and nonorganic causes (Burklow, Phelps, Schultz, McConnell, & Rudolph, 1998) or have used a multidimensional approach, combining descriptive and etiological categories (Kedesdy & Budd, 1998; Linscheid, 1992). However, there has been little uniformity in terms, and because of vague definitions of symptoms, confusion continues among clinicians and researchers regarding what constitutes a feeding disorder. Researchers continue to use different terminology to describe similar disorders, or use the same name when referring to very different disorders (see table 15.1). Differences in the description and labeling of feeding disorders have also caused confusion over how to treat children with feeding disorders. Moreover, the testing of effective treatments is limited by the tendency to consider specific problematic feeding behaviors (e.g., food refusal), rather than children's overall feeding patterns. In fact, in a review of empirically supported treatments for severe feeding problems, Kerwin (1999) concluded that such treatments exist, and that "it is now time to turn to the question for whom they are appropriate, and when, and why" (p. 193). To address these difficulties, we propose a classification system that presents clear diagnostic criteria for a variety of feeding disorders, and which has an empirical foundation. However, before addressing the different feeding disorders, we describe the developmental progression of feeding during infancy and early childhood, and discuss child and parent characteristics that can disrupt feeding at various stages of feeding development.

THE DEVELOPMENT OF INTERNALLY REGULATED FEEDING

An important task of the first years of life is the development of autonomous internal regulation of feeding, including young children's capacities to detect their internal hunger and satiety cues and to respond accordingly by eating or ceasing to eat. This seems like a fairly simple task, but even for many adults, internal regulation of eating

Table 15.1 Types of Food Refusal Identified by Previous Studies

Food Refusal Subtype	Description	Names Used in Previous Studies
Unpredictable food refusal	Intense food refusal varies from meal to meal, leading to an overall inadequate caloric intake	Infantile anorexia (Chatoor et al., 1998) Food refusal (Dahl et al., 1994; Lindberg et al., 1994)
Selective food refusal	Intense refusal of specific foods during all meals	Sensory food aversions (Chatoor et al., 2000) Taste aversion (Garb & Stunkard, 1974; Kalat & Rozin, 1973; Logue et al., 1981) Food neophobia (Birch, 1999; Hursti & Sjödén, 1997; Pliner & Lowen, 1997) Choosy eaters (Rydell et al., 1995) Selective eaters (Kern & Marder, 1996; Shore et al., 1998; Timimi et al., 1997)
Consistent food refusal	Refusal to drink milk, eat solids, or all foods during all meals	Posttraumatic feeding disorder (Benoit & Coolbear, 1998; Chatoor, Conley, & Dickson, 1988; Chatoor et al., 2001) Traumatically acquired conditioned dysphagia (DiScipio et al., 1978) Food aversion (Archer & Szatmari, 1990; Handen et al., 1986; Siegel, 1982) Feeding resistance (Dellert et al., 1993) Choking phobia (McNally, 1994) Food phobia (Singer et al., 1992)

remains very difficult. For example, anorexia nervosa in adults has been associated with poor awareness of hunger and emotional cues (Bruch, 1974). Obese adults also demonstrate confusion over hunger and satiation (Schlundt, Hill, Sbrocco, Pope-Cordle, & Kasser, 1990). In many cases, eating is not controlled by hunger sensations, but by emotions (Arnow, Kenardy, & Agras, 1995; Striegel-Moore et al., 1999).

We propose that the basis for internally regulated eating is established during the first years of life. The key to internal regulation is the development of an infant-parent communication system that requires the infant to signal hunger and satiety states, and the parents to respond to these cues accordingly. By responding appropriately to their infant's hunger and satiety cues, caregivers act as external scaffolds to their infant's emerging ability to self-regulate eating. They support their infant's conscious detection of his or her own hunger and satiety states by responding differentially and contingently to the infant's cues. Through their responses, caregivers also reinforce

and teach their infant appropriate responses to these internal states: that is, seek out and eat food when hungry, and cease eating when sated. Thus, parents help infants to regulate eating in response to hunger and satiety, and prepare them for the eventual transition from mutual regulation of eating to internally self-regulated eating. This development parallels the emergence of self-regulation in other domains, including emotions (Kopp, 1989; Tronick, 1989) and behavioral control (Kopp, 1982), and is part of a major developmental transition to autonomy during the toddler years. We propose that the development of internally regulated, autonomous feeding occurs in three stages: (1) homeostasis, (2) dyadic reciprocity, and (3) transition to self-feeding.

Stage 1: Achieve Homeostasis

Stage 1 occurs during the first few months of life. During this time, infants must establish basic cycles and rhythms of sleep and wakefulness, and of feeding and elimination (Greenspan & Lieberman, 1980). In regard to feeding, the major developmental task for the infant is to reach and maintain a calm state of alertness for feeding. If an infant cannot do this, then feeding attempts will be unsuccessful. For example, the infant will frequently be too irritable or too sleepy to feed. Another critical component of this stage is the development of an infant-parent communication system through which the infant's hunger and satiety cues are expressed and understood by the caregivers. Establishment of such a system is key to maintaining *nutritional homeostasis*—a state in which the infant's nutritional needs for growth and development are met. While in utero, the fetus's nutritional demands are met automatically through the umbilical cord. However, once born, infants must actively and clearly signal hunger and satiety to caregivers. In turn, the caregiver must perceive and read the infant's signals accurately, and respond contingently.

Fortunately, most infants emit hunger cries that are qualitatively distinct from other types of cries. In optimal cases, parents become increasingly adept at understanding these cues during the first few weeks of life, and infants and parents begin to develop a communication system by which infants can communicate their needs. If the caregivers are able to differentiate between the infant's hunger and satiety cues, and they respond appropriately, they foster the infant's internal regulation of feeding by (a) reinforcing that hunger and satiety are two different states, and (b) reinforcing that these states require different responses. However, if parents have difficulties understanding or attending to the infant's cues, they may feed or not feed the infant irrespective of the infant's internal states of hunger and satiety. Consequently, the infant's distinctions between hunger and satiety may become confused and the infant's nutritional needs may not be met.

Stage 2: Achieve Dyadic Reciprocity

By the beginning of stage 2, most infants have become adept at state regulation. Starting at 2 to 4 months of age, infants become active social partners (Greenspan & Lieberman, 1980). At this time, infant-parent interactions are characterized by mutual eye contact and gazing, reciprocal vocalizations, and mutual physical closeness expressed through touching and cuddling. The adaptive infant actively mobilizes and engages caretakers, and interactions become increasingly reciprocal in nature. Significant changes are also apparent during feeding interactions. Reflexive hunger cries are replaced by intentional cries and vocalizations for food, and by body language that clearly communicates satiation (e.g., refusing to open the mouth, turning the head). At this time, infants begin to regulate caregivers actively and purposefully during feeding interactions via signals of hunger and satiation. In response, caregivers regulate the presentation and withdrawal of food. Through this process feeding, interactions are mutually regulated by infants and caregivers (Tronick, 1989).

In optimal situations, infants emit clear hunger and satiety cues, and caregivers accurately interpret and respond contingently to infants' cues. However, if infants give weak signals of their inner state and/or parents are distracted by their own needs, the mutual regulation of infant and parent may not develop. These infants are fed sporadically, and their nutritional needs are not met adequately. In severe cases, these infants will develop a feeding disorder of failed reciprocity, as described below.

Stage 3: Transition to Self-Feeding

Between 6 months and 3 years of age, the infant progresses through a developmental process characterized by Mahler, Pine, and Berman (1975) as separation and individuation. Both motoric and cognitive maturation enable the infant to function with increasing physical and emotional independence. As the infant becomes physically more competent, issues of autonomy and dependency are played out daily in the feeding situation, where mother and infant have to negotiate who is going to place the spoon in the infant's mouth. In addition, the infant's increasing understanding of cause and effect takes on special meaning in the feeding situation. During this stage, the infant not only needs to understand the difference between hunger and fullness, but also needs to differentiate these physical sensations from emotional experiences (e.g., wish for affection, feelings of anger or frustration). Consequently, it is of utmost importance that caregivers differentiate the infant's hunger and satiety cues from emotional cues and respond contingently, for example, offering food when the infant signals hunger but not offering food when the infant needs affection or calming; and terminating the meal when the infant appears satiated, and not insisting that the infant keeps eating until the plate is empty. This will facilitate the infant's independent internal regulation of eating. On the other hand, if the parent responds to the infant's emotional needs by feeding the infant, the infant will confuse hunger with emotional experiences and learn to eat or refuse to eat when sad, lonely, frustrated, or angry. The infant's eating will be externally regulated by the infant's emotional experiences.

In optimal cases, the infant gives clear signals and the parents interpret them correctly and allow the infant increasing autonomy during feeding. However, if the infant gives poor hunger cues, as is seen in infantile anorexia, the parents may become anxious and confused as to how to get their infant to eat adequate amounts of food for necessary growth, and they try to override their infant's satiety cues. This may result in battles of will with the infant over eating, which only exacerbate the infant's food refusal. On the other hand, if the infant emits weak signals of satiety and calms itself if food is offered when it is upset, parents may teach their infant to eat in response to emotional needs and fall into a pattern of overfeeding. Consequently, these early years are critical in the development of internal versus external regulation of eating.

As pointed out above, during each of the three developmental stages, the infant's and caregiver's characteristics can interfere with the mutual regulation of feeding. When this occurs, maladaptive feeding patterns emerge. When taken to the extreme, a child's nutritional status and long-term health is threatened, and the feeding difficulties become a disorder. In the following section, we discuss three feeding disorders that are tied to specific developmental stages, and three feeding disorders that can disrupt feeding at any stage of feeding development.

A PROPOSED DIAGNOSTIC CLASSIFICATION OF FEEDING DISORDERS

In this section, we present diagnostic criteria for six individual feeding disorders. Each feeding disorder is characterized by a specific feeding pattern and, in some cases, associated with specific medical conditions. Moreover, as described below, each disorder is associated with distinct parent-infant interactional patterns that can be used to differentiate various feeding disorders from each other and from healthy eating habits. Last, we relate our diagnostic classification scheme to existing clinical and empirical studies in an attempt to develop a common language for feeding disorder symptoms and subtypes. The six feeding disorders are (1) feeding disorder of state regulation; (2) feeding disorder of caregiver-infant reciprocity; (3) infantile anorexia; (4) sensory food aversions; (5) feeding disorder associated with a concurrent medical condition; and (6) posttraumatic feeding disorder.

Feeding Disorder of State Regulation

Diagnostic Criteria

1. Has difficulty reaching and maintaining a state of calm alertness for feeding; is either too sleepy or too agitated and/or distressed to feed.
2. The feeding difficulties start in the newborn period.
3. Shows significant growth deficiency.[1]

Clinical Description

Infants with this disorder start to demonstrate significant problems with feeding during the first months of life. Typically, parents report that the infant has extraordinary difficulties reaching and maintaining a state of alert calmness, and appears to be too sleepy, excited, or distressed to feed. As a result, the parents have a difficult time determining when the infant is hungry or full. Young infants with immature central nervous systems or medical illnesses, such as cardiac or pulmonary disease, may be at greatest risk for this disorder.

Such infants may tire quickly and terminate feedings without taking adequate amounts of milk to grow. Some mothers can compensate for the infant's poor state regulation by helping the infant reach and maintain calm and alert arousal states by reducing external stimuli. However, mothers who are depressed, anxious, or overwhelmed with stressors may have difficulty dealing with the infant's irritability or unresponsiveness. As such, they may inadvertently intensify the infant's state-regulation difficulties and feeding difficulties.

Empirical Literature

Virtually no empirical research has focused on this subgroup of infants. The only study that exists found that infants diagnosed as having a feeding disorder of state regulation (homeostasis) demonstrated less positive reciprocal interactions with their mothers than infants who were healthy eaters (Chatoor, Getson, et al., 1997). Further studies are clearly required to better understand infant and parent characteristics that are associated with this feeding disorder.

Feeding Disorder of Caregiver-Infant Reciprocity

Diagnostic Criteria

1. Shows lack of developmentally appropriate signs of social reciprocity (e.g., visual engagement, smiling, babbling) during feeding with primary caregiver.
2. Shows significant growth deficiency.
3. The growth deficiency and lack of relatedness are not solely due to a physical disorder or a pervasive developmental disorder.

Clinical Description

Most infants with feeding disorder of caregiver-infant reciprocity are detected when they become acutely ill and require emergency treatment. The infants are malnourished, weak, feed poorly, and avoid eye contact. When picked up, they scissor their legs and hold up their arms in a surrender posture to balance their heads, which appear too heavy for their weak bodies. When held, they do not cuddle like healthy, well-fed infants, but draw up their legs or appear hypotonic and limp like a rag doll.

This disorder is most likely to arise if an effective infant-caregiver communication system has not developed. In many cases, the primary caregivers seem unaware that there is a problem, and may report that the infant sleeps for long periods of time without requiring feeding. Additionally, some caregivers may admit to propping bottles for feeding and to spending minimal time with their infant. These interactional patterns suggest that the caregivers do not attend to their infant's cues and are unable to interpret their infant's hunger and satiety cues or to distinguish them from other cues. This disorder is usually only diagnosed when the infant becomes severely malnourished and requires hospitalization, because frequently the caregivers are distrustful and difficult to engage, elusive, and avoidant of any contact with professionals. In most cases these infants' feeding behavior tends to improve in the hospital if they are given consistent attention by staff members.

Empirical Literature

This feeding disorder has been described in the early literature as the consequence of maternal deprivation (Fischhoff, Whitten, & Pettit, 1971; Patton & Gardner, 1963), and has also been described as deprivation dwarfism (Silver & Finkelstein, 1967). In line with these findings, the DSM-III (American Psychiatric Association, 1980) included failure to thrive in its diagnostic criteria for reactive attachment disorder of infancy. However, the DSM-IV (American Psychiatric Association, 1994) modified reactive attachment disorder to encompass only problems in relatedness of young children without an emphasis on growth failure of the child. With the present diagnostic system of the DSM-IV, these infants frequently fall into the broad category of neglect.

In the past, Chatoor and colleagues referred to this feeding disorder as feeding disorder of attachment (Chatoor, 1991, 1997, 2000; Chatoor, Dickson, Schaefer, & Egan, 1985). Chatoor, Getson, et al. (1997) reported that infants with this disorder and their mothers showed less positive engagement and dyadic reciprocity during feeding than healthy eaters. In addition, their mothers received higher maternal noncontingency ratings than mothers of healthy eaters. Infants with this feeding disorder also exhibit high rates of attachment insecurity (Gordon & Jameson, 1979; Valenzuela, 1990; Ward, Kessler, & Altman, 1993).

Mothers of these infants are frequently described as suffering from character disorders, affective illness, alcohol abuse, and drug abuse (e.g., Fischhoff et al., 1971). They are also more likely to experience poverty and unemployment (e.g., Drotar & Malone, 1982) and have a history of abuse by their partners (e.g., Weston & Colloton, 1993). Clinicians and researchers have reported that this type of feeding disorder is related to the mothers' own past and present relationship difficulties (Benoit, Zeanah, & Barton, 1989; Drotar & Sturm, 1987; Fraiberg, Anderson, & Shapiro, 1975).

Infantile Anorexia

Diagnostic Criteria

1. Refusal to eat adequate amounts of food for at least 1 month.
2. Onset of the food refusal before 3 years of age, most commonly between 9 and 18 months during the transition to spoon and self-feeding.
3. Does not communicate hunger and lacks interest in food, but shows strong interest in exploration and/or interaction across caregiving contacts.
4. Shows significant growth deficiency.
5. The food refusal did not follow a traumatic event.
6. The food refusal is not due to an underlying medical illness.

Clinical Description

Infants with infantile anorexia are usually referred for a psychiatric evaluation because of their intense food refusal and growth failure. In some cases, caregivers spontaneously report that since birth the infant appeared disinterested in feeding, and was easily distracted by external stimuli during feeding interactions (e.g., sounds, visual stimuli). They may also report that the infant consumed only small amounts of milk and had to be fed frequently during the first months

of life. Most commonly, by the end of the first year, these infants take a few bites of food only and then refuse to eat. In contrast to parents of infants who show a feeding disorder of reciprocity, caregivers of infantile anorectics are painfully aware of the infant's feeding problems and poor nutritional status. They try to enhance their infant's food intake by coaxing, distracting, offering different foods, feeding while playing, feeding at night, threatening, and even force feeding when desperate. However, the caregivers report that these methods work only temporarily, if at all, and that they are unable to increase their infant's food intake.

Most commonly, the infant's food refusal and poor growth becomes a matter of concern when the infant is between the ages of 9 and 18 months, during the transition to spoon and self-feeding. Initially, the infants fail to gain adequate weight. After several weeks or months of poor food intake, their linear growth slows down and they develop chronic malnutrition, characterized by low weight and stunted linear growth. Interestingly, in most cases, their heads continue to grow at a normal rate. Consequently, their bodies appear small and thin, but the children have relatively larger heads and normal cognitive development.

Empirical Literature

Chatoor, Egan, Getson, Menvielle, and O'Donnell (1988) referred to this feeding disorder as infantile anorexia because food refusal appeared to be related to a lack of appetite. More recently, Chatoor, Ganiban, Hirsch, Borman-Spurrell, and Mrazek (2000) have developed a transactional model for infantile anorexia. Specifically, they postulated that infantile anorexia will emerge when a toddler who has a difficult temperament (i.e., is emotionally reactive, demanding, willful, and has irregular rhythms of eating and sleeping) is raised by a parent who sets weak or ineffective limits upon the toddler's challenging behaviors that interfere with eating. This combination leads to poorly structured, conflictual feeding interactions that interfere with the toddler's sensation of hunger and capacity to eat.

Chatoor and colleagues explored the mother-infant interactional patterns associated with infantile anorexia and the differential diagnosis of infantile anorexia in a series of studies. In the first study, Chatoor, Egan, et al. (1988) found that toddlers with infantile anorexia demonstrated less dyadic reciprocity, less maternal contingency, more dyadic conflict, and more struggle for control than toddlers who were healthy eaters. These findings were recently replicated within a different sample (Chatoor, Hirsch, Ganiban, Persinger, & Hamburger, 1998).

Clinical observations indicate that during feeding interactions, toddlers with infantile anorexia are curious about their surroundings, willful, and demanding of attention, while their mothers are very anxious (Chatoor, 1989). These clinical observations were supported by a study by Chatoor and colleagues (2000). They found that when compared to healthy eaters, toddlers with infantile anorexia were rated by their parents as more emotionally intense, negative, irregular in eating and sleeping patterns, dependent, unstoppable, and difficult. Importantly, difficult temperament was also associated with a lower percentage of ideal weight, suggesting that the most difficult infants demonstrated the highest levels of growth failure. In regard to associated parent characteristics, mothers of infantile anorectics were more likely to describe insecure attachment to their own parents than mothers whose infants did not have a feeding disorder (Chatoor et al., 2000). Moreover, mothers' insecure attachments as well as their own drive for thinness correlated significantly with mother-infant conflict during feeding. In turn, mother-infant conflict during feeding was positively associated with low percentage of ideal weight within the infantile anorectic toddlers, and within nonclinical groups of infants. Collectively, these studies suggest that although infantile anorexia is associated with growth failure, it has little else in common with the infant and parent characteristics associated with the feeding disorder secondary to poor caregiver-infant reciprocity, which has also been described as maternal deprivation in the research and clinical literature.

Sensory Food Aversions

Diagnostic Criteria

1. Consistently refuses to eat specific foods with specific tastes, textures, and/or smells.

2. Onset of the food refusal during the introduction of a different type of food (e.g., may drink one type of milk but refuse another; may eat carrots, but refuse green beans; may eat crunchy foods but refuse pureed food or baby food).

3. Eats without difficulty when offered preferred foods.

4. The food refusal causes specific nutritional deficiencies and/or delay of oral motor development.

Clinical Description

Sensory food aversions are common and occur along a spectrum of severity. Some children refuse to eat only a few types of food, and the parents accommodate the child's food preferences. Others may refuse most foods and cause serious parental concern. The diagnosis of a feeding disorder should only be made if the food selectivity results in nutritional deficiencies and/or has led to delay of oral motor development.

Within this disorder, food refusal is related to the texture, taste, or smell of particular foods. When specific foods are placed in an infant's mouth, the infant's aversive reactions range from grimacing to gagging, vomiting, or spitting out the food. Sensory food aversions become apparent when infants are introduced to baby food or table food with a variety of tastes and textures. After an initial aversive reaction, infants usually refuse to continue eating that particular food and become distressed if forced to do so. Some infants generalize their reluctance to eat one food to other foods that look or smell similarly (e.g., an aversion to green beans may generalize to all green vegetables). Parents frequently report that these children are reluctant to eat new foods. Some children may even refuse to eat any food that has touched another food on the plate, while others will only eat food prepared by a specific restaurant or company. Older children with sensory food aversions may experience social anxiety when their peers discover that they eat only certain foods, while some older children may avoid altogether social situations that include eating.

If children refuse many foods or whole food groups (e.g., vegetables and fruits), their limited diet may lead to specific nutritional deficiencies (e.g., vitamins, zinc, iron). If infants reject foods that require significant chewing (e.g., meats, hard vegetables or fruits), they will fall behind in their oral motor development due to lack of experience with chewing. Frequently, the infant's refusal to eat a variety of foods creates parental concern and conflict within the family during mealtime.

In addition to their sensitivity to certain foods, many of these children experience hypersensitivities in other sensory areas as well. For example, parents frequently report that these infants become distressed when asked to walk on sand or grass, and that they do not like to wear socks, certain types of fabric, or labels in clothing. Many of these children are also hypersensitive to odors and sounds.

Empirical Literature

Some authors have referred to this feeding disorder as *food selectivity* (e.g., Shore, Babbitt, Williams, Coe, & Snyder, 1998; Timimi, Douglas, & Tsiftsopoulou, 1997); others have called it *choosy eaters* (Rydell, Dahl, & Sundelin, 1995), *picky eaters* (Marchi & Cohen, 1990), *food neophobia* (Birch, 1999; Pliner & Lowen, 1997), or *food aversion* (Archer & Szatmari, 1990). We chose the term *sensory food aversions* because these children experience specific foods as strongly aversive in taste, texture, and/or smell, and they frequently have other sensory difficulties, as described above.

Food selectivity is fairly common. Marchi and Cohen (1990) found that 27% of mothers they surveyed reported that their children were very choosy when it came to food. In a questionnaire survey that included 1,523 parents of toddlers, Chatoor, Hamburger, Fullard, and Rivera (1994) reported that 20% of the parents indicated that their children were eating only a few types of food "often" or "always." Of these parents, 6% expressed concerns that their children were eating only a few types of food and were not eating enough to grow. Timimi et al. (1997) indicated that older children who exhibit food selectivity can also suffer from anxiety, fear of eating with others, and obsessive-compulsive symptoms.

Feeding Disorder Associated With Concurrent Medical Condition

Diagnostic Criteria

1. Readily initiates feeding, but over the course of feeding, shows distress, and refuses to continue feeding.
2. Has concurrent medical condition that is believed to cause the distress.
3. Medical management improves but does not fully alleviate the feeding problems.
4. Fails to gain adequate weight or may even lose weight.

Clinical Description

Infants with medical conditions that cause pain or respiratory distress may develop feeding problems. Some medical conditions are not readily diagnosed, and food refusal may be the leading symptom. For example, food allergies can be difficult to diagnose in this young age group, and silent reflux is often overlooked by pediatricians because the infant does not vomit (vomiting is usually the leading symptom of reflux). Infants with gastroesophageal reflux can typically drink 1 to 2 ounces of milk before reflux is activated. However, once reflux occurs, some infants show signs of discomfort (e.g., wiggling, arching, crying) and push the bottle away. These infants are usually well engaged with their caretakers and willing to feed, but they refuse to continue feeding when they appear to experience pain or discomfort. Some infants can calm themselves and resume feeding until they experience a new episode of pain. However, some infants cry in distress and become increasingly agitated while their caretakers try to continue feeding them. Some infants with respiratory distress may feed for a while and take a few ounces until they tire out and stop feeding. In general, these infants consume inadequate amounts of food, fail to gain weight, or lose weight. Although medical management frequently improves the infants' feeding difficulties, the feeding disorder does not fully remit with treatment of the medical condition.

Empirical Literature

Severe feeding problems such as food refusal and taking more than an hour per feeding have been reported in infants with gastroesophageal reflux (Nelson, Chen, Syniar, & Christoffel, 1998). Dellert, Hyams, Treem, and Geertsma (1993) reported that food refusal was so severe that infants had to be tube fed. Even after successful surgery, the severe feeding difficulties and growth failure continued (Lemons & Dodge, 1998). However, further studies are required to examine how gastrointestinal illnesses lead to feeding problems and which infants are most vulnerable to react to pain with food refusal.

Posttraumatic Feeding Disorder (PTFD)

Diagnostic Criteria

1. Food refusal follows a traumatic event or repeated traumatic insults to the oropharynx or gastrointestinal tract (e.g., choking, severe vomiting, insertion of nasogastric or endotracheal tubes, suctioning) that trigger intense distress in the infant.
2. Consistent refusal to eat manifests in one of the following ways:
   - Refuses to drink from the bottle, but may accept food offered by spoon or finger food. (Although consistently refuses to drink from the bottle when awake, may drink from the bottle when sleepy or asleep.)
   - Refuses solid food, but may accept the bottle.
   - Refuses all oral feedings.
3. Reminders of the traumatic events cause distress, as manifested by one or more of the following:
   - May show anticipatory distress when positioned for feeding.
   - Shows intense resistance when approached with bottle or food.
   - Shows intense resistance to swallowing food placed in the mouth.
4. The food refusal poses an acute or long-term threat to the child's nutrition.

Clinical Description

Parents may report that their infants refused to eat any solid foods after an incident of choking, or after one or more episodes of severe gagging. Some parents may have observed that the food refusal followed intubation, the insertion of na-

sogastric feeding tubes, or major surgery requiring vigorous oropharyngeal suctioning. Depending on the mode of feeding that the infants appear to associate with the traumatic event, some may refuse to eat solids, but will continue to drink from the bottle, whereas others may refuse to drink from the bottle, but are willing to eat solids (e.g., an infant who choked on a Cheerio may refuse to eat solids, but drinks from the bottle; and an infant who experienced reflux while drinking from the bottle may refuse the bottle, but will continue to eat from the spoon). Reminders of the traumatic event such as the bottle or the high chair may cause intense distress. Some infants become fearful and distressed as soon as they are positioned for feedings and presented with feeding utensils and food. They resist being fed by crying, arching, and refusing to open their mouths. If food is placed in their mouths, they intensely resist swallowing. They may gag or vomit, let the food drop out, actively spit out food, or store food in their cheeks and spit it out later. The fear of eating seems to override any awareness of hunger, and infants who refuse all food, liquids and solids, require acute intervention due to dehydration and starvation.

Empirical Literature

The term posttraumatic eating disorder was first coined by Chatoor, Conley, and Dickson (1988) in an article on food refusal in five latency-age children who experienced episodes of choking or severe gagging and later refusal to eat any solid food. These children were preoccupied with the fear of choking to death, afraid of choking in their sleep, and had frightening dreams about choking or being threatened by monsters. Several other clinicians have reported that children and adults can develop eating problems after choking on food or experiencing trauma to the oropharynx and to the esophagus (e.g., Bernal, 1972; McNally, 1994; Solyom & Sookham, 1980). Handen, Mandell, and Russo (1986) and Culbert, Kajander, Kohen, and Reaney (1996) describe case series of children with "food aversions" that include children with "conditioned fear of eating (phagophobia)." Dellert and colleagues (1993) reported that 5% of infants with gastroesophageal reflux developed "feeding resistance" to oral feedings severe enough to require tube feedings for nutritional support. Chatoor, Ganiban, Harrison, and Hirsch (2001) found that toddlers with a posttraumatic feeding disorder exhibited more resistance to swallowing food during feeding interactions than healthy eaters and toddlers diagnosed with infantile anorexia.

ASSESSMENT OF FEEDING PROBLEMS

The diagnostic criteria for each disorder include a description of the specific pattern of feeding difficulties infants exhibit, as well as possible associated medical conditions. Therefore, diagnostic assessments of feeding disorders should include extensive assessments of the infants' feeding patterns and comprehensive medical evaluations (see table 15.2).

Assessments of feeding problems should always begin with an extensive interview with caregivers to evaluate the infant's feeding difficulties, developmental history, medical history, and family history. This interview is critical for establishing when feeding problems began, as well as identifying medical conditions that may interfere with feeding or traumatic experiences that may have triggered feeding problems. As described previously, gastroesophageal reflux can make feeding painful and thus disrupt feeding interactions. Neurological conditions can interfere with the child's capacity to chew and swallow. Last, traumatic choking or gagging experiences can render some infants fearful of placing food in their mouths or swallowing.

This interview should be followed by direct observation of the infant with the primary caregiver during feeding and play. The purpose of this assessment is to evaluate when and how feeding interactions go awry (Chatoor, Conley, & Dickson, 1988; Chatoor, Getson, et al., 1997; Chatoor et al., 1998, 2001). As such, these observations are key to the clinician's understanding of how to foster mutually regulated feeding interaction. Feeding and play observations are best done from behind a one-way mirror, since some infants and young children become easily distracted by an observer in the room, which can also make caregivers feel self-conscious and uncomfortable.

As a result, their feeding interactions may be artificially altered. It is also helpful to remind parents before they start feeding the infant that the feeding is not meant to be a star performance, and that they should do things in the same way they would at home in order to allow the diagnostician to observe the distinct behaviors of the infant that make feeding so difficult.

The observation of play interactions enables the clinician to determine whether problematic feeding interactions are also associated with more fundamental problems within the infant-parent relationship. For example, signs of maternal intrusiveness and dyadic conflict during play usually indicate a much more serious relationship problem that needs to be taken into consideration in making the diagnosis and in planning treatment for all feeding disorders.

Since many feeding disorders are associated with nutritional problems, medical illnesses, and impairment of oral motor or general development, a multidisciplinary assessment is usually necessary to address the various aspects of feeding disorders. In addition to the assessment outlined above, it is important that the infant's medical status is assessed and that current medical illnesses that may contribute to the infant's feeding difficulties are addressed. Because serious feeding difficulties are commonly associated with growth deficiency or deficiency of specific nutrients in the child's diet, a nutritional assessment is also essential in the diagnostic process. In addition, an oral motor assessment is often indicated to understand whether the feeding difficulties have been caused by an oral motor dysfunction, or whether the infant's avoidance of foods that need to be chewed has resulted in oral motor delay because of lack of practice.

The multidisciplinary assessments can be arranged individually, but are done most effectively by a team that works together on a regular basis. In our experience, the team works best if most of the assessments are performed on the same day, and the family is given feedback and diagnostic information with all team members in the room. Within our clinic, a child psychiatrist or psychologist integrates the diagnostic assessments of all the team members and presents the parents with a specific diagnosis and treatment plan for their child. At the end of the meeting, each family is

Table 15.2 Diagnostic Procedures and Measures

Assessment	Personnel	Measures	Purpose
Psychiatric assessment of feeding disorder	Psychiatrist or clinical psychologist	Gather information regarding the feeding, medical, and developmental history of infant or toddler. Observe parent-infant interactions during feeding and play	To assess symptoms of specific feeding disorders
Psychiatric assessment of comorbidity	Psychiatrist or clinical psychologist	Semistructured interview or questionnaire to assess additional child behavior/emotional problems	To identify psychiatric disorders associated with feeding disorders
Evaluation of medical illnesses	Pediatrician, gastroenterologist, or nurse practitioner	Infant's physical status	To evaluate medical conditions associated with feeding disorder
Nutritional assessment	Nutritionist	Infant's height, weight, head circumference. Infant's 3-day food intake	To assess infant's degree of growth deficiency and/or specific nutritional deficiencies
Oral motor assessment	Occupational therapist or speech pathologist	Oral motor development and presence of pathological reflexes	To evaluate oral motor delay or oral motor disorder
Developmental assessment	Clinical psychologist	Developmental testing	To assess current developmental status
Assessment of parent characteristics	Parent report	Parents' attachment styles. Parents' general mental health, anxiety level, history of eating disorders/problems. Marital relationship, social support system	To assess parent characteristics associated with specific feeding disorders
Assessment of infant temperament	Parent report	Assessment of temperament via parent report measures	To assess temperament characteristics associated with specific feeding disorders

assigned a primary therapist or case manager who helps to coordinate the personnel involved in the treatment plan.

FUTURE DIRECTIONS

In this chapter, we have outlined a theory for the development of feeding and presented a diagnostic classification scheme for feeding disorders. This classification scheme is based upon clinical observations as well as existing empirical studies.

However, it is clear that more work needs to be done to establish its validity.

Robins and Guze (1989) have outlined five phases of validation of psychiatric disorders:

1. Clinical description of the disorder
2. Laboratory studies
3. Delineation from other disorders
4. Follow-up studies to determine whether or not the original patients are suffering from some other defined disorder that may account for the original picture
5. Family studies

Robins and Guze postulate that independent of the question of hereditary or environmental causes, the finding of an increased prevalence of the same disorder among the close relatives of the original patients strongly indicates that one is dealing with a valid entity.

Although progress has been made in steps 1 through 3, additional prospective research and family studies are needed to truly understand the etiological roots of each disorder as well as the developmental paths that lead to each disorder. Such research will enhance our ability to better understand the various feeding disorders and to distinguish disorders from each other. To date, few studies have followed children with feeding disorders over time. Moreover, existing longitudinal studies have focused on the development of children with feeding problems but have not attempted to differentiate between subtypes of feeding problems (Marchi & Cohen, 1990; Stice et al., 1998). As a result, it is unknown how specific feeding disorders are related to eating disorders or other disorders in adolescence and adulthood. Last, to our knowledge no study has attempted to examine whether familial contributions to feeding disorders are solely made via "experiential" avenues (e.g., parenting styles), or whether genes also contribute to these disorders.

SUMMARY

This chapter presents a classification system for feeding disorders of infancy and early childhood. It describes specific stages of feeding development during which some of the feeding disorders arise, presents diagnostic criteria and a clinical description of the various feeding disorders, lists studies of parent-infant interactions that characterize the various feeding disorders, and describes specific infant and parent characteristics that have been found to be associated with a specific feeding disorder, infantile anorexia. However, further research is needed to test the reliability of the diagnostic categories and to validate the various feeding disorder diagnoses through follow-up studies and through family studies of feeding and eating disorders. These studies will shed light on the relationship of feeding disorders of infancy

and early childhood to eating disorders of later childhood, adolescence, and adulthood.

Above all, studies of infant and parent characteristics associated with the various feeding disorders are needed to gain a better understanding of how to prevent and treat the various feeding disorders. Preliminary studies show that a treatment that is effective for one type of feeding disorder may be ineffective or even contraindicated for another feeding disorder. Chatoor, Hirsch, and Persinger (1997) demonstrated that facilitating internal regulation of eating through parent training is an effective intervention for toddlers with infantile anorexia. However, this treatment is ineffective for infants with a posttraumatic feeding disorder. On the other hand, infants with a posttraumatic feeding disorder can overcome their feeding resistance through a behavioral approach (extinction) described by Benoit, Wang, and Zlotkin (2000). However, this behavioral approach would lead to external regulation of eating in children with infantile anorexia and further interfere with their awareness of hunger and fullness. In her review of treatments for severe feeding problems, Kerwin (1999) concluded that, although small case studies have demonstrated that empirically supported treatments for severe feeding problems exist, "it is now time to turn to the question for whom they are appropriate, and when, and why" (p. 193). Our diagnostic delineation of the various feeding disorders is a first step in addressing these questions.

Note

1. Growth deficiency can be measured in the following ways. *Acute malnutrition* according to Waterlow et al. (1977) criteria reflects current or acute nutritional status. The reference "normal" is 50th percentile weight for height (Hamill et al., 1979). This number divided by current weight gives the percentage of ideal body weight. Mild, moderate, and severe acute malnutrition correspond with 80 to 89%, 70 to 79%, and less than 70% of ideal body weight respectively. *Chronic malnutrition* according to Waterlow et al. (1977) criteria defines stunting of linear growth. The child's actual height is divided by the height that corresponds to the 50% NCHS percentile for age of the child or "ideal height." Mild, moderate, and severe chronic malnutrition corresponds with 90 to 95%, 85 to 89%, and less than 85% of ideal height, respectively. Addi-

tional parameters that can be used include z scores less than −1.68, faltering growth, percentage change of weight greater than 5% over baseline (percentile change/percentile at baseline = percentage of change over baseline).

References

American Psychiatric Association (1980). *Diagnostic and statistical manual of mental disorders* (3rd ed.). Washington, DC: Author.

American Psychiatric Association (1994). *Diagnostic and statistical manual of mental disorders* (4th ed.). Washington, DC: Author.

Archer, L. A., & Szatmari, P. (1990). Assessment and treatment of food aversion in a four-year-old boy: A multidimensional approach. *Canadian Journal of Psychiatry, 35*(6), 501–505.

Arnow, B., Kenardy, J., & Agras, W. S. (1995). The emotional eating scale: The development of a measure to assess coping with negative affect by eating. *International Journal of Eating Disorders, 18*(1): 79–90.

Benoit, D. (1993). Phenomenology and treatment of failure to thrive. *Child and Adolescent Psychiatric Clinics of North America, 2*(1), 61–73.

Benoit, D., & Coolbear, J. (1998). Post-traumatic feeding disorders in infancy: Behaviors predicting treatment outcome. *Infant Mental Health Journal, 19*, 409–421.

Benoit, D., Wang, E. E., & Zlotkin, S. H. (2000). Discontinuation of enterostomy tube feeding by behavioral treatment in early childhood: A randomized control trial. *Journal of Pediatrics, 137*, 498–503.

Benoit, D., Zeanah, C. H., & Barton, M. L. (1989). Maternal attachment disturbances in failure to thrive. *Infant Mental Health Journal, 10*, 185–202.

Bernal, M. E. (1972). Behavioral treatment of a child's eating problem. *Journal of Behavioral Therapy and Experimental Psychiatry, 3*, 43–50.

Birch, L. L. (1999). Development of food preferences. *Annual Review of Nutrition, 19*, 41–62.

Bruch, H. (1974). *Eating disorders: Obesity, anorexia nervosa, and the person within*. London: Routledge and Kegan Paul.

Burklow, K. A., Phelps, A. N., Schultz, J. R., McConnell, K., & Rudolph, C. (1998). Classifying complex pediatric feeding disorders. *Journal of Pediatric Gastroenterology and Nutrition, 27*(2), 143–147.

Chatoor, I. (1989). Infantile anorexia nervosa: A developmental disorder of separation and indi-

viduation. *Journal of the American Academy of Psychoanalysis, 17*, 43–64.

Chatoor, I. (1991). Eating and nutritional disorders of infancy and early childhood. In J. Wiener (Ed.), *Textbook of child and adolescent psychiatry* (pp. 357–361). Washington, DC: American Psychiatric Press.

Chatoor, I. (1997). Feeding and other disorders in infancy. In A. Tasman, J. Kay, & J. Lieberman (Eds.), *Psychiatry* (pp. 683–701). Philadelphia: W.B. Saunders.

Chatoor, I. (2000). Feeding and eating disorders of infancy and early childhood. In H. I. Kaplan & B. J. Saddock (Eds.), *Comprehensive textbook of psychiatry* (Vol. 7). Baltimore: Williams and Wilkins.

Chatoor, I., Conley, C., & Dickson, L. (1988). Food refusal after an incident of choking: A posttraumatic eating disorder. *Journal of the American Academy of Child and Adolescent Psychiatry, 27*, 105–110.

Chatoor, I., Dickson, L., Schaefer, S., & Egan, J. (1985). A developmental classification of feeding disorders associated with failure to thrive: Diagnosis and treatment. In D. Drotar (Ed.), *New directions in failure to thrive: Research and clinical practice* (pp. 235–238). New York: Plenum.

Chatoor, I., Egan, J., Getson, P., Menvielle, E., & O'Donnell, R. (1988). Mother-infant interactions in infantile anorexia nervosa. *Journal of the American Academy of Child and Adolescent Psychiatry, 27*, 535–540.

Chatoor, I., Ganiban, J., Harrison, J., & Hirsch, R. (2001). The observation of feeding in the diagnosis of the posttraumatic feeding disorder of infancy. *Journal of American Academy of Child and Adolescent Psychiatry, 40*(5), 595–602.

Chatoor, I., Ganiban, J., Hirsch, R., Borman-Spurrell, E., & Mrazek, D. (2000). Maternal characteristics and toddler temperament in infantile anorexia. *Journal of American Academy of Child and Adolescent Psychiatry, 39*(6), 743–751.

Chatoor, I., Getson, P., Menvielle, E., O'Donnell, R., Rivera, Y., Brasseaux, C., & Mrazek, D. (1997). A feeding scale for research and clinical practice to assess mother-infant interactions in the first three years of life. *Infant Mental Health Journal, 18*, 76–91.

Chatoor, I., Hamburger, E., Fullard, R., & Rivera, Y. (1994). A survey of picky eating and pica behaviors in toddlers. *Scientific Proceedings of* the Annual Meeting of American Academy of Child and Adolescent Psychiatry, 10, 50.

Chatoor, I., Hirsch, R., Ganiban, J., Persinger, M., & Hamburger, E. (1998). Diagnosing infantile anorexia: The observation of mother-infant interactions. Journal of the American Academy of Child and Adolescent Psychiatry, 37(9), 959–967.

Chatoor, I., Hirsch, R., & Persinger, M. (1997). Facilitating internal regulation of eating. Infants and Young Children, 9(4), 12–22.

Culbert, T. P., Kajander, R. L., Kohen, D. P., & Reaney, J. B. (1996). Hypnobehavioral approaches for school-age children with dysphagia and food aversion: A case series. Developmental and Behavioral Pediatrics, 17, 335–341.

Dahl, M., Rydell, A. M., & Sundelin, C. (1994). Children with early refusal to eat: Follow-up during primary school. Acta Paediatricia Scandinavia, 83, 54–58.

Dellert, S. F., Hyams, J. S., Treem, W. R., & Geertsma, M. A. (1993). Feeding resistance and gastroesophageal reflux in infancy. Journal of Pediatric Gastroenterology and Nutrition, 17, 66–71.

Di Scipio, W. J., Kaslon, K., & Ruben, R. J. (1978). Traumatically acquired conditioned dysphagia in children. Annals of Otology, Rhinology, and Laryngology, 87, 509–514.

Drotar, D., & Malone, C. A. (1982). Family-oriented intervention in failure to thrive. In M. Klaus & M. O. Robertson (Eds.), Birth interaction and attachment (6th ed., pp. 104–112). Skillman, NJ: Johnson & Johnson Pediatric Roundtable.

Drotar, D., & Sturm, L. (1987). Paternal influences in nonorganic failure to thrive: Implications for psychosocial management. Infant Mental Health Journal, 8, 37–50.

Duniz, M., Scheer, P. J., Trojovsky, A., Kaschnitz, W., Kvas, E., & Macari, S. (1996). Changes in psychopathology of parents of NOFT (nonorganic failure to thrive) infants during treatment. European Child and Adolescent Psychiatry, 5, 93–100.

Emde, R., Bingham, R., & Harmon, R. (1993). Classification and the diagnostic process in infancy. In C. Zeanah (Ed.), Handbook of infant mental health (pp. 225–235). New York: Guilford Press.

Fischhoff, J., Whitten, C. F., & Pettit, M. G. (1971). A psychiatric study of mothers of infants with growth failure secondary to maternal deprivation. Journal of Pediatrics, 79, 209–215.

Fraiberg, S., Anderson, E., & Shapiro, U. (1975). Ghosts in the nursery. Journal of the American Academy of Child Psychiatry, 14, 387–421.

Galler, J. R., Ramsey, R. L., Solimano, G., Lowell, W. E., & Mason, E. (1988). The influence of early malnutrition on subsequent behavioral development: I. Degree of Impairment in Intellectual Performance, 22, 8–15.

Garb, J. L., & Stunkard, A. J. (1974). Taste aversions in man. American Journal of Psychology, 131, 1204–1207.

Goldbloom, R. (1987). Growth in infancy. Pediatrics Review, 9, 57–61.

Gordon, A. H., & Jameson, J. C. (1979). Infant-mother attachment in patients with nonorganic failure to thrive syndrome. Journal of the American Academy of Child Psychiatry, 18, 251–259.

Greenspan, S., & Lieberman, A. (1980). Infants, mothers, and their interaction: A quantitative clinical approach to developmental assessment. In S. I. Greenspan & G. H. Pollock (Eds.), The course of life: Psychoanalytic contributions toward understanding personality development (Vol. 1, pp. 271–312). Washington, DC: NIMH.

Hamill, P. V. V., Drizd, T. A., Johnson, C. L., Reed, R. B., Roche, A. F., & Moore, W. M. (1979). Physical growth: National Center for Health Statistics percentiles. American Journal of Clinical Nutrition, 32, 607–629.

Handen, B. L., Mandell, F., & Russo, D. C. (1986). Feeding induction in children who refuse to eat. American Journal of Diseases in Childhood, 140, 52–54.

Homer, C., & Ludwig, S. (1981). Categorization of etiology of failure to thrive. American Journal of Diseases in Childhood, 135, 848–851.

Hursti, U. K. K., & Sjödén, P. O. (1997). Food and general neophobia and their relationship with self-reported food choice: Familial resemblance in Swedish families with children of ages 7–17 years. Appetite, 29, 89–103.

Kalat, J. W., & Rozin, P. (1973). "Learned safety" as a mechanism in long delay taste aversion learning in rats. Journal of Comparative and Physiological Psychology, 83, 198–207.

Kedesdy, J. H., & Budd, K. S. (Eds.) (1998). Childhood feeding disorders. Baltimore: Paul H. Brookes.

Kern, L., & Marder, T. J. (1996). A comparison of simultaneous and delayed reinforcement as treatments for food selectivity. *Journal of Applied Behavior Analysis, 29*(2), 243–246.

Kerwin, M. E. (1999). Empirically supported treatments in pediatric psychology: Severe feeding problems. *Journal of Pediatric Psychology, 24,* 193–214.

Kessler, D. (1999). Failure to thrive and pediatric undernutrition: Historical and Theoretical Context. In D. B. Kessler & P. Dawson (Eds.), *Failure to thrive and pediatric undernutrition* (pp. 3–18). Baltimore: Paul H. Brookes.

Kopp, C. B. (1982). Antecedents of self-regulation: A developmental perspective. *Developmental Psychology, 18,* 199–214.

Kopp, C. B. (1989). Regulation of distress and negative emotions: A developmental view. *Developmental Psychology, 25,* 343–354.

Lemons, P. K., & Dodge, N. N. (1998). Persistent failure-to-thrive: A case study. *Journal of Pediatric Health Care, 12*(1), 27–32.

Lindberg, L., Bohlin, G., & Hagekull, B. (1991). Early feeding problems in a normal population. *International Journal of Eating Disorders, 10,* 395–405.

Lindberg, L., Bohlin, G., Hagekull, B., & Thunstrom, M. (1994). Early food refusal: Infant and family characteristics. *Infant Mental Health Journal, 15,* 262–277.

Linscheid, T. R. (1992). Eating problems in children. In C. E. Walker & M. C. Roberts (Eds.), *Handbook of clinical child psychology* (2nd ed., pp. 451–473). New York: John Wiley.

Logue, A. W., Ophir, I., & Strauss, K. (1981). The acquisition of taste aversions in humans. *Behaviour Research and Therapy, 19,* 319–333.

Mahler, M. S., Pine, F., & Berman, A. (1975). *The psychological birth of the human infant.* New York: Basic Books.

Marchi, M., & Cohen, P. (1990). Early childhood eating behaviors and adolescent eating disorders. *Journal of the American Academy of Child and Adolescent Psychiatry, 29,* 112–117.

McNally, R. J. (1994). Choking phobia: A review of the literature. *Comprehensive Psychiatry, 35,* 83–89.

Nelson, S. P., Chen, E. H., Syniar, G. M., & Christoffel, K. K. (1998). One-year follow-up of symptoms of gastroesophageal reflux during infancy. Pediatric Practice Research Group. *Pediatrics, 102*(6), E67.

Patton, R. G., & Gardner, L. L. (1963). *Growth failure in maternal deprivation.* Springfield, IL: Charles C. Thomas.

Pliner, P., & Lowen, E. R. (1997). Temperament and food neophobia in children and their mothers. *Appetite, 28*(3), 239–254.

Reif, S., Beler, B., Villa, Y., & Spirer, Z. (1995). Long-term follow-up and outcome of infants with non-organic failure to thrive. *Israel Journal of Medical Sciences, 31*(8), 483–489.

Reilly, S. M., Skuse, D. H., Wolke, D., & Stevenson, J. (1999). Oral-motor dysfunction of children who fail to thrive: Organic or nonorganic? *Developmental Medicine and Child Neurology, 41*(2), 115–122.

Robins, E., & Guze, S. B. (1989). Establishment of diagnostic validity in psychiatric illness: Its application to schizophrenia. *American Journal of Psychiatry, 126*(7), 107–111.

Rydell, A. M., Dahl, M., & Sundelin, C. (1995). Characteristics of school children who are choosy eaters. *Journal of Genetic Psychology, 156*(2), 217–229.

Schlundt, D. G., Hill, J. O., Sbrocco, T., Pope-Cordle, J., & Kasser, T. (1990). Obesity: A biogenetic or biobehavioral problem. *International Journal of Obesity, 14,* 815–828.

Shore, B. A., Babbitt, R. L., Williams, K. E., Coe, D. A., & Snyder, A. (1998). Use of texture fading in the treatment of food selectivity. *Journal of Applied Behavioral Analysis, 31*(4), 621–633.

Siegel, L. J. (1982). Classical and operant procedures in the treatment of a case of food aversion in a young child. *Journal of Clinical Child Psychology, 11,* 167–172.

Silver, H. K., & Finkelstein, M. (1967). Deprivation dwarfism. *Journal of Pediatrics, 70,* 317–324.

Singer, L. T., Ambuel, B., Wade, S., & Jaffe, A. C. (1992). Cognitive-behavioral treatment of health-impairing food phobias in children. *Journal of American Academy of Child and Adolescent Psychiatry, 31*(5), 847–852.

Solyom, L., & Sookham, D. (1980). Fear of choking and its treatment. *Canadian Journal of Psychology, 24,* 30–34.

Stice, E., Agras, W. S., & Hammer, L. D. (1998). Risk factors for the emergence of childhood eating disturbances: A five-year prospective study. *International Journal of Eating Disorders, 25,* 375–387.

Striegel-Moore, R. H., Morrison, J. A., Schreiber, G., Schumann, B. C., Crawford, P. B., & Obarzanek, E. (1999). Emotion-induced eating and sucrose intake in children: The NHLBI growth and health study. *International Journal of Eating Disorders, 25,* 389–398.

Timimi, S., Douglas, J., & Tsiftsopoulou, K. (1997). Selective eaters: A retrospective case note study. *Child: Care, Health, and Development, 23*(3), 265–278.

Tronick, E. Z. (1989). Emotions and emotional communication in infants. *American Psychologist, 44,* 112–119.

Valenzuela, M. (1990). Attachment in chronically underweight young children. *Child Development, 61,* 1984–1996.

Ward, M. J., Kessler, D. B., & Altman, S. C. (1993). Infant-mother attachment in children with failure to thrive. *Infant Mental Health Journal, 14,* 208–220.

Waterlow, J. C., Buzina, R., Keller, W., Lan, J. M., Nichaman, M. Z., & Tanner, J. M. (1977). The presentation and use of height and weight data for comparing the nutritional status of groups of children under the age of 10 years. *Bulletin of the World Health Organization, 55,* 489–498.

Weston, J., & Colloton, M. (1993). A legacy of violence in nonorganic failure to thrive. *Child Abuse and Neglect, 17,* 709–714.

Wittenberg, J. V. (1990). Feeding disorders in infancy: Classification and treatment considerations. *Canadian Journal of Psychiatry, 35*(6), 529–533.

VI

SPECIFIC AREAS OF DISTURBANCE: APPLYING DIAGNOSTIC CRITERIA TO DISORDERS WITH AN ONSET IN THE PRESCHOOL YEARS

It is now widely acknowledged that there is a need to improve the classification of disorders that arise in young children. The chapters included in this section review empirical work in an attempt to do just that. By using the *DSM* approach as a starting point, the authors evaluate the validity of *DSM* criteria for young children and make important recommendations for modifying the criteria to reflect the dynamic developmental changes that occur in early childhood. In addition, some authors make an attempt to integrate their conceptualizations with the DC:0–3 criteria, which are examined in relation to the *DSM* criteria, and integration is proposed. One of the major strengths of these chapters is that the authors provide developmentally based conceptual models of the specific disorders and describe how these conceptual models inform assessment. Not only are the approaches highly regarded and empirically driven, they also are conceptually quite innovative in that they attempt a full integration of clinical and developmental perspectives.

Ami Klin and his colleagues present a developmental approach for the assessment and diagnosis

of autism in early childhood. They outline the components of a comprehensive, empirically derived approach, including developmental assessment measuring intellectual and other resources; a speech, language, and communication assessment; evaluation of functional adjustment; and a diagnostic formulation. The authors recommend evaluating supplemental information about self-regulation and genetic liability. Diagnostic assessment of autism in young children is advanced relative to diagnostic assessment of other areas of young child psychopathology. Advances in diagnostic assessment in autism are in large part due to the development and wide acceptance of structured parent interview and child observation methods (i.e., Autism Diagnostic Interview, Autism Diagnostic Observational Scales) that, when used in combination, have been shown to be reliable with toddlers and preschool-aged children. The authors recommend that in addition to focusing on autism symptomatology it is critical to study early mechanisms of communication and socialization.

Joan Luby has developed a state-of-the-art, comprehensive program to study the identification of affective disorders in infants and young children. She argues that current *DSM-IV* criteria can be applied to preschool children when the assessment is modified to account for age-appropriate manifestations of symptom states. She notes that identification of affective disorders in infancy and the preschool period may be critical to early and potentially more effective interventions. She asserts that the significance of early intervention is heightened due to the fact that many affective disorders are known to have a chronic, relapsing, and relatively treatment-resistant course when identified and treated in later childhood. The author makes empirically based recommendations for modification of *DSM-IV* criteria for major depressive disorders for preschoolers, including modified symptom manifestations (for example, pertinent themes observed in play rather than overtly expressed thoughts) as well as quantitative differences in diagnostic criteria (for example, duration of symptoms for a portion of the day for several days rather than 2 weeks in a row). To assess affective disorders, the author recommends the inclusion of direct observational assessment of and interviews with the child as well as parent interviews probing for developmental manifestation of affective symptoms in this age group. Dimensional measures are also reviewed. Further, the author recommends greater attention to the assessment of impairment, given the lack of consensus on diagnostic criteria in this age group. Finally, for a comprehensive assessment the author also recommends a neurocognitive assessment. The author provides excellent illustrative case examples, including one for bipolar disorder.

Like many of the disorders presented in this section, anxiety disorders are not only disabling conditions in their own right but also can lead to even more severe forms of psychopathology if left untreated. Susan Warren has been working on an extensive research program designed to clarify developmental pathways contributing to childhood anxiety disorders. Using a high-risk paradigm (e.g., studying infants of mothers with anxiety disorders), she has been looking at infant predispositions, the mother-infant relationship, and how their interaction may contribute to the development of anxiety in toddlers. She presents compelling evidence for the manifestation of anxiety dis-

orders in infants and preschoolers. She examines the challenges associated with diagnosing anxiety disorders in the early years and recommends longitudinal studies to establish the long-term significance and developmental trajectories of fearfulness and anxiety in early childhood.

Michael Scheeringa has been working on research with preschoolers suffering from posttraumatic stress disorder (PTSD). He discusses the developmental appropriateness of the PTSD construct and presents a review of the developmental capacities necessary to manifest PTSD. His research has established that children less than 4 years of age do develop PTSD following exposure to trauma. He outlines which symptoms are most often observed in preschoolers and presents his work on creating an alternative set of criteria for PTSD in infants and young children. In addition, he provides a discussion of relationship issues as they relate to PTSD, suggesting that, as is seen in many other disorders in this age group, the clinically relevant literature on trauma and PTSD supports a relationship-based perspective of the disorder. Based on a review of the relevant research as well as extensive clinical experience in this area, the author proposes a conceptual model of parent-child relationship disturbances relevant to PTSD. Most interesting is the presentation of a "vicarious traumatization effect" in which a symptomatic child does not directly experience a trauma but suffers a disturbance in response to exposure to a parent's traumatic experience. Further, the author describes three qualitative patterns of parent-child disturbances that appear relevant to the development and maintenance of PTSD. He recommends prospective studies to assess how the diagnosis of PTSD in young children relates to future symptoms as well as impairment and more sophisticated studies to explore whether and how certain family characteristics combine with genetic vulnerabilities to predispose children to this disorder. This impressive line of research is exemplary in that it presents clear diagnostic criteria based on a developmental and relational model with direct clinical implications.

William Pelham, Anil Chacko, and Brian Wymbs present a critical review of the research relevant to diagnosing and assessing attention deficit/hyperactivity disorder (ADHD) in the preschool child. Based upon a developmental framework, they describe in detail the limitations of the *DSM* system for the young child. In particular, they note that high activity levels and impulsivity are common in young children and that a strong reliance on the hyperactive-impulsive dimension can lead to diagnoses of many children without the true disorder. In addition, although the *DSM* criteria involve assessing symptoms across multiple settings, this requirement presents unique challenges with young children who may not yet attend school. Thus, the authors provide a balanced discussion of situations in which the *DSM-IV* criteria can be validly applied to young children (e.g., when the child is in a highly structured preschool setting) and those aspects that must be used with care (such as heavy reliance on symptom levels for the impulsivity/hyperactivity dimension or on only one informant). They also suggest that impulsivity, inattentiveness, and hyperactivity in very young children in the absence of impairment across family and peer contexts may reflect a transient developmental problem. Given these problems, the authors underscore the importance of assessing impairment for valid diagnosis of ADHD in preschool children and suggest that standardized instruments that assess impairment need to be developed for this young age group. The authors recommend that future research address several important issues, including diagnosis for children under the age of 4 years, specific modifications in *DSM* definitions for younger children, particularly in the criteria of multiple settings for children not yet in school, and the question of whether early identification and treatment can result in improved outcomes.

Lauren Wakschlag and Barbara Danis have been supported by NIMH to develop a developmentally informed framework for the clinical assessment of disruptive behavior problems in young children. Drawing on fields of infant mental health, developmental psychopathology, and clinical science, they base their work on the assumption that while clinical problems may mani-

fest differently at different developmental periods, this difference reflects heterotypic continuity rather than discontinuity of fundamentally different types of problems. At the outset, the authors acknowledge that although clinically significant disruptive behaviors can be reliably identified in preschoolers, currently there is no standardized approach to assess disruptive behavior problems in young children. They recommend a thoughtful, conceptually rich, multimethod approach that is firmly grounded in knowledge of normative development, including the assessment of the parent-child relationship as well as issues of impairment.

The work described in this section represents impressive research programs designed to incorporate existing *DSM* criteria into more developmentally sensitive frameworks in conceptualizing these disorders in the preschool years. To some extent, these studies also attempt to integrate a relational perspective into their recommendations for assessment, and all research programs described in this section involve parents as an essential component of the assessment protocol. It is also important to note that the authors in this section highlight the importance of impairment in assessing the various disorders in this young age group. The relational perspective, along with the suggested emphasis on impairment, is particularly useful to generate information that can link assessment to treatment. All authors also point to the serious shortage of empirical data, not only in validating the core symptomatology for the disorders but also addressing these important relational and impairment issues as they relate to the manifestation of the disorders in this age group. Finally, most authors in this section point to research findings suggesting a more treatment-resistant course when diagnosing these disorders in later childhood and highlight an urgency in establishing appropriate diagnostic criteria and instrumentation to assess these disorders, impairment, and related relational functioning in the early years.

16

Clinical Assessment of Young Children at Risk for Autism

Ami Klin

Katarzyna Chawarska

Emily Rubin

Fred Volkmar

Autism is a developmental disorder marked by severe deficits in reciprocal social interaction, communication, and imagination, as well as repetitive and restricted patterns of interests and behaviors (Volkmar & Klin, 2000). Its early onset, symptom profile, and chronicity strongly argue for a biological basis and, in fact, several lines of research implicate core biological mechanisms. For example, autism is one of the most strongly genetic psychiatric disorders (Rutter, 2000), and preliminary linkage data have already identified susceptibility regions likely to contain genes involved in the condition (Rutter, 2000). About a quarter of individuals with autism will develop a seizure disorder (Volkmar & Nelson, 1990), and a similar number of individuals have abnormal EEGs, which typically indicate bilateral abnormalities. Functional neuroimaging work has yielded well-replicated findings indicating abnormalities in a series of highly interconnected brain regions subserving social cognitive skills such as face perception and social attribution, with a focus on midtemporal and mesiofrontal structures (Schultz & Klin, 2002). These findings notwithstanding, the absence of biological markers present across all cases and the pronounced heterogeneity of its manifestations signify that the diagnosis of autism and related conditions is still based on observations of the confluence of behavioral abnormalities in the social, communication, play, and imagination domains (Volkmar, Cook, Pomeroy, Realmuto, & Tanguay, 1999).

Previously thought to be a rather rare disorder, with prevalence rates of maybe 5 per 10,000, more recent epidemiological studies indicate much higher rates of 16 children per 10,000 for more narrowly defined autism, and up to 40 children per 10,000 for the more broadly defined family of conditions marked by significant socialization deficits (Chakrabarti & Fombonne, 2001). Given the need for very intensive and long-term educational and other interventions required to address these children's needs, autism and related conditions have become a much more central point of discussion in social policy than hitherto, bringing to the fore issues of early identification, early intervention, and the nature and intensity of educational services that need to be provided to this substantial minority of children (National Research Council [NRC], 2001).

Yet, although first described by Leo Kanner in 1943 as a congenital disorder of "affective contact," it was not until the past 10 years or so that a large number of children under the age of 3 years began to be seen by mental health professionals specializing in the field of autism. In the 1980s, parents typically expressed concerns about their children's development in the first two years of life, but their children did not receive a diagnosis of autism until about the age of 4½ years (Siegel, Piner, Eschler, & Elliott, 1988). Knowledge about the early development of children with autism was restricted to parental reports (Volkmar, Stier, & Cohen, 1985) and to studies based on home movies and videotapes made of children prior to their diagnosis (Osterling & Dawson, 1994). This gap in knowledge became all the more alarming with the advent of the first studies of the utility of interventions in autism, which consensually highlighted the importance of early intervention in maximizing treatment effectiveness (Filipe et al., 1999; NRC, 2001). As recognition of the condition was taking place at later stages of development, the vast majority of children were not receiving early intervention services. The mean age of diagnosis of autism is now around 40 months in epidemiological studies (Chakrabarti & Fombonne, 2001), and this is likely to be lowered to even younger ages as the field as a whole catches up with what are known to be best practices in the identification and evaluation of young children with this and related conditions (Volkmar et al., 1999), including the more aggressive use of population-based early screening (Baird et al., 2000; Briggs-Gowan, Carter, Moye Skuban, & McCue Horwitz, 2001; Robins, Fein, Barton, & Green, 2001), heightened awareness of autism in higher functioning children, and the increased sophistication of first-line service providers such as pediatricians and early childhood mental health workers. Many factors appear to underlie this shift into earlier identification, including the advocacy work of increasingly influential parent support organizations, more effective dissemination of information by the media, the advocacy of prominent infant mental health organizations, and the establishment of governmental agencies with a strong mandate to identify and provide services to infants and toddlers. This trend was fully substantiated with the advent of the initial longitudinal studies in autism (Lord, 1995) and of studies evaluating model early intervention programs (Rogers & Lewis, 1989). Collectively, this emerging body of research has been unequivocal in revealing the importance of early identification of children at risk of having autism, as we stand the best chance of altering the natural course of the disorder the earlier we are able to put in place adequate programs for these children. This conclusion is fully consistent with what we know about neuroplasticity and the importance of early experiences in shaping behavioral and brain development (Dawson, Ashman, & Carver, 2000).

The need to see and evaluate increasing numbers of children under the age of 3 years provides excellent opportunities for research into autism, as one may explore early social predispositions, the unfolding of communication, and the onset of deviant patterns of behavior in a state of nature without the confounds of long-term treatment effects. It makes us rely more heavily on more precise knowledge of normative development, because behavioral deviations in early childhood are likely to be less stark than what is observed in later childhood, particularly because the usual discrepancies we look for, such as higher cognitive functioning relative to lower social skills, are observed within a more restricted (i.e., chronological and developmental) range. Equally important, the still small number of studies of toddlers with autism have shown that standardized diagnostic instruments are not as effective in identifying the condition in young children as they are in older children (Lord & Risi, 2000). This may be so because the most visible (if not specific) markers of autism (such as repetitive motor mannerisms) do not typically emerge until later in development. Hence, in early childhood there is a need for clinical reliance on symptoms affecting social reciprocity and social communication, for which reliable assessment has been repeatedly shown to be more challenging, particularly for the less experienced clinician (Volkmar et al., 1994).

This chapter summarizes principles and elements of clinical assessment of toddlers at risk for autism. While some of these principles can build on proven experience in the assessment of older children (Klin, Carter, & Sparrow, 1997), there is an emphasis on unique challenges and opportunities associated with our attempt to intuit, measure, and explain social development at these tender ages. Accordingly, we preface the discussion of the essential elements of evaluation with a brief description of expectations derived from our knowledge of normative development. Clearly, to fully appreciate delay and deviance in small children, there is a need to have typical paths of development clearly landmarked. We conclude with a vision of the impact of ongoing and future research on the way we assess small children, with a focus on novel techniques attempting to trace the origins of autism all the way to the first weeks of life and on neurobiological approaches that may allow us to identify the condition even before there are any symptoms to be observed.

PRINCIPLES OF CLINICAL ASSESSMENT IN YOUNG CHILDREN

A Comprehensive Developmental Approach

Autism is the paradigmatic condition among a class of disorders marked by social and communication deficits and behavioral rigidities called the pervasive developmental disorders (PDDs; American Psychiatric Association, 2000). The term *PDD* was chosen because it implies disruptions in multiple areas of development, including not only social and communication disabilities but also play patterns and cognitive development among many others. There is a need, therefore, to adopt a comprehensive developmental approach (Sparrow, Carter, Racusin, & Morris, 1995) that emphasizes the assessment of multiple areas of functioning and the reciprocal impact of abilities and disabilities. As a substantial proportion of children with autism also present with mental retardation (Fombonne, 1999), it is important to cast both quantified and informal observations in terms of a developmental perspective. Hence, the overall developmental or intellectual level establishes the frame within which one may interpret more meaningfully both the performance obtained and the behaviors observed during the assessment. By explicitly framing the assessment in terms of the normative course of development, it

is possible to appreciate delays in the acquisition of skills that emerge systematically in typical children. This information allows the clinician to fully appreciate the departures from normal expectations that delineate autistic symptomatology. Because the more obvious markers of autism may not be present in toddlers (e.g., "mechanical voice," motor stereotypies), it is often the absence of normative behaviors (e.g., reduced social orientation and rate of communicative approaches) rather than the display of aberrant behaviors that becomes the hallmark of risk for autism in this young age group (Wetherby, Prizant, & Schuler, 2000).

The need for assessment of multiple areas of functioning requires the involvement of professionals with different areas of expertise. To avoid multiple views of a child (which can be conflicting, thus confusing parents and service providers), there is an equal need for transdisciplinary cohesion in which a single coherent picture can emerge and be translated into a set of intervention recommendations. An interdisciplinary format also encourages discussion among the clinicians involved, with the beneficial effects of creating a more complex and accurate view of the child (e.g., due to variability of presentation across people, time, and setting), reconciling meaningful differences, and fully appraising the impact of findings in one area upon other areas of functioning (e.g., language level and social presentation).

Variability Across Settings

The settings in which the child is observed and tested can vary greatly in terms of familiarity, degree of structure, intrusion adopted by the adult interacting with the child, and complexity of the physical environment. If these factors are not fully considered, highly discrepant views of the child may emerge, leading to conflicting impressions or narrowly framed observations. Given that the child's presentation in different settings informs clinicians more comprehensively about areas of strengths and weaknesses and about optimal and less helpful educational environments, it is important to consider these factors explicitly and to deliberately alter them in order to obtain a more complete view of the child. Clinicians involved in different sections of the assessment may adopt different approaches. Thus the assessment of intellectual functioning may require a highly structured, adult-directed approach within a very bare testing environment in order to yield the child's "best" performance (e.g., maximizing attention and minimizing distractions).

In contrast, the assessment of social presentation may require a much less intrusive approach to create opportunities to observe the extent to which the child spontaneously initiates social contact, requests desired objects, shares experiences with others, and seeks socially salient aspects of the environment. This more naturalistic approach is likely to create the greatest social interaction demands, given that in the absence of the typical adult scaffolding that takes place whenever a young child interacts with an adult, the spontaneous social predispositions of the child and absence thereof are more likely to be observed (e.g., tendency for self-isolation, exploration of extraneous physical stimuli such as lights and shadows rather than representational toys or people). It is also useful to explore the extent to which a child is able to profit from therapeutic interventions, intrusively interfering with what a child is doing and redirecting him or her to more socially engaged situations, while providing augmentative forms of communication such as pictures or modeled gestures. This approach can greatly inform the kinds of interventions that are likely to be of help in the child's daily treatment plan.

Toddlers' presentation can vary greatly as a function of time of day and state (including level of fatigue, minor illness), among a host of other factors. The potential misleading effect of such conditions can be addressed by continuously seeking information from parents or caregivers as to how representative the child's behaviors are relative to what they are used to seeing in other settings. Equally informative is a systematic comparison of observations among the clinicians involved, who can outline discrepancies in observations as a function of the underlying factors creating the setting for each observation (e.g., early in the morning versus later in the day; first day versus second day; clinic-based versus day care versus home-based observations; nonverbal problem-solving tasks versus language and communication tasks).

Parental Involvement

An understanding of findings related to specific skills measured in the assessment must be qualified in terms of the child's adjustment to everyday situations and real-life demands. This can only be achieved through the participation of parents in the assessment as a source of information. During the toddler years, parents are typically the only adults who have an opportunity to observe the child in multiple environments. Although parents may not have the objectivity to appreciate the extent to which their child conforms to normative expectations (e.g., this might be their first child or they might have developed a style of interaction in which the adult's approach masks the child's more marked social disabilities), the information they can provide has been shown to be both useful and sufficiently reliable to inform the diagnostic process (Lord, Rutter, & LeCouteur, 1994). This includes historical data, observations of the child in naturalistic settings such as home and day care program, and incidental observations such as a visit to the playground or a birthday party. By grounding the findings obtained during the assessment in this contextual base of information, many advantages follow, including a better sense of the child's developmental path, a validation of clinical observations, and the opportunity for comparisons across environments and situations.

Parental involvement is also advantageous from other perspectives. The clinician's intervention is likely to be much more effective if parents have the opportunity to directly observe what takes place in the evaluation and then to discuss specific behaviors (rather than more vague concepts or symptoms) with the clinicians afterward. It is in the context of this understanding, as well as in the process of discussing a child's strengths and weaknesses and the required interventions emerging from this profile, that parents are optimally prepared to become advocates and coordinators of the child's intervention program.

Profile Scatter

Even during the tender ages of toddlerhood, one typically observes great scatter in the skills displayed by toddlers with suspected autism relative to typical children or children with other developmental conditions (Stone, 1997). In the majority of cases, there are relative strengths on sensorimotor and visual-perceptual tasks that contrast with significant weaknesses on tasks involving language, particularly those that involve language use for the purpose of sharing information. It is important, therefore, to delineate a profile of assets and deficits rather than simply presenting an overall (often misleading) summary score or measure, because such global scores may represent the average of highly discrepant skills. Similarly, it is important not to generalize from an isolated performance (e.g., knowledge of letters and numbers) to an overall impression of the level of functioning. This too may be a gross misrepresentation of the child's capacities for learning and adaptation, given that this group of children often display "splinter skills" (isolated peaks or strengths in performance), which are often acquired in ways that differ from normative acquisition and which typically fail to serve social adjustment and growth.

NORMATIVE DEVELOPMENT OF SOCIAL AND COMMUNICATIVE SKILLS

The comprehensive developmental approach described above calls for the need to compare observations of deviant behaviors to the normative course of development. Although this principle applies to all areas of development assessed (e.g., cognitive, motor, language acquisition), the central developmental domains for comparison are social orientation and social communication.

Typical infants exhibit a series of predispositions that prompt them to seek social stimuli; in turn, adults reciprocate in kind, seeking their child by prompting and reinforcing further social contact. It is out of this mutually reinforcing choreography that so many social and communication skills appear to emerge (Klin, Schultz, & Cohen, 2000). For typically developing infants, the human voice appears to be one of the earliest and most effective stimuli conducive to social engagement (Eimas, Siqueland, Jusczyk, & Vigorito, 1971; Mills & Melhuish, 1974). This is evidenced in the effects of speech sounds upon their attention mechanisms. This spontaneous orientation is not seen in young children with autism (Klin, 1991). In fact, the lack of orientation to speech sounds (e.g., when another person makes a statement) is one of the most robust predictors of a diagnosis of autism in children first seen at the age of 2 years (Lord, 1995). In the visual modality, human faces have been emphasized as one of the most potent facilitators of social engagement (Bryant, 1991). A very large number of studies have demonstrated infants' preferential sensitivity to and salience-driven perceptual processing of faces as well sensitivity to gaze direction (Haith, Bergman, & Moore, 1979; Symons, Hains, & Muir, 1998). In autism, a large number of face-processing studies have demonstrated deficits (Klin et al., 1999; Langdell, 1978) and abnormalities (Hobson, Ouston, & Lee, 1988; Tantam, Monaghan, Nicholson, & Stirling, 1989). These deficits are not seen when these children are processing other visual objects such as buildings (Boucher & Lewis, 1992), and one study showed that when children with autism were asked to sort people who varied in terms of age, sex, facial expressions of emotion, and the type of hat they were wearing, they gave priority to type of hat, which contrasted with typical children, who grouped pictures by emotional expression (Weeks & Hobson, 1987). Such studies indicate not only abnormalities in face processing but also preferential orientation to inanimate objects, a finding corroborated in other studies (Dawson, Meltzoff, Osterling, Rinaldi, & Brown, 1998; Klin, Jones, & Schultz, 2003).

Neither human voice nor human face processing, however, appears in a context-free environment. Rather, they are deeply immersed in a social-affective context, and infants are very sensitive to this context. For example, very young infants can discriminate between happy and sad faces (Field & Walden, 1981); 5-month-olds can discriminate between happy and sad vocalizations (Walker-Andrews & Grolnick, 1983), and between happy and angry vocal expressions (Walker-Andrews & Lennon, 1991); 5-month-olds are also capable of matching facial and vocal expressions on the basis of congruity (Walker-Andrews & Lennon, 1991). Children with autism, in contrast, have been repeatedly shown to exhibit abnormalities in the perception of facial emotions (Hobson, 1986a, 1986b).

Not only are infants sensitive to affective salience, they also react appropriately to emotional signals (Haviland & Lelwica, 1987). For example, they react negatively to their mothers' depressed affect (Tronick, Cohn, & Shea, 1986) and appropriately to the emotional content of praise or prohibition (Fernald, 1993). In fact, they soon learn to expect contingency between their actions and those of their partners (Tarabulsy, Tessier, & Kappas, 1996). In the affective domain, this phenomenon has been shown through a series of studies using the still-face paradigm (Tronick, Als, Adamson, Wise, & Brazelton, 1978). Infants' expectation of social reciprocity has also been shown in studies of imitative games of infancy such as peekaboo (Trevarthen, 1979), where babies as young as 9 months understand the roles involved in the joint activity and work to maintain their reciprocal structure (Ross & Lollis, 1987). Precursors of such reciprocal engagements can be seen in the emergence of imitation in young infants. Newborn infants imitate facial and manual gestures (Meltzoff & Moore, 1977) and emotional expressions (Field, Goldstein, Vega-Lahr, & Porter, 1982) modeled by an adult; they also react with great interest to an adult who imitates their own actions (Field, 1977). The notion that early imitation corresponds to an infant's attempt to elicit a response from another person (Meltzoff & Moore, 1992) would suggest that infants not only expect reciprocity on the part of the social partner (as in peekaboo) but also try to elicit it themselves. Such social-affective expectations also translate into specific expectations about the world of people and that of inanimate objects (Legerstee, 1994). These various forms of emotional attunement and engagement in social action, and the clear separation between the social and inanimate world, are important deficits in individuals with autism of all ages (Klin, Jones, Schultz, Volkmar, & Cohen, 2002a, 2002b; Klin et al., 2003; Rogers & Bennetto, 2000; Volkmar, Carter, Grossman, & Klin, 1997).

As the infant approaches the end of the first year of life, there is an important shift from simply seeking others to trying to share a common focus of attention and to direct the other person's attention toward a desired target. These behaviors—so-called joint-attention skills (Mundy & Neal, 2000; Mundy & Sigman, 1989)—are important building blocks of language and communication, as well as of "theory of mind" skills (i.e., the capacity to attribute mental states such as beliefs, intentions, and motivations to others, and then to predict their behaviors on the basis of these internal states) (Carpenter & Tomasello, 2000; Mundy & Stella, 2000). All of these skills are greatly reduced in young children with autism (Baron-Cohen, 1995). Beginning in the second year with simple forms of role play (e.g., pretending to be asleep, pretending to be daddy), and becoming increasingly sophisticated in the next two years with instances of pretend social routines (e.g., playing with miniature people or dolls) and object substitution (e.g., pretending that an object is something other than it really is), pretend play is evidenced in typical young children (Fein, 1981). The absence of pretend play in young children with autism is one of the hallmarks of this condition in preschool years (Leslie, 1987).

As an integral part of social development, the early onset of communication skills builds on an overlapping body of developmental accomplishments. Thus, a child's orientation to social stimuli plays an essential role in his or her development of more sophisticated communicative skills. In fact, a child's ability to consider the attentional focus of another and to draw another's attention toward objects and events of mutual interest is a foundation for the development of language, social-conversational skills, and social relationships and is often firmly established within the first year of life. These capacities provide the foundation for a child to begin interpreting and sharing emotional states (which develops within the first 6 months of life), to begin interpreting and sharing intentions (which develops within the first 10 months of life), and to consider another's prior experiences and perspective in relation to events or conversational topics (which emerges within the second and third year of life). These capacities are evidenced by the emergence of role-play within symbolic play, a child's ability to convey information across contexts, and a child's ability to initiate communicative bids related to a listener's preferences (Carpenter & Tomasello, 2000).

At prelinguistic stages of language acquisition, a child's development of joint attention is typically evidenced by his or her ability to orient to a social partner, to coordinate and shift attention between people and objects, to share and interpret affect or emotional states, and eventually to use gestures and vocalizations paired with physical contact or gaze to deliberately send a message to another person. In assessing communicative competence, it is essential to recognize that a child's abilities to monitor the social environment by shifting his or her gaze between people and objects and to share his or her emotional state through facial expressions, gestures, and changes in vocal quality typically precede the developmental milestone of intentional communication. Prior to the development of verbal language, a child's capacity for joint attention also underlies his or her ability to communicate not only for need-based instrumental purposes (e.g., using push away or "give me" gestures to protest and make requests), but also for more social purposes (e.g., using showing or pointing gestures to comment, share observations, and relay experiences). Consequently, to simplify the assessment process by tallying the number of words and the emergence of expressive language milestones overlooks the many developmental processes that precede the emergence of single words and verbal language.

Next, as a child makes the transition to the use of expressive language as a primary means of communication, the capacity for joint attention facilitates the development of a more sophisticated and explicit system of communication. At this point in time, a child often experiences a rapid expansion of vocabulary and linguistic concepts, an emergence of more sophisticated sentence structures for the purposes of sharing intent and affect, and the use of additional strategies for establishing another's attention (e.g., calling out a caregiver's name) (Wetherby et al., 2000). Last, as a child approaches his or her third birthday and more advanced stages of language acquisition, the emergence of more sophisticated joint attention capacities typically involve communication about past and future events and enable a child to consider, in a sense, what information is novel, interesting, and important to the listener based on previous communicative exchanges with that communicative partner (Carpenter & Tomasello, 2000).

The symbolic development of gestures and language is an active process in which children acquire shared meanings based on interactions with people and experiences in their environment (Bates, 1979; Bloom, 1993; Lifter & Bloom, 1998). Several transitions capture the developmental path of typical children who are in the process of developing more sophisticated symbolic language skills to effectively communicate shared meanings with communicative partners. By the first year of life, a child typically makes a transition to intentional communication, a developmental shift toward the systematic use of conventional gestures (e.g., giving, waving, showing, and pointing), and vocalizations. Next, in the second year, a child makes the transition to early symbolic communication, as evidenced by a shift toward the acquisition of single-word vocabulary (e.g., first words, signs, or picture symbols), which serves a variety of communicative functions. Last, a child in the second and third year typically makes the transition to linguistic communication, as evidenced by the emergence of multiword combinations, early grammar, and simple conversational discourse. These transitions are also observed in a child's use of objects, which are used initially for conventional, functional purposes and then in symbolic play involving elaborate role-play. The subsequent growth in conversation abilities and representational play continue to be affected by continuously evolving capacities for joint attention, as evidenced in the acquisition of increasingly sophisticated linguistic and gestural means to clarify intent to the conversational or play partner (Wetherby et al., 2000). These verbal and nonverbal abilities serve increasingly demanding social functions, also becoming important tools to solve problems, to organize experiences, to plan and regulate behavior, and to regulate arousal and emotional state (Prizant, Wetherby, & Rydell, 2000).

ESSENTIAL ELEMENTS OF A CLINICAL ASSESSMENT OF TODDLERS AT RISK FOR AUTISM

The comprehensive developmental approach outlined above calls for a highly integrated, and to some extent necessarily overlapping, group of procedures aimed at obtaining information necessary for diagnostic determination and for outlining a comprehensive profile of assets and deficits needed to design and implement a program of treatment and intervention.

The first element is a thorough developmental assessment capable of describing and measuring the child's current intellectual and other resources. These measures should frame subsequent observations in terms of the child's current potential as well and inform decisions as to the kinds of intervention strategies from which the child is developmentally ready to profit. The overall goal of the developmental assessment is not only to establish a benchmark against which other measures and observations can be judged, but also to characterize the child's specific style of learning and relative assets that need to be capitalized upon in treatment.

The second element is a speech, language, and communication assessment. Particularly during early childhood, communication patterns are inextricably tied to global social development. It is, therefore, not surprising that this area of development is invariably impaired in children with autism, and represents a core aspect of assessment and possibly the most central area of intervention (Prizant et al., 2000; Wetherby et al., 2000).

The third essential element is the assessment of the child's demonstrated functional adjustment in day-to-day situations. Universally, children with autism have adaptive skills that significantly lag behind their best performance in laboratory-based evaluations (Carter et al., 1998). The discrepancy between intellectual potential and consistently displayed skills in naturalistic settings can be pronounced even within the context of the reduced parameters of toddler development, with some children failing to achieve skills that are normatively acquired in the first few months of life (Klin, Volkmar, & Sparrow, 1992). Given that children with autism typically acquire many skills, spontaneously or as result of structured intervention, but fail to use them in real life—indeed, difficulties in generalization are probably one of the most entrenched challenges in autism—it is crucial that detailed measures of adaptive behavior are obtained in such a way that a plan for addressing disparities between potential and real-life capacities is fully outlined for service providers.

The fourth essential element of assessment is what can be described as a diagnostic workup. This process should use and integrate the data of all of the other components of assessment to better understand the child's developmental history and current presentation. Although one aspect of this component is diagnostic assignment of a syndrome label—for example, based on *DSM-IV* (American Psychiatric Association [APA], 1994) or ICD-10 (World Health Organization [WHO], 1992)—this is hardly its most important role. Given the heterogeneity of autism along all dimensions (cognitive, social, and communication, in both display of normative skills and severity of symptoms), a diagnostic label (while necessary for communication among professionals and for deeming children eligible for specialized services) can hardly provide the basis for programmatic recommendations for intervention. Such recommendations are built upon detailed, individualized profiles of relative strengths and significant deficits revealed through comprehensive assessments of the kind described here. These four domains of assessment—developmental, communication, adaptive, and diagnostic—are supplemented by additional information that may help clinicians understand better the child's developmental vulnerabilities. Chief among these are aspects of self-regulation (which can be crucial in maximizing the effectiveness of learning strategies taught to the child) and genetic liability (which can further inform clinicians about the risk for autism and help them counsel the family as to recurrence rates in subsequent offspring).

Developmental Assessment

The developmental assessment focuses on measurements and descriptions of a child's various emerging skills and capacities in the context of a structured task-oriented interaction with an adult. For some young children with autism and related conditions, particularly those who have already experienced several months of structured intervention, this setting may enhance compliance and level of performance. For others, the structure of the setting may be too demanding and rigid. For example, they may have difficulty tolerating the proximity of the adult, sitting at a table and following the adult lead, or they may become overly focused on extraneous aspects of the environment or may engage in repetitive movements. For these children, great care has to be taken to modify the test administration without compromising its standardized presentation so as not to invalidate the usage of normed measures.

The purpose of developmental testing is to (1) assess current levels of skills in the cognitive, language, and motor domains relative to other children of the same age; (2) determine the presence of any sensory, attentional, motivational, or other factors that may interfere with the child's ability to learn and function adaptively; and (3) provide information necessary for diagnostic considerations and for the formulation of an individualized intervention plan.

The developmental assessment of young children with autism involves components similar to those included in the assessment of young children with other developmental disabilities. It includes a combination of structured instruments and nonstructured clinical observations of the child's responses to testing materials, as well as to the social and physical environment (Gilliam & Mayes, 2000; see also chapter 10). Just like other young children, children with autism are less predictable, less guided by social rules, and more likely to follow their immediate interests (e.g., an attractive toy) or needs (e.g., being hungry or restless) than older children. Hence the need to keep the testing situation interesting and engaging from the child's standpoint, while moving seamlessly through individual tasks and transitions. Young children with autism, however, also present with a set of unique challenges originating from their social and communicative disability. These challenges can significantly interfere with their ability to conform to testing requirements, which in turn can have a deleterious impact on their performance. These challenges include a diminished ability to orient to naturally occurring social stimuli such as voice or facial expressions and to both initiate social contact and respond consistently to the bids of others (Lord, 1995; Osterling & Dawson, 1994; Stone, 1997). Specifically, they are unlikely to respond to the kinds of behaviors that adults typically use to attract the attention of young children (e.g., calling the child's name). They are also unlikely to respond consistently to adult efforts to guide their attention to a specific object or to guide the adult to their object of attention or desire (Mundy, Sigman, & Kasari, 1990). Although children with autism may smile with joy upon completion of a puzzle or a similar task, they usually do not share their enjoyment with others, thus making it difficult to use these episodes of success to promote compliance with additional testing. Physical means such as gentle touch, or explicit requesting supported by gesture (e.g., "Look at me") may need to be used to redirect the child's attention. In general, therefore, there is a need to make the requirements of the task quite explicit and intrinsically rewarding, particularly because the child may not make eye contact or profit from facial expressions of encouragement and support.

An additional challenge to the examiner comes from the great heterogeneity, in terms of developmental capacities and social presentation, evidenced in young children with autism. They differ in terms of their ability to regulate arousal and attention, availability of verbal and gestural means of communication, responsivity to social overtures, curiosity about the environment, and level of sensory-seeking and self-stimulatory behaviors. Poor regulation of arousal may lead to severe tantrums in response to novelty. Attentional difficulties may manifest as glancing at random objects or overfocus on parts of objects. Constantly shifting attention may result in visual focus that is not long enough to register the nature of a task or to complete a brief learning cycle (e.g., appreciating the various materials involved in a given task or imitation of an adult's action on an object). Such challenges can be equally or more disruptive in the social and communication domain. Some children may not initiate or tolerate eye contact, withdrawing upon more direct approaches on the part of the adult. The absence of speech or the presence of language that is primarily echolalic and noncommunicative poses difficulties in both directing and maintaining the child's attention and explaining the requirements of a given task or in modeling or supporting effective performance behaviors. Although self-stimulatory behaviors are more likely to be present in children over 3 years of age, a wide range of stereotypic behaviors may already be present at a younger age, including sensory-seeking or ritualistic behaviors (e.g., focusing on lights, exploring objects for their texture, spinning a top or anything that is spinnable) and motor mannerisms (e.g., flicking objects over and over). Such behaviors may divert the child's attention to extraneous aspects of the environment or diminish the child's ability to handle objects in a way that facilitates task performance. Naturally occurring reinforcers that can be very effective with typical and with nonautistic developmentally delayed children (e.g., social praise, a sense of mastery) may not be of intrinsic interest to children with autism. In the absence of such forms of motivation, there may be a need for tangible reinforcers such as edibles or controlled opportunities to play with a favorite toy. Even having the time to engage in a repetitive activity (e.g., spinning a top) may promote optimal performance.

A number of developmental scales are available for testing children under the age of 3 years (see chapter 10 for reviews). While some of the scales rely purely on parental report, others involve direct sampling of the child's skills across a number of relevant domains. Only the latter are discussed here, given that it is essential that direct assessment of developmental skills is performed. Scales based on parental report can be used to further contextualize and validate clinic-based data, or if for any reason direct assessment cannot be conducted. Direct observation is necessary not only to obtain information about levels of performance (e.g., scores) but also to document styles of learning and a wide range of factors that impact on the child's learning potential. Two developmental scales have been used most frequently in the assessment of young children with autism: the Bayley Scales of Infant Development II (Bayley) (Bayley, 1993) and the Mullen Scales of Early Learning (Mullen) (Mullen, 1995). Although both scales allow for scoring some low-frequency or difficult-to-elicit behaviors based on parental report, these are primarily performance-based scales assessing the child's development in several domains. This is done in the context of direct interaction with the child around goal-oriented activities.

The Bayley is the most widely used measure of developmental skills in both clinical and research settings. Its scales range from 1 to 42 months of age. The test consists of three main components: the Mental Development Index (MDI), Psycho-motor Development Index (PDI), and Behavior Rating Scale (BRS). While the MDI provides information about the child's problem-solving and language skills, the PDI assesses the child's fine and gross motor skills. The BRS is a form designed to be used by the evaluators to rate the child's behavior during the testing, including attentional capacities, social engagement, affect, and emotions, as well as the quality of movement and motor control. Although the Bayley provides a method for obtaining age-equivalent scores for four facets of development, namely cognitive, language, social, and motor, empirical support for the validity of these facet scores is limited (Bayley, 1993). The Bayley takes about 60 minutes to administer for children over 15 months. Despite its excellent statistical properties (e.g., Bayley, 1993) and its sensitivity to high-risk childhood conditions (e.g., Allessandri, Bendersky, & Lewis, 1998; Ross, 1985), the Bayley's value for the assessment of young children with autism can be limited. The primary reason for this is that the summary scores are likely to be averages of highly discrepant skills in the various domains, thus creating a great misrepresentation of the child's developmental skills. For example, the MDI summarizes scores in nonverbal problem solving and expressive and receptive language, as well as personal-social functioning. Children with autism typically present with a highly scattered profile of skills, with higher level nonverbal problem-solving skills (e.g., color matching, assembling puzzles), lower level expressive language skills (although this score may still be inflated due to these children's higher single-word vocabulary relative to typically lower sentence construction skills), and lowest scores in receptive language (due to their difficulty in responding consistently to spoken language). Thus any composite index score summarizing performance across a number of domains is likely to misrepresent the child's developmental profile. In many respects, the average of these scores will hardly convey the most important information to the special educators whose mission is to address the child's needs while capitalizing on the child's strengths. For this purpose, the profile, in all its variability and scatter, is more informative than overall scores. Similarly, in the motor domain, a child may have relatively good gross motor skills but score poorly on fine motor tasks due to difficulties in motor imitation inherent to autism (Rogers & Pennington, 1991).

For these reasons, the popularity of the Mullen has increased dramatically in the past few years. The Mullen is a multidomain assessment scale that emphasizes the measurement of distinct abilities rather than developmental summaries. Its range is from birth to 62 months of age. It contains five domains: visual reception (primarily nonverbal visual discrimination, perceptual categorization, and memory), receptive language, expressive language, fine motor, and gross motor. The Mullen yields standard *t* scores in all five domains and an early learning composite score based on the first four domains. The Mullen takes between 15 and 60 minutes to administer, depending on the child's age. Its separation of visual perceptual abilities from expressive and receptive language, as well as the separation of fine and gross motor skills, serves very well the assessment of young children with autism who, as noted, typically display highly scattered profiles.

Speech, Language, and Communication Assessment

The assessment of speech, language, and communicative development should include not only a determination of a child's achievement of early language milestones (e.g., acquisition of specific gestures, single words, and multiword combinations), but also a child's ability to use these communicative strategies at the frequency one might expect given his or her language stage, to both initiate and respond to communicative bids and to effectively convey a variety of messages to a communicative partner (e.g., requesting, protesting, showing off, commenting, and requesting information). These latter aspects of development are often referred to as the development of communicative competence. Communicative competence is highly correlated with positive long-term outcomes for children with autism, especially in longitudinal studies documenting the effectiveness of early intervention for toddlers at risk (Garfin & Lord, 1986; Koegel, Koegel, Yoshen, & McNerney, 1999; NRC, 2001; Venter, Lord, & Schopler, 1992).

The development of communicative competence is best viewed as a set of capacities that arise from the interplay between social-cognitive and language development. These include the capacities to establish and follow the attentional focus of communicative partners, to maintain a communicative interaction by initiating a high frequency of communicative bids and responding to the communicative bids of others, to use more sophisticated gestures and symbolic language, to recognize and repair communicative breakdowns, and to respond to contextual and interpersonal cues (Carpenter & Tomasello, 2000; Wetherby, Prizant, & Hutchinson, 1998). Several core challenges may compromise this developmental process. These difficulties fall under two primary dimensions: (a) the capacity for establishing shared attention (i.e., joint attention skills), which underlies a child's ability to follow another's attentional focus and establish shared attention, share affect, express intentions, and engage in reciprocal social interactions (e.g., vocal and gestural imitation as well as nonverbal and verbal communicative exchanges); and (b) the capacity for symbol use, which refers to a child's acquisition of gestures learned within reciprocal exchanges with caregivers (e.g., pointing, giving, and waving), a child's acquisition of symbolic word forms and more advanced linguistic forms, and a child's ability to engage in appropriate use of objects (e.g., functional object use and representational play schemes) (Wetherby et al., 2000).

These core challenges provide the clinician with a set of expectations to determine whether a child is at risk of having autism (NRC, 2001). First, children with autism are likely to exhibit limitations in coordinating attention and affect, a vulnerability reflected in difficulties orienting and attending to a social partner, shifting gaze between people and objects in order to monitor another person's attentional focus and to share intentions, sharing affect or emotional states with others, following and drawing another person's attention toward objects or events for the purpose of sharing experiences, and participating in reciprocal interactions over multiple turns within a social interactional exchange, especially when communicative breakdowns occur (Prizant & Wetherby, 1987). Second, although children with autism may exhibit an ability to send a message to a communicative partner, they typically exhibit a very restricted range of communicative functions, as evidenced by a reduced frequency of communication for more social purposes (Wetherby, Prizant, & Hutchinson, 1998). Thus a child may exhibit a variety of nonverbal and verbal strategies for requesting objects (e.g., favorite toys and snacks) and protesting nonpreferred activities, but his or her ability to show off, seek praise, initiate social routines, comment, share experiences, and express emotions may be significantly reduced in relation to typical children or children with language delays at the same stage of language acquisition. Last, children at risk of autism are likely to demonstrate difficulties inferring another's perspective or emotional state. These difficulties, though quite subtle within the first 3 years, are often evidenced in a compromised ability to respond appropriately to others' emotional expressions (e.g., gestures, faces, vocal quality, and words) as well as in a difficulty to recognize topics of conversation that are of interest to another person. Underlying these various challenges are the ubiquitous difficulties in establishing and maintaining shared attention and in interpreting and expressing intentions (Carpenter & Tomasello, 2000; Wetherby et al., 2000). Thus, identifying a child's relative strengths and areas of need in this domain of functioning early in development will likely provide a more pinpointed course of action and may, likewise, have a positive impact on a child's future developmental course.

Similarly, there is a strong correlation between early foundation skills in joint attention and communicative reciprocity and the eventual development of more sophisticated and conventional gestures and expressive language (Wetherby et al., 2000). Thus, a child's early symbolic communication should be assessed primarily within opportunities for that child to demonstrate a capacity to establish and share intentions with others using target words and language forms. For example, although a child may present with a broad repertoire of single words on formal testing or in other isolated contexts, he or she may have significant difficulty using these words to share communicative intents. Thus, these words cannot be considered well established, as they may actually reflect minimal semantic understanding and will likely be poorly generalized across environments and communicative partners. As a result, assessment of a child's symbolic capacities should be conducted across contexts (e.g., formal testing, caregiver interview, and naturalistic observation) and with an understanding of typical developmental processes in mind.

Challenges in the capacity for symbol use typically compromise the development of very specific capacities in the speech and language profile of children with autism. Thus, the clinician conducting the assessment should have a strong awareness of these aspects of communicative functioning. First, a child with autism is likely to exhibit limitations in his or her use of conventional gestures (e.g., showing, waving, and pointing) and other nonverbal conventional communicative means (e.g., head nods and headshakes) during the speech, language, and communication assessment. This vulnerability often results in a reliance on very concrete and presymbolic motor-based gestures such as manipulating a caregiver's hand, leading another person toward a desired item, and reenacting desired actions. Additionally, this limitation often leads to maladaptive patterns of communication such as the use of less desirable communicative means or challenging behaviors for communication (e.g., screaming, aggression, tantrums). Second, a child with autism may exhibit unconventional vocal development at a very young age. This vulnerability may be marked by a paucity of vocal communication or the use of difficult-to-read, unconventional sounds. Vocal play or vocal turn taking is also an area of vulnerability secondary to limitations in reciprocal imitation of both nonverbal and verbal behaviors (Wetherby et al., 2000). Third, a child with autism may develop more unconventional verbal behavior (e.g., immediate or delayed forms of echolalia) (Rydell & Prizant, 1995). Last, a child with autism is likely to demonstrate significant limitations in functional object use and symbolic play, as evidenced by a tendency to use objects in an unconventional manner as well as limitations in the underlying symbolic capacity to represent social events through basic role play (Wolfberg, 1999). As noted, deficits in symbolic play are often considered hallmarks of the social disability found in children with autism in the preschool years. Thus, recognition of these vulnerabilities is critical for assessing risk prior to 3 years of age as well as establishing a course of intervention and therapeutic management.

A variety of both formal and informal strategies should be used for collecting information on a child's communicative competence, including direct behavioral sampling, naturalistic observation across contexts, caregiver interview, and ongoing monitoring and assessment (Prizant & Bailey, 1992). While formal testing can be useful for assessing the structural aspects of language (e.g., a child's gestural repertoire, depth of vocabulary, and speech sound repertoire), assessment of a child's use of language actually requires observations in less structured settings, making it possible for the clinician to observe the child's ability to spontaneously initiate communicative bids.

In this context, the utility of a variety of formal language assessment batteries designed to identify language delays when assessing young children with autism is questionable, given that these measures typically focus on specific aspects of language development (e.g., vocabulary, grammar, and linguistic form) rather than providing a context to assess a child's ability to use communicative strategies across contexts, communicative partners, and for a variety of communicative purposes. Additionally, many formal language assessments have, at least historically, been less suited for assessing the conventionality of a child's nonverbal communicative means (e.g., gestures, facial expressions, etc.) (NRC, 2001). As a result, the protocol adopted should capitalize on the available tools designed specifically for children with autism, and which focus on abilities such as sharing attention (i.e., joint attention skills) and using conventional gesture.

In this light, the Communication and Symbolic Behavior Scales (CSBS; Wetherby & Prizant, 1993) is a standardized assessment tool for children whose functional communication age is between 8 and 24 months (chronological ages from 9 months to 6 years). This tool provides a format to engage a child in a semistructured sampling of behavior. The framework of this tool establishes a developmental profile of communicative functions, gestural communicative means, vocal communicative means, social reciprocity, social-affective signaling, and symbolic behavior.

Unlike traditional assessment tools, the CSBS provides specific guidelines for collecting a spontaneous rather than elicited communicative sample.

This behavioral sample can then be complemented with a means to gather information about the child's communicative competence in more naturalistic environments, that is, the CSBS Caregiver Questionnaire (Wetherby & Prizant, 1993). Additionally, the MacArthur Communicative Development Inventories (Fenson et al., 1993) can be incorporated into the assessment protocol as a method for gathering information regarding a child's use of gestures, comprehension, and single-word vocabulary (e.g., familiar objects, actions, attributes, people, etc.) and, eventually, comprehension and use of early semantic relations and grammatical structures. Caregivers at home or a child's early intervention team members can complete this questionnaire.

Assessment of Adaptive Functioning

Adaptive functioning refers to capacities for personal and social self-sufficiency in real-life situations. The importance of this component of the clinical assessment cannot be overemphasized. Its aim is to obtain a measure of child's typical patterns of functioning in familiar and representative environments, such as the home or day care environment, which may contrast markedly with patterns of behavior and skills observed in the more artificial environment of the clinic. As noted, adaptive functioning is an essential indicator of the extent to which the child is able to utilize his or her potential (as demonstrated during the more formal sections of the evaluation) in the process of adaptation to environmental demands. More specifically, it delineates the challenges faced by service providers in helping the child to generalize from the display of skills that are learned through adult scaffolding or in structured intervention to skills that are consistently shown in response to typical demands in more naturalistic settings, a core difficulty in individuals with autism not only in early childhood but throughout the lifespan (Klin et al., 2002a).

The most widely employed instrument to assess adaptive behavior is the Vineland Adaptive Behavior Scales (Sparrow, Balla, & Cicchetti,

1984). The Vineland assesses capacities for self-sufficiency in various domains of functioning, including communication (receptive, expressive, and written language), daily living skills (personal, domestic, and community), socialization (interpersonal relationships, play and leisure time, and coping skills), and motor skills (gross and fine). These capacities are assessed on the basis of the child's current daily functioning, using a semistructured interview administered to a parent or primary caregiver. Besides characterizing and measuring a child's profile of adaptive challenges, the Vineland has also been shown to have diagnostic value (Gillham, Carter, Volkmar, & Sparrow, 2000; Klin et al., 1992; Volkmar et al., 1987; Volkmar, Carter, Sparrow, & Cicchetti, 1993), and there are supplementary norms for children with autism (Carter et al., 1998), although not as yet for children under the age of 3 years.

Although the Vineland comes in three editions, the most relevant one is the expanded form (Sparrow et al., 1984), given that it can be used for the development of individual education planning. Using a child's developmental level as a point of reference, this form makes it possible for the clinician to plan intervention on the basis of skills that the child should have acquired given his or her cognitive level. Because the items of the Vineland were selected on the basis of their immediate relevance to real-life adaptation, the skills described therein can be readily incorporated into the child's intervention plan (see Carter, Gillham, Sparrow, & Volkmar, 1996, for a sample case exemplifying this profile obtained with the Vineland Expanded Edition).

The Vineland is currently undergoing revision and restandardization. A major effort is being made to expand greatly the areas of coverage in the scales that could be valuable to clinicians and researchers in the field of autism. For example, the number of items in the socialization domain that are applicable to infants and toddlers has been greatly expanded with a view to providing wider distributions and more sampling of this central aspect of development in autism and related conditions. This process is also making possible the development of screening instruments based on deficits in the normative acquisition of adaptive behaviors, an approach that is likely to enrich the currently available armory of instruments based on early symptoms (Baird et al., 2000; Robins et al., 2001), and to further validate screening instruments that aim at integrating both symptom-based and normatively acquired skills (Briggs-Gowan et al., 2001) in the detection of early problems in socialization.

Profiles of toddlers with autism on the Vineland are marked by great scatter across the various domains, typically including significant deficits in the socialization domain, particularly in interpersonal relationships, and relatively higher daily living and motor skills. Overall scores in the communication domain can be misleading as a result of inflated scores on the written subdomain, given that in this age bracket such skills refer primarily to interest in and knowledge of letters and numbers, which is often observed in young children with autism. Thus it is important to carefully analyze subdomain profiles and, in many cases, to conduct a more thorough item analysis.

Diagnostic Workup

It is important to provide parents with a diagnostic formulation that captures the constellation of difficulties exhibited by their child. A diagnostic formulation, in addition to a diagnostic label, should provide some information regarding the nature and intensity of needed remediating services, as well as some indication of outcome. Parents are often perplexed about their interactions with their autistic child and often experience a sense of great anxiety, isolation, and at times guilt. By capturing the child's difficulties within the context of clinical science, parents are typically reassured despite the initial and the continuous hardships associated with the announcement. Given the great availability of information about autism (e.g., through the Internet) and dissemination of knowledge through the media, some parents are already well informed about the characteristics of autism and have already considered the possibility that their child has the condition. A discussion with professionals serves to sanction their concerns while moving their thoughts in the direction of a plan of action. This discussion also helps them correct misleading information that they may have obtained informally, such as, for example, information about nonconventional (and potentially harmful) forms of treatment. In many situations, a diagnosis also helps parents in their effort to document eligibility for services, recover some of their medical expenses, connect with other parents and resources that can be of help, and avail themselves of a straightforward and well-proven strategy to advocate for their child's treatment program.

Clearly, to have a child with disabilities is fraught with mixed emotions and anxieties, but, particularly in light of advances in clinical science, it makes little sense to withhold this information from parents and thus virtually preclude a plan of immediate action that is now known to be absolutely necessary to maximize the child's potential (Filipe et al., 1999; NRC, 2001; Volkmar et al., 1999). It is, nevertheless, equally important to appreciate the limitations of diagnostic labels and to share this information with parents. The vast heterogeneity witnessed in autism and related conditions (in terms of developmental patterns, challenges, and outcome), the child-specific nature of intervention programs that need to capitalize on individual strengths while addressing the child's needs, the rapid and variable rate of growth in the first few years of life, and the individual nature of response to treatment are all factors that need to be explored with parents in the context of a diagnostic discussion about their child. In fact, a label is best provided at the end of an exhaustive description of the child's profile of development and challenges (Rutter, 1978), when diagnostic categories can be discussed as ways to best capture (or not) the child's history and current presentation. In this discussion, it is also important to share with parents the limitations of current nosologic knowledge, and the extent to which diagnostic assignments are predictive of future diagnostic formulations and the individualized factors pertinent to this prediction (Lord, 1995). This discussion sets the stage for outlining the most important aspect of this experience, namely the translation of findings into an individualized, comprehensive, and practical intervention plan (Klin et al., 1997). By conceptualizing diagnostic assignment in young children as first and foremost a statement about the child's present challenges, and by highlighting the need for a conservative approach (i.e., it is better to be more than less concerned at this age), the diagno-

sis is more likely to energize parents and involve them in the creation of a plan for action.

The diagnostic process needs to integrate every aspect of the child revealed through the assessment (Lord & Risi, 2000). Cognitive level frames expectations as to social, communicative, and play skills. Speech and language levels qualify difficulties in social interaction, learning, and communication. Levels of adaptive functioning reveal discrepancies between demonstrated potential and real-life functional adjustment, highlighting challenges in spontaneous adjustment, particularly in the social domain, as well as areas for focal intervention when specific adaptive behaviors have not been mastered despite sufficient cognitive skills. This body of knowledge provides the necessary canvas for a careful delineation of departures from normalcy, in terms of both developmental history and current presentation. The diagnostic process is by necessity composed of two complementary strategies of data acquisition. First, parents need to provide a detailed view of their child's history and current representative behaviors. Second, direct observations are necessary to explore the parents' concerns and to obtain an independent sampling of the child's social, communication, and play behaviors, as well as other behavioral patterns related to exploration of the environment, self-regulation and self-stimulation, and reaction to environment stimuli.

The first part of the diagnostic process is thus to involve parents as a welcome and important source of information about the given child. Well before the visit to the clinic, parents should be engaged to provide information about their child. This process primes them to think about developmental history, allows them to consult materials (e.g., videotapes, baby books) that can refresh their memory and to solicit the thoughts of other pertinent adults (e.g., grandparents, day care providers), promotes more detached observations of the child in naturalistic settings, and otherwise prepares them for the kind of interviews that they will complete during the evaluation. One efficient way of accomplishing this goal is to provide parents with detailed forms that include developmental inventories (e.g., information on gestation, birth, developmental milestones, typical patterns of normative behaviors, and lists of developmental concerns). Such inventories may also include screening instruments for the purpose of further preparing the clinicians to explore specific areas of concern. Additional areas to be covered include medical information, behaviors or symptoms of grave concern to parents, and family history (given the need to explore genetic liabilities).

Many young children have already been seen by other professionals (e.g., developmental pediatricians, Birth to Three providers) prior to the more specialized developmental disabilities evaluation. Their findings and insights are important and need to be considered, as is information about any forms of intervention and the child's rate of progress as a result of treatment. Collectively, all of this information can promote greater reliability of parents as informants, save time during direct contact, and prioritize further direct interviews to elaborate, clarify, or otherwise substantiate areas of specific concern.

From a diagnostic perspective, direct interviews with parents are aimed at collecting a body of information on social, communication, play, and other forms of behavioral functioning that are of particular importance in diagnostic formulation. Although this can be achieved more informally, to ensure that major symptom areas are covered in conversation with parents, there are specific instruments that help structure these interviews to cover all relevant behavioral features. Chief among these is the Autism Diagnostic Interview–Revised (ADI-R; Lord, Rutter, & LeCouteur, 1994). This instrument was developed as a way of standardizing diagnostic procedures in multisite genetic research projects (Lord, 1997). It follows a semistructured format of interview with the parent or primary caregiver and includes an exhaustive list of items related to onset patterns, communication, social development and play, and restricted patterns of interests and behaviors that are pertinent to the diagnosis of autism. Besides standardizing the acquisition of developmental history and current presentation, the ADI-R also provides a diagnostic algorithm that is keyed to *DSM-IV* (APA, 1994) criteria for autism.

Although the ADI-R offers these various advantages, it is important to note that in the case of young children with autism, it does have some limitations relative to the gold standard of diagnosis by experienced clinicians (Lord, 1995). For example, it tends to overdiagnose children with significant cognitive delays as having autism at age 2 years, but to underdiagnose a small proportion of children who at age 2 do not show symptoms in the restricted patterns of interests and behaviors (thus failing to meet *DSM-IV* criteria for autism). The ADI-R contrasts somewhat unfavorably with the stability obtained with diagnostic assignment obtained by experienced clinicians. For example, in one study (Lord & Risi, 2000), clinicians' diagnoses of autism at ages 2 and 3 remained the same for about 70% of children, with the majority of the other children maintaining a diagnosis within the autism spectrum (i.e., PDD-NOS). Clinicians' diagnosis of the subthreshold PDD-NOS was much less stable. For about 40% of those children at age 3 years, the diagnosis was shifted to autism. This may have occurred because they were initially speaking and this fact masked somewhat the level of their social disability, which became clearer later on. The other 60% or so moved out of the spectrum of autism conditions (possibly because their symptoms improved). These data are fairly consistent with data on clinicians' diagnostic assignment in regard to older children (Klin, Lang, Cicchetti, & Volkmar, 2000). While experienced clinicians' interrater agreement for the diagnosis of autism versus a non-PDD condition is very high, the rates are much lower for distinctions among the PDDs (e.g., between autism and Asperger syndrome or PDD-NOS).

In many respects, the limitations of the ADI-R in the case of children under 3 years speak to the difficulties in using parental reports as sources of specific information relevant to a diagnosis of autism. What might not be obvious signs of abnormality to a parent in the way the child explores the environment or plays with toys may be seen very differently in direct observation by an experienced clinician. Hence the importance of both framing questions in a way that will make sense from the perspective of a parent's experience with the child, and supplementing this information with direct observations. For example, parents may answer "yes" to the question of whether the child responds to his or her name being called, although to obtain such a response the parent may have gotten used to coming very close to the child and intruding upon what he or she is doing. In contrast, they are very likely to answer in the negative if asked, "Does your child usually respond to a neutral statement that does not involve active and intrusive pursuit of the child's attention?" (Lord, 1995). This item has been found to be most helpful in differentiating children with autism-spectrum disorders from other clinic referrals (Lord, 1995), together with an item that focuses on the degree to which a child spontaneously directs other people's attention (e.g., by gesturing or vocalizing in a way that is directed at the adult).

These issues can be largely overcome through further probing on the part of the well-trained interviewer and through direct observations of the child. In other words, the ADI-R limitations are vastly outstripped by its advantages if the instrument is used as one component (not the only one) of the diagnostic process. The ADI-R probes cover primarily four areas of diagnostic information. The early development domain focuses on onset patterns including developmental milestones and age of recognition of specific concerns. The communication domain covers information on speech and language acquisition, and typical autistic symptomatology (e.g., immediate echolalia, stereotyped utterances and delayed echolalia, social vocalization and reciprocal conversation, nonverbal communication and attention to the human voice). The social development and play domain covers aspects of gaze behavior (e.g., eye contact, directing other people's attention through pointing), sensitivity to and appropriateness to social approaches, nature and range of facial expressions, prosocial behaviors (e.g., offering comfort), peer interaction, and play patterns (e.g., imitative play, pretend play alone and with others). The restricted interests and behaviors domain covers behaviors associated with circumscribed interests, unusual preoccupations, repetitive use of objects or interest in parts of objects, ritualistic behavior, unusual sensory interests, and motor mannerisms. A toddler version of the ADI-R is available that serves to eliminate items that are not applicable to this age group, while offering detail on behaviors that are of particular interest

to clinicians working with children in this age bracket (Lord, LeCouteur, & Rutter, 1991).

The second part of the diagnostic process involves direct observation of the child. Just as one cannot take clinic-based data in isolation from information obtained through parents and others who observe the child in more naturalistic environments, so do parental reports need to be validated in terms of direct observations of the child's behavioral presentation. Parents cannot be expected to ground their accounts on the basis of extensive experience with children with normative and socially disordered development, nor can they be expected to recognize early signs of derailed socialization. The corollary of this statement is that clinical assessment of toddlers at risk for autism requires extensive knowledge of, as well as training and experience with, typically developing infants and toddlers as well as developmentally disabled young children. With probably no other age group is this expertise more necessary than in the assessment of toddlers at risk. As autism is first and foremost a social disorder (Waterhouse et al., 1996), it is in the context of spontaneous social interaction that deviant patterns of socialization become most tangible. The sampling of spontaneous social, communication, and play skills is probably best done in the context of a diagnostic play session. This should be set in as naturalistic a fashion as can be contrived in the context of a clinic environment. One standardized approach to create such an environment is through the use of the Autism Diagnostic Observation Schedule (ADOS; Lord, Rutter, DiLavore, & Risi, 1999). Just like the ADI-R, the ADOS was developed with a view to standardize diagnostic procedures in multisite genetic projects (Lord, 1997). The instruments are complementary in that one focuses on parents as sources of information (ADI-R), whereas the other focuses on direct observations (ADOS).

The ADOS consists of a series of playlike "presses" that generate opportunities for the toddler to display his or her spontaneous patterns of social, communicative, and play behaviors. It starts with a free play session that allows the observer to sample the child's preferential patterns of attention (e.g., focusing on people versus things) and play behaviors (e.g., focus on cause-

and-effect versus representational play materials or solitary versus socially engaged play). Opportunities for showing sensitivity to social cues (e.g., calling the child's name, trying to elicit a smile without touching the child), joint-attention behaviors (e.g., pointing to distant objects, creating highly attractive stimuli such as soap bubbles and waiting for the child to bring another person's attention to the bubbles), patterns of request and showing (e.g., bringing in attractive objects and then placing them out of the child's reach), imitative skills and familiarity with social routines (e.g., modeling actions on miniatures, creating a pretend birthday party), among others, are all created in a playful and seamless fashion. These observations are coded according to detailed criteria in the various clusters defining autism. In the language and communication domain, the sample of communicative behaviors is coded in terms of frequency of vocal approaches, intonation of voice, presence of echolalia and idiosyncratic uses of words and phrases, use of the other person's body to communicate, and gestural communication. In the social domain, eye contact and sensitivity to gaze cues, sensitivity to the other person's facial expressions, range of emotional expressions, integration of communicative behaviors, giving and showing behaviors, and joint-attention skills, among other social behaviors, are coded. Play behaviors are coded in terms of presence of pretend skills, whereas stereotyped behaviors and restricted interests are coded in terms of unusual sensory interests (e.g., feeling of texture, focusing on lights or shiny objects), motor mannerisms (e.g., hand flapping, finger mannerisms), and repetitive or perseverative behaviors (e.g., spinning wheels or lining things up).

The ADOS provides a diagnostic algorithm that is keyed to *DSM-IV* (APA, 1994). In contrast to the ADI-R, which only makes possible a distinction between autism and a non-PDD condition, the ADOS makes a distinction between autism and PDD-NOS on the basis of level of severity. ADOS data on 2-year-olds (Lord & Risi, 2000; Lord et al., 1999) showed that if anything, ADOS results were more predictive of a diagnosis of autism at age 5 than the parental reports obtained with the ADI-R. However, more higher-functioning toddlers (e.g., those with some language) were sometimes misidentified as nonautistic. Importantly, summaries of impressions were more effective than specific behaviors (e.g., presence or absence of joint-attention skills), which appeared to be influenced greatly by level of cognitive functioning (DiLavore, Lord, & Rutter, 1995). Overall impressions of a child's social reciprocity were more consistently associated with a diagnosis across development than with scoring of specific behaviors. In other words, there were no simple tests for autism that were equally effective across age ranges in the discrimination of autism from other developmental disorders (e.g., global developmental delay). Nevertheless, by standardizing the way the data are collected and coded and by creating summary impressions, the ADOS is of great help in the diagnostic process.

Our experience with this instrument is consistent with the benefits expected from using a quasi-experimental and yet observational tool to collect samples of spontaneous social, communicative, and play behaviors. By observing from close proximity a child's initial exploration of the room, there are opportunities to experience the extent to which the adult is a salient aspect of the child's environment, as well as to observe unusual preferential patterns of attention (e.g., to parts of objects, ceiling lights, or reflective or shiny surfaces). By using "presses" for social interaction, one may observe the child's sensitivity to social cues (e.g., exaggerated tone of voice, gaze cues, pointing, facial gestures, and posture) and social context (e.g., social referencing behaviors; Emde, 1992). By creating exciting situations and then withdrawing or distancing objects of the child's desire, one may observe the child's repertoire of requesting, giving, and showing behaviors. By eliciting play and modeling actions on miniatures, one may observe the child's capacity for imitation at different levels of social sophistication (e.g., action on physical object, pretend action on representational object, social action). Within this wealth of sampled behaviors, the ADOS scoring criteria force the clinician to cover core areas of autistic symptomatology. It is still the case that the sampled behaviors are as meaningful as the clinician is knowledgeable and trained to recognize them as such. Thus, usage of the instrument without a thorough grounding in normative child development and without expertise in autistic social behaviors in young children is unlikely to generate equally useful information.

Diagnostic Formulation

The main reason for developmental disabilities evaluations is to give parents and service providers a practical, specific, and comprehensive set of guidelines for intervention. Even when parents present as seeking primarily a diagnosis, an isolated diagnostic label can be both unhelpful and disheartening. A more constructive approach is to frame, from the outset, the purpose of the evaluation as a way of delineating a detailed profile of assets and deficits exhibited by the child relative to other children of the same age and/or developmental level. By focusing on how the observations and measures obtained in the evaluation are translated into a specific plan of action, parents are encouraged to go beyond a diagnosis, to translate some of the inevitable anxiety into advocacy with very specific goals and timelines, and thus to reach a broader understanding of their child's condition.

The setting for the discussion of this information is the parent conference that should follow the evaluation. Parents come to these conferences with different sets of expectations, needs, intrafamily cohesion, and views, among other family-specific concerns and resiliencies. The clinical approach extended to the child should also encompass the entire family, prioritizing what to focus on, how much, and in what manner. Some families might welcome as much detail as possible, whereas others become easily overwhelmed with lengthy discussions. With that in mind, it is essential that the clinicians treat the parent conference as an opportunity to establish an ongoing relationship with the family, so that the inevitable questions and requests for clarifications that will follow the initial meeting can be addressed in a timely fashion. While some formats may be helpful to some families (e.g., when every team member provides an exhaustive account of results and implications for intervention), it can be indeed overwhelming to others. This fine tuning, just like the evaluation itself, needs to be tailored to the individual characteristics of a given child and

family, an important factor to consider in order to maximize the effectiveness of the team as a whole. A rule of thumb is to consider what seems to be the most helpful approach to maximize the parents' understanding of their child and their effectiveness as advocates for services. A thorough document in the form of a clinical report should follow, summarizing observations and findings and providing an extensive program of intervention building on the child's strengths while addressing the child's needs. Reevaluations aimed at gauging rate of progress after a reasonable period of time (e.g., 1 year for a toddler) are excellent ways of nurturing a relationship with parents and conveying to them a sense of support and partnership in the journey they are about to embark on. As the team produces a clinical report, it is essential that sufficient detail about practical recommendations be provided, as such reports not only summarize findings to parents but also, and quite frequently, serve as blueprints of goals and how to achieve them to special educators and others involved in the child's care.

Other Areas of Assessment

Although the decision as to whether to pursue additional areas of assessment is child specific, the following considerations should be covered when making such a decision. The first consideration is whether there should be a medical follow-up. Although autism and related conditions are developmental disorders with strong neurobiological and genetic underpinnings, exhaustive medical workups usually have limited clinical benefit (Klin et al., 1997). Therefore, in the absence of clinical indicators, brain and metabolic studies are unlikely to be helpful. Nevertheless, a small number of medical exams should be considered. These include hearing assessments (this has to be done for any child with speech, language, and communication impairments), blood screening for fragile X syndrome (because a small number of individuals with autism also exhibit fragile X syndrome), and a child neurology assessment if there is any concern about possible absence spells (e.g., staring into the distance for long periods, being irresponsive to calls and touch). The neurology assessment may be necessary to rule out seizure disorders or focal abnormalities. When there is a family history of mental retardation or the presence of cognitive delays and dysmorphic features a visit to a geneticist may be warranted to rule out a possible genetic syndrome of mental retardation.

After general medical consideration, the second important consideration for additional assessment relates to family history (and related genetic liabilities). As noted, autism has a strong genetic basis, with recurrence rates of maybe 2 to 5% for a similar condition, with rates higher still for more broadly defined social disabilities or learning difficulties (Rutter, 2000). Parents of toddlers are often considering having more children or may be already quite anxious about the developmental status of a younger sibling (whether or not there are reasons for concern). By systematically collecting data about genetic liabilities while being knowledgeable about up-to-date information on the genetic basis of autism, clinicians can be very helpful in clarifying and framing the discussions that will inevitably take place between parents (Simonoff, 1998).

A last essential area of assessment to consider has to do with occupational and physical therapy. During toddlerhood and throughout the preschool years, the effectiveness of educational interventions can suffer greatly if enough consideration is not given to factors impacting on the child's attention to tasks, compliance, capacity for self-regulation, sensory-seeking behaviors, self-stimulatory behaviors, or otherwise child-specific characteristics that are not necessarily part of the core features of autism but which can be equally impairing. Professionals trained in assessing these factors and devising ways of addressing them in the educational environment play a very important role in intervention programs. The primary goal of these forms of assessment and intervention is to maximize the effectiveness of social, communicative, and cognitive activities by treating disruptive behaviors, optimizing the learning environment, fostering more competence in the areas of self-awareness, motor planning, and visual-motor exploration of the environment, and otherwise pairing with communication specialists and special educators within a common effort to create the best fit between environmental conditions and child-specific characteristics.

FUTURE DIRECTIONS

At present, the greatest challenge at the frontier of clinical assessment of young children at risk of having autism and related disorders is to push back identification to the earliest of ages, so that attempts at early intervention are maximized and fully evaluated. The initial studies of outcome in autism (Rutter & Lockyer, 1967) presented a rather bleak picture, which, by most accounts, no longer applies. The number of individuals who are mute or noncommunicative appears to have grown smaller (Howlin & Goode, 1998), and earlier and adequate intervention seem to be the factors accounting for this major development (NRC, 2001). Large early screening projects, some adopted by state programs, will ensure the continuity of this trend. However, the symptoms of autism, as currently conceptualized in diagnostic instruments, are unlikely to be the final border in this effort. Social isolation, stereotyped language, cognitive disabilities, and stereotypic movements, for example, may be, at least to some extent, the results of more basic abnormalities affecting fundamental and highly conserved mechanisms of socialization (Klin et al., 2003). Supporting this notion is the most successful animal model of autism (Bachevalier, 1994, 1996), which has shown that infant primates with ablated brain areas thought to subserve social adaptation do not immediately develop symptoms that mimic those of autism. Rather, they "grow" into them, maybe as the result of the interaction between faulty brain circuitry and the demands of social life. If so, focusing on the more basic mechanisms of social predisposition, rather than on the resulting symptomatology, might help us identify abnormalities conducive to autism at even earlier stages of development than previously thought possible. For example, while joint-attention deficits are now considered to be among the earliest indicators of vulnerabilities (Mundy & Neal, 2000), from an infancy development perspective, these skills are but the crowning event culminating a fairly long sequence of achievements. Sensitivity and reflexive reactions to gaze direction are phenomena observed in the first 3 months of life. Our research group has preliminary documentation of this effect in toddlers with autism (Chawarska, Klin, & Volkmar, 2003), and it is only a question of time

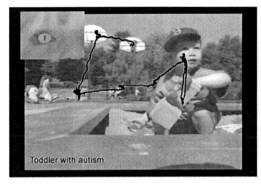

Figure 16.1 Eye-tracking studies of social visual pursuit in toddlers viewing simple social scenes. This figure illustrates the scanpaths or visual traces left by the viewing of 10 seconds of a social scene by a toddler with autism and typically developing toddler. The scanpaths (dark and light lines in each photo) indicate the focus of visual attention of these children as they viewed a video clip of a little boy playing in a sandbox within the context of a playground. The visual fixation patterns of the toddler with autism reveal marked differences in how he engages with the social aspects of the scene. Despite the foreground placement of the video's subject (the child at play) and the active behavior of the child (which included occasional glances toward the camera), the toddler with autism spends a significant portion of his time focusing on objects and unrelated events in the background of the scene (a distant toy truck, the basketball backboards). In contrast, the typically developing toddler focused on the child's face and on monitoring the child's actions (looking down at the truck and at what the child's hands are doing). (*Source*: Ami Klin & Warren Jones, unpublished data).

before this method is adopted for screening children who may carry a genetic liability for autism and yet do not present with symptoms. Other promising areas of research include preferential attentional patterns to social stimuli, such as the human voice and the human face. New techniques to characterize and measure visual scanning of naturalistic, complex social stimuli are already on-line (Klin et al., 2002a, 2002b), focusing on predispositions that emerge in the first months of life. Figure 16.1 illustrates preliminary findings in a 2-year-old with autism and a typical comparison child. Given the early onset of these phenomena, the potential for tracing the ontology of these early social predispositions and for utilizing tools to identify abnormalities in these areas is great.

Finally, thanks to large, concerted efforts in molecular genetics, established findings of susceptibility regions (International Molecular Genetic Study of Autism Consortium, 1998) may soon bring about the identification of the first genes involved in autism. Although the road to understanding the pathophysiology of autism may still be a long one (e.g., in understanding the func-

tions of the putative genes), there will be an immediate impact on our ability to detect vulnerabilities, maybe even before the child is born.

References

Allessandri, S., Bendersky, M., & Lewis, M. (1998). Cognitive functioning in 8- to 18-month-old drug-exposed infants. *Developmental Psychology, 34*, 656–573.

American Psychiatric Association (1994). *Diagnostic and statistical manual of mental disorders* (4th ed.). Washington, DC: Author.

American Psychiatric Association (2000). *Diagnostic and statistical manual of mental disorders* (4th ed., text revision). Washington, DC: Author.

Bachevalier, J. (1994). Medial temporal lobe structures and autism: A review of clinical and experimental findings. *Neuropsychologia, 32*(6), 627–648.

Bachevalier, J. (1996). Medial temporal lobe and autism: A putative animal model in primates. *Journal of Autism and Developmental Disorders, 26*(2), 217–220.

Baird, G., Charman, T., Baron-Cohen, S., Cox, A., Swettenham, J., Wheelwright, S., & Drew, A.

(2000). A screening instrument for autism at 18 months of age: A 6-year follow-up study. *Journal of the American Academy of Child and Adolescent Psychiatry, 39*(6), 694–702.

Baron-Cohen, S. (1995). *Mindblindness: An essay on autism and theory of mind.* Cambridge, MA: MIT Press.

Bates, E. (1979). *The emergence of symbols: Cognition and communication in infancy.* San Diego, CA: Academic Press.

Bayley, N. (1993). *Bayley scales of infant development* (2nd ed.). San Antonio, TX: Psychological Corporation.

Bloom, L. (1993). *The transition from infancy to language.* New York: Cambridge University Press.

Boucher, J., & Lewis, V. (1992). Unfamiliar face recognition in relatively able autistic children. *Journal of Child Psychology and Psychiatry, 33*(5), 843–859.

Briggs-Gowan, M. J., Carter, A. S., Moye Skuban, E., & McCue Horwitz, S. (2001). Prevalence of social-emotional and behavioral problems in a community sample of 1- and 2-year-old children. *Journal of the American Academy of Child and Adolescent Psychiatry, 40*(7), 811–819.

Bryant, P. E. (1991). Face to face with babies. *Nature, 354,* 19.

Carpenter, M., & Tomasello, M. (2000). Joint attention, cultural learning, and language acquisition: Implications for children with autism. In A. M. Wetherby & B. M. Prizant (Eds.), *Autism spectrum disorders: A transactional developmental perspective* (pp. 31–54). Baltimore: Paul H. Brookes.

Carter, A. S., Gillham, J. E., Sparrow, S. S., & Volkmar, F. R. (1996). Adaptive behavior in autism. *Child and Adolescent Psychiatric Clinics of North America: Mental Retardation, 5,* 945–961.

Carter, A., Volkmar, F. R., Sparrow, S. S., Wang, J.-J., Lord, C., Dawson, G., Fombonne, E., Loveland, K., Mesibov, G., & Schopler, E. (1998). The Vineland Adaptive Behavior Scales: Supplementary norms for individuals with autism. *Journal of Autism and Developmental Disorders, 28*(4), 287–302.

Chakrabarti, S., & Fombonne, E. (2001). Pervasive developmental disorders in preschool children. *JAMA, 285*(24), 3093–3099.

Chawarska, K., Klin, A., & Volkmar, F. R. (2003). Automatic attention cueing through eye movement in 2-year-old children with autism. *Child Development, 74*(4), 1108–1122.

Dawson, G., Ashman, S. B., & Carver, L. J. (2000). The role of early experience in shaping behavioral and brain development and its implications for social policy. *Development and Psychopathology, 12*(4), 695–712.

Dawson, G., Meltzoff, A. N., Osterling, J., Rinaldi, J., & Brown, E. (1998). Children with autism fail to orient to naturally occurring social stimuli. *Journal of Autism and Developmental Disorders, 28*(6), 479–485.

DiLavore, P., Lord, C., & Rutter, M. (1995). Prelinguistic Autism Diagnostic Observation Schedule (PL-ADOS). *Journal of Autism and Developmental Disorders, 25,* 355–379.

Eimas, P., Siqueland, E., Jusczyk, P., & Vigorito, J. (1971). Speech perception in infants. *Science, 171,* 303–306.

Emde, R. (1992). Social referencing research: Uncertainty, self, and the search for meaning. In S. Feinman (Ed.), *Social referencing and the social construction of reality in infancy* (pp. 79–94). New York: Plenum Press.

Fein, G. G. (1981). Pretend play in childhood: An integrative review. *Child Development, 52,* 1095–1102.

Fenson, L., Dale, P. S., Reznick, J. S., Thal, D., Bates, E., Hartung, M. S., Pethick, S., & Reilly, J. S. (1993). *MacArthur Communicative Development Inventories.* San Diego, CA: Singular.

Fernald, A. (1993). Approval and disapproval: Infant responsiveness to vocal affect in familiar and unfamiliar languages. *Child Development, 64,* 657–674.

Field, T. (1977). Effects of early separation, interactive deficits, and experimental manipulation on infant-mother face-to-face interaction. *Child Development, 48,* 763–771.

Field, T., Goldstein, S., Vega-Lahr, N., & Porter, K. (1982). Discrimination and imitation of facial expressions by neonates. *Science, 218,* 179–181.

Field, T., & Walden, T. (1981). Production and perception of facial expressions in infancy and early childhood. In H. W. Reese & L. P. Lipsitt (Eds.), *Advances in child development and behavior* (pp. 181–204). New York: Academic Press.

Filipe, P. A., Accardo, P. J., Baranek, G., Cook, E. H., Jr., Dawson, G., Gordon, B., Gravel, J. S., Johnson, C. P., Kallen, R. J., Levy, S. E., Minshew, N. J., Prizant, B. M., Rapin, I., Rogers, S. J., Stone, W. L., Teplin, S., Tuchman, R. F., & Volkmar, F. R. (1999). The screening and diagnosis of autistic spectrum disorders.

Journal of Autism and Developmental Disorders, 29(6), 439–484.

Fombonne, E. (1999). The epidemiology of autism: A review. *Psychological Medicine, 29*(4), 769–786.

Garfin, D., & Lord, C. (1986). Communication as a social problem in autism. In E. Schopler & G. Mesibov (Eds.), *Social behavior in autism* (pp. 237–261). New York: Plenum Press.

Gillham, J. E., Carter, A. S., Volkmar, F. R., & Sparrow, S. S. (2000). Toward a developmental operational definition of autism. *Journal of Autism and Developmental Disorders, 30*(4), 269–278.

Gilliam, W., & Mayes, L. (2000). Developmental assessment of infants and toddlers. In C. H. Zeanah, Jr. (Ed.), *Handbook of infant mental health* (2nd ed., pp. 236–248). New York: Guilford Press.

Haith, M. M., Bergman, T., & Moore, M. J. (1979). Eye contact and face scanning in early infancy. *Science, 198*(4319), 853–855.

Haviland, J. M., & Lelwica, M. (1987). The induced affect response: 10-week-old infants' responses to three emotional expressions. *Developmental Psychology, 23*, 97–104.

Hobson, R. (1986a). The autistic child's appraisal of emotion: A further study. *Journal of Child Psychology and Psychiatry, 27*(5), 671–680.

Hobson, R. (1986b). The autistic child's appraisal of expressions of emotion. *Journal of Child Psychology and Psychiatry, 27*(3), 321–342.

Hobson, R.P., Ouston, J., & Lee, A. (1988). What's in a face? The case of autism. *British Journal of Psychology, 79*, 441–453.

Howlin, P., & Goode, S. (1998). Outcome in adult life for people with autism and Asperger's syndrome. In F. R. Volkmar (Ed.), *Autism and pervasive developmental disorders* (pp. 209–241). Cambridge: Cambridge University Press.

International Molecular Genetic Study of Autism Consortium. (1998). A full genome screen for autism with evidence for linkage to a region on chromosome 7q. *Human Molecular Genetics, 7*(3).

Kanner, L. (1943). Autistic disturbances of affective contact. *Nervous Child, 2*, 217–250.

Klin, A. (1991). Young autistic children's listening preferences in regard to speech: A possible characterization of the symptom of social withdrawal. *Journal of Autism and Developmental Disorders, 21*(1), 29–42.

Klin, A., Carter, A., & Sparrow, S. S. (1997). Psychological assessment. In D. J. Cohen & F. R. Volkmar (Eds.), *Handbook of autism and pervasive developmental disorders* (2nd ed., pp. 418–427). New York: Wiley.

Klin, A., Jones, W., & Schultz, R. (2003). The enactive mind—from actions to cognition: Lessons from autism. *Philosophical Transactions of the Royal Society, Biological Sciences, 358*, 345–360.

Klin, A., Jones, W., Schultz, R., Volkmar, F. R., & Cohen, D. J. (2002a). Defining and quantifying the social phenotype in autism. *American Journal of Psychiatry, 159*(6), 895–908.

Klin, A., Jones, W., Schultz, R., Volkmar, F. R., & Cohen, D. J. (2002b). Visual fixation patterns during viewing of naturalistic social situations as predictors of social competence in individuals with autism. *Archives of General Psychiatry, 59*(9), 809–816.

Klin, A., Lang, J., Cicchetti, D. V., & Volkmar, F. R. (2000). Interrater reliability of clinical diagnosis and DSM-IV criteria for autistic disorder: Results of the DSM-IV autism field trial. *Journal of Autism and Developmental Disorders, 30*(2), 163–167.

Klin, A., Schultz, R., & Cohen, D. (2000). Theory of mind in action: Developmental perspectives on social neuroscience. In S. Baron-Cohen, H. Tager-Flusberg, & D. Cohen (Eds.), *Understanding other minds: Perspectives from developmental neuroscience* (2nd ed., pp. 357–388). Oxford: Oxford University Press.

Klin, A., Sparrow, S. S., de Bildt, A., Cicchetti, D. V., Cohen, D. J., & Volkmar, F. R. (1999). A normed study of face recognition in autism and related disorders. *Journal of Autism and Developmental Disorders, 29*(6), 497–507.

Klin, A., Volkmar, F.R., and Sparrow, S. (1992). Autistic social dysfunction: Some limitations of the theory of mind hypothesis. *Journal of Child Psychology and Psychiatry, 33*(5), 861–876.

Koegel, L., Koegel, R., Yoshen, Y., & McNerney, E. (1999). Pivotal response intervention. II. Preliminary long-term outcome data. *Journal of the Association for Persons with Severe Handicaps, 24*, 186–198.

Langdell, T. (1978). Recognition of faces: An approach to the study of autism. *Journal of Child Psychology and Psychiatry, 19*, 255–268.

Legerstee, M. (1994). Patterns of 4-month-old infant responses to hidden silent and sounding people and objects. *Early Development and Parenting, 3*, 71–80.

Leslie, A. (1987). Pretence and representation: The

origins of "theory of mind." *Psychological Review*, 94, 412–426.

Lifter, K., & Bloom, L. (1998). Intentionality and the role of play in the transition to language. In A. M. Wetherby, S. F. Warren, & J. Reichle (Eds.), *Communication and language intervention series: Vol. 7. Transitions in prelinguistic communication* (pp. 161–195). Baltimore: Paul H. Brookes.

Lord, C. (1995). Follow-up of two-year-olds referred for possible autism. *Journal of Child Psychology and Psychiatry*, 36, 1365–1382.

Lord, C. (1997). Diagnostic instruments in autism spectrum disorders. In D. J. Cohen & F. R. Volkmar (Eds.), *Handbook of autism and pervasive developmental disorders* (pp. 460–483). New York: Wiley.

Lord, C., LeCouteur, A., & Rutter, M.(1991). *Autism diagnostic interview–toddler version*. Unpublished manuscript, University of Chicago.

Lord, C., & Risi, S. (2000). Diagnosis of autism spectrum disorders in young children. In A. M. Wetherby & B. M. Prizant (Eds.), *Autism spectrum disorders: A transactional developmental perspective* (pp. 11–30). Baltimore: Paul H. Brookes.

Lord, C., Rutter, M., DiLavore, P., & Risi, S. (1999). *Autism diagnostic observation schedule*. Los Angeles, CA: Western Psychological Services.

Lord, C., Rutter, M., & LeCouteur, A. (1994). Autism Diagnostic Interview–Revised: A revised version of a diagnostic interview for caregivers of individuals with possible pervasive developmental disorders. *Journal of Autism and Developmental Disorders*, 24(5), 659–685.

Meltzoff, A. N., & Moore, M. K. (1977). Imitation of facial and manual gestures by human neonates. *Science*, 198, 75–78.

Meltzoff, A. N., & Moore, M. K. (1992). Early imitation within a functional framework: The importance of person identity, movement, and development. *Infant Behavior and Development*, 15, 479–505.

Mills, M., & Melhuish, E. (1974). Recognition of mother's voice in early infancy. *Nature*, 252, 123–124.

Mundy, P., & Neal, R. (2000). Neural plasticity, joint attention and autistic developmental pathology. In L. Glidden (Ed.), *International review of research in mental retardation* (Vol. 23, pp. 141–168). New York: Academic Press.

Mundy, P., & Sigman, M. (1989). The theoretical implications of joint attention deficits in autism. *Development and Psychopathology, 1*, 173–183.

Mundy, P., Sigman, M., & Kasari, C. (1990). A longitudinal study of joint attention and language development in autistic children. *Journal of Autism and Developmental Disorders*, 20, 115–128.

Mundy, P., & Stella, J. (2000). Joint attention, social orienting, and communication in autism. In A. M. Wetherby & B. M. Prizant (Eds.), *Autism spectrum disorders: A transactional developmental perspective* (pp. 55–78). Baltimore: Paul H. Brookes.

National Research Council (2001). *Educating children with autism*. Washington, DC: National Academy Press.

Osterling, J., & Dawson, G. (1994). Early recognition of children with autism: A study of first birthday home video tapes. *Journal of Autism and Developmental Disorders*, 24, 247–257.

Prizant, P., & Bailey, D. (1992). Facilitating the acquisition and use of communication skills. In D. Bailey & M. Wolery (Eds.), *Teaching infants and preschoolers with handicaps* (pp. 112–148). Columbus, OH: Merrill.

Prizant, B. M., & Wetherby, A. M. (1987). Communicative intent: A framework for understanding social-communicative behavior in autism. *Journal of the American Academy of Child Psychiatry*, 26, 472–479.

Prizant, B. M., Wetherby, A. M., & Rydell, P. J. (2000). Communication intervention issues for young children with autism spectrum disorders. In A. M. Wetherby & B. M. Prizant (Eds.), *Autism spectrum disorders: A transactional developmental perspective* (pp. 193–224). Baltimore, MD: Paul H. Brookes.

Robins, D. L., Fein, D., Barton, M. L., & Green, J. A. (2001). The Modified Checklist for Autism in Toddlers: An initial study investigating the early detection of autism and pervasive developmental disorders. *Journal of Autism and Developmental Disorders*, 31(2), 131–144.

Rogers, S. J., & Bennetto, L. (2000). Intersubjectivity in autism: The roles of imitation and executive function. In A. M. Wetherby & B. M. Prizant (Eds.), *Autism spectrum disorders: A transactional developmental perspective* (pp. 79–108). Baltimore: Paul H. Brookes.

Rogers, S. J., & Lewis, H. (1989). An effective day treatment model for young children with pervasive developmental disorders. *Journal of the American Academy of Child and Adolescent Psychiatry*, 28, 207–214.

Rogers, S. J., & Pennington, B. F. (1991). A theoretical approach to the deficits in infantile autism. *Development and Psychopathology, 3,* 137–162.

Ross, G. (1985). Use of the Bayley scales to characterize abilities of premature infants. *Child Development, 56,* 835–842.

Ross, H. S., & Lollis, S. P. (1987). Communication within infant social games. *Developmental Psychology, 23,* 241–248.

Rutter, M. (1978). Diagnosis and definitions of childhood autism. *Journal of Autism and Childhood Schizophrenia, 8,* 139–161.

Rutter, M. (2000). Genetic studies of autism: From the 1970s into the millennium. *Journal of Child Psychology and Psychiatry, 28*(1), 3–14.

Rutter, M., & Lockyer, L. (1967). A five to fifteen year follow-up study of infantile psychosis. II. Social and behavioral outcome. *British Journal of Psychiatry, 113,* 1183–1199.

Rydell, P., & Prizant, B. (1995). Assessment and intervention strategies for children who use echolalia. In K. Quill (Ed.), *Teaching children with autism: Strategies to enhance communication and socialization* (pp. 105–129). Albany, NY: Delmar.

Schultz, R. T., & Klin, A. (2002). The neural foundations of autism. *Journal of the American Academy of Child and Adolescent Psychiatry, 41*(10), 1259–1262.

Siegel, B., Piner, C., Eschler, J., & Elliott, G. R. (1988). How children with autism are diagnosed: Difficulties in identification of children with multiple developmental delays. *Journal of Developmental and Behavioral Pediatrics, 9*(4), 199–204.

Simonoff, E. (1998). Genetic counseling in autism and pervasive developmental disorders. *Journal of Autism and Developmental Disorders, 28*(5), 447–456.

Sparrow, S., Carter, A. S., Racusin, G., & Morris, R. (1995). Comprehensive psychological assessment through the life span: A developmental approach. In D. Cicchetti & D. J. Cohen (Eds.), *Developmental psychopathology* (Vol. 1., pp. 81–108). New York: John Wiley & Sons.

Sparrow, S. S., Balla, D., & Cicchetti, D. (1984). *Vineland Adaptive Behavior Scales* (expanded ed.). Circle Pines, MN: American Guidance Service.

Stone, W. L. (1997). Autism in infancy and early childhood. In D. J. Cohen & F. R. Volkmar (Eds.), *Handbook of autism and pervasive developmental disorders* (2nd ed., pp. 266–282). New York: Wiley.

Symons, L. A., Hains, S. M. J., & Muir, D. W. (1998). Look at me: Five-month-old infants' sensitivity to very small deviations in eye-gaze during social interactions. *Infant Behavior and Development, 21*(3), 531–536.

Tantam, D., Monaghan, L., Nicholson, H., & Stirling, J. (1989). Autistic children's ability to interpret faces: A research note. *Journal of Child Psychology and Psychiatry, 30*(4), 623–630.

Tarabulsy, G. M., Tessier, R., & Kappas, A. (1996). Contingency detection and the contingent organization of behavior in interactions: Implications for socioemotional development in infancy. *Psychological Bulletin, 120*(1), 25–41.

Trevarthen, C. (1979). Communication and cooperation in early infancy: A description of primary intersubjectivity. In M. Bullowa (Ed.), *Before speech: The beginning of interpersonal communication* (pp. 321–347). Cambridge: Cambridge University Press.

Tronick, E., Als, H., Adamson, L., Wise, S., & Brazelton, T. B. (1978). The infant's response to entrapment between contradictory messages in face-to-face interaction. *Journal of the American Academy of Child and Adolescent Psychiatry, 17,* 1–13.

Tronick, E. Z., Cohn, J., & Shea, E. (1986). The transfer of affect between mothers and infants. In T. B. Brazelton & M. W. Yogman (Eds.), *Affective development in infancy* (pp. 11–25). Norwood, NJ: Ablex.

Venter, A., Lord, C., & Schopler, E. (1992). A follow-up study of high-functioning autistic children. *Journal of Child Psychology and Psychiatry, 33,* 489–507.

Volkmar, F., Cook, E. H., Jr., Pomeroy, J., Realmuto, G., & Tanguay, P. (1999). Practice parameters for the assessment and treatment of children, adolescents, and adults with autism and other pervasive developmental disorders. *Journal of the American Academy of Child and Adolescent Psychiatry, 38*(12), 32S–54S.

Volkmar, F. R., Carter, A., Grossman, J., & Klin, A. (1997). Social development in autism. In D. J. Cohen & F. R. Volkmar (Eds.), *Handbook of autism and pervasive developmental disorders* (2nd ed., pp. 173–194). New York: Wiley.

Volkmar, F. R., Carter, A., Sparrow, S. S., & Cicchetti, D. V. (1993). Quantifying social development of autism. *Journal of Child and Adolescent Psychiatry, 32,* 627–632.

Volkmar, F. R., & Klin, A. (2000). The pervasive developmental disorders. In H. Kaplan & B.

Sadock (Eds.), *Comprehensive textbook of psychiatry* (7th ed., pp. 2659–2678). Philadelphia: Lippincott Williams & Wilkins.

Volkmar, F. R., Klin, A., Siegel, B., Szatmari, P., Lord, C., Campbell, M., Freeman, B. J., Cicchetti, D. V., Rutter, M., Kline, W., Buitelaar, J., Hattab, Y., Fombonne, E., Fuentes, J., Werry, J., Stone, W., Kerbeshian, J., Hoshino, Y., Bregman, J., Loveland, K., Szymanski, L., & Towbin, K. (1994). *DSM-IV* autism/pervasive developmental disorder field trial. *American Journal of Psychiatry, 151*, 1361–1367.

Volkmar, F. R., & Nelson, D. S. (1990). Seizure disorders in autism. *Journal of the American Academy of Child and Adolescent Psychiatry, 29*(1), 127–129.

Volkmar, F. R., Sparrow, S. A., Goudreau, D., Cicchetti, D. V., Paul, R., & Cohen, D. J. (1987). Social deficits in autism: An operational approach using the Vineland Adaptive Behavior Scales. *Journal of the American Academy of Child and Adolescent Psychiatry, 26*, 156–161.

Volkmar, F. R., Stier, D. M., & Cohen, D. J. (1985). Age of recognition of pervasive developmental disorder. *American Journal of Psychiatry, 142*(112), 1450–1452.

Walker-Andrews, A. S., & Grolnick, W. (1983). Infants' discrimination of vocal expressions. *Infant Behavior and Development, 6*, 491–498.

Walker-Andrews, A. S., & Lennon, E. (1991). Infants' discrimination of vocal expressions: Contributions of auditory and visual information. *Infant Behavior and Development, 14*, 131–142.

Waterhouse, L., Fein, D., & Modahl, C. (1996). Neurofunctional mechanisms in autism. *Psychological Review, 103*, 457–489.

Weeks, S., & Hobson, R. (1987). The salience of facial expression for autistic children. *Journal of Child Psychology and Psychiatry, 28*(1), 137–151.

Wetherby, A., & Prizant, B. (1993). *Communication and symbolic behavior scales.* Chicago: Riverside.

Wetherby, A., Prizant, B., & Hutchinson, T. (1998). Communicative, social-affective, and symbolic profiles of young children with autism and pervasive developmental disorder. *American Journal of Speech-Language Pathology, 7*, 79–91.

Wetherby, A. M., Prizant, B. M., & Schuler, A. L. (2000). Understanding the nature of communication and language impairments. In A. M. Wetherby & B. M. Prizant (Eds.), *Autism spectrum disorders: A transactional developmental perspective* (pp. 109–142). Baltimore, MD: Paul H. Brookes.

Wolfberg, P. (1999). *Play and imagination in children with autism.* New York: Teachers College Press.

World Health Organization (1992). *The ICD-10 classification of mental and behavioral disorders.* Geneva: Author.

17

Affective Disorders

Joan L. Luby

This chapter discusses assessment strategies that are useful for the research assessment of affective disorders in infants and toddlers. Consideration of the use of these assessment strategies for clinical evaluation is discussed. Empirical data supporting *Diagnostic and Statistical Manual of Mental Disorders*, Fourth Edition (*DSM-IV*; American Psychiatric Association, 1994) criteria for the diagnosis of major depression in preschoolers when age-adjusted symptom manifestations are assessed has been established and are presented (Luby et al., 2002). Related to this, the need for empirically supported age-adjusted assessment and criteria for all infant and preschool affective disorders is discussed. Case examples of preschool-aged children with depressive syndromes and a presumptive bipolar or bipolarlike syndrome or subsyndrome are presented. Due to the lack of data on the age-adjusted nosology of bipolar disorder in very young children, the need for future study in this area is emphasized.

EARLY INVESTIGATIONS

In this section, early investigations of clinical affective disorders in young children are reviewed.

To date, data on the clinical manifestations of affective disorders in infants and toddlers have been remarkably scarce. Accordingly, the field has been lacking the tools and validated developmentally specific diagnostic criteria to identify a population of infants and toddlers with manifest affective disorders. As a result, studies of the neurobiology and etiology of early-onset affective disorders, as well as treatment studies of these disorders in very young children, have been nonexistent. A few studies have looked at the application of *DSM-III* (American Psychiatric Association, 1980) criteria for major depressive disorders (MDD) in preschool children. These case studies and small-scale investigations looked for preschool children who met *DSM-III* criteria for MDD and found few (Kashani, 1982; Kashani & Carlson, 1985; Kashani, Ray, & Carlson, 1984; Poznanski & Zrull, 1970). An epidemiological survey found significant numbers of children with "concerning symptoms," but few meeting formal *DSM-III* criteria for MDD or dysthmia, suggesting the possible need for developmental modifications (Kashani & Ray, 1983; Kashani, Allan, Beck, Bledsoe, & Reid, 1997). Prior to our ongoing investigation described below, there have been no controlled studies of the age-specific developmental nosology of MDD in these very young children. Further, the literature offers nothing more than isolated case studies to inform the question of whether bipolar disorders occur in children younger than 6 years of age and, if so, how they can be identified.

The concept of clinical mental disorders in young children is in general one that meets with resistance as it is difficult and disturbing to imagine a young child suffering from a psychiatric disorder. Further, the notion of an affective disorder offends our hope and belief that childhood is an inherently joyful time of life. The greater vicissitudes of emotion that occur with normal development create ambiguity in our efforts to distinguish clinical disorders from normative developmental difficulties; however, proper study design and measurement strategies can address this critical distinction.

STUDIES OF INFANTS AT RISK FOR AFFECTIVE DISORDERS

In this section, the developmental literature on infants and toddlers at risk for affective disorders is reviewed, and the implications for the detection of early-onset clinical disorders are considered. Despite the dearth of data on clinical manifestations of affective disorders, there has been substantial attention to and much controlled investigation of possible early signs of risk and precursors of affective disorders. These studies, which have been highly suggestive of the need for clinical investigations, have focused on normal and aberrant development of mood and affect in early life. Investigators have approached the problem by looking at various parameters of social and emotional development in young children who are at high risk for the development of affective illness. These studies of high-risk children have focused predominantly on the infant offspring of mothers experiencing mood disturbances, compared to the offspring of control mothers. This approach is likely to be fruitful, since family studies have shown that the children of parents with affective disorders have significantly higher rates of these disorders than do children in the general population (Kovacs, Devlin,

Pollock, Richards, & Mukerji, 1997). In addition to genetic risk factors, psychosocial factors may also be salient, given that the primary caretaker plays such a key role in the regulation of infant and toddler affective states and serves as a model and teacher for affect development. Along these lines, a number of studies have suggested that caretakers with mood disturbances may be more impaired than controls in their ability to act effectively in this role (Gelfand & Teti, 1990; Radke-Yarrow, Zahn-Waxler, Richardson, & Susman, 1994).

Studies of high-risk children have demonstrated a number of impairments in emotional expression in the offspring of mothers with major depressive disorders or varying degrees of depressed mood states. Several investigations have found evidence of significantly higher levels of negative emotional expression and lower levels of positive emotional expression (measured by facial expression) in the infants of depressed mothers compared to controls (Cohn, Matias, Tronick, Connell, & Lyons-Ruth, 1986; Cohn, Campbell, Matias, & Hopkins, 1990; Field, 1984; Field et al., 1985; Murray, 1992; Pickens & Field, 1993). Several groups have also shown that the infants of depressed mothers demonstrate more difficult temperamental features. In particular, they are rated as having greater difficulty in self-soothing, displaying more irritability and lower levels of activity (Cummings & Davies, 1994; Field, 1984). Evidence of more complex depressive symptoms such as excessive guilt (measured using story completion tasks) and empathic overinvolvement in the problems of others have been found in the preschool offspring of depressed mothers compared to controls (Zahn-Waxler, Kochanska, Krupnick, & McKnew, 1990). Preschool children of depressed parents also have been observed to demonstrate increased inhibition to unfamiliar situations (Kochanska, 1991). These findings suggest that impairments in mood and affect as well as biological changes are already occurring in young children at high risk for depression very early in development.

Using a research paradigm in which mothers were asked to be artificially unresponsive to their infants (the so-called still face procedure), Field and colleagues compared 3-month-old infants of control mothers to the infants of mothers experiencing postpartum depression (Field, 1984). Consistent with the original findings of Cohn and Tronick (1983), the infants of control mothers demonstrated anger and protestation in response to the unresponsive facial expressions of their mothers. However, in notable contrast to these findings, the infants of the mothers with postpartum depression demonstrated an absence of these responses. The authors hypothesize that these high-risk infants did not respond with the typical show of protest because they had accommodated to the expression of flat or negative emotions in their primary caregivers. This work suggests that there may be more enduring effects of exposure to caretakers with depression that extend beyond the immediate interactions between mother and child. Indeed, alterations in the infant's expectation of a depressed caregiver's behavior may be different, which could imply differences in the infant's expectations of the emotional responsiveness of others in general.

BIOLOGICAL CORRELATES IN INFANTS OF DEPRESSED MOTHERS

In addition to changes in the behavioral expression of emotions, a number of associated biological findings have also been reported in the high-risk infant offspring of depressed mothers. Numerous psychophysiological alterations have been identified in these high-risk infants. In particular, decreased vagal tone (Field, Pickens, Fox, Nawrocki, & Gonzalez, 1995) and right frontal electroencephalogram (EEG) asymmetry in the infant offspring of depressed mothers has been demonstrated (Dawson et al., 1992; Field, Fox, Pickens, & Nawrocki, 1995). High-risk infants demonstrated reduced left frontal activation both at rest and during dyadic play with their mothers compared to controls. In addition, control infants demonstrated greater right frontal activation upon a distress-inducing separation from their mothers, but this pattern was not observed in the infants of symptomatic mothers. The potential clinical importance of these changes is underscored by similar EEG findings in depressed adults during episodes of depression (Henriques & Davidson,

1990). An equivalent pattern of asymmetry has also been observed in 10-month-old infants in response to happy and sad videotapes (Davidson & Fox, 1982). Further, this right frontal EEG asymmetry has also been found to be associated with expressions of negative affect in infants. These biological findings in infants at high risk for depression might also suggest that central nervous system changes are already occurring at this very early stage of development, even in advance of the overt behavioral manifestation of depressive symptoms in these very young children.

Findings from these studies are highly suggestive of the presence of very early and identifiable alterations in affective development in young children at high risk. The related question of whether such alterations also occur among young children in the general population and whether these signs and symptoms reach clinical significance and are impairing is critical to defining clinical affective disorders in young children. A fundamental impediment to progress in this area to date has been the lack of developmentally appropriate assessments of symptom manifestations and criteria to identify depressive disorders in preschool children. Neither epidemiological nor treatment studies can be done until valid diagnostic criteria are established for the identification of appropriate clinical groups. The few studies that have been done to date have concluded that preschool depression may not be an important clinical phenomenon, as few cases were found utilizing the standard adult-based assessment for *DSM* criteria (Kashani, Holcomb, & Orvaschel, 1986). However, reliance on the standard assessment for *DSM* criteria may have been a critical design flaw, as some of the adult symptom manifestations lack face validity for very young children. A number of the symptom states as they are described in the current *DSM* are not developmentally pertinent to the life experiences of young children. Further, the requirement for a 2-week duration of sustained symptoms may be unreasonable for this age group, based on the greater affective range and variation that can occur normatively in young children. It stands to reason that this normative pattern of mood and affective instability would also be salient in psychopathological states among young children.

DEFINING DEVELOPMENTALLY SPECIFIC CRITERIA FOR EARLY MAJOR DEPRESSIVE DISORDER

The age-adjusted manifestations of clinical depression in young children are considered in this section, and findings from our ongoing investigation of the nosology of preschool depression are presented. At the Washington University School of Medicine Early Emotional Development Program, my colleagues and I have been conducting the first large-scale controlled study, to our knowledge, of the developmentally specific manifestations of MDD in preschool children. Findings from this study have demonstrated that the "typical" symptoms of MDD can be identified in preschool children. However, importantly, to capture these typical symptoms of depression, the assessment for *DSM-IV* symptom states was modified. To do this, an age-appropriate version of the Diagnostic Interview Schedule for Children, Version IV (DISC-IV; Shaffer, Fisher, Lucas, & NIMH DISC Editorial Board, 1998) was developed for parent informants about young children, the DISC-IV-Young Child (DISC-IV-YC; Lucas, Fisher, & Luby, 1998). Several DISC-IV items were modified in the DISC-IV-YC to account for their age-appropriate developmental manifestations. This was deemed necessary at face value since some items as they were described in the DISC-IV did not apply to the life experiences of young children. The most obvious were the items that applied to school behavior. Because preschoolers are not in academic school settings, all items that addressed schoolwork were modified to address "activities and play." A more subtle modification was that the phrase "sad or depressed" on the DISC-IV was changed to "sad or unhappy" to better express how parents tend to view the dysthymic or depressed mood state of a young child. Along these lines, for the assessment of concentration, "decisions" were described as "choices." Further, because preschool children are less verbally competent than older children, items that addressed preoccupation with death and suicidality were modified to account for the possibility that these symptoms might be manifested as persistent themes in play (in addition to the possibility that they might be verbally expressed). All

items pertaining to anhedonia in the DISC-IV (described as "nothing was fun"), a highly specific symptom of depression in preschoolers, were unchanged in the DISC-IV-YC. All remaining MDD items on the DISC-IV were also unchanged.

Young children are less inclined to verbally express their internal thoughts, and may not even be aware of these thoughts and feelings based on the normative limitations of their emotional development. Therefore, it is important to look for other more indirect expressions of depressed mental state in young children through the observation of play. Such negative or depressive themes have been observed by parents in the play of depressed young children, while the children themselves do not necessarily spontaneously report feeling depressed (Luby et al., 2002). Thematic play has long been hypothesized to be an accurate representation of the child's internal mental preoccupations, and this hypothesis has more recently been supported by empirical data (Warren, Oppenheim, & Emde, 1996). Therefore, the assessment of pertinent play themes in lieu of overtly expressed thoughts (which occur less commonly in young children) is well supported developmentally. Similar developmental modifications were applied to the symptoms of "feelings of worthlessness or excessive or inappropriate guilt." It was our hypothesis that these feelings were more likely to be observed indirectly in the child's play preoccupations.

All *DSM-IV* symptoms of MDD are assessed by the DISC-IV-YC. Figure 17.1 demonstrates the proportion of these core *DSM-IV* symptoms of depression, translated from developmentally specific manifestations as they occurred in our depressed preschoolers compared to both psychiatric (who met *DSM-IV* criteria for attention deficit/hyperactivity disorder and/or oppositional defiant disorder) and no-disorder comparison groups.

In addition to developmentally modified symptom manifestations along the lines described above, a number of other algorithmic and quantitative differences in the diagnostic criteria for MDD in young children are suggested by our investigation. Using principles that formed the basis of the current *DSM* system outlined by Robins and Guze (1970) for the validation of psychiatric nosology, we investigated the validity of age-specific criteria for MDD in children ages 3 years 0 months to 5

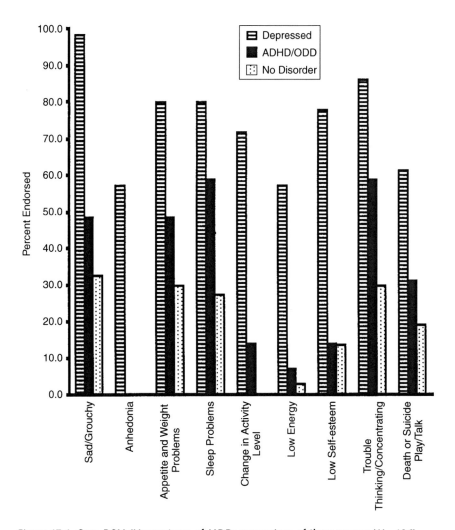

Figure 17.1 Core *DSM-IV* symptoms of MDD: comparison of three groups (*N* = 136). (ADHD/ODD, attention deficit hyperactivity disorder/oppositional defiant disorder)

years 6 months. Our findings indicated that young children with 5 criteria and those who had only 4 criteria (*n* = 2) but who had both core symptoms of depression, sadness and anhedonia, currently required by the *DSM-IV* also had numerous other markers of clinical significance. Further, while parents endorsed the presence of the developmentally modified (and some unmodified as above) symptoms of MDD as defined by *DSM-IV*, they did not endorse that the symptoms were persistently present over a 2-week period (as is required by *DSM-IV* criteria). Because a detailed assessment of the duration of symptoms was not addressed by the structured diagnostic interview used (DISC-IV-YC), the significance of this finding remains unclear. A detailed investigation of symptom duration among depressed preschoolers is now underway in our laboratory.

The group of preschoolers who demonstrated *DSM-IV* symptoms of depression (when the assessment was modified for age-appropriate manifestations) "for most of the day" and "almost every day" but apparently without persistence for "2 weeks in a row" had other markers of clinical significance. These included a significantly greater family history of affective disorders, suicidality,

PRESCHOOL DIAGNOSTIC CRITERIA
FOR MDD:

(modifications from standard
DSM-IV criteria are shown in italics)

A. Five (or more) of the following symptoms have been present *but not necessarily persistently* over a 2-week period and represent a change from previous functioning; at least one of the symptoms is either (1) depressed mood or (2) loss of interest or pleasure *in activities or play. If both (1) and (2) are present a total of only 4 symptoms are needed.*

1. Depressed mood *for a portion of the day for several days, as observed (or reported) in behavior. Note: may be irritable mood.*

2. Markedly diminished interest or pleasure in all, or almost all, activities *or play for a portion of the day for several days (as indicated by either subjective account or observation made by others).*

3. Significant weight loss when not dieting or weight gain or decrease or increase in appetite nearly every day.

4. Insomnia or hypersomnia nearly every day.

5. Psychomotor agitation or retardation nearly every day (observable by others, not merely subjective feelings of restlessness or being slowed down).

6. Fatigue or loss of energy nearly every day.

7. Feelings of worthlessness or excessive or inappropriate guilt (which may be delusional) *that may be evident in play themes.*

8. Diminished ability to think or concentrate, or indecisiveness, *for several days* (either by subjective account or as observed by others).

9. Recurrent thoughts of death (not just fear of dying), recurrent suicidal ideation without a specific plan, or a suicide attempt or a specific plan for committing suicide. *Suicidal or self-destructive themes are persistently evident in play only.*

and bipolar disorder, significant impairment according to an independent measure of social development, and higher scores of both internalizing and externalizing symptoms on an independent rating scale when compared to no-disorder and psychiatric controls. The depressed group also demonstrated a unique pattern of cortisol reactivity in response to a psychosocial stressor (Luby, Heffelfinger, et al., in press). In addition, children with this modified symptom constellation also showed stability of depressive symptoms over a 6-month period; another marker of a valid psychiatric syndrome using the Robins and Guze (1970) model. When the 2-week duration criterion was strictly upheld, 78% of preschoolers in the clinical group failed to meet *DSM-IV* criteria on this basis (Luby et al., 2003). The issue of duration appears to need further investigation.

METHODS FOR THE ASSESSMENT OF AFFECTIVE DISORDERS

Informants

Methods for the research assessment of clinical affective disorders are considered in this section. The possible uses of some of these measures for clinical evaluations are also considered. A central and critical issue for the assessment of affective symptoms in young children is the limitation of the use of adult reporters. The traditional reliance on the adult reporter in investigations of child psychopathology, and the greater challenge of assessing the young child reporter, may have contributed to our relative lack of data in this area. The limitations of sole reliance on the parent informant are underscored by the potential biases of caretakers, who may lack both awareness of and sensitivity to the child's internal feeling states, as well as objectivity in their judgments of the child's behavior. Such a phenomenon may be particularly salient in families in which there is parental psychopathology, as studies have shown that respondents' reports about others are influenced by their own mental condition (Kendler, Neale, Kessler, Heath, & Eaves, 1992). While parents and teachers are more likely to be reliable and valid reporters for externalizing or disruptive symptoms, it is widely believed that they may fail to recognize symptoms of anxiety and depression in children. For this reason, age-appropriate direct interview of the child may be an invaluable component of a valid assessment of internalizing psychopathology in general and affective disorders in particular.

The issue of obtaining valid and reliable information from young children about their own internal emotions is a complex and controversial one. A primary question is whether (and at what point) young children have the developmental maturity to recognize and label their own internal emotional states. Looking at a higher-level emotional construct such as self-worth, Harter (1986) suggests that children younger than 9 years are not accurate informants, as evidenced by their tendency to overrate themselves in the areas of competence and to report idealized images of themselves. Further, some experts in development theorize that certain complex and distressing emotional states may not be experienced or understood by children until specific cognitive milestones are met. Cowan (1978) suggests, for example, that guilt is not experienced by children until an awareness of the difference between the real and idealized self are achieved. Contrary to traditional cognitive (e.g., Piagetian) notions, however, several recent investigations have found that children as young as preschool age were able to understand and label a wide range of basic emotions (Gobbo & Chi, 1986; Markman, 1989; Russell, 1990). These preschool children were also able to explain the causes and consequences of these emotions. Additionally, Beizer, Stipek, and Deitch (1985) showed that 5-year-olds were able to understand the more complex feelings of pride and embarrassment, evidenced by their ability to give accurate examples of each. These more recent data suggest that young children are more emotionally competent than previously believed, suggesting that they can serve as reliable informants if age-appropriate interview methods are employed. From a clinical standpoint, it is important to consider that there may be significant individual differences and a wide range of abilities in this area. Other more general developmental issues such as limited receptive and expressive language as well as capacity for sustained atten-

tion are also issues that must be considered in any direct assessment that utilizes the young child as an informant (for review, see Measelle, Ablow, Cowan & Cowan, 1998).

Interview of the Young Child: The Berkeley Puppet Interview– Symptoms Scales

The Berkeley Puppet Interview–Symptom Scales (BPI-S; Ablow & Measelle, 1993) utilize a novel assessment methodology developed to directly assess young children's perceptions of their own internal emotional states. This is a puppet interview, designed to allow young children to label their own emotions by utilizing displacement. This is done by asking a child to endorse one of the expressed feelings of the puppets, thereby bypassing any need for the ability to identify and label his or her own emotional states directly (e.g., insight). The BPI-S is an interactive interview with known reliability and validity, which blends structured and clinical interviewing techniques to elicit young children's self-perceptions (Ablow et al., 1999; Measelle et al., 1998). The BPI-S is composed of nine separate mental health subscales that address age-adjusted symptom manifestations, are designed for easy comprehension by the young child, and map onto the current diagnostic system for childhood disorders (DSM-IV). The BPI-S has modules for the assessment of the majority of DSM-IV disorders, including both depressive and anxiety disorders. An experimental mania section is currently undergoing reliability testing in our laboratory. This measure is one part of a larger comprehensive assessment battery for young children that encompasses biological, neuropsychological, personality, and contextual aspects of development thought to contribute to adaptation and impairment during the preschool and early school-age years (ages 4–8) developed by the MacArthur Network on Psychopathology and Development (chair, David Kupfer, MD). A parallel parent and teacher report measure, the Health and Behavioral Questionnaire (HBQ, described below) was developed in tandem and is fully compatible with the BPI-S.

The validity of the BPI-S for the assessment of depressive symptoms is suggested by the finding that depressed preschoolers reported more depressive symptoms on the BPI than control children (Luby et al., 2002). Further, data from this investigation have also shown an association between BPI-S scores and salivary cortisol measures, lending additional support for the validity of the measure (Luby, Heffelfinger, & Mrakotsky, 2001).

While the BPI-S was designed for use in standardized research settings, it may also be useful in a modified form for clinical evaluations as well. Pertinent sections of the interview may be used with the puppets to elicit key aspects of the mental status exam from the young child in the clinical setting. The puppet format may facilitate the young child's ability to express to an unfamiliar examiner his or her fears, anxieties, and mood state, issues that the young child in an unfamiliar clinical setting is unlikely to be comfortable discussing directly. The BPI may be useful in a highly verbal child as young as age 3; however, the measure has established reliability for children older than 4 years and, in our experience, children younger than 4 often do not understand, or seem unable to meaningfully reflect upon, many of the questions. Standardized coding would not be necessary for the clinical use of the BPI-S; however, many of the coding parameters may be useful to the interpretation of the child's responses. Of course, in either the research or clinical setting, the BPI-S must be considered as one part of a multidimensional assessment that includes observational play assessment and an extensive history from a parent or primary caregiver.

Observational Measures of Emotional Reactivity

While the direct interview of the young child using the BPI-S appears to be a valid, unique, and important component of an assessment for early-onset affective disorders, developmental limitations in young children's ability to recognize and report on their own mental state suggests that observation of behavior remains a critical component of any affective disorder assessment. In the research setting, this is an invaluable but labor-intensive (and therefore expensive) process. It requires the use of standardized emotionally evocative or "incentive events" under controlled conditions. The procedure is videotaped and the child's reactions (verbal, facial, and bodily) are coded using standardized procedures by coders blind to diagnostic status. The Laboratory Temperament Assessment Battery (Lab-TAB; Goldsmith & Rothbart, 1996) was originally conceptualized and designed for objectively assessing temperament or behavioral style in infants and young children. Depending upon which age-appropriate version is utilized, Lab-TAB is composed of multiple "episodes" that are combined to fall into six to eight core dimensions of temperament. Several of these temperament dimensions appear at face value to have clinical relevance to the risk for, or overt manifestations of, affective disorders. In particular, the tendency to experience anger/frustration, fear, sadness/disappointment, and exuberance/joy are all highly relevant to the manifestation of affective disorders. The tendency to experience exuberance or the lack of ability to experience it falls into the negative versus positive affective continuum. Theoretically, this measure provides an objective assessment of the child's tendency to experience negative and positive emotions in reaction to evocative events designed to recapitulate such experiences as they may be encountered in daily life. While these temperament dimensions have been well established as early risk factors for later behavioral problems (Caspi & Silva, 1995), their relationship to manifest psychiatric disorders remains unclear at this time, pending analysis of the data we have collected in our ongoing 5-year study.

Diagnostic Interview: Parent Report

Recognizing the limitations of parent report previously discussed and the fact that parent report alone is unlikely to be sufficient to identify affective disorders in young children, the parent interview remains a vital source of information. Until very recently, all available validated structured and semistructured diagnostic interviews were designed and tested for children older than 6 years. Despite this, they have been used for younger children in some studies, although the specificity and sensitivity of these measures in these populations has not been established and is questionable at face value. Preschool versions of several standardized diagnostic interviews are now available and are in various stages of development and testing (see chapter 12). The DISC-IV-YC was used in our first study of preschool depression. It performed well in capturing age-adjusted symptoms of depression in these young children. This is a fully structured diagnostic interview and as such the lack of probes may limit its utility to comprehensively assess affective disorders in young children, who have been traditionally assessed using semistructured measures. This measure does not currently contain a mania section, largely due to the lack of data on this disorder in young children. The Preschool Age Psychiatric Assessment (PAPA; Egger, Ascher, & Angold, 1999; see chapter 12) is a semistructured interview designed for young children. It contains a comprehensive section on mood disorders, including an experimental section on mania. Reliability and validity testing of this measure is under way at Duke University.

Many investigators have regarded the Kiddie Schedule for Affective Disorders (K-SADS) as an optimal semistructured diagnostic interview for the assessment of childhood mood disorders. A modified version of the measure that includes the assessment of childhood mania, the so-called Wash U K-SADS, has demonstrated validity and reliability for this purpose and is now widely used in studies of childhood bipolar disorder. To date, modifications of this measure for use in children under the age of 6 years have not been available.

Dimensional Measures of Psychopathology

In addition to the diagnostic interviews mentioned above, parent and teacher report versions of dimensional measures of psychopathology in young children are also available. These measures are comprehensive checklist-style questionnaires that also capture affective symptoms and disorders. The Child Behavior Checklist (CBCL; Achenbach & Edelbrock, 1983) has been widely used in research on young child psychopathology. This measure has been modified to achieve greater developmental specificity. A version has been created for children between the ages of 18 months and 5 years, and another version for those between 5 and 18 years. While this measure has been very useful in the identification of internal-

izing symptoms in general, using "broad band" scales that have well-established validity, it has had less utility in the identification and differentiation of specific DSM internalizing disorders such as affective disorders.

A novel dimensional measure that is compatible with the DSM system, developed by the MacArthur Network on Development and Psychopathology, is also available. The Health and Behavior Questionnaire (HBQ) has both parent and teacher versions, is a part of a larger comprehensive assessment battery for young children that encompasses biological, neuropsychological, personality, and contextual aspects of development, and is designed to be compatible with the BPI child report measure described above. Reliability and validity of this measure have been established (Boyce et al., 2002; Essex et al., 2002). Further, evidence suggests that the HBQ may be more sensitive for the identification of internalizing disorders in young children, including MDD, than the DISC-IV (Luby et al., 2002).

ASSESSMENT OF IMPAIRMENT

Impairment is an important clinical indicator for any psychiatric disorder and is currently a core criterion for caseness for affective disorders (as well as all other psychiatric disorders) according to the DSM system. The issue of the assessment of impairment in young children is a complex one that is beyond the scope of this chapter (see epilogue). However, some comments about capturing impairment in young children with affective disorders are warranted. As clear criteria for affective disorders have not been well established, the standard method employed by structured interviews of assessing the level of impairment only when criteria for caseness are met is not useful for young children (since many young children with clinically significant affective disorders will fall short of full DSM-IV criteria on the basis of duration). Therefore, at this juncture when clear and well-validated algorithms are not yet available, it is necessary to assess impairment in a broader range of children who manifest symptoms. Impairment in young children must be considered in terms of the age-appropriate challenges and demands that they face. For this reason, the Vineland (Sparrow, Carter, & Cicchetti, 1987) is an excellent and developmentally sensitive measure that addresses levels of functioning across a variety of pertinent domains. In preschool children with MDD, the Vineland socialization scale was used to investigate impairment in the depressed, psychiatric, and no-disorder comparison groups. Significant differences were found between the depressed and normal groups, with the preschool MDD group showing significantly lower functioning than controls and higher functioning at a trend level than the psychiatric controls (Luby et al., 2002). This suggests that this Vineland subscale is a valid and useful measure of impairment in the assessment of preschool MDD. Despite the apparent utility of the Vineland, it is also clear that further measurement development in the area of impairment in young children is needed.

ASSESSMENT OF THE PARENT-CHILD RELATIONSHIP

The parent-child relationship is a central area of emotional functioning for young children. Because the young child is not emotionally autonomous and relies heavily on the caregiver for basic support, nurturance, and direction, the nature and quality of the caregiving relationship must be a primary component of the assessment of the mental status of the young child (Benham, 2000; Thomas et al., 1997). While the dyadic relationship serves as an important and in some areas optimal context for any meaningful assessment of psychopathology in young children, it may be the object of observation as well. The child's level of comfort and security, competence, and ability for self-assertion within that relationship is highly pertinent to the assessment of psychopathology in general and to an assessment of affective regulation and reactivity more specifically. The central emotional issue, as above, depends upon the developmental and chronological age of the young child and therefore the salient developmental challenges.

Settings in which the child and the primary caregiver are observed in free play are very useful for clinical assessments. Free play serves both as an optimal setting in which to observe other aspects of the child's mental status and as a good way to assess the parent-child relationship itself. The unstructured format offers the advantage of allowing the child to choose play themes and therefore express his or her thought content, allowing the expression of a personal narrative. The predominant play themes of the young child appear to be a good representation of thought content. Warren et al. (1996) have demonstrated that play can be interpreted as a valid mental representation in young children in general. Pertinent to affective disorders specifically, the group of children with developmentally modified symptoms of depression demonstrated play that had traumatic or suicidal themes (as reported by parents) at very high rates that were significantly greater than either psychiatric or no-disorder comparison groups (Luby et al., 2002).

Semistructured dyadic assessments are also very useful tools to measure the child's mental status within the context of the dyadic relationship. There are numerous measures of this kind, used to varying degrees in both clinical and research settings (Clark, 1985; Egeland et al., 1995). Most of these measures include teaching tasks, brief separations, and free play, and some include a snack scenario. These semistructured interviews provide incentive events that may stress the dyad mildly and therefore bring out underlying conflictual elements of the relationship that could be missed in a free play setting. As such, these interviews are useful to bring out either harmonious or disharmonious elements of the parent-child relationship that are pertinent to the young child's emotional development. Mental health intervention in young children is also done in a dyadic format and there is a substantial descriptive literature on such approaches (see Fraiberg, 1981).

COGNITIVE AND NEUROPSYCHOLOGICAL MEASURES

A number of specific neuropsychological deficits have been demonstrated in adults and older children with MDD. These include deficits in visual-spatial abilities and specific deficits in facial affect perception, emotion recognition, and emotion discrimination (Asthana, Mandal, Khurana, & Haque-Nazamie, 1998; Cooley & Nowicki, 1989; Gur et al., 1992). Similar to the adult findings, studies have found specific visual-spatial deficits in depressed children, evidenced by poorer performance on block design and anagram tasks, while no deficits were evident in expressive language and verbal intelligence (Blumberg & Izard, 1985; Seligman & Peterson, 1985). Findings from our study have revealed deficits in visual-spatial skills and differences in the ability to recognize facial affect in preschool children with MDD compared to controls (Mrakotsky, 2001). These findings suggest an early pattern of neuropsychological deficits in very young children similar to those seen in older children and adults. These findings suggest that a comprehensive assessment for affective disorders should include specific cognitive and neuropsychological tasks that address these areas of functioning. While age-appropriate standardized measures are available to assess visual-spatial skills (e.g., Differential Ability Scales; Elliott, 1990), the assessment of facial affect recognition in the young child is a newer area of investigation. The Facial Affect Comprehension Evaluation (FACE; Mrakotsky & Luby, 2001) is a novel measure that addresses several areas of facial affect recognition using pictorial images as well as a computerized component that measures the child's ability to rate the intensity of emotional expression, designed for young children (Emodiff-K; Gur et al., unpublished). This measure has been shown to be highly feasible and appropriate for children between the ages of 3 years and 5 years 6 months and has been used in our sample of clinically depressed, psychiatric, and no-disorder comparison children (Mrakotsky, 2001). Measures of facial affect recognition and labeling have been developed for older children. However, the FACE is the only comprehensive measure of this kind to our knowledge that is specifically designed for very young children.

CLINICAL PRESENTATION AND CASE DESCRIPTIONS

In this section, an overview of clinical features as well as several clinical cases of young children diagnosed with affective disorders are described. In contrast to adults with MDD, our clinical experience and empirical data suggest that young chil-

dren with MDD do not appear as obviously withdrawn and vegetative as severely depressed older children and adults often are. However, it is important to note that neurovegetative signs are observed by the parents of these depressed children, although they do not appear pervasive. These children are more likely to appear and to describe themselves as "less happy" than same age nondepressed peers. They also display changes in activity, problems with appetite and sleep, and, importantly, seem to derive less pleasure from activities and play. That is, depressed preschoolers in our study displayed notable anhedonia. Consistent with this, the symptom of anhedonia appears to be a highly specific marker of clinical depression in young children. This symptom was reported in 57% of children with depression and, in sharp contrast, was not observed in any child in either of the two comparison groups (0% incidence in control groups) (Luby et al., 2002). This suggests that anhedonia does not typically occur as a part of normal development in a young child, nor does it occur in children suffering from externalizing disorders. Rather, it may be a highly specific marker of MDD. Our data also suggest that this symptom may be a marker of a more severe melancholic sybtype of depression (Luby, Mrakotsky, et al., in press). The notion that an inability to experience pleasure and joy from activities and play would be a serious symptom in a young child and suggestive of psychopathology meets with our experience and intuition that young children are inherently joyful and pleasure seeking.

Our finding of the relatively high frequency and greater specificity of anhedonia in young children is notable and contrasts with the suggestion of Ryan et al. (1987), who reported a significantly lower frequency of anhedonia with younger age when he compared depressed adolescents to prepubertal children. One issue may be the different assessment strategies used. It is not clear whether the assessment of the presence of anhedonia, which is geared toward adult life experiences in standard interviews, was sufficiently sensitive to capture this symptom in prepubertal children. This is clearly an important area for future investigation.

Along these lines (see figure 17.1), findings from our ongoing study reveal that 98% of depressed children were described by their parents as "often appearing sad," or "often appearing grouchy"; 86% had trouble thinking or concentrating and 78% were observed to have low self-esteem. Only 55% of depressed preschoolers in the study sample whined or cried excessively. The presence of neurovegetative signs in these very young depressed children was evidenced by the finding that 80% of depressed preschoolers showed changes in sleep, 80% had weight or appetite changes, and 71% demonstrated changes in activity. Highly notable was the finding that 74% of young children with MDD demonstrated play themes involving death or killing (and occasional suicidal themes), representing a significantly higher incidence than was observed in either of the two control groups. Symptoms historically referred to as "depressive equivalents" were also found but in somewhat lower incidences. Along these lines, 51% had multiple somatic complaints, a symptom that was hypothesized to be a key depressive equivalent in children in the early 1970s, prior to the empirical finding that typical symptoms characterized the clinical picture (Carlson & Cantwell, 1980; Luby et al., 2003). Only 37% of depressed preschoolers displayed the more nonspecific symptom of regression in development (Luby et al., 2003).

Two notable cases of major depressive syndromes in preschool children are described here. L.R. was a 4-year-old White female who presented to the clinic at the referral of her mother due to concerns about persistent irritability and sad mood. Mother reported that L.R. would wake up in a tearful and irritable mood multiple days a week for no apparent reason and would stay in this mood state for at least half of the day. This mood state was characterized by crying and sadness as well as expressions of extreme anger without apparent precipitant (e.g., expressing the desire to kill her younger sister). At the same time, L.R. displayed excessive guilt and expressed negative self-appraisals if she had done something wrong, repeating "I am bad" or "I am stupid." These negative self-appraisals would arise when she was reprimanded for even a very minor infraction. This negative mood state would last for several hours but notably was interrupted by periods of bright mood during which she seemed to run and play displaying relative euthymia. Her parents reported a family history of diagnosed

and treated depression in her maternal uncle and grandmother. Mother observed L.R. to demonstrate repeated play themes involving death and tragedy.

T.W. was a 3-year-old White male who was brought into the clinic due to severe separation anxiety and periods of intense sad mood during which he expressed negative self-evaluations, preoccupation with death, and overt anxiety about the anticipated death of loved ones (who were in no physical or health jeopardy). Parents reported that this low or negative mood appeared to have a cyclic pattern, worse in the fall and winter and relatively improved in the spring and summer. T.W. suffered from severe separation anxiety as well and articulately expressed fears of catastrophic outcomes. These fears were evident in his representational play themes, in which family members were killed or placed in perilous situations. Another associated symptom was periods during which he displayed low appetite, lack of interest in play, and significant difficulty falling asleep with middle insomnia. These changes in sleep and appetite occurred concurrently with periods of depressed and irritable mood.

BIPOLAR DISORDER

Beyond case studies, there have been little to no data on the issue of whether bipolar disorders can be detected and how they might manifest in infants and toddlers. However, clinical experience suggests they may manifest at least as early as 4 years of age. The following case studies describe their possible manifestations; however, it should be noted that many of these observations remain clinical speculation and that this is an important area for future research.

K.M. was a 5-year-old White female who was referred by her mother due to concerns about excessive energy, precocity, talkativeness, and apparent periods of lack of need for sleep and, at times, food. Mother reported that the child woke up routinely at 3 or 4 a.m. full of energy and wanting to play. She described her as talking incessantly at home, inclined to engage complete strangers in a grocery store, and showing excessive talkativeness and directiveness both at school and home. Mother described these symptoms as occurring on a daily basis, although she noted that they were worse in the afternoon. In addition to this baseline behavior, there were periods during which K.M. had a decreased need for sleep associated with a decreased interest in food, resulting in significant weight loss that caused health concerns. During these periods, K.M. seemed to need to sleep only 3 to 4 hours a night and did not appear obviously fatigued during the day but displayed increased irritability and activation. These periods were interrupted by periods in which normal eating and sleeping patterns returned. However, the patient had a persistent decreased need for sleep, which the parents believed had been present since birth. On exam, the patient entered the unfamiliar setting of the clinic and immediately began to taunt an unfamiliar physician examiner. The child teased this doctor about "eating eyeballs for dinner" and tauntingly accused him of "asking the secretary out for a date" while laughing with great intensity and obviously amusing herself (despite her mother's admonitions about appropriate social behavior and obvious embarrassment). During the interview, when asked about her future plans, K.M. indicated that she was going to be a "better singer than Britney Spears" when she grew up, as she confidently explored the playroom while periodically taunting the examiner further. Family history was significant for several individuals with unusually high levels of energy, decreased need for sleep and histories of unusually bold behavior in early childhood, but no formal psychiatric diagnoses. Most notable was the history of a paternal grandfather who at the age of 5 years held onto the bumper of a stranger's car and rode 10 miles into town (sliding all the way) during a snowstorm. He had been known to "retile the kitchen floor at 3 a.m." and now, at age 75, routinely went to the grocery store in the middle of the night to do his shopping.

J.E. was a 4-year-old White male who was referred by his teacher. He had received the diagnosis of pervasive developmental disorder, not otherwise specified from a pediatric neurologist. While his teacher acknowledged significant behavioral problems in school, she was adamant that something more was going on. J.E. was described as very active, constantly on the go, and socially promiscuous and engaging of family, friends, and strangers. He also had periods of decreased need for sleep. He had a history of periods in which he was constantly in need of physical contact with a parent. During these times, he had a seemingly persistent need to press his body up against his mother's and expressed the need to be in constant physical contact with her. This was interspersed with periods in which he seemed relatively aloof and withdrawn and uninterested in engagement. His parents also described him as excessively friendly to strangers, both adults and children. His play was characterized as unusual and his parents described that he had a tendency to personify inanimate objects such as a tube of toothpaste with Barney on it, or cereal boxes, and to line them up as though they were stuffed animals. During the mental status exam, he immediately jumped into the unfamiliar examiner's lap seconds after she entered the room. After just meeting her, he began to hug her, to tell her that he loved her, and to attempt several kisses on her face and lips. There was no history of sexual abuse or premature sexual stimulation. Mother was being treated for depression but also described periods of elevated mood and excessive energy with decreased need for sleep.

CONCLUSION

A large body of developmental evidence is highly suggestive of early alterations in neurobiology and affect development in infants and preschoolers at high risk for MDD. However, prior to our ongoing study, very little empirical data has informed the question of whether clinical affective disorders can occur in very young children and, if so, how symptoms manifest themselves developmentally at this early stage. Preliminary data from our ongoing study suggest that children as young as 3½ years can display the signs and symptoms of clinical depression. Our data suggest that the current *DSM-IV* criteria can be applied to preschool children when the assessment is modified to account for age-appropriate manifestations of the symptom states.

Content validity for *DSM-IV* criteria for MDD has been established; however, questions remain about the application of the 2-week duration criterion. Age-appropriate assessment tools are now available for the assessment of depressive disorders in young children. These include developmentally modified parental interviews, age-appropriate direct interviews of the child using puppets, and observational measures of emotional reactivity and parent-child relationship quality. A novel measure of affect recognition and labeling, as well as other cognitive and neuropsychological measures, may also be a useful component of a comprehensive assessment of affective disorders in young children.

While these data will be useful to advance the identification and assessment of MDD in very young children, there are unfortunately no comparable data to inform the recognition and assessment of bipolar disorders in young children. There have been exciting data on the nosology and longitudinal course of bipolar disorders in school-age children and adolescents (Biederman et al., 2000; Geller, Warner, Williams, & Zimmerman, 1998; Geller, Williams, et al., 1998; Geller et al., 2001; National Institute of Mental Health Research Roundtable, 2001). However, there are currently no controlled studies of the phenomenology of bipolar disorders arising in the preschool period. Two case studies are described (and numerous others have been observed) that lend anecdotal support to the hypothesis that these disorders can begin at this early age. The clinical observation of putative bipolar symptoms among preschool children with increasing frequency by the author as well as other clinicians also supports this hypothesis. A number of the measurement strategies described above might also be applicable to the assessment of early-onset bipolar disorders, inasmuch as they target the assessment of mood and affect as well as emotional reactivity. However, the feasibility and utility of most of the measures described for capturing the early manifestations of mania or hypomania currently remain unclear and will hopefully be the focus of future study.

References

Ablow, J. C., & Measelle, J. R. (1993). *The Berkeley puppet interview*. Berkeley, CA: University of California at Berkeley.

Ablow, J. C., Measelle, J. R., Kraemer, H. C., Harrington, R., Luby, J., Smider, N., Dierker, L.,

Clark, V., Dubicka, B., Heffelfinger, A., Essex, M. J., & Kupfer, D. J. (1999). The MacArthur Three-City Outcome Study: Evaluating multi-informant measures of young children's symptomatology. *Journal of the American Academy of Child and Adolescent Psychiatry, 38,* 1580–1590.

Achenbach, T. M., & Edelbrock, C. (1983). *Manual for the child behavior checklist and revised behavior profile*. Burlington, VT: University of Vermont, Department of Psychiatry.

American Psychiatric Association (1980). *Diagnostic and statistical manual of mental disorders* (3rd ed.). Washington, DC: Author.

American Psychiatric Association (1994). *Diagnostic and statistical manual of mental disorders* (4th ed.). Washington, DC: Author.

Asthana, H. S., Mandal, M. K., Khurana, H., & Haque-Nizamie, S. (1998). Visuospatial and affect recognition deficit in depression. *Journal of Affective Disorders, 48,* 57–62.

Beizer, S. L, Stipek, D. J., & Deitch, F. N. (1985). A developmental analysis of elementary school-aged children's concepts of pride and embarrassment. *Child Development, 59,* 367–377.

Benham, A. L. (2000). The observation and assessment of young children including use of the infant-toddler mental status exam. In C. H. Zeanah, Jr. (Ed.), *Handbook of infant mental health* (pp. 249–265). New York: Guilford Press.

Biederman, J., Mick, E., Faraone, S. V., Spencer, T., Wilens, T. E., & Wozniak, J. (2000). Pediatric mania: A developmental subtype of bipolar disorder? *Biological Psychiatry, 48,* 458–466.

Blumberg, S. H., & Izard, C. E. (1985). Affective and cognitive characteristics of depression in 10- and 11-year-old children. *Journal of Personality and Social Psychology, 49,* 194–202.

Boyce, W. T., Essex, M. J., Woodward, H. R., Measelle, J. R., Ablow, J. C., & Kupfer, D. J. (2002). The confluence of mental, physical, social, and academic difficulties in middle childhood. I. Exploring the "headwaters" of early life morbidities. *Journal of the American Academy of Child and Adolescent Psychiatry, 41,* 580–587.

Carlson, G. A., & Cantwell, D. P. (1980). Unmasking masked depression in children and adolescents. *American Journal of Psychiatry, 137,* 445–449.

Caspi, A., & Silva, P. A. (1995). Temperamental qualities at age 3 predict personality traits in young adulthood. *Child Development, 66,* 486–498.

Clark, R. (1985). *The parent-child early relational assessment: Manual and instrument.* Madison, WI: University of Wisconsin Medical School, Department of Psychiatry.

Cohn, J. F., Campbell, S. B., Matias, R., & Hopkins, J. (1990). Face-to-face interactions of postpartum depressed and nondepressed mother-infant pairs at 2 months. *Developmental Psychology, 26,* 15–23.

Cohn, J. F., Matias, R., Tronick, E. Z., Connell, D., & Lyons-Ruth, K. (1986). Face-to-face interactions of depressed mothers and their infants. *New Directions for Child Development, 34,* 31–45.

Cohn, J. F., & Tronick, E. Z. (1983). Three-month-old infants' reaction to simulated maternal depression. *Child Development, 54,* 185–193.

Cooley, E. L., & Nowicki, S. (1989). Discrimination of facial expressions of emotion by depressed subjects. *Genetic, Social, and General Psychology Monographs, 115,* 449–465.

Cowan, P. (1978). *Piaget with feeling: Cognitive, social and emotional dimensions.* New York: Holt, Rinehart, and Winston.

Cummings, E. M., & Davies, P. T. (1994). Maternal depression and child development. *Journal of Child Psychology and Psychiatry, and Allied Disciplines, 35,* 73–112.

Dawson, G., Klinger, L. G., Panagiotides, H., Hill, D., & Spieker, S. (1992). Frontal lobe activity and affective behavior of infants of mothers with depressive symptoms. *Child Development, 63,* 725–737.

Davidson, R. J., & Fox, N. A. (1982). Asymmetrical brain activity discriminates between positive and negative affective stimuli in human infants. *Science, 218,* 1235–1237.

Egeland, B., Weinfield, N., Hiester, M., Lawrence, C., Pierce, S., Chippendale, K., & Powell, J. (1995). *Teaching tasks administration and scoring manual.* Minneapolis, MN: University of Minnesota.

Egger, H. L., Ascher, B. H., & Angold, A. (1999). *The preschool age psychiatric assessment (PAPA).* Durham, NC: Duke University Medical Center.

Elliott, C. D. (1990). *Differential ability scales (DAS).* San Antonio, TX: Psychological Corporation.

Essex, M. J., Boyce, W. T., Goldstein, L. H., Armstrong, J., Kraemer, H. C., & Kupfer, D. J. (2002). The confluence of mental, physical, social, and academic difficulties in middle childhood. II. Developing the MacArthur Health and Behavior Questionnaire. *Journal of the American Academy of Child and Adolescent Psychiatry, 41,* 588–603.

Field, T., Fox, N. A., Pickens, J., & Nawrocki, T. (1995). Relative right frontal EEG activation in 3- to 6-month-old infants of "depressed" mothers. *Developmental Psychology, 31,* 358–363.

Field, T., Pickens, J., Fox, N. A., Nawrocki, T., & Gonzalez, J. (1995). Vagal tone in infants of depressed mothers. *Developmental Psychopathology, 7,* 227–231.

Field, T., Sandberg, D., Garcia, R., Vega-Lahr, N., Goldstein, S., & Guy, L. (1985). Pregnancy problems, postpartum depression and early mother-infant interactions. *Developmental Psychology, 21,* 1152–1156.

Field, T. M. (1984). Early interactions between infants and their postpartum depressed mothers. *Infant Behavior and Development, 7,* 517–522.

Fraiberg, S. (Ed.). (1981). *Clinical studies in infant mental health: The first year of life.* New York: Basic Books.

Gelfand, D. M., & Teti, D. M. (1990). The effects of maternal depression on children. *Clinical Psychology Review, 10,* 329–353.

Geller, B., Craney, J. L., Bolhofner, K., DelBello, M. P., Williams, M., & Zimmerman, B. (2001). One-year recovery and relapse rates of children with a prepubertal and early adolescent bipolar disorder phenotype. *American Journal of Psychiatry, 158,* 303–305.

Geller, B., Warner, K., Williams, M., & Zimmerman, B. (1998). Prepubertal and young adolescents bipolarity versus ADHD: Assessment and validity using the WASH-U-KSADS, CBCL and TRF. *Journal of Affective Disorders, 51,* 93–100.

Geller, B., Williams, M., Zimerman, B., Frazier, J., Beringer, L., & Warner, K. L. (1998). Prepubertal and early adolescent bipolarity differentiate from ADHD by manic symptoms, grandiose delusions, ultra-rapid or ultradian cycling. *Journal of Affective Disorders, 51,* 81–91.

Gobbo, C., & Chi, M. T. (1986). How knowledge is structured and used by expert and novice children. *Cognitive Development, 1,* 221–237.

Goldsmith, H. H., & Rothbart, M. K. (1996). *The laboratory temperament assessment battery, version 3.0.* Eugene, OR: University of Oregon, Department of Psychology.

Gur, R. C., Erwin, R. J., Gur, R. E., Zwil, A. S., Heimberg, C., & Kraemer, H. C. (1992). Facial emotion discrimination. II. Behavioral findings in depression. *Psychiatry Research, 42,* 241–251.

Harter, S. (1986). Processes underlying the construction, maintenance, and enhancement of self-concept in children. In J. Suis & A. Greenwald (Eds.), *Psychological perspectives on the self* (pp. 137–181). Hillsdale, NJ: Lawrence Erlbaum.

Henriques, J. B., & Davidson, R. J. (1990). Regional brain electrical asymmetries discriminate between previously depressed and healthy control subjects. *Journal of Abnormal Psychology, 99,* 22–31.

Kashani, J. H. (1982). Depression in the preschool child. *Journal of Children in Contemporary Society, 15,* 11–17.

Kashani, J. H., Allan, W. D., Beck, N. C., Bledsoe, Y., & Reid, J. (1997). Dysthymic disorder in clinically referred preschool children. *Journal of the American Academy of Child and Adolescent Psychiatry, 36,* 1426–1433.

Kashani, J. H., & Carlson, G. A. (1985). Major depressive disorder in a preschooler. *Journal of the American Academy of Child and Adolescent Psychiatry, 24,* 490–494.

Kashani, J. H., Holcomb, W. R., & Orvaschel, H. (1986). Depression and depressive symptoms in preschool children from the general population. *American Journal of Psychiatry, 143,* 1138–1143.

Kashani, J. H., & Ray, J. S. (1983). Depressive related symptoms among preschool-age children. *Child Psychiatry and Human Development, 13,* 233–238.

Kashani, J. H., Ray, J. S., & Carlson, G. A. (1984). Depression and depressive-like states in preschool-age children in a child development unit. *American Journal of Psychiatry, 141,* 1397–1402.

Kendler, K. S., Neale, M. C., Kessler, R. C., Heath, A. C., & Eaves, L. J. (1992). Major depression and generalized anxiety disorder: Same genes, (partly) different environments? *Archives of General Psychiatry, 49,* 716–722.

Kochanska, G. (1991). Patterns of inhibition to the unfamiliar in children of normal and affectively ill mothers. *Child Development, 62,* 250–263.

Kovacs, M., Devlin, B., Pollock, M., Richards, C., & Mukerji, P. (1997). A controlled family history study of childhood-onset depressive disorder. *Archives of General Psychiatry, 54,* 613–623.

Luby, J. L., Heffelfinger, A., & Mrakotsky, C. (2001, April). *Salivary cortisol in depressed preschoolers: Relationship to children's self-reports of depression.* Paper presented at the Society for Research of Child Development Conference, Minneapolis, MN.

Luby, J. L., Heffelfinger, A. K., Mrakotsky, C., Brown, K., Hessler, M., & Spitznagel, E. (in press). Alterations in salivary cortisol in depressed preschoolers relative to psychiatric and no disorder comparison groups. *Archives of General Psychiatry.*

Luby, J. L., Heffelfinger, A. K., Mrakotsky, C., Brown, K., Hessler, M., Wallis, J., & Spitznagel, E. (2003). The clinical picture of depression in preschool children. *Journal of the American Academy of Child and Adolescent Psychiatry, 42*(3), 340–348.

Luby, J. L., Heffelfinger, A. K., Mrakotsky, C., Hessler, M. J., Brown, K., & Hildebrand, T. (2002). Preschool major depressive disorder (MDD): Preliminary validation for developmentally modified DSM-IV criteria. *Journal of the American Academy of Child and Adolescent Psychiatry, 41*(8), 928–937.

Luby, J. L., Mrakotsky, C., Heffelfinger, A., Brown, K., Hessler, M., & Spitznagel, E. (in press). Characteristics of preschoolers with anhedonic vs. hedonic DSM-IV MDD: Evidence for a melancholic sub-type of depression in young children. *American Journal of Psychiatry.*

Lucas, C., Fisher, P., & Luby, J. (1998). *Young-child DISC-IV research draft: Diagnostic interview schedule for children.* New York: Columbia University Division of Child Psychiatry, Joy and William Ruane Center to Identify and Treat Mood Disorders.

Markman, E. M. (1989). *Categorization and naming in children: Problems in induction.* Cambridge, MA: MIT Press.

Measelle, J. R., Ablow, J. C., Cowan, P. A., & Cowan, C. P. (1998). Assessing young children's views of their academic, social, and emotional lives: An evaluation of the self-perception scales of the Berkeley Puppet Interview. *Child Development, 69,* 1556–1576.

Mrakotsky, C. (2001). *Visual perception, spatial cognition and affect recognition in preschool depressive syndromes.* Doctoral dissertation, University of Vienna, Austria and Washington University, St. Louis, MO.

Mrakotsky, C., & Luby, J. (2001). *The facial affect*

comprehension evaluation (FACE): A test for emotion perception and emotion recognition in the preschool age. Vienna: University of Vienna; St. Louis, MO: Washington University.

Murray, L. (1992). The impact of postnatal depression on infant development. Journal of Child Psychology and Psychiatry, and Allied Disciplines, 33, 543–561.

National Institute of Mental Health research roundtable on prepubertal bipolar disorder. (2001). Journal of the American Academy of Child and Adolescent Psychiatry, 40, 871–878.

Pickens, J., & Field, T. (1993). Facial expressivity in infants of depressed mothers. Developmental Psychology, 29, 986–988.

Poznanski, E. O., & Zrull, J. P. (1970). Childhood depression. Archives of General Psychiatry, 23, 8–15.

Radke-Yarrow, M., Zahn-Waxler, C., Richardson, D. T. & Susman, A. (1994). Caring behavior in children of clinically depressed and well mothers. Child Development, 65, 1405–1414.

Robins, E., & Guze, S.B. (1970). Establishment of diagnostic validity in psychiatric illness: Its application to schizophrenia. American Journal of Psychiatry, 126, 983–987.

Russell, J. A. (1990). The preschooler's understanding of the causes and consequences of emotions. Child Development, 61, 1872–1881.

Ryan, R. D., Puig-Antich, J., Ambrosini, P., Rabinovich, D., Nelson, B., Iyengar, S., & Twomey, J. (1987). The clinical picture of major depression in children and adolescents. Archives of General Psychiatry, 44, 854–861.

Seligman, M., & Peterson, C. (1985). Depressive symptoms, attributional style, and helplessness deficits in children. In M. Rutter, C. E. Izard, & P. Read (Eds.), Depression in children: Developmental perspectives. New York: Guilford Press.

Shaffer, D., Fisher, P., Lucas, C., & NIMH DISC Editorial Board (1998). Diagnostic interview schedule for children, version IV. New York: Columbia University, Division of Psychiatry.

Sparrow, S. S., Carter, A. S., & Cicchetti, D. V. (1987). Vineland screener: Overview, reliability, validity, administration and scoring. New Haven, CT: Yale University, Department of Psychology.

Thomas, J. M., Benham, A. L., Gean, M., Luby, J., Minde, K., Turner, S., & Wright, H. H. (1997). Practice parameters for the psychiatric assessment of infants and toddlers (0–36 months). Journal of the American Academy of Child and Adolescent Psychiatry, 36, 21S–36S.

Warren, S. L., Oppenheim, D., & Emde, R. N. (1996). Can emotions and themes in children's play predict behavior problems? Journal of the American Academy of Child and Adolescent Psychiatry, 34, 1331–1337.

Zahn-Waxler, C., Kochanska, G., Krupnick, J., & McKnew, D. (1990). Patterns of guilt in children of depressed and well mothers. Developmental Psychology, 26, 51–59.

18

Anxiety Disorders

Susan L. Warren

Anxiety disorders are extremely prevalent poten-tially chronic and disabling conditions that affect adults, adolescents, and children (Cantwell & Baker, 1989; Hettema, Neale, & Kendler, 2001; Ost & Treffers, 2001; Woodward & Fergusson, 2001). Emerging research suggests that without treatment, anxiety disorders in children and ado-lescents may lead to depression and other types of psychopathology (Cole, Zahn-Waxler, Fox, Usher, & Welsh, 1996; Woodward & Fergusson, 2001). Despite this, little research has focused on anxiety disorders during the infant and toddler period. Part of this omission results from the fact that fears and fearfulness in infants and toddlers are common and are therefore thought to be in-nocuous. However, little research has actually de-termined whether high levels of fearfulness, cer-tain types of fears, or specific types of fearful behavioral responses in young children could ac-tually be indicators of psychopathology.

This chapter reviews current descriptions and data concerning fearfulness and anxiety in infants and toddlers. First, definitions and typical fears in infants and toddlers are described. Then, early

evidence showing associations between specific toddler behaviors and the development of later anxiety disorders is reviewed. Because parenting behaviors are important to early development (Bornstein, 1995), parenting behaviors that could potentially contribute to or reduce risk for anxi-ety disorders are described. Finally, classification of anxiety disorders for infants and toddlers is dis-cussed, along with several clinical examples for illustrative purposes. The chapter concludes with a review of assessment measures and approaches, prevalence studies, conclusions, and future direc-tions for the investigation of anxiety disorders in young children.

DEFINITIONS

Although different definitions have been used for the terms *fear*, *anxiety*, and *anxiety disorders*, sev-eral authors have defined fear as the feeling aris-ing in response to danger (Marks, 1987b; Rosen & Schulkin, 1998). In contrast, anxiety has been viewed as an emotion similar to fear, but arising without any objective source of danger (Marks, 1987b). Spielberger, Gorsuch, and Lushene (1970) described two types of anxiety: (1) state anxiety, which is viewed as a transitory emotional state or condition of the human organism that is characterized by subjective feelings of tension, apprehension, and heightened autonomic nervous system activity; and (2) trait anxiety, which is viewed as a relatively stable individual difference in general anxiety proneness and tendency to respond with elevations of state anxiety intensity to situations perceived as threatening. Pathological anxiety or anxiety disorders have been defined as exaggerated fear or anxiety that is characterized by a sense of uncontrollability (Barlow, 1988; Rosen & Schulkin, 1998) and interference in daily routines or functioning (American Psychiatric Association, 1994; Rosen & Schulkin, 1998).

Several different types of anxiety disorders in children have been described, based upon clusters of clinical symptoms and research. These include separation anxiety disorder (anxiety in response to separation from caregivers), specific phobia (anxiety in response to a specific feared object or situation), social phobia (anxiety in response to social situations), and generalized anxiety disorder (persistent and excessive anxiety concerning a number of events or activities) (American Psychiatric Association, 1994). Each of these anxiety disorders is further described in later sections. Obsessive-compulsive disorder, posttraumatic stress disorder, panic disorder, and agoraphobia have also been classified as anxiety disorders (American Psychiatric Association, 1994), but the assessment of these disorders in infants and toddlers is not addressed in this chapter.

One of the difficulties with the identification of anxiety disorders in young children is the fact that anxiety involves subjective feelings of distress, which may be difficult to recognize because young children may not be able to clearly report such symptoms. In contrast, fearful affect and behaviors in response to fear-inducing situations are much more readily observed. Thus, fears and fearful responses have been more extensively studied in early childhood. Examining data concerning typical fears for infants and toddlers could provide information that might aid the assessment of anxiety disorders in young children.

TYPICAL FEARS IN INFANTS AND TODDLERS

Rates of fearfulness change over the course of development. In a sample of approximately 600 mothers, 58% reported seeing fears in their infants between 1 and 3 months of age (Johnson, Emde, Pannabecker, Stenberg, & Davis, 1982), which increased to 90% between 16 and 18 months of age. Shy behaviors were less frequent (9%) between 1 and 3 months of age, but increased to 41% for 4- to 6-month-olds, 66% for 7- to 9-month-olds, and up to 90% for 16- to 18-month-olds (Johnson et al., 1982). These data suggest that some children appear to be fearful within the first few months of life but that almost all children can be seen as demonstrating at least some fearful and shy behaviors by 18 months of age.

Types of fears and anxiety also change over the course of development. Table 18.1 lists the most frequent childhood fears reported by parents during the first two years of life (Jersild & Holmes, 1935). Young infants between 1 and 3 months of age show fearful reactions to impending collisions (Ball & Tronick, 1971). Fear of heights emerges at approximately 6 months of age (Bertenthal, Campos, & Barrett, 1984; Marks, 1987a), and is related to experience with crawling (Scarr & Salapatek, 1970). Walking also tends to increase fear of heights (Bertenthal et al., 1984), suggesting that fears can develop as children face new experiences and challenges. Fears

Table 18.1 Most Frequent Fears Reported by Parents Within the First Two Years of Life

Noises and objects, agents, and events associated with noise	25%
Strange, unfamiliar, or novel situations, objects, and persons	24%
Pain and tactual sensory shock, including persons and objects associated with pain and sensory shock	18%
Falling, high places, sudden displacement, immediate possibility of falling	13%
Animals	7%
Sudden, unexpected visual phenomena, sudden movement, light, flashes	6%

Note. From Jessild & Holmes, 1935.

of strange adults and separation begin from 4 to 9 months of age, as children begin to differentiate between their primary caretakers and others (Bronson, 1972; Marks, 1987a). Both of these fears tend to peak between 8 and 22 months of age, and decline toward the end of the second year (Marks, 1987a). Unfamiliar peers tend to evoke fear later than unfamiliar adults, with fear of unfamiliar peers peaking from 20 to 29 months of age (Marks, 1987a). At older ages, children tend to develop fears of imaginary creatures (e.g., monsters) (Jersild & Holmes, 1935). It is interesting to speculate as to why certain fears tend to appear at certain ages and then fade. Emerging capabilities on the part of the child and new experiences are likely to contribute to the onset and decline of specific types of fear (Warren & Sroufe, in press). However, if the fears do not decline as expected, it is possible that the child is suffering from an anxiety disorder.

TODDLER BEHAVIORS AND THE DEVELOPMENT OF LATER ANXIETY DISORDERS

Toddler behaviors in two different contexts have been linked to later anxiety disorders: (a) behaviors in responses to new situations and strangers, and (b) behaviors in response to separation and reunion with the primary caregiver. Identifying such associations between toddler behaviors and later anxiety disorders is important because it can provide developmentally based information that is useful for early identification and intervention. In addition, such investigations may offer clues concerning the etiology of anxiety disorders.

Behaviors in Response to New Situations and Strangers

Behaviors in response to new situations and strangers have often been investigated in the context of studying temperament. The term *temperament* refers to relatively enduring behavioral and emotional reactions that appear early, differ among individuals, and are thought to be associated with genetic constitution (Goldsmith et al., 1987). The type of temperament that has been most consistently studied in relation to later anxiety disorders is behavioral inhibition. Behavioral inhibition refers to a child's tendency to exhibit quiet withdrawal in novel situations (Kagan, 1994). When a child with behavioral inhibition is presented with an unfamiliar object, person, or situation, the child is quiet, retreats to the caregiver, and withdraws from the unfamiliar stimulus (Kagan, 1994). Kagan and his colleagues have measured behavioral inhibition by examining the latency of the child to talk to and interact with an unfamiliar examiner, tendency to retreat from novel objects and unfamiliar people, cessation of vocalization in new situations, and long periods of proximity to the caregiver, especially when not playing.

Several studies have reported that young children of parents with anxiety disorders are more likely to show behavioral inhibition (Manassis, Bradley, Goldberg, Hood, & Swinson, 1995; Rosenbaum et al., 1988, 2000). This is significant because anxiety disorders tend to run in families (Biederman, Faraone et al., 2001; Biederman, Rosenbaum, Bolduc, Faraone, & Hirshfeld, 1991; Hettema et al., 2001), and suggests that behavioral inhibition may be an early risk factor for anxiety disorders or perhaps an early manifestation of an anxiety disorder.

Rosenbaum and colleagues (1988) studied 2- to 7-year-old children of parents with and without panic disorder and agoraphobia (PDAG). Almost half of the children were younger than 4 years. Children were given age-appropriate cognitive tasks, and behavioral inhibition was rated by measuring the number of spontaneous comments and latency to first, second, and third spontaneous comment. Children of parents with PDAG were 2.5 times more likely to show behavioral inhibition than children of parents without psychopathology.

In a later study, Rosenbaum and colleagues (2000) assessed a much larger group of children of parents with panic disorder, with or without depression, but only about 20% were younger than 4 years. Ratings of behavioral inhibition for the 2-year-old children were slightly different from those for the older children, including displays of distress (crying and fretting) and distractibility, in addition to avoidance and decreased vocalizations. Panic disorder in the parents, in combination with lifetime major depression, conferred a twofold risk for behavioral inhibition in the children (all ages combined).

Manassis et al. (1995) similarly studied children of parents with anxiety disorders (mostly panic disorder). The youngest child was 18 months of age, in a group with a mean age of 3 years. Behavioral inhibition was assessed by counting the number of episodes during which the child displayed crying, approaching the mother, or avoidance of the novel stimuli. Sixty percent of the children showed behavioral inhibition (Manassis et al., 1995), as compared to estimates of approximately 15% in the general population (Kagan, 1994).

Although research concerning children of parents with anxiety disorders supports an association between behavioral inhibition and anxiety disorders, longitudinal investigations have provided even more compelling evidence linking the two variables. Biederman et al. (1990) studied 41 children who had been evaluated as behaviorally inhibited or uninhibited at 21 months of age by Kagan and colleagues (Kagan, Reznick, Snidman, Gibbons, & Johnson, 1988). When the children reached 7 to 8 years of age, psychiatric interviews concerning the child were administered to the parents. Although the inhibited children displayed higher rates of overanxious disorder, separation anxiety disorder, and avoidant disorder (see Social Phobia below for a description of avoidant disorder), statistical significance was established only for phobic disorder at that age, with higher rates of phobic disorder in the school-age children who had been behaviorally inhibited as toddlers. Three years later, 33 of these children were reassessed (Biederman et al., 1993), and 44% of the inhibited children, compared to 7% of the uninhibited children, displayed multiple anxiety disorders. Avoidant disorder, separation anxiety disorder, and agoraphobia were the most common disorders in the inhibited children, as compared to the uninhibited children. Schwartz, Snidman, and Kagan (1999) followed these children further, reassessing them at 13 years of age. An additional and similar group was added (Snidman, 1989), resulting in 79 subjects who had been classified as inhibited or uninhibited at 2 years of age. Adolescents who had been behaviorally in-

hibited at 2 years of age were significantly more likely to have generalized social anxiety at 13 years of age than adolescents who had been uninhibited at 2 years of age, with a greater than twofold increase in risk (Schwartz et al., 1999).

Overall, these studies demonstrate that children who show extremely shy or inhibited behaviors as toddlers are at risk for anxiety disorders at older ages. The study conducted by Schwartz et al. (1999) suggests that there are specific associations between inhibited behavior and social anxiety, which is supported by additional research with older children (Biederman, Hirshfeld, et al., 2001; Hayward, Killen, Kraemer, & Taylor, 1998). Thus, children with shy or inhibited behaviors may have a greater likelihood to be on a particular developmental trajectory leading to social phobia. It is also possible that some children with shy or inhibited behaviors are already manifesting symptoms of a social anxiety disorder.

Behaviors in Response to Separation and Reunion

Behaviors in response to separation and reunion have often been investigated in the context of studying attachment relationships. Attachment behaviors become organized around specific caregivers during the second half of the first year of life. After that time, infants will feel threatened if their attachment figures are not readily available, especially in the face of danger in the immediate environment. In such a situation, the infant will seek help from the attachment figure using behaviors such as crying, signaling, clinging, and, with locomotion, proximity seeking. Maladaptive anxiety may develop in the context of repeated experiences of anxiety that do not appear to be resolvable from the perspective of the child. If the caregiver comes to the child's aid regularly when the child is in need, the child develops confidence in the caregiver and a sense of safety. Such a child is less likely to feel anxious chronically and is said to have a secure attachment relationship. In contrast, a child who has not experienced the relief of anxiety with the caregiver's aid and support is said to have an insecure attachment relationship. An insecurely attached child may be anxious frequently in benign circumstances because of not believing that threatening situations can be readily resolved. Chronic vigilance and anxiety resulting from an insecure attachment relationship may contribute to the development of an anxiety disorder.

Ainsworth, Blehar, Waters, and Wall (1978) described two types of insecure attachment relationships and the mother-infant interactional patterns that preceded and were associated with them. Infants with mothers who responded consistently to their needs were found to have secure attachment relationships (Type B: 66%). Such infants explored confidently in their mother's presence in an unfamiliar situation and were easily comforted after separation from the mother. Infants whose mothers frequently rejected them when the infant sought contact were found to have a type of insecure attachment relationship called *avoidant attachment* (Type A: 22%). These infants did not explore as confidently and tended to avoid their caregiver upon reunion after a brief separation, perhaps as a way of avoiding the feelings they experienced in relation to their mother's unavailability (Sroufe, 1996). Infants who had experienced inconsistent or intrusive care were found to have a different type of insecure attachment relationship called *resistant attachment* (Type C: 12%). These infants also did not explore confidently but showed angry, resistant, and ambivalent behavior upon reunion, appearing to experience and display both anxiety and anger toward the mother. Both A and C infants were said to be insecurely attached, although one showed explicit anxiety (Type C) and the other did not (Type A).

Several studies have linked insecure infant attachment relationships to anxiety disorders. In a sample that has been previously described in this chapter, Manassis, Bradley, Goldberg, Hood, and Swinson (1994) reported higher rates than expected of resistant attachment (30%) in the young children of parents with anxiety disorders (as compared to 12% reported by Ainsworth et al., 1978). This research follows the model described previously of investigating infants of parents with anxiety disorders for risk factors and therefore suggests that resistant attachment may be a risk factor for anxiety disorders. In terms of longitudinal follow-up of toddler behaviors, Bohlin, Hagekull, and Rydell (2000) observed that infants who were insecurely attached at 15 months

of age were more socially anxious at 8 to 9 years of age. This research suggests more general associations between insecure attachment and later anxiety disorders.

In a longitudinal study measuring attachment in infancy and anxiety disorders in adolescence, Warren, Huston, Egeland, and Sroufe (1997) established an even more specific association between insecure attachment and anxiety disorders. Infants with resistant attachment relationships at 12 months of age were two times more likely than expected to develop diagnosed anxiety disorders at 17 years of age. Specific associations were also found between separation anxiety disorder and resistant attachment. Of the eight adolescents who were diagnosed with lifetime separation anxiety disorder, five (62%) had demonstrated resistant attachment relationships in infancy, which was significantly different from that for adolescents not diagnosed with separation anxiety disorder, who showed more typical rates for resistant attachment ($\chi^2 = 10.47$, $p < .003$). This research suggests that toddler behaviors in response to maternal separation and reunion can provide important information concerning the risk for later anxiety disorders.

Taken together, these findings highlight the role of attachment processes in the development of anxiety disorders. Since parenting behaviors play a role in the development of the attachment relationship (Ainsworth et al., 1978) and are also an essential aspect of infant development more generally (Bornstein, 1995), parenting influences may also play an important role in the development of anxiety disorders.

PARENTAL INFLUENCES

Research concerning the attachment relationship suggests that the parenting behaviors most likely to contribute to childhood anxiety would be insensitive and intrusive parenting behaviors. These parenting behaviors have been associated with insecure attachment relationships (Ainsworth et al., 1978), have been found to be more common in anxious parents as compared to controls (Warren et al., 2003; Weinberg & Tronick, 1998), and have also been seen to contribute to increased anxiety/depressive symptoms in preschoolers, especially for more temperamentally vulnerable children (Warren & Simmens, 2003).

Several other theories and research approaches have also provided relevant information concerning parenting behaviors that could contribute to anxiety disorders. In a review of the literature concerning parenting dimensions, Grolnick and Gurland (2002) reported that multiple studies have identified two separate parenting dimensions: (a) warmth, and (b) control. Warmth refers to love and compassion for the child (Baumrind, 1971). Control can refer to making age-appropriate demands and setting limits *or* placing paramount value on compliance and pressuring children toward specified outcomes. The former is considered beneficial while the latter has predicted adverse outcomes (Becker, 1964). Rapee (1997) reviewed the literature concerning anxiety disorders and reported that anxiety disorders are associated with low warmth (or more rejection) and more control (pressuring children toward specified outcomes). Most of the research has focused on retrospective reports by adults or on older children. For example, several studies with anxious children have found evidence of controlling and overprotective parenting behaviors (Krohne & Hock, 1991; Siqueland, Kendall, & Steinberg, 1996) and parental encouraging of avoidant strategies (Dadds & Roth, 2001). Kagan, Rubin, and Fox (Fox & Calkins, 1993; Kagan, 1994; Rubin & Burgess, 2001; Rubin, Burgess, & Hastings, 2002; Rubin, Hastings, Stewart, Henderson, & Chen, 1997; Rubin & Mills, 1991) have similarly proposed that high parental control may contribute to the maintenance of behavioral inhibition, which has been linked to later anxiety disorders (Hirshfeld et al., 1992). Other types of parenting behaviors that may be important in the development of anxiety disorders include: (a) modeling anxiety (Gerull & Rapee, 2002; Muris, Steerneman, Merckelbach, & Meesters, 1996), (b) reinforcing anxiety through disproportionate attention to anxiety (suggested in Kagan, 1994), and (c) inconsistent parenting behaviors (Kohlmann, Schumacher, & Streit, 1988). Prospective longitudinal research is needed to clarify whether parenting behaviors definitely contribute to anxiety or are merely associated.

One clear parental influence on children's anxiety is genetic. Anxiety disorders have been found to show significant heritabilities, which appear to account for one third of the variance, increase with age, and are greater for girls than boys (Eley, 2001). Although these genetic influences could account for the associations between parenting behaviors and children's anxiety, behavioral genetic studies suggest a significant shared environmental influence as well (Eley, 2001). In other words, shared family experiences, which are likely to involve parenting behaviors, have been found to be influential in the development of anxiety disorders.

CLASSIFICATION OF ANXIETY DISORDERS IN YOUNG CHILDREN

Because fears in infants and toddlers are developmentally common and have been thought to reflect temperament and parent-child relationships, the classification of anxiety disorders in infants and toddlers has been somewhat difficult and controversial. To address problems concerning the assessment of infants and toddlers, the task force of the Washington, DC–based Zero to Three, National Center for Infants, Toddlers, and Families developed new diagnostic criteria (Zero to Three, 1994) and published cases (Lieberman, Wieder, & Fenichel, 1997) to clarify diagnosis in infants. This work has been extremely useful and important. However, it combined all types of anxiety into one category, providing little guidance for the study of particular types of anxiety problems, which may be important given possible differences in developmental trajectories (such as for behavioral inhibition and social anxiety, for example).

In contrast, the *Diagnostic and Statistical Manual of Mental Disorders*, Fourth Edition (*DSM-IV*; American Psychiatric Association, 1994) does describe separate types of anxiety disorders. However, little research has used this system systematically with infants and toddlers.

The following subsections review issues related to the classification of specific types of anxiety disorders in infants and young children. In addition, descriptions of clinical cases are provided for illustration.[1]

Separation Anxiety Disorder

The diagnosis of separation anxiety disorder according to the *DSM-IV* (American Psychiatric Association, 1994) requires that a child show three out of eight symptoms related to separation anxiety disorder (the first eight symptoms listed in table 18.2, excluding italic notes). Four of these symptoms require good verbal skills (complaints, worry about attachment figures, worry about separation, and reports of nightmares), making it difficult for an infant or toddler to meet the criteria. In addition, clinicians are warned not to diagnose developmentally appropriate levels of separation anxiety, although little guidance is provided.

Because of these issues and other concerns related to diagnosing young children, a group was formed to develop diagnostic criteria for disorders in young children, the Research Diagnostic Criteria–Preschool Age (RDC-PA).[2] Alternative criteria for separation anxiety disorder in young children were created and are listed in table 18.2. Because of developmental shifts in the formation of the attachment relationship and responses to separation, clinicians have been reluctant to diagnose separation anxiety disorder in infants and toddlers (American Psychiatric Association, 1994). Yet some children as young as 17 months appear to meet criteria and are experiencing significant distress and impairment in family life.

Separation Anxiety Disorder: A Clinical Example

Mary was 17 months old when she was brought into the clinic because of difficulties sleeping. She

---

Table 18.2 Diagnostic Criteria for Separation Anxiety Disorder as Defined by the Research Diagnostic Criteria–Preschool Age (RDC-PA)

A. Developmentally inappropriate and excessive anxiety concerning separation from home or from those to whom the individual is attached, as evidenced by three (or more) of the following:

1. Recurrent excessive distress when separation from home or major attachment figures occurs or is anticipated.
2. Persistent and excessive worry about losing, or about possible harm befalling, major attachment figures.
3. Persistent and excessive worry that an untoward event will lead to separation from a major attachment figure (e.g., getting lost or being kidnapped).
4. Persistent reluctance or refusal to go to school or elsewhere because of fear of separation.
   Note: In young children, this may appear as
   (a) fear or subjective anxious affect related to leaving home for day care or school,
   (b) anticipatory fear or subjective anxious affect related to day care or school situation, or
   (c) the child stays out of day care or school because of fear, anxiety, or emotional disturbance.
5. Persistently and excessively fearful or reluctant to be alone or without major attachment figures at home or without significant adults in other settings.
6. Persistent reluctance or refusal to go to sleep without being near a major attachment figure or to sleep away from home.
7. Repeated nightmares involving the theme of separation. *(Note: in preverbal or barely verbal children, there may be frightening dreams without recognizable content.)*
8. Repeated complaints *or expression* of physical symptoms (such as headaches, stomachaches, nausea, or vomiting) when separation from major attachment figures occurs or is anticipated.
9. *Persistent preoccupation or worrying about the whereabouts of attachment figures (e.g., looking out a window or stopping play).*

B. The duration of the disturbance is at least four weeks.

C. The onset is before age 18 years.

D. The disturbance causes clinically significant distress or impairment in social, academic (occupational), or other important areas of functioning. *Note: In young children, the disturbance may cause parents to significantly modify their behavior to modify the child's behaviors.*

E. The disturbance does not occur exclusively during the course of . . . *(no change from DSM-IV).*

Note: Changes to *DSM-IV* are in italic.

Source: Diagnostic criteria for Separation Anxiety Disorder reprinted with permission from the *Diagnostic and Statistical Manual of Mental Disorders*, Fourth Edition. Copyright 1994 American Psychiatric Association.

showed recurrent excessive distress with crying when separated from her mother, persistent reluctance to separate from her mother, and persistent refusal to go to sleep without being near her mother. The separation anxiety was so severe that the mother could not go to the bathroom or take a shower alone. The mother also wanted to return to work but could not. Mary could take hours to settle even after a brief separation and also had nightmares. Most of these difficulties had been present for approximately 8 months. In addition, the sleep difficulties were causing marital problems, as the father wanted the child to sleep in a separate room.

Mary was born at term and was a planned and desired baby. Her developmental milestones were normal and she had no medical problems. The mother, a designer, had stayed home to care for Mary. The father, an architect, had missed weeks at work to support his wife and child with the continuing sleep and separation difficulties. The couple reported no other stresses or difficulties in their lives.

A Strange Situation procedure was conducted as part of the evaluation. Mary showed a resistant attachment relationship (Type C) with her mother. In free play the mother appeared somewhat irritable (she reported that this was from lack of sleep) but otherwise played appropriately with her child.

This brief vignette illustrates some of the difficulties with diagnosing separation anxiety in young children. Mary's distress at separation was developmentally appropriate. However, it was causing sustained suffering for Mary and her family. Alternative diagnoses could include a sleep disorder and parent-child relationship problem. Yet the separation anxiety was significant, warranting clinical attention as well.

Specific Phobia

Infants and toddlers can meet the criteria for specific phobia as outlined in *DSM-IV*, although the requirement of a duration of 6 months signifies that this diagnosis would not be met by a child who experiences multiple specific fears that could be quite distressing and disabling but are not of long enough duration. Further research is needed regarding these criteria in young children, as well

as for the situation in which a child moves from one extreme and disabling fear to another over the course of development but does not meet the 6-month duration criteria for any one fear.

Social Phobia

The diagnosis of social phobia for infants and toddlers involves some of the same difficulties as described for separation anxiety disorder. Because fears of strangers are generally considered to be developmentally appropriate until the end of the second year of life, clinicians are reluctant to diagnose social anxiety in young children (Rapoport & Ismond, 1996). In addition, children generally develop the capacity for being concerned about the evaluation of others at approximately 4 years of age (Asendorpf, 1989). This makes the diagnosis of social phobia for infants and toddlers virtually impossible, because the diagnosis of social phobia requires that an individual must fear that he or she will act in a way that will be humiliating or embarrassing. Previous versions of *DSM* included a diagnosis called avoidant disorder of childhood, which did not require such capabilities. This diagnosis was eliminated in *DSM-IV*, perhaps because of the overlap with social phobia in older children (Francis, Last, & Strauss, 1992; Rapoport & Ismond, 1996). As a result of these issues, the RDC-PA includes criteria for a disorder of inhibition/avoidance (table 18.3), which may describe an early form of social phobia. The criteria are almost identical to those for social phobia and could perhaps eventually be combined descriptively with that disorder, if this is supported by research. The case below describes a boy with these characteristics who also meets criteria for social phobia.

Disorder of Inhibition/Avoidance and Social Phobia: A Clinical Example

Steven was a 3-year-old boy who was brought to the clinic because of long-standing concerns about social anxiety. The patient was fussy and irritable as a young infant and began to display extreme withdrawal behaviors in the presence of strangers toward the end of his first year. Although he interacted in a socially appropriate way with his family from a young age, Steven did

Table 18.3 Disorder of Inhibition/Avoidance

A. Excessive shrinking from contact with and persistent reluctance to approach unfamiliar people or novel stimuli (e.g., new toys, new smells, new tastes, new sounds, new situations).

B. Exposure to unfamiliar people or to novel stimuli almost invariably provokes the behaviors in A which may also be expressed in crying, tantrums, freezing, or shrinking from the situation.

C. Desire for social involvement with familiar people (family members and peers the person knows well) and generally warm and satisfying relations with family members and other familiar figures.

D. The situations in A are avoided or else are endured with intense anxiety or distress.

E. The avoidance, anxious anticipation, or distress in the situation interfere significantly with the child's normal routine, functioning, play, or social activities or relationships, or there is marked distress concerning these reactions.

F. Symptoms occur for a period of 3 months or longer.

G. The avoidance is not due to the direct physiological effects of a substance (e.g., a medication) or a general medical condition and is not better accounted for by another mental disorder (e.g., separation anxiety disorder, posttraumatic stress disorder, social phobia).

Note: This is a category for research purposes to describe children who are likely to later show social phobia or selective mutism but are not yet at the age at which they can report symptoms related to humiliation or embarrassment.

not talk until he was almost 2 years old. However, at that point he spoke in complete sentences and appeared to be quite advanced verbally. His mother reported that it was as if he was unwilling to talk until he had mastered it. When Steven started preschool, he was frozen and withdrawn in the social setting. He would not interact or play with the other children and would frequently cry and resist going at all. The mother also tried to get Steven to engage in a variety of outdoor and indoor activities, which she thought he would enjoy, with other children, but Steven refused to participate. Steven did not have difficulty separating from either of his parents, as long as he did not have to go into peer situations.

Steven was also fearful of novelty and changes. In addition, Steven's mother said that Steven did not like to receive praise, and would in fact cry if he were praised. Steven refused to perform in front of others at preschool, indicating concerns about how the other children would react. These fears of social situations caused a great deal of distress for Steven and his family and prevented his participation in a program for gifted children, despite his extraordinary intelligence.

Steven was born at term and was a planned and desired baby. He had no medical problems except for a small abdominal hernia. Because of his social anxiety, Steven had a very difficult time being examined by doctors. As a result of his crying and refusal behaviors, he had not been adequately evaluated for the abdominal hernia, though

surgery was recommended. His mother, who was a social worker, worked part-time while Steven was in preschool. His father was an engineer. Steven played well with his younger brother (15 months old) and had not shown distress or changed his behaviors after his brother's birth. The family reported no other stresses or difficulties in their lives and no marital problems.

In the initial evaluation, Steven appeared shy but made eye contact eventually. He spoke to his parents in front of the clinician but would not talk directly with the clinician, and when the clinician addressed him directly, he appeared to withdraw.

This case describes a child who could have been diagnosed with disorder of inhibition/avoidance at a younger age because he had a long-standing history of those symptoms. At the time of presentation to the clinic, however, he seemed to meet criteria for social phobia because of his reactions to praise (suggesting fears of disapproval) and fears of performing in front of peers.

Generalized Anxiety Disorder

The diagnosis of generalized anxiety disorder requires that the individual experience excessive anxiety or worry occurring more days than not for at least 6 months about a number of events or activities, with the person finding it difficult to control the worry or anxiety. For children, only one additional symptom related to the worry or anxiety is needed from a list that includes restlessness, difficulty concentrating, irritability, muscle tension, and sleep disturbance. Generalized anxiety disorder can be difficult to diagnose in infants and toddlers because the hallmark of the disorder is worry, which must be reported by the child. However, anxiety can be observed in young children, who repeatedly bring up issues related to fears and concerns about immediate and impending situations. In addition, young children can easily meet criteria for restlessness, irritability, or sleep disturbance in reaction to the pervasive fears or anxiety.

Generalized Anxiety Disorder: A Clinical Example

Rachel, a 2-year-old girl, was brought to the clinic by her mother because of difficulties sleeping. These concerns had been present for most of her life. She had difficulties both with falling asleep and with frequent awakenings. At 2 years of age, she was still awakening up to three times per night and would appear quite anxious upon awakening, crying and calling for her mother. During the day, Rachel frequently expressed several types of anxiety. She regularly was concerned about dirt or damage to her toys (which was apparent to others but was so minor that it would not have distressed most children) and spent much of the day complaining about these things and her concerns that she would not be able to engage in fun activities later in the day (such as getting a new toy or going to the park). She also refused to take baths because she was afraid she would get hurt in the bathtub (although this had never happened). This caused major problems for Rachel and her mother. In addition, Rachel would become irritable and restless when anxious, which greatly distressed both mother and child and interfered with her acceptance at an exclusive preschool.

Rachel did not have any difficulties separating from her mother, who, in fact, had worked long hours since Rachel was 2 months old. Rachel's mother was a physician and had experienced a major depressive episode after Rachel's father had died, shortly before Rachel's birth. A full-time nanny had cared for Rachel since her mother had returned to work. Rachel had a very good relationship with the nanny, and showed the anxiety symptoms with both her mother and the nanny. Rachel had been born by cesarean section because of maternal preeclampsia but otherwise had not experienced any trauma, developmental delays, or medical problems. In addition, Rachel was comfortable meeting strangers and peers and played well with other children.

This case illustrates that it is possible for a toddler to meet criteria for generalized anxiety disorder. However, this was partly because the toddler was quite articulate and could describe the issues that were causing her distress. Rachel also met criteria for a sleep disorder, and her prenatal experiences and/or parenting issues could have contributed to her anxiety symptoms. However, Rachel's anxiety symptoms were causing significant distress and interfering with her development, warranting clinical attention and intervention.

Anxiety Disorder Not Otherwise Specified

The diagnosis of anxiety disorder not otherwise specified was initially proposed to address situations with prominent anxiety or phobic avoidance that did not meet criteria for another disorder. Unfortunately, because infants and toddlers often do not meet criteria for the other anxiety disorders, this diagnosis is commonly used with such populations.

Anxiety Disorder Not Otherwise Specified: A Clinical Example

Amy was a 6-month-old who was brought to the clinic by her mother. The mother's major concern was that she needed to constantly carry and distract Amy, or Amy would become upset. The mother reported that whenever she put Amy down and did not interact with her, Amy would cry until her mother picked her up again. This could continue for many hours. The mother was extremely distressed about this, as she felt that she could not adequately attend to her other child, her husband, or the household tasks. The mother was also concerned that Amy seemed to be somewhat delayed in comparison to her 2-year-old sister when the sister was the same age. Amy could not roll over, was not interested in crawling or playing independently, and was not trying to make sounds.

Amy was born at term and was a planned and desired baby. She had no medical or growth problems but slept almost all the time for the first month of her life. The mother reported that Amy's desire to be carried developed after the first month. In addition, Amy required an extremely quiet and dark environment to nurse. She could not nurse with bright lights, the TV, or if her mother talked with anyone during that time. The mother stayed home to care for the children, and the father was a salesman who traveled frequently. Amy refused to sleep without her mother, so the parents did not sleep together. The couple also reported some marital tension related to managing the children and household tasks (and were in therapy for this) but denied other stresses, violence, or difficulties in their lives.

In the first session, the mother's description of Amy was supported. The infant initially appeared to be very passive and did not vocalize. She was not interested in playing by herself but could be distracted and engage with the clinician. If Amy was not actively engaged, she became distressed, reaching for her mother. Amy also appeared to be very sensitive and fearful of bright lights and loud sounds.

Because of her clinical presentation, Amy was tested by an experienced occupational therapist for hypersensitivity and hyposensitivity. In addition, a psychologist administered the Bayley Scales of Infant Development to quantify Amy's developmental levels. Both assessments did not show any deficits.

The Working Model of the Child Interview (Benoit, Parker, & Zeanah, 1997; Zeanah, Benoit, & Barton, n.d.) was administered to the mother, who realized during the course of the interview that she was very angry with Amy. The mother felt that Amy was extremely demanding, which reminded the mother of her own mother. Amy's mother decided that it did not make sense for her to feel so negatively toward her daughter. She became aware that she had been projecting the anger she felt toward her mother onto her daughter. She decided to focus on and resolve the anger she felt toward her mother and to separate those feelings from her feelings toward Amy. After this session, the mother became more relaxed, acknowledged her own needs, and was able to view her child more clearly; and Amy's behavior

started to change. Amy began to roll over, sit, and crawl on her own, vocalize, and explore toys. She was able to separate from her mother for brief periods and was less sensitive to lights and sounds.

This case provides many diagnostic challenges because it seems to incorporate several different domains. In the DC:0–3 system (Zero to Three, 1994), the child could possibly have been diagnosed with a regulatory disorder. However, testing did not reveal any clear developmental or sensory problems. There was definitely a relationship problem between the mother and child, and the major symptoms resolved when this was treated. However, the child also showed fearfulness in response to lights and sounds and anxiety in response to separation. Acknowledging such symptoms could be important because such symptoms could indicate a particular predisposition or tendency in terms of anxiety disorders. With additional research, specifying such problems with fearfulness and anxiety in infants may prove useful in order to further clarify prognosis and refine treatment approaches.

ASSESSMENT METHODS FOR ANXIETY IN YOUNG CHILDREN

Although research concerning typical fears, behavioral inhibition, and insecure attachment relationships in infants and toddlers has been conducted, little research has focused on the assessment of anxiety disorders in such young children (Warren & Dadson, 2001). Several instruments have been used to assess anxiety problems in young children but have not, in general, differentiated between different types of anxiety and fearful responses.

Questionnaires

The Child Behavior Checklist (CBCL) and Caregiver-Teacher Report Form are questionnaires that have been widely used to assess emotional and behavioral problems in children and adolescents (Achenbach, 1991a, 1991b). Newer versions of these questionnaires have been developed, which can be used for children as young as 18 months of age (Achenbach & Rescorla, 2000). In addition, a specific anxiety scale has now been created to explicitly target anxiety symptomatology (Achenbach & Rescorla, 2000). Symptoms on this scale mostly seem to characterize generalized and separation anxiety disorders.

Designed to assess even younger children, the Infant-Toddler Social and Emotional Assessment (ITSEA; Briggs-Gowan & Carter, 1998; Carter & Briggs-Gowan, 1999) is a questionnaire that is completed by parents of 1- to 3-year-old children. This questionnaire includes subscales for anxiety (includes 10 items concerning specific fears, general anxiety, and obsessive-compulsive symptoms), separation distress (6 items), and inhibition to novelty (5 items). Although this questionnaire has shown excellent psychometric properties (Briggs-Gowan & Carter, 1998; Carter & Briggs-Gowan, 1999), it has not yet been specifically tested in relation to anxiety disorders.

The Preschool Anxiety Scale (PAS; Spence, Rapee, McDonald, & Ingram, 2001) is a promising measure for examining anxiety problems in young children. The questionnaire, which was developed for children 2 through 5 years of age, has confirmed separate factors for social phobia, separation anxiety, generalized anxiety, and fears of physical injury. Children studied thus far have ranged in age from 31 to 83 months (mean = 55 months), so additional research is needed for younger children.

The Fear Survey Schedule for Infants and Preschoolers (Warren & Ollendick, 2001) and the Infant-Preschool Scale for Inhibited Behaviors (Warren, 2001a) are questionnaires currently undergoing investigation. The first questionnaire is structured in a manner similar to the Fear Survey Schedule (Gullone & King, 1992; Ollendick, 1983; Scherer & Nakamura, 1968), listing specific types of fears that an infant or toddler might experience. The second questionnaire focuses on behaviors suggestive of disorder of inhibition/avoidance and social anxiety. A screening instrument for use in pediatric settings has also been developed (Warren, 2001b).

Structured Diagnostic Interviews

Several structured diagnostic interviews have been developed but require further examination. Mammen, Scholle, Jennings, and Popper (1995) and Scheeringa (1995) have developed diagnostic interviews focused on the DC:0–3 diagnostic criteria

(Zero to Three, 1994). However, since different types of anxiety disorders are not distinguished in this system, these interviews are of limited usefulness for the identification of specific types of anxiety disorders.

Lucas, Fisher, and Luby have modified the Diagnostic Interview Schedule for Children (DISC) for use with children down to 3 years of age. However, except for a study of depression (see chapter 17), little research has yet been reported regarding this interview.

The Preschool Age Psychiatric Assessment (PAPA; Egger, Ascher, & Angold, 1999) is the most promising interview because it assesses multiple discrete symptoms individually and thus can be used in epidemiological studies to define the best diagnostic criteria for children. It can be used for children as young as 2 years of age. Research is currently underway to further validate this instrument (H. Egger, personal communication, March 2002) and an additional supplement designed specifically to study anxiety (Warren, 2003).

The Diagnostic Interview for Infants to Preschoolers for Anxiety (DIIPA; Warren, 2000) was developed to specifically assess anxiety disorders in infants and toddlers. Research is currently underway on the validity of this interview. One disadvantage of the interview is that it does not assess psychopathology other than anxiety disorders. However, one advantage is that it does include an observational assessment of the child.

Behavioral Observations

Because young children cannot easily report anxiety symptoms, and because the reports of parents could be biased, an observational measure for anxiety disorders would be extremely beneficial. The research described previously concerning toddler behavioral responses to new situations and strangers and to separation and reunion has provided important information that could contribute to the development of such an instrument. Research has also been conducted concerning such an observational measure for older children (Kaminer, Feinstein, Seifer, Stevens, & Barrett, 1990). However, further work is needed to develop a measure for younger children; although the DIIPA (Warren, 2000) includes an observational scale, it has not been validated yet.

Physiological Measurements

If physiological measures could diagnose anxiety disorders, the assessment process would be greatly facilitated. Unfortunately, at this time there are no such measures. Some potential candidates for infants and toddlers have arisen from the research concerning behaviors in response to new situations and strangers; Kagan and colleagues have identified multiple physiological differences associated with behaviorally inhibited temperament (Kagan, 1994). These physiological differences include higher and less variable heart rates, increased blood pressure changes to challenge, increased pupillary dilation, increased muscle tension in the vocal cords, increased urinary norepinephrine, increased salivary cortisol, increased startle, differences in skin conductance, temperature differences, and greater right frontal electroencephalogram (EEG) activation (Kagan, 1994). Thus far, greater heart rate in response to novel stimuli and greater right frontal EEG activation have shown the most consistent relations with behavioral inhibition (Schmidt & Fox, 1998; Turner & Beidel, 1996). However, both have been associated with psychopathology other than anxiety disorders and do not appear to provide information specific to anxiety. Salivary cortisol has also shown some promise, with earlier measures of elevated salivary cortisol predicting later internalizing symptoms (Ashman, Dawson, Panagiotides, Yamada, & Wilkinson, 2002; Essex, Klein, Cho, & Kalin, 2002; Goldsmith & Lemery, 2000; Smider et al., 2002). In addition, more disturbed sleep in young infants could also be a potential early marker for risk for anxiety disorders (Warren et al., 2003). However, additional research is needed to clarify whether any of these physiological measures, or some combination of them, could reliably be used to specifically identify anxiety disorders in infants and toddlers.

CLINICAL ASSESSMENT OF ANXIETY DISORDERS IN YOUNG CHILDREN

This section offers recommendations, based on clinical experience and on research whenever possible, to aid clinicians in the assessment of anxiety disorders for young children. This section is not meant as a comprehensive assessment guide; many excellent books provide chapters concerning assessment for infants and toddlers (Greenspan, 1992; Zeanah, 2000) and for anxiety disorders (March, 1995; Ollendick & March, in press). Rather, the focus is specifically on the issues that seem to be most relevant for the clinical assessment of anxiety disorders in infants and toddlers.

Typically, the assessment process includes interviews with caregivers and play sessions with the child. Observations of the child are important and should be done in multiple contexts including in the waiting room, during play and clean-up with the caregivers, separating from caregivers, and in a new setting with a stranger (the clinician). Observations at home and in day care or school can also provide valuable information. Administering the Working Model of the Child Interview (Benoit et al., 1997; Zeanah et al., n.d.) to the caregivers can also elicit useful information concerning the parents' views of the child and possible relationship issues. The assessment is usually conducted over multiple sessions in order to observe the child on several different occasions.

Table 18.4 provides an overview of major assessment issues. As is typical in clinical practice, the clinician must obtain complete information concerning the presenting symptoms. It is important to examine the specific time of onset of symptoms in relation to the timing of family changes and potential stresses. Parents may miss such connections, but these connections can provide important clues concerning sources of distress for the child. Because anxiety disorders may involve disturbances in relations with others (e.g., separation anxiety disorder and social phobia), the clinician should also gather information concerning social development, including the child's interest in and behaviors toward parents, siblings, other adults, and peers. Feeding difficulties can accompany temperamental reactivity and anxiety disorders (Chatoor, Ganiban, Hirsch, Borman-Spurrell, & Mrazek, 2000), so the clinician should inquire about feeding practices and problems. In addition, difficulties with sleep are an integral part of several anxiety disorders (American Psychiatric Association, 1994). Thus, obtaining in-

Table 18.4 Major Issues for the Clinical Assessment of Anxiety Disorders in Infants and Toddlers

Assessment Topic	Major Issues for Assessment
Chief complaint and history of present illness	Onset, duration, and expression of symptoms Exacerbating and alleviating factors Social, feeding and sleep behaviors
Past history	Pregnancy, delivery, development milestones, traumas Previous interventions
Family history	Psychiatric symptoms, particularly parental anxiety and depression Family conflict or stresses Cultural and community context
Medical history and medications	Medical conditions or medications that could cause or contribute to anxiety
Mental status examination	Child's affect, attention, motor, language, and social abilities Child's response to different types of sensory stimuli Child's response to new situations and strangers
Parent-child relationship	Child's level of interaction and comfort with caregivers Child's reactions to separation and reunion with caregivers Caregiver sensitivity, intrusiveness, warmth, control, inconsistency, introducing anxiety themes, modeling anxiety, reinforcing anxiety
Day care and/or preschool	Presence of symptoms Social interactions with adults and peers
Differential diagnosis and comorbidity	Pervasive developmental disorder or autism Posttraumatic stress disorder Reactive attachment disorder Depression Attention deficit/hyperactivity disorder Regulatory disorder[a] Medically or substance-induced anxiety disorder

[a]From DC:0–3 (Zero to Three, 1994).

formation about problems initiating or maintaining sleep is crucial. In addition, the clinician should make inquiries concerning where the child sleeps and with whom. Some children sleep with their parents because of separation anxiety, and parents do not always volunteer this information if it does not cause difficulties for them.

In terms of past history, the clinician should elicit descriptions of pregnancy or delivery difficulties because they could provide information concerning medical issues and life experiences that might contribute to anxiety. A history of medical problems and medication use is similarly important, because it could account for anxiety symptoms. History concerning developmental milestones might show the impact of anxiety on development, but such a history is even more necessary to identify developmental problems or a pervasive developmental disorder requiring inter-

ventions. Traumatic experiences could contribute to anxiety and might suggest a diagnosis of posttraumatic stress disorder, depending on the child's symptoms. History concerning previous interventions could also aid the design of new treatments for the child.

Because anxiety disorders run in families, eliciting a family history for anxiety disorders is crucial. Parents will frequently have such a history, or a history of depression, and often are not receiving treatment but could benefit from it. Sometimes parents will deny a history of psychiatric illness for all family members. Inquiring about phobic symptoms and social anxiety in those cases will often elicit information concerning untreated anxiety disorders. Marital conflict and family stress could also contribute to internalizing symptoms (Shaw, Keenan, Vondra, Delliquadri, & Giovannelli, 1997), so assessing these issues is important. Cultural and community contexts could influence the expression or tolerance of anxiety symptoms and thus should be included in the assessment.

In terms of the mental status examination, it is important to carefully observe the child in the waiting room and the child's initial response to the clinician, watching for shy or inhibited behaviors. Anxious children could also show heightened startle in response to sudden noises or movements. Observing the child's reactions to different types of stimuli can often provide useful information about particular fears and sensitivities.

Caregiver-child interactions should be examined with all caregivers independently and in multiple contexts including free play, cleanup (or some other type of structured task), and separation and reunion. It is also useful to view the entire family together. The comfort of the child with the parent should be observed as well as the child's responses to separation from and reunion with the parent. In addition, caregivers' behaviors should be observed for sensitivity, intrusiveness, warmth, overcontrol, inconsistency, modeling of anxiety, and reinforcing anxiety through disproportionate attention to anxiety over other emotional responses. Parents of anxious children will frequently introduce anxiety themes into the play (such as a child doll becoming injured or in danger). Identifying such issues is important to help with the design of treatment interventions.

Because some children may manifest anxiety only in day care or preschool, it is important to gather information from day care providers and teachers concerning the child's behaviors. It is best if the clinician can observe the child in these settings, although that is not always possible.

In terms of differential diagnosis and comorbidity, it sometimes can be difficult to differentiate pervasive developmental disorder from social anxiety when a child does not have clear-cut symptoms of pervasive developmental disorder. Early social developmental history, including the child's desire for interactions with others, can often help with this distinction. A history of trauma or posttraumatic-type symptoms with a sudden onset can signal posttraumatic stress disorder. A child who is withdrawn not only with strangers but also with parents could be experiencing reactive attachment disorder or depression. Attention

deficit disorder is often comorbid with anxiety disorders, and it can be difficult to differentiate inattentiveness from anxiety in young children. Objective tests can be useful in this case. Although not part of *DSM-IV*, regulatory disorders should also be considered. Thorough evaluations are important for designing individualized treatment interventions for the child, addressing all areas in which difficulties are identified (e.g., social relationships, feeding, sleep, parental psychopathology, marital and family relationships, developmental delays, problems with attention, increased sensitivity to stimuli, parent-child relationships). Child anxiety can involve multiple domains of functioning, and it is important to identify and address each one.

PREVALENCE OF ANXIETY DISORDERS IN YOUNG CHILDREN

Because assessment measures have not yet been fully tested and because classification is not entirely clear, prevalence estimates for anxiety disorders in young children have not yet been established. Lavigne and colleagues (1993, 1996) conducted unstructured clinical interviews of parents concerning their young children. Rates of 3 to 5% were found for anxiety disorders in this pediatric sample (Lavigne et al., 1993, 1996). Wright et al. (2002) used *DSM-IV* to diagnose anxiety disorders in infants 1 and 2 years of age. They reported rates of 2% for *DSM-IV* anxiety disorders in a community clinic and 17% in a specialty infant clinic. The authors reported that although the prevalence rates appeared to differ, they thought that the community clinic had actually underdiagnosed anxiety disorders in the infants and toddlers.

CONCLUSIONS AND FUTURE DIRECTIONS

Assessment of anxiety disorders in infants and young children is extremely challenging at this time but critically important. Developmental changes in fears and behaviors in response to fear-inducing situations contribute to difficulties with making early diagnoses. The tendency has been for clinicians not to diagnose anxiety disorders in young children, because fearfulness and anxiety are viewed as developmentally appropriate. However, undiagnosed, these disorders create a great deal of suffering for children and their families (Hettema et al., 2001; Woodward & Fergusson, 2001), and a delayed diagnosis may unnecessarily prolong these difficulties. Many children do not grow out of these disorders and, in fact, may go on to develop additional psychopathology (Cole, Peeke, Martin, Truglio, & Seroczynski, 1998; Woodward & Fergusson, 2001).

Research concerning behavioral inhibition in toddlers and young children has shown linkages with later social anxiety. However, it is possible that in some extreme cases, toddlers with behavioral inhibition may actually be experiencing an early form of social anxiety. Similarly, it is feasible that the symptoms and suffering of some children with resistant attachment relationships may actually qualify for a diagnosis of separation anxiety disorder.

Some clinicians have been reluctant to diagnose infants and toddlers because of concerns about labeling young children and discounting the significance of primary relationships. Yet dismissing suffering is certainly not helpful, and characterizing early difficulties with fearfulness and anxiety may help with refinement of prognosis and treatment. Researchers and clinicians have also been reluctant to make diagnoses in infants and toddlers because the symptoms may remit over time without intervention. However, this is also true for major depression in adults (Endicott, 1998; Judd & Akiskal, 2000), which is clearly a treatable disorder (Bakish, 2001) and can even occur in the presence of normal developmental transitions (Bedi, 1999; Kessler, 1997).

Longitudinal research is needed to further establish the long-term significance and developmental trajectories of fearfulness and anxiety in early childhood. It would be useful if clinicians had more precise cutoff ages for defining when a given fear could represent increased risk. In addition, further investigations are needed to clarify whether children who show multiple fears are at greater risk than children with only one or two fears.

Additional research is also needed concerning the assessment of anxiety, as current measures are not yet fully validated, and anxiety has traditionally been difficult to study (Perrin & Last, 1992). Multimodal noninvasive biological measures (such as salivary cortisol, heart rate, or skin conductance) may prove useful as infants and toddlers cannot directly report symptoms, and parent reports may not be objective (Seifer, Sameroff, Barrett, & Krafchuk, 1994). Furthermore, since sleep is a frequent symptom of anxiety disorders, further investigations of the relations between sleep disturbances and anxiety disorders may be beneficial.

A major issue that concerns all diagnoses in infants and toddlers, including anxiety disorders, is the assessment of impairment. Further research is needed to characterize and measure the disability that results from problems in early childhood. Refinement of current diagnostic criteria and assessment approaches for identifying anxiety disorders in young children, along with a better understanding of impairment, is crucial to reducing current suffering and preventing additional psychopathology.

ACKNOWLEDGMENT   This work was supported by NIMH Scientist Award for Clinicians MH01532.

Notes

1. Names and identifying information have been changed for the cases to protect confidentiality.

2. The group met twice in January 2001 and July 2001 with seed funding provided by the American Academy of Child and Adolescent Psychiatry Work Group on Research. Participants included: Chair, Michael Scheeringa, MD, MPH; Thomas Anders, MD; Neil Boris, MD; Alice Carter, PhD; Irene Chatoor, MD; Helen Egger, MD; Kate Keenan, PhD; Joan Luby, MD; Jean Thomas, MD; Lauren Wakschlag, PhD; Susan Warren, MD; Harry Wright, MD; Charles Zeanah, MD; with additional consultation from Adrian Angold, MRCPsych; Cheryl Boyce, PhD; E. Jane Costello, PhD; Rebecca DelCarmen-Wiggins, PhD; Della Hann, PhD; and Serena Weider, PhD.

References

Achenbach, T. M. (1991a). *Manual for the child behavior checklist/4–18 and 1991 profile.* Burlington, VT: University of Vermont, Department of Psychiatry

Achenbach, T. M. (1991b). *Manual for the teacher's report form and 1991 profile.* Burlington, VT: University of Vermont, Department of Psychiatry

Achenbach, T. M., & Rescorla, L. A. (2000). *Manual for the ASEBA preschool forms and profiles.* Burlington, VT: University of Vermont, Department of Psychiatry.

Ainsworth, M., Blehar, M., Waters, E., & Wall, S. (1978). *Patterns of attachment.* Hillsdale, NJ: Lawrence Erlbaum.

American Psychiatric Association. (1994). *Diagnostic and statistical manual of mental disorders* (4th ed.). Washington, DC: Author.

Asendorpf, J. (1989). Shyness as a final common pathway for two different kinds of inhibition. *Journal of Personality and Social Psychology, 57,* 481–492.

Ashman, S. B., Dawson, G., Panagiotides, H., Yamada, E., & Wilkinson, C. W. (2002). Stress hormone levels of children of depressed mothers. *Development and Psychopathology, 14*(2), 333–349.

Bakish, D. (2001). New standard of depression treatment: Remission and full recovery. *Journal of Clinical Psychiatry, 62*(suppl. 26), 5–9.

Ball, W., & Tronick, E. (1971). Infant responses to impending collision: Optical and real. *Science, 171,* 818–820.

Barlow, D. H. (1988). *Anxiety and its disorders.* New York: Guilford Press.

Baumrind, D. (1971). Harmonious parents and their preschool children. *Developmental Psychology, 4*(1, Pt. 1), 99–102.

Becker, W. C. (1964). Consequences of different kinds of parental discipline. In M. L. Hoffman & L. W. Hoffman (Eds.), *Review of child development research* (Vol. 1, pp. 169–208). New York: Russel Sage Foundation.

Bedi, R. P. (1999). Depression: An inability to adapt to one's perceived life distress? *Journal of Affective Disorders, 54*(1–2), 225–234.

Benoit, D., Parker, K. C., & Zeanah, C. H. (1997). Mothers' representations of their infants assessed prenatally: Stability and association with their infants' attachment classification. *Journal of Child Psychology and Psychiatry and Allied Disciplines, 38*(3), 307–313.

Bertenthal, B. I., Campos, J. J., & Barrett, K. C. (1984). Self-produced locomotion: An organizer of emotional, cognitive, and social development in infancy. In R. N. Emde & R. J. Harmon (Eds.), *Continuities and discontinuities in development* (pp. 175–210). New York: Plenum Press.

Biederman, J., Faraone, S. V., Hirshfeld-Becker, D. R., Friedman, D., Robin, J. A., & Rosenbaum, J. F. (2001). Patterns of psychopathology and dysfunction in high-risk children of parents with panic disorder and major depression. *American Journal of Psychiatry, 158*(1), 49–57.

Biederman, J., Hirshfeld, D. R., Rosenbaum, J. F., Herot, C., Friedman, D., Snidman, N., Kagan, J., & Faraone, S. V. (2001). Further evidence of association between behavioral inhibition and social anxiety in children. *American Journal of Psychiatry, 158*(10), 1673–1679.

Biederman, J., Rosenbaum, J. F., Bolduc, E. A., Faraone, S. V., Chaloff, B. A., Hirschfeld, D. R., & Kagan, J. (1993). A 3 year follow-up of children with and without behavioral inhibition. *Journal of the American Academy of Child and Adolescent Psychiatry, 32*(4), 814–821.

Biederman, J., Rosenbaum, J. F., Bolduc, E. A., Faraone, S. V., & Hirshfeld, D. R. (1991). A high risk study of young children of parents with panic disorder and agoraphobia with and without comorbid major depression. *Psychiatry Research, 37,* 333–348.

Biederman, J., Rosenbaum, J. F., Bolduc, E. A., Faraone, S. V., Hirschfeld, D. R., Gerster, M., Meminger, S. R. J. K., Snidman, N., & Reznick, J. S. (1990). Psychiatric correlates of behavioral inhibition in young children of parents with and without psychiatric disorders. *Archives of General Psychiatry, 47,* 21–26.

Bohlin, G., Hagekull, B., & Rydell, A.-M. (2000). Attachment and social functioning: A longitudinal study from infancy to middle childhood. *Social Development, 9*(1), 24–39.

Bornstein, M. H. (1995). Parenting infants. In M. H. Bornstein (Ed.), *Handbook of parenting: Vol. 1. Children and parenting* (pp. 3–39). Mahwah, NJ: Lawrence Erlbaum.

Briggs-Gowan, M. J., & Carter, A. S. (1998). Preliminary acceptability and psychometrics of the Infant-Toddler Social and Emotional Assessment (ITSEA): A new adult-report questionnaire. *Infant Mental Health Journal, 19*(4), 422–445.

Bronson, G. W. (1972). Infants' reactions to unfamiliar persons and novel objects. *Monographs of the Society for Research in Child Development, 37,* 1–45.

Cantwell, D. P., & Baker, L. (1989). Stability and natural history of DSM-III childhood diagnoses. *Journal of the American Academy of Child and Adolescent Psychiatry, 28*(5), 691–700.

Carter, A. S., & Briggs-Gowan, M. (1999). *The infant-toddler social and emotional assessment (ITSEA).* New Haven, CT: Yale University, Department of Psychology.

Chatoor, I., Ganiban, J., Hirsch, R., Borman-Spurrell, E., & Mrazek, D. A. (2000). Maternal characteristics and toddler temperament in infantile anorexia. *Journal of the American Academy of Child and Adolescent Psychiatry, 39*(6), 743–751.

Cole, D. A., Peeke, L. G., Martin, J. M., Truglio, R., & Seroczynski, A. D. (1998). A longitudinal look at the relation between depression and anxiety in children and adolescents. *Journal of Consulting and Clinical Psychology, 66,* 451–460.

Cole, P. M., Zahn-Waxler, C., Fox, N. A., Usher, B. A., & Welsh, J. D. (1996). Individual differences in emotion regulation and behavior problems in preschool children. *Journal of Abnormal Psychology, 105*(4), 518–529.

Dadds, M. R., & Roth, J. H. (2001). Family processes in the development of anxiety problems. In M. W. Vasey & M. R. Dadds (Eds.), *The developmental psychopathology of anxiety* (pp. 278–303). New York: Oxford University Press.

Egger, H. L., Ascher, B. H., & Angold, A. (1999). *The preschool age psychiatric assessment* [1.1 ed.]. Durham, NC: Center for Developmental Epidemiology, Duke University Medical Center.

Eley, T. C. (2001). Contributions of behavioral genetics research: Quantifying genetic, shared environmental and nonshared environmental influences. In M. W. Vasey & M. R. Dadds (Eds.), *The developmental psychopathology of anxiety* (pp. 45–59). New York: Oxford University Press.

Endicott, J. (1998). Gender similarities and differences in the course of depression. *Journal of Gender-Specific Medicine, 1*(3), 40–43.

Essex, M. J., Klein, M. H., Cho, E., & Kalin, N. H. (2002). Maternal stress beginning in infancy may sensitize children to later stress exposure: Effects on cortisol and behavior. *Biological Psychiatry, 52,* 776–784.

Fox, N. A., & Calkins, S. D. (1993). Pathways to aggression and social withdrawal: Interactions among temperament, attachment, and regulation. In K. H. Rubin & J. B. Asendorpf (Eds.), *Social withdrawal, inhibition, and shyness in childhood* (pp. 81–100). Hillsdale, NJ: Lawrence Erlbaum.

Francis, G., Last, C. G., & Strauss, C. C. (1992). Avoidant disorder and social phobia in children and adolescents. *Journal of the American Academy of Child and Adolescent Psychiatry, 31*(6), 1086–1089.

Gerull, F. C., & Rapee, R. M. (2002). Mother knows best: The effects of maternal modeling on the acquisition of fear and avoidance behaviour in toddlers. *Behaviour Research and Therapy, 40*(3), 279–287.

Goldsmith, H. H., Buss, A. H., Plomin, R., Rothbart, M. K., Thomas, A., Chess, S., Hinde, R. A., & McCall, R. B. (1987). Roundtable: What is temperament? *Child Development, 58,* 505–529.

Goldsmith, H. H., & Lemery, K. S. (2000). Linking temperamental fearfulness and anxiety symptoms: A behavior-genetic perspective. *Biological Psychiatry, 48,* 1199–1209.

Greenspan, S. I. (1992). *Infancy and early childhood: The practice of clinical assessment and intervention with emotional and developmental challenges.* Madison, WI: International Universities Press.

Grolnick, W. S., & Gurland, S. T. (2002). Mothering: Retrospect and prospect. In J. P. McHale & W. S. Grolnick (Eds.), *Retrospect and prospect in the psychological study of families* (pp. 5–33). Mahwah, NJ: Lawrence Erlbaum.

Gullone, E., & King, N. J. (1992). Psychometric evaluation of a revised fear survey schedule for children and adolescents. *Journal of Child Psychology and Psychiatry, 33*(6), 987–998.

Hayward, C., Killen, J. D., Kraemer, H. C., & Taylor, C. B. (1998). Linking self-reported childhood behavioral inhibition to adolescent social phobia. *Journal of the American Academy of Child and Adolescent Psychiatry, 37,* 1308–1316.

Hettema, J. M., Neale, M. C., & Kendler, K. S. (2001). A review and meta-analysis of the genetic epidemiology of anxiety disorders. *American Journal of Psychiatry, 158,* 1568–1578.

Hirshfeld, D. R., Rosenbaum, J. F., Biederman, J., Bolduc, E. A., Faraone, S. V., Snidman, N., Reznick, J. R., & Kagan, J. (1992). Stable behavioral inhibition and its association with anxiety disorder. *Journal of the American Academy of Child and Adolescent Psychiatry, 31*(1), 103–111.

Jersild, A. T., & Holmes, F. B. (1935). *Children's*

fears. (Child Development Monographs no. 12). New York: Teacher's College, Columbia University Bureau of Publications.

Johnson, W. F., Emde, R. N., Pannabecker, B. J., Stenberg, C. R., & Davis, M. H. (1982). Maternal perception of infant emotion from birth through 18 months. *Infant Behavior and Development, 5,* 313–322.

Judd, L. L., & Akiskal, H. S. (2000). Delineating the longitudinal structure of depressive illness: Beyond clinical subtypes and duration thresholds. *Pharmacopsychiatry, 33*(1), 3–7.

Kagan, J. (1994). *Galen's prophecy.* New York: Basic Books.

Kagan, J., Reznick, J. R., Snidman, N., Gibbons, J., & Johnson, M. O. (1988). Childhood derivatives of inhibition and lack of inhibition to the unfamiliar. *Child Development, 59,* 1580–1589.

Kaminer, Y., Feinstein, C., Seifer, R., Stevens, L., & Barrett, R. P. (1990). An observationally based rating scale for affective symptomatology in child psychiatry. *Journal of Nervous and Mental Disease, 178*(12), 750–754.

Kessler, R. C. (1997). The effects of stressful life events on depression. *Annual Review of Psychology, 48,* 191–214.

Kohlmann, C.-W., Schumacher, A., & Streit, R. (1988). Trait anxiety and parental child-rearing behavior: Support as a moderator variable? *Anxiety Research, 1,* 53–64.

Krohne, H. W., & Hock, M. (1991). Relationships between restrictive mother-child interactions and anxiety of the child. *Anxiety Research, 4,* 109–124.

Lavigne, J. V., Binns, H. J., Christoffel, K. K., Rosenbaum, D., Arend, R., Smith, K., Hayford, J. R., McGuire, P. A., & Group, P. P. R. (1993). Behavioral and emotional problems among preschool children in pediatric primary care: Prevalence and pediatricians' recognition. *Pediatrics, 91*(3), 649–655.

Lavigne, J. V., Gibbons, R. D., Christoffel, K. K., Arend, R., Rosenbaum, D., Binns, H., Dawson, N., Sobel, H., & Isaacs, C. (1996). Prevalence rates and correlates of psychiatric disorders among preschool children. *Journal of the American Academy of Child and Adolescent Psychiatry, 35*(2), 204–214.

Lieberman, A. F., Wieder, S., & Fenichel, E. (Eds.). (1997). *DC:0–3 Casebook.* Washington, DC: Zero to Three, National Center for Clinical Infant Programs.

Mammen, O., Scholle, R., Jennings, K., & Popper, S. (1995). *Semi-structured interview for assessing NCCIP diagnoses in children under 3 years.* Unpublished manuscript.

Manassis, K., Bradley, S., Goldberg, S., Hood, J., & Swinson, R. P. (1994). Attachment in mothers with anxiety disorders and their children. *Journal of the American Academy of Child and Adolescent Psychiatry, 33*(8), 1106–1113.

Manassis, K., Bradley, S., Goldberg, S., Hood, J., & Swinson, R. P. (1995). Behavioural inhibition, attachment and anxiety in children of mothers with anxiety disorders. *Canadian Journal of Psychiatry, 40,* 87–92.

March, J. S. (1995). *Anxiety disorders in children and adolescents.* New York: Guilford Press.

Marks, I. (1987a). The development of normal fear: A review. *Journal of Child Psychology and Psychiatry, 28*(5), 667–697.

Marks, I. (1987b). *Fears, phobias, and rituals.* New York: Oxford University Press.

Muris, P., Steerneman, P., Merckelbach, H., & Meesters, C. (1996). The role of parental fearfulness and modeling in children's fear. *Behaviour Research and Therapy, 34*(3), 265–268.

Ollendick, T. H. (1983). Reliability and validity of the Revised Fear Survey Schedule for Children (FSSC-R). *Behaviour Research and Therapy, 21,* 685–692.

Ollendick, T. H., & March, J. S. (in press). *Phobic and anxiety disorders in children and adolescents: A clinician's guide to effective psychosocial and pharmacological interventions.*

Ost, L.-G., & Treffers, P. D. A. (2001). Onset, course, and outcome for anxiety disorders in children. In W. K. Silverman & P. D. A. Treffers (Eds.), *Anxiety disorders in children and adolescents* (pp. 293–312). New York: Cambridge University Press.

Perrin, S., & Last, C. G. (1992). Do childhood anxiety measures measure anxiety? *Journal of Abnormal Child Psychology, 20*(6), 567–578.

Rapee, R. M. (1997). Potential role of childrearing practices in the development of anxiety and depression. *Clinical Psychology Review, 17*(1), 47–67.

Rapoport, J. L., & Ismond, D. R. (Eds.). (1996). *DSM-IV training guide for diagnosis of childhood disorders.* New York: Brunner/Mazel.

Rosen, J., & Schulkin, J. (1998). From normal fear to pathological anxiety. *Psychological Review, 105*(2), 325–350.

Rosenbaum, J. E., Biederman, J., Hirshfeld-Becker, D. R., Kagan, J., Snidman, N., Friedman, D., Nineberg, A., Gallery, D. J., & Faraone, S. V.

(2000). A controlled study of behavioral inhibition in children of parents with panic disorder and depression. *American Journal of Psychiatry, 157,* 2002–2020.

Rosenbaum, J. F., Biederman, J., Hirschfeld, D. R., Meminger, S. R., Herman, J. B., Kagan, J., Reznick, J. S., & Snidman, N. (1988). Behavioral inhibition in children of parents with panic disorder and agoraphobia. *Archives of General Psychiatry, 45,* 463–470.

Rubin, K. H., & Burgess, K. B. (2001). Social withdrawal and anxiety. In M. W. Vasey & M. R. Dadds (Eds.), *The developmental psychopathology of anxiety* (pp. 407–434). New York: Oxford University Press.

Rubin, K. H., & Burgess, K. B. (2002). Parents of aggressive and withdrawn children. In M. Bornstein (Ed.), *Handbook of parenting: Vol. 1. Children and parenting* (2nd ed., pp. 383–418). Hillsdale, NJ: Lawrence Erlbaum.

Rubin, K. H., Burgess, K. B., & Hastings, P. D. (2002). Stability and social-behavioral consequences of toddlers' inhibited temperament and parenting. *Child Development, 73,* 483–495.

Rubin, K. H., Hastings, P. D., Stewart, S. L., Henderson, H. A., & Chen, X. (1997). The consistency and concomitants of inhibition: Some of the children, all of the time. *Child Development, 68*(3), 467–483.

Rubin, K. H., & Mills, R. S. L. (1991). Conceptualizing developmental pathways to internalizing disorders in childhood. *Canadian Journal of Behavioral Differences, 23,* 300–317.

Scarr, S., & Salapatek, P. (1970). Patterns of fear development during infancy. *Merrill-Palmer Quarterly, 16*(1), 53–90.

Scheeringa, M. (1995). *Semi-structured interview for DC:0–3 diagnoses for clinicians.* Unpublished work, New Orleans, LA.

Scherer, M. W., & Nakamura, C. Y. (1968). A fear survey schedule for children (FSS-FC): A factor analytic comparison with manifest anxiety (CMAS). *Behaviour Research and Therapy, 6,* 173–182.

Schmidt, L. A., & Fox, N. A. (1998). Electrophysiological studies. I: Quantitative electroencephalography. In C. E. Coffey & R. A. Brumback (Eds.), *Textbook of pediatric neuropsychiatry. Section II. Neuropsychiatric assessment of the child and adolescent* (pp. 315–329). Washington, DC: American Psychiatric Press.

Schwartz, C. E., Snidman, N., & Kagan, J. (1999). Adolescent social anxiety as an outcome of inhibited temperament in childhood. *Journal of the American Academy of Child and Adolescent Psychiatry, 38*(8), 1008–1015.

Seifer, R., Sameroff, A. J., Barrett, L. C., & Krafchuk, E. (1994). Infant temperament measured by multiple observations and mother report. *Child Development, 65,* 1478–1490.

Shaw, D. S., Keenan, K., Vondra, J. I., Delliquadri, E., & Giovannelli, J. (1997). Antecedents of preschool children's internalizing problems: A longitudinal study of low-income families. *Journal of the American Academy of Child and Adolescent Psychiatry, 36*(12), 1760–1767.

Siqueland, L., Kendall, P. C., & Steinberg, L. (1996). Anxiety in children: Perceived family environments and observed family interaction. *Journal of Clinical Child Psychology, 25*(2), 225–237.

Smider, N. A., Essex, M. J., Kolin, N. H., Buss, K. A., Klein, M. H., Davidson, R. J., & Goldsmith, H. (2002). Salivary cortisol as a predictor of socioemotional adjustment during kindergarten: A prospective study. *Child Development, 73*(1), 75–92.

Snidman, N. (1989). Behavioral inhibition and sympathetic influence on the cardiovascular system. In J. S. Resnick (Ed.), *Perspectives on behavioral inhibition* (pp. 51–69). Chicago: University of Chicago Press.

Spence, S. H., Rapee, R., McDonald, C., & Ingram, M. (2001). The structure of anxiety symptoms among preschoolers. *Behaviour Research and Therapy, 39,* 1293–1316.

Spielberger, C. D., Gorsuch, R. L., & Lushene, R. I. (1970). *Manual for the state-trait anxiety inventory.* Palo Alto, CA: Psychologists Press.

Sroufe, L. A. (1996). *Emotional development.* New York: Cambridge University Press.

Turner, S. M., & Beidel, D. C. (1996). Is behavioral inhibition related to the anxiety disorders? *Clinical Psychology Review, 16*(2), 157–172.

Warren, S. L. (2000). *Diagnostic interview for infants to preschoolers for anxiety (DIIPA).* Washington, DC: George Washington University.

Warren, S. L. (2001a). *The infant-preschool scale for inhibited behaviors.* Washington, DC: George Washington University.

Warren, S. L. (2001b). *Infant-toddler anxiety screener.* Washington, DC: George Washington University.

Warren, S. L. (2003). *Anxiety PAPA addendum.* Washington, DC: George Washington University.

Warren, S. L., & Dadson, N. (2001). Assessment

of anxiety in young children. *Current Opinion in Pediatrics, 13*, 580–585.

Warren, S. L., Gunnar, M. R., Kagan, J., Anders, T. F., Simmens, S. J., Rones, M., Wease, S., Aron, E., Dahl, R. E., & Sroufe, L. A. (2003). Maternal panic disorder: Infant temperament, neurophysiology and parenting behaviors. *Journal of the American Academy of Child and Adolescent Psychiatry, 42*, 814–825.

Warren, S. L., Huston, L., Egeland, B., & Sroufe, L. A. (1997). Child and adolescent anxiety disorders and early attachment. *Journal of the American Academy of Child and Adolescent Psychiatry, 36*(5), 637–644.

Warren, S. L., & Ollendick, T. H. (2001). *The fear survey schedule for infants and preschoolers.* Washington, DC: George Washington University.

Warren, S. L., & Simmens, S. J. (2003). *Predicting toddler anxiety/ depressive symptoms: Effects of caregiver sensitivity on temperamentally reactive children.* Unpublished manuscript.

Warren, S. L., & Sroufe, L. A. (in press). Developmental issues. In T. H. Ollendick & J. S. March (Eds.), *Phobic and anxiety disorders in children and adolescents: A clinician's guide to effective psychosocial and pharmacological interventions.*

Weinberg, M. K., & Tronick, E. Z. (1998). Emotional care of the at-risk infant: Emotional characteristics of infants associated with maternal depression and anxiety. *Pediatrics, 102* (5), 1298–1304.

Woodward, L. J., & Fergusson, D. M. (2001). Life course outcomes of young people with anxiety disorders in adolescence. *Journal of the American Academy of Child and Adolescent Psychiatry, 40*(9), 1086–1093.

Wright, H., Penny, R., Wieduwilt, K., Cuccaro, M., Leonhardt, T., & Abramson, R. (2002). *DSM-IV diagnoses for infants and toddlers seen in an infant mental health clinic and community mental health center.* Paper presented at the International Conference for Infant Studies, Toronto, Canada.

Zeanah, C. H. (Ed.). (2000). *Handbook of infant mental health* (2nd ed.). New York: Guilford Press.

Zeanah, C. H., Benoit, D., & Barton, M., n.d. *Working model of the child interview (VI).* New Orleans: Louisiana State University School of Medicine, Division of Infant, Child, and Adolescent Psychiatry.

Zero to Three, National Center for Clinical Infant Programs. (1994). *Diagnostic classification of mental health and developmental disorders of infancy and childhood.* Washington, DC: Author.

19

Posttraumatic Stress Disorder

Michael S. Scheeringa

For a variety of possible reasons, professionals and parents in the past have not readily acknowledged that young children can be affected by trauma. The persistence of the ancient tabula rasa notion of infancy (i.e., that infants do not possess sufficient developmental capacities to perceive, remember, or be affected by their environment) may have effectively blinded many to children's symptoms. Also, the intrusion of trauma during the period of infancy is incompatible with our wishful thinking that this be a time of peaceful development. Life-threatening trauma during the early childhood years may be a shattering experience that sends ripples through an entire family and possibly through the long-term development of the individual child. Partly for these reasons, then, families in the preschool years tend to believe that they should be able to cope on their own without professional assessment or intervention. These factors often hinder families from seeking help, except perhaps under extreme duress or in special situations such as legal cases.

We, as clinicians and researchers, are hampered by the dearth of theoretical and research attention to posttraumatic stress disorder (PTSD) in this age group compared to the relatively longer tradition of research on PTSD on older children and adults. Research efforts are further complicated by the necessary ethical limitations on invasive or anxiety-provoking laboratory procedures with young children who are unable to give voluntary consent. Nevertheless, more rigorous research studies have begun to emerge over the last decade, and an extensive case report literature has built up over the last quarter century that is reviewed in this chapter.

DEFINITIONS AND DEVELOPMENT

It is worthwhile to clarify the definition of *trauma* since this term has been used with a wide range of meaning in the last century. The *Diagnostic and Statistical Manual of Mental Disorders*, Third Edition (*DSM-III*; American Psychiatric Association [APA], 1980) introduced the definition of a trauma in relation to a disorder in the first publication of PTSD as an "event that is generally outside the range of usual human experience" (p. 236). The *DSM-IV* definition is that an event "in-

volved actual or threatened death or serious injury, or a threat to the physical integrity of self
or others" (APA, 1994, p. 428). This definition
represents the highest possible threshold for defining a trauma. However, other authors have
used the term in relation to a wide variety of
non–life-threatening events, such as divorce (e.g.,
Dreman, 1991) and living with a parent who has
an alcohol or drug problem (e.g., Joseph, Mynard, & Mayall, 2000). This loose application of
the term *trauma* is not a new phenomenon but
seems to be more common when young children
are involved. For example, witnessing parents engage in consensual intercourse was considered "psychic trauma" for a preschool child in one early
article (Greenacre, 1949). On one hand, a lenient
definition of trauma seems reasonable in the early
stages of research as we are learning what types
of events truly are traumatic to young children.
When dealing with preverbal and nonverbal children who cannot tell us if an event was perceived
by them as life threatening, it may be wise to err
on the side of calling an event a trauma even
when it is not certain that it was traumatic. In
addition, it is understandable that researchers may
try to draw connections between certain events
and PTSD in order to draw on the extensive body
of familiar research on PTSD. On the other hand,
this strategy in the end obscures the meaning of
trauma and trivializes the phenomenon for those
who suffer truly traumatic events.

The term *traumatized* also must be carefully
defined. *Traumatized* is an adjective and describes
the impact of the event on the individual. An
event can be a trauma but may have no impact
on the individual. In fact, when all types of traumatic events are considered, on average, approximately 70% of exposed persons show no lasting
symptoms (Kessler, Sonnega, Bromet, Hughes, &
Nelson, 1995). Studies have indicated that it is
the persons who experienced higher levels of
perceived threat that are more likely to develop
PTSD (reviewed in March, 1993). This concept
was behind the impetus in *DSM-IV* to add an additional gatekeeper criterion to the diagnostic criteria for PTSD. The item which states that the
person's response at the time "involved fear, helplessness, or horror" (APA, 1994, p. 428) was added to capture the person's subjective experience
during the trauma.

Developmental Appropriateness of the PTSD Construct

Unfortunately, it has not always been evident to
all physicians, psychologists, counselors, health
program administrators, or the lay public that infants and toddlers can and do suffer from PTSD.
While this issue is not overt in the scientific literature, it is apparent in day-to-day clinical and legal
arenas. I have evaluated new cases and discovered
that the child suffered symptoms for years and
the onset could be traced to a traumatic event.
Sometimes the parents did not seek mental health
treatment earlier because they did not make the
connection between traumatic event and symptoms. Sometimes pediatricians, relatives, or friends
told them that the child would "grow out of it,"
even though the parents harbored the notion that
something was really wrong with the child. Another too common scenario occurs when the clinician is asked to evaluate an extremely symptomatic young child only because the evaluation
is needed for a lawsuit. For example, one mother
sued a person who molested her child but sought
help only because the attorney needed expert
documentation to show that the child had been
psychologically harmed by the molestation. The
lack of researchers qualified and interested in
studying young children has also hindered progress in these areas.

Salient Developmental Issues

One can approach the issue of whether PTSD is
an appropriate construct for young children from
a different direction and ask what minimum developmental capacities are needed to develop
PTSD and how early these capacities emerge.

First, a child must be able to perceive the existence of a traumatic event in the environment.
Perception is achieved through the five senses, although sight and hearing are usually the primary
avenues of traumatic input. Vision is extremely
nearsighted at birth and develops steadily to 20/
20 by approximately 6 months of age. Depth perception, or binocular vision, emerges around 3
months of age. Auditory and tactile sensations are
near the adult level of sensitivity at birth (Haith,
1986). Faces cannot be distinguished as a class of

stimuli until around 5 months of age (reviewed in Cohen, DeLoache, & Strauss, 1979).

Infants can discriminate fear from other affects in others by around 5 months of age (Schwartz, Izard, & Ansul, 1985). They can discriminate happy from sad vocalizations by 5 months (Walker-Andrews & Gronlick, 1983) and can discriminate happy from angry vocalizations at 7 months (Caron, Caron, & MacLean, 1988). Classic social referencing paradigms have shown that the recognition of affect (Balaban, 1995; Sorce, Emde, Campos, & Klinnert, 1985) and vocalizations in others (Mumme, Fernald, & Herrera, 1996) can influence their actions. It is noteworthy that infants typically can recognize fear in others before they can express fear themselves, much as children can usually comprehend much more language than they can produce during the second and third years of life.

Second, some form of memory for the event must be recorded and stored in the child's brain to serve as the reservoir for reexperiencing symptomatology. Memory scholars agree that there are at least two types of memory—nondeclarative (implicit) and declarative (explicit) (Schacter, 1987). Nondeclarative memory capacities are evident usually by around 9 months of age, when infants can behaviorally reproduce events from one day prior (reviewed in Mandler, 1990). Declarative memories are knowable to a second person, by definition, only by verbalizations from the child. Hence, the assessment of declarative memory is highly dependent on the emergence of speech and language capacities. Verbal recall is rare before 18 months of age, spotty for events that occur between 18 and 36 months, and finally present in coherent narrative style by around 36 months. Prior to 36 months of age, children may be able to produce more recall when provided with contextual cues or prompted by an adult (Fivush, Pipe, Murachver, & Reese, 1997). This schema also fits nicely with Terr's timeline, which was arrived at through the assessment of clinical cases (Terr, 1988).

Third, the manifestation of many PTSD symptoms can be known only through verbalizations of the patient, because it requires knowing internal thoughts and feelings. Therefore, language development is the rate-limiting factor for some symptomatology. Children generally begin to say their first single words around 12 months of age, combine words into two-word phrases by 20 months, and construct grammatically correct sentences by around 36 months.

Fourth, the manifestations of many PTSD symptoms also depend on affective displays. That is, the child must be able to display sadness, irritability, or fear in order for certain symptoms to be apparent to clinicians. The last to emerge of these basic emotions is fear, which typically emerges around 9 months of age, although a precursor of fear, wariness, is present earlier, around 4 months (Sroufe, 1979).

Fifth, purposeful motor movements, while not the rate-limiting factor for the manifestation of any PTSD symptoms, are an integral component of many of them, such as flashbacks, play reenactments, avoidance behaviors, loss of interest in usual activities, and outbursts of anger. The motor components needed to create intentional movements include purposeful arm movements (evident to some degree at birth), multistep coordinated means-end behavior (evident around 7 to 9 months) (reviewed in Gratch & Schatz, 1987), walking (evident by 12 months), and imaginative play (evident around 18 months).

Socioemotional relational capacities are integral to several of the PTSD criteria, such as detachment and estrangement from others and restricted range of affect, and may also be crucial for the ability to experience certain events as traumatic or not, such as witnessing domestic violence or witnessing the injury of family members in accidents. The sequence of emergence of relationship-specific capacities starts with the period of 2 to 7 months of age and the social smile, enhanced eye contact, and longer periods of engagement with a partner. At the 7- to 9-month biobehavioral shift, two important capacities develop. One capacity is the cognitive capacity called intersubjectivity, or the ability to understand that one's own inner experiences can be appreciated by others. Another capacity is the social capacity for attachment. Infants have unique relations with each attachment figure (reviewed in Zeanah, Boris, & Scheeringa, 1997).

In summary, the full package of developmental capacities needed to manifest PTSD symptomatology is not present until 9 months of age, with the rate-limiting capacity probably being the emergence of nondeclarative memory. Of course, that does not imply that infants cannot be symptomatic prior to 9 months of age. However, it is more likely that the manifestations of symptoms prior to 9 months are better thought of as a conditioned response to repetitive stimuli rather than the abstract type of symptoms associated with PTSD (Scheeringa & Gaensbauer, 2000).

SCOPE OF THE PROBLEM

In this section, I briefly overview the prevalence of traumatic events that strike young children. The main sources of trauma include physical abuse, sexual abuse, accidents involving motor vehicles, accidental injuries, dog bites, witnessing community violence, and witnessing domestic violence.

Epidemiology of Trauma in Infants and Toddlers

Statistics on child abuse from the National Child Abuse and Neglect Reporting System estimated that in 1999 there were 826,000 victims of maltreatment (U.S. Department of Health and Human Services, 2001). However, only 21% suffered physical abuse, and 11% suffered sexual abuse, while 58% suffered neglect, which would not usually constitute a life-threatening trauma. The age group with the highest victimization rate was the birth to 3-year age group (13.9 maltreatments per 1,000 children). Based on this conservative database of screened and reported cases, this suggests that over 40,000 children in the birth to 3-year age group suffer physical abuse, and over 20,000 suffer sexual abuse annually. More disturbing perhaps is the fact that fatalities occur more often by far in younger children. Of the estimated 1,100 children who died from abuse and neglect in 1999, 43% were less than 1 year old and 86% were less than 6 years old.

There is no nationwide system in place for reporting children who witness domestic violence. However, the National Violence Against Women Survey (Tjaden & Thoennes, 1998) estimated that 1.9 million women are physically assaulted annually, and each assaulted woman averaged 3.1 assaults, but this survey did not provide data on

how often children of these women witnessed the attacks. A survey of attendees at a Boston pediatric primary care clinic estimated that 1 of every 10 children had witnessed a shooting or stabbing before the age of 6 years, and half of those had occurred in the home (Taylor, Zuckerman, Harik, & Groves, 1992). A survey of fourth, fifth, and sixth graders in another city found that 30% of the mothers reported spouse abuse during their children's lifetimes (Spaccarelli, Sandler, & Roosa, 1994). Overall, a conservative estimate of the number of newborn to 3-year-old children who witness domestic violence annually is in the millions, although data are lacking on the severity of violence the children actually witness.

Surveys of exposure to community violence have not traditionally asked respondents to distinguish between violence that children witnessed among strangers or family members (Bell & Jenkins, 1993; Osofsky, Wewers, Hann, & Fick, 1993), so it is difficult to know how much of what is reported as community violence is actually domestic violence. Because it is doubtful that the limited locomotor abilities of young children put them at high risk for witnessing neighborhood violence, it is problematic at this point to try to estimate a separate prevalence for exposure to community (i.e., nonfamily) violence.

There are no systematic surveys of the number of young children exposed to war or terrorism, but there are ample reports of the symptomatology that follows these events. In fact, the first documentation of posttraumatic symptomatology in children under 4 years of age was Carey-Trefzer's (1949) landmark report on children affected by the German bombing of London during World War II. Subsequent studies have shown the tremendous impact that war (Dybdahl, 2001) and terrorism (Laor et al., 1996) can have on young children.

The rate of death due to accidental injuries is higher in the newborn to 4 age group (18.6 per 100,000) than all of the child and adolescent age groups except for the 15- to 19-year-old group (National Center for Health Statistics, 1998). In 1997, this amounted to 3,559 deaths of newborn to 4-year-old children. Since nonfatal injuries are far more common than fatal injuries following accidents, the number of young children significantly injured from accidents is in the thousands every year. The most common type of fatal accidental injury to children, by far, involves motor vehicles, whether children are occupants in cars that crash, or pedestrians that are struck.

Dog attacks are a type of trauma that is uniquely salient to young children because of their small size and relative helplessness. There is no national reporting system on the prevalence of dog bites, but the case report literature is over-represented with cases of severely symptomatic young children who have been attacked by dogs (Gaensbauer, 1994; Gaensbauer & Siegel, 1995; Gislason & Call, 1982).

Epidemiology of PTSD

The prevalence of PTSD in the general adult population has ranged from 1% (Helzer, Robins, & McEvoy, 1987) to 2.6% (Shore, Tatum, & Vollmer, 1986). Two medium-size surveys of adolescents found rates of 3% (Cuffe et al., 1998) and 6% (Reinherz, Giaconia, Lefkowitz, Pakiz, & Frost, 1993). The only large survey that included preschool children and assessed for PTSD found only 2 cases out of 3,860 (0.1%) 2- to 5-year-old children screened at pediatric office visits (Lavigne et al., 1996).

LIMITATIONS AND CONCEPTUAL CHALLENGES

Making the diagnosis of PTSD traditionally requires knowing with a high degree of certainty when a traumatic event occurred in the life of the patient. We can ascertain the exact day and time of events with adults and older children, and all changes in signs and symptoms are tracked from that point. This is a methodological advantage for researchers in the PTSD field in comparison to most other *DSM-IV* disorders in that a specific etiologic agent is identifiable. However, it becomes a distinct problem when trying to assess preverbal or barely verbal children if a reliable adult historian is not available. Such is often the case for abused and neglected children in foster care homes. Sometimes, even when reliable biological parents are available, the onset of symp-tomatology is still unclear because traumatic events may have occurred repeatedly since the child's birth and it is unclear when the events started to have an impact. This is the case in children who have witnessed chronic domestic violence or community violence or suffered repeated child abuse.

Furthermore, following the individual threads of multiple traumas is difficult in preverbal children. Unfortunately, children who are exposed to one kind of violence are often exposed to other kinds of violence, whether it is physical abuse, sexual abuse, domestic violence, community violence, or motor vehicle accidents. For example, one child witnessed a woman being raped in her house at 12 months of age, then witnessed her cousin shooting at a man during a fight at 2 years of age, and then witnessed another cousin beating a neighbor woman unconscious at 3 years of age (Osofsky & Scheeringa, 1997). How do we know which event was more salient to the child? Or, when children witnessed their mother murdered by their father and then had to endure the additional loss of the father when placed in foster care (e.g., Pruett, 1979), which event was more traumatic? It is at the least clinically important to know because treatment could plausibly be focused in extremely different directions depending on the correct answer.

The previous example touches on another vexing issue that is unfortunately too common in traumatic events that affect young children. Is the sudden loss of the primary attachment figure equivalent to a life-threatening event for a young child? Young children are extremely dependent on caregivers for their lives, and the loss of such a caregiver, in the absence of another caregiver, puts the child's life at risk in a literal sense. But how much can a young child appreciate the abstract notion of his or her life being dependent on another? Is the symptomatology following the sudden loss of a caregiver better conceptualized as an attachment disorder, grief reaction, or PTSD? A conscious perception of the threat is mandatory for the diagnosis (and presumably the development) of PTSD, which would seem to make the distinction rather easy clinically. Yet the emotional and behavioral disturbances described by Bowlby in his classic work on attachment and loss

(Bowlby, 1973) sound remarkably similar to PTSD, even though PTSD had not been formulated at the time of that writing. Given that there is a rich history of research on attachment and loss, the complete lack of empirical research on the overlap between attachment, grief reactions, and PTSD is unfortunate.

Another limitation that we must deal with when trying to assess PTSD in young children is the fact that the majority of what we know about PTSD comes from research on adults and older children. Application of diagnostic criteria and associated findings requires the downward extension from adult to young child, a proposition that has been empirically challenged (Scheeringa, Zeanah, Drell, & Larrieu, 1995).

NEW APPROACHES AND THEORETICAL ADVANCES

In this section, I consider the relevant issues for diagnosing PTSD in young children. These issues include the validity of the construct in very young children, different diagnostic schemes, developmental considerations, the available diagnostic instruments, procedural validity, and differential diagnoses.

Are the *DSM-IV* criteria developmentally appropriate to capture PTSD in young children? *DSM* definitions of PTSD, as is the case with most disorders, have not been informed by research studies that included this age group. Our work (Scheeringa et al., 1995; Scheeringa, Peebles, Cook, & Zeanah, 2001; Scheeringa, Zeanah, Myers, & Putnam, 2003) has established that children less than 4 years of age unquestionably do develop PTSD following exposure to trauma. Further, the traditional triad of reexperiencing symptoms, numbing/avoidance symptoms, and hyperarousal symptoms are unmistakable in young children, although detecting their presence in preverbal children may be more difficult, as their clinical manifestations sometimes differ from those of older children and adults. For example, flashbacks in young children are rarely observed (Scheeringa et al., 1995), in contrast to the fact that they are common among traumatized adults (Kilpatrick & Resnick, 1993). This work led to the creation of an alternative set of criteria for

PTSD for infants and young children, which is discussed in more detail below.

Diagnostic Criteria

Every incarnation of PTSD (APA, 1980, 1987, 1994) has been based on a three-factor structure that includes reexperiencing items, avoidance and numbing of responsiveness items, and hyperarousal items. These three factors have been empirically supported by factor analyses in children (e.g., Pynoos et al., 1987) and adults (e.g., Foa, Riggs, & Gershuny, 1995). The *DSM-IV* criteria are presented in table 19.1.

My colleagues and I (Scheeringa et al., 1995, 2001, 2003) have proposed an alternative set of criteria, also in table 19.1, for infants and young children based on empirical work. The alternative criteria are modifications of the *DSM-IV* criteria in two important ways. First, some of the criteria in the *DSM-IV* version were too dependent on describing the internal thoughts and feelings of patients. Young children with limited verbal and abstract cognitive capacities cannot yet express their internal experiences. Therefore, some items that were never observed empirically (and we concluded were impossible ever to be manifest in this age group) were deleted, such as foreshortened sense of the future and partial psychological amnesia for the event. Some items were modified to be less dependent on verbalizations and more dependent on behavioral observations of the children (e.g., behaviors and affective displays that look like a flashback are sufficient regardless of whether the child is able to verbalize the internal content). Second, the alternative criteria contain new items that are more developmentally sensitive to this age group. The items "new separation anxiety," "new onset of aggression," "loss of previously acquired developmental skills," and "new fears that have no apparent relation to the trauma" were added. In addition, other items were modified to reflect appropriate developmental levels, such as noting that play is the main significant activity in which patients may lose interest. In total, the wording of five symptoms was modified.

The conclusion from two studies on diagnostic validity (Scheeringa et al., 1995, 2001) is that the diagnostic criteria would be more sensitive for

Table 19.1 Comparison of the Alternative Criteria to the *DSM-IV* Criteria for PTSD

DSM-IV Criteria	Alternative Criteria
A. (1) The person experienced, witnessed, or was confronted with an event or events that involved actual or threatened death or serious injury, or a threat to the physical integrity of self or others.	Same as *DSM-IV*.
(2) The person's response involved fear, helplessness, or horror. Note: In children, this may be expressed instead by disorganized or agitated behavior.	This item may not be known for preverbal children if an adult did not witness their reaction.
B. At least one of the following reexperiencing items:	B. At least one of the following reexperiencing items:
(1) Recurrent and intrusive distressing recollections of the event, including images, thoughts, or perceptions. Note: In young children, repetitive play may occur in which themes or aspects of the trauma are expressed.	Same as *DSM-IV* but the distress aspect is not necessarily apparent.
(2) Recurrent distressing dreams of the event. Note: In children, there may be frightening dreams without recognizable content.	Same as *DSM-IV*.
(3) Acting or feeling as if the traumatic event were recurring (includes a sense of reliving the experience, illusions, hallucinations, and dissociative flashback episodes, including those that occur on awakening or when intoxicated). Note: In young children, trauma-specific reenactment may occur.	Objective, behavioral manifestations of a flashback are observed, but the individual may not be able to verbalize the content of the experience.
(4) Intense psychological distress at exposure to internal or external cues that symbolize or resemble an aspect of the traumatic event.	Same as *DSM-IV*.
(5) Physiological reactivity on exposure to internal or external cues that symbolize or resemble an aspect of the traumatic event.	Same as *DSM-IV*.
C. At least three of the following avoidance or numbing of responsiveness items:	C. At least one of the following avoidance or numbing of responsiveness items:
(1) Efforts to avoid thoughts, feelings, or conversations associated with the trauma.	Same as *DSM-IV*
(2) Efforts to avoid activities, places, or people that arouse recollections of the trauma.	Same as *DSM-IV*.
(3) Inability to recall an important aspect of the trauma.	(The *DSM-IV* C. (3) item cannot be known in very young children.)
(4) Markedly diminished interest or participation in significant activities.	Same as the *DSM-IV*, but this likely to manifest mainly in constriction of play activities.
(5) Feeling of detachment or estrangement from others.	The *DSM-IV* C. (5) item is reworded as: Increased social withdrawal.
(6) Restricted range of affect.	Same as *DSM-IV*.
(7) Sense of a foreshortened future.	(The *DSM-IV* C. (7) item cannot be known in very young children.)
D. At least two increased arousal items:	D. At least two increased arousal items.
(1) Difficulty falling or staying asleep.	Same as *DSM-IV*.
(2) Irritability or outbursts of anger.	Modify the *DSM-IV* D. (2) item to include severe temper tantrums.
(3) Difficulty concentrating.	Same as *DSM-IV*.
(4) Hypervigilance.	Same as *DSM-IV*.

(continued)

Table 19.1 Continued

DSM-IV Criteria	Alternative Criteria
(5) Exaggerated startle response.	Same as DSM-IV.
	Common associated features: Loss of previously acquired developmental skills, such as toilet training or speech. New onset of aggression. New separation anxiety. New fears that have no apparent relation to the trauma, such as fear of the dark or fear of entering the bathroom alone.

Note: DSM-IV criteria reprinted with permission from the *Diagnostic and Statistical Manual of Mental Disorders*, Text Revision. Copyright 2000 American Psychiatric Association; alternative criteria from Scheeringa et al., 2003.

young children if two changes were made: modify a portion of items as described above to be more developmentally sensitive and reduce the number of items required. These studies did not address whether making only one or the other of those changes would have a sufficient impact by itself.

My colleagues and I retested this set of alternative criteria on a larger sample of 20-month through 6-year-old children (Scheeringa et al., 2003). We assessed 62 children who had experienced motor vehicle collisions, accidental injuries, or abuse, or witnessed domestic violence. Even though these children were often highly symptomatic, none of them could meet the diagnosis of PTSD by the *DSM-IV* criteria. For the first time, we tested whether the single change of having the new items (loss of developmental skills, new aggression, new separation anxiety, and new fears) improved diagnostic sensitivity. Contrary to expectations, the diagnosis rate did not substantially increase with the inclusion of these items. We also tested whether the single change of modifying the algorithm improved diagnostic sensitivity. Contrary to expectations, lowering the threshold for the D cluster (hyperarousal symptoms) from two symptoms to one symptom did not markedly increase the diagnosis rate.

However, as expected, lowering the threshold for the C cluster (avoidance/numbing symptoms) made a drastic difference. If three symptoms were required (as in *DSM-IV*), zero cases could be diagnosed with PTSD. If two symptoms were required, five cases could be diagnosed. If one symptom was required, 16 cases could be diagnosed.

Using these revisions for the alternative criteria, 16 out of the 62 subjects could be diagnosed with PTSD, for a rate of 26%. The PTSD group ($n = 16$) had significantly more symptoms ($M = 6.1$) than the trauma/no PTSD group ($n = 46$, $M = 2.3$), Wilcoxon pairwise (1, $N = 62$), $p < .0001$. Therefore, more current recommendations would be to not require item A(2), maintain the alternative wording for five symptoms, and lower the number of avoidance and numbing items required from three to one. This ought to be considered a tentative finding. Whether these suggestions hold up in larger samples with a predictive validity design and better measures of convergent validity remains to be seen.

Associated Signs and Symptoms

Other important signs and symptoms that develop following trauma have not made their way into the PTSD criteria. The 17 items of PTSD are considered the essential elements of the diagnosis but are not the whole story. Associated features may include survivor guilt, self-destructive behavior, somatic complaints, shame, despair, feeling permanently damaged, loss of previously sustained beliefs, and change from the individual's previous personality characteristics (APA, 1994).

Our work has identified several behaviors that may or may not be critical for the diagnosis, as discussed above, but occur frequently (see previous section). In Scheeringa et al. (2001), the most frequently occurring criterion in a sample of severely traumatized young children was one of the alternative items, new aggression. In Scheeringa et al. (2003), three of the seven most common symptoms were new aggression, new fears that appeared unrelated to the trauma (e.g., fear of the dark, fear of going to the bathroom alone), and new separation anxiety. The cluster of avoidance and numbing of responsiveness items were the least common.

Instruments

The only diagnostic instrument with published results for preschool children is the clinician-based semistructured measure created by Scheeringa and Zeanah (1994). Interrater reliability between two blind raters who watched the same videotapes of a clinician using this interview was high regardless of whether the raters were scoring for *DSM-IV* (Cohen's kappa .74) or the alternative criteria (.74) (Scheeringa et al., 2001). Similar interrater reliability was obtained in the Scheeringa et al. (2003) study. In an earlier study, when four raters scored the criteria from written vignettes of cases that covered these same criteria, the mean kappa between pairs of raters was good when using the *DSM-IV* criteria (.50) and better using the alternative criteria (.75) (Scheeringa et al., 1995). These studies used veteran clinicians with extensive experience with infants. It is not known how replicable these results would be with lay interviewers using more structured research interviews as is typically done in large epidemiological studies.

The Preschool Age Psychiatric Assessment (PAPA) is a measure under development that covers a wide range of disorders, including PTSD, in preschool age children (see chapter 12). The PAPA is a lengthy, interviewer-based measure that is likely to become one of the standards for large-scale epidemiological surveys of preschool children using nonclinician interviewers. The PTSD criteria include both the *DSM-IV* criteria and alternative items suggested by previously published empirical studies. Finally, the Infant-Toddler Social and Emotional Assessment (ITSEA; Briggs-Gowan & Carter, 1998; Carter, Garrity-Rokous, Chazan-Cohen, Little, & Briggs-Gowan, 2001) is a recently developed instrument that is not meant to be a diagnostic instrument but may be relevant for screening and related research uses. The ITSEA is a lengthy parent-report checklist on a variety of dimensions, analogous to the familiar Achenbach Child Behavior Checklist scales but with much more explicit PTSD items.

Procedural Validity for Assessment

Procedural validity refers to the extent to which a new procedure yields results similar to the results of an established procedure (Spitzer & Williams, 1980). An example in psychiatric diagnosis would be a comparison of the diagnoses made by lay interviewer students using highly structured interviews to the diagnoses made by experienced clinicians using all available data. This term is infrequently used in psychiatric research, but the concept seems particularly useful when studying infants and young children. The lack of verbal capacities of the identified patient makes direct assessment more challenging.

Child psychiatric assessments have always promoted the use of multiple methods for obtaining information, such as observation of parent-child interaction, comparison to examiner-child interaction, and assessment of the reliability and biases in parental reports. A major challenge to the investigation of procedural validity, however, is the lack of an established standard to use for comparison. Gaensbauer and Harmon (1981) proposed a paradigm for a general psychiatric evaluation of young children using a sequence of structured and unstructured observations, but it was never tested formally. Crowell, Feldman, and Ginsberg (1988) focused on parent-child interaction by studying clinic-referred children and controls in a highly structured sequence of tasks, based on the tool task model (Matas, Arend, & Sroufe, 1978). This remains the only known study that differentiated clinic-referred from control children based on parent-child interaction ratings. However, the usefulness of these various modalities in relation to diagnostic validity had never been systematically quantified until recently.

Scheeringa et al. (2001) evaluated 15 severely traumatized and symptomatic children and 12 at-risk (low income) comparison children under 48 months of age. Subjects were videotaped during a standardized evaluation of five observational sequences: (1) interview of the caregiver while the child plays on the floor (approximately 60 minutes), (2) caregiver-child free play (10 minutes), (3) examiner-child free play (10 minutes), (4) examiner-guided reenactment of the trauma with dolls and toy props (10 minutes), and (5) interview of the caregiver about her own PTSD symptoms (approximately 30 minutes). We found that child behaviors that represented diagnostic criteria were evident during all five sequences but that it was only necessary to observe three sequences to observe all of the relevant behaviors. These three sequences included: (1) the interview of the caregiver while the child plays on the floor, (2) caregiver-child free play, and (3) examiner-guided trauma reenactment play. The remaining two sequences (interview of the caregiver about herself and examiner-child free play) did not add unique diagnostic information but might be useful for other clinical purposes such as predicting prognosis or ability to utilize play therapy.

In addition, of all the PTSD signs and symptoms that were present (132) in the 15 traumatized subjects, only 12% could be detected through observation. Information about the remaining signs and symptoms (88%) was obtained only through parent report. While not terribly surprising, this quantified for the first time how limited are the sources and quality of information for young children when compared to those for older children and adults.

Last, this study also investigated in a preliminary way whether the criteria were more accurately reflected by the clinician observer/raters than by maternal report. This gets to the issue of whether parents may be biased reporters. There were only 12 instances in which raters felt confident that their observations of the child were more accurate than the parental report. The overwhelming direction of this finding was that the mothers tended to endorse the presence of a symptom but raters tended to believe that the symptom was not present (i.e., the raters saw the children as less symptomatic). This occurred with seven different criteria: irritability and outbursts ($n = 3$), restricted range of affect ($n = 2$), social withdrawal ($n = 2$), decreased interest in significant activities ($n = 2$), psychological distress upon exposure to the trauma ($n = 1$), constricted play ($n = 1$), and detachment or estrangement from others ($n = 1$).

Relational Perspectives on PTSD

Relationship disturbances have been acknowledged as legitimate issues for clinical intervention as V codes in the various editions of the *DSM* (i.e., parent-child relational problem), described in detail in speculative works (Sameroff & Emde, 1989), and taken to the next level of being operationalized at the disorder level in the *Diagnostic Classification of Mental Health and Developmental Disorders* nosology of early childhood disorders (Zero to Three, 1994).

The importance of the parent-child relationship for normal socioemotional development is well documented (Crockenberg & Leerkes, 2000). Important domains of child development can even be predicted before the child is born based on parental characteristics (Fonagy, Steele, & Steele, 1991; Heinecke, Diskin, Ramsey-Klee, & Oates, 1986; Steele, Steele, & Fonagy, 1996). In addition, relationship quality is predictive of some forms of psychopathology. For example, being classified with an insecure attachment at 12 months of age is predictive of later childhood behavior problems (Fagot & Kavanagh, 1990) and adolescent anxiety disorders (Warren, Huston, Egeland, & Sroufe, 1997). The clinically relevant literature on trauma and PTSD also supports this relationship perspective. In fact, the theme of infant mental health treatment in general centers on managing the limitations of caregivers (Fraiberg, 1989).

Scheeringa and Zeanah (2001) reviewed all of the studies that simultaneously assessed parents and children following traumas. All but one of these 17 studies found that less adaptive parental functioning was associated with worse outcomes in their children. Whether there is any causal relationship in this association and, if so, what the actual mechanism is through which parents impact their children are still speculative, however.

Based on this review of studies and our own clinical experience, my colleagues and I have proposed a conceptual model of parent-child relationship disturbances that may be uniquely salient to PTSD (table 19.2). This model may be useful both for clinical purposes of evaluation and treatment and for research purposes to generate testable hypotheses. The impact of the parent-

Table 19.2 Conceptual Model of Parent-Child Relationship Effects on Child PTSD Symptomatology

Type of Effect	Child Experienced a Trauma	Parent Experienced a Trauma[a]	Parent Impacts on Child's Symptoms
Minimal effect	Yes (child had no or few symptoms)	Maybe, but not necessary	Minimal or none
Moderating effect	Yes	Maybe, but not necessary	Yes
Vicarious traumatization effect	No	Yes	Yes
Compound effect	Yes	Yes	Yes

[a]The parent's trauma may be the same or different from the child's.

child relationship on the child following trauma may take one of several forms.

There may be a *minimal effect* (or even no effect). Estimates from adult studies are that the majority of individuals exposed to trauma (70%) do not become symptomatic (e.g., Kessler et al., 1995), and there is no known reason to suspect that this would not be true also for young children.

There may be a *moderating effect* in a situation in which a child experienced a trauma and the parent may or may not also have experienced the same trauma. The trauma itself has an adverse impact on the child, but the subsequent quality of the caregiver's responsiveness to the child has an additional impact. That is, we propose that the caregiver's ability to read the child and respond sensitively to the child's symptomatology is the moderating effect. Sensitive responding may include helping the child to anticipate distress when a reminder of a trauma is going to occur or physically removing a child from a distressing situation and soothing the child. Caregivers who respond sensitively may alleviate their child's distress, and caregivers who do not respond sensitively may exacerbate their child's distress. Such was the situation in a case I treated of a 2-year-old boy who was mauled by a rottweiler dog in front of his parents. The mother had no history of other traumas in her own life. The child initially had symptoms consistent with PTSD, but the mother was the most symptomatic of the pair. A substantial amount of the boy's symptoms improved over time, but residual symptoms of aggression, outbursts of anger, and fear of dogs seemed to be at least in part maintained by the mother's intense

psychological and physiological distress at any type of reminder of the event. For example, she forbade the child to be around even the smallest and most harmless dog, and her anxiety level was palpable to everyone around her. She was preoccupied by her own symptomatology and was not able to respond sensitively to her child's needs. She was not able to help her child endure experiences with small dogs and had limited emotional reserves left over to soothe the boy when he became upset.

There may be a *vicarious traumatization effect* in a situation in which a child does not directly experience a trauma but the mother does. The mother's relationship with the child alone accounts for any effect of the traumatic event on the child. This effect is supported in a case reported by Terr (1990) of a 4-year-old girl who claimed to have visual memories of her older sister's accident even though she did not witness any part of it. The girl's "memories" of the event were drawn from family conversations. Due to the speculative nature of this model, it is not clear what conditions are necessary for this to occur. For example, it is not clear whether there needs to be high level of anxiety in the family during these conversations or whether there needs to be a high level of anxiety in the nonexposed child, or both.

Last, there may be a *compound effect* that involves aspects of both moderating and vicarious traumatization. Both the child and parent directly experience a traumatic event (not necessarily the same event) and the symptomatic behavior of each exacerbates that of the other. An example comes from a case of my own in which a young girl was sexually molested by her day care provider. This event by itself seemed to affect the child. However, the event triggered deep feelings in the mother in relation to her own experience of being molested as a child (an event not experienced by the child). The mother had sworn to herself that she would never let such a thing happen to her child. When it did, the mother's sense of guilt and failure were at times overwhelming, led to her crying in front of the girl, and at times restricted her ability to sensitively and flexibly respond to the girl's needs. Furthermore, we speculated further on the compound effect and described three qualitative patterns of parent-child disturbance that appeared salient to PTSD symptoms in young children.

First is the *withdrawn/unresponsive/unavailable pattern*. Avoidance and withdrawal symptoms in the parent limit her or his ability to respond to the child's needs for listening, acknowledging feelings, soothing, and providing structure. This is the case in the example cited above of the mother whose feelings about her own childhood abuse were triggered by the molestation of her daughter. This mother withdrew from interactions with her child at times.

Second is the *overprotective/constricting pattern*, in which the parent is preoccupied with the fear that the child may be victimized again. In this scenario, the parent has some capacity to engage in conversations with the child about the trauma and to respond at times to the child's distress but physically restricts the child from participating in activities that carry any risk. The parent's anxiety during these times is palpable to the child and adversely effects the child's recovery process. For example, a 2-year-old boy fell from the second floor of a mall onto an escalator. His face was severely cut and he suffered several facial bone fractures. Afterward, his mother would not let him return to the mall or walk on any floor above ground level, despite his apparent comfort with heights. This sheltered existence and his mother's obvious anxiety seemed to foster a sense in the child that he was continually vulnerable.

Third is the *reenacting/endangering/frightening pattern*. A parent may become so preoccupied with the traumatic event that she or he repeatedly asks the child questions or tries to discuss the event. The pressured and uncensored nature of these intense interactions represent unwelcome, and perhaps bewildering, intrusions to the child. At a different level, the parent may actually place the child at risk in new dangerous situations. One interpretation of this parental behavior is that the parent is unconsciously reenacting the traumatic exposure through the child as a way to try to master the experience, although this level of coping is not typically a mature or effective way to deal therapeutically with one's symptoms. Another interpretation may be that this behavior is the most active form of projective identification; that is, for example, a mother cannot tolerate her own level of discomfort, so she actively places her child in situations that make the child feel like she does. Thus, in the mother's mind it is not herself who feels terror, it is her child, which is the easier option to cope with at the time. This seemed to be the case in the situation of a 3-year-old boy who was sexually molested by slightly older boys in his neighborhood (Scheeringa & Zeanah, 2001). The molestation event itself did not seem terribly traumatic, as the boys were fairly close in age and it involved only fondling of the genitalia and rectum. However, the mother of this boy was convinced of the traumatic nature of this event and pressured her son to reveal more and more details of the event. When the boy had nothing else to tell her, she insisted he say more, even threatening to call the police to take him away if he did not talk. This repeated scene was predictably distressing to the child, who could only react by crying and shrinking into a corner of the room. The mother's behavior seemed driven by her own childhood history of severe abuse. In fact, this particular mother had full-blown PTSD at the time, including flashbacks of her own abuse.

All of these patterns in the model, while they appear to be very important in the clinical cases described above, are still to be confirmed by empirical data and provide key directions for future research.

CLINICAL RECOMMENDATIONS FOR ASSESSMENT

The information from the preceding sections has direct implications for the clinical assessment of young children who are symptomatic following trauma exposure. First, the tendency in some parents to underappreciate the impact of trauma on young children means that the clinician must systematically and diligently search for the traumatic event. Some parents may either be ignorant of the fact that young children may be affected by trauma or they may want to strongly avoid talking about the event and bringing up painful memories. The clinician ought to ask parents about the occurrence of every main type of trauma, regardless of whether the parent has hinted about it. The main types include physical abuse, sexual abuse, motor vehicle accidents, dog bites, witnessing domestic violence, witnessing accidental harm to family members, and invasive medical procedures.

Second, while the clinician ought to be persistent in exploring the occurrence of traumas despite the distress this may arouse in some parents, the clinician simultaneously ought to address this distress during the assessment phase. I have found it extremely helpful in clinical experience to tell parents that I know they find this discussion difficult. I anticipate with them that they will have serious second thoughts about coming back for further appointments because of this distress. I ask them to remember that this distress is normal and somewhat unavoidable but not to let that stop them from coming back. This type of discussion normalizes their reaction and validates their feelings of insecurity.

Third, again realizing that many parents will not be fully aware of how their young children can experience and suffer from trauma, I highly recommend educating parents about PTSD as part of the first assessment session. Naming the disorder, verbally describing the symptom criteria, and perhaps even giving them written information on PTSD serves to validate the existence of their children's symptoms. This step is crucial to shaping an informed parent and to strengthening the therapeutic alliance that will be needed when dealing with painful topics in therapy.

Fourth, the limited research on procedural validity for the assessment of PTSD in young children suggests that the observational sequences of watching the child while the mother is being interviewed, mother-child free play, and examiner-guided trauma reenactment are the most salient for witnessing diagnostic signs in the child.

Fifth, substantial research on parental and family variables is highly suggestive that parent-child relationship quality is a crucial component in the development and maintenance of symptoms in children. While the exact mechanism of parent-to-child transmission is mostly speculative at this point, the data have consistently shown that the worse the parents and family function following trauma, the worse the children adapt. We have proposed a relational construct with three different possible relationship patterns (Scheeringa & Zeanah, 2001). A clinician ought to know, for example, if a mother is highly avoidant of talking about the trauma with her child or, in contrast, is preoccupied with the event to the extent that she constantly reminds the child of the trauma.

Sixth, another way to evaluate the parental and family component is to directly inquire about symptomatology that each parent is currently experiencing. If substantial, this may preclude the possibility of therapeutic progress with the child, and the parent may need to be the focus of treatment (Scheeringa, 1999). The foregoing discussion of the relational aspects of PTSD in young children emphasizes the absolutely imperative need to assess the parents concurrently in every case where parents bring their child in for treatment following trauma. At first, this may seem unnecessarily intrusive and awkward to parents who do not perceive themselves as the ones needing help. However, in actual practice, when the assessment is prefaced with a comment by the clinician that it is well known that parental reactions are important for how children cope, the parents nearly always intuitively grasp this concept. In fact, the overwhelming reaction I have received from parents is a sign of validation and relief that I already understand what they have been thinking themselves about the impact of their own behavior on their children.

The assessment of the parents should certainly include standard interviewing about their own symptomatology, PTSD-related and otherwise. An additional method that I have found extremely helpful in research is to ask parents to fill out self-report checklists on PTSD symptoms, such as the Davidson Trauma Scale (Davidson, 1995). In clinical treatment cases, I have found that tracking parent and child symptoms on a weekly basis is not only helpful to me as a therapist but is a way of documenting for the parents in black and white each time the critical importance of the relationship for the child's recovery. We have developed a one-page checklist rating scale that asks the parent to rate the child's behavior on nine symptoms over the previous week on one side, and rate the parent's behavior on eight symptoms on the other side (Peebles & Scheeringa, 1996; see figure 19.1).

Seventh, the interview of the parent about the child's PTSD symptoms ought to include symptoms that have been empirically identified as common following trauma but are not part of the *DSM-IV*. These include loss of previously acquired developmental skills, new aggression, new separation anxiety, and new fears that are not obviously related to the trauma. In addition, the *DSM-IV* symptoms ought to be inquired about with the flexibility required of an infant mental health clinician in knowing that some symptoms

Parent-Child PTSD Weekly Rating Scale
Peebles CD & Scheeringa MS, 1996

Child's Name:_____   Child's Age:_____
Parent's Name:_____   Date:_____

Please circle the number that best describes how severe your **child's** symptoms were over the last week. Circle **0** only if it has **NOT** been a problem for your **child**.

1. Sleep problems (circle: trouble falling asleep, staying asleep, nightmares):
0 __1_____2_____3_____4_____5
       much less   less severe   no change   more severe   much more
       severe   severe

2. Irritable, fussy, temper tantrums:
0 __1_____2_____3_____4_____5

3. Fears (of the dark, of toileting alone, of strangers):
0 __1_____2_____3_____4_____5

4. Separation anxiety (clingy to you, gets upset when you leave him/her):
0 __1_____2_____3_____4_____5
       much less   less severe   no change   more severe   much more
       severe   severe

5. Aggression (hitting, kicking, pushing):
0 __1_____2_____3_____4_____5

6. Avoiding reminders of the trauma (conversations, photos, places):
0 __1_____2_____3_____4_____5

7. Distress at being reminded of the trauma:
0 __1_____2_____3_____4_____5
       much less   less severe   no change   more severe   much more
       severe   severe

8. Always on the lookout for danger (hypervigilance):
0 __1_____2_____3_____4_____5
       much less   less severe   no change   more severe   much more
       severe   severe

9. Loss of developmental skills (speech, toileting, acting like a baby):
0 __1_____2_____3_____4_____5
       much less   less severe   no change   more severe   much more
       severe   severe

Figure 19.1 Parent-Child PTSD Weekly Rating Scale.

may manifest slightly differently than described in the *DSM-IV*. For example, loss of interest in significant activities is likely to be manifest in only one arena, play. Detachment and estrangement from others cannot be directly asked about because it requires knowing the child's internal thoughts and feelings, but this symptom may be reliably detected from observing social behavior with family members. The avoidance symptoms may be particularly difficult to detect because young children are highly dependent on their caregivers with regard to where they travel. If they are never exposed to potential reminders of the trauma, then opportunities to manifest this symptom are limited.

Differential Diagnoses/Diagnostic Difficulties

A number of diagnoses may overlap on several symptoms with PTSD. Specific phobia may develop in reaction to potentially traumatic events. This less severe condition ought to be easily differentiated from PTSD by the lack of the full algorithm of PTSD signs and symptoms. An attachment disorder could plausibly appear concomitantly with PTSD when the traumatic event

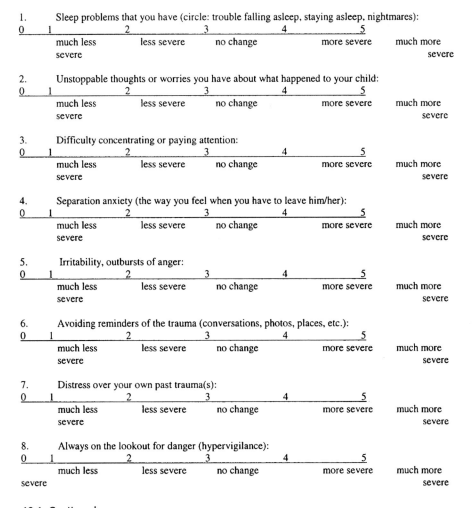

Caregiver Questions: Circle the number that best describes how severe **YOUR OWN** symptoms were over the last week. Circle **0** only if it has **NOT** been a problem for **you**.

1. Sleep problems that you have (circle: trouble falling asleep, staying asleep, nightmares):
    0   1   2   3   4   5
         much less   less severe   no change   more severe   much more
         severe   severe

2. Unstoppable thoughts or worries you have about what happened to your child:
    0   1   2   3   4   5
         much less   less severe   no change   more severe   much more
         severe   severe

3. Difficulty concentrating or paying attention:
    0   1   2   3   4   5
         much less   less severe   no change   more severe   much more
         severe   severe

4. Separation anxiety (the way you feel when you have to leave him/her):
    0   1   2   3   4   5
         much less   less severe   no change   more severe   much more
         severe   severe

5. Irritability, outbursts of anger:
    0   1   2   3   4   5
         much less   less severe   no change   more severe   much more
         severe   severe

6. Avoiding reminders of the trauma (conversations, photos, places, etc.):
    0   1   2   3   4   5
         much less   less severe   no change   more severe   much more
         severe   severe

7. Distress over your own past trauma(s):
    0   1   2   3   4   5
         much less   less severe   no change   more severe   much more
         severe   severe

8. Always on the lookout for danger (hypervigilance):
    0   1   2   3   4   5
         much less   less severe   no change   more severe   much more
    severe   severe

Figure 19.1 Continued.

involves either abuse from a caregiver or the loss of a caregiver through violence. However, no known case report or empirical group study has yet described such a case. This is potentially an extremely important condition to study in relation to PTSD in young children because anecdotal descriptions of children who suffered maternal deprivation are remarkably similar to PTSD symptoms (Bowlby, 1973). On the one hand, one could speculate that attachment disorders and PTSD ought to be easily distinguished from one another because attachment disorders require the manifestation of disturbed attachment behaviors (i.e., lack of seeking or responding to comfort from a caregiver or indiscriminate sociability). On the other hand, one could also plausibly speculate that some attachment disorders and PTSD are indistinguishable because some disturbed attachment behaviors are equivalent to either the reexperiencing or avoidance symptoms of PTSD (e.g., inability to develop closeness to the new substitute caregiver). The resolution of these speculations awaits empirical data collection.

Likewise, complicated grief reactions to the death of a parent may also resemble PTSD. Intrusive thoughts of the deceased, avoidance of reminders of the parent, restricted range of affect, loss of interest in activities, difficulty concentrating, and sleep difficulties are all symptoms that overlap in both conditions. It ought to be possible to distinguish complicated grief reactions from PTSD by the predominantly sad mood in grief compared to the more anxious, frightened, and vigilant emotions in PTSD. Similarly, depressive disorders include symptoms that overlap with PTSD, such as restricted range of affect, sleep problems, difficulty concentrating, and decreased interest in activities. Again, the predominantly sad mood and the lack of reexperiencing-type symptoms in depression ought to distinguish it from PTSD. Last, PTSD may be confused with the disruptive behavior disorders, namely attention deficit/hyperactivity disorder and oppositional defiant disorder, if a child's disruptive outbursts are driven by unappreciated intrusive recollections of the trauma (Thomas & Guskin, 2001). However, a routine psychiatric evaluation ought to easily distinguish these syndromes, since they actually overlap on few criteria.

Comorbidity

Adults with PTSD are comorbid for at least one other disorder approximately 80% of the time (Kessler et al., 1995). Depression, generalized anxiety, and alcohol abuse are the most frequent diagnoses. In contrast, disruptive behavior disorders are common in traumatized children (Famularo, Kinscherff, & Fenton, 1992). Comorbidity is an extremely important issue because it may help differentiate subtypes, denote different neurobiological underpinnings, predict treatment responses, and predict long-term course. I report here on the first known study to analyze diagnostic comorbidity with PTSD in a sample of preschool children.

In the previously mentioned study, my colleagues and I assessed 62 traumatized children and 63 healthy control children who were 20 months through 6 years of age (Scheeringa et al., 2003). In addition to PTSD, we conducted structured diagnostic interview modules for major depressive disorder (MDD), separation anxiety disorder (SAD), attention deficit/hyperactivity disorder (ADHD), and oppositional defiant disorder (ODD). Because the interview instrument was not validated for this age group, we considered that continuous symptom scores of the comorbid disorders might be more valid measures than categorical diagnostic status. Nonetheless, the data were analyzed both ways. The diagnosis of PTSD was made by the revised alternative criteria (see table 19.1). Sixteen subjects were diagnosed with PTSD, which left 46 subjects in the trauma/no PTSD category. The PTSD group had significantly more symptoms of all four disorders than the healthy controls, and significantly more symptoms of SAD and ODD than the trauma/no PTSD group. When categorical disorders were assigned, the rate of having at least one comorbid disorder in the PTSD group was 92.9%, in the trauma/no PTSD group was 28.2%, and in the healthy control group was 16.1%.

Perhaps most important, we assessed when the onset of symptoms started for each condition. In 12 of the 16 PTSD cases (75%), the comorbid symptomatology began after the traumatic event. This contrasts with the expectation from studies on adults that subjects with premorbid mental illness are the ones at greatest risk for developing PTSD.

DIRECTIONS FOR
FUTURE RESEARCH

Two key aspects of diagnostic validity have yet to be studied in PTSD in young children. First, predictive validity must be established by following prospectively a cohort of children from the time of trauma into the future. PTSD in adults is a chronic debilitating condition. While the case report literature on young children is filled with severe, chronic cases, this may reflect referral and reporting biases, and it is yet to be established whether a diagnosis of PTSD by *DSM-IV* criteria portends the same degree of chronicity and severity in young children that it does in adults. Prospective studies are needed to assess how the diagnosis of PTSD relates to future symptoms, future impairment, and future impacts on developmental domains.

Second, differential correlates of PTSD must be demonstrated that distinguish it from other disorders on more than just diagnostic criteria including factors such as familial patterns, neurobiological variables, and relevant associated features. Family studies have already documented the relationship between poorer parental functioning and child functioning, as noted above, but more sophisticated studies are needed to explore whether and how certain family characteristics combine with genetic vulnerabilities to predispose children to this disorder.

The association between neurobiological abnormalities and PTSD in adults is among the strongest of any psychiatric disorder and is based on a well-defined neural and hormonal stress response system. There is overwhelmingly consistent evidence for overreactivity of the sympathetic nervous system in response to trauma-related stimuli, including elevated heart rate, blood pressure (e.g., Blanchard, Kolb, Gerardi, Ryan, & Pallmeyer, 1986), skin conductance (e.g., Pallmeyer, Blanchard, & Kolb, 1986), and startle response (e.g., Orr, Lasko, Shalev, & Pitman, 1995). The evidence is also impressive for a tonic baseline elevation of sympathetic activity. Cortisol is an important stress hormone that has wide-ranging and potent impacts throughout the body. The majority of studies on cortisol regulation have found abnormal levels, but the direction of findings is inconsistent. Almost as many studies have found

higher levels (Lemieux & Coe, 1995) as have found lower levels (Mason, Kosten, Southwick, & Giller, 1990). Despite this controversy, the prevailing opinion in the field appears to be that the real risk comes from having abnormally low levels of cortisol during the acute aftermath of a trauma. Cortisol exerts a powerful protective negative feedback effect on many systems in the body, and the absence of cortisol allows stress reactions to continue unabated. A handful of studies have shown abnormal preliminary results for thyroid function, serotonin levels, opioid responsiveness, and immune system indicators. Brain imaging studies have made provocative discoveries such as a smaller hippocampus in structural imaging (e.g., Bremner et al., 1995) and abnormal limbic system activity in functional imaging (e.g., Rauch, van der Kolk, Fisler, & Alpert, 1996).

Abnormalities in brain processing capacities have also been shown in electroencephalograph (EEG) studies (e.g., Paige, Reid, Allen, & Newton, 1990). Based on these findings and animal studies, some authors have speculated that trauma in the preverbal period profoundly and permanently damages the brain (Kolb, 1987; Perry, Pollard, Blakley, Baker, & Vigilante, 1995; Schore, 2001). This presumes the existence of critical periods of development in the first 3 years. Other authors have noted the tenuous links in this chain of reasoning and the lack of actual data in children and suggested that these dire predictions are overstating the case (Bruer, 1999; Harris, 1998). Given an advanced understanding of the neural and hormonal stress response systems in adults and the suggestion that the first 3 years of life may represent a critical period of development, defining the neural and hormonal stress response in young children is a promising avenue of research.

Associated features of PTSD that are relevant to study in young children include attentional and concentration deficits, short- and long-term memory impairments, the development of aggression and disruptive behavior disorders, and socioemotional problems related to attachment security and the development of close relationships. All of these features are closely connected to one or more of the diagnostic criteria of PTSD, and several of them have already been documented in adult studies. In addition, large-scale epidemiological surveys are needed to estimate the community prevalence and course of PTSD in young children. Finally, we need better methods to estimate prognosis of symptomatic children with randomized intervention studies.

Overall, this is a large research agenda that is complicated relative to older children and adults due to the developmental considerations that are needed for diagnosis, the unique salience of the parent-child relationship, and the difficulty in translating research methods and measures for use in this age group. While much is known already, much remains unanswered for this vulnerable population.

References

American Psychiatric Association. (1980). *Diagnostic and statistical manual of mental disorders* (3rd ed.). Washington, DC: Author.

American Psychiatric Association. (1987). *Diagnostic and statistical manual of mental disorders* (3rd ed., rev.). Washington, DC: Author.

American Psychiatric Association. (1994). *Diagnostic and statistical manual of mental disorders* (4th ed.). Washington, DC: Author.

Balaban, M. T. (1995). Affective influences on startle in five-month-old infants: Reactions to facial expressions of emotion. *Child Development, 66,* 28–36.

Bell, C. C., & Jenkins, E. J. (1993). Community violence and children on Chicago's southside. *Psychiatry, 56,* 46–54.

Blanchard, E. B., Kolb, L. C., Gerardi, R. J., Ryan, P., & Pallmeyer, T. P. (1986). Cardiac response to relevant stimuli as an adjunctive tool for diagnosing post-traumatic stress disorder in Vietnam veterans. *Behavior Therapy, 17,* 592–606.

Bowlby, J. (1973). *Separation: Anxiety and anger.* New York: Basic Books.

Bremner, J. D., Randall, P., Scott, T. M., Bronen, R. A., Seibyl, J. P., Southwick, S. M., Delaney, R. C., McCarthy, G., Charney, D. S., & Innis, R. B. (1995). MRI-based measurement of hippocampal volume in patients with combat-related posttraumatic stress disorder. *American Journal of Psychiatry, 152,* 973–981.

Briggs-Gowan, M. J., & Carter, A. S. (1998). Preliminary acceptability and psychometrics of the infant-toddler social and emotional assessment (ITSEA): A new adult-report questionnaire. *Infant Mental Health Journal, 19,* 422–445.

Bruer, J. T. (1999). *The myth of the first three years: A new understanding of early brain development and lifelong learning.* New York: Free Press.

Carey-Trefzer, C. J. (1949). The results of a clinical study of war-damaged children who attended the child guidance clinic, the Hospital for Sick Children, Great Ormond Street, London. *Journal of Mental Science, 95,* 535–559.

Caron, A. J, Caron, R. F., & MacLean, D. J. (1988). Infant discrimination of naturalistic emotional expressions: The role of face and voice. *Child Development, 59,* 604–616.

Carter, A. S., Garrity-Rokous, F. E., Chazan-Cohen, R., Little, C., & Briggs-Gowan, M. J. (2001). Maternal depression and comorbidity: Predicting early parenting, attachment security, and toddler social-emotional problems and competencies. *Journal of the American Academy of Child and Adolescent Psychiatry, 40,* 18–26.

Cohen, L. B., DeLoache, J. S., & Strauss, M. S. (1979). Infant visual perception. In J. D. Osofsky (Ed.), *Handbook of infant development* (pp. 393–438). New York: Wiley.

Crockenberg, S., & Leerkes, E. (2000). Infant social and emotional development in family context. In C. H. Zeanah, Jr. (Ed.), *Handbook of infant mental health* (pp. 60–90). New York: Guilford Press.

Crowell, J. A., Feldman, S. S., & Ginsberg, N. (1988). Assessment of mother-child interaction in preschoolers with behavior problems. *Journal of the American Academy of Child and Adolescent Psychiatry, 27,* 303–311.

Cuffe, S. P., Addy, C. L., Garrison, C. Z., Waller, J. L., Jackson, K. L., McKeown, R. E., & Chilappagari, S. (1998). Prevalence of PTSD in a community sample of older adolescents. *Journal of the American Academy of Child and Adolescent Psychiatry, 37,* 147–154.

Davidson, J. R. T. (1995). *Davidson trauma scale.* North Tonowanda, NY: Multi-Health Systems.

Dreman, S. (1991). Coping with the trauma of divorce. *Journal of Traumatic Stress, 4,* 113–121.

Dybdahl, R. (2001). Children and mothers in war: An outcome study of a psychosocial intervention program. *Child Development, 72,* 1214–1230.

Fagot, B. L., & Kavanagh, K. (1990). The prediction of antisocial behavior from avoidant attachment classifications. *Child Development, 61,* 864–873.

Famularo, R., Kinscherff, R., & Fenton, R. (1992). Psychiatric diagnoses of maltreated children: Preliminary findings. *Journal of the American Academy of Child and Adolescent Psychiatry, 31*, 863–867.

Fivush, R., Pipe, M., Murachver, T., & Reese, E. (1997). Events spoken and unspoken: Implications of language and memory development for the recovered memory debate. In M. Conway (Ed.), *Recovered memories and false memories: Debates in psychology* (pp. 34–62). Oxford, UK: Oxford University Press.

Foa, E. B., Riggs, D. S., & Gershuny, B. S. (1995). Arousal, numbing, and intrusion: Symptom structure of PTSD following assault. *American Journal of Psychiatry, 152*, 116–120.

Fonagy, P., Steele, H., & Steele, M. (1991). Maternal representations of attachment during pregnancy predict the organization of infant-mother attachment at one year of age. *Child Development, 62*, 891–905.

Fraiberg, S. (Ed.). (1989). *Assessment and therapy of disturbances in infancy.* Northvale, NJ: Jason Aronson.

Gaensbauer, T. J. (1994). Therapeutic work with a traumatized toddler. *Psychoanalytic Study of the Child, 49*, 412–433.

Gaensbauer, T. J., & Harmon, R. J. (1981). Clinical assessment in infancy utilizing structured and playroom situations. *Journal of the American Academy of Child Psychiatry, 20*, 264–280.

Gaensbauer, T. J., & Siegel, C. H. (1995). Therapeutic approaches to posttraumatic stress disorder in infants and toddlers. *Infant Mental Health Journal, 16*, 292–305.

Gislason, I. L., & Call, J. D. (1982). Dog bite in infancy: Trauma and personality development. *Journal of the American Academy of Child Psychiatry, 21*, 203–207.

Gratch, G., & Schatz, J. A. (1987). Cognitive development: The relevance of Piaget's infancy books. In J. D. Osofsky (Ed.), *Handbook of infant development* (2nd ed., pp. 204–237). New York: Wiley.

Greenacre, P. (1949). A contribution to the study of screen memories. *Psychoanalytic Study of the Child, 3/4*, 73–84.

Haith, M. M. (1986). Sensory and perceptual processes in early infancy. *Journal of Pediatrics, 109*, 158–171.

Harris, J. R. (1998). *The nurture assumption: Why children turn out the way they do.* New York: Free Press.

Heinecke, C. M., Diskin, S. D., Ramsey-Klee, D. M., & Oates, D. S. (1986). Pre- and post-birth antecedents of 2-year-old attention, capacity for relationships, and verbal expressiveness. *Developmental Psychology, 22*, 777–787.

Helzer, J. E., Robins, L. N., & McEvoy, L. (1987). Posttraumatic stress disorder in the general population: Findings of the Epidemiologic Catchment Area survey. *New England Journal of Medicine, 317*, 1630–1634.

Joseph, S., Mynard, H., & Mayall, M. (2000). Life-events and post-traumatic stress in a sample of English adolescents. *Journal of Community and Applied Social Psychology, 10*, 475–482.

Kessler, R. C., Sonnega, A., Bromet, E., Hughes, M., & Nelson, C. B. (1995). Posttraumatic stress disorder in the National Comorbidity Survey. *Archives of General Psychiatry, 52*(12): 1048–1060.

Kilpatrick, D. G., & Resnick, H. S. (1993). Posttraumatic stress disorder associated with exposure to criminal victimization in clinical and community populations. In J. R. T. Davidson & E. B. Foa (Eds.), *Posttraumatic stress disorder: DSM-IV and beyond* (pp. 113–143). Washington, DC: American Psychiatric Press.

Kolb, L. C. (1987). Neurophysiological hypothesis explaining posttraumatic stress disorder. *American Journal of Psychiatry, 144*, 989–995.

Laor, N., Wolmer, L., Mayes, L. C., Golomb, A., Silverberg, D. S., Weizman, R., & Cohen, D. J. (1996). Israeli preschoolers under Scud missile attacks. *Archives of General Psychiatry, 53*, 416–423.

Lavigne, J. V., Gibbons, R. D., Christoffel, K. K., Arend, R., Rosenbaum, D., Binns, H., Dawson, N., Sobel, H., & Isaacs, C. (1996). Prevalence rates and correlates of psychiatric disorders among preschool children. *Journal of the American Academy of Child and Adolescent Psychiatry, 35*, 204–214.

Lemieux, A. M., & Coe, C. L. (1995). Abuse-related posttraumatic stress disorder: Evidence for chronic neuroendocrine activation in women. *Psychosomatic Medicine, 57*, 105–115.

Mandler, J. M. (1990). Recall and its verbal expression. In R. Fivush & J. A. Hudson (Eds.), *Knowing and remembering in young children* (pp. 317–330). Cambridge: Cambridge University Press.

March, J. S. (1993). What constitutes a stressor? The "Criterion A" issue. In J. R. T. Davidson & E. B. Foa (Eds.), *Posttraumatic stress disorder: DSM-IV and beyond* (pp. 37–54). Washington, DC: American Psychiatric Press.

Mason, J. W., Kosten, T. R., Southwick, S. M., & Giller, E. L. (1990). The use of psychoendocrine strategies in post-traumatic stress disorder. *Journal of Applied Social Psychology,* 20(21, Part 1), 1822–1846.

Matas, L., Arend, R. A., & Sroufe, L. A. (1978). Continuity of adaptation in the second year: The relationship between quality of attachment and later competence. *Child Development, 49,* 547–556.

Mumme, D. L., Fernald, A., & Herrera, C. (1996). Infants' responses to facial and vocal emotional signals in a social referencing paradigm. *Child Development, 67,* 3219–3237.

National Center for Health Statistics, Centers for Disease Control. (1998). *National Mortality Data, 1997.* Hyattsville, MD: Author.

Orr, S. P., Lasko, N. B., Shalev, A. Y., & Pitman, R. K. (1995). Physiologic responses to loud tones in Vietnam veterans with posttraumatic stress disorder. *Journal of Abnormal Psychology, 104,* 75–82.

Osofsky, J. D., & Scheeringa, M. S. (1997). Community and domestic violence exposure: Effects in development and psychopathology. In D. Cicchetti & S. L. Toth (Eds.), *Rochester symposium on developmental psychopathology:. Vol. 8. Developmental perspectives on trauma: Theory, research, and intervention* (pp. 155–180). Rochester, NY: University of Rochester Press.

Osofsky, J. D., Wewers, S., Hann, D. M., & Fick, A. C. (1993). Chronic community violence: What is happening to our children? *Psychiatry, 56,* 36–45.

Paige, S. R., Reid, G. M., Allen, M. G., & Newton, J. E. (1990). Psychophysiological correlates of posttraumatic stress disorder in Vietnam veterans. *Biological Psychiatry, 27,* 419–430.

Pallmeyer, T. P., Blanchard, E. B., & Kolb, L. C. (1986). The psychophysiology of combat-induced post-traumatic stress disorder in Vietnam veterans. *Behaviour Research and Therapy, 24,* 645–652.

Peebles, C. D., & Scheeringa, M. S. (1996). *Parent-child PTSD weekly rating scale.* Unpublished manuscript.

Perry, B. D., Pollard, R. A., Blakley, T. L., Baker, W. L., & Vigilante, D. (1995). Childhood trauma, the neurobiology of adaptation, and "use-dependent" development of the brain: How "states" become "traits." *Infant Mental Health Journal, 16,* 271–291.

Pruett, K. D. (1979). Home treatment for two infants who witnessed their mother's murder. *Journal of the American Academy of Child and Adolescent Psychiatry, 18,* 647–657.

Pynoos, R. S., Frederick, C., Nader, K., Arroyo, W., Steinberg, A., Eth, S., Nunez, F., & Fairbanks, L. (1987). Life threat and posttraumatic stress in school-age children. *Archives of General Psychiatry, 44,* 1057–1063.

Rauch, S. L., van der Kolk, B. A., Fisler, R. E., & Alpert, N. M. (1996). A symptom provocation study of posttraumatic stress disorder using positron emission tomography and script-driven imagery. *Archives of General Psychiatry, 53,* 380–387.

Reinherz, H. Z., Giaconia, R. M., Lefkowitz, E. S., Pakiz, B., & Frost, A. K. (1993). Prevalence of psychiatric disorders in a community population of older adolescents. *Journal of the American Academy of Child and Adolescent Psychiatry, 33,* 369–377.

Sameroff, A. J., & Emde, R. N. (Eds.). (1989). *Relationship disturbances in early childhood.* New York: Basic Books.

Schacter, D. L. (1987). Implicit memory: History and current status. *Journal of Experimental Psychology: Learning, Memory, and Cognition, 13,* 501–518.

Scheeringa, M. S. (1999). Treatment for posttraumatic stress disorder in infants and toddlers. *Journal of Systemic Therapies, 18,* 20–31.

Scheeringa, M. S., & Gaensbauer, T. J. (2000). Posttraumatic stress disorder. In C. H. Zeanah, Jr. (Ed.), *Handbook of infant mental health* (pp. 369–381). New York: Guilford Press.

Scheeringa, M. S., Peebles, C. D., Cook, C. A., & Zeanah, C. H. (2001). Toward establishing procedural, criterion, and discriminant validity for PTSD in early childhood. *Journal of the American Academy of Child and Adolescent Psychiatry, 40,* 52–60.

Scheeringa, M. S., & Zeanah, C. H. (1994). *Posttraumatic stress disorder semi-structured interview and observational record for infants and young children (0–48 months).* New Orleans: Tulane University Health Sciences Center.

Scheeringa, M. S. & Zeanah, C. H. (2001). A relational perspective on PTSD in young children. *Journal of Traumatic Stress, 14,* 799–815.

Scheeringa, M. S., Zeanah, C. H., Drell, M. J., & Larrieu, J. A. (1995). Two approaches to the diagnosis of posttraumatic stress disorder in infancy and early childhood. *Journal of the American Academy of Child and Adolescent Psychiatry, 34,* 191–200.

Scheeringa, M. S., Zeanah, C. H., Myers, L., & Putnam, F. W. (2003). New findings on alternative criteria for PTSD in preschool children. *Journal of the American Academy of Child and Adolescent Psychiatry, 42*(5), 561–570.

Schore, A. N. (2001). The effects of early relational trauma on right brain development, affect regulation, and infant mental health. *Infant Mental Health Journal, 22*(1–2), 201–269.

Schwartz, G. M., Izard, C. E., & Ansul, S. E. (1985). The 5-month-old's ability to discriminate facial expressions of emotion. *Infant Behavior and Development, 8,* 65–77.

Shore, J. H., Tatum, E., & Vollmer, W. M. (1986). Psychiatric reactions to disaster: The Mt. St. Helen's experience. *American Journal of Psychiatry, 143,* 590–595.

Sorce, J. F., Emde, R. N., Campos, J., & Klinnert, M. D. (1985). Maternal emotional signaling: Its effect on the visual cliff behavior of 1-year-olds. *Developmental Psychology, 21,* 195–200.

Spaccarelli, S., Sandler, I. N., & Roosa, M. (1994). History of spouse violence against mother: Correlated risks and unique effects in child mental health. *Journal of Family Violence, 9,* 79–98.

Spitzer, R. L. & Williams, J. B. W. (1980). Classification of mental disorders and DSM-III. In H. I. Kaplan, A. M. Freedman, & B. J. Sadock (Eds.), *Comprehensive textbook of psychiatry* (3rd ed., pp. 1035–1072). Baltimore: Williams and Wilkins.

Sroufe, L. A. (1979). Socioemotional development. In J. D. Osofsky (Ed.), *Handbook of infant development* (pp. 462–516). New York: Wiley.

Steele, H., Steele, M., & Fonagy, P. (1996). Associations among attachment classifications of mothers, fathers, and their infants: Evidence for a relationship-specific perspective. *Child Development, 67,* 541–555.

Taylor, I., Zuckerman, B., Harik, V., & Groves, B. (1992). Exposure to violence among inner city parents and young children. *American Journal of Diseases of Children, 146,* 487.

Terr, L. (1990). *Too scared to cry.* New York: Basic Books.

Terr, L. C. (1988). What happens to early memories of trauma? A study of twenty children under age five at the time of documented traumatic events. *Journal of the American Academy of Child and Adolescent Psychiatry, 27,* 96–104.

Thomas, J. M., & Guskin, K. A. (2001). Disruptive behavior in children: What does it mean? *Journal of the American Academy of Child and Adolescent Psychiatry, 40,* 44–51.

Tjaden, P., & Thoennes, N. (1998, November). Prevalence, incidence, and consequences of violence against women: Findings from the National Violence Against Women Survey. *Research in Brief.* Washington, DC: U.S. Department of Justice.

U.S. Department of Health and Human Services. (2001). *Child maltreatment 1999: Reports from the states to the national child abuse and neglect data system.* Washington, DC: U.S. Government Printing Office.

Walker-Andrews, A. S., & Gronlick, W. (1983). Discrimination of vocal expressions by young infants. *Infant Behavior and Development, 6,* 491–498.

Warren, S. L., Huston, L., Egeland, B., & Sroufe, L. A. (1997). Child and adolescent anxiety disorders and early attachment. *Journal of the American Academy of Child and Adolescent Psychiatry, 36,* 637–644.

Zeanah, C. H., Boris, N. W., & Scheeringa, M. S. (1997). Infant development: The first 3 years of life. In A. Tasman, J. Kay, & J. A. Lieberman (Eds.), *Psychiatry* (pp. 75–100). Philadelphia: Saunders.

Zero to Three, National Center for Clinical Infant Programs. (1994). *Diagnostic classification of mental health and developmental disorders of infancy and early childhood.* Washington, DC: Author.

20

Diagnostic and Assessment Issues of Attention Deficit/ Hyperactivity Disorder in the Young Child

William E. Pelham, Jr.

Anil Chacko

Brian T. Wymbs

Attention deficit/hyperactivity disorder (ADHD), the most common mental health disorder of childhood, is characterized by developmentally inappropriate, excessive levels of inattention, hyperactivity, and impulsivity. School-aged children with ADHD display significant impairment in many areas of daily life functioning, including school, family, and peer domains. ADHD is a chronic disorder, with symptoms generally emerging early in development (i.e., in the toddler to preschool period) and with problems continuing through adolescence and into adulthood. The level of impairment for the child with ADHD, the impact upon the family, and the costs of ADHD to families, schools, and communities are substantial (NIH Consensus Statement, 1998) and therefore warrant attention from health, mental health, and educational professionals. Given the early age of onset, understanding the early course of ADHD may inform prevention and early intervention efforts.

The majority of ADHD children are referred for services in early elementary school, and the vast majority of research on ADHD has been conducted on elementary-aged children. Indeed, recent guidelines for identification and treatment of ADHD are specifically designed for children between the ages of 6 and 12 years (American Academy of Pediatrics [AAP], 2000, 2001). However, it is likely that a large portion and perhaps even the majority of ADHD children can be identified at the preschool age (Barkley, 1997; Campbell, 1995). The dramatic increase in the use of psychoactive medication to treat young children in the 1990s (Zito et al., 2000) heightened public awareness of the need to recognize and intervene with ADHD children before they reach school (Vitiello, 2001). In addition, this trend points out the importance of ensuring that diagnosis of ADHD in very young children is a valid construct. In this chapter, we discuss basic information about ADHD in young children, including diagnosis, prevalence, correlates, and long-term outcomes, as well as implications for intervention. We also discuss effective assessment when validated diagnostic procedures may not be feasible. Before turning to these issues, it is appropriate to begin with a discussion of the validity of the diagnosis of ADHD in preschoolers. Can ADHD be reliably and validly identified in young children?

VALIDITY OF ADHD IN YOUNG CHILDREN

Particularly in the media and in day care and early education settings, the validity of ADHD as a diagnosis in young children has been a hot-button issue. Many have argued that the core symptoms of the disorder are phenomena that may be typical of the functioning of young children, as attention and impulse regulation skills are not yet well developed in very young children, and have therefore questioned the validity of the diagnosis (McClellan & Speltz, 2003). Indeed, the vast majority of 2-year-olds have shorter attention spans, poorer impulse control, and higher activity levels than their parents or teachers would like. Thus, it is argued, many young children with basically normal but not yet well-developed levels of the adaptive components of these core criteria may be misidentified as ADHD, casting doubt on the validity of the diagnosis in preschoolers. Others, arguing from a different perspective, have suggested that there are normative variations in the core symptoms of ADHD that reflect normal variation in temperament. These authors argue that cutoff points are inappropriate that define psychopathology in what is a normal distribution of temperamental characteristics (e.g., Carey, 1998). Fortunately, research has addressed these criticisms.

In a handful of studies, ADHD children have been identified at the preschool age, and they are discussed below. One study used the *Diagnostic and Statistical Manual of Mental Disorders*, Fourth Edition (*DSM-IV*; American Psychiatric Association, 1994) definition of ADHD. Lahey et al. (1998), in the first wave of a longitudinal study examining the development of children with ADHD and comparison children, recruited children mostly at the ages of 4 and 5 years. In their first report, they utilized the diagnostic algorithms specified in the *DSM-IV* and compared children who met ADHD diagnostic criteria with those who did not meet criteria on multiple measures of functioning (e.g., intelligence and academic achievement, social behavior, and peer relationships) to examine concurrent validity. They demonstrated quite clearly that, when the *DSM-IV* algorithms employing parent and teacher reports were used to define ADHD, young children with

ADHD were as different from comparison children on measures of concurrent validity (e.g., academic functioning, peer relationships, family functioning) as has been extensively reported for older children. As discussed below (see sections Limitations of the DSM and Future Directions), the team of investigators has not yet reported whether a variant of the *DSM-IV* algorithm would have been better at this age than the existing definition—but the current definition "worked." Thus, there is strong evidence that ADHD is a valid diagnosis in older preschool children when these children can be assessed in a structured preschool setting. We now turn to a review of important issues to consider in the study of ADHD in young children.

PREVALENCE

Given that the core symptoms of ADHD are constructs that frequently occur at high levels in young children and that change with development, it is reasonable to ask whether the prevalence of ADHD in young children is different than in older children. Several studies using community and clinic samples have investigated the prevalence of ADHD or its symptoms in preschool-aged children. Using maternal responses to a mass mailing of the ADHD Rating Scale (DuPaul, Power, Anastopoulos, & Reid, 1994) sent to families with 2- to 6-year-old children in preschool ($N = 253$), one study found that nearly 1 in 10 mothers reported that their child exhibited symptoms of ADHD (Gimpel & Kuhn, 2000). An earlier study with a larger sample ($N = 1,037$) found that about 2% of 3-year-old preschool children were inappropriately hyperactive across settings, while another 3% were hyperactive only at home (McGee, Partridge, Williams, & Silva, 1991). A more recent study by Gadow, Sprafkin, and Nolan (2001) using both parent and teacher reports in a community sample of children between the ages of 3 and 5 years found that 8% of males and 4% of females met symptom criteria for ADHD as reported by parents. Teacher reports indicated that 22% of males and 13% of females met symptom criteria in the community sample. Similar to work done with school-aged children (Goldman, Genel, Bezman, & Slanetz, 1998), community-based studies (Gadow et al., 2001; Miller, Koplewicz, & Klein, 1997) demonstrate that ADHD is more prevalent in preschool boys than girls. Specifically, Gimpel and Kuhn (2000) noted that two out of three children with ADHD symptoms were boys, and all of the preschoolers that were determined to have ADHD-combined type were boys. Furthermore, studies that have analyzed age effects within the preschool period (Miller et al., 1997) have found that younger preschool children (i.e., 3-year-olds) present with more symptoms of ADHD than older preschool children (i.e., 4- to 5-year-olds).

Not surprisingly, clinic-based studies of preschool populations have found that clinic-referred children typically present higher rates of ADHD than nonreferred children (Gadow et al., 2001; Keenan, Shaw, Walsh, Delliquadri, & Giovannelli, 1997; Keenan & Wakschlag, 2000). Specifically up to 60% (Keenan & Wakschlag, 2000) of clinic-referred preschool children exhibited symptoms of ADHD. These high rates of ADHD symptomatology have also been found across gender within clinic samples (Gadow et al., 2001).

Collectively, the above research indicates the prevalence rate of ADHD symptoms in young children as rated by parents to be between 2% and 10%. Teacher reports of symptomatology, however, show an increased prevalence of ADHD symptomatology compared to parental reports (Gadow et al., 2001). Furthermore, the gender ratio is two boys for every one girl. Notably, these prevalence rates and gender ratios are comparable to what has been extensively reported for elementary-aged children (Barbaresi et al., 2002; Barkley, 1997; Rowland et al., 2002).

COMORBIDITY

Comorbidity has been a particularly widely studied aspect of child psychopathology for the past decade (Angold, Costello, & Erkanli, 1999; chapter 7). Although ADHD is a distinct disorder, it is often comorbid with other disruptive behavior disorders of childhood, including oppositional defiant disorder (ODD) and conduct disorder (CD; August, Realmuto, MacDonald, & Nugent, 1996; Biederman, Faraone, & Lahey, 1992; Bird, Canino, Rubio-Stipec, & Gould, 1988; Bird, Gould,

& Staghezza, 1993; Pelham, Evans, Gnagy, & Greenslade, 1992; Pelham, Gnagy, Greenslade, & Milich, 1992). For some time, it has been clear that comorbidity with ODD and CD is also present in preschool samples (Campbell, Szumowski, Ewing, Gluck, & Breaux, 1982). Using a large community sample ($N = 3,860$) in which 2.0% of the preschool children sampled presented ADHD symptoms, Lavigne et al. (1996) discovered that 90% of the ADHD children presented symptoms of other disruptive behavior disorders. Notably, internalizing problems appear to be considerably less comorbid with ADHD in preschoolers (Lavigne et al., 1996), as has been reported in older samples (MTA Cooperative Group, 1999). Comorbidity is also prevalent in clinic-referred samples. Studies have shown that between 39% (Speltz, McClellan, DeKlyen, & Jones, 1999) and 81% (Keenan & Wakschlag, 2000) of the clinic-referred preschool children with ADHD have at least one other disruptive behavior disorder (ODD/CD), with as many as 45% of them presenting symptoms of ADHD, ODD, and CD. Last, young children diagnosed with comorbid disruptive behavior disorders typically have the worst long-term outcome (Pierce, Ewing, & Campbell, 1999; Speltz et al., 1999).

In a longitudinal study begun two decades ago, Campbell and colleagues broadened the scope of considering psychopathology in young children by investigating both the immediate and the long-term effects of disruptive behavior symptomatology in preschoolers. Campbell and others have focused on four coexisting symptoms that consistently result in present and future functional impairment across settings: inattention, hyperactivity, impulsivity, and noncompliance (Campbell, 1987; Campbell, Breaux, Ewing, & Szumowski, 1986; Campbell, Ewing, Breaux, & Szumowski, 1986; Campbell et al., 1982; Pierce et al., 1999). Despite noting the difficulty in differentiating between hyperactivity and aggression in younger children due to similar correlates and precursors (Campbell, 1985), Campbell and colleagues also found that aggression tends to contribute to both immediate and long-term negative outcomes (Campbell, Breaux, et al., 1986; Campbell, Ewing, et al., 1986; Campbell et al., 1982). In sum, rates of comorbidity with other disruptive behavior disorders in preschoolers with ADHD appear to be substantial and similar to those that have been reported for older children.

ASSOCIATED PROBLEMS

In addition to the core symptoms and comorbidities present in young children with ADHD, many additional conditions are commonly associated with functional impairment across settings. As in samples of older children, these include low levels of cognitive functioning, developmentally immature peer relationships, and negative family interactions. Research has shown that the precursors of childhood ADHD can be traced to infancy and are often manifested as early temperamental difficulties such as age-inappropriate levels of irritability and hyperactivity (Campbell et al., 1982). Preschoolers who present symptoms of ADHD also tend to have poor language skills (McGee et al., 1991) and are more likely to receive special education services (Lahey et al., 1998). In addition, young children with ADHD tend to have more problems with friendships and are less popular, less prosocial, and less cooperative with their peers (Lahey et al., 1998), all patterns that have long been known in school-aged samples of ADHD children (Pelham & Bender, 1982).

Similar to older children with ADHD, numerous familial stressors are also prevalent with younger children exhibiting symptoms of ADHD (Campbell, Breaux, et al., 1986; Campbell & Ewing, 1990; McGee et al., 1991; Moffitt, 1990), including the absence of the father (Keenan & Wakschlag, 2000), low socioeconomic status (Campbell, Breaux, et al., 1986; Campbell & Ewing, 1990), and maternal distress (Mash & Johnston, 1990). Research has indicated that these stressors are associated with negative long-term outcomes for preschool children. In particular, maternal depression, the frequency of stressful life events for parents, lower marital satisfaction, and marital discord predict ongoing behavioral difficulties for children (Campbell, 1994; Campbell, Breaux, et al., 1986; Campbell, Pierce, March, & Ewing, 1991; Johnston, 1996).

Furthermore, research has demonstrated a link between impaired parenting practices and behavioral impairments in young ADHD children (Mash & Johnston, 1982). Using a behavioral observational system to classify parent-child interactions, Mash and Johnston found that during structured activities with their ADHD preschool children, mothers were more negative and directive of their child's behavior and less involved with their child during play activities. In response to their mother's direction, ADHD preschool children were more likely than children not diagnosed with ADHD and school-aged ADHD children to be noncompliant. As illustrated in the Mash and Johnston study, mother-child interactions are typically impaired, with more serious difficulties observed in mothers with low tolerance for noncompliance or those with a comorbid hyperactive/aggressive child (Stormont-Spurgin & Zentall, 1995). Researchers have noted that inconsistent, unresponsive, controlling, and power-assertive parenting can maintain or exacerbate a child's disruptive behavior (Chamberlain & Patterson, 1995; Miller, Cowan, Cowan, Hetherington, & Clingempeel, 1993; Patterson, DeBaryshe, & Ramsey, 1989; Snyder, 1991; Webster-Stratton, 1990). Although the subjects in these studies are typically labeled conduct problem children, ADHD has been a very common comorbidity, accounting for up to two thirds of the samples (Lahey & Loeber, 1997; Webster-Stratton, Reid, & Hammond, 2001). Futhermore, it has been shown (e.g., Fletcher, Fischer, Barkley, & Smallish, 1996) that the greatest levels of impaired parenting are among parents of comorbid children.

Taken together, research has indicated a bidirectional pathway between children's behavior problems and parental stress and psychopathology. Gillberg, Carlstrom, and Rasmussen (1983) noted that mothers of children with ADHD sought treatment for stress or psychopathology more often than mothers of children without behavior disorders. Befera and Barkley (1985) found that ratings of parental stress were associated with maternal depression, and the severity of difficulty was associated with the child's ADHD symptoms. Studies have suggested that mothers of comorbid ADHD/ODD children are more likely than mothers of children with a single diagnosis of ADHD or ODD to exhibit symptoms of depression (Barkley, Fischer, Edelbrock, & Smallish, 1991; Befera & Barkley, 1985; Cunningham, Benness, & Siegel, 1988). It is important to note that findings of this study suggest that symptom count alone does not predict associated problems in the mother, but severity does. Maternal depression is also found to occur at a very high rate in families of children with ADHD (Biederman, Faraone, Keenan, & Tsuang, 1991). Depression in mothers of ADHD children often complicates and reduces parenting efficacy (Forehand & McMahon, 1981) by increasing the frequency of commands, increasing the amount of controlling behaviors, and increasing and maintaining stress (Fischer, 1990). These negative parenting methods are usually met with noncompliance from the child (Barkley & Cunningham, 1980; Campbell, 1975), thereby reducing parenting self-efficacy. This bidirectional effect may maintain parental stress and psychopathology over long periods of time, with parents developing inappropriate coping styles, particularly coping with problematic child behavior by using alcohol. For example, we have conducted several controlled experiments examining alcohol consumption of parents with children diagnosed with ADHD (Lang, Pelham, Atkeson, & Murphy, 1999; Pelham & Lang, 1999; Pelham et al., 1997, 1998). In these studies we have manipulated both (a) alcohol administration and its effects on parenting and (b) ADHD/oppositional behavior and its effects on parental alcohol consumption. These studies collectively demonstrate a bidirectional influence of parental alcohol consumption and child problematic behavior, such that alcohol negatively influences parenting behaviors (e.g., lax monitoring), which mediate the development of conduct problems in children (Chamberlain & Patterson, 1995), and that deviant child behaviors cause increased parental alcohol consumption. Although these results were found in elementary-aged child-parent dyads, one would assume that the bidirectional influence is no less and arguably more severe in younger child-parent dyads, as research has shown that these dyads typically involve more stress for parents (Mash & Johnston, 1982).

LONG-TERM OUTCOME

Whereas past research has stressed the importance of concurrent factors influencing the long-term outcome of young children, Campbell and colleagues suggest that the severity of initial impairment predicts future behavioral problems (Campbell, Breaux, Ewing, & Szumowski, 1984; Campbell et al., 1982). Longitudinal studies investigating the relationship between behaviors characteristic of ADHD (i.e., inattention, hyperactivity, impulsivity) present in preschoolers and their long-term outcome have shown that, while continuous and age-inappropriate difficulties with hyperactive, aggressive, or other antisocial behaviors are important, it is the initial severity of the behavioral impairment that tends to predict persistent, stable problems (Campbell, 1987; Pierce et al., 1999; Sonuga-Barke, Thompson, Stevenson, & Viney, 1997). The presence of overactivity, inattention, and disobedience in young children, in the absence of impairment across family and peer contexts, may reflect a transient developmental problem. However, young children who present with both ADHD symptoms and greater functional impairment, such as antisocial behavior, peer relationship difficulties, or a dysfunctional family climate, tend to have more pervasive and persistent behavioral problems across settings (Campbell, 1987; Pierce et al., 1999). These problems persist from preschool to middle childhood and through adolescence (Campbell, 1987; Campbell & Ewing, 1990; Campbell, Ewing, et al., 1986; Chamberlain & Patterson, 1995; Moffitt, 1990; Pierce et al., 1999). The role of functional impairment in addition to symptoms is important to highlight in these outcomes, a point discussed in greater detail below.

Finally, it is important to note that longitudinal studies have followed the course of ADHD symptoms present in young children until school age (Campbell, 1994; Campbell et al., 1984; Campbell & Ewing, 1990; Campbell, Ewing, et al., 1986) and adolescence (McGee et al., 1991). These studies and others (e.g., Cantwell & Baker, 1989) attest to the stability of the problem behavior during preschool. For instance, Cantwell and Baker (1989) found that 80% of the young children in their study previously diagnosed with ADHD in preschool continued to meet criteria for ADHD 5 years later. Similarly, aggression, ODD, CD, and social skills deficits in children presenting signs of ADHD in preschool have been shown to persist through middle childhood (Campbell, 1994; Campbell et al., 1984; Campbell &

Ewing, 1990; Speltz et al., 1999). Furthermore, studies have shown that preschoolers diagnosed with ADHD often develop additional behavioral impairments throughout childhood, including internalizing behavior problems (e.g., social anxiety and feelings of incompetence; Campbell, 1994; Cantwell & Baker, 1989; Speltz et al., 1999), comorbidity with CD (Campbell et al., 1982), ODD (Pierce et al., 1999; Speltz et al., 1999) or antisocial behavior and criminal offending (Moffitt, 1990), and other psychiatric disorders, including transient tic disorder and pervasive developmental disorder (Cantwell & Baker, 1989). One study also found that preschoolers diagnosed with ADHD frequently develop poorer language skills, lower levels of reading ability, and poorer cognitive abilities (McGee et al., 1991).

Given the prevalence, stability, associated difficulties, and poor outcomes for very young children with ADHD, the task of early identification is crucial. The early identification of young children with ADHD may lead to earlier intervention at school (e.g., special education services) and home (e.g., parent training) that may not only improve current functioning but also prevent the development of later problems, as we discuss below (see Early Identification and Early Intervention).

LIMITATIONS OF THE DSM FOR YOUNG CHILDREN

Psychological disorders are constructs that are developed to describe individual behavior, cognitions, and emotions that occur in daily life. For some disorders (e.g., schizophrenia), the defining characteristics are unique and vivid (e.g., delusions and hallucinations). The construct of ADHD, however, is less distinctive and salient. In particular, the defining core symptoms—inattention, impulsivity, and hyperactivity—are developmentally changing phenomena that are quite common, especially in young children. This is particularly true given the specific descriptors that have been used in the DSMs to operationalize the core symptoms (see table 20.1 for the DSM-IV definition of ADHD). What 2-year-old does *not* often fidget or squirm? It is not surprising that many professionals and media outlets have disputed the

existence of ADHD, particularly in young children. Researchers and clinicians alike have noted the developmental insensitivity of the DSM-IV (Cummings, Davies, & Campbell, 2000). What is normative behavior for a very young child is a question of importance, particularly when using the DSM-IV as a classification system. As the DSM-IV itself states, "It is especially difficult to establish this diagnosis in children younger than age 4 or 5 years, because their characteristic behavior is much more variable than that of older children" (American Psychiatric Association, 1994, p. 81). High levels of activity, inability to sustain attention, and impulsive behavior are more normative in this young age group than for the remainder of the developmental spectrum.

Campbell (1995) lists suggested requirements for a definition of a disorder in young children:

> (1) the presence of a pattern or constellation of symptoms; (2) a pattern of symptoms with at least short-term stability that goes beyond a transient adjustment to stress or change, such as that subsequent to the birth of a sibling or entry into child care; (3) a cluster of symptoms that is evident in several settings and with other people other than the parent(s); (4) symptoms that are relatively severe; and (5) symptoms that interfere with the child's ability to negotiate developmental challenges, thereby reflecting some impairment in functioning. (p. 117)

The DSM-IV specifies that developmental issues, as Campbell suggests, need to be considered. However, it is reasonable to ask how well the DSM-IV is really serving the diagnostic needs of young children.

First, Campbell refers to a "pattern or constellation of symptoms." The DSM-IV obviously lists such a pattern of symptoms in its diagnostic criteria, but there are major limitations of the symptom lists with regard to young children. The first issue is whether these lists of symptoms are relevant to the young age range. For example, many DSM-IV criteria consist of "school-specific" symptoms—symptoms that may be inappropriate or difficult to assess for very young children (examples include "often avoids, dislikes, or is reluctant to engage in tasks that require sustained mental effort")—a limitation noted in the DSM-IV text.

Table 20.1 *DSM-IV* Diagnostic Criteria for Attention Deficit/Hyperactivity Disorder

A. Either (1) or (2):
  (1) Six (or more) of the following symptoms of inattention have persisted for at least 6 months to a degree that is maladaptive and inconsistent with developmental level:
  Inattention
  (a) Often fails to give close attention to details or makes careless mistakes in schoolwork, work, or other activities
  (b) Often has difficulty sustaining attention in tasks or play activities
  (c) Often does not seem to listen when spoken to directly
  (d) Often does not follow through on instructions and fails to finish schoolwork, chores, or duties in the workplace (not due to oppositional behavior or failure to understand instructions)
  (e) Often has difficulties organizing tasks and activities
  (f) Often avoids, dislikes, or is reluctant to engage in tasks that require sustained mental effort (such as schoolwork or homework)
  (g) Often loses things necessary for tasks or activities (e.g., toys, school assignments, pencils, books, or tools)
  (h) Is often easily distracted by extraneous stimuli
  (i) Often forgetful in daily activities
  (2) Six (or more) of the following symptoms of hyperactivity-impulsivity have persisted for at least 6 months to a degree that is maladaptive and inconsistent with developmental level:
  Hyperactivity
  (a) Often fidgets with hands or feet or squirms in seat
  (b) Often leaves seat in classroom or in other situations in which remaining seated is expected
  (c) Often runs about or climbs excessively in situations where it is inappropriate (in adolescents or adults, may be limited to subjective feelings of restlessness)
  (d) Often has difficulty playing or engaging in leisure activities quietly
  (e) Is always "on the go" or acts as if "driven by a motor"
  (f) Often talks excessively
  Impulsivity
  (g) Often blurts out answers before questions have been completed
  (h) Often has difficulty awaiting turn
  (i) Often interrupts or intrudes on others (e.g., butts into conversations or games)
B. Some hyperactive-impulsive or inattentive symptoms that caused impairment were present before age 7
C. Some impairment from the symptoms is present in two or more settings (e.g., at school [or work], and at home).
D. There must be clear evidence of clinically significant impairment in social, academic, or occupational functioning
E. The symptoms do not occur exclusively during the course of a pervasive developmental disorder, schizophrenia or other psychotic disorder, and is not better accounted for by a mood disorder, anxiety disorder, dissociative disorder, or a personality disorder.

Code Based on Type:
  314.01 Attention Deficit/Hyperactivity Disorder, Combined Type: If both Criteria A1 and A2 are met for the past 6 months
  314.00 Attention Deficit/Hyperactivity Disorder, Predominantly Inattentive Type: if Criterion A1 is met but Criterion A2 is not met for the past 6 months
  314.01 Attention Deficit/Hyperactivity Disorder, Predominantly Hyperactive-Impusive Type: If Criterion A2 is met but Criterion A1 is not met for the past 6 months
  Coding Note: For individuals (especially adolescents and adults) who currently have symptoms that no longer meet full criteria, "In Partial Remission" should be specified.

If the presence of these symptoms is necessary to meet diagnostic criteria, an underestimation of the prevalence of ADHD in younger populations may occur unless the child is in a preschool setting in which structured tasks are conducted and monitored. The second major issue with regard to the *DSM-IV* symptom lists is that the symptom count requirements are identical for all ages—six symptoms from each dimensional list. Because younger children generally display relatively higher levels of activity, inattention, and impulsive behavior than older children, cutoffs that employ absolute criteria (e.g., does the behavior occur "pretty much") will result in a higher number of symptom counts for younger than for older children. Thus, a straightforward application of these criteria should identify a higher proportion of young children as having ADHD than would be the case for older children (a point discussed further below), with a likely increase in the number of false positives.

Campbell's second point refers to a pattern of symptoms with at least short-term stability. The *DSM-IV*'s requirement that symptoms have persisted for at least 6 months addresses this point. However, the stability of the *DSM-IV* diagnosis of ADHD in young children has yet to be demonstrated. As an illustration, consider the *DSM-IV* subtypes of ADHD—in particular the hyperactive-impulsive subtype. This subtype was noted as having a skewed age distribution in the *DSM-IV* field trials (Lahey, Applegate, McBurnett, & Biederman, 1994), with 76% of children diagnosed with the hyperactive-impulsive subtype being younger than 6 years old. Moreover, Lahey and colleagues (in preparation) have demonstrated that some young children meeting criteria for the hyperactive-impulsive subtype may in fact no longer meet criteria for ADHD when assessed 1 year later. They found that nearly 30% of young children diagnosed with the hyperactive-impulsive type failed to meet diagnostic criteria for *any* subtype over the following three waves of longitudinal data. Only 22% of these children retained a classification of hyperactive-impulsive subtype over all three waves, with classifications shifting either to no diagnosis or to a different subtype.

Although greater stability was found in the combined and inattentive subtypes, a great deal of shifting occurred across three waves, with 67% of children meeting combined-type criteria in wave 1 retaining that classification, and 36% of inattentive-type children retaining that classification for all three waves. However, when an overall diagnosis of any subtype of ADHD is considered, the numbers are more stable: 87% of the children who met symptom criteria for ADHD (any subtype) in wave 1 continued to meet criteria for ADHD (any subtype) in at least two subsequent waves. Thus, the major problem with stability was for children with the hyperactive/impulsive subtype. As noted above, high activity levels are common in young children, and reliance on a sole dimension derived largely from items reflecting excessive activity levels (see table 20.1) to define the disorder ends up diagnosing many children without the true disorder. Notably, this study included 4- to 6-year-olds, with two thirds of the sample being of school age, raising the question of whether this problem is even more apparent for children in the preschool and toddler years.

Campbell's third requirement is that symptoms are evident in several settings and with people other than the parent. Again, the *DSM-IV* addresses this point by requiring impairment caused by symptoms in two or more settings. Home and school are the two settings for which the symptoms have been written and in which they are most commonly observed. However, assessing multiple settings presents unique difficulties with young children, because many young children do not yet attend school. Studies have indicated that using parent-only reports of behavior (Pineda et al., 1999) can increase the prevalence of ADHD in a preschool sample beyond rates identified when both parents and teachers are required to note symptom presence. Pineda and colleagues, using a *DSM-IV* checklist of ADHD symptoms administered to parents only, found the prevalence of ADHD to be 18.2% of the preschool sample surveyed, a prevalence rate much higher than what is expected with school-aged children in the community. Other researchers have demonstrated the importance of teacher reports as a means of validating disruptive behavior disorders in children (Hinshaw, Han, Erhardt, & Huber, 1992). Considering these two findings, a clinician is left to grapple with the question of how to diagnose ADHD in children when there are limited settings to evaluate. It may be possible to assess other settings (e.g., playground), but this does not address the limitation of relying on only one informant (i.e., the child's parents) to assess the child's behavior. With the increasing use of child care, child care providers may serve as a second, cross-setting informant for many toddlers and preschoolers. As we discuss below, however, research has not yet been conducted that validates rating scales of ADHD symptoms in informant samples of child care providers.

Campbell's fourth and fifth points both refer to impairment. Relying solely on a *DSM-IV* symptom count is clearly insufficient to classify children, and the *DSM-IV* criteria recognize this fact, with their requirement that symptoms must be present to a degree that is maladaptive and that impairment must be present across settings. We regard impairment in daily life functioning as the gold star indicator for the necessity of treatment—which is the intended purpose of both assessment and diagnosis (e.g., Angold, Costello, Farmer, Burns, & Erkanli, 1999; Scotti, Morris, McNeil, & Hawkins, 1996). Indeed, impairment is why children are referred for treatment (e.g., for problems in peer relations, noncompliance, academic functioning), is what mediates long-term outcome, and is what determines who receives mental health services (Angold, Costello, Farmer, et al., 1999; Pelham & Fabiano, 2000). High levels of motor activity, impulsivity, and inattention in young children are not in and of themselves sufficient to warrant diagnosis, especially in young children when they may be confused with nondeviant behavior, as is apparently the case with the hyperactive/impulsive subtype. The symptoms must be associated with impairment in daily life functioning to justify diagnosis and intervention. Campbell's longitudinal studies discussed above demonstrate that severity of impairment rather than symptom level predicts stable problems in young children, highlighting the importance of adaptive functioning versus symptoms in the assessment of young children. The limitation of the *DSM-IV* in this area is that although it requires impairment, it does not provide explicit guidelines for assessing or defining impairment (Scotti et al., 1996). As we discuss below, most instruments for assessing ADHD in children emphasize measuring symptoms more

than and sometimes to the exclusion of impairment in functioning. ADHD appears to be unique among childhood disorders in that *DSM-IV* symptoms (e.g., excessive motor activity or talking) can readily occur in the *absence* of impairment in daily life functioning, especially, as we have discussed above, in young children. In contrast, other childhood externalizing disorders (ODD/CD) are defined according to symptoms that in and of themselves imply impairment (e.g., disrupted parent-child communication, aggression, willful violations of authority). Still other disorders are defined in the *DSM-IV* with symptoms that *are* impairment (e.g., substance use disorder and abuse). Thus, for ADHD, more so than other disorders, assessment needs to go beyond symptoms to impairment to allow accurate decisions regarding diagnosis (and intervention) in young children.

HOW SHOULD WE ASSESS AND DIAGNOSE ADHD IN YOUNG CHILDREN?

It is commonly accepted that diagnostic information for ADHD should be gathered from adults in the natural environment regarding (1) the degree to which the child displays developmentally inappropriate levels of the core symptoms (inattention, hyperactivity, impulsivity) and (2) associated impairment in daily life functioning (AAP, 2000). However, the implementation of these guidelines varies across experts and for different ages of children. The process of assessment for ADHD must take into account the limited time and financial resources of the professionals conducting these assessments. Considering that clinicians are increasingly limited in the time they are able to spend with a family, the use of rating scales and brief parent interviews conserves both time and cost when compared with more elaborate psychological tasks, structured objective observations, and structured psychiatric interviews. Furthermore, it is of paramount importance to acquire information regarding the child's symptoms and impairment from adults who interact with the child in the natural settings of home and school or preschool. The emphasis on assessing impairment relative to symptoms cannot be overstated. Parents simply do not come to treatment complaining that their young child is often on the go or acts as if driven by a motor but instead are concerned that they cannot do their grocery shopping without having to constantly work on keeping the child next to them, both for the child's safety and to minimize their stress and embarrassment.

Given the limitations of the *DSM-IV* in addressing the specific needs of very young children, the process of diagnosis may need to be different from what it is for school-aged children. For 4- to 6-year-old children who are in a structured preschool setting, symptom identification can be based on *DSM-IV* criteria, as research has shown that *DSM-IV* criteria can be validly applied to such children (Lahey et al., 1998). However, the hyperactivity/impulsivity dimension must be used with care, as discussed above. Children must exhibit maladaptive and age-inappropriate symptoms of inattention and/or hyperactivity/impulsivity for at least 6 months, although some authors have argued to extend this time criteria to 9 months to make the inclusionary criteria more restrictive (Vitiello, 2001). In addition, some symptoms must cause clinically significant impairment across two or more settings (e.g., home, school, and recreational activities). In situations in which parents and teachers have discrepant reports, weight is given to the teacher's rating in children of elementary age. Ideally, the same logic should apply for preschool children when a teacher or child care provider is available. However, the clinician needs to be confident that the preschool teacher or child care provider does not have a bias against labeling children as having a mental health problem, a common bias in teachers of young children. In such cases, teachers might minimize problems that parents are reporting accurately, especially when they believe that identification might lead to treatment such as medication.

In a recent survey (nonclinical) study, Gadow et al. (2001) found that teachers rated 22% of preschool males and 13% of preschool females in a community sample as meeting *DSM-IV* symptom criteria for ADHD. However, teachers rated only 43% of these children as being significantly impaired. Therefore, using teacher report only, less than half (approximately 6 to 11%) of preschool children who met symptom criteria would have actually met diagnostic criteria when impairment is included as part of the diagnostic classification system. It is important to note that these rates are similar to those found in elementary-aged children (Pelham et al., 1992; Wolraich, Hannah, Pinnock, Baumgaertel, & Brown, 1996). Although these results are promising, more research on the reliability of preschool teacher/day care provider ratings of behavior and impairment is sorely needed. Specifically, we are not aware of studies documenting the validity of teacher ratings of ADHD symptoms in preschoolers compared to other objective indices, as has been conducted with elementary-aged children (Atkins, Pelham, & Licht, 1985, 1989). When a child is not in a structured school setting, the clinician should seek out reports from other adults (in addition to parents) who have interacted with the child. Direct observations in natural or clinic settings may also help resolve discrepancies between evaluators despite their complexities and expense (see discussion below).

Clinical interviews can be administered to parents. However, instead of the traditional emphasis on prenatal history and developmental milestones, the emphasis should be on information directed at understanding the domains of impairment, target behaviors for intervention (which derive directly from domains of impairment rather than from core symptoms), and factors that influence the targets (e.g., various antecedents, consequences, and setting events) and that will be changed during intervention. The goal of such clinical interviews should be to perform a functional analysis (albeit verbal) of the behaviors that will be targeted in treatment. In contrast to interviews focused on functional analysis, systematic structured interviews have been widely used in research settings (e.g., K-SADS, Chambers et al., 1985; Diagnostic Interview Schedule for Children, Shaffer et al., 1996). Such interviews ask not about target behaviors and domains of impairment but instead about *DSM-IV* symptoms of disorders; they are intended to yield a *DSM-IV* diagnosis of ADHD (for the present purposes), while also diagnosing comorbid disorders and ruling out others. Although these instruments have not been constructed for use in young children, researchers have reliably administered them to 4- to 6-year-old preschool samples (i.e., Keenan &

Wakschlag, 2000; Lahey et al., 1998). Their high degree of structure makes them very reliable, but their length (60 to 120 minutes) and training requirements make them impractical for routine clinical use. In addition, they have not been validated in very young children.

Standardized rating scales (see table 20.2) should be administered to parents and others who deal directly with the child (e.g., day care supervisors, preschool teacher) to obtain information regarding ADHD symptoms as well as associated problems. Some of these rating scales address specific ADHD symptoms (e.g., DBD, ADHD Rating Scale, ECBI, PBQ, WWPAS), while others ask about a broad range of childhood behavior (e.g., Conners Parent Rating Scale–Revised, CBCL). Although each of these rating scales has been used in the assessment of ADHD, several issues regarding the relative usefulness of each scale and their use in younger children should be considered.

As mentioned previously, the *DSM-IV* lists several symptoms for the diagnosis of ADHD that may be developmentally insensitive in teacher rating scales due to context specificity of the items—that is, being related exclusively to a structured school setting. For example, it is not clear that a preschool teacher's or child care worker's evaluation of sustained attention or following through on tasks means the same thing as an elementary school teacher's rating, because young children in these settings are typically not required to engage in lengthy academic-like tasks. Instead, they engage in play activities for brief periods of time that might well not tax the difficulties that ADHD children have sustaining attention in tasks that are not intrinsically motivating. Instead of independent seatwork assignments to be done at a desk—the most problematic aspect of school for ADHD children—preschool children engage in small-group activities under the teacher's supervision, a setting less problematic for the typical ADHD child. These scales may thus not be appropriate for younger children who do not attend a structured preschool where school-specific symptoms can be adequately assessed. Other scales

Table 20.2 Measures Assessing Child Symptomatology and Impairment Across Domains

Domain and Measures	Age Validated
Symptomatology	
ADHD Rating Scale (DuPaul et al., 1994; Gimpel & Kuhn, 2000)	2–5+
Behar Preschool Behavior Questionnaire (PBQ; Behar, 1977; Campbell, 1987)	2–5
Child Behavior Checklist (CBCL; Achenbach, 1991, 1992)	2–5+
Disruptive Behavior Disorder (DBD; Pelham et al., 1992; Lahey et al., 1998)	4–5+
Conners Teacher Rating Scale–Revised (CTRS-R; Goyette et al., 1978; Conners et al., 1998)	3–5+
Werry-Weiss-Peters Activity Scale (WWPAS; Routh et al., 1974; Campbell, 1987)	2–5
Eyberg Child Behavior Inventory (ECBI; Boggs et al., 1990)	2–5+
Conners Parent Rating Scale–Revised (CPRS-R; Goyette et al., 1978; Conners et al., 1998b)	3–5+
Global functioning	
Children's Global Assessment Scale (CGAS; Lahey et al., 1998; Setterberg et al., 1992)	4–5+
Children's Impairment Rating Scale (CIRS; Fabiano et al., 1999)	4–5+
Global Assessment of Function Scale (GAF; American Psychiatric Association, 1994; Keenan et al., 1997)	4–5+
Peer relationships	
Social Skills Rating System–Preschool Level (SSRS; Gresham & Elliott, 1990)	4–5
Impact on school performance	
Teacher Assessment of Social Behavior (TASB; Cassidy & Asher, 1992; Lahey et al., 1998)	4–5+

Note: Rating scales and other measures should be administered to the parent and teacher for information regarding ADHD as well as associated problems and functional impairment.
+Denotes that the measure has demonstrated validity across school-age and/or adolescent populations in addition to preschool children.

(i.e., PBQ, ECBI) do not have items that are so heavily dependent on school-based behaviors and therefore may be more useful for younger children.

An important issue when using the *DSM-IV*–based rating scales, particularly for younger children, is the method used to score the scale. Two approaches are commonly taken in scoring rating scales. One approach involves counting the items that were endorsed by the rater as occurring at a high frequency (e.g., "pretty much" or "very much" of the time). Although this ballpark method is useful particularly for school-aged children, as we have previously discussed, it may overestimate the prevalence of ADHD in younger children (e.g., Pineda et al., 1999). This is not surprising, considering that younger children display elevated levels of the core symptoms—particularly symptoms of hyperactivity. An alternative and more conservative approach is to compare scale scores (totals or averages across items) to developmental norms. This approach takes into account age differences in symptom expression and allows the clinician to compare a child's behavior to what is typical for that age group. Using developmental norms will more accurately identify children who are displaying significant levels of a behavior that is outside of the norm for that age group, in particular reducing the number of children who will be falsely identified as having high symptom levels in a ballpark count. As shown in table 20.2, several scales (i.e., CBCL, Conners Parent Rating Scale–Revised, PBQ, ECBI) have normative data for younger children.

The Eyberg Child Behavior Inventory (Boggs, Eyberg, & Reynolds, 1990) is one of the more unusual rating scales used in the assessment of children for disruptive behavior problems in that it not only asks about the frequency of problem behavior but also asks, "Is this a problem for you?" In other words, this checklist assesses for the impairment associated with symptoms. The ECBI, although primarily designed for the assessment of conduct and oppositional problems, appears to be useful for assessing ADHD as well. Ten of the 36 items in the ECBI are directly related to ADHD symptoms, and these items are all developmentally appropriate in that they can be assessed in younger children. Other advantages of the ECBI

include the availability of normative data for children as young as 2 years of age and the opportunity to assess for both oppositional and conduct problems, both of which are highly comorbid with ADHD.

In addition to DSM symptoms, measures must be administered to assess for clinically significant and cross-situational impairment for a child to meet *DSM-IV* criteria for ADHD. Because the *DSM-IV*–based rating scales do not assess impairment, other measures have been developed that assess impairment, including global functioning (e.g., CGAS, GAF) and specific functioning within particular domains (e.g., TASB, SSRS). The global measures do not provide sufficiently precise information to guide intervention, while the domain-specific scales are generally rather lengthy and target only a single aspect of impairment. Useful measures of impairment must yield information that can guide intervention but are feasibly administered in clinical and educational settings.

One current scale used to operationalize impairment is the Impairment Rating Scale (IRS; Fabiano et al., 1999). This scale for parents and teachers has six Likert-scale questions asking about the degree to which the child has problems that warrant treatment, intervention, or special services in specific areas of functioning (e.g., playmates, siblings, parent-child relationship, academic progress, self-esteem of child, and family/classroom in general). The scale shows psychometric properties (e.g., reliability, validity, predictive power) comparable to other much more lengthy indices of functioning. More important for our purposes, it has empirically derived cutoff points that are identical for young children (ages 4 and 5) and older children (ages 6 through 12), as well as the same psychometrics across this age range. In addition, over the elementary age range from kindergarten (age 5) through grade 5 (age 11), age does not influence scores. Thus, impairment, as operationalized in this scale, appears to be a very stable construct across ages 4 to 12. This is noteworthy relative to symptoms because, as discussed above, symptoms of ADHD, as operationalized in rating scales and structured interviews, change dramatically over the young age range (Lahey et al., in preparation). Although adjustments in cutoff criteria can be made for different ages, the clinical utility of an instrument is heavily influenced by the ease with which it can be used in practice. A scale with empirically derived cutoff points that remain constant over age and that has only a small number of easily completed items will be adopted in community mental health and school settings in preference to more complex scales, particularly if its psychometric properties are comparable. No such measure has been constructed for children under the age of 4 years. Given the IRS's practicality and utility with school-aged children, validation of this measure is clearly needed in children younger than 4. Researchers and clinicians who work with very young children often have used other measures to assess for the functional impairment of ADHD. Many of these measures have focused on the parent-child dyad (e.g., structured parent-child interactions), owing to the importance of this relationship for very young children (Campbell, 1990; Patterson et al., 1989; Webster-Stratton, 1990) and the usefulness of this assessment method with younger (Mash & Johnston, 1982) rather than older (Cunningham & Barkley, 1979) children. The aim in conducting structured parent-child interactions (e.g., cleanup task) is to observe the relationship between the child's disruptive behavior and the parenting skills of the parent. Although structured parent-child tasks have been widely used in research settings and yield very useful information, their expense and complexity make them impractical or not always possible for standard clinical practice. An alternative approach, which includes observing parent-child interactions, that enhances the clinical utility of these observations has been the use of a functional analytic approach to the assessment of problematic behavior. Functional analyses using dyadic interactions, a procedure that has often been employed in the treatment of children with developmental disabilities (Carr & Durand, 1985), combines assessment of the quality of the interactions between a child and an adult (e.g., parent) but also lends itself to making treatment recommendations. Specifically, a parent-child interaction can be observed, and behaviors of both parents and children can be assessed. Furthermore, the contingencies placed on the behavior can be manipulated such that the function of the behavior can be ascertained. Knowing the function of

and the contingencies maintaining a particular behavior is one of the most important types of information to be gathered in an assessment, and it is the foundation for sound treatment recommendations (Boyajian, DuPaul, Handler, Eckert, & McGoey, 2001; Scotti et al., 1996).

Similarly, direct observations in school settings are the gold standard in research but have been used exclusively in elementary schools rather than preschools or day care settings. This may be due to the structure of elementary school settings, which, as discussed above, allow for more accurate assessment of the difficulties experienced by ADHD children in classroom settings. Typically, problematic behavior is assessed in elementary school settings when children are engaged in structured activities (e.g., on-task behavior seatwork; DuPaul & Stoner, 1994). For the same reason that teacher ratings may not be as valid in the preschool setting, the unstructured nature of day care/preschool settings and less clear rules and expectations for performance of young children make it more difficult to assess problematic behavior through direct observations. In fact, studies have shown that elementary-aged children with ADHD are indistinguishable from their peers when observed in informal, unstructured settings (Jacob, O'Leary, & Rosenblad, 1978).

It is important to note that no medical (e.g., neurological exam, magnetic resonance imaging, electroencephalogram) or psychological tests (e.g., intelligence and achievement testing, continuous performance tasks, neuropsychological testing) have yet been developed that are useful for diagnosing ADHD at any age (AAP, 2000; Goldman et al., 1998). Further, the absence of symptoms during a doctor's office visit, a one-to-one testing session, or while watching television does not indicate the absence of symptoms or the disorder. For example, physicians who base diagnosis on the presence of symptoms during an office visit often miss a large portion of true ADHD cases (Sleator, 1982). Furthermore, assessing for symptoms during television viewing is uninformative, as ADHD children watch television with little difficulty under most situations (Milich & Lorch, 1994). Although the risk of false negatives may be lower when assessing younger children for ADHD in office or one-to-one testing sessions, it should warrant concern.

EARLY IDENTIFICATION
AND EARLY INTERVENTION

Impairment in the child's life and the life of the family, not whether the child meets a symptom cutoff score, is of paramount importance when assessing young children's need for treatment. A young child who might be subthreshold for ADHD symptoms warrants intervention if impairment in daily life functioning is present, and if symptoms exceed threshold but impairment is absent, treatment is not warranted. Angold, Costello, Farmer, et al. (1999) conducted interviews to assess for 29 well-defined psychiatric diagnoses as well as impairment in a group of 1,015 school-aged children. Of those children, 104 were diagnosed and had impairment, 143 were given a diagnosis yet were without impairment, and 205 had no diagnosis but were still impaired. Results indicated that approximately 52% of treatment users of specialty mental health centers were children without a formal diagnosis but with impairments in daily life functioning. Furthermore, at 1-year follow-up, impaired-only children were considered to have problems that were in need of services and exhibited levels of impairment equal to those of the diagnosed and impaired group. Considering that an official diagnosis usually determines the availability of services, this study has important implications for young ADHD children. If one focuses exclusively or even mostly on ADHD symptoms instead of problems in daily life functioning, some young children who are in need of intervention may not receive services, while others (those with transient symptoms but no impairment) will receive valuable resources that they do not need.

ADHD is a pervasive disorder that necessitates chronic, pervasive treatment (AAP, 2001; Pelham & Fabiano, 2000). One argument in favor of identifying ADHD in young children is that early identification can lead to early intervention. Clinicians who identify young ADHD children have an opportunity to begin to intervene in critical domains at a crucial period in the development of the child, during which intervention may be more effective than at older ages. Relative to older children, parents and teachers of very young children often have better control over the environmental contingencies of the child and have

not experienced long periods of failure resulting in a low sense of caretaker efficacy and vicious cycles of transactionally escalating negative adult-child interactions. Parents, for example, are less likely to have begun the pathway leading to parental stress and psychopathology that many parents of older ADHD children experience (Pelham & Lang, 1999). In addition, ADHD children's relations with other children are just developing, and they have not yet built up years of negative interactions with peers that inevitably result in reputations that are difficult to change. Here we consider these two domains in which early intervention may be especially critical—parent-child relationships and peer relationships.

Regarding parent-child relationships, consider the problems of noncompliance and oppositional behavior—often the major complaints of parents (as well as teachers) in dealing with their young ADHD children (Barkley, Karlsson, & Pollard, 1985; Cunningham & Barkley, 1979; Tallmadge & Barkley, 1983). Chamberlain and Patterson (1995) have described the coercive cycle of noncompliance, ineffective parental response, and escalating oppositional behavior and coercive interactions that begins in toddlerhood. If parents fail to follow through and to obtain compliance from the child early in the child's life, over time the parent will experience failure in parenting and a loss of parenting efficacy, and therefore be less persistent in future interactions with the child (Johnston & Mash, 1989; Mash & Johnston, 1990), which in turn results in increased noncompliance and defiance. Inconsistent monitoring and inappropriately harsh punishments are parenting styles that have been shown to contribute to escalating child behavior problems (Chamberlain & Patterson, 1995). Thus, ADHD and noncompliance in young children are viewed as setting the stage for the development of ODD, which then evolves into antisocial behavior and CD for many children (Chamberlain & Patterson, 1995; Coie & Dodge, 1998). The stability and refractory nature of antisocial behavior are well known. It is far simpler and more effective to intervene in negative parent-child interactions with very young children than it is with adolescents and their parents. Further, intervention in the very early stages of coercive parent-child interactions should interrupt the development of the coercive process at an early stage, reducing the probability of the development of later antisocial behaviors.

The same argument can be made for the domain of peer relationships. ADHD children have serious disturbances in their relationships with other children, ranging from interruptions in the classroom and class clowning to verbal and physical aggression (Milich & Landau, 1982; Pelham & Bender, 1982). They routinely receive a high rate of negative nominations and a low rate of positive nominations from peers in school settings. It is well known that such dysfunctional peer relations are risk factors for the development of a variety of serious negative outcomes in adulthood (Coie & Dodge, 1998; Rubin, Bukowski, & Parker, 1998). It has also been known for some time that negative peer interactions and negative reputations among peers are quite refractory. If the negative behaviors that give rise to negative peer reputations and nominations could be modified before school entry, then these later factors that contribute to the refractoriness of aggression could be avoided. Indeed, there is evidence that very early intervention even in school settings (kindergarten) can have a beneficial effect on negative peer relationships among children with disruptive behavior disorders (Conduct Problems Prevention Research Group, 1999; Tremblay, LeMarquand, & Vitaro, 1999).

Implicit in our discussion regarding the factors that are important to assess when determining the need for early intervention is that the focus should not be on symptom identification or symptom counts. Rather, the focus should be on problems in daily life functioning (i.e., parenting skills, parent-child interactions, peer relationship difficulties) that have been shown to predict future difficulties in children. As mentioned earlier, research with younger children identified with ADHD is beginning to demonstrate that symptoms and diagnostic categories are less stable in this age group (Lahey et al., in preparation). Given this lack of stability, a greater emphasis in assessing impairment in this age group appears to be warranted.

By identifying ADHD children at an early age and providing early intervention, professionals may have a unique opportunity to change the trajectory of many of these children and their families, thereby decreasing the need for future services for both the parent and the child. In particular, treatment starting at this age may have a cumulative effect over time in changing domains of impairment (e.g., antisocial behavior) that are more refractory at later ages.

FUTURE DIRECTIONS

While we believe that it is both possible and desirable to identify young children with ADHD problems, there are clear avenues that require additional work to maximize the utility of diagnostic schemes for ADHD in young children. The most glaring need for research is in the area of how to evaluate and diagnose children under the age of 4 years. The research reviewed herein includes almost exclusively children aged 4 and above, and it is not clear whether simple downward extensions of the results will apply. Given the dramatic increase in the rates of psychoactive medication use in very young (3 years and younger) ADHD children (Vitiello, 2001), information about diagnosis in these toddlers is clearly needed.

Another area for future research is whether the diagnosis and assessment of young children could be improved beyond what currently exists in *DSM-IV*. As we have noted, the current *DSM-IV* definition, while not developmentally sensitive, works. However, none of the studies of its validity to date has addressed the question of whether modifications in the *DSM-IV* definition would yield better diagnoses for younger children. For example, would a change in the number of symptoms required for diagnosis result in a group of children with greater stability of the diagnosis into elementary school? Would such a change be differential for the two dimensions of ADHD? Would elimination of the requirement for multiple settings facilitate diagnosis in young children not yet in school settings, or would that increase the heterogeneity of the diagnosis? Would such changes improve predictive validity of diagnosis with respect to impaired functioning? Do the specific symptoms listed in the *DSM-IV* need to be modified for young children, who, for example, have not yet been exposed to the structure of school? Does the length of time symptoms are displayed need to be modified to rule out transient developmental stages that mimic ADHD?

Further, standardized instruments that assess impairment need to be developed for the preschooler and young child. This would include observational procedures for unstructured settings, standardized parent-child interaction protocols, impairment rating scales, and standardized protocols for conducting functional analyses in preschoolers (Boyajian et al., 2001). The need for such instrumentation and procedures follows from the importance of assessing impairment in daily life functioning versus symptomatic functioning in the young child.

Finally, will early identification and resulting intervention in ADHD result in improved outcomes for ADHD children? This is the $64,000 question regarding diagnosis of ADHD in young children. If early intervention had no differentially beneficial impact on ADHD children compared to later intervention, then early identification would have no point. There is hope that early intervention will be beneficial, but to date there is no demonstration of this presumption. Evidence from a handful of studies shows that behavioral interventions such as parent training (Pisterman, McGrath, Firestone, & Goodman, 1989; Sonuga-Barke, Daley, Thompson, Laver-Bradbury, & Weeks, 2001) and school interventions (Barkley et al., 2000; Tremblay et al., 1999), as well as medication with psychostimulants (Barkley, Karlsson, Strzelecki, & Murphy, 1984) are acutely beneficial with young children. None of these studies has extended to long-term outcomes, however. While some have called for more research with psychoactive medications in this age group with the assumption that early treatment with a central nervous system stimulant would be differentially beneficial on outcomes compared to later treatment (Vitiello, 2001), that belief is not universally shared (cf. Pelham, 1999), and we know of no data suggesting that differential benefits would accrue. In our opinion, it would be unfortunate if better identification and diagnosis of young ADHD children led to more widespread use of medication as the primary mode of intervention.

CONCLUSION

ADHD is one of the most frequently diagnosed mental health disorders of childhood. It is a major public health problem that is encountered with increasing frequency by professionals in educational, health, and mental health settings. Recent conceptualizations of ADHD (e.g., AAP, 2001) have emphasized its chronic nature. ADHD children tend not to improve with time and in fact typically have worsening impairment with increasing age. This fact argues that a chronic disease model of treatment needs to be developed for ADHD and that intervention needs to begin as early as possible to prevent the deterioration of functioning that typically ensues in ADHD. For example, deviant peer relationships are common and strong predictors of negative outcomes for ADHD children; these become increasingly difficult to change with age. Thus, early identification and diagnosis of ADHD may not only set the stage for a chronic care model of treatment but may also prevent later refractory problems.

Unfortunately, virtually all of the voluminous research literature on ADHD—including studies of diagnosis, etiology, mechanisms, and treatment—has concentrated on the elementary-aged child. If a successful chronic care model of treatment is to be developed, the issues discussed in this chapter need to be resolved so that intervention can begin as early as possible. We have argued that the current *DSM-IV* approach to diagnosis has limitations, particularly when considering issues concerning younger children, but that current guidelines and instrumentation can be used with validity in the young child aged 4 years and above who is in a structured school setting. At the same time, we have noted that the core symptoms of ADHD change so much with development that care needs to be exercised in their application to young children. In contrast, impairment in daily life functioning (also part of the *DSM-IV* definition) can be validly measured in young children, does not appear to be so changeable across ages, is the main reason for referral, is a better predictor and mediator of long-term outcomes, and forms the basis (e.g., target domains and behaviors) for treatment. Thus, a relative emphasis on impairment in daily life functioning may be of considerably more benefit for the children and their families than an emphasis on *DSM-IV* symptoms. Such a reorientation in approach in mental health, primary care, and educational settings should result in more effective intervention for young ADHD children while the necessary research outlined above is conducted.

References

Achenbach, T. M. (1991). *Manual for the child behavior checklist/4–18 and 1991 profile*. Burlington, VT: University of Vermont, Department of Psychiatry.

Achenbach, T. M. (1992). *Manual for the child behavior checklist/2–3 and 1992 profile*. Burlington, VT: University of Vermont, Department of Psychiatry.

American Academy of Pediatrics. (2000). Clinical practice guideline: Diagnosis and evaluation of the child with attention-deficit/hyperactivity disorder. *Pediatrics, 105,* 1158–1170.

American Academy of Pediatrics. (2001). Clinical practice guideline: Treatment of the school-aged child with attention-deficit/hyperactivity disorder. *Pediatrics, 108,* 1033–1044.

American Psychiatric Association. (1994). *Diagnostic and statistical manual of mental disorders* (4th ed.). Washington, DC: Author.

Angold, A., Costello, E. J., & Erkanli, A. (1999). Comorbidity. *Journal of Child Psychology and Psychiatry and Allied Disciplines, 40,* 57–87.

Angold, A., Costello, E. J., Farmer, E. M. Z., Burns, B., & Erkanli, A. (1999). Impaired but undiagnosed. *Journal of the American Academy of Child and Adolescent Psychiatry, 38,* 129–137.

Atkins, M. S., Pelham, W. E., & Licht, M. H. (1985). A comparison of objective classroom mesures and teacher ratings of attention deficit disorder. *Journal of Abnormal Child Psychology, 13,* 155–167.

Atkins, M. S., Pelham, W. E., & Licht, M. H. (1989). The differential validity of teacher ratings of inattention/overactivity and aggression. *Journal of Abnormal Child Psychology, 17,* 423–435.

August, G. J., Realmuto, G. M., MacDonald, A. W., & Nugent, S. M. (1996). Prevalence of ADHD and comorbid disorders among elementary school children screened for disruptive behavior. *Journal of Abnormal Child Psychology, 24,* 571–595.

Barbaresi, W. J., Katusic, S. I., Colligan, R. C., Pankratz, V. S., Weaver, A. L., Weber, K. J., Mrazek, D. A., & Jacobsen, S. J. (2002). How common is attention-deficit/hyperactivity disorder? Incidence in a population-based birth cohort in Rochester, Minn. *Archives of Pediatrics and Adolescent Medicine, 156,* 217–224.

Barkley, R. A. (1997). Attention-deficit/hyperactivity disorder. In E. J. Mash & R. A. Barkley (Eds.), *Treatment of childhood disorders* (2nd ed., pp. 55–110). New York: Guilford Press.

Barkley, R. A., & Cunningham, C. E. (1980). The parent-child interactions of hyperactive children and their modification by stimulant drugs. In R. Knights & D. Baker (Eds.), *Treatment of hyperactive and learning disabled children* (pp. 219–236). Baltimore: University Park Press.

Barkley, R. A., Fischer, M., Edelbrock, C., & Smallish, L. (1991). The adolescent outcome of hyperactive children diagnosed by research criteria—III. Mother-child interactions, family conflicts and maternal psychopathology. *Journal of Child Psychology and Psychiatry, 32,* 233–255.

Barkley, R. A., Karlsson, J., & Pollard, S. (1985). Effects of age on the mother-child interactions of ADD-H and normal boys. *Journal of Abnormal Child Psychology, 13,* 631–637.

Barkley, R. A., Karlsson, J., Strzelecki, E., & Murphy, J. V. (1984). Effects of age and ritalin dosage on the mother-child interactions of hyperactive children. *Journal of Consulting and Clinical Psychology, 52,* 750–758.

Barkley, R. A., Shelton, T. L., Crosswait, C., Moorehouse, M., Fletcher, K., Barrett, S., Jenkins, L., & Metevia, L. (2000). Multi-method psycho-educational intervention for preschool children with disruptive behavior: Preliminary results at post-treatment. *Journal of Child Psychology and Psychiatry and Allied Disciplines, 41,* 319–332.

Befera, M. S., & Barkley, R. A. (1985). Hyperactive and normal girls and boys: Mother-child interaction, parent psychiatric status and child psychopathology. *Journal of Child Psychology and Psychiatry, 26,* 439–452.

Behar, L. B. (1977). The preschool behavior questionnaire. *Journal of Abnormal Child Psychology, 5,* 265–275.

Biederman, J., Faraone, S. V., Keenan, K., & Tsuang, M. T. (1991). Evidence of familial association between attention deficit disorder and major affective disorders. *Archives of General Psychiatry, 48,* 633–642.

Biederman, J., Faraone, S. V., & Lapey, K. (1992). Comorbidity of diagnosis in attention-deficit hyperactivity disorder. *Child and Adolescent Psychiatric Clinics of North America, 1,* 335–360.

Bird, H. R., Canino, G., Rubio-Stipec, M., & Gould, M. S. (1988). Estimates of the prevalence of childhood maladjustment in a community survey in Puerto Rico: The use of combined measures. *Archives of General Psychiatry, 45,* 1120–1126.

Bird, H. R., Gould, M. S., & Staghezza, B. M. (1993). Patterns of diagnostic comorbidity in a community sample of children aged 9 through 16 years. *Journal of the American Academy of Child and Adolescent Psychiatry, 32,* 361–368.

Boggs, S. R., Eyberg, S. M., & Reynolds, N. A. (1990). Concurrent validity of the Eyberg Child Behavior Inventory. *Journal of Clinical Child Psychology, 19,* 75–78.

Boyajian, A. E., DuPaul, G. J., Handler, M. W., Eckert, T. L., & McGoey, K. E. (2001). The use of classroom-based brief functional analyses with preschoolers at-risk for attention deficit hyperactivity disorder. *School Psychology Review, 30,* 278–293.

Campbell, S. B. (1975). Mother-child interaction: A comparison of hyperactive, learning disabled, and normal boys. *American Journal of Orthopsychiatry, 45,* 51–57.

Campbell, S. B. (1985). Hyperactivity in preschoolers: Correlates and prognostic implications. *Clinical Psychology Review, 5,* 405–428.

Campbell, S. B. (1987). Parent-referred problem three-year-olds: Developmental changes in symptoms. *Journal of Child Psychology and Psychiatry, 28,* 835–845.

Campbell, S.B. (1990). Hard-to manage preschoolers: Adjustment at age nine and predictors of continuing symptoms. *Journal of Child Psychology and Psychiatry, 31,* 871–889.

Campbell, S. B. (1994). Hard-to-manage preschool boys: Externalizing behavior, social competence, and family context at two-year follow-up. *Journal of Abnormal Child Psychology, 22,* 147–166.

Campbell, S. B. (1995). Behavior problems in preschool children: A review of recent research. *Journal of Child Psychology and Psychiatry, 36,* 113–149.

Campbell, S. B., Breaux, A. M., Ewing, L. J., & Szumowski, E. K. (1984). A one-year follow-up study of parent-referred hyperactive preschool children. *Journal of the American Academy of Child Psychiatry, 23,* 243–249.

Campbell, S. B, Breaux, A. M., Ewing, L. J., & Szumowski, E. K. (1986). Correlates and predictors of hyperactivity and aggression: A longitudinal study of parent-referred problem preschoolers. *Journal of Abnormal Child Psychology, 14,* 217–234.

Campbell, S. B., & Ewing, L. J. (1990). Follow-up of hard-to-manage preschoolers: Adjustment at age 9 and predictors of continuing symptoms. *Journal of Child Psychology and Psychiatry, 31,* 871–889.

Campbell, S. B., Ewing, L. J., Breaux, A. M., & Szumowski, E. K. (1986). Parent-referred problem three-year-olds: Follow-up at school entry. *Journal of Child Psychology and Psychiatry, 27,* 473–488.

Campbell, S. B., Pierce, E. W., March, C. L., & Ewing, L. J. (1991). Noncompliant behavior, overactivity, and family stress as predictors of negative maternal control with preschool children. *Development and Psychopathology, 3,* 175–190.

Campbell, S. B., Szumowski, E. K., Ewing, L. J., Gluck, D. S., & Breaux, A. M. (1982). A multidimensional assessment of parent-identified behavior problem toddlers. *Journal of Abnormal Child Psychology, 10,* 569–592.

Cantwell, D. P., & Baker, L. (1989). Stability and natural history of DSM-III childhood diagnoses. *Journal of the American Academy of Child and Adolescent Psychiatry, 28,* 691–700.

Carey, W. B. (1998). Is attention deficit hyperactivity disorder a valid disorder? In National Institute of Health (Ed.), *NIH consensus conference: Diagnosis and treatment of attention deficit hyperactivity disorder* (pp. 33–36). Bethesda, MD: NIH.

Carr, E. G. & Durand, V. M. (1985). Reducing behavior problems through functional communication training. *Journal of Applied Behavior Analysis, 18,* 111–126.

Cassidy, J., & Asher, S. Z. R. (1992). Loneliness and peer relations in young children. *Child Development, 63,* 350–365.

Chamberlain, P., & Patterson, G. R. (1995). Discipline and child compliance in parenting. In M. H. Bornstein (Ed.), *Handbook of parenting: Applied and practical parenting* (Vol. 4, pp. 205–225). Hillsdale, NJ: Lawrence Erlbaum.

Chambers, W. J., Puig-Antich, J., Hirsh, M., Paez, P., Ambrosini, P. J., Tabrizi, M. A., & Davies, M. (1985). Test-retest reliability of the schedule for affective disorders and schizophrenia for school-age children, present episode version. *Archives of General Psychiatry, 42,* 696–702.

Coie, J. D., & Dodge, K. A. (1998). Aggression and

antisocial behavior. In W. Damon (Series Ed.) & N. Eisenberg (Vol. Ed.), *Handbook of child psychology: Vol. 3. Social, emotional, and personality development* (5th ed., pp. 779–862). New York: Wiley.

Conduct Problems Prevention Research Group. (1999). Initial impact of the fast track prevention trial for conduct problems. I. The high-risk sample. *Journal of Consulting and Clinical Psychology, 67*, 631–647.

Conners, C. K., Sitarenios, G., Parker, J. D. A., & Epstein, J. N. (1998a). Revision and restandardization of the Conners Teacher Rating Scale (CTRS-R): Factor structure, reliability, and criterion validity. *Journal of Abnormal Child Psychology, 26*, 279–291.

Conners, C. K., Sitarenios, G., Parker, J. D. A., & Epstein, J. N. (1998b). The revised Conners Parent Rating Scale (CPRS-R): Factor structure, reliability, and criterion validity. *Journal of Abnormal Child Psychology, 26*, 257–268.

Cummings, E. M., Davies, P. T., & Campbell, S. B. (2000). *Developmental psychopathology and family process: Theory, research, and clinical implications.* New York: Guilford Press.

Cunningham, C. E., & Barkley, R. A. (1979). The interactions of normal and hyperactive children with their mothers in free play and structured tasks. *Child Development, 50*, 217–224.

Cunningham, C. E., Benness, B. B., & Siegel, L. S. (1988). Family functioning, time allocation, and parental depression in the families of normal and ADDH children. *Journal of Clinical Child Psychology, 17*, 169–177.

DuPaul, G. J., Power, T. J., Anastopoulos, A. D., & Reid, R. (1994). *ADHD rating scale–IV: Checklists, norms, and clinical interpretation.* New York: Guilford Press.

DuPaul, G. J., & Stoner, G. (1994). *ADHD in the school: Assessment and intervention strategies.* New York: Guilford Press.

Fabiano, G. A., Pelham, W. E., Gnagy, E. M., Kipp, H., Lahey, B. B., Burrows-MacLean, L., Chronis, A. M., Onyango, A. N., & Morrisey, S. (1999, November). *The reliability and validity of the children's impairment rating scale: A practical measure of impairment in children with ADHD.* Poster presented at the annual meeting of the Association for the Advancement of Behavior Therapy, Toronto, Ontario.

Fischer, M. (1990). Parenting stress and the child with attention deficit hyperactivity disorder. *Journal of Clinical Child Psychology, 19*, 337–346.

Fletcher, K. E., Fischer, M., Barkley, R. A., & Smallish, L. (1996). A sequential analysis of mother-adolescent interactions of ADHD, ADHD/ODD, and normal teenagers during neutral and conflict discussions. *Journal of Abnormal Child Psychology, 24*, 271- 297.

Forehand, R. C., & McMahon, R. J. (1981). *Helping the noncompliant child.* New York: Guilford Press.

Gadow, K. D., Sprafkin, J., & Nolan, E. E. (2001). DSM-IV symptoms in community and clinic preschool children. *Journal of the American Academy of Child and Adolescent Psychiatry, 40*, 1383–1392.

Gillberg, C., Carlstroem, G., & Rasmussen, P. (1983). Hyperkinetic disorders in seven-year-old children with perceptual, motor and attentional deficits. *Journal of Child Psychology and Psychiatry and Allied Disciplines, 24*, 233–246.

Gimpel, G. A., & Kuhn, B. R. (2000). Maternal report of attention deficit hyperactivity disorder symptoms in preschool children. *Child: Care, Health and Development, 26*, 163–179.

Goldman, L. S., Genel, M., Bezman, R. J., & Slanetz, P. J. (1998). Diagnosis and treatment of attention deficit/hyperactivity disorder in children and adolescents. *Journal of the American Medical Association, 279*, 1100–1107.

Goyette, C. H., Conners, C. K., & Ulrich, R. F. (1978). Normative data for revised Conners parent and teachers rating scales. *Journal of Abnormal Child Psychology, 6*, 221–236.

Gresham, F. M., & Elliott, S. N. (1990). *Social skills rating system: Preschool level.* Circle Pines, MN: American Guidance Services.

Hinshaw, S. P., Han, S. S., Erhardt, D., & Huber, A. (1992). Internalizing and externalizing behavior problems in preschool children: Correspondence among parent and teacher ratings and behavior observations. *Journal of Clinical Child Psychology, 21*, 143–150.

Jacob, R. G., O'Leary, K. D., & Rosenblad, C. (1978). Formal and informal classroom settings: Effects on hyperactivity. *Journal of Abnormal Child Psychology, 6*, 47–59.

Johnston, C. (1996). Parent characteristics and parent-child interactions in families of nonproblem children and ADHD children with higher and lower levels of oppositional-defiant behavior. *Journal of Abnormal Child Psychology, 24*, 85–104.

Johnston, C. & Mash, E. J. (1989). A measure of parenting satisfaction and efficacy. *Journal of Clinical Child Psychology, 18(2)*, 167–175.

Keenan, K., Shaw, D. S., Walsh, B., Delliquadri, E., & Giovannelli, J. (1997). "DSM-IIIR" disorders in preschool children from low-income families. *Journal of the American Academy of Child and Adolescent Psychiatry, 36*, 620–627.

Keenan, K., & Wakschlag, L. S. (2000). More than the terrible twos: The nature and severity of behavior problems in clinic-referred preschool children. *Journal of Abnormal Child Psychology, 28*, 33–47.

Lahey, B. B., Applegate, B., McBurnett, K., & Biederman, J. (1994). DMS-IV field trials for attention deficit hyperactivity disorder in children and adolescents. *American Journal of Psychiatry, 151*, 1673–1685.

Lahey, B. B., & Loeber, R. (1997). Attention-deficit/hyperactivity disorder, and adult antisocial behavior: A life span perspective. In D. M. Stoff, J. Breiling, & J. D. Maser (Eds.), *Handbook of antisocial behavior* (pp. 51–60). New York: Wiley.

Lahey, B. B., Pelham, W. E., Loney, J., Kipp, H., Ehrhardt, A., Lee, S., Willcutt, E., & Hartung, C. (in preparation). *Three-year predictive validity of DSM-IV attention-deficit/hyperactivity disorder first diagnosed at 4 through 6 years of age.*

Lahey, B. B., Pelham, W. E., Stein, M. A., Loney, J., Trapani, C., Nugent, K., Kipp, H., Schmidt, E., Lee, S., Cale, M., Gold, E., Hartung, C. M., Willcutt, E., & Baumann, B. (1998). Validity of DSM-IV attention-deficit/hyperactivity disorder for younger children. *Journal of the American Academy of Child and Adolescent Psychiatry, 37*, 695–702.

Lang, A. R., Pelham, W. E., Atkeson, B. M., & Murphy, D. A. (1999). Effects of alcohol intoxication on parenting behavior in interactions with child confederates exhibiting normal or deviant behaviors. *Journal of Abnormal Child Psychology, 27*(3), 177–189.

Lavigne, J. V., Gibbons, R. D., Christoffel, K. K., Arend, R., Rosenbaum, D., Binns, H., Dawson, N., Sobel, H., & Issacs, C. (1996). Prevalence rates and correlates of psychiatric disorders among preschoolers. *Journal of the American Academy of Child and Adolescent Psychiatry, 35*, 204–214.

Mash, E. J., & Johnston, C. (1982). A comparison of the mother-child interactions of younger and older hyperactive and normal children. *Child Development, 53*, 1371–1381.

Mash, E. J., & Johnston, C. (1990). Determinants of parenting stress: Illustrations from families of hyperactive children and families of physi-

cally abused children. *Journal of Clinical Child Psychology, 19*, 313–328.

McClellan, J. M., & Speltz, M. L. (2003). Psychiatric diagnosis in preschool children. *Journal of the American Academy of Child and Adolescent Psychiatry, 42*, 127–128.

McGee, R., Partridge, F., Williams, S., & Silva, P. A. (1991). A twelve-year follow-up of preschool hyperactive children. *Journal of the American Academy of Child and Adolescent Psychiatry, 30*, 224–232.

Milich, R., & Landau, S. (1982). Socialization and peer relations in hyperactive children. *Advances in Learning and Behavioral Disabilities, 1*, 283–339.

Milich, R., & Lorch, E. P. (1994). Television viewing methodology to understand cognitive processing of ADHD children. In T. H. Ollendick & R. J. Prinz (Eds.), *Advances in clinical child psychology* (Vol. 16, pp. 177–201). New York: Plenum Press.

Miller, L. S., Koplewicz, H. S., & Klein, R. G. (1997). Teacher ratings of hyperactivity, inattention, and conduct problems in preschoolers. *Journal of Abnormal Child Psychology, 25*, 113–119.

Miller, N. B., Cowan, P. A., Cowan, C. P., Hetherington, E. M., & Clingempeel, W. G. (1993). Externalizing behavior in preschoolers and early adolescents: A cross-study replication of a family model. *Developmental Psychology, 29*, 3–18.

Moffitt, T. E. (1990). Juvenile delinquency and attention deficit disorder: Boys' developmental trajectories from age 3 to age 15. *Child Development, 61*, 893–910.

MTA Cooperative Group. (1999). A 14-month randomized clinical trial of treatment strategies for attention-deficit/hyperactivity disorder. *Archives of General Psychiatry, 56*, 1073–1086.

NIH Consensus Statement. (1998). *Diagnosis and treatment of attention deficit hyperactivity disorder (ADHD)*. Washington, DC: National Institutes of Health.

Patterson, G. R., DeBaryshe, B. D., & Ramsey, E. (1989). A developmental perspective on antisocial behavior. *American Psychologist, 44*, 329–335.

Pelham, W. E. (1999). The NIMH Multimodal Treatment Study for attention-deficit hyperactivity disorder: Just say yes to drugs alone? *Canadian Journal of Psychiatry, 44*, 981–990.

Pelham, W. E., & Bender, M. E. (1982). Peer relationships in hyperactive children: Description and treatment. *Advances in Learning and Behavioral Disabilities, 1,* 365–436.

Pelham, W. E., Evans, S. W., Gnagy, E. M., & Greenslade, K. E. (1992). Teacher ratings of DSM-III-R symptoms for the disruptive behavior disorders: Prevalence, factor analyses, and conditional probabilities in a special education sample. *School Psychology Review, 21,* 285–299.

Pelham, W. E., & Fabiano, G. A. (2000). Behavior modification. *Child and Adolescent Psychiatric Clinics of North America, 9,* 671–688.

Pelham, W. E., Gnagy, E. M., Greenslade, K. E., & Milich, R. (1992). Teacher ratings of DSM-III-R symptoms for the disruptive behavior disorders. *Journal of the American Academy of Child and Adolescent Psychiatry, 31,* 210–218.

Pelham, W. E., & Lang, A. R. (1999). Can your children drive you to drink? Stress and parenting in adults interacting with children with ADHD. *Alcohol Research and Health, 23,* 292–298.

Pelham, W. E., Lang, A. R., Atkeson, B., Murphy, D. A., Gnagy, E. M., Greiner, A. R., Vodde-Hamilton, M., & Greenslade, K. E. (1997). Effects of deviant child behavior on parental distress and alcohol consumption in laboratory interactions. *Journal of Abnormal Child Psychology, 25,* 413–424.

Pelham, W. E., Lang, A. R., Atkeson, B., Murphy, D. A., Gnagy, E. M., Greiner, A. R., Vodde-Hamilton, M., & Greenslade, K. E. (1998). Effects of deviant child behavior on parental alcohol consumption: Stress-induced drinking in parents of ADHD children. *American Journal on Addictions, 7,* 103–114.

Pierce, E. W., Ewing, L. J., & Campbell, S. B. (1999). Diagnostic status and symptomatic behavior of hard-to-manage preschool children in middle childhood and early adolescence. *Journal of Clinical Child Psychology, 28,* 44–57.

Pineda, D., Ardila, A., Rosselli, M., Arias, B. E., Henao, G. C., Gomez, L. F., Mejia, S. E., & Miranda, M. L. (1999). Prevalence of attention-deficit/hyperactivity disorder symptoms in 4 to 17-year-old children in the general population. *Journal of Abnormal Child Psychology, 27,* 455–460.

Pisterman, S., McGrath, P. J., Firestone, P., & Goodman, J. T. (1989). Outcome of parent-mediated treatment of preschoolers with attention deficit disorder with hyperactivity.

Journal of Consulting and Clinical Psychology, 57, 628–635.

Routh, D. K., Schroeder, C. S., & O'Tuama, L. A. (1974). Development of activity level in children. *Developmental Psychology, 10,* 163–168.

Rowland, A. S., Umbach, D. M., Stallone, L., Naftel, A. J., Bohlig, E. M., & Sandler, D. P. (2002). Prevalence of medication treatment for attention-deficit-hyperactivity disorder among elementary school children in Johnston County, North Carolina. *American Journal of Public Health, 92,* 231–234.

Rubin, K. H., Bukowski, W., & Parker, J. G. (1998). Peer interactions, relationships, and groups. In W. Damon (Series Ed.) & N. Eisenberg (Vol. Ed.), *Handbook of child psychology: Vol. 3. Social, emotional, and personality development* (5th ed., pp. 619–700). New York: Wiley.

Scotti, J. R., Morris, T. L., McNeil, C. B., & Hawkins, R. P. (1996). DSM-IV and disorders of childhood and adolescence: Can structural criteria be functional? *Journal of Consulting and Clinical Psychology, 64,* 1177–1191.

Setterberg, S., Bird, H., & Gould, M. (1992). *Parent and interviewer version of the children's global assessment scale.* New York: Columbia University.

Shaffer, D., Fisher, P., Dulcan, M., Davies, M., Piacentini, J., Schwab-Stone, M., Lahey, B. B., Bourdon, K., Jensen, P., Bird, H., Canino, G., & Regier, D. (1996). The NIMH Diagnostic Interview Schedule for Children (DISC 2.3): Description, acceptability, prevalences, and performance in the MECA study. *Journal of the American Academy of Child and Adolescent Psychiatry, 35,* 865–877.

Sleator, E. K. (1982). Office diagnosis of hyperactivity by the physician. *Advances in Learning and Behavioral Disabilities, 1,* 341–364.

Snyder, J. (1991). Discipline as a mediator of the impact of maternal stress and mood on child conduct problems. *Development and Psychopathology, 3,* 263–276.

Sonuga-Barke, E. J. S., Daley, D., Thompson, M., Laver-Bradbury, C., & Weeks, A. (2001). Parent-based therapies for preschool attention-deficit/hyperactivity disorder: A randomized, controlled trial with a community sample. *Journal of the American Academy of Child and Adolescent Psychiatry, 40,* 402–408.

Sonuga-Barke, E. J. S., Thompson, M., Stevenson, J., & Viney, D. (1997). Patterns of behavior problems among pre-school children. *Psychological Medicine, 27,* 909–918.

Speltz, M. L., McClennan, J., DeKlyen, M., & Jones, K. (1999). Preschool boys with oppositional defiant disorder: Clinical presentation and diagnostic change. *Journal of the American Academy of Child and Adolescent Psychiatry, 38*, 838–845.

Stormont-Spurgin, M., & Zentall, S. S. (1995). Contributing factors in the manifestation of aggression in preschoolers with hyperactivity. *Journal of Child Psychology and Psychiatry, 36*, 491–509.

Tallmadge, J., & Barkley, R. A. (1983). The interactions of hyperactive and normal boys with their fathers and mothers. *Journal of Abnormal Child Psychology, 11*, 565–580.

Tremblay, R. E., LeMarquand, D., & Vitaro, F. (1999). The prevention of oppositional defiant disorder and conduct disorder. In H. Quay & A. Hogan (Eds.), *Handbook of disruptive behavior disorders* (pp. 525–555). New York: Kluwer.

Vitiello, B. (2001). Psychopharmacology for young children: Clinical needs and research opportunities. *Pediatrics, 108*, 983–989.

Webster-Stratton, C. (1988). Mothers' and fathers' perceptions of child deviance: Roles of parent and child behaviors and parent adjustment. *Journal of Consulting and Clinical Psychology, 56*, 909–915.

Webster-Stratton, C. (1990). Stress: A potential disruptor of parent perceptions and family interactions. *Journal of Clinical Child Psychology, 19*, 302–312.

Webster-Stratton, C., Reid, J., & Hammond, M. (2001). Social skills and problem-solving training for children with early-onset conduct problems: Who benefits? *Journal of Child Psychology, Psychiatry, and Allied Disciplines, 7*, 943–952.

Wolraich, M. L., Hannah, J. N., Pinnock, T. Y., Baumgaertel, A., & Brown, J. (1996). Comparison of diagnostic criteria for ADHD in a county-wide sample. *Journal of the American Academy of Child and Adolescent Psychiatry, 35*, 319–324.

Zito, J. M., Safer, D. J., dosReis, S., Gardner, J. F., Boles, M., & Lynch, F. (2000). Trends in the prescribing of psychotropic medications to preschoolers. *Journal of the American Medical Association, 283*, 1025–1030

21

Assessment of Disruptive Behavior in Young Children: A Clinical-Developmental Framework

Lauren S. Wakschlag

Barbara Danis

The complexity of distinguishing normative from problematic behavior during early childhood, a period marked by normative behavioral disruption, has called into question whether disruptive behavior problems can be reliably assessed during this period (Campbell, 2002). Unfortunately, this debate has often appeared to split along the lines of developmentalists versus clinicians. Developmentalists fear pathologizing normative developmental perturbations. Within this framework, premature labeling is a concern because of the worry that it may pigeonhole a child as disordered when developmental righting may yet occur. Furthermore, diagnostic approaches are seen as too confining because they dichotomize behaviors that often appear to fall along a continuum (Silk, Nath, Siegel, & Kendall, 2000). In contrast, clinicians face the pragmatic issue that disruptive behavior is the most common reason for referral of young children to mental health clinics (Keenan & Wakschlag, 2000; Luby & Morgan, 1997; Thomas & Guskin, 2001) and the reality is that parents, teachers, and physicians report that the problems are real and that they need help.

While there is increasing evidence that behavior disorders can be validly diagnosed in preschoolers (Keenan & Wakschlag, 2002a), these assessments have occurred primarily within a research context. Consequently, clinicians trained to diagnose disruptive behavior disorders in older children, for whom the presence of a behavior per se is often symptomatic, may have difficulty determining whether a behavior is symptomatic in a young child. The absence of a standardized, well-validated set of clinical tools developed specifically for assessment of behavior in young children also presents challenges to the clinician because there is such rapid change and variability within this period. Thus, although assessment of disruptive behavior problems in young children requires integration of clinical information and knowledge of normal development during this period, there is no systematic method for doing so. As such, a developmentally informed framework for the clinical assessment of disruptive behavior problems in young children is of great theoretical and practical significance.

The goal of this chapter is the delineation of

such a framework. We first discuss conceptual issues in the assessment of disruptive behavior in young children, followed by a clinical description of their manifestations. We next discuss methods of assessment and finally highlight clinical process issues in this domain.

Our framework draws upon theory and research from the fields of infant mental health, developmental psychopathology, and clinical science (e.g., Sameroff, Lewis, & Miller, 2000; Silverman, 1999; Zeanah, 2000). Accordingly, we believe that behavior must be assessed within developmental and social contexts (Shaw, Gilliom, & Giovannelli, 2000). For example, assessment of a child's language functioning is important for accurate assessment of behavior. Similarly, assessment of the parent-child relationship is fundamental to understanding the nature of the child's behavior problems.

Behavior that is outside the realm of expectable functioning within a developmental period and that interferes with normative developmental tasks and progression is seen as an adaptational failure (Sroufe, 1997), that is, a clinical problem. For example, while mild aggression toward peers is not a symptom in young children, aggressive behavior that interferes with peer relationships and school attendance is symptomatic. This developmental approach suggests that, while clinical problems may manifest differently at different developmental periods, this reflects heterotypic continuity rather than fundamentally different types of problems (Keenan & Wakschlag, 2002a). We also draw on our collective experience with hundreds of preschoolers referred for disruptive behavior problems in the Preschool Behavior Problems Clinic (PBC). The PBC is a specialty clinic in the Section of Child and Adolescent Psychiatry at the University of Chicago, which serves children ages 18 months to 5½ years, with disruptive behavior problems. The PBC is a clinical research program designed to develop systematic methods for assessment of disruptive behavior in young children and to study developmental pathways, including predictive validity of early-onset disruptive behavior disorders (DBDs) and the role of parenting and family factors in these trajectories (Keenan & Wakschlag, 2000; Wakschlag & Keenan, 2001).

WHAT IS DISRUPTIVE ABOUT DISRUPTIVE BEHAVIOR PROBLEMS?

In this section, we discuss the clinical and developmental aspects of disruptive behavior disorders in young children.[1] The development of self-control is a hallmark of the toddler and preschool periods.[2] Frustration tolerance, delay of gratification, the use of verbal negotiation strategies, internalization of standards, sensitivity to the divergent needs of self and other, and behavioral flexibility are all skills that emerge and are consolidated during this period (Keenan & Wakschlag, 2002a). Salient developmental contexts and demands also shift during this period. For example, the child's social world expands beyond the family to include peers and entry into the preschool environment, involving a host of new expectations and routines. In meeting the child's burgeoning capacities, optimal parental behavior also shifts during this period, from a primary emphasis on emotional responsiveness to one that also includes expectations, limits, and demands (Shaw et al., 2000; Wakschlag & Keenan, 2001). As all of these processes converge, there is a normative increase in assertions of autonomy, resulting in heightened noncompliance (e.g., "I want to do it my way"), aggression (e.g., forceful efforts to assert one's will), and negative emotionality (e.g., tantrums) in the face of frustration.

The defining feature of DBDs is a pattern of negative behaviors that interfere with social interactions with others (American Psychiatric Association, 1994). The hallmarks of oppositional defiant disorder (ODD) are defiance and negative emotionality. The essential features of conduct disorder (CD) are aggression and rule violation. At the surface, it would appear that these patterns of disordered behavior are virtually identical to the normative behavioral disruption described above. There are several fundamental differences, however. First, within a normative context, behavioral disruption is not *pervasive*. We mean this not only in the usual sense of the word (i.e., across multiple contexts such as school and home) but also in the sense of pervasiveness across multiple interactions with the same caregiver. Second, within a normative context, behaviors tend to be relatively flexible and well-modulated, whereas symptomatic behaviors are more likely to be *intransigent and dysregulated*. Finally, normative behaviors during this period generally do not interfere with developmental or family functioning (e.g., going to school, playing with friends, having a family member baby-sit). In contrast, clinically significant behaviors are *developmentally impairing*.

Manifestations of Disruptive Behavior in Preschoolers

The clinical presentation of preschoolers referred for disruptive behavior problems is quite varied. It is not clear whether there are distinct disruptive behavior constellations (i.e., separate oppositional and conduct patterns) at this age or whether there is a more nonspecific disruptive behavior disorder in preschoolers. In the PBC, the vast majority of preschoolers referred for disruptive behavior problems exhibit both oppositional and conduct problems. For example, in our PBC sample, over 90% of the children who met criteria for ODD had at least one conduct symptom; conduct symptoms were in the clinically significant range for more than half (57.4%) of these children. On the other hand, we have also identified some differences, both in presentation and correlates, for preschoolers with ODD alone compared to preschoolers with ODD who also have clinically significant conduct symptoms. Preschoolers with combined symptoms were significantly more impaired than preschoolers with ODD symptoms alone and were more likely to exhibit aggression in interaction with their parents. Their family contexts were also riskier; they were more likely to have mothers with an early first birth and absent fathers than preschoolers with ODD symptoms alone. Although many clinical studies of preschool disruptive behavior have not assessed conduct symptoms, perhaps because of discomfort with the notion that these symptoms can appear at such a young age, our own experience suggests that such behaviors are present and their assessment critically important for clarifying clinical issues and for treatment planning.

Clinical Prototype of DBDs in the Young Child

We describe below clinical prototypes of preschool children with DBD symptoms, to highlight how these differ from normative behaviors during this period. We focus on behavioral and emotional constructs that are central to preschool manifestation of DBDs rather than symptoms per se. These prototypes are intended to provide a general characterization of the clinical picture of young children with DBD symptoms. However, it is important to note that there is a great deal of heterogeneity in clinical presentation, and we do not yet know whether these different clinical constellations differ in terms of correlates or in terms of continuity with later disorders.

One defining characteristic of ODD is a pervasive pattern of resistance to caregivers, which can include either noncompliant or provocative behavior or both. The quality of noncompliance distinguishes clinically significant oppositionality from normative noncompliance. In preschoolers, normative noncompliance reflects a child's self-assertion as part of burgeoning autonomy (Crockenberg & Litman, 1990). Assertive noncompliance is generally short-lived and is elicited by a desire to do something other than what is being asked. In contrast, *defiance* reflects "negativism for its own sake" (Wenar, 1982), that is, active refusal that is first and foremost resistance toward the caregiver's request, with the particular context or activity of secondary importance. This defiant behavior may include both active defiance (e.g., "no") and passive noncompliance (e.g., grudging compliance, ignoring) (e.g., Kochanska & Aksan, 1995). Defiance is often intransigent, whereas assertive noncompliance tends to be responsive to caregiver guidance. In addition, assertive noncompliance is rarely elicited during positive interactions that do not involve limit setting or transition, whereas defiance tends to occur pervasively, that is, a "reflexive no." As a result, the child whose noncompliance is normative will also have frequent positive social interchanges, whereas defiance predominates in the interactions of the child with oppositional-defiant symptoms.

Provocativeness reflects deliberate attempts to

annoy caregivers and "push their buttons," that is, purposefully engaging in prohibited activities with the goal of eliciting a reaction from the caregiver. The deliberateness of provocative behavior is often evident in visual referencing or taunting of the person toward whom the behavior is directed as well as in the fact that the behavior often occurs in direct response to a prohibition. Although assertive noncompliance may involve doing something in a manner different than that suggested by the caregiver, this is driven by the desire to do something autonomously and does not involve deliberate attempts to provoke.

The other defining feature of ODD is negative emotionality. The negative emotionality that characterizes oppositional-defiant symptoms has two distinct aspects, *chronic negative mood* and *emotional dysregulation*. There is substantial variability in whether children present with one or both of these dimensions. The child with chronic negative mood may be described as "sulky," "sullen," "angry," or "rarely cheerful." Moodiness and irritability are described as typical and long-standing and are not contingent on limits or frustration. (This must be distinguished from moodiness due to emotional problems, such as depression. See Differential Diagnosis and Co-occurring Disorders). Such children are often described as "difficult." However, many children with oppositional-defiant symptoms do not exhibit chronic negative mood but present only with emotional dysregulation. The child who is emotionally dysregulated may be described as "easily set off," "out of control," and "reactive." Although tantrums are common during this period, normative manifestations are generally brief in duration and mild to moderate in intensity, with relatively rapid recovery. They are likely to occur in response to frustration and when the child is fatigued. In contrast, young children with oppositional-defiant symptoms tend to have frequent, emotionally intense tantrums. Tantrums are easily elicited (caregivers often feel like they are "walking on eggshells" to avoid setting them off), and prolonged and disorganized (e.g., pushing over chairs or breaking objects when upset). Once a preschooler with oppositional-defiant symptoms gets upset, he or she will often require significant input from the caregiver to calm down.

A defining feature of CD is aggression and cruelty to others. Normative aggression during this period is generally directed toward peers in the context of disputes (Tremblay, 2000). It may involve mild hitting or kicking in response to frustration and often appears to be an immature strategy for resolving conflict rather than an action deliberately aimed at hurting another. In contrast, aggressive behavior in the preschool child with conduct symptoms tends to be proactive as well as reactive. Preschool children with conduct symptoms are often described as hitting others for "no reason," and they may display aggression as often in the context of positive interactions as in reaction to negative ones. This aggression has a driven quality to it, with the aim of deliberately being cruel to another person. Its manifestations are more varied and intense than normative aggression, including choking, biting, scratching, and pulling hair, as well as purposeful use of objects to harm others and intentional destructiveness. Physical and verbal aggression toward adults, which is rarely seen in a normative context during the preschool period, may also be present. Less common but also present in the young child with conduct problems are more serious forms of aggression including throwing things, slapping, hitting, and stabbing with objects.

The other hallmark of CD is deliberate violation of rules and norms. Although preschoolers may break rules when testing limits and may typically lie to avoid punishment, these behaviors are infrequent and generally "corrected" via adult prompting. In contrast, clinically significant rule violation is more deliberate, pervasive, frequent, and severe. Lying about intentional rule breaking is common, as are behaviors such as taking other children's belongings by force or threatening to do so.

Preschool children with clinically significant disruptive behavior problems not only exhibit more negative behaviors but also fewer social and behavioral competencies. They tend to be less likely to utilize verbal negotiation to solve problems, to be less behaviorally flexible, and to have difficulty sustaining positive social interactions (Webster-Stratton & Lindsay, 1999).

In the next section, we discuss methods and approaches for distinguishing normative from clinically significant behaviors in this age group.

THE SCIENCE OF ASSESSING DBD SYMPTOMS: MULTIPLE CONTEXTS

In this section, we present fundamental principles that underlie developmentally based clinical assessment of behavior in young children and outline a multimethod, contextually based approach to assessment.

Basic Assessment Principles

Developmentally Sensitive Instruments

Methods that are specifically designed for this age group (rather than those that tag on preschoolers at the low end of a measure, e.g., "4–16-year-olds") are most sensitive for distinguishing atypical and normative behaviors.

Multimethod Approach

A multimethod approach, which includes both parent report and observation, is essential. It is often difficult to obtain reports from multiple informants when assessing young children, since many are not yet attending school, because young children cannot serve as informants about their own symptoms, and/or because many high-risk young children are being raised in single-parent environments. Thus, observation may be the only supplementary source of information available. Relying on parent report alone to identify behavior problems in preschoolers also has inherent limitations, since the necessary distinctions between normative and problematic behavior during this period are often subtle, and many factors may influence parental judgments of preschoolers' behavior including lack of knowledge about developmentally appropriate expectations, parental stress, and parental psychopathology.

Assessing Behavior in Developmental Context

Assessment of the child's developmental functioning is vital to accurate clinical assessment of disruptive behavior in the young child (Keenan & Wakschlag, 2002). This is essential in ruling out alternative explanations for symptoms and to determine how developmental delays (e.g., lags in language development) may be contributing to the behavioral difficulties.

Assessment of Child Behavior in the Clinical Context

Although a variety of methods for assessing behavior problems in preschoolers exist, there is currently no standard diagnostic battery for assessing preschool disruptive behavior. In particular, there is (a) no comprehensively validated method for clinical interviewing, (b) no standardized observational method for assessing clinically significant disruptive behavior problems, and (c) no method for integrating (often disparate) information into clinical judgment. In this section, we highlight methods and issues in the clinical assessment of disruptive behavior in preschool children, drawing on the protocol we have developed within the PBC as an illustration (see table 21.1). Our focus is on methods and contexts of behavioral assessments. However, understanding the nature and function of the child's behavior problems also necessitates an assessment of the broader family environment. Table 21.1 illustrates key domains of family context to be assessed, including parental psychopathology,[3] social supports and stressors, exposure to violence, and parental relationship history (past and present).

Parent-Report Methods

A number of behavior checklists have been developed and validated for toddlers and preschoolers. These include the Child Behavior Checklist (CBCL), which has both a toddler and preschool version (Achenbach, 1991; Achenbach & Edelbrock, 1983), the Preschool Behavior Questionnaire (Behar, 1977) and the Eyberg Child Behavior Inventory (ECBI; Eyberg & Ross, 1978). The Infant-Toddler Social and Emotional Assessment (ITSEA) has been developed to assess both competencies and problem behaviors in infants and toddlers (Carter, Briggs-Gowan, Jones, & Little, in press). Although not a diagnostic measure per se, the ITSEA has substantially advanced our ability to examine problematic behaviors in young children by systematically assessing domain-specific problems (e.g., aggression, negative emotionality) in infants and toddlers in a manner that can

Table 21.1 A Multimethod, Multi-Informant, Contextual Approach to Assessment of Disruptive Behavior Problems in Young Children

Domain	Context		
	Clinic		School
Child's behavioral symptoms	Diagnostic Observation of Child (e.g., DB-DOS[a])	Parent interview (e.g., K-DBDS[b]) Parent questionnaire (e.g., ECI[c])	Observation of child (Classroom Observation Ratings[d]) Teacher questionnaire (e.g., SCBE[e], ECI[c])
Child's developmental functioning	Developmental Testing (e.g., DAS[f])	Parent report of milestones	
Parent-child relationship	Structured observation of parent-child interaction (e.g, DB-DOS[a])	Parent questionnaire (e.g., Parenting Styles Questionnaire[g])	
Broader family context Psychopathology Exposure to violence Parental childhood history Stressors/supports		Parent interview (SCID[h], Childhood Experiences Interview[i]) Parent questionnaire (e.g., PSI[j], DLC[k], CTS[l])	

[a]Disruptive Behaviors Diagnostic Observation Schedule; [b]Kiddie Disruptive Behavior Disorders Schedule for Preschool Children (Keenan & Wakschlag, 2002b); [c]Early Childhood Symptom Inventory (Gadow & Sprafkin, 1996); [d]Classroom Observation Ratings (Webster-Stratton, 2002); [e]Social Competence and Behavior Evaluation–Preschool Edition (Le Freniere & Dumas, 1995); [f]Differential Abilities Scale (Elliot, 1983); [g]Parenting Styles Questionnaire (Greenberger et al., 1994); [h]Structured Clinical Interview for *DSM-IV* Axis I (Spitzer & Endicott, 1978; Spitzer et al., 1987); [i]Childhood Experiences Interview (Lyons-Ruth et al., 1989); [j]Parenting Stress Index (Abidin, 1995); [k]Difficult Life Circumstances Questionnaire (Barnard et al., 1988); [l]Conflict Tactics Scale (McGuire & Earls, 1993).

be coherently mapped to clinical constellations as children enter the preschool years.

Behavior checklist questionnaires generally ask parents to rate behaviors along a frequency continuum (e.g., rarely, somewhat, a lot). The advantage of behavior checklists is that they are easy to administer and provide a broad picture of whether the child has problematic behavior. Checklists provide a clinical cutoff to indicate whether behaviors are in the problematic range and as such are often a good first step in clinical evaluation of behavior in the young child. However, their overall clinical utility is limited by their focus on broad domains (e.g., externalizing problems) rather than discrete disorders (but see the Early Childhood Inventories [ECI]; Gadow & Sprafkin, 1996) and frequency, such that they do not take qualitative aspects of the behavior into account. Questionnaire methods to assess these qualitative aspects of behavior problems (e.g., confrontational versus sneaky noncompliance) have been developed (Drabick, Strassberg, & Kees, 2001).

In contrast, parent interviews have the advantage of being specifically designed to assess child symptoms and, with semistructured interviews, provide the opportunity for probing and determining clinical significance. However, there are currently no comprehensively validated diagnostic interviews for children as young as 3 years. We are currently in the process of validating a preschool version of the disruptive behavior module of the K-SADS, the Kiddie Disruptive Behavior Disorders Schedule for Preschool Children (K-DBDS; Keenan & Wakschlag, 2002b). In the K-DBDS, standardized probes are used to assess behavior within developmental context (see table 21.2). Since the determination of whether a be-

Table 21.2 Examples of Developmentally Sensitive Probes From the Kiddie Disruptive Behavior Disorders Schedule for Preschool Children (K-DBDS)

Assessing Symptoms
  Oppositional Defiant
  Disorder

Symptom	Specific Probes
Often loses temper	How often
	How severe
	How long does it last
	How long to recover

Conduct Disorder

Symptom	Specific Probes
Physically aggressive	Only with siblings
	Toward adults
	How often
	Ever seriously hurt anyone

havior is symptomatic during this period does not rest on presence or absence of a specific behavior, both qualitative and quantitative aspects of the behavior must be assessed to establish symptom thresholds. Clinically, we have found that the use of probes such as those illustrated in table 21.2, which systematically assess frequency, intensity, severity, and the contexts in which the behaviors occur, are critically important in distinguishing normative from problematic behavior during this period. For example, it is likely that a substantial proportion of parents of preschoolers would endorse the symptom "frequently loses temper." Probes that establish (a) actual frequency and timing; (b) intensity; (c) duration of these episodes, particularly the child's capacity to "recover"; and (d) the contexts in which they occur are extremely useful for establishing whether such behavior is symptomatic. This measure will be further validated in a National Institutes of Mental Health (NIMH)-funded study we have initiated, the Chicago Preschool Project, which is designed to systematically establish thresholds of clinical significance during this period and to identify the functional equivalence of preschool manifestations of particular symptoms (Keenan, 2002). Another effort currently underway is the validation of a comprehensive diagnostic interview for 2½- to 6-year-olds, the Preschool Age Psychiatric Assessment (PAPA; see chapter 12).

While emerging methods for diagnostic interviewing about young children's behavioral symptoms are critically important, we argue that they should not be used in isolation. Although multi-informant methods are typically the standard in assessment of older children, preschool children cannot serve as informants about their own behavior, and the parent is often the sole informant about the behavior. In the next section, we discuss the importance of supplementing parental reports with information gathered from standardized observation and describe a clinical/observational tool for the assessment of disruptive behavior that we are developing for this purpose.

Observational Methods

A major contribution of the infant mental health and developmental psychopathology perspectives has been underscoring the importance of understanding young children's behavior within social context, with particular emphasis on observations of the child in interaction with the parent (Cicchetti & Aber, 1998; Zeanah, Boris, & Scheeringa, 1997). These perspectives also strongly emphasize the importance of developmentally informed clinical observation and judgment in the assessment of problematic versus normative behavior during early childhood. *Clinical observation* goes beyond observation of discrete behaviors per se to an integrated examination of multiple facets of the child's behavior (such that the whole is more than the sum of its parts). Building on such observations, *clinical judgment* is an overall assessment of the atypicality of the child's behaviors, which weights the salience of particular behaviors based on age appropriateness and context. The clinician's experience of, and with, the child is a vital dimension of this process. However, there is a disconnect between the importance of observation within these theoretical and clinical perspectives and existing methods for the assessment of preschool behavior problems (see chapter 11). Currently, there are no standardized methods for incorporating clinical observations or observations of parent-child interaction into the clinical decision-making process.

Many studies of preschool disruptive behavior have included observations of parent-child interactions, but as correlates rather than clinical indicators (e.g., Greenberg, Speltz, DeKlyen, & Jones, 2001; Wakschlag & Keenan, 2001; Webster-Stratton & Lindsay, 1999). Existing paradigms for assessing parent-child interaction were not specifically developed for clinical purposes (with the Dyadic Parent-Child Interaction Coding System–Revised, or DPICS-R, a notable exception; Webster-Stratton & Lindsay, 1999). While existing observational methods do distinguish referred from nonreferred preschoolers (Keenan & Wakschlag, 2000; Webster-Stratton & Lindsay, 1999), they are not clinically sensitive; that is, they are not diagnostically oriented and do not have clinical cutoffs. For example, in the PBC, we assessed parent-child interaction with the widely used puzzle and cleanup tasks (Berlin, Brooks-Gunn, Spiker, & Zaslow, 1995; Campbell, Pierce, March, Ewing, & Szumowski, 1994). Although nearly half of the referred preschoolers were reported by their parents to be exhibiting serious aggressive symptoms, less than 5% of the children observed displayed significant aggression during the puzzle task. Thus, it was difficult to map maternal report of symptoms onto observed behaviors.

Standardized clinically based observational assessment has been utilized very effectively in the validation of another early-onset disorder, autism (Lord et al., 2000). To develop a diagnostic observation tool for disruptive behavior disorders in young children, we turned to the Autism Diagnostic Observation Schedule (ADOS) as a model upon which to draw. The ADOS has been widely used in conjunction with the Autism Diagnostic Interview (ADI) and has substantially contributed to the widespread consensus on the validity of the diagnosis of autism in young children (Klinger & Renner, 2000; Lord et al., 2000). However, there are no standardized diagnostic observation tools for the assessment of preschool disruptive behavior. The development of such methods for clinical assessment of preschool behavior is especially critical because:

- They will provide clinicians with a systematic means of incorporating their clinical judgment into the assessment of young children.
- They will provide a standard and consistent metric for diagnosis. In conjunction with standardized diagnostic interviews, this will

enable systematic comparison across studies, which is fundamental to resolving the ongoing debate about the validity of preschool disruptive behavior disorders.
- They will gather rich, detailed information that will help the field move beyond "crude" descriptions of disruptive behavior in preschoolers (e.g., aggression, noncompliance) to a more refined understanding of the qualitative differences between normative and disruptive behaviors during this period.

To address these issues, we have developed the Disruptive Behavior Diagnostic Observation Schedule (DB-DOS; Wakschlag et al., 2002). The DB-DOS is designed to yield information on the boundaries between atypical and typical behavior in preschoolers by getting "underneath symptoms" via assessment of qualitative and quantitative dimensions of child emotional and behavioral functioning in multiple domains. The DB-DOS was designed to be clinically sensitive and specific, with the aim of generating diagnostic algorithms that can identify children with DBDs (as well as children with clinically concerning but not severe disruptive behavior problems) and to meaningfully characterize the heterogeneity that is evident among preschool children with disruptive behavior problems. The DB-DOS was developed and piloted within the PBC, and we have submitted a grant to NIMH for a large-scale validation of the DB-DOS measure. As illustrated in figure 21.1, the DB-DOS assesses multiple dimensions of child disruptive behavior, modulation of negative affect, and competence. Thus, the DB-DOS is designed to move beyond assessment of disruptive behaviors in isolation to examine the pattern of child functioning across multiple domains, domains that we hypothesize to be the core domains impaired in preschoolers with disruptive behaviors.

In developing the DB-DOS, we drew on the ADOS model of utilizing a series of developmentally salient situations to provide "presses" designed to spontaneously elicit diagnostically relevant behaviors within a standardized context (Lord et al., 2000). A typical DB-DOS task presses for the child's capacity to flexibly modulate behavior according to task demands, such as tolerating the disappointment of not winning a prize, completing a series of relatively uninteresting compliance

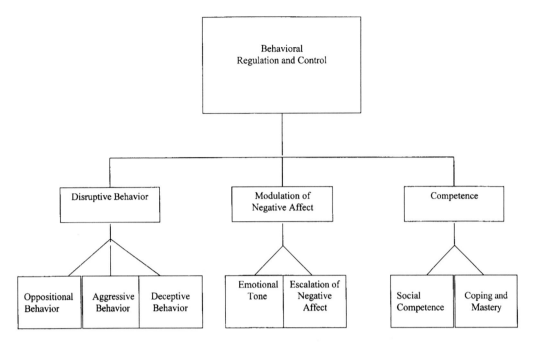

Figure 21.1 Illustration of domains of functioning and the types of behaviors coded in the Disruptive Behavior Diagnostic Observation Schedule (DB-DOS).

tasks, and turn-taking during a play task. (In contrast, ADOS tasks press for social communication skills such as socially directed gaze.)

The DB-DOS has both examiner and parent modules and lasts approximately 1 hour. The inclusion of a parent module is in contrast to the ADOS paradigm, and its rationale is worth noting in regard to complexities of assessment specific to DBDs. Whereas the atypicalities of children with autism tend to be pervasively impairing, children with early-onset disruptive behavior may have very impairing behavior problems that are only manifest within specific social contexts. Although we do not yet know the nosological or prognostic implications of such problems manifesting solely within the parent-child interaction (see Parent-Child Relationship Problems below), it is clear that assessment of the child's social behavior within and outside of the parent-child context is critically important for eliciting the range of behaviors that are diagnostically relevant. Since the DB-DOS is specifically designed to elicit such behaviors, the parent module also provides an excellent opportunity to assess parental flexibility,

emotional responsiveness, and capacity to effectively manage the child's behavior.

DB-DOS tasks last approximately 5 minutes and include tasks that tap into compliance ("do" and "don't"), disappointment, social engagement, frustration, and internalization of rules (see table 21.3). The examiner modules include examiner present with active support and examiner present with minimal support modules. Tasks in the parent module are parallel to those in the examiner modules, although the examiner modules are more systematically scripted than is possible (or desirable) with the parent. A total of 27 behaviors are coded on the DB-DOS within the domains of disruptive behavior, modulation of negative affect, and competence. DB-DOS ratings integrate quantitative (e.g., frequency) and qualitative (e.g., how intransigent the behavior is in response to examiner prompts) dimensions of behavior. Modeled after the ADOS, ratings range from 0 to 3; a broad range of typical behaviors are included in the zero category. A score of 1 reflects mild forms of the behavior, which may or may not be typical and scores of 2 to 3 indicate

Table 21.3 Modules of the Disruptive Behavior Diagnostic Observation Schedule (DB-DOS)

Modules	Task Description
I. Tasks with examiner present, with active support	
Compliance	Child is asked to do three consecutive sorting tasks
Frustration	Child is given toy that doesn't work
Social interaction	Examiner plays with child
II. Tasks with examiner present, with minimal support	Child is asked to do boring task with prohibited toys
Compliance	near
Frustration	Child works to win prize with rigged task
	Child prohibited from touching toys (examiner out of
Internalization of rules	room)
III. Tasks with parent	
Compliance	Parent asks child to do a sorting task
	Parent has child complete challenging, multiple-step
Frustration	task
	Parent asks child to work independently (parent
Compliance	occupied)
Social interaction	Parent and child play together

moderate to severe problems (reversed for competence).

Preliminary use of the DB-DOS has been very encouraging. We have successfully trained clinicians at a variety of levels to administer it reliably, and it has been very informative—enabling us to characterize the complex and varied presentation of disruptive preschoolers in new and meaningful ways. Pilot data on a sample of referred and non-referred preschoolers has also provided preliminary evidence of the reliability and clinical validity of the DB-DOS ($N = 47$) (Wakschlag et al., 2003). Evidence of reliability includes good interrater reliability (mean weighted kappa = .79) and internal consistency (mean alpha for domains = .84). In terms of clinical validity, discriminant function analysis indicated very good to excellent sensitivity and specificity (92.9 and 85.7%, respectively).

Assessment of Child Behavior in the School Context

Information gleaned in a preschool or day care setting about the child's behavior is a valuable adjunct to parent report and clinical observations for a number of reasons. First, many young children with disruptive behavior problems manifest their most significant difficulties with other children, difficulties that may not be apparent within the clinical context. In fact, some children with disruptive behavior do quite well one-on-one with an adult but have substantial difficulty when they must modulate their own behavior without this level of adult input or engage in the flexible, fast-paced social interactions that characterize peer relationships during this period. Second, this is an important, ecologically valid source of information about the child's daily functioning and can be especially clarifying when there is a discrepancy between parent report of child behavior and behavioral assessment of the child in the clinic.

As with clinic-based assessment, ideally school assessment will include both teacher report and observations of child behavior. Teacher report provides an assessment of the teacher's day-to-day experience with the child. Preschool teachers are an excellent source of information because, in contrast to many parents, they are very familiar with the typical preschooler and have a solid basis for comparison. A number of teacher checklists have been developed for preschoolers including the Response Style Questionnaire (Drabick et al., 2001) and a teacher version of the CBCL 2–3. A teacher form of the preschool version of the ECI also exists and can be useful for the purposes of obtaining parallel information about symptoms from parents and teachers (Gadow & Sprafkin, 1996). However, a disadvantage of many of the above checklists is that they focus exclusively on misbehavior. In our clinical experience, preschool children with disruptive behavior problems also have concomitant deficits in social competence (see also Webster-Stratton & Lindsay, 1999). Conversely, children with disruptive behavior problems who also have social competencies may be clinically and prognostically quite different than those with both problem behaviors and social deficits (Carter, 2002; Wakschlag et al., 2003). For this reason, in the PBC we use the Social Competence and Behavior Evaluation (SCBE; Le Freniere & Dumas, 1995), which yields both narrow and broadband measures of problem behavior and competence. Broadband scores include internalizing, externalizing, social competence, and general adaptation scores.

A limitation of relying solely on teacher report is that teachers have different thresholds for misbehavior, and the classroom management skills of the teacher may influence perceptions of the child. The behavioral demands of day care and preschool may vary substantially, in contrast to the relatively standard demands in elementary school, making it difficult to validly compare teacher reports across school settings. As such, when possible, systematic observation of the child in the school setting is very helpful. There are no standard observational systems that have been specifically designed as clinical tools, although a number of systems assessing preschoolers' peer interactions have been utilized in studies of preschool behavior problems (e.g., Webster-Stratton, 2002). Both disruptive and prosocial behaviors have been assessed. We are also currently adapting the DB-DOS ratings for use in preschool observations (Hill, Keenan, Davis, & Wakschlag, 2003.

Assessment of Impairment

The assessment of impairment in young children has received little attention, but is vitally important to the determination of whether behaviors are problematic during this age period. Measures such as the Children's Global Assessment Scale

(C-GAS; Shaffer et al., 1983), have been validly utilized with preschool populations (Lahey et al., 1998; Lavigne et al., 1998; Wakschlag & Keenan, 2001); however, they do not have developmentally specific anchors. One fundamental aspect of impairment on the C-GAS is the pervasiveness of the behavior across contexts. However, many preschoolers are not in multiple contexts either because of their age, family circumstances, or precisely because of their behavior (e.g., parents avoid sending a child to preschool because they fear the child will be expelled). As such, primary emphasis in assessing impairment in preschoolers should be on assessing the extent to which the behaviors interfere with normative developmental tasks of this period. Such tasks are centered primarily on the development of behavioral control and social competencies, including behavioral flexibility, frustration tolerance, increased independence, internalization of rules, the use of higher level problem-solving strategies to modulate upset and negotiate conflict (e.g., verbal rather than aggressive), and the capacity for sustained social interactions and cooperation. They also include the child's capacity to expand his or her social world beyond the family into school and other peer contexts (e.g., birthday parties).

Another fundamental, but often overlooked, aspect of impairment with young children is the extent to which the child's behavior interferes with the family's capacity to make developmentally appropriate shifts in their own behavior toward the child that would be consistent with normative expectations for preschoolers (e.g., establishing rules, enforcing limits, reducing supervision, and increasing expectations for independence), as well as the extent to which the child's behavior detracts from the family's capacity to have pleasurable interactions with the child (e.g., "everything is a battle") and as a family (e.g., "we can't do anything that he doesn't like because he'll get so angry we'll have to stop anyway"). In fact, a major indication of a clinical problem is that the family devotes substantial energy to avoid setting off or crossing the child (e.g., no set bedtime because the child is resistant, telling siblings to give in to the child to avoid upset, not going out because they are afraid to leave the child with a baby-sitter). Because of this ten-

Table 21.4 Examples of Developmentally Sensitive Probes to Assess Impairment From the Kiddie Disruptive Behavior Disorders Schedule for Preschool Children (K-DBDS)

Assessing Impairment	Specific Probes
Interferes with parent/family functioning	To go out in public
	To set limits
	To leave him or her with sitter
Interferes with child's functioning	To play with other children
	To go to school and learn
	Get along with family members

dency to dance around the child's behavior, serious impairment may be missed if questions are not asked directly about the effects of the child's behavior on the family. For example, if asked whether the behavior interferes with the child's functioning with other adults, the parent may reply "no," but further probing may reveal that the parent rarely leaves the child with anyone because of fear that the child's behavior will be uncontrollable. Table 21.4 illustrates developmentally salient impairment questions. Both the PAPA and the ITSEA also include developmentally based impairment questions.

THE ART OF ASSESSMENT OF DBD SYMPTOMS: INTEGRATION AND PROCESS

Too often, discussions of assessment of preschool disruptive behavior focus solely on the science and fail to elaborate on the art. The PBC is a training clinic, and it is our students who have most effectively brought home to us the importance of articulating the principles and process of a clinically skillful assessment of the disruptive preschooler. In particular, our psychiatry fellows and psychology interns have brought to our attention the ways in which clinical assessment of young children differs from their experience with older children and have helped us to understand how helpless even a very experienced clinician can feel in the face of a willful toddler's refusal to listen or a seemingly endless tantrum at the close of a session. In addition, as outlined above,

data must be gathered across methodology, across informants, and across contexts. It is often the case that interviews and clinical observations do not map cleanly onto each other. When this is the case, the clinician faces the difficult task of weighting the information gathered, resolving discrepancies, and integrating this into a meaningful, developmentally based clinical formulation. In this section, we discuss issues related to clinical decision making and the process of assessment.

Clinical Decision Making

Disruptive behavior is the most common reason for referral to mental health clinics, but not all children who present with behavior problems have a disruptive behavior disorder. Although an extensive discussion of differential diagnosis is beyond the scope of this chapter, we briefly highlight important issues for consideration and primary alternative explanations to be explored. (Detailed discussion of these types of clinical problems and their manifestations are found throughout this volume.)

Differential Diagnosis and Co-occurring Disorders

Our general approach to sorting out this issue of differential diagnosis is to examine whether the behavior problems are primary and indicative of a behavioral disorder or whether there is another underlying problem that may drive the behavioral presentation. Figure 21.2 illustrates this clinical decision-making process.[4] Although the presence of another primary problem does not in and of itself indicate that the behavior problems are not clinically significant, it does substantially influence diagnostic formulation and treatment planning. As is common with older children, many referred preschoolers have co-occuring problems. The task for the clinician is to determine whether a behavioral presentation (a) reflects a primary behavioral disturbance, (b) is masking another underlying problem, or (c) is one of a constellation of co-occurring problems. In our experience in the PBC, the following are the most common clinical problems that must be considered in diagnostic assessment of behavior problems:

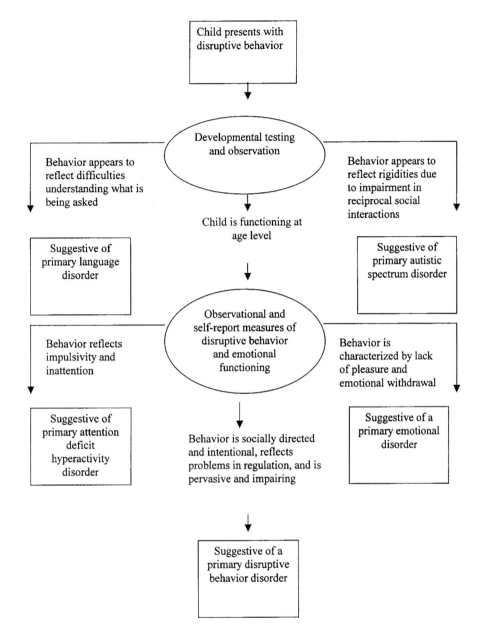

Figure 21.2 Illustration of clinical decision-making process for preschoolers presenting with disruptive behavior.

1. *Behavior problems in the context of language disorder.* Signs of primary language problems include (a) behavior problems that are primarily reactive to frustration, and (b) clinical observation that noncompliance appears to be due to not understanding what is being asked rather than willfulness or provocativeness. Since such language problems may be either obvious or subtle, standardized developmental assessment is critical to determining whether there are language deficits. If so, core assessment issues are (a) determination of whether the behavior problems are inconsistent with

the child's developmental level rather than chronological age (e.g., several daily tantrums for a 3-year-old functioning at a 24-month language level are likely within normal age limits); and (b) examining the extent to which the parent's interactions with the child are appropriately geared to developmental age. Parental language and expectations that are not attuned to the child's developmental level are likely to contribute to high levels of noncompliance and frustration.

2. *Behavior problems in the context of developmental disorder, particularly autism spectrum disorders.* Clinical indications that behaviors reflect an underlying autism spectrum disorder include (a) aggression that seems designed to protect against intrusions on the child's world rather than a reflection of angry or hostile intent, and behaviors that (b) reflect rigidities (e.g., insistence on doing things a certain way) and (c) are not socially directed. There is a strong social connection, albeit a negative one, in the behaviors of a child with disruptive behavior problems that is much less evident in the behaviors of a child with an autism spectrum disorder. For example, the child with a disruptive behavior disorder will often reference an adult provocatively before doing something prohibited and when the child ignores adult directives, it will seem deliberate rather than seeming that the adult is not getting through to the child.

3. *Behavior problems in the context of emotional problems.* Behavior problems secondary to emotional problems are likely to manifest primarily as irritability and negative mood. Here observations of parent-child interaction are especially useful, as such children often appear sad and withdrawn rather than disruptive. Since parents are far less likely to be attuned to the subtler signs of depression or anxiety than to annoying behaviors, problems in emotional functioning may not be initially reported and often require further probing to bring them to light.

4. *Behavior problems in the context of inattention and hyperactivity.* Many children with disruptive behavior problems also have problems with inattention and hyperactivity. For children with clinically significant attentional problems, it is important for the clinician to explore whether the disruptive behavior is primarily a result of impulsivity or distractibility or whether it has socially directed, intentional elements of the disruptive behavior above and beyond this.

Parent-Child Relationship Problems

Observations of parent-child interactions with disruptive preschoolers often reveal harsh, helpless, or reactive parenting styles. At times, this parental behavior is in response to feelings of helplessness in the face of the child's behavior; at other times, it reflects a longstanding pattern of problematic parenting. The notion that behavior problems in young children reflect a relationship disturbance rather than an individual clinical problem has been suggested (Anders, 1989). Our own view is that if a child has fundamental problems in regulating his or her behavior within a social context that are pervasive and impairing *and* such behaviors are discrepant from age-expected capacities for behavior and social functioning, this represents disordered behavior for the child (Keenan & Wakschlag, 2002a). This does not detract from the importance of understanding the contribution of relational dynamics for accurate assessment, and for the development of targeted interventions, as is also true for older children (Frick, 1994).

There is, however, a subgroup of preschool children whose disruptive behavior problems are not pervasive and appear to manifest only within the context of the parent-child relationship. With such children, we often find a substantial discrepancy between parental report of severely impairing symptomatology at home (e.g., extreme and pervasive defiance) versus the absence of behavior problems during clinical assessment and by teacher report. The behavioral difficulties may or may not be exhibited in structured observational assessments of parent-child interaction in the clinic. Although this would technically be diagnosable as a DBD within the *Diagnostic and Statistical Manual of Mental Disorders*, Fourth Edition, framework (American Psychiatric Association, 1994), it is not clear to us whether such cases actually reflect a somewhat different type of clinical problem. The assessment of child behavior both within and outside of the parent-child context in the

DB-DOS is designed to begin to examine the clinical significance of disruptive behavior problems that occur within the parent-child relationship exclusively, and to examine whether such children systematically differ from children with more pervasive problems in terms of the pattern and nature of problems and competencies across the DB-DOS domains. Empirically, this question also requires longitudinal investigation to establish whether the clinical trajectory of this subgroup differs from that of preschoolers with more pervasive behavior problems.

Although parent-child relationship problems are multidimensional and complex, in broad terms we mention two basic patterns that characterize those observed within the clinical context. While we cannot determine the specific contribution of parenting to child behavior problems when these are assessed concurrently, it appears that some relational problems are a reaction to the child's disruptive behavior and others reflect more pervasive parenting dysfunction. Reactive parents may appear responsive to the child's needs and exhibit many competencies when the child is behaving well. However, when the child misbehaves or becomes distressed, reactive parents may exhibit skill deficits (either because this is an area of vulnerability for them or because the child's behavior is so challenging). Typically these include becoming helpless, having trouble generating alternative solutions with the child, feeling overwhelmed by the child's upset, and/or rapidly escalating behavior. In talking about the child's behavior, reactive parents are more likely to show a capacity for reflection and perspective on their own contribution to the child's problems than are parents with pervasive parenting difficulties. In contrast, parents who exhibit pervasive parenting dysfunction tend to exhibit problematic parenting behavior (e.g., harshness) across multiple contexts and are less likely to show fundamental capacity for responsiveness and empathy with the child. Identifying these patterns informs treatment planning, such as determining the capacity of a dyad to benefit from short-term behavioral intervention—a technique that is likely to be far more effective with the reactive than the pervasive group. As we discuss in the final section, further exploration of these issues is an important direction for future research.

Clinical Process

Techniques for managing the disruptive preschooler's behavior within the clinic context and for engaging parents as effective partners in the assessment are fundamental to the therapeutic process of evaluation (Clark, Paulson, & Conlin, 1993). We articulate below basic principles of our clinical approach to assessment of preschoolers with disruptive behavior and their families.

Behavior as Communication

Fundamental to understanding the nature of disruptive behavior and its clinical significance is getting "underneath" the behavior to identify its adaptive significance for the child. Rather than just viewing behavior as out of control, we work to deconstruct the behaviors and understand the purpose they serve for the child and the contexts in which they occur. For example, does a tantrum reflect low frustration tolerance or an attempt to control the environment? Is aggressive behavior provocative, hostile, or reactive?

We use this principle not only to guide our observations but also to "bring it into the room" over the course of the assessment, by labeling our understanding of the behavioral communication (e.g., "you get so mad when you have to wait"). While we communicate to the child that he or she is understood and we model a more adaptive means of communication, the child's response to labeling and interpreting also provides us with valuable insights into the flexibility and responsiveness of the child's behavior. In addition, very often families who are struggling with a difficult-to-manage child have trouble seeing him or her empathically and lack perspective on what underlies the behavior. Responding to the behaviors differentially and as meaningful communications during the assessment lays out the framework with which we will conceptualize the problem with the family at the conclusion of the assessment.

Striking a Balance Between Clinical Exploration and Structuring and Containing the Child's Behavior

Preschoolers presenting with disruptive behavior may be aggressive, provocative, highly dysregulated, or extremely oppositional in the clinic. Play materials may be used as a weapon, the child may openly defy the examiner during testing, and tantrums may be prolonged and intense. Consequently, one of the biggest challenges of this type of assessment is finding a way to manage the child's behavior in a manner that is clinically skillful and informative while at the same keeping the child from being inappropriate or very out of control in the clinic. This is truly an art: stepping in too quickly may prevent the clinician from learning about the range and severity of the behaviors as well as the child's capacity for self-regulation, whereas allowing the child to engage in excessive and highly inappropriate behavior (e.g., cursing at the examiner) does not provide an environment that feels safe or therapeutic for parent or child.

In the PBC, we approach this issue flexibly but with a clear understanding that the clinician, not the child, is in control of the session. We avoid imposing too much structure at the outset but gradually increase structure to support more regulated behavior if a child begins to escalate or lose control. There is a very active and deliberate use of the self (e.g., rapid pacing, high level of animation) to keep the child positively engaged. But there is also a conscious reduction of these supports over the course of the evaluation in order to test the limits of the behavior and to learn what the child requires to function well. Limits are paired with labeling and reflection. For example, when a child curses at the clinician, a response might be, "I know you are mad, but we don't use those words here," followed by a prompt such as, "You need to say 'I am mad' or 'I don't want to clean up.'" The tone used is firm but calm—with the goal of containing and modeling alternatives, while not responding in the angry, escalated manner that such behaviors typically elicit.

Building Bridges: Intergenerational Legacies and Helping Parents Join in the Process

Developing an empathic understanding of the roots of child and parent behavior and talking to parents in a way that they can "hear" is essential to a meaningful assessment of the child's behavior in context. It also provides the clinician with

a meaningful language with which to convey his or her understanding of the ways in which the parent's own history and struggles may contribute to the child's behavior problems. Sensitivity to these issues is enormously helpful in helping the parent gain an understanding of this dynamic without eliciting feelings of guilt or inadequacy.

Since many parents feel hopeless and helpless, the clinician must also strike a balance between modeling and taking over (thus further increasing the parents' sense of ineffectiveness). Combining modeling, reflection, and guidance during the assessment provides valuable information about parents' capacity for behavioral change but also helps parents to begin to feel that what they do affects how the child behaves—which will serve as a cornerstone in treatment planning discussions focused on changing the child's behavior via changing environmental contingencies.

CONCLUSION AND IMPLICATIONS FOR FUTURE RESEARCH AND PRACTICE

Although the methods necessary to conduct epidemiological studies to provide prevalence estimates on disruptive behavior disorders in preschoolers are still in the validation stages, the public health significance of this mental health issue is evident from the relatively high rates of parent-reported problems in this age group. With 9 to 25% of parents reporting behavioral concerns in epidemiological studies (Campbell, 2002), disruptive behavior is the most common reason for referral of preschoolers to mental health clinics, and a substantial number of youths with DBDs are reported to have onset in the preschool years (Keenan & Wakschlag, 2000). While it is increasingly clear that clinically significant disruptive behaviors can be reliably identified in preschoolers (Keenan & Wakschlag, 2002a), making such a diagnosis is complex and requires a thoughtful, multimethod approach that is firmly grounded in knowledge of normative development. Continuing efforts to develop standardized methods that distinguish normative from problematic behavior for this age group are vitally important to providing clinicians and researchers with a standard metric for clinical decision making.

Whether oppositional and conduct symptoms in preschoolers are functionally equivalent to these symptoms in older children requires further longitudinal investigation, a primary aim of the Chicago Preschool Project. But while this nosological issue remains in question, there can be little doubt that disruptive behaviors that burden families, prevent young children from engaging in activities of daily living, and interfere with the acquisition of the behavioral and social skills fundamental to development represent a serious clinical problem. From our perspective, resistance to using disruptive behavior diagnoses in young children as a means of avoiding the stigma of labeling, while perhaps well-intentioned, is actually detrimental to, rather than protective of, the mental health and well-being of young children and their families. It is unfortunate that many families and children who are struggling mightily with these problems are told by pediatricians and mental health clinicians that they should wait until the child is in elementary school because accurate clinical assessment is not possible during the preschool period. This approach is also contrary to fundamental beliefs in the critical influence of children's experience in the first few years of life on pathways to adaptation and psychopathology. Recognizing early identification of such problems as an opportunity for early intervention and prevention will enable us to draw on the rich traditions of infant mental health and developmental psychopathology to improve the lives of children and families.

ACKNOWLEDGMENTS   The writing of this chapter was supported in part by grant support to Lauren Wakschlag from the National Institute of Drug Abuse (1 K08 DA00330) and the National Institute of Mental Health (1 R01 MH62437–01), and grants from the Walden and Jean Young Shaw Foundation and the Irving B. Harris Center for Developmental Studies to the Department of Psychiatry. A seed grant from the Robert Wood Johnson foundation to Zero to Three National Center for Infants, Toddlers, and Families provided support for the development of the DB-DOS. We gratefully acknowledge critical review on earlier drafts of this manuscript by Kate Keenan and Bennett Leventhal. This work has also been profoundly influenced by ongoing collaboration with our colleagues in the Section of Child and Adolescent Psychiatry. Kate Keenan is an integral partner in our work on preschool disruptive behavior disorders. The rigor and clarity of her thinking are reflected throughout our work. Bennett Leventhal's passion for translating clinical thinking into testable scientific questions continually inspires and challenges us to expand the boundaries of our thinking. His generous and steadfast support for the work of PBC has been vital to the realization of our scientific mission. Chaya Roth set the stage for this work through the development of a theoretical framework that conceptualizes clinical observations of young children within a life-span context. Finally, we thank our students for caring enough to ask the hard questions and the children and families of PBC for teaching us so eloquently that their struggles cannot wait.

Notes

1. Although historically attention deficit/hyperactivity disorder (ADHD) has been included within the broader rubric of behavior problems, *DSM-IV* differentiates disruptive behavior disorders (DBDs, i.e., oppositional and conduct) from attentional problems. This distinction is supported by research showing different correlates, developmental pathways, and comorbidities (Hinshaw, Lahey, & Hart, 1993). The DBDs are of special interest from an infant mental health perspective because, in contrast to ADHD, they are fundamentally social in nature (e.g., defiance, aggression toward others) and problems in the parent-child relationship appear to play an etiological role, which is not the case for ADHD (Frick, 1994; Shaw & Bell, 1993; Wakschlag & Hans, 1999). Although many of the principles delineated here are also relevant to the assessment of early attentional problems, our primary focus is on oppositional and conduct problems.

2. We refer to children ages 18–35 months as toddlers and children aged 3–5½ years as preschoolers. Although, relative to other age groupings of children (e.g., school age, 6–12 years), this is a rather narrow age range within which to be making developmental distinctions, we believe such a distinction is warranted because differences in the developmental capacities of preschoolers versus toddlers are substantial and have direct implications for the assessment of clinical problems. Of particu-

lar relevance here is the substantially more advanced capacity for behavioral control, internalization of rules, and linguistic skill of the preschool-age child relative to the toddler. These developmental differences make it possible to conceptualize behavior disorder in preschoolers, whereas the far more limited capacities of the toddler make it difficult to do so. This is not to say that atypical behavior cannot be identified in toddlers. For example, multiple prolonged tantrums in a 2-year-old are not normative. Rather, the distinction lies in our capacity to infer from these behaviors that they represent a behavior disorder per se, which is not possible to do when the behaviors of relevance rest on skills that may not even have been acquired (e.g., defiance requires understanding of what is being asked). As such, our discussion focuses primarily on preschool-age children.

3. In assessing relationship of maternal psychiatric history to child disruptive behavior, we have found it very clinically informative to include interviewing about maternal history of conduct problems, a domain often overlooked in clinical interviews about maternal history. The utility of this information lies not only in the identification of increased familial risk but also the identification of maternal problems in behavioral regulation, which often has direct implications for a mother's capacity to help a child learn how to modulate his or her own behavior.

4. We highlight here clinical indications and avenues for exploration based on the child's presentation. Clearly, additional comprehensive evaluation specifically designed to assess these alternative problems or disorders must be conducted to make a definitive diagnosis.

References

Abidin, R. (1995). *Parenting stress index manual* (3rd ed.). Odessa, FL: Psychological Assessment Resources, Inc.

Achenbach, T. M. (1991). *Manual for the child behavior checklist/4–18 and 1991 profile.* Burlington, VT: University of Vermont, Department of Psychiatry.

Achenbach, T. M., & Edelbrock, C. S. (1983). *Manual for the child behavior checklist and revised child behavior profile.* Burlington, VT: University of Vermont, Department of Psychiatry.

American Psychiatric Association. (1994). *Diagnostic and statistical manual of mental disorders* (4th ed.). Washington, DC: Author.

Anders, T. (1989). Clinical syndromes, relationship disturbances and their assessment. In A. Sameroff & R. Emde (Eds.), *Relationship disturbances in early childhood: A developmental approach* (pp. 125–145). New York: Basic Books.

Barnard, K., Magyary, D., Sumner, G., Booth, C., Mitchell, S., & Spieker, S. (1988). Prevention of parenting alterations for women with low social support. *Psychiatry, 51,* 248–253.

Behar, L. (1977). The preschool behavior problem questionnaire. *Journal of Abnormal Child Psychology, 5,* 265–275.

Berlin, L. J., Brooks-Gunn, J., Spiker, D., & Zaslow, M. J. (1995). Examining observational measures of emotional support and cognitive stimulation in black and white mothers of preschoolers. *Journal of Family Issues, 16,* 664–686.

Campbell S. (2002). *Behavior problems in preschool children: Clinical and developmental issues* (2nd ed.). New York: Guilford Press.

Campbell, S., Pierce, E., March, C., Ewing, L., & Szumowski, E. (1994). Hard-to-manage preschool boys: Symptomatic behavior across contexts and time. *Child Development, 65,* 836–851.

Carter, A. (2002). Assessing social-emotional and behavior problems and competencies in infancy and toddlerhood: Available instruments and directions for application. In N. A. Fox, B. Zuckerman, & A. Lieberman (Eds.), *Socioemotional regulation: Dimensions, developmental trends, and influences* (pp. 277–299). New York: Johnson and Johnson Pediatric Institute.

Carter, A., Briggs-Gowan, S., Jones, S., & Little, T. (in press). The Infant-Toddler Social and Emotional Assessment (ITSEA): Factor structure, reliability, and validity. *Journal of Abnormal Psychology.*

Cicchetti, D., & Aber, J. L. (1998). Contextualism and developmental psychopathology. *Development and Psychopathology, 10,* 137–142.

Clark, R., Paulson, A., & Conlin, S. (1993). Assessment of developmental status and parent-infant relationships: The therapeutic process of evaluation. In C. Zeanah (Ed.), *Handbook of infant mental health* (pp. 191–209). New York: Guilford Press.

Crockenberg, S., & Litman, C. (1990). Autonomy as competence in 2 year olds: Maternal correlates of child defiance, compliance, and self assertion. *Developmental Psychology, 26,* 961–971.

Drabick, D., Strassberg, Z., & Kees, M. (2001).

Measuring qualitative aspects of preschool boys' noncompliance: The response style questionnaire (RSQ). *Journal of Abnormal Child Psychology*, 29(2), 129–140.

Elliot, C. (1983). *Differential abilities scale–preschool version*. New York: Psychological Corporation.

Eyberg, S. M., & Ross, A. W. (1978). Assessment of child behavior problems: The validation of a new inventory. *Journal of Clinical Child Psychology*, 113–116.

Frick, P. (1994). Family dysfunction and the disruptive behavior disorders: A review of recent empirical findings. In T. Ollendick & R. Prinz (Eds.), *Advances in clinical child psychology* (Vol. 16, pp. 203–226). New York: Plenum.

Gadow, K., & Sprafkin, J. (1996). *Early childhood inventories (ECI) manual*. Stony Brook, NY: Checkmate Plus.

Greenberg, M. T., Speltz, M. L., DeKlyen, M., & Jones, K. (2001). Correlates of clinic referral for early conduct problems: Variable- and person-oriented approaches. *Development and Psychopathology*, 13(2), 255–276.

Greenberger, E., O'Neil, R., & Nagel, S. (1994). Linking workplace and homeplace: Relations between the nature of adults' work and their parenting behaviors. *Developmental Psychology*, 30, 990–1002.

Hill, C., Keenan, K., Davis, B., & Wakschlag, L. (2003, August). *The use of clinical observation in the assessment of behavior in preschool children*. Paper presented at the meetings of the American Psychological Association. Toronto, Ontario, Canada.

Hinshaw, S. P., Lahey, B. B., & Hart, E. L. (1993). Issues of taxonomy and comorbidity in the development of conduct disorder. *Development and Psychopathology*, 5, 31–50.

Keenan, K., & Wakschlag, L. (2000). More than the terrible twos: The nature and severity of behavior problems in clinic-referred preschool children. *Journal of Abnormal Child Psychology*, 28, 33–46.

Keenan, K., & Wakschlag, L. (2002a). Can a valid diagnosis of disruptive behavior disorder be made in preschool children? *American Journal of Psychiatry*, 59, 351–358.

Keenan, K., & Wakschlag, L. (2002b). *Kiddie disruptive behavior disorders schedule for preschool children (K-DBDS)*. Unpublished manuscript, University of Chicago.

Klinger, P., & Renner, P. (2000). Performance based measures in autism: Implications for diagnosis, early detection and identification of cognitive profiles. *Journal of Clinical Child Psychology*, 29, 479–492.

Kochanska, G., & Aksan, N. (1995). Mother-child mutual positive affect, the quality of child compliance to requests and prohibitions, and maternal control as correlates of early internalization. *Child Development*, 66, 236–254.

Lahey, B. B., Pelham, W. E., Stein, M. A., Loney, J., Trapani, C., Nugent, K., Kipp, H., Schmidt, E., Lee, S., Cale, M., Gold, E., Hartung, C. M., Willcutt, E., & Baumann, B. (1998). Validity of DSM-IV attention-deficit/hyperactivity disorder for younger children. *Journal of the American Academy of Child and Adolescent Psychiatry*, 37(7), 695–702.

Lavigne, J., Arend, R., Rosenbaum, D., Binns, H., Christoffel, K., & Gibbons, R. (1998). Psychiatric disorders with onset in the preschool years. I. Stability of diagnoses. *Journal of the American Academy of Child and Adolescent Psychiatry*, 37, 1246–1254.

Le Freniere, P., & Dumas, J. (1995). *Social competence and behavior evaluation (SCBE)–Preschool edition*. Los Angeles: Western Psychological Services.

Lord, C., Risi, S., Lambrecht, L., Cook, E., Leventhal, B., DiLavore, P., Pickles, A., & Rutter, M. (2000). The Autism Diagnostic Observation Schedule–Generic: A standard measure of social and communication deficits associated with the spectrum of autism. *Journal of Autism and Developmental Disorders*, 30, 205–223.

Luby, J., & Morgan, K. (1997). Characteristics of an infant/preschool psychiatric clinic sample: Implications for clinical assessment and nosology. *Infant Mental Health Journal*, 18, 209–220.

Lyons-Ruth, K., Zoll, D., Connell, D., & Grunebaum, H. (1989). Family deviance and family disruption in childhood: Associations with maternal behavior and infant maltreatment during the first two years of life. *Development and Psychopathology*, 1, 219–236.

McGuire, J., & Earls, F. (1993). Exploring the reliability of measures of family relations, parental attitudes, and parent-child relations in a disadvantaged minority population. *Journal of Marriage and the Family*, 55, 1042–1046.

Sameroff, A., Lewis, M., & Miller, S. (Eds.). (2000). *Handbook of developmental psychopathology*. New York: Kluwer.

Shaffer, D., Gould, M., Brasic, J., Ambrosini, P.,

Fisher, P., Bird, H., & Aluwahlia, S. (1983). A Children's Global Assessment Scale (CGAS). *Archives of General Psychiatry, 4*, 1228–1231.

Shaw, D., & Bell, R. (1993). Developmental theories of parental contributors to antisocial behavior. *Journal of Abnormal Child Psychology, 21*, 493–518.

Shaw, D., Gilliom, M., & Giovannelli, J. (2000). Aggressive behavior disorders. In C. Zeanah (Ed.), *Handbook of infant mental health* (2nd ed., pp. 397–411). New York: Guilford Press.

Silk, J., Nath, S., Siegel, L., & Kendall, P. (2000). Conceptualizing mental disorders in children: Where have we been and where are we going? *Development and Psychopathology, 12*, 713–735.

Silverman, W. (Ed.). (1999). Special section: Importance of incorporating developmental theory into clinical child training. *Journal of Clinical Child Psychology, 28*, 426–489.

Spitzer, R., & Endicott, J. (1978). *Schedule for affective disorders and schizophrenia.* New York: New York State Psychiatric Institute.

Spitzer, R., Williams, J., & Gibbon, M. (1987). *Structured clinical interview for DSM-III-R nonpatient version.* New York: New York State Psychiatric Institute.

Sroufe, A. L. (1997). Psychopathology as outcome of development. *Development and Psychopathology, 9*, 251–268.

Thomas, J., & Guskin, K. (2001). Disruptive behavior in young children: What does it mean? *Journal of the American Academy of Child and Adolescent Psychiatry, 40*, 44–51.

Tremblay, R. (2000). The development of aggressive behavior during childhood: What have we learned in the past century? *International Journal of Behavioral Development, 24*, 129–134.

Wakschlag, L., & Hans, S. (1999). Relation of maternal responsiveness during infancy to the development of behavior problems in high risk youths. *Developmental Psychology, 37*, 569–579.

Wakschlag, L., & Keenan, K. (2001). Clinical significance and correlates of disruptive behavior symptoms in environmentally at-risk preschoolers. *Journal of Clinical Child Psychology, 30*, 262–275.

Wakschlag, L., Leventhal, B., Briggs-Gowan, M., Danis, B., Hill, C., Keenan, K., Egger, E., Cicchetti, D., & Carter, A. (2003). *What makes preschool behavior disruptive: A conceptual framework and preliminary validation of the Disruptive Behavior Diagnostic Observation Schedule (DB-DOS).* Manuscript submitted for publication.

Wakschlag, L., Leventhal, B., Danis, B., Keenan, K., Egger, H., & Carter, A. (2002). *The disruptive behavior diagnostic observation schedule (DB-DOS), Version 1.1.* Unpublished manuscript, University of Chicago.

Webster-Stratton, C. (2002). *Evaluation tools for classroom observation.* Available: http://www.son.washington.edu/centers/parenting-clinic.

Webster-Stratton, C., & Lindsay, D. (1999). Social competence and conduct problems in young children: Issues in assessment. *Journal of Clinical Child Psychology, 28*, 25–43.

Wenar, C. (1982). On negativism. *Human Development, 25*, 1–23.

Zeanah, C. (Ed.). (2000). *Handbook of infant mental health* (2nd ed). New York: Guilford Press.

Zeanah, C., Boris, N., & Scheeringa, M. (1997). Psychopathology in infancy. *Journal of Child Psychology, Psychiatry and Allied Disciplines, 38*, 81–99.

VII

VARIED APPLIED SETTINGS FOR ASSESSMENT

It has been suggested that to improve validity, assessment must be conducted within and across the various settings in which children develop. Yet ways of collecting and integrating assessment information from community settings such as the primary care office, the community mental health clinic, and the day care center or preschool are not well developed. In addition, as we learned in chapter 20, assessing in multiple settings often presents unique challenges with young children because many young children do not yet attend school (i.e., most of their time is spent with a primary caregiver at home). In this section, the authors discuss measurement issues across various applied settings for young children and provide important research and clinical recommendations.

Ruth Feldman and Miri Keren present a community-based model of mental health assessment that incorporates a strong program of research. The chapter provides an illustrative example of comprehensive, multilayered assessment in an applied community setting that incorporates the DC:0–3 diagnostic system. The authors review the theoretical background of a community-based

perspective for infant mental health assessment, suggesting that the target for assessment be not only the individual, including his or her adaptation, change over time, and caregiving environment, but also the entire community. Their work is based on extensive experience in establishing and operating a community-based infant mental health clinic in Israel. Assessment is conducted in both the home (for example, observations are conducted in the home of the mother and child in free play or in a feeding session) and the clinic. The clinic now serves as an exemplary training center for several new infant mental health centers across that country. To advance the thinking in this field, they identify the chasm between the medical-psychiatric tradition, which calls for discrete categories or "disorders," and developmental science, which deals with phenomena measured on a continuum. They suggest that the community-based model calls for the integration of the medical and developmental approaches within a developmental framework. Such integration, for example, would utilize continuous developmental information to reach and verify a final discrete categorical diagnosis. The authors also recommend a focus on prevention, awareness work, and understanding of the normative processes of child adaptation in relation to dysfunction. While their setting is unique in that it utilizes a well-established well-baby system not currently available in this country (including home visits), their work may pave the way for broadening assessment of infants and young children to meaningful community settings.

In contrast to this well-established system of care for infants, Lynne Huffman and Mary Nichols describe the challenges in addressing the need for more systematic mental health care screening in primary care settings in this country. While it has been acknowledged that primary care physicians may hold great influence in the early identification and referral of young children with behavioral problems, this potential is still unrealized. The authors provide a table that summarizes screening instruments that may be used in the primary care setting. They identify the challenges for mental health screening in the primary care setting. They also note strategies that can facilitate the screening and early identification of young children's behavioral problems in primary care settings. Finally, the authors provide recommendations for both service utilization and directions for future research.

Lisa McCabe, Pia Rebello-Britto, Magdalena Hernandez, and Jeanne Brooks-Gunn describe work in assessing self-regulation in infants and pre-schoolers across varied ecological settings. Drawing on data collected in community-based projects such as the Early Head Start Research and Evaluation Program, the authors discuss challenges such as the standardization and meaning of measures across settings. They suggest that researchers and clinicians pay greater attention to environmental issues such as socioeconomic factors (e.g., the presence of certain technologies or toys) that may confound conclusions concerning areas of functioning (e.g., delay of gratification) and compromise validity of findings. Despite these challenges, the authors conclude that assessment conducted across multiple settings at multiple levels provides the richest picture of individual-environment transactions over time.

The authors in this section all attempt to expand the scope of assessment to meaningful, community-based settings in order to both increase service utilization and to increase validity of assessment. It has been suggested by the authors in this section that community settings, such as the pediatrician's office or the preschool, hold great promise for early identification and referral of young children with behavioral problems. Not surprisingly, the authors also stress the importance of understanding the sociocultural and economic influences on the reliability and validity of infant, toddler, and preschool mental health assessment procedures.

22

Expanding the Scope of Infant Mental Health Assessment: A Community-Based Model

Ruth Feldman
Miri Keren

When clinical theory is first applied to a new patient population, the encounter leads to the enrichment of both theory and technique (Stern, 1995). The recent application of clinical theory to the population of infants and toddlers, who have not been traditional consumers of mental health services, and the attempt to construct systems for evaluating the preverbal child have opened new theoretical and practical vistas. This new infant-toddler population has not only stimulated the development of innovative assessment tools; the encounter between the clinical setting and the infant patient has added important dimensions to general theory and practice. Such contributions include consideration of the nonverbal components in the patient-therapist exchange, or the focus on dyadic, systemic, or multilevel perspectives on the development of the self (Beebe & Lachman, 1994; Sander, 1987; Stern et al., 1998). Thus, the psychological assessment of infants and young children, itself an emerging field of inquiry, may open new insights into the origins of the self and the study of psychopathology.

Assessment constitutes the process that most reflects the mental health practitioner's philosophy of health and pathology, as it requires a clear definition of deviant behavior from a range of related behavior. In this chapter, we present a community-based model of infant mental health assessment that is consistent with our philosophy on the interconnectedness of the infant and the larger social context. The chapter is divided into three main sections. The first section provides the theoretical background of the community-based model. It begins by discussing (1) adaptation, (2) the caregiving context, and (3) focus on change over time, issues that we consider central to infant mental health assessment. Next, we discuss the need for expanding the *context* of infant assessment to the entire community and for expanding the *scope* of the assessment process to a comprehensive multilevel evaluation. The theoretical section concludes by addressing the integration of the medical and developmental perspectives into a unitary model. The second section presents the application of the model at our community-based infant mental health clinic. Consistent with the theoretical propositions, we address both the community work aimed at sensitizing parents and professionals to the psychological needs of infants (context) and the specific evaluation tools used for our multilevel assessment (scope). The final section presents a case study that describes the process of assessment as it unfolds at the clinic and highlights the usefulness of a community-based evaluation in gaining understanding of the child's symptoms and in planning effective intervention.

The community-based model is based on our experience in establishing and operating a community-based infant mental health clinic in a middle-size Israeli town (Petah-Tikva). This clinic now serves as a training center for several new infant mental health centers across the country modeled after the same approach. The community centers, which target the detection, assessment, and treatment of infants and their families, hold a community-based philosophy and their goal is reaching the broadest possible ecological context—the entire community.

THEORETICAL BACKGROUND OF A COMMUNITY-BASED MODEL

The community-based approach reflects the position that emotional disorders in infancy should be examined in relation to three central topics. First, we consider the main focus of the assessment process to be the level of infant adaptation to the age-appropriate demands of the environment. Second, as child adaptation evolves within the context of early relationships, the caregiving environment needs to be specifically and broadly evaluated. Specificity relates to the specific conditions under which maladaptive behavior appears (e.g., only during feeding). Broad assessment refers to different manifestations of maladaptive patterns in different contexts (child noncompliance at home versus at nursery school). Third, assessment should be carried out from a developmental perspective that takes into account normative developmental processes and examines the child and family's propensity for change, in addition to providing a comprehensive picture of the present state. We use evaluation tools, observational techniques, and theoretical perspectives borrowed from the fields of developmental psychology and psychopathology, infant psychiatry, and child

psychoanalysis—each of which provides a different interpretation of observed data. These topics—the focus on adaptation, the attention to person in context, and the consideration of the degree of malleability in addition to current symptomatology—may offer important contributions from the field of infant assessment to the general process of psychological evaluation for children and adults.

Adaptation

Adaptation is a construct that has been emphasized in various fields from evolutionary psychology (Bjorklund & Pellegrini, 2000) to cognitive epistemology (Piaget, 1952) to social-emotional development (Sander, 1987). In each field, adaptation denotes maturity and appropriate functioning and highlights the fit of the infant and the environment as an index of well-being. In the area of emotional development, a closely related construct—regulation—has gained increasing theoretical and empirical attention (Calkins & Fox, 2002). Regulation addresses the infant's ability to organize physiological, cognitive, social, and emotional processes in order to respond to the age-appropriate demands of the social and nonsocial environment. Perhaps a slight distinction between the two constructs is the emphasis in *regulation* on the self-organization of various internal systems as a precondition for functioning, whereas *adaptation* is more closely related to actual performance. Schore (2001) suggested that regulation is the construct that defines the field of infant mental health, as it indicates the child's capacity to manage developmental demands. Along these lines, our approach considers the child's adaptation to different persons, situations, contexts, and skills as the hallmark of the assessment process.

Caregiving Context

The embedded nature of child adaptive functioning is never as obvious as it is during infancy, when the dependence of the infant on the caregiver is nearly absolute. Whether or not one agrees with Winnicott's (1965) statement that "there is no such thing as an infant without mother and mother care" (p. 233), assessing an infant's own disorder apart from disordered relationships and disturbed environments is an issue of continuous debate (Emde & Sameroff, 1989). As a central component of the assessment process, therefore, it is necessary to define the caregiving context. At our community-based center, infants are observed with the primary caretaker—typically the mother—in various settings (home, laboratory, playground, pediatric clinic), during routine daily activities (play, feeding), and in several structured tasks and interactions. Mother and child are evaluated both as a dyad and within the family context. Further, because the parent's behavior and mental representations of the infant are separate but equally important components of the caregiving context (Stern, 1995), the evaluation includes both parental behavior and mental representations. Finally, the assessment addresses the several cycles of ecology (Bronfenbrenner, 1986): the parent-infant dyad, the family, the community, and the larger context of cultural values, child-rearing philosophies, and norms of proper social conduct, against which deviant behavior is measured.

Change Over Time

Apart from the focus on child adaptation within the caregiving matrix, deviant infant behavior must be evaluated in relation to normative developmental processes, as infants are the most rapidly changing human beings. Psychopathology in the first years of life cannot be assessed, understood, or treated without considering the typical developmental course (Cicchetti & Cohen, 1995; Sroufe & Rutter, 1984). Nearly all infants exhibit signs of emotional distress in infancy, and whether a specific behavior sufficiently disrupts the developmental process to merit intervention is a question that must be evaluated in relation to the dynamic nature of development at this stage. Although the central argument in favor of early assessment is the consistency of behavior over time and the tendency of early emotional disturbances to persist into later childhood and adolescence, researchers have questioned whether consistency or change characterizes the typical course of early social-emotional development (Emde, 1994). Assessment processes, therefore, should be developmentally sensitive—attentive to newly emerging

abilities and to critical periods in the development of certain skills—and at the same time find new techniques to evaluate the child's and family's propensity for change. It is important to consider not only the malleability of behavior in general but, consistent with the goal of specificity, the specific behaviors that improve following intervention and the domains in which disturbed patterns tend to persist. The application of dynamic systems thinking to the study of early social-emotional development is illuminating in this context (Fogel, 1993). This perspective considers the dyadic system as a single functional unit, focuses on the self-organizational and adaptive properties of the system, and attempts to quantify its change over time. In the evaluation process, important questions to consider include whether the presenting symptom has changed its expression over time, how different behaviors in diverse contexts cohere into a unified symptom constellation, and how resistant these behaviors are to positive change.

Expanding the Context of Infant
Mental Health Assessment

Apart from the diagnosis of disorders, the community-based model emphasizes teaching, prevention, and awareness work on the topic of infant mental health. The assessment process is not limited to the microsystem but aims to affect the macrosystem of the child's ecology by increasing public awareness and changing social policies. Consistent with the "person-in-context" ecological perspective (Cicchetti & Aber, 1998; Sameroff, 1997), we consider the embedded nature of infant development, and address the child's disposition, the parenting style, family structure, and cultural milieu as important determinants in the development of health and pathology. To date, the application of the person-in-context perspective in infant mental health has been mainly limited to mother-child relations, and few clinicians have gone beyond the dyad. Little effort has been directed to include the broader social context, such as day care settings or pediatric clinics, as a routine part of the assessment process or as partners for a dialogue on issues of infant mental health. The goal of the community-based model is to involve the entire community in the concern for infants through raising public awareness of mental health concerns. Awareness is viewed initially as an assessment issue, directed at sensitizing professionals who come in immediate contact with infants, such as nurses, pediatricians, and care providers, to the early manifestations of emotional distress. Awareness work continues with providing information to the general public on the types of child behaviors that should raise parental concern. Assessment viewed from this broad perspective also removes infant mental health from its exclusive reliance on a medical model and on the diagnosis of disease and affords a broader view on the entire range of maladaptive symptoms—normal and pathological—typical of this age range.

In addition, our approach calls for the integration of empirical tools into the clinical process. By using developmental research methods, such as videotaped interactions, self-report measures, interviews, and formal developmental instruments, clinicians can gain a more comprehensive picture of the infant, the family, the relationship context, and the child's adaptation strategies. The infant mental health clinic is closely connected with a university developmental laboratory, and the clinical and empirical approach are assimilated into a unified model.

Expanding the Scope of the Assessment Process

The community-based approach proposes an expansion of the scope of assessment by evaluating a wide range of behaviors and skills. Assessment is a multidimensional process (Cicchetti & Cohen, 1995); thus, our model of assessment includes behaviors and mental representations, reactions to relaxed as well as stressful situations, formal tasks and informal dialogues, and concrete behaviors in addition to global interactive styles. Such a definition echoes Stern's (1995) notion of the "ports of entry." As social-emotional disorders in infancy are multilevel conditions, consisting of child liabilities, parental psychological profiles, and family patterns, clinicians must attempt a variety of entry points into the representational and behavioral meaning of the symptom for the infant and the family, in order to define the best roads for intervention.

In addition, cultural settings and customs need to be considered in the assessment process (for further discussion, see chapter 2). A behavior that constitutes a problem in the regulation of a basic function may be, to some extent, culturally defined. For instance, the regularity with which the child eats may be considered more or less normative in different cultures, as will more or less aggressive behavior. However, when infants are referred to a mental health clinic for maladaptive behavior, this is often preceded by the parents' struggle to resolve the problem on their own, by feelings of helplessness, shame, and distress, and by negative cycles of parent-child interactions, regardless of the cultural context. Such feelings often affect the parent-child and family relationships and hamper the child's social-emotional growth; thus the underlying feelings of incompetence and struggle may be universal regardless of the cultural specificity of the particular behavioral expression. Cultural belief systems also dictate how parents perceive the referral, assessment, and proposed treatment in mental health clinics, and should thus be considered prior to devising the treatment plan.

Integrating the Medical and Developmental Traditions Into a Comprehensive Assessment

While attempting to establish a unified framework for the psychological assessment of infants, the field needs to integrate two opposing traditions—the medical-psychiatric tradition and the tradition of developmental science. The medical tradition calls for discrete categories, a clear distinction between healthy and pathological states, and a conceptualization of abnormal processes in terms of disorders. Assessment in the medical tradition involves diagnosing individuals with specific disorders, defining clinical and subclinical thresholds, and aiming to detect groups at risk for various disorders. The final assessment typically appears in the form of a single heading and may rely on formal standardized assessment tools, often in combination with the clinician's impressions. The clinician often reaches categorical judgments on the basis of a long tradition of clinical practice and reported case histories. From a scientific viewpoint, although clinical case reports may or may not have the same empirical validity as larger scale research—depending on the researcher's outlook—they have been instrumental in theory construction. In particular, case descriptions have been central to the assessment process in terms of the fine-tuning of existing classifications, the definition of new syndromes, and the substantiation of differential diagnoses.

Developmental science, on the other hand, has emerged from a different scientific tradition. It deals with developmentally relevant phenomena that are often measured on a continuum. Empirical attention is paid to the amount and quality of behaviors, their appropriateness to infant age, and their correlates. The study of social-emotional development often relies on observations in various tasks and settings, during daily interactions between the infant and his or her significant others. Most important to the topic of mental health assessment is the fact that developmental science does not focus on disorders but rather on the understanding of normative behavior patterns, their developmental course, and their differential expressions at various ages and contexts. This viewpoint, therefore, lends a normative, spectrum-like perspective to the assessment of observed and reported behavior, placing child and communicative parent-child actions within a developmental meaning system rather than within a framework of illness and its remedy. In an attempt to construct a psychology of positive emotional experience, leading personality researchers critically noted that psychology has drifted along a medical line, focusing most of its effort on malfunction and negative experiences, and paying less attention to the assessment of healthy, growth-promoting experiences (Seligman & Csikszentmihalyi, 2000). Models on assessments of adaptive functioning should thus afford a better understanding of adaptation, predictors and concomitants of resilience, and the role of cultural values and extrafamilial relationships in promoting mental health.

Kagan (1989) suggested that the decision whether to use a categorical or continuum approach to data collection is the scientist's choice, often reflecting the specific research framework of the observer. The complex task of evaluating the largely preverbal infant from a person-in-context perspective may benefit from the integration of these two traditions. In the medical tradi-

tion, infant assessment can benefit from a differential, multiaxial diagnosis, from the epidemiological description of specific risk groups for various disorders, and from the attempt to devise treatment with measurable outcomes. Categorical assessment may be enhanced by multidimensional developmental information. Such information may include different levels of data collection (behaviors, representations), multiple informants, various contexts, and several settings that may provide convergent evidence on child adaptation and on the caregiving context.

The community-based model calls for the integration of the medical and developmental approaches within a comprehensive framework. Most important, such integration implies the ability to wear two types of lenses concurrently while looking at observed information. Categorical diagnostic evaluations are often necessary for practical purposes: They are typically required by health care agencies, serve as the basis for treatment, and sharpen the distinction between sets of maladaptive behaviors. In line with the medical-psychiatric tradition, a categorical classification is reached at the end of the assessment process. In the community-based clinic, the integration of the developmental perspective into the medical framework involves the use of developmental information to reach and verify a final diagnosis, as well as the focus on normative processes, prevention, and awareness work as part of the dialogue on infant mental health.

Four dimensions of infant mental health assessment are examined. (a) The parent-child relational profile provides a multidimensional assessment of the parent-child relationship. (b) The child's social-emotional adaptation profile provides a multidimensional evaluation of child adaptation to developmental demands. These two dimensions aim to create a comprehensive picture of the parent-child communicative system and the child's adaptive functioning in various domains. (c) Correlates of the child's adaptive functioning provide a broader person-in-context assessment. In our model, correlates include family factors (family functioning and interactive patterns), child factors (child temperament and developmental level), maternal factors (maternal psychopathology, history, and support), and the sociocultural context. (d) The diagnosis is formulated in nosological terms: In the final stage, data from coded sessions, observed visits, interviews, clinical summaries, and self-reports are summarized into a multiaxial psychiatric evaluation using the *Diagnostic Classification of Mental Health and Developmental Disorders of Infancy and Early Childhood* (DC:0–3) (Zero to Three, 1994).

APPLICATION OF THE COMMUNITY-BASED MODEL

Stage I: Broader Community Context

Illustrated Example: Israeli Well-Baby Care

To broaden the context of assessment to the entire community, we capitalize on the existing Israeli infant Well-Baby care system (Tipat Halav), in a collaborative project between the university's developmental laboratory, the community infant mental health clinic, and the Well-Baby stations. The development of observational tools, coding of videotapes, and data analysis are conducted at the university; clinical assessments, therapeutic work, and the ongoing relations with parents are carried out by the clinic's team; and the outreach program to the general population and the referral of at-risk dyads to the clinic are carried out by the Well-Baby stations' nurses. Graduate students in clinical psychology and child psychiatry carry out some of the clinical evaluation and data management under supervision, thus serving as a bridge between the three agencies.

The Well-Baby system is a nationwide infant care system that provides medical care and developmental follow-up to nearly all Israeli infants and their families in their immediate neighborhoods. The philosophy of the Well-Baby care system is community based: Stations are located within the community; mothers receive medical follow-up from pregnancy; and infants are followed periodically through the first 3 years of life. Most Israeli infants receive their vaccinations at the stations, and at several time points across infancy infants are evaluated for gross disturbances in motor and mental development. Contact between nurses and families is personalized. Each community nurse is assigned to a specific district and is responsible for developing long-term contact with its families, often following families from their first to last infant. The stations also afford nurses the opportunity to meet the extended family, when grandparents accompany pregnant mothers or take infants of working parents for follow-ups. Under risk conditions, for instance in the case of very young or unsupported mothers, nurses make home visits. The Well-Baby nurses are typically middle-aged women with considerable experience in raising their own children and in community work. They serve the function of the experienced women who, in every culture, assume the role of training and counseling young mothers at the sensitive postbirth period (Stern, 1995).

Training Community Nurses

Over many years of experience, community nurses developed considerable skills in spotting motor or cognitive delays, but paid little attention to early signs of emotional disorders. As a first step in establishing the first infant mental health clinic, we developed a training program for the Well-Baby nurses in the town of Petah-Tikva (including 19 stations) to sensitize nurses to signs of emotional distress in infancy. These nurses then served as the main referral source of clients for the new infant mental health center, where referred infants were diagnosed and treated. The training program focused on raising the nurses' awareness of the existence of social-emotional disturbances in infancy, directing their focus toward specific signs of risk, and pointing out potentially informative situations for infant, maternal, or relational problems. The training incorporated up-to-date knowledge of the pervasive nature and the correlates of social-emotional problems in infancy, emphasizing the importance of early detection. Nurses were instructed to attend to and ask directly about the child's predominant mood, sleep and feeding patterns, aggressive behavior, relations to family members, sibling rivalry, stranger anxiety, and adaptability to new places, foods, or activities. Common emotional problems of new mothers were mentioned, such as depression, anxiety, child abuse and neglect, and lack of social support, while delineating specific risk groups for each condition. Nurses learned to consider the mother's mood, signs of aggression toward the infant, or a gross misunderstanding of the infant's communications or developmental stage.

In addition, we discussed informal situations that are most useful for parent-child observations. For instance, nurses can observe mothers in the toy-filled waiting room, when they are not on their best behavior, and assess whether and how the mother engages the infant or responds to his or her signals. The way a mother undresses and dresses the child for a check-up, calms the infant after injections, and divides her attention between infant and nurse are also important indicators of the mother's caretaking skills. Nurses were also directed to listen for gross misperceptions in the mother's narrative (e.g., "Every time I change his diaper he dirties it. He does it on purpose to annoy me," about a 3-month-old). Such information on the infant, mother, and relationship is invaluable not only for the process of assessment but also for theory development. Winnicott's (1965) formulations on the "good enough mother" and the "facilitating environment," central to current thinking about early relationships, emerged from his keen observations in a public pediatric clinic, much like the community Well-Baby station. The specific risk signals that were discussed in the nurses' training program appear in table 22.1.

We (Keren, Feldman, & Tyano, 2001) found that the Well-Baby nurses provide valid assessment of early relational difficulties. Comparing mother-infant dyads who were referred by the nurses to our center with nonreferred dyads from the same neighborhoods, reliable differences in mother-child interaction patterns were found. Mothers of referred infants were less sensitive, warm, and consistent and provided less efficient limits and direction for their children. Referred dyads also engaged in less reciprocal play, and referred children were more negative and withdrawn and showed less social involvement.

Public Education and Lobbying

In parallel with the provision of awareness training to the nurses, we continuously work at the general public level through nationwide forums of psychiatrists, pediatricians, general practitioners, government officials, day care center workers, and psychologists. The goal of these talks is to raise awareness about infant mental health issues, discuss options for referral to infant clinics, and sensitize health professionals to social-emotional problems, thus delegating the responsibility for early detection to the entire health community. The results of such public awareness work are reflected in the number and sources of referral. Whereas at the beginning most infants were referred by the well-baby nurses, pediatricians, social workers, and adult psychiatrists currently initiate many referrals. In addition, the number of self-referrals has increased, suggesting the growing awareness among parents of early signs of social-emotional distress (Keren, Feldman, & Tyano, 2003).

The second goal of the community-based work at the general public level was to achieve a meaningful change in social policy and in the allocation of public funds to infant mental health. The success of these efforts is evident in the Ministry of Health's allocation of funds to the development of five new infant mental health centers across the country, guided by a community approach and modeled after our original center. The clinical team now also provides training to a range of professionals working with small children: child psychiatrists, social workers, and clinical and developmental psychologists—for the assessment and treatment of young children and families.

Stage II: Expanding the Scope of Infant Mental Health Assessment

As stated, the evaluation process includes four components: the parent-child relationship, the child's adaptive functioning; maternal, child, and family correlates; and the final diagnosis. In the majority of cases, most of the assessment procedures are routinely conducted, as part of a research program. When the entire assessment is not possible, there is an attempt to carry out at least one component from each dimension, often the more global assessments. A summary of the four dimensions and the specific measures used in our assessment process is presented in table 22.2. The assessment utilizes well-known assessment

Table 22.1 Observation of Caregiver-Infant Interaction at Community Well-Baby Stations

General guidelines for the observing nurse

1. The observation takes place during any routine visit of the infant to the station. One may observe the interaction in the waiting room or the office. Any routine caregiving activity, such as feeding, diaper changing, dressing, and holding are valuable opportunities for observation of the caregiver-child interaction.
2. In addition to the observation, please ask the caregiver the following specific questions:
   What are the child's sleep habits (when, where, and how)?
   What are the child's eating habits (when, where, and how)?
   To what extent is the child's father routinely involved in caregiving?
3. Please note the specific populations at risk for a maladaptive parent-infant relationship:
   a. Infant's risk factors
      Small and very small birthweight premature babies, with long hospitalization in neonatal intensive care
         unit
      Infants with congenital malformations and/or chronic medical conditions
      Difficult temperament/regulatory problems
   b Mother's risk factors
      High-risk pregnancy with difficult course
      Known emotional difficulties
      Known losses of significant figures in recent past
      Chronic physical illness
   c. Environmental risk factors
      Poverty
      Chronic marital conflict with verbal/physical aggression
      Recent immigration
      Recent grief
4. Guidelines for observation:

	Indicators of at-risk development during first year of life	Indicators of at-risk development during second and third years of life
Infant	Persistent crying	Extreme stranger anxiety
	Lack of eye contact	Extreme shyness
	Lack of smile	Aggression toward self/others
	Lack of interest	Lack of interest
	Lack of vocalizations	Sadness
	Self-induced vomiting	Irritability
	Breath-holding spells	Lack of speech
		Lack of self-control
		Self-endangerment
Mother	Looks sad/anxious/tense	Poor limit setting
	Feeds baby every time it fusses or cries	Feelings of helplessness
	Isolates herself at home with baby	Looks angry/sad/tense
	Perceives baby as difficult/bad	Lack of praising
	Poor quality of touch	
	Poor quality of talk	
	Lack of praising baby	
Dyad	Lack of mutual gaze	Control struggle
	Lack of mutual pleasure	Aggressiveness
	Lack of kisses/touch	Lack of mutual pleasure

tools and measures developed at our lab for this and other studies.

Parent-Child Relational Profile

Assessment of the parent-child relationship is conducted in two contexts: home and clinic, with several observations conducted in each setting. Interactions are coded, and the level of analysis includes both global rating scales and microanalytic codes. In addition, maternal representations are assessed during maternal interviews. Fathers also take part in the treatment process, but do so on a less regular basis. Videotaped observation of dyadic father-child interactions (except within the family assessment described below) is, unfortunately, not routinely conducted.

The home setting

Assessment in the home setting involves observation of the home environment, mother-child free play, and a mother-child feeding session.

Observation of the home environment The parent's sensitivity and discipline, environmental provision and organization, and the opportunities for age-appropriate learning are assessed via the Home Assessment for Measurement of the Environment (HOME, Caldwell & Bradley, 1978). The HOME is an hour-long observation of the child's natural environment conducted by trainees in clinical psychology, which yields scores on six scales and a total score.

Mother-child free play Mothers and infants are videotaped in a 10-minute free play session. The session is coded using the Coding Interactive Behavior (CIB; Feldman, 1998), a global coding scheme that includes 42 parent, infant, and dyadic codes summarized into six composites relating to maternal sensitivity, limit setting, intrusiveness, dyadic engagement, child involvement, and withdrawal. In the clinic-referred group, special attention is paid to the maternal sensitivity construct, considered a central element in children's social-emotional development (Sroufe, 1996). The parental sensitivity composite includes codes relating to the parent's acknowledgment of the child's signals, adaptation to change in state, elab-

orating and expanding on child communications, and maintaining positive affect, warm vocal quality, consistent style, and synchronous interactions. The CIB system has been used in various studies and has been shown to delineate differences in behavior related to parent gender, infant's age, cultural background, and biological and emotional risk factors (Feldman, 2000; Feldman, Eidelman, Sirota, & Weller, 2002; Feldman, Greenbaum, Mayes, & Erlich, 1997; Feldman & Klein, 2003; Feldman, Masalha, & Nadam, 2001; Keren, Feldman, & Tyano, 2001).

Mother-child microregulatory patterns of proximity and touch Touch is considered an important component of the parent-infant coregulatory system, although touch has not been explored in depth compared to micropatterns of visual, vocal, and affective communications (Tronick, 1995). The mother's supportive physical presence—addressing the degree of physical closeness, touch, and proximity in the mother-infant dyad—is not only an important aspect of the mother-child relationship but also may be used as a diagnostic tool. In particular, because proximity and touch are often not under the mother's conscious control, these behaviors may provide a window to mother-infant physical intimacy, the basis of the attachment relationship (Field, 1996). The mother-infant play session is coded for the degree of physical proximity and the patterns of touch in second-by-second frames. Coding addresses the degree of proximity, gaze, type of touch, maternal responsivity to the child's bids for closeness, the appropriateness of the mother's touch, and the degree of physical intrusiveness. Using microanalytic methodology in a triadic family session, we have shown that the degree of maternal and paternal affectionate touch predicted both parent-child and family-level interaction patterns between parents and their premature infants (Feldman, Weller, Sirota, & Eidelman, 2003).

Feeding session Finally, mothers and infants are observed during a feeding session. Visits are scheduled to coincide with the child's regular evening meal. Feeding is a maternal function that involves the fulfillment of a basic infant need and feeding interactions were found to be especially stressful for clinic-referred dyads. During feed-

Table 22.2 The Community-Based Four-Dimension Model of Infant Mental Health Assessment

Parent-Child Relational Profile	Child Social-Emotional Adaptation Profile	Correlates of Child Adaptation	Final Diagnosis
A. Parent-child interactive behavior (setting: home)	A. Child adaptation during social interactions (setting: home)	A. Family functioning (settings: home and clinic)	A. Psychodynamic formulation
1. Home Observation for Measurement of the Environment (HOME; Caldwell & Bradley, 1978)	1. Free play: child involvement and creativity, child withdrawal (CIB)	1. Structured family interview: McMaster Model of Family Functioning; Roles, system management, control of behavior, problem solving, communication, affective responsiveness (Epstein et al., 1978)	1. Underlying conflict (maternal): Precursors or indicators for child conflict
2. Free play: Maternal sensitivity and responsiveness (CIB; Feldman, 1998)	2. Free play: Microregulatory patterns of child proximity and touch	2. Videotaped triadic interactions: Lausanne Triadic Play (LTP): Disordered, collusive, stressed, and cooperative family alliance (Fivaz-Depeursinge & Corboz-Warnery, 1999)	2. Defense mechanisms (maternal): Precursors or indicators for child defenses
3. Free play: Microregulatory patterns of maternal proximity and touch	3. Feeding: Child acceptance, initiative, and withdrawal (CIB)		3. Maternal representations of the child (flexibility, anger management, acknowledgment of feelings)
4. Feeding: Maternal sensitivity, intrusiveness, and limit setting (CIB)			4. Nature of object relations (maternal provision of holding environment, acknowledgment of dependence)
			5. Issues related to the development of the self (providing boundaries, mirroring)
B. Parent-child interactive behavior (setting: clinic)	B. Child adaptation during social interactions (setting: clinic)	B. Maternal psychopathology	B. Diagnostic classification
1. Free play: Maternal sensitivity and responsiveness	1. Free play: Child involvement and creativity, withdrawal (CIB)	1. Maternal clinical interview developed by the clinical team: Maternal history of mental health, substance abuse, support system, bereavement, work functioning, conflict, current relations with parents.	1. Formal multi-axis diagnosis using the *Diagnostic Classification of Mental Health and Developmental Disorders of Infancy and Early Childhood* (DC:0–3; Zero to Three, 1994)
2. Free play: Maternal facilitation of child symbolic play	2. Free play: Child symbolic play: level of symbolic complexity and topics expressed during free play	2. Maternal self-report: SCL-90-R (Derogatis, 1983)	Axis I. Child primary diagnosis
3. Maternal support of child's exploratory skills			Axis II. Parent-child relational disorder
4. Maternal disciplinary techniques			Axis III. Medical/developmental conditions

5. Maternal regulation of child separation distress

3. Child persistence, motivation, and skill in exploring new toys
4. Child self-regulated compliance
5. Management of separation distress and reaction to reunion

C. Maternal representations of child and parent-child relationship
1. Parent Developmental Interview (PDI; Slade et al., 1999)

C. Child developmental level and temperament
1. Maternal report: Infant-Toddler Behavior Questionnaire (Rothbart, 1981)
2. Maternal report: TBAQ (Goldsmith, 1996)
3. Emotion regulation: Coded from the feeding, separation-reunion, and toy pickup situations
4. Bayley Scales of Infant Development (Bayley, 1993)

C. Child adaptation to daily living skills
1. Interview of mother: Vineland Adaptive Behavior Scales (VABS; Sparrow et al., 1984)

D. Child adaptation to day care or nursery
1. Observation of child in nursery: Nursery Assessment Scale (Feldman & Alony, 1998)

ings, referred infants demonstrated higher levels of withdrawal, negative emotionality, and resistance as compared to the free play session, and sustained withdrawal was particularly high among infants with feeding problems (Keren et al., 2001). The feeding sessions were coded with the CIB (Feldman, 1998) adapted for feeding sessions, and several codes were added to address the special characteristics of the feeding situation, including the location and duration of the feeding session, independence during feeding, struggle for control, and the efficacy of the feeding session.

The clinic setting

In the third or fourth visit to the clinic, as the treatment alliance is beginning to develop and the evaluation phase has not been completed, mothers and infants are videotaped in four interactive contexts that range from relaxed to emotionally taxing situations: free play, teaching task, toy pickup, and separation-reunion. Five aspects of maternal style are addressed: global sensitivity, facilitation of the child's symbolic play, skill in introducing new cognitive tasks, disciplinary techniques, and the mother's ability to manage her child's separation distress.

Mother-child free play   Because mother and child social behavior is sensitive to the interactive context (Feldman et al., 1997), there is clinical value in pinpointing the optimal context for each specific dyad. Thus, in the clinic, mothers and infants are observed in a free play session with a set of simple toys, similar to the play session conducted in the home. This videotaped interaction is similarly coded with the CIB (Feldman, 1998).

Maternal facilitation of the child's symbolic play
The mother-child free play session is also subjected to microanalytic assessment of infant symbolic play for infants aged 10 months and above. Coding is conducted in 5-second frames, using eight mutually exclusive and hierarchical levels of mother and child symbolic play, ranging from no play to functional play to complex symbolic combinatory play (Feldman & Greenbaum, 1997). Codes addressing the mother's facilitation of the child's symbolic expression include offering play material, reframing the child's symbolic output,

redirecting attention, and providing apprenticeship by expanding the child's symbolic level within the zone of proximal development (Vygotsky, 1978).

Mother's support of the child's cognitive development   In the second interactive context, mother and child are videotaped in a teaching task. Mothers are asked to introduce two toys to the child—one developmentally easy and one difficult. The quality of maternal assistance, ability to give the child space for exploration, efficiency in offering help, and affective quality are coded (Chase-Lansdale, Brooks-Gunn, & Zamsky, 1994).

Maternal disciplinary techniques   The third context examines the mother's socialization technique during a toy pickup task. Microanalysis examines the type of child compliance, whether it is self-motivated or externally regulated, and modes of noncompliance (Feldman, Greenbum, & Yirmiya, 1999; Kochanska & Aksan, 1995). Maternal control techniques are also assessed, especially whether the mother is able to provide a warm but firm style that is considered optimal in facilitating socialization.

Mother's management of separation distress
The last observation is a separation-reunion episode. Microanalysis and global codes examine the mother's behavior upon reunion; her reengagement style, maintenance of proximity and full attention to the infant, affective expression, acknowledgment of the separation's effect on the child, ability to accept the child's anger and dependency, and skill in consoling emotional distress.

Maternal representations

Mental representations of intimate relationships are complex cognitive-affective schemata that are constructed on the basis of repeated experiences within the relationship and are colored by specific affective valance (Blatt, 1995; Bowlby, 1969). The mother's mental representations of the child and the relationship are assessed through the Parent Developmental Interview (PDI; Aber, Belsky, Slade, & Crnic, 1999). The PDI is an hour-long semistructured interview that assesses the mother's representations of the child and the relationship. Questions call for maternal descriptions of daily experiences, feelings, memories, sense of parenting, modes of handling positive and negative emotions, and the management of guilt and separation distress. Analysis considers the parent's expressed feelings, such as anger, dependency, guilt, and joy, the parent's ability to acknowledge negative and positive feelings, and the capacity to self-regulate and modulate intense emotions. In line with the attachment literature, the quality of the narrative is considered, and its coherence, richness, and affective valance are assessed. Mothers' responses on the PDI were found to be associated with observed maternal behavior toward the child and were related to the mother's attachment security to her own mother (Aber et al., 1999; Slade, Belsky, Aber, & Phelps, 1999). The PDI is a relatively new instrument, and data on clinic-referred infants are still emerging.

Child Social-Emotional Adaptation Profile

Three levels of child adaptation are examined to assess the child's adaptive functioning: during social interactions with the caretaker, to the demands of daily life, and to the day care or nursery environment.

Child adaptation during social interactions with the caretaker

Child adaptation during social interactions is coded from the same four interactive situations (free play, teaching task, pickup, separation-reunion).

Child social engagement and withdrawal During free play, two composites from the CIB are considered: the child's social engagement (including creativity, alertness, positive affect and enthusiasm, vocal quality, initiative and autonomy) and withdrawal (including negative affect, withdrawn behavior, gaze break, and labile or depressed mood).

Child adaptation to situations of physical intimacy Microanalysis examines the child's adaptation in the domain of physical intimacy, including the capacity to flexibly approach and recede from physical contact, usage of the mother's proximity for comfort and refueling, and ability to give and receive affectionate touch.

Child attention regulation and motivation During the teaching task, adaptation refers to the child's skill in solving problems, working diligently and persistently, showing motivation, and using the mother for assistance.

Child self-regulated compliance In the toy pickup, the central assessment relates to whether the child's compliance is adaptive and is of the self-regulated, self-motivated type (e.g., child picks up the toy enthusiastically, with positive affect, and needs no reminders to complete the task).

Child management of separation and the regulation of stressful events During separation, adaptive functioning refers to the child's acknowledgment of maternal absence on the one hand, and the ability to self-regulate distress on the other. During reunion, adaptation is expressed in the child's positive emotional response to the mother's return and the ability to find comfort in her presence.

Child adaptation to the demands of daily life

Adaptation to daily demands is assessed with the Vineland Adaptive Behavior Scales (VABS; Sparrow, Balla, & Cicchetti, 1984), a maternal interview that considers the child's daily behavior and communication. The instrument provides information on child adaptive functioning in the domains of daily skills, communication, socialization, motor functioning, and maladaptive behavior patterns in daily life.

Child adaptation to the day care or nursery environment

Child adaptation to the larger social context is assessed using the Nursery Assessment Scale (Feldman & Alony, 1998), a coding scheme for child socialization in the nursery or day care setting that has been developed and validated at our laboratory on a sample of healthy Jewish and Arab toddlers in Israel. The assessment is conducted in a 45- to 60-minute visit to the kindergarten and includes observation during indoor activity and free outdoor play. The observer marks the setting and rates the child's appearance, activities, and interactions with the adults and children along 27 scales, such as the style of behavior (e.g., activity level, self-regulation), sociability (e.g., prefers being alone, functions as a social center), ego skills (e.g., persists, concentrates), interactions with peers (e.g., approaches children, maintains eye contact, initiates, cooperates, is aggressive), and relations with adults (e.g., relies on adults for help, is independent, seeks contact). The observer also marks the areas where child behavior is most adaptive and maladaptive.

During this multilevel assessment of child adaptation—in mother-child interaction, daily life, and in the kindergarten—particular attention is paid to areas of strength as well as to areas of maladaptive functioning, along the developmental perspective. The multicontext developmental assessment is then integrated into the process of differential diagnosis, the formulation of treatment goals, and the evaluation of treatment outcomes.

Correlates of Child Adaptive Functioning: Family, Mother, and Child Factors

Family functioning

We use two models for the assessment of the whole-family process in clinic-referred families: the McMaster Model of Family Functioning (Epstein, Bishop, & Levin, 1978) and the Lausanne Triadic Play (LTP) model (Fivaz-Despeursinge & Corboz-Warnery, 1999). The first is a structured interview, and the second measure is employed to observe and code triadic interaction.

1. The McMaster Model of Family Functioning (Epstein et al., 1978) draws upon the family systems perspective, which emphasizes that the child's social-emotional functioning is influenced by the general family atmosphere and by specific alliances within the family system. In accordance with the systems perspective (Minuchin, 1985), the family is viewed as a single functional unit, and interactive patterns, resources, integrative forces, and elements disruptive to the system's functioning are evaluated. The McMaster is a structured interview conducted at the home with the entire family. Areas of functioning include role definitions, allocation of resources, management, control of behavior, problem-solving skills,

communication, and affective responsiveness within the family system. Specific areas of family function and dysfunction are delineated and serve as a basis for intervention. The family assessment is used to examine links between child symptoms, specific social-emotional problems, and areas of family dysfunction.

2. The LTP (Fivaz-Despeursinge & Corboz-Warnery, 1999) is a structured paradigm that evaluates the mother-father-child communication and family alliances on the basis of videotaped interactions. The LTP consists of four episodes. There are three "two plus one" episodes, in which two partners are interacting and the third person is a passive observer (mother-infant, father-infant, and mother-father). Finally, there is a triadic family play with all members. Each episode and the transitions between episodes are coded to evaluate four types of family alliance: disordered, collusive, stressed, and cooperative.

Although the LTP procedure has mainly been used for research purposes, we have found the paradigm clinically useful in the assessment process. We assess whether difficulties in the family setting appear in the form of excluding one partner, one partner dominates the interaction, parents interfere with each other's interaction with the child, or there is a lack of energy and joy in the triadic situation. Information from the mother-child interaction is then compared with the patterns of the triadic play for a more comprehensive evaluation of the child's social environment.

Maternal psychopathological profile

To assess maternal psychopathology, we utilize a clinical interview and self-report measures.

Maternal clinical interview The semistructured clinical interview was developed by our therapeutic team. Mothers are interviewed with regard to their family history of mental health, areas of conflict in their life, past episodes of depression or mood disorder, previous losses of close people, anxiety and panic, substance abuse, accident proneness, functioning at work, social support networks and friendships, and current relations with parents. The interview also explores the pregnancy and postbirth period of the referred child.

Maternal self-reported psychopathology In the third or fourth session, mothers are asked to complete the Symptom Checklist–90-R (SCL-90-R; Derogatis, 1983). This is a widely used instrument with good reliability and validity that provides information on nine subscales of psychopathology. Information from the treatment sessions, the home visits, and the mother's mode of responding to the VABS and the family interview provide additional information on the mother's psychological profile.

Child's developmental level and temperament

The child's developmental level and temperament are assessed during the intake period.

Child developmental level The child's mental and psychomotor development are assessed with the Bayley Scales of Infant Development (Bayley, 1993), by a developmental psychologist. In addition to information on the child's cognitive and motor skills, the testing situation provides information on the child's cognitive style, such as motivation, relation to the examiner, mode of problem solving, and frustration tolerance.

Child temperament In assessing child temperament—an important predictor of maladaptive social-emotional development—we are particularly interested in the child's emotion regulation capacities. Emotion regulation is assessed from the home visit, at the kindergarten, at the clinic (particularly during the stressful pickup and separation-reunion procedures), and at home. Particular attention is paid to the child's emotion regulation in the context of cognitive testing. At the end of the intake, mothers complete the Infant-Toddler Behavior Questionnaire (IBQ; Rothbart, 1981), which provides information on the child's reactivity and regulation.

Formulation of the Diagnosis in Nosological Terms

DC:0–3

The DC:0–3 (Zero to Three, 1994) has been suggested as a standardized way of summarizing all clinical information collected through the various assessment procedures (for a comprehensive discussion of the DC:0–3, see chapter 8). The formulation is multiaxial, based on the concept that the young child is both influenced by and shapes the rearing environment. The child's primary diagnosis (Axis I) reflects the main clinical symptoms of the child. The presence of a relational parent-child disorder, as reflected in the videotaped interactions, is marked as an Axis II diagnosis. Medical and/or developmental conditions are recorded as Axis III diagnoses. Environmental stressors, including parental psychopathology, parental conflict, and family dysfunction are noted on Axis IV. Finally, the actual level of the child's adaptive functioning is recorded on Axis V.

Based on the DC:0–3 formulation and on the developmental information, a strategy for intervention is planned. Assessment, as the foundation for treatment, is continuously integrated with new information emerging from the intervention. During the treatment process, we evaluate the mother and child's propensity to change and note the areas that are resistant to change. The clinician pays continous attention to change in the areas described during the evaluation process. Has the mother's narrative of the child become more coherent and positive during the treatment? Has her interactive style become more adaptive and reciprocal? Have family patterns become more functional? Finally, considering that a major treatment goal is to increase child adaptation, areas in which maladaptation have been successfully or unsuccessfully treated are continuously monitored.

CLINICAL CASE ILLUSTRATION

This section presents the case of a young boy who was self-referred to the infant mental health clinic. The mother came for treatment following the recommendation of a friend who was referred by the Well-Baby station's nurse and was successfully treated at our center. Such referrals point to the links between the community work conducted at the level of the general public and the clinical situation in promoting awareness of infant mental health issues. We describe the assessment process as it actually unfolded stage by stage, and as information was gathered through standard tests, observed behavior, and maternal interviews at the home, clinic, and kindergarten. This multi-level evaluation helped us form a final diagnosis and devise a plan for treatment. The reason for selecting this case as an illustration for our model was that the final diagnosis differed substantially from the presenting complaint symptom. The case thus illustrates the role of community-based assessment in reaching a differential diagnosis from several alternatives.

History

Ben (names are fictitious), aged 2 years, 4 months, was an only child of a single mother. The mother, Donna, an intelligent and educated 43-year-old journalist, sought help because Ben was biting and hitting children at the kindergarten over the previous 2 months and had recently begun to hit and bite her. Donna mentioned that she came to the clinic following the advice of a friend who had been successfully treated there.

Donna had been romantically involved with Ben's father, a married man, for several years. When she became pregnant, the father urged her to terminate the pregnancy, but Donna refused, considering her chances slim to get pregnant again at her age. The two kept in touch throughout the pregnancy, and the father was present during part of labor. During the first months of Ben's life, the father secretly maintained occasional contact and sporadic involvement in child rearing, but when Ben was 8 months old the father suddenly disappeared from their lives. At the same time as the father's departure, Donna's mother committed suicide by hanging herself at the main entrance of her apartment building and was found by Donna. Donna became preoccupied by a search for reasons for her mother's suicide, spending hours searching scientific literature on the Internet, and was mostly unavailable for Ben during that time. She described her mother as cold and distant, and was generally reluctant to discuss her mother's suicide.

Following his wife's death, Donna's father moved in with her, while Ben was moved to a separate room for the first time. Two months prior to referral, around the time of symptom onset, Ben's grandfather left the house and Ben's fa-

ther resurfaced with sporadic visits. At the time of evaluation and treatment, the grandfather remained involved in his daughter's life, coming in and out of her home and driving her and Ben to the assessment sessions.

Child's Developmental and Functional Assessment

Ben's general development appeared normative. On the Bayley Scales of Infant Development (Bayley, 1993), his mental development score was 112 and his psychomotor developmental score was 86, both within normal limits. The examiner described a smart, curious child, who was often stubborn but seemed able to concentrate on the tasks. Although his global behavior rating score was within normal limits, the emotion regulation subscale, which refers to the child's negative affect, adaptation, on-task persistence, frustration when unable to complete a task, cooperation, and hyperactivity during testing was below normal limits (score of 70).

Ben's adaptation to daily living, as expressed in the VABS (Sparrow et al., 1984), was normative in the motor domain, and no overt maladaptive patterns were reported. Indicators for concern appeared in the daily living and socialization domains. Ben was not yet toilet trained, and Donna had not yet begun talking about the topic or introducing the first stages of toilet habits. (It should be noted that most Israeli mothers have already begun introducing toilet habits at this stage, using books or introducing toilet-training devices such as a toilet seat.) Ben also did not put toys or objects back in their place, nor did Donna demand it, suggesting a problem in limit setting. Ben did not show preference for a specific friend, indicated no desire to please his attachment figure, and did not spontaneously describe emotions or experiences in simple words. At the period when toddlers begin to give words to thoughts and feelings and to develop personal friendships, Ben was described as socially withdrawn with limited capacities to give words to internal experiences.

Family Functioning Assessment

The McMaster structured family interview (Epstein et al., 1978), typically conducted at home with all family members and adapted to single-parent families, was conducted with Donna and Ben. On both the HOME (Caldwell & Bradley, 1978) and the McMaster visits, observers described the home as functionally clean but surprisingly barren, with no signs of personal taste and little opportunity for a variety of experiences. Ben's room had few age-appropriate toys but contained a computer, a recent gift from his father. Ben's participation in the interview was minimal, but he did not disrupt the conversation. The mother described this situation as typical, because she worked at home and her son had learned to occupy himself. The family interview revealed a woman who stressed the functional elements of family life. She refrained from issues of conflict or discomfort, minimized the difficulties of single parenthood, and avoided the expression of emotions as a coping mechanism. Donna described herself as relatively consistent in her responses to Ben, but admitted yelling and throwing things when seized by sudden anger, which she subsequently regretted. Although highly competent in solving practical problems, when problems involved interpersonal relations she reported feeling helpless, for instance, in demanding alimony from Ben's father or insisting that her own father leave the house. She complained of putting other people's agendas before her own and admitted to being afraid to raise a child alone, particularly since her mother's death. The interview defined Ben's immediate environment as marked by practical functionality, diminished emotional expressiveness, avoidance of negative emotions, and allowing for little expression of dependency needs. We considered filming an LTP session with the grandfather, but decided that fostering a triadic constellation with the grandfather would go against the treatment goal of enabling Donna's separation from her father.

Mother-Child Relationship

Maternal Personality Profile

The McMaster interview (Epstein et al., 1978) revealed signs of the mother's withdrawal and underlying hostile style, manifested in her flatness of affect, self-victimization, sense of parenting incompetence, inability to regulate anger, and guilt over hostility. Information from the maternal self-report using the SCL-90-R (Derogatis, 1983) further illuminated the mother's psychological profile. General maternal psychopathology was indicated by the existence of two subscales with scores above the clinical cutoff: hostility, in which she scored extremely high (above the 99th percentile), and anxiety.

Mother-Child Interaction

As indicated by the global CIB codes (Feldman, 1998) during free play at both home and clinic, interactions were characterized by medium-to-low maternal sensitivity, inability to read and respond to child cues, emotional distance, ineffectiveness in providing appropriate limits, and an inconsistent style characterized by rapid shifts between intrusiveness and withdrawal. Ben's social behavior showed low responsiveness; little enthusiasm, initiative, or creativity; few initial attempts to engage the mother, which were quickly frustrated; passive noncompliance; and little reliance on the mother for help. The dyadic atmosphere was characterized by minimal fluency, little mutual adaptation, and nearly no reciprocity or shared positive affect, creating a general feeling of dyssynchrony between mother and child.

Each of the observed settings highlighted a different viewpoint on the mother-child relational profile. Microanalysis of mother-child proximity and touch during the videotaped home interactions showed that the dyad spent most of the time within arm's reach of each other but with no physical closeness (94.8% of the time). Their attention was mostly (92.6%) directed toward an object of mutual engagement, with nearly no episodes of social gaze (.03%). During most of the interaction (97.2%), there was no maternal touch of any sort, with only one short episode (0.02%) of loving touch. Similarly, there was no child touch of mother, and only a single short episode of child unintentional touch (0.06%). Mother's response to child touch was coded as intrusive, whereas the child showed no response to maternal touch. This analysis highlighted the mother's difficulty in providing a supportive presence, a holding environment for maturation and play. The dyad was occupied in functional play, needs for physical closeness were not expressed, and when expressed were not reciprocated properly. These patterns placed Ben at risk for developing social withdrawal and future difficulties with physical intimacy.

During the presentation of a cognitive task in the structured task at the clinic, the mother's inability to respond to the child's developmental needs and her difficulties in reading his cues for help became more apparent. Donna's ability to give Ben space was medium-range during the developmentally easy task, but very low in the difficult task. She provided inefficient help, unadapted to the child's cues and needs, with inappropriate timing and a rigid, intrusive style. She demanded that the task be completed her way, and there was little emotional support, enthusiasm, or emotional restructuring of the learning situation. The child's adaptation to the problem-solving situation was relatively low, with low scores on persistence, compliance to maternal suggestions, and enthusiasm. Although Ben was able to work on his own, his requests for assistance were frustrated, leading to a false independence. Ben expressed neither positive nor negative affect toward the task or the mother. Similar to his emotion regulation subscale on the Bayley scales, Ben's cognitive-regulatory functioning here was lower than his actual cognitive ability.

A similar picture was revealed in the assessment of Ben's symbolic play. Ben spent most of the playtime in functional play (65%), manipulating objects with no symbolic expansion. During periods of symbolic play, his symbolic level remained low and rarely reached the level of combinatory or hierarchical symbolic play. Mother was ineffective in guiding, elaborating, or expanding the child's symbolic output and provided little apprenticeship in symbolic skills. In the cognitive and social-cognitive domain, although intelligent, Ben seemed to be at risk for developing limited cognitive complexity, a poor internal world, and diminished attention regulation.

Ben's self-regulation capacities were further examined in two contexts at the clinic, toy pickup and separation-reunion. During pickup, Ben did not show any signs of self-regulated compliance, the enthusiastic, self-motivated compliance with maternal demands. There were two episodes of externally regulated compliance, in which Ben unwillingly complied with his mother's nagging (24.65%). Otherwise, Ben demonstrated passive noncompliance (39.6%) or took a time-out (26.3%). Maternal separation did not seem to have any effect on the child. Ben remained preoccupied with toys during the entire separation (94.3%) and maintained neutral affect (100%). During reunion, mother and child maintained neutral affect, the child wandered away from the mother, there was no comforting touch, and mother directed her speech to the examiner. This information highlighted potential disturbances in the attachment scheme, with avoidant overtones. Ben's self-regulatory strategies were not optimal: compliance was enforced from the outside, and there was a disavowal of dependency toward the attachment figure. The fact that Ben was growing up with a single mother exacerbated the problem, in that no alternative attachment relationships or agents for socialization were available. The finding, however, that no overt aggression toward mother was observed in any of the situations at home or in the clinic precluded the diagnosis of aggressive attachment.

Mother's Mental Representations of the Child

Mother's representations were assessed with the PDI (Aber et al., 1999) by the primary clinician. The narrative revealed a global tendency to minimize needs, experiences, and both positive and negative emotions. Donna seemed unable to modulate negative emotions or needs, which possibly led to defensive distancing. She expressed considerable anger when talking about her explosive outbursts, but denied feeling angry when asked directly and belittled the significance of those angry outbursts ("I get very angry and then I tell myself, this is so stupid, why should I get so angry?"). Similarly, she renounced feeling guilty when asked directly but mentioned several times that she tended to "ask Ben's forgiveness" after her outbursts. Donna talked about her fears of leaving Ben, in particular of letting someone else take him to the playground.

She managed separation by working from home and limiting her activities out of the house, but expressed little recognition the child's need for separation, nor did she acknowledge dependency needs. There was little expressed joy and pleasure, although she spoke of positive emotions, with limited capacity to use vivid descriptions, remember specific events, or relate to special moments. Thus, although the representational level was akin to the behavioral level by its minimization of emotions, defensiveness, and maternal withdrawal, the behavioral observations revealed the intrusive and uncoordinated components in the maternal style, whereas the representational level provided a window into its internal dynamics. It appeared that the mother was struggling to control intense anger, hostility, and dependence that she was unable to self-regulate, nor could she allow room for such feelings in her son.

Child Adaptation at Kindergarten

Ben's general affect during the observations at home and in the clinic seemed depressed and withdrawn, which raised the question of whether he suffered from an affective disorder. To finalize such a diagnosis, the clinician needs to determine whether the child's withdrawal is specific to the mother-child dyad or has become a generalized behavioral pattern. For a single child living with a single mother with no other stable attachment figures, the only other context in which to assess depressive symptomatology is the nursery school. An hour-long observation in the nursery school revealed Ben's depressed and withdrawn behavior. He preferred being alone, made no eye contact with peers, displayed passive behavior toward peers, and imitated others' activities with no initiation. Some of his behaviors in the nursery school significantly contrasted with those observed with his mother. Ben showed no aggressive behavior; to the contrary, he would often desist during conflicts over a specific toy or play area. Ben's avoidant, dependent behavior often resulted in social rejection by his peers. He was obedient and clinging toward the adults in the nursery school.

Diagnostic Formulation

The combined information derived from videotaped interactions, formal assessments, clinical interviews with the mother, and observations at home and in kindergarten revealed a discrepancy between the stated reasons for referral (aggression toward mother and peers) and the underlying dynamics. Aggression did not appear to be a major component in any of the observations at the home, clinic, or kindergarten. To the contrary, we observed resignation and withdrawal in the kindergarten, indifference to maternal separation and reunion, lack of positive involvement in the free play, lack of attempts to gain physical closeness, and little mobilization of resources during cognitive testing despite good abilities. This discrepancy led us to search for potentially distorted representations of the child in the mother's mind. Donna's apparent perception of Ben as aggressive perhaps comprised a projective mechanism of her own aggression and ambivalence toward her son. As reflected in the PDI and McMaster, the mother herself was often struggling with intense anger and conflicting feelings toward the child. Stern's (1995) work on the "clinical infant" relates to a similar phenomenon. The child may be the recipient of distorted parental projections, which may shape the parent's representations of the child and color parental interactive behavior.

The observational tools, therefore, reinforced the clinical impression that a gap existed between the reported and underlying maternal emotions and representations and pointed to the nature of this discrepancy. On the basis of these observations, we were able to characterize the parent-child relational disorders in terms of underinvolved relational style, and not as aggressive relational disorders as would have been suggested by the presenting symptoms. Similarly, the child's underlying constellation was defined more within the affective/depressed constellation than within the disruptive behavior complex. We reframed all of the above evaluations in accordance with the DC:0–3 classification system (Zero to Three, 1994). On Axis I, the differential diagnosis was finalized as disorder of affect with a depressive component masked by aggression. On Axis II, there were definite signs of a mother-child relationship disorder, underinvolved type. On Axis III, no developmental disorder nor medical condition was recorded. On Axis IV, both maternal personality profile and family structure were considered as psychosocial stressors. On Axis V, the child's level of adaptive functioning was assessed as lower than expected.

Using a Comprehensive Assessment to Devise a Developmentally Sensitive Intervention

Between the ages of 2 and 3 years, children's social, symbolic, and cognitive worlds expand, leading to new mechanisms of self-regulation and more advanced adaptation. As seen, Ben's adaptive functioning was considerably compromised, possibly due to the interaction of genetic liability, disturbed parent-child relationship, and the family's limited social support. Disturbances in self-regulation emerged in the cognitive domain and manifested in the mechanisms of persistence, motivation, concentration, and attention. In the peer group, there were disruptions in the child's initiative, cooperative play, sharing, the development of close friendships, and in the appearance of victimized behavior. In terms of self-control, Ben was not self-motivated to internalize maternal rules of conduct. Finally, during this stage, children develop the ability to talk about thoughts and feelings and are able to describe simple emotional experiences and enact them during symbolic play. In general, the mother's intrusiveness, affective flatness, and insensitivity to her son's cues limited Ben's symbolic and emotional expression, provided little supportive physical presence, and did not furnish the necessary secure base. Both the parent-child profile and the child adaptive functioning profile indicate that intervention should focus on the dyadic relationship (Sameroff & Fiese, 1993).

In selecting the port of entry for the treatment of early mother-child relationship disorders (Stern, 1995), one needs to take into consideration the kind of working alliance the parent would be able to develop. Donna displayed a very aloof stance, with no interest in examining the links between her motherhood and her experiences with her mother. Therefore, psychoanalytically oriented mother-child psychotherapy would not seem to be the best port of entry. The child's depressed affect and general withdrawal conveyed a sense of urgency, and it was important to allow the child's voice to be heard in the treatment room. We therefore decided to choose the present child-mother interactions as the main port of entry for therapy, in accordance with the interaction guidance therapy approach (McDonough, 2000). Once-a-week dyadic therapy was recommended. The first goal of therapy was to help the mother reframe her perceptions of her son and to help the child become more present in the room. For example, instead of describing his avoidant, self-sufficient behavior as independent and mature, we suggested calling it "a way Ben copes at times when you are unavailable to him and work at your computer." Ben's aggressive behavior toward his mother was noted each time it occurred in the treatment room, and the therapist helped Donna understand how her interactive patterns may have led to the child's aggression. Because of her dismissal, treatment was predicted to be slow, with many ups and downs.

CONCLUSION

In this chapter, we elaborate on the fundamentals of assessing young children and their families in a specific context—the community-based infant mental health setting. We attempted to demonstrate the way in which the community-based setting offers the opportunity to expand the scope of assessment from the traditional mental health evaluation to the interactive exposure of community health professionals to the field of infant mental health. The clinical case illustrated the dynamic interplay between our multifaceted assessment paradigm and treatment planning, underscoring the benefits of a community-based approach to the field of infant mental health.

Given the constraints and limited resources of most clinics, we would suggest using the aforementioned research tools not necessarily for empirical purposes, which would involve tedious microlevel coding, but as frameworks for observations. The coding systems described above address various conceptual perspectives, each with a unique clinical utility. These different perspectives may direct the clinician's attention to the degree of proximity and touch in the parent-child or spousal relationship, the disciplinary techniques mothers use, how creative the child's symbolic output is, or how the child reacts to moments of maternal separation. In the realm of representations, the PDI may direct the clinician's attention to how coherent the mother's descriptions are of positive and negative episodes and child characteristics, how vivid her memories are of moments with the child, and how appropriate her representations are to the child's age. Such use of empirical tools for clinical purposes may broaden the clinicians' perspective on the child's symptom and its communicative meaning.

In sum, the goal of the community-based model is to provide a broad framework for the prevention, detection, and treatment of emotional difficulties in infants and their parents. Such a model involves broadening the scope of infant mental health assessment to the entire community, to normative as well as disturbed behavior, and to the child and family's propensity for change. Although modern society has long neglected the notion that it takes a village to raise a child, when the concern for children's well-being is shared by the entire community, young infants may have a better opportunity for optimal social-emotional growth.

ACKNOWLEDGMENT Data reported in this chapter were collected with the kind assistance of Dr. Mona Ackerman at the Ricklis Family Foundation and the joint support of the Ministry of Health and Sacta-Rashi Foundation.

References

Aber, J. L., Belsky, J., Slade, A., & Crnic, K. (1999). Stability and change in mothers' representations of their relationship with their toddlers. *Developmental Psychology, 35*, 1038–1047.

Bayley, N. (1993). *Bayley scales of infant development: Administering and scoring manual*. New York: Psychological Corporation.

Beebe, B., & Lachman, F. (1994). Representation and internalization in infancy: Three principles of salience. *Psychoanalytic Psychology, 11*, 127–165.

Bjorklund, D. F., & Pellegrini, A. D. (2000). Child development and evolutionary psychology. *Child Development, 71*, 1687–1708.

Blatt, S. J. (1995). Representational structures in psychopathology. In D. Cicchetti & S. Toth (Eds.), *Rochester symposium on developmental psychopathology: Vol. VI. Emotion, cognition, and representation* (pp. 1–33). Rochester, NY: University of Rochester Press.

Bowlby, J. (1969). *Attachment and loss: Vol. 1. Attachment*. New York: Basic Books.

Bronfenbrenner, U. (1986). Ecology of the family as a context for human development: Research perspectives. *Developmental Psychology, 22*, 723–742.

Caldwell, B. & Bradley, R. (1978). *Home observation for measurement of the environment*. Little Rock: Arkansas University Press.

Calkins, S. D., & Fox, N. A. (2002). Self-regulatory processes in early personality development: Multilevel approach to the study of childhood social withdrawal and aggression. *Development and Psychopathology, 14*, 477–498.

Chase-Lansdale, P. L., Brooks-Gunn, J., & Zamsky, E. (1994). Young African-American multigenerational families in poverty: Quality of mothering and grandmothering. *Child Development, 65*, 373–393.

Cicchetti, D., & Aber, L. (1998). Contextualism and developmental psychopathology. *Development and Psychopathology, 10*, 137–141.

Cicchetti, D., & Cohen, D. J. (1995). *Developmental psychopathology*. New York: Wiley.

Derogatis, L. R. (1983). *SCL-90-R Manual* (2nd ed.). Towson, MD: Clinical Psychometric Research.

Emde, R. N. (1994). Individuality, context, and the search for meaning. *Child Development, 65*, 719–737.

Emde, R. N., & Sameroff, A. J. (1989). Understanding early relationship disturbances. In R. N. Emde & A. J. Sameroff (Eds.), *Relationship disturbances in early childhood: Developmental approach* (pp. 3–16). New York: Basic Books.

Epstein, N. B., Bishop, D. S., & Levine, S. (1978). The McMaster model of family functioning. *Journal of Marriage and Family Counseling, 4*, 19–31.

Feldman, R. (1998). *Coding manual for parent-child separation and reunion*. Unpublished manuscript, Bar-Ilan University.

Feldman, R. (2000). Parents' convergence on sharing and marital satisfaction, father involvement, and parent-child relationship at the transition to parenthood. *Infant Mental Health Journal, 21*, 176–191.

Feldman, R., & Alony, D. (1998). *The nursery as-

sessment scale. Unpublished manuscript, Bar-Ilan University.

Feldman, R., Eidelman, A. I., Sirota, L., & Weller, A. (2002). Comparison of skin-to-skin (kangaroo) and traditional care: Parenting outcomes and preterm infants' development. *Pediatrics, 110*, 16–26.

Feldman, R., & Greenbaum, C. W. (1997). Affect regulation and synchrony in mother-infant play as precursors to the development of symbolic competence. *Infant Mental Health Journal, 18*, 4–23.

Feldman, R., Greenbaum, C. W., Mayes, L. C., & Erlich, H. S. (1997). Change in mother- infant interactive behavior: Relations to change in the mother, the infant, and the social context. *Infant Behavior and Development, 20*, 153–165.

Feldman, R., Greenbaum, C. W., & Yirmiya, N. (1999). Mother-infant affect synchrony as an antecedent to the emergence of self-control. *Developmental Psychology, 35*, 223–231.

Feldman, R., & Klein, P. S. (2003). Toddlers' self-regulated compliance with mother, caregiver, and father: Implications for theories of socialization. *Developmental Psychology, 39*, 680–692.

Feldman, R., Masalha, S., & Nadam, R. (2001). Cultural perspective on work and family: Dual-earner Jewish and Arab families at the transition to parenthood. *Journal of Family Psychology, 15*, 492–509.

Feldman, R., Weller, A., Eidelman, A.I., & Sirota, L. (2003). Testing a family intervention hypothesis: The contribution of mother-infant skin-to-skin contact (kangaroo care) to family interaction and touch. *Journal of Family Psychology, 17*, 94–107.

Field, T. M. (1996). Attachment and separation in young children. *Annual Review of Psychology, 47*, 541–561.

Fivaz-Despeursinge, E., & Corboz-Warnery, A. (1999). *The primary triangle: A developmental systems view of mothers, fathers, and infants.* New York: Basic Books.

Fogel, A. (1993). *Developing through relationships: Origins of communication, self, and culture.* Chicago: University of Chicago Press.

Fox, N. A. (Ed.). (1994). The development of emotion regulation: Biological, and behavioral considerations. *Monographs of the Society for Research in Child Development, 59* (2–3, Serial No. 240).

Goldsmith, H. H. (1996). Studying temperament via construction of the Toddler Behavior Assessment Questionnaire. *Child Development, 67*, 218–235.

Kagan, J. (1989). *Unstable ideas.* Cambridge MA: Harvard University Press.

Keren, M., Feldman, R., & Tyano, S. (2001). Emotional disturbances in infancy: Diagnostic classification and interactive patterns of infants referred to a community-based infant mental health clinic. *Journal of the American Academy of Child and Adolescent Psychiatry, 40*, 27–35.

Keren, M., Feldman, R., & Tyano, S. (2003). Israeli experience with the DC:0–3 classification. *Infant Mental Health Journal, 24*, 337–348.

Kochanska, G., & Aksan, N. (1995). Mother-child mutually positive affect, the quality of child compliance to requests and prohibitions and maternal control as correlates of early internalization. *Child Development, 66*, 236–254.

McDonough, S. (2000). Interaction guidance: An approach for difficult-to-engage families. In C. H. Zeanah, Jr. (Ed.), *Handbook of infant mental health* (2nd ed., pp. 485–493). New York: Guilford Press.

Minuchin, P. (1985). Families and individual development: Provocations from the field of family therapy. *Child Development, 56*, 289–302.

Piaget, J. (1952). *The origins of intelligence in children.* New York: International Universities Press.

Rothbart, M. K. (1981). Measurement of temperament in infancy. *Child Development, 52*, 569–578.

Sander, L. W. (1987). Awareness of inner experience. *Child Abuse and Neglect, 2*, 339–346.

Sameroff, A. J. (1997). Understanding the social context of early psychopathology. In J. Noshpitz (Ed.), *Handbook of child and adolescent psychiatry* (pp. 224–235). New York: Wiley.

Sameroff, A. J., & Fiese, B. H. (1993). Models of development and developmental risk. In C. H. Zeanah (Ed.), *Handbook of Infant Mental Health* (pp. 3–13). New York: Guilford Press.

Schore, A. N. (2001). The effects of a secure attachment relationship on right brain development, affect regulation, and infant mental health. *Infant Mental Health Journal, 22*, 6–66.

Seligman, M. E. P., & Csikszentmihalyi, M. (2000). Positive psychology: An introduction. *American Psychologist, 55*, 5–15.

Slade, A., Belsky, J., Aber, J. L., & Phelps, J. L. (1999). Mothers' representations of their relationships with their toddlers: Links to adult attachment and observed mothering. *Developmental Psychology, 35*, 611–619.

Sparrow, S., Balla, D., & Cicchetti, D. (1984). *Vineland adaptive behavior scales (VABS): Extended form manual.* Circle Pines, MN: American Guidance Services.

Sroufe, L. A. (1996). *Emotional development: The organization of emotional life in the early years.* New York: Cambridge University Press.

Sroufe, L. A., & Rutter, M. (1984). The domain of developmental psychopathology. *Child Development, 55,* 17–29.

Stern, D. N. (1985). *The interpersonal world of the infant.* New York: Basic Books.

Stern, D. N. (1995). *The motherhood constellation.* New York: Basic Books.

Stern, D. N., Sander, L. W., Nahum, J. P., Harrison, A. M., Lyons-Ruth, K., Morgan, A. C., Bruschweiler-Stern, N., & Tronick, E. Z. (1998). Non-interpretive mechanisms in psychoanalytic therapy. *International Journal of Psycho-Analysis, 79,* 903–921.

Tronick, E. Z. (1995). Touch in mother-infant interaction. In T. M. Field (Ed.), *Touch in early development* (pp. 53–65). Mahwah, NJ: Lawrence Erlbaum.

Vygotsky, L. S. (1978). *Mind in society.* Cambridge, MA: Harvard University Press.

Winnicott, D. W. (1965). *The maturational process and the facilitating environment.* London: Hogarth Press.

Zero to Three, National Center for Clinical Infant Programs. (1994). *Diagnostic classification of mental health and developmental disorders of infancy and early childhood.* Washington, DC: Author.

23

Early Detection of Young Children's Mental Health Problems in Primary Care Settings

Lynne C. Huffman
Mary Nichols

Behavioral issues can emerge in children as early as infancy and be clearly apparent by toddlerhood (12–18 months). These issues include social relationship problems, excessive fears, sleeping, feeding, and toileting problems, parenting skill deficits, and family transition problems, as well as trauma, abuse, and neglect. Frequently, however, such problems are not appreciated or identified by primary care providers. While pediatricians are important professionals involved in the care of infants and young children, seeing them for as many as a dozen well-child visits during the first two years of life, traditionally there has been a lack of opportunity and focus on these behavioral issues. Given the pediatric developmental surveillance and anticipatory guidance models, these visits provide an important opportunity for both prevention and early intervention efforts in the behavioral health domains (U.S. Department of Health and Human Services, 2001). A few screening tools that reliably identify behavioral health problems in young children can help pediatricians substantiate parental concerns, validate clinical impressions, inform immediate care, and facilitate appropriate referrals.

In this chapter, we first describe the primary health care context and examine the role of the primary care pediatrician in caring for young children with behavioral health problems. Next, we provide a brief overview of those behavioral health problems that are typically seen in this age range. Then, we review the screening tools that are available to the primary care pediatrician, commenting on the reliability and validity data that have been collected for each tool. Based upon this review, we make recommendations for useful screening strategies and address the limits of what is available to primary care providers. Finally, we make suggestions regarding important goals for future clinical research in this area.

The topic of mental health screening and evaluation in the context of general pediatric medicine settings has been the focus of wide-reaching discussion. To date, in the United States, we lack a systematic approach to screening and referral for mental health problems that is easily employed in primary care contexts. Repeatedly, in national conferences (e.g., the Surgeon General's Conference on Children's Mental Health; the Administration for Children, Youth, and Families/Head-

Start Infant Mental Health Forum), it has been recommended that mental health services be integrated more thoroughly into primary health care. In this chapter, we seek to inform this developing agenda by reviewing the history of assessment of mental health problems in primary care settings, assessing the scope of mental health problems in young children, highlighting conceptual and methodological advances in assessment and diagnostic strategies in this clinical arena, and making summary recommendations on this topic to those involved in pediatric primary care.

ROLE OF THE PEDIATRICIAN IN ADDRESSING MENTAL HEALTH PROBLEMS IN PEDIATRIC PRIMARY CARE SETTINGS

In this section, we highlight primary care–based estimates of mental health problems in older infants and preschoolers. Then we examine the characteristics of the primary care context, the processes inherent in the recognition and assessment of mental health problems in this context, and the challenges to these processes. In addition, we clarify the use of relevant terms in this context, such as screening, detection, assessment, referral, prevention, and intervention.

Mental Health Problems in Infants and Young Children

The late infancy and preschool years are characterized by significant alterations in language, cognition, social behavior, motor abilities, and the development of peer relationships and independent behavior. Changes in these basic psychological processes can affect the emergence, modification, or remission of early-onset psychiatric disorders (Lavigne et al., 1998). In one large study of the emotional and behavioral problems of preschoolers who were cared for in private primary care pediatric settings (Lavigne et al., 1993), the most common diagnoses included oppositional defiant disorder (51%), parent-child relationship problems (10%), attention deficit/hyperactivity disorder (9%), depressive disorder (3%), and separation anxiety disorder (2%). Many of the disruptive disorders also manifest their symptoms in the class-

room and increasingly are being identified by educators as children progress through school.

Diagnostic estimates of the prevalence of child psychiatric disorders in school-age children and adolescents document rates for moderate to severe disorder of 16 to 20% (Bird, Shaffer, et al., 1993; Costello, 1989). Comorbidity appears to be as high as 40 to 50% (Bird, Gould, & Staghezza, 1993; Offord, Boyle, & Racine, 1989). We know less about the prevalence of mental health disorders among preschool children, though our level of knowledge is increasing (Lavigne et al., 1996). A small number of reports describe the occurrence of behavior problems in young children (Campbell, Breaux, Ewing, Szumowski, & Pierce, 1986; Offord, 1987), often with modest convenience or clinical samples (Pianta & Castaldi, 1989; Rose, 1989). Even fewer studies examine the occurrence of preschool children's psychiatric disorders in primary care settings (Earls, 1980; Lavigne et al., 1996). One of those few reports suggested an overall prevalence rate for Axis I disorders of approximately 20% (9% for severe Axis I disorders) with rates for problem behaviors above the 90th percentile on Child Behavioral Checklist (CBCL) norms at 8 to 10% of the evaluated sample (Lavigne et al., 1996). Another report showed that 22% of children aged 3 to 6 years screened at a pediatric outpatient clinic had significant behavior problems (Rai, Malik, & Sharma, 1993), where "fearfulness" and "attention-seeking" were problems found exclusively in girls. An additional study comparing parent-reported 3-year-old behavior problem prevalence rates in urban and suburban communities indicated no differences in prevalence (13.2%) by location (Thompson et al., 1996). Briggs-Gowan, Carter, Moye Skuban, and McCue Horwitz (2001) reported that the weighted prevalence of parent-reported subclinical/clinical CBCL/2–3 scores was 11.8% for 2-year-olds. Further, approximately 6% of parents of 1- and 2-year-olds reported clinical-level scores on the Parenting Stress Index/Difficult Child (PSI/DC) scale. The authors used the PSI/DC scale as a proxy for behavior problems among 1-year-olds, for whom measures are limited.

A range of prevalence rates has been reported in European studies, depending on the country in which the studies were performed (e.g., Britain

22% and Netherlands 7.8%). This variance suggests that culture (including parenting practices, social child care institutions, etc.), as well as macro factors such as socioeconomic status, may influence early problem behavior detection and prevalence rates. In fact, some researchers reset cutoff points for "cultural" reasons when determining prevalence rates (Pavuluri, Luk, Clarkson, & McGee, 1995).

Primary Health Care Context

Physician-parent communication about psychosocial problems has become important as primary care physicians (a) begin to have some awareness of the factors, including family stress, substance abuse, gun safety, and television, that have an effect on physical health (Cheng, DeWitt, Savageau, & O'Connor, 1999); and (b) assume their role as gatekeepers to more expensive services, including mental health interventions (Horwitz, Leaf, & Leventhal, 1998). These communications may be facilitated or thwarted by the pragmatics of the primary health care context. A child's well-child visit with a physician usually is characterized by a brief duration and multiple tasks that include a review of medical and psychosocial history, physical examination, and vaccinations/immunizations. Further, the visit can comprise developmental surveillance with the assessment of developmental milestones, screening for medical problems, and anticipatory guidance. Thus, each well-child visit has multiple goals, such as early identification of problems, prevention of disorder, and referral for additional evaluation of new problems (see table 23.1 for more elaborated definitions and distinctions among these terms). In general, the visit takes place within an examining room.

A report by Minkovitz, Mathew, and Strobino (1998) described pediatric practices and physician approaches to addressing developmental and behavioral issues in primary care contexts. They further considered the differences in provider practices and satisfaction concerning children's development (based on length of time in practice). The authors' survey of physicians in 30 pediatric practices compared physicians in training, recently in practice, or more experienced. In general, pediatricians did not conduct routine behavioral or developmental screening in the early months of life, and most discussed safety, as opposed to development and mental health, concerns with parents of infants. While all three groups of physicians were satisfied with the amount of time to discuss growth, development, behavior, and parenting issues, more experienced physicians were more satisfied with their own and their staff's abilities to meet new parents' needs on these issues.

In another set of publications, Cheng and colleagues (1999) described pediatrician goals and practice in preventive counseling, and attempted to use social learning theory to examine physician attitudes about preventive health issues, time, and reimbursement to explain physician counseling behavior. In a random sample survey of 1,620 American Academy of Pediatrics fellows, 556 pediatricians who had finished training and who currently performed child health supervision were asked about their goals in health supervision. They also were asked about the prevalence of counseling, importance of specific topics, their self-efficacy, outcome expectation in these areas, and their concerns about time and reimbursement for preventive counseling. For this group, assurance of physical health and normal development were the most important goals of child health supervision, while goals involving behavior, family, and safety issues were less important and less likely to be addressed in practice. Most did not regularly discuss family and environmental stressors. In these areas, physicians had less confidence that they could provide guidance, and lower expectations regarding their ability to prevent problems. Multiple regression analyses established that the primary predictors of physician counseling were an issue's importance, a physician's perceived self-efficacy, and perceived effectiveness of counseling; in contrast, concerns about time and reimbursement were secondary.

The same group of investigators also collected home interviews of parents of young children being seen at a health maintenance organization (Cheng, Savageau, DeWitt, Bigelow, & Charney, 1996). Mothers stated that physicians were their main source of parenting information. Assurances of physical health and normal development were more important than discussion of behavior, family, or safety issues. Compared to mothers of higher socioeconomic status, mothers of lower socio-

Table 23.1 Definition of Important Terms

Term	Definition	Characteristics of Effective Implementation	Relevant References
Screening	A brief assessment procedure designed to identify children who should receive more intensive diagnosis or assessment	1. Brief and easy to complete 2. Readily administered as questionnaire or interview 3. High sensitivity and specificity when compared to a gold standard	Carter, 2002
Developmental surveillance	An ongoing process that involves well-informed professionals performing skilled observations of children during health care visits	1. Elicitation and attention to parental concerns 2. Collection of relevant history 3. Accurate and informative observations 4. Sharing of concerns with other professionals	Dworkin, 1993
Early detection	Timely identification of children with clinical problems or children who are at risk for clinical problems, to promote participation in early intervention programs or services	Tools include 1. Screening tests 2. Evidence-based techniques of professional elicitation and interpretation of parental concerns	Glascoe, 1999
Anticipatory guidance	Physician description to parent and child of expected developmental changes	Consideration of: 1. Biomedical issues 2. Development 3. Behavior 4. Family functioning 5. Safety education 6. Supportive interpersonal interaction	American Academy of Pediatrics, 2001
Preventive intervention	The early identification and intervention of maladaptive behaviors in preschool children as a precedent to the prevention of psychiatric disorders across the life span	1. Universal models of prevention 2. Selective models of prevention 3. Indicated models of prevention	U.S. Department of Health and Human Services, 2000

economic status were more likely to feel that physical aspects of health should be the focus and were less interested in psychosocial issues. The authors suggested either that mothers do not feel that psychosocial and safety issues are the highest priorities in health supervision or that physicians are not effectively reaching mothers on these issues.

Challenges to Mental Health Assessment in Infants and Preschoolers

Mental health services information suggests that behavioral and emotional disorders still are pediatric problems in need of additional attention. The rates of utilization of behavioral health services are substantially lower than might be estimated from community prevalence rates of childhood mental health problems, and, in particular, pediatricians and other primary care providers appear to underidentify children with behavior problems (Lavigne et al., 1993). Past research has determined that the identification of behavioral and psychosocial problems within pediatric primary care practices is complicated by numerous issues, including but not limited to: brevity of physician-family interaction duration (Horwitz,

Leaf, Leventhal, Forsyth, & Speechley, 1992), sensitivity and specificity issues in the identification of problems, and absence of information from sources outside of the family (e.g., preschool or school teachers).

In the Minkowitz et al. (1998) study described above, over one third of physicians reported that factors affecting their ability to deliver the best-quality care in this clinical area were shortage of support staff, limited referral sources, managed care restrictions on referrals for special services, excessive paperwork, and lack of time for follow-up, teaching parents, and answering questions. Compared to physicians in training or recently in practice, pediatricians with more experience believed they were better meeting new parents' needs and were less likely to cite systems and organizational factors as limiting their ability to deliver high-quality psychosocial care.

In addition, it is clear that pediatricians need to be well trained in clinical skills that allow interviewing in clinically sensitive and developmentally appropriate ways. Studies of patient-physician communication suggest that specific aspects of pediatrician interview style increase disclosure of sensitive information. In a study of pediatric residents, Wissow, Roter, and Wilson (1994) audiotaped and coded pediatric primary care visits. They determined that simple communication skills (i.e., questions about psychosocial issues, statements of support and reassurance, and statements indicating sympathetic and attentive listening) were associated with parental disclosure of specific concerns relevant to child mental health. Training pediatricians to use these skills would help to better detect and diagnose children's mental health problems.

Finally, pediatricians appear to underrefer mental health problems even when those problems are brought to their attention (Briggs-Gowan, Horwitz, Schwab-Stone, Leventhal, & Leaf, 2000); such underreferral presumably results in fewer families seeking mental health services for their children. Other factors that are associated with limited mental health service use include parental reluctance to discuss behavioral and emotional concerns with their pediatricians, child depressive symptoms, and physicians' lack of knowledge regarding patients' stressful life events, as well as low levels of perceived parental burden, and two-parent households (Angold et al., 1998; Briggs-Gowan et al., 2000; Wu et al., 1999).

Summary

It is clear that we need to identify factors that distinguish children with unmet needs for behavioral health services from the rest of the pediatric population. These factors may overlap substantially with the identified barriers to accurate identification of childhood behavioral problems. Additional factors that may adversely affect identification in the primary care physician's office include (1) lack of physician or other staff experience with approaches appropriate for assessment of child mental health in the context of the primary care practice (for example, brief interviews, observation of pediatric practices, telephone follow-up interviews); and (2) inadequate professional training with regard to risk factors for mental health problems and psychosocial adversity.

MENTAL HEALTH PROBLEMS IN INFANTS AND YOUNG CHILDREN (AGES 1 TO 5 YEARS)

In this section, we briefly describe the mental health problems of older infants, toddlers, and preschoolers and address the importance of early identification and referral of young children in this age range.

Types of Problems

Since the mid-1990s, several articles have included extensive reviews of the behavior problems and psychopathology of older infants and young children (e.g., Bjornholm, Moszkowicz, & Skovgaard, 2001; Briggs-Gowan et al., 2001; Keenan, Shaw, Walsh, Delliquadri, & Giovanelli, 1997; Lavigne et al., 1996). For this reason, we do not attempt to include a comprehensive review in this chapter. We briefly note that prevalence rates of serious and persistent socioemotional and behavioral problems in older infants and young children range from 7 to 24% (e.g., Lavigne et al., 1996; Thompson et al., 1996; Zeanah, 2000). These problems include externalizing disorders (e.g., hyperactivity); internalizing disorders (e.g., anxiety disorders, prolonged bereavement/grief reactions); relationship disorders (e.g., reactive attachment disorder, pervasive developmental disorder); and regulatory disorders (e.g., sleep and eating behavior disorders). We also note that the establishment of a diagnosis in infancy and early childhood requires an understanding of very young children's adaptive capabilities as well as their emotional and developmental problems.

Scope and Importance

As noted above, many behavioral problems begin to emerge in late infancy and early childhood, with prevalence rates of up to 20% reported for emotional problems and disruptive behaviors in 4- and 5-year-olds. It also is clear that there are longitudinal pathways from specific early preschool behavioral problems to internalizing and externalizing problems in preadolescence (Mesman, Bongers, & Koot, 2001). It has been proposed that early identification of young children's mental health problems by pediatricians, resulting in appropriate referrals to mental health care specialists, will yield more positive outcomes: less severe behavioral symptoms, improved functioning in home and school environments, and enhanced psychological well-being and quality of life.

To date, however, early identification of behavioral problems has been hindered in several ways. First, we lack a systematic approach to screening and referral that is easily employed in primary care contexts. Second, for all children, but particularly young children, developmental effects are noteworthy. For example, developmentally appropriate anxiety, noncompliance, or activity can blur the boundaries between what is normative, what is a risk factor, and what is pathological or disorder. Third, the issue of cultural salience is not always addressed; in culturally diverse populations, we must discuss with parents both their level of concern and the meaning that they attribute to their children's behavior. In addition, there are suggestions that the assessment of mental health problems in preschool-aged children is complicated by factors including overreporting of child symptoms by mothers with psychopathology (Frick, Silverthorn, & Evans, 1994). To a lessening extent over the past decade, there are continued concerns about a dearth of reliable and valid questionnaire, interview, and observational measures (Bernstein, Borchardt, & Perwien, 1996).

The utility of early identification may seem an obvious point. Early identification can spotlight behavioral problems before they solidify into disorders that may be less responsive to intervention; further, early and precise identification presumably results in more appropriate referral and mental health care. In a study measuring the outcomes of 130 preventive community mental health interventions for children and adolescents, early identification of child maladjustment (before full-blown disorders had developed) significantly reduced problems and increased competencies in participating children, particularly those with subclinical-level behavioral problems (Durlak & Wells, 1998). Similar results have been previously reported among young Mexican American school-aged children (5–8 years), where boys showed fewer teacher-reported acting-out problems and aggressive behaviors after a primary prevention program intervention (Johnson & Walker, 1987).

Summary

Prevalence rates of socioemotional and behavioral problems in older infants and young children range from 7% to 24%. Important diagnostic categories in this age range incorporate developmental and relational aspects and include variations in attachment patterns; disorders of neurophysiological regulation such as eating disorders; failure to thrive; emotional, affective, and behavioral problems (externalizing and internalizing); disorders of relating and communication; and parent-child relationship disorders. In addition, predictors of stability and change in psychiatric disorders occurring among preschool children in primary care populations include family cohesion, life events, and maternal psychopathology (Lavigne et al., 1998). Evidence suggests that a primary care provider's awareness of these diagnostic possibilities, as well as knowledge of the important risk factors for and correlates of these diagnoses, can result in early identification of child maladjustment, reduction in severity of problems, and increase in child competency.

CONCEPTUAL ADVANCES IN ASSESSMENT AND DIAGNOSIS

In this section, we describe two classification systems for describing emotional, behavioral, and social problems of young children: (1) the *Diagnostic and Statistical Manual for Primary Care, Child and Adolescent Version* (DSM-PC; American Academy of Pediatrics, 1996), and (2) the *Diagnostic Classification of Mental Health and Developmental Disorders of Infancy and Early Childhood* (DC:0–3; Zero to Three, 1994).

Diagnostic and Statistical Manual for Primary Care, Child and Adolescent Version

A classification system for diagnosing psychosocial problems in primary care settings has been developed by the American Academy of Pediatrics Task Force on Mental Health Coding for Children. This classification system, DSM-PC, represents a more prevention-oriented, developmentally based system for classifying psychosocial diagnoses of children with mental health symptoms than the standard *Diagnostic and Statistical Manual of Mental Disorders*, Fourth Edition (*DSM-IV*; American Psychiatric Association, 1994; Kelleher & Wolraich, 1996). Drotar (1999) notes that the conceptual framework and goal for the DSM-PC is to address the need for a comprehensive, developmentally appropriate method to facilitate primary care pediatricians' recognition, management, and referral of a wide spectrum of children's behavioral and developmental problems, as well as stressful situations. Further, Costello and Shugart (1992) state that there is an aim of establishing a set of criteria for disorders that do not meet the severity requirements of the American Psychiatric Association's current *DSM-IV*. An element in the argument for the DSM-PC is that there is a high level of functional impairment and need for treatment in children with mental health problems below the *DSM-IV* threshold; this may be particularly true for young children.

While the impact of this system on identification of behavioral problems remains to be established, limited research (Costello & Shugart, 1992) has suggested that the DSM-PC diagnostic system is sensitive to clinical and threshold levels of behavioral symptoms. In a sample of 789 children (age 7–11 years), who were recruited sequentially from the pediatric clinics of a health maintenance organization, 22% had one or more clinical-level *DSM-III* (American Psychiatric Association, 1980) diagnoses, and 42% had a threshold-level disorder. This compared to 134 age-matched children seen in a psychiatric clinic, in which 65% had one or more clinical-level *DSM-III* diagnoses and 34% had a threshold-level disorder. In the pediatric sample, most threshold-level and all clinical-level disruptive behavior disorders were associated with significant levels of functional impairment. In contrast, anxiety and depression, even at the clinical level, were not associated with significant impairment. The authors concluded that one implication of these results is that pediatricians can expect one child in five to have a clinical-level *DSM* disorder. A second is that intervention at low levels of disruptive behavioral symptomatology may be needed if significant functional impairment is to be avoided.

Diagnostic Classification of Mental Health and Developmental Disorders of Infancy and Early Childhood (DC:0–3)

The DC:0–3 represents a comprehensive guide to assessment, diagnosis, and treatment planning for mental health problems in children, from infants to toddlers. DC:0–3 offers a comprehensive, multiaxial framework for diagnosing emotional and developmental problems in the first 3 years of life. DC:0–3 is based on an understanding of emotional, intellectual, motor, and sensory patterns in infancy and makes it possible to pinpoint very young children's adaptive capacities as well as their emotional and developmental difficulties (see chapter 8 for a more extensive discussion). DC:0–3 diagnostic categories include the following:

> Axis I: Primary diagnosis (e.g., traumatic stress disorder, disorders of affect; childhood gender identity disorder; reactive attachment deprivation/maltreatment disorder of infancy and early childhood, adjustment disorder, regulatory disorders, sleep behavior disorder, eating behavior disorder, and disorders of relating and communicating)

Axis II: Relationship disorder classification (e.g., overinvolved, underinvolved, anxious/tense, mixed, abusive, verbally abusive, physically abusive, sexually abusive)

Axis III: Medical and developmental disorders and conditions

Axis IV: Psychosocial stressors

Axis V: Functional emotional developmental level

Intuitively, the DC:0–3 disorders that would seem to be most apparent in primary care settings, where the largest number of well-child visits occur between birth and age 2 years, include regulatory disorders and relationship disorders. To some degree, this intuition is supported by a study of referral patterns of primary care physicians to an infant mental health clinic (Keren, Feldman, & Tyano, 2001). In this study, two peaks of referral were found for children aged 0 to 6 months and children aged 12 to 18 months. Further, the DC:0–3 was used to characterize the main reasons for referral, which were eating problems, sleep problems, aggressive behavior, irritability, and maternal depression. Another study conducted by Thomas and Guskin (2001) evaluated young children presenting with disruptive behavior to an early childhood psychiatry clinic. The authors determined that children with relationship and affect disorders (as determined by DC:0–3) had more externalizing and internalizing symptoms. These data suggest that primary care providers might utilize the DC:0–3 diagnoses to focus discussion with parents on specific behavioral symptom sets.

Summary

Both the DSM-PC and the DC:0–3 diagnostic classification strategies appear to have utility in primary care settings and have provided further clarification of what constitutes disorder in this age group. However, it should be remembered that it is not necessarily sufficient for primary care physicians to establish a diagnosis and refer for a mental health intervention; diagnosis is only one aspect of a broader range of assessment strategies.

In any event, there is little evidence that pediatricians are systematically employing the available categorical systems (nor any dimensional classification procedure). Strategies to enhance utilization of the DSM-PC or the DC:0–3 system include more widespread dissemination of information concerning the classification systems and their practical utility, promotion of reimbursement for their use, and documenting applications of the DSM-PC and DC:0–3 diagnostic classifications in teaching, practice, and research.

METHODOLOGICAL ADVANCES IN ASSESSMENT AND DIAGNOSIS

In this section, we review the literature concerning screening instruments for mental health problems in young children. The review is described in tabular form for the reader's ease of reference. We have included definitions of psychometric terms (table 23.2). We have created several categories of screening measures: instruments primarily behavioral[1] in focus (see table 23.3), instruments primarily developmental[2] in focus (see table 23.4), diagnosis-specific instruments[3] (see table 23.5), and instruments focused on screening for family psychosocial problems (see table 23.6). For each instrument, we summarize the appropriate age range for use, the respondent required, a short description (including dimensions, number of items, and time to complete), psychometrics (including reliability and validity, if available), and cross-cultural applicability (if known). Finally, we note our own assessment of the utility of each instrument in pediatric practice, and apparent strengths and weaknesses.

Some of the most widely used behavioral instruments, the versions of the CBCL (Achenbach & Rescorla, 2000a) provide useful measures of both adaptive functioning and impairment (see table 23.3). They have a number of features common to all the Achenbach System of Empirically Based Assessment (ASEBA) forms that deserve special mention here. The versions for parents and teachers/caregivers are translated into 58 languages with comparison scores published for children from 12 different cultures. ASEBA also offers the *Medical Practitioners' Guide for the ASEBA* forms that provide a standardized basis for comparing the problems and language reported for a sick child with those reported for normal age mates (Achenbach & Rescorla, 2000b). Their cross-informant information and *DSM-IV–*

Table 23.2 Definition of Psychometric Terms

Reliability

Interrater or alternate form: The extent of agreement between examiners or alternate forms.

Test-retest: The extent of agreement between readministrations of a measure by the original examiner after a short interval (2–6 weeks).

Stability agreement: The extent of agreement between readministrations of a measure after longer intervals (3–12 months).

Excellent	kappa > 0.9
Very good	kappa > 0.8
Good	kappa = 0.7–0.8
Fair	kappa = 0.5–0.7
Poor	kappa < 0.5

Reliability

Internal consistency: The extent to which items interrelate and are assessing a well-defined construct.

High	alpha > 0.7
Moderate	alpha = 0.5–0.7
Low	alpha < 0.5

	Criterion-Related: Categorical Measures, Diagnoses, or Continuous Measures With a Cutoff Point				
Validity	Sensitivity	Specificity	Concurrent	Construct	Discriminant
Definition	Tests the ability to identify true cases, or true positive rate	The test's accuracy in identifying noncases, the false positive rate	The degree to which a test is related to other similar measures	Determining whether test items are representative of the domain or construct the test purports to measure	The degree to which a test can discriminate unique patterns or problems
Analytic Strategy	Percentages of Cases Correctly Identified	Percentages of Noncases Who Are Identified	Usually by Eta Correlations	Correlation Coefficient	Logistic Regression
Good	>.75	>.75	eta ≥. 60	Depending on the data, the appropriate strength of association statistic will vary	Odds ratios attaining statistical significance
Fair	.65–.75	.65–.75	eta < .60		
Poor	<.65	<.65			

oriented scales are useful additions. The forms may be hand scored or computer scored by a program that provides clinical profiles, narrative summaries, and comparisons of problem items and subscale scores for up to eight forms per child.

The Child Development Inventories (CDI; Ireton, 1992) are another set of instruments that offer a systematic approach in obtaining information from parents about their children's functioning (see table 23.4). These inventories have been used in a variety of cultural settings and have been translated into Spanish, Russian, Chinese, Arabic, and several other languages. Research and practice have established their validity since the inventories were constructed. Excellent sensitivity and good specificity for the CDIs have been reported.

Please note that, under psychometrics in each

Table 23.3 Screening Instruments Primarily Behavioral in Focus

Screening Instrument	Child Behavior Checklist–Revised (CBCL-R; Achenbach & Rescorla, 2000)	Caregiver-Teacher Report Forms–Revised (Achenbach & Rescorla, 2000)	Burks' Behavior Rating Scales, Preschool and Kindergarten Edition (Burks, 1977)
Age range	1½–5 years	1½–5 years	3–6 years
Respondent	Parent	Caregiver or teacher	Parent or teacher
Number of items or description	99 items	99 items	105 items
Domains covered	Behavioral/emotional/social	Emotional/behavioral	Behavioral/emotional
Psychometrics	Scales derived from factor analyses of correlations among items. Test-retest reliability high for most subscales. Good cross-informant agreement. Content, criterion-related, and construct validity of problem scales acceptable.	Good test-retest reliability and stability correlations.	High test-retest reliability. Validity based on criterion-related, content, and factorial validity. The 25% overlap of 3 factors does not support division of items into 18 categories of behavior.
Cross-cultural validity	The final normative sample consists of nonreferred children from all socioeconomic status groups, 4 ethnic groups, 40 states, and both mother and father as respondents.	The strategy of forming normative samples was the same as for the CBCL, with caregiver or teacher as respondents.	Cross-cultural information not available from research sample. No behavior pattern differences were found between a small sample of Mexican American and White children in a later study.
Utility in pediatric primary care setting	The CBCL can help monitor psychoactive medication and determine whether certain behavioral or emotional problems accompany a particular medical condition.	See CBCL Parent Version.	Has some ability to identify patterns of disturbed behavior where further evaluation might be needed. Also has some ability to show changes in behavior patterns over time.
Stengths and weaknesses	Spanish versions available. Includes language development survey feature. The CBCL can be used to guide clinical interviews.	Spanish versions available. No language development survey.	The scales' standardization sample consisted of a small group lacking cross-cultural information. Conceptual model of behavioral problems appears to be outdated.

Behavior Assessment System for Children (BASC; Reynolds & Kamphaus, 1992)	Infant-Toddler Social and Emotional Assessment (ITSEA; Carter & Briggs-Gowan, 1993)	Brief Infant-Toddler Social and Emotional Assessment (BITSEA; Carter, 2000)	The Toddler Behavior Screening Inventory (TBSI; Mouton-Simien et al., 1997)	Pediatric Symptom Checklist (Jellinek et al., 1988)
2½–5 years	1–3 years	1–3 years	12–41 months	4–16 years
Parent or teacher	Parent	Parent	Parent	Parent
10–20 minutes to complete	139 items	60 items	40 items	35 items
Aspects of behavior and personality, adaptive and clinical dimensions	Externalizing, internalizing, dysregulation, and competencies domains covered	Problem index and competence index	Frequently occurring toddler behaviors that cause mothers concern; problems scale and frequency scale	Behavioral/ emotional
High internal consistency and test-retest reliability; atypicality and conduct problems subscale reliabilities are relatively low; high correlations obtained with the CBCL and externalizing scales of the Conners' Parent Rating Scale (Conners, 1997). Norms differentiated according to age, gender, and status.	High internal consistency for domains and moderately high internal consistency for subscales. Excellent test-retest reliability. Good criterion-related and construct validity.	Fair to good sensitivity and specificity in identifying children with extreme scores on ITSEA and CBCL/2–3. Good criterion-related and construct validity (as described in Carter, 2002).	Adequate intrascale and test-retest reliability. Concurrent validity was relatively strong between the TBSI frequency scale and the CBCL/2–3 but less so with the problem scale, suggesting the two scales should be used together.	Good internal consistency and very good test-retest reliability. Over time, good sensitivity and specificity. Good validity demonstrated.
Norms based on large, representative samples weighted within gender so distributions of race/ethnicity and parental education would match 1988 U.S. Census.	Normative data established in a community birth cohort sample of >1,300 "ethnically and socioeconomically diverse" families.	Data collected from an early intervention sample.	Measure developed with samples of mothers who were primarily married, middle-class Caucasians. Further research with special populations needed.	Normative data established from a large, representative sample.
Scales are highly interpretable from clearly specified constructs; easy to administer and quick to score.	Longer measure intended for second-stage screening of problem behaviors.	Shorter measure intended for first-stage screening of problem behaviors.	Promising screening measure to quickly detect toddlers at risk for long-term problems. Brief and easy to use.	A useful, quick screening tool for assessing psychosocial dysfunction.
Consists of useful composite scales (externalizing problems, internalizing problems, school problems, other problems, and adaptive skills). Spanish versions available.	Combined problem and competence items in an effort to reduce response set biases.	Items selected from ITSEA; selection based on highest loading items in factor analysis plus judgment by expert of items' "clinical importance."	Attempts to measure the range of problems unique to the entire toddler period. More extensive research needed in cross-cultural area and with nonclinical populations.	Cutoff scores for preschool children indicating psychosocial impairment have been empirically developed.

Table 23.4 Screening Instruments Primarily Developmental in Focus

Screening Instruments	Child Development Inventory (CDI; Ireton, 1992)	Infant Development Inventory (IDI; Ireton, 1992)	Early Child Development Inventory (Ireton, 1992)
Age range	4–16 years	0–18 months	15 months–3 years
Respondent	Parent	Parent	Parent
Number of items, time to complete	300 items.	The parent questionnaire is one page, two sides with a child development chart on the back.	Consists of a one-page two-sided questionnaire with 60 items that measure overall development; 24 items pertain to behavioral symptoms and problem behaviors.
Domains covered	Developmental, including strengths and delays in social and self-help	Developmental	Developmental and problem behaviors checklist
Psychometrics	Internal consistency of each of the developmental scales by age varies from .33 to .96. Separate scales are not supported by factor analysis or cluster analysis. The General Development Scale is highly correlated with most of the CDI scales. Valid for age changes with exception of Letters and Numbers Scales, which should be interpreted with caution below age 5. Correlations between parents' CDI scale results and kindergarten achievement range from not significant to .69.	The IDI items were drawn from the Minnesota Child Developmental Inventory that has stable age norms. It has good overall agreement with the Bayley Scale scores and has demonstrated good sensitivity in detecting delay with fair specificity in identifying normal development.	The total score on the development subscale is highly age discriminating and 90% predictive of significant developmental problems.
Cross-cultural validity	The initial standardization sample, which was 95% White, is inappropriate for comparison to parents of some racial and cultural groups and for parents with less than a high school education.	See CDI.	See CDI.
Utility in pediatric primary setting	Provides a systematic and in-depth measure of development. Also serves as a useful screening measure for various symptoms and behavior problems.	A child development chart, used as an observation guide, provides benchmarks for the first 21 months. Below-age guidelines are provided to identify infants who are possibly delayed.	Includes a brief manual for the professional; provides indicators of need for follow-up evaluation. Additionally, parents describe their child, report any special problems or concerns, and report status of parent.
Strengths and weaknesses	Widely used in pediatric settings. Recent revision provides a more representative normative sample. Number of infant items is limited.	Measures development in 5 areas: social, self-help, gross motor, fine motor, and language.	Covers areas of general development, possible problems, child description, special problems, or handicaps. The accuracy of the possible problem items for identifying current problems has not yet been studied.

Preschool Development Inventory (PDI; Ireton, 1992)	Child Development Review (CDR; Ireton, 1992)	Parents' Evaluations of Developmental Status (PEDS; Glascoe, 1998)
3 years–Kindergarten	18 months–5 years	0–8 years
Parent	Parent	Parent
PDI format is the same as the Early Child Development Inventory.	The parent questionnaire includes 6 questions and a 25-item problem checklist.	10 questions eliciting parents' concerns.
Developmental and problems checklist	Developmental and problems checklist	Learning, development, and behavior
Sensitivity of .68; specificity of .88.	Research shows parents' responses to this questionnaire are accurate indicators of children's developmental and behavioral problems	PEDS has high interrater and test-retest reliability. Intercorrelations among concerns are modest. It has high degree of internal consistency. Discriminant validity is high. Concurrent validity correlations are high but not always in the expected domain.
See CDI.	See CDI.	Standardization sample included from diverse geographic regions, racial backgrounds, and parents' levels of education.
Provides indicators of need for follow-up evaluation.	Useful for well child care visits. A developmental chart covering birth to age 5 years. The IDI and CDR complement each other and are standardized based on established norms.	Identifies when to refer, screen further, give parents advice, or monitor vigilantly.
See Early Child Development Inventory.	Measures development in 5 areas: social, self-help, gross motor, fine motor, and language.	Spanish versions available.

Table 23.5 Diagnosis-Specific Screening Instruments

Screening Instruments	Conners Parent and Teacher Rating Scales–Revised: Short (Conners, 1997)	Eyberg Child Behavior Inventory (Eyberg, 1980)	Childhood Autism Rating Scale (CARS; Schopler et al., 1988)	Checklist for Autism in Toddlers (CHAT; Baron-Cohen et al., 1992)	Pervasive Developmental Disorders Screening Test (PDDST-II; Siegel, 1996)
Age range	3–17 years	2–16 years	>36 months	>18 months	0–3 years
Respondent	Parent and teacher	Parent	Parent, teacher, or clinician	Parent	Parent self-administered and self-explanatory. Can be administered by clinician without autism expertise.
Number of items, time to complete	Parent, 27 items; Teacher, 28 items. Both 5–10 minutes to complete.	36	15 items, 10–15 minutes to complete.	9-item parent report and 5-item observation-based measure. 10–15 minutes to administer.	Full form can be administered or as one of three-stage set, depending upon clinical setting or purpose of assessment. Full form takes 10 minutes to complete.
Domains covered	Measures specific symptom patterns related to ADHD, cognitive problems, oppositional, hyperactivity-impulsivity, anxious-shy, perfectionism, social problems, and psychosomatic subscales.	Behavioral/emotional	Identifies children with autism and distinguishes them from developmentally handicapped children without autism.	Autism	Autism

Psychometrics	Confirmatory factor analysis established a definitive 7-factor model. Good internal reliability coefficients, high test-retest reliability, and effective discriminatory power demonstrated.	Very good internal consistency, test-retest, and reliability have been demonstrated for this scale. Good concurrent and discriminant validity. A recent factor analysis produced 3 meaningful factors (oppositional behavior toward adults, inattentive behavior, and conduct problem behavior), a better fit than earlier 2- and 1-factor models.	Positive predictive validity = 75%. Poor sensitivity.	Early studies suggest reliability can be improved by reviewing questions with parent. Test includes sufficient PDD signs to provide good predictability (combining specificity and sensitivity). Errors tend to be in false positives. The PDDST-II has acceptably high levels of accuracy.	
Cross-cultural validity	Normative data derived from a large, representative sample of North American children. Reliability high for measuring scale constructs for gender, age, groups, and certain ethnic groups.	Recent normative sample (1999) included adequate number of children at different age levels and broad range ethnic and socioeconomic groups, and family structures as well as children from urban and rural settings.	Ten years of scale development and revision based on 1,500 children reflecting the racial distribution served by the public schools in North Carolina.	Sensitivity and validity tested in a large-scale, longitudinal, population-based study.	Nearly 1,200 children have been studied in the outpatient child psychiatry clinic of a major university in a large city during the time this test was developed. No racial or ethnic information reported on the sample at this time.

(continued)

Table 23.5 Continued

Screening Instruments	Conners Parent and Teacher Rating Scales–Revised: Short (Conners, 1997)	Eyberg Child Behavior Inventory (Eyberg, 1980)	Childhood Autism Rating Scale (CARS; Schopler et al., 1988)	Checklist for Autism in Toddlers (CHAT; Baron-Cohen et al., 1992)	Pervasive Developmental Disorders Screening Test (PDDST-II; Siegel, 1996)
Utility in pediatric primary setting	Provides an effective screening tool for assessing parental reports of childhood behavior problems with an emphasis on ADHD and related behaviors. Has updated item content to reflect recent knowledge of childhood behavior problems.	Easy to administer and score. Widely used to measure disruptive behavior problems in children.	A widely used behavioral rating system for autism symptomatology that can be scored with unstructured observations in a clinic.	Observation-based instrument designed to be used in primary care settings at well-child visits.	Observation section considered a brief, performance-based measure of autism symptomatology. Best used as a 2-stage screener, but continues to have poor sensitivity.
Strengths and weaknesses	Scale development and refinement based on a large number of children over 10 years' use of the scale and based on behavioral and empirical data. Effective at discriminating ADHD children from normal children.	Discriminates adequately between clinic-referred and nonreferred children.	Distinguishes between mild to moderate range and moderate to severe range. Does not use the same triad or differentiate between the different subtypes of PDD defined by the DSM-IV but functions well as a screening device.	Designed for use in primary care settings to identify children who may meet criteria for a PDD including autistic disorder, PDD-NOS, and Asperger's disorder.	A useful addition to the area of developmental disorders assessment. Manual providing information regarding clinical samples, test construction, and test administration and interpretation in preparation.

Note: ADHD, attention deficit/hyperactivity disorder; PDD, pervasive developmental disorder; NOS, not otherwise specified.

Table 23.6 Family Psychosocial Screening Instruments

Screening Instruments	Parenting Stress Index/Short Form (PSI/SF; Abidin, 1990)	Family Psychosocial Screening (Kemper & Kelleher, 1996)
Age range	1 month–12 years	Parents of young children
Respondent	Parent	Parent
Number of items or time to complete	36 items	Two-page clinic intake form; takes about 10 minutes to complete
Domains covered	Identifies parent-child systems that are under stress. Provides global measure of total stress and specific measure of parental distress, parent-child dysfunctional interaction, and difficult child subscales.	Psychosocial risk factors of parent.
Psychometrics	The PSI/SF is a direct derivative of the long form. The original, large standardization sample was primarily on mothers from a variety of settings and a broad range of socioeconomic groups with a much smaller sample of fathers. A number of more recent independent research samples have extended the clinical utility of this instrument. The correlations of the short form with the full-length PSI are high. A number of recent studies provide evidence for the construct and predictive validity of the long form of the PSI. Empirical validity in terms of predictive validity in relation to observed parent-child interactions has been demonstrated in the PSI/SF.	Good sensitivity and specificity.
Cross-cultural validity	The factor structure of the PSI has been replicated not only in a variety of U.S. samples but also in transcultural research involving samples from a half dozen other countries.	No information.
Utility in pediatric primary setting	The PSI serves as a first-gate diagnostic and triaging measure that flags a dyad for attention and provides direction to the areas for further assessment or where intervention is needed.	Screens for parental history of physical abuse as a child, parental substance abuse, and maternal depression.
Strengths and weaknesses	Captures the primary components of the parent-child system by focusing on the parent, the child, and their interactions. Conversion of raw scores into percentile scores is available on the profile of the test form. Translated into over 15 languages with replication studies of the PSI factor structure.	Identification of psychosocial risk factors associated with developmental and behavioral problems of the child.

table, we have used the descriptors in table 23.2 to provide a shorthand estimate of validity and reliability for each instrument. Even though we suggest these criteria, certain factors must be taken into account that affect reliability or validity, such as the relative stability of the trait or behavior being measured, the method of estimating reliability or validity, or perhaps the test format itself. Thus, certain questions must be asked when evaluating whether or not to use a test, for example, will the test be accurate within the context and purpose for which it is to be used?

As a brief reminder to the reader, *reliability* refers to the consistency of a measurement, a vital characteristic of a test. The three types of reliability are test-retest, alternate form or interexaminer, and internal consistency. They are usually expressed by a reliability coefficient or by the standard error of measurement. These refer to whether the test results have stability over time, whether identical results are obtained from different forms of the test or examiners, and how well the items interrelate, that is, relate to the same broad idea. High reliabilities are especially needed for tests used for individual assessment. Several factors affect reliability, including test length, test-retest interval, variability of scores, guessing, and situational factors.

Even though a test might have high reliability (consistency), it may not be valid. The validity of a test is concerned with the extent to which a test measures what it is supposed to measure, in a particular setting with a particular population. Thus, when the issue of validity is addressed, evidence is being established for the validity of the scores on that test for a particular purpose, and not the validity of the test per se. The three principal types are content, criterion-related, and construct validity. They involve, respectively, evaluation of test content, correlations with specific criteria, and evaluation of concepts underlying the development of the test. Because tests are used for many different purposes, no single type of validity is appropriate for all testing purposes. Establishing reliability requires only several independent replicated measures on a sample of subjects. To establish validity, one or more gold standards or criteria related to the purpose of the test are needed.

Summary

While several instruments have been described as screening tools that can serve in the early identification of behavioral problems in young children, few focus on behavioral (in contrast to developmental) issues and satisfy the stringent requirements of brevity, established reliability and validity, and cross-cultural appropriateness. Based on our review, the Brief Infant-Toddler Social and Emotional Assessment (BITSEA; Briggs-Gowan et al., 2001) and Behavior Assessment System for Children (BASC; Reynolds & Kamphaus, 1992) meet these criteria for toddlers and preschoolers, while the Pediatric Symptom Checklist (PSC;

Jellinek et al., 1999) meets these criteria for slightly older children (4- and 5-year-olds).

In addition to a few satisfactory measures that exist to screen for global mental health problems in the young child, our review highlights measures that address the parent-child relationship and assess some psychological and social aspects of the parents and family. Measures are also available for the specific diagnosis of autism spectrum disorders and externalizing behavioral problems, specifically for attention deficit/hyperactivity disorder (ADHD) and related problems, in the young child. These instruments have good psychometric properties and norms with clinical utility. Unfortunately, screening tools for the internalizing disorders of anxiety and depression in the young child are largely absent. One reason for this absence may be that researchers agree that internalizing symptoms involve interacting response domains rather than a unitary construct. Thus, screening for anxiety and depression is likely to require multiple assessments to tap each domain.

IMPORTANT GOALS FOR PRIMARY CARE PRACTICE AND CLINICAL RESEARCH

In this section, we speculate on ways to facilitate the initiation of systematic mental health screening during pediatric primary care visits. Further, we highlight the challenges that must be addressed to implement these routines. Finally, we reflect on logical next steps in related clinical research.

Strategies and Challenges for Mental Health Screening

Screening Young Children During Primary Care Visits

The following strategies can facilitate the screening and early identification of young children's behavioral problems in primary care settings.

- A short screening protocol for all children older than 18 months might include parent-completed developmental and behavioral problems screeners (e.g., PEDS and PSC).

- Screening might be initiated by office staff and facilitated by adjunct mental health professionals.
- Early identification strategies could make use of waiting room time to have parents complete carefully selected screening instruments.
- Based on results of initial screen, further information could be collected from caregivers on more extensive questionnaires by a mailout-mailback process or by phone follow-up.
- Primary care providers should receive more extensive training in the arena of early childhood behavior problems and the importance of parent-physician communication about psychosocial issues. This training should include increasing skills in: (1) the elicitation of parent opinions and concerns, (2) the observation of parent and child behavior during well-child and acute care visits, and (3) the consideration of the opinions of other professionals (such as preschool teachers and day care providers).
- Primary care providers should acquire more knowledge of the need to manage and/or refer positive screening results, the utility of tracking outcomes, and the importance of cost benefits.

Difficulty of Screening During Primary Care Visits

The following challenges must be addressed:

1. Limited time is available to care for increasing numbers of patients.
2. There is inadequate reimbursement for preventive efforts, such as addressing psychosocial problems.
3. An administrative burden is inherent in systematically implementing screening procedures that must be sustained by the practitioner.
4. The primary care provider may feel that management options (including referral after screening) are constrained by (a) the limited number of qualified child mental health clinicians, especially clinicians trained in the evaluation and treatment of younger children; and (b) the complicated, lengthy,

and duplicative processes required for children to receive mental and behavioral health services.

Important Directions for Clinical Research in this Area

We have suggested that pediatricians may hold great influence in the early identification and referral of young children with behavioral problems. However, very little research has explored these issues systematically. Further, mental health service utilization research historically has focused on older school-aged and adolescent children, and has not adequately addressed the referral processes that lead young children into such services or the effects of pediatricians on these processes. Future research might address some of these insufficiencies by doing the following:

- Identifying young children's behavioral problems across multiple contexts, especially home, preschool, and primary care settings—the situations in which young children spend most of their time and in which they cross paths with trained professionals who can facilitate access to appropriate subspecialist care.
- Exploring the feasibility of screening instruments for the identification of mental health problems in young children, considering the critical issues of cultural validity and working within real-life contexts, including and extending beyond primary health care.
- Including multiple respondents. It is important to collect various sources of data concerning behavioral problems described by parents in the doctor's office. Research procedures that validate parental report with responses from other more objective reporters will assist in determining appropriate referrals and may help avoid unnecessary and costly overreferrals.
- Understanding pediatrician-initiated referrals. It is critical to begin to clarify the factors that contribute to parents' pursuit of recommended treatment for children identified as being in need of subspecialist mental health care. It is likely that different factors contribute to pediatricians' decision making about referrals. Assessment of the referral process is challenging. Collecting in

formation based on maternal recall of professional recommendations is one strategy; corroboration of this information with data from medical information systems is another strategy. Information gleaned via medical information systems can provide the absolute amount of services recommended as well as a clearer description of the time interval between identification, referral, and pursuit of referral.

Another goal for future research will be to evaluate whether early identification, per se, of preschoolers' mental health problems by primary care pediatricians will result in improved child behavioral and educational outcomes. It has been suggested that pediatricians' increased mental health–related skills and improved strategies for identification of children with mental health problems will have a positive effect on at-risk children and families. However, little prospective research to date has systematically examined these effects (Yoshikawa, 1994; Yoshikawa & Knitzer, 1997). It will be important to use mental health problem data collected in clinics to begin cost-effectiveness analyses and to assess whether early mental health screening is feasible, beneficial, and justified. These conclusions can be established by ascertaining (a) the frequency of mental health problems; (b) the accuracy of screening tests, measuring the performance characteristics of the screening tests against a gold standard; (c) the ability of primary health care providers to appropriately refer children for subspecialty mental health care; (d) the capacity of mental health specialists to provide early intervention; (e) the documentation of improved outcomes that are attributable to early intervention; (f) confirmation of the type and intensity of interventions; and (g) the potential for recovery of all screening costs in the prevention of future intervention costs.

These clinical research topics are important and relevant to child health broadly. Studies that integrate sociocultural and educational theory, developmental psychopathology research, and clinical service investigation have the potential to dramatically increase our knowledge in this arena. Such research can contribute to the improvement of current primary care practices, the advancement of relations between primary pediatric care and specialty mental health services, and to an understanding of the social and economic aspects of primary care.

Notes

1. *Behavioral* constitutes a focus on contextual relationships and functions, the biological and psychosocial factors that enhance or disturb them, and the resulting variations and deviations in a child's growth, behavior, and emotions.

2. *Developmental* constitutes a focus on the manifestations of the maturation of the central nervous system and how it is affected by biology and environment, resulting in abilities and/or disabilities.

3. *Diagnosis-specific* constitutes behavioral, emotional, and developmental issues that are particular to an individual disorder.

References

Abidin, R. R. (1990). *Parenting stress index: Manual.* Charlottesville, VA: University of Virginia, Pediatric Psychology Press.

Achenbach, T. M., & Rescorla, L. A. (2000a). *Manual for the ASEBA preschool forms and profiles.* Burlington, VT: University of Vermont, Department of Psychiatry.

Achenbach, T. M., & Rescorla, L. A. (2000b). *Medical practitioners' guide for the ASEBA.* Burlington, VT: University of Vermont, Research Center for Children, Youth & Families.

American Academy of Pediatrics. (1996). *Diagnostic and statistical manual for primary care (DSM-PC): Child and adolescent version.* Elk Grove Village, IL: Author.

American Academy of Pediatrics. (2001). Developmental surveillance and screening of infants and young children. *Pediatrics, 108*(1), 192–196.

American Psychiatric Association (1980). *Diagnostic and statistical manual of mental disorders* (3rd ed.). Washington, DC: Author.

American Psychiatric Association (1994). *Diagnostic and statistical manual of mental disorders* (4th ed.). Washington, DC: Author.

Angold, A., Messer, S. C., Stangl, D., Farmer, E. M., Costello, E. J., & Burns, B. J. (1998). Perceived parental burden and service use for child and adolescent psychiatric disorders. *American Journal of Public Health, 88*(1), 75–80.

Baron-Cohen, S., Allen, J., & Gillberg, C. (1992). Can autism be detected at 18 months? The needle, the haystack, and the CHAT. *British Journal of Psychiatry, 168,* 839–843.

Bernstein, G. A., Borchardt, C. M., & Perwien, A. R. (1996). Anxiety disorders in children and adolescents: A review of the past 10 years. *Journal of the American Academy of Child and Adolescent Psychiatry, 35*(9), 1110–1119.

Bird, H. R., Gould, M. S., & Staghezza, B. M. (1993). Patterns of diagnostic comorbidity in a community sample of children aged 9 through 16 years. *Journal of the American Academy of Child and Adolescent Psychiatry, 32*(2), 361–368.

Bird, H. R., Shaffer, D., Fisher, P., Gould, M. S., Staghezza, B., Chen, J. V., et al. (1993). The Columbia Impairment Scale (CIS): Pilot findings on a measure of global impairment for children and adolescents. *International Journal of Methods in Psychiatric Research, 3*, 167–176.

Bjornholm, K. I., Moszkowicz, M., & Skovgaard, A. M. (2001). [Infant psychiatry]. *Ugeskr Laeger, 163*(8), 1107–1111.

Briggs-Gowan, M. J., Carter, A. S., Moye Skuban, E., & McCue Horwitz, S. (2001). Prevalence of social-emotional and behavioral problems in a community sample of 1- and 2-year-old children. *Journal of the American Academy of Child and Adolescent Psychiatry, 40*(7), 811–819.

Briggs-Gowan, M. J., Horwitz, S. M., Schwab-Stone, M. E., Leventhal, J. M., & Leaf, P. J. (2000). Mental health in pediatric settings: Distribution of disorders and factors related to service use. *Journal of the American Academy of Child and Adolescent Psychiatry, 39*(7), 841–849.

Burks, H. F. (1977). *Burks' behavior rating scales, preschool and kindergarten edition.* Los Angeles: Western Psychological Services.

Campbell, S. B., Breaux, A. M., Ewing, L. J., Szumowski, E. K., & Pierce, E. W. (1986). Parent-identified problem preschoolers: Mother-child interaction during play at intake and 1-year follow-up. *Journal of Abnormal Child Psychology, 14*(3), 425–440.

Carter, A. S. (2002). Assessing social-emotional and behavior problems and competencies in infancy and toddlerhood: Available instruments and directions for application. In B. Zuckerman, A. Lieberman, & N. Fox (Eds.), *Emotion regulation and developmental health: Infancy and early childhood (pp. 277–299).* New York: Johnson and Johnson Pediatric Institute.

Carter, A., & Briggs-Gowan, M. (1993). *The infant-toddler social and emotional assessment (ITSEA).*
New Haven, CT: Yale University Department of Psychology.

Cheng, T. L., DeWitt, T. G., Savageau, J. A., & O'Connor, K. G. (1999). Determinants of counseling in primary care pediatric practice: Physician attitudes about time, money, and health issues. *Archives of Pediatric and Adolescent Medicine, 153*(6), 629–635.

Cheng, T. L., Savageau, J. A., DeWitt, T. G., Bigelow, C., & Charney, E. (1996). Expectations, goals, and perceived effectiveness of child health supervision: A study of mothers in a pediatric practice. *Clinical Pediatrics (Philadelphia), 35*(3), 129–137.

Conners, C. K. (1997). *Conners' rating scales-revised manual.* North Tonawanda, NY: Multi-Health Systems.

Costello, E. J. (1989). Child psychiatric disorders and their correlates: A primary care pediatric sample. *Journal of the American Academy of Child and Adolescent Psychiatry, 28*(6), 851–855.

Costello, E. J., & Shugart, M. A. (1992). Above and below the threshold: Severity of psychiatric symptoms and functional impairment in a pediatric sample. *Pediatrics, 90*(3), 359–368.

Drotar, D. (1999). The diagnostic and statistical manual for primary care (DSM-PC), child and adolescent version: What pediatric psychologists need to know. *Journal of Pediatric Psychology, 24*(5), 369–380.

Durlak, J. A., & Wells, A. M. (1998). Evaluation of indicated preventive intervention (secondary prevention) mental health programs for children and adults. *American Journal of Community Psychology, 26*, 775–802.

Dworkin, P. H. (1993). Detection of behavioral, developmental, and psychosocial problems in pediatric primary care practice [review]. *Current Opinion in Pediatrics, 5*(5), 531–536.

Earls, F. (1980). The prevalence of behavior problems in 3-year-old children. *Journal of the American Academy of Child and Adolescent Psychiatry, 19*(3), 439–452.

Eyberg, S. (1980). Eyberg child behavior inventory. *Journal of Clinical Child Psychology, 54*, 587–599.

Frick, P. J., Silverthorn, P., & Evans, C. (1994). Assessment of childhood anxiety using structured interviews: Patterns of agreement among informants and association with maternal anxiety. *Psychological Assessment, 6*, 372–379.

Glascoe, F. (1998). *Collaborating with parents.* Nashville, TN: Ellsworth and Vandermeer Press.

Glascoe, F. (1999). Early detection of developmental and behavioral problems [review]. *Pediatrics Review, 21*(8), 272–279.

Horwitz, S. M., Leaf, P. J., & Leventhal, J. M. (1998). Identification of psychosocial problems in pediatric primary care: Do family attitudes make a difference? *Archives of Pediatric and Adolescent Medicine, 152*(4), 367–371.

Horwitz, S. M., Leaf, P. J., Leventhal, J. M., Forsyth, B., & Speechley, K. N. (1992). Identification and management of psychosocial and developmental problems in community-based, primary care pediatric practices. *Pediatrics, 89*(3), 480–485.

Ireton, H. R. (1992). *Child development inventories.* Minneapolis, MN: Behavior Science Systems.

Jellinek, M. S., Murphy, J. M., Robinson, J., Feins, A., Lamb, S., & Fenton, T. (1988). Pediatric symptom checklist: Screening school-age children for psychosocial dysfunction. *Pediatrics, 112,* 201–209.

Jellinek, M. S., Murphy, J. M., Little, M., Pagano, M. E., Comer, D. M., & Kelleher, K. J. (1999). Use of the Pediatric Symptom Checklist to screen for psychosocial problems in pediatric primary care: A national feasibility study. *Archives of Pediatrics and Adolescent Medicine, 153*(3), 254–260.

Johnson, D. L., & Walker, T. (1987). Primary prevention of behavior problems in Mexican-American children. *American Journal of Community Psychology, 15*(4), 375–385.

Keenan, K., Shaw, D. S., Walsh, B., Delliquadri, E., & Giovanelli, J. (1997). DSM-III-R disorders in preschool children from low-income families. *Journal of the American Academy of Child and Adolescent Psychiatry, 36*(5), 620–627.

Kelleher, K. J., & Wolraich, M. L. (1996). Diagnosing psychosocial problems. *Pediatrics, 97*(6, Pt. 1), 899–901.

Kemper, K. J., & Kelleher, K. J. (1996). Family psychosocial screening: Instruments and techniques. *Ambulatory Child Health, 112,* 201–209.

Keren, M., Feldman, R., & Tyano, S. (2001). Emotional disturbances in infancy: Diagnostic classification and interactive patterns of infants referred to a community-based infant mental health clinic. *Journal of the American Academy of Child and Adolescent Psychiatry, 40*(1), 27–35.

Lavigne, J. V., Arend, R., Rosenbaum, D., Binns, H. J., Christoffel, K. K., & Gibbons, R. D. (1998). Psychiatric disorders with onset in the preschool years. I. Stability of diagnoses. *Journal of the American Academy of Child and Adolescent Psychiatry, 37*(12), 1246–1254.

Lavigne, J. V., Binns, H. J., Christoffel, K. K., Rosenbaum, D., Arend, R., Smith, K., Hayford, J. R., McGuire, P. A., & Pediatric Practice Research Group. (1993). Behavioral and emotional problems among preschool children in pediatric primary care: Prevalence and pediatricians' recognition. Pediatric Practice Research Group. *Pediatrics, 91*(3), 649–655.

Lavigne, J. V., Gibbons, R. D., Christoffel, K. K., Arend, R., Rosenbaum, D., Binns, H., Dawson, N., Sobel, H., & Issacs, C. (1996). Prevalence rates and correlates of psychiatric disorders among preschool children. *Journal of the American Academy of Child and Adolescent Psychiatry, 35*(2), 204–214.

Mesman, J., Bongers, I. L., & Koot, H. M. (2001). Preschool developmental pathways to preadolescent internalizing and externalizing problems. *Journal of Child Psychology Psychiatry, 42*(5), 679–689.

Minkovitz, C., Mathew, M. B., & Strobino, D. (1998). Have professional recommendations and consumer demand altered pediatric practice regarding child development? *Journal of Urban Health, 75*(4), 739–750.

Mouton-Simien, P., McCain, A. P., & Kelley, M. L. (1997). The development of the toddler behavior screening inventory. *Journal of Abnormal Child Psychology, 2,* 59–61.

Offord, D. R. (1987). Prevention of behavioral and emotional disorders in children. *Journal of Child Psychology Psychiatry, 28*(1), 9–19.

Offord, D. R., Boyle, M. H., & Racine, Y. (1989). Ontario Child Health Study: Correlates of disorder. *Journal of the American Academy of Child and Adolescent Psychiatry, 28*(6), 856–860.

Pavuluri, M. N., Luk, S. L., Clarkson, J., & McGee, R. (1995). A community study of preschool behaviour disorder in New Zealand. *Australian and New Zealand Journal of Psychiatry, 29*(3), 454–462.

Pianta, R., & Castaldi, J. (1989). Stability of internalizing symptoms from kindergarten to first grade and factors related to instability. *Development and Psychopathology, 1*(4), 305–316.

Rai, S., Malik, S. C., & Sharma, D. (1993). Behavior problems among preschool children. *Indian Pediatrics, 30*(4), 475–478.

Reynolds, C. R., & Kamphaus, R. W. (1992). *Behavior assessment system for children manual.* Circle Pines, MN: American Guidance Service.

Rose, S. A. (1989). Stability of behavior problems in very young children. *Development and Psychopathology, 1*(1), 5–19.

Schopler, E., Reichler, R., & Renner, B. R. (1988). *The childhood autism rating scale (CARS)*. Los Angeles: Western Psychological Services.

Siegel, B. (1996). *Pervasive developmental disorders screening test (PDDST)*. Unpublished manuscript.

Thomas, J. M., & Guskin, K. A. (2001). Disruptive behavior in young children: What does it mean? *Journal of the American Academy of Child and Adolescent Psychiatry, 40*(1), 44–51.

Thompson, M. J., Stevenson, J., Sonuga-Barke, E., Nott, P., Bhatti, Z., Price, A., & Hudswell, M. (1996). Mental health of preschool children and their mothers in a mixed urban/rural population. I. Prevalence and ecological factors. *British Journal of Psychiatry, 168*(1), 16–20.

U.S. Department of Health and Human Services. (2000). *Relationships, resiliency, and readiness: Building a system of care and education mental health services*. Proceedings, Healthy Child Care New England Conference, Brewster, Massachusetts, April 10–11. Washington, DC: Author.

U.S. Department of Health and Human Services. (2001). *Report of a surgeon general's working meeting on the integration of mental health services and primary health care: 2000 Nov. 30–Dec. 1; Atlanta, Georgia*. Rockville, MD: U.S. Department of Health and Human Services, Public Health Service, Office of the Surgeon General.

Wissow, L. S., Roter, D. L., & Wilson, M. E. (1994). Pediatrician interview style and mothers' disclosure of psychosocial issues. *Pediatrics, 93*(2), 289–295.

Wu, P., Hoven, C. W., Bird, H. R., Moore, R. E., Cohen, P., Alegria, M., Dulcan, M. K., Goodman, S. H., Horwitz, S. M., Lichtman, J. H., Narrow, W. E., Rae, D. S., Regier, D. A., & Roper, M. D. (1999). Depressive and disruptive disorders and mental health service utilization in children and adolescents. *Journal of the American Academy of Child and Adolescent Psychiatry, 38*(9), 1081–1092.

Yoshikawa, H. (1994). Prevention as cumulative protection: Effects of early family support and education on chronic delinquency and its risks. *Psychology Bulletin, 115*(1), 28–54.

Yoshikawa, N., &Knitzer, J. (Eds.). (1997). *Lessons from the field: Head Start mental health strategies to meet changing needs*. New York: National Center for Children in Poverty.

Zeanah, C. H. (2000). Disturbances of attachment in young children adopted from institutions. *Journal of Developmental and Behavioral Pediatrics, 21*(3), 230–236.

Zero to Three, National Center for Clinical Infant Programs. (1995). *Diagnostic classification of mental health and developmental disorders of infancy and early childhood*. Arlington, VA: Author.

24

Games Children Play: Observing Young Children's Self-Regulation Across Laboratory, Home, and School Settings

Lisa A. McCabe

Pia Rebello-Britto

Magdalena Hernandez

Jeanne Brooks-Gunn

Early difficulties in self-regulation have been conceptualized as precursors of childhood and adolescent mental health and behavioral problems (Shonkoff & Phillips, 2000). Similarly, challenges in early self-regulation predict externalizing symptoms in middle childhood, adolescence, and young adulthood (Bates, Pettit, Dodge, & Ridge, 1998; Hart, Hofmann, Edelstein, & Keller, 1997; Newman, Caspi, Moffitt, & Silva, 1997) and underlie many childhood disorders, including attention deficit/hyperactivity disorder (ADHD), oppositional defiant disorder (ODD), and externalizing behaviors more broadly conceived (Aman, Roberts, & Pennington, 1998; Barkley, 1997; Campbell, Pierce, March, Ewing, & Szumowski, 1994; Pierce, Ewing, & Campbell, 1999). Self-regulatory capacities have also been implicated in the ontogeny of a variety of constructs, including conscience, aggression, and substance abuse (Block, Block, & Keyes, 1988; Kochanska, Murray, Jacques, Koenig, & Vandergeest, 1996). For these reasons, it comes as no surprise that researchers have turned their attention to self-regulation as an attractive prospect for further investigation in large, nonclinical samples.

How are later mental health problems manifested in early childhood and how can these early manifestations be measured reliably and validly across diverse populations? This chapter addresses the need for valid and reliable observational instruments to assess the development of children's self-regulation abilities in large-scale studies. We begin by examining the extant laboratory and clinical research and methods addressing the development and expression of self-regulation in young children. We then turn our attention to the development of naturalistic situational assessments for observing self-regulatory capacities including delay of gratification, cognitive control, motor control, and sustained attention. Finally, we highlight efforts to examine self-regulation in ecologically valid contexts as part of several large-scale, multisite studies: the Early Head Start Research and Evaluation Program, the Project on Human Development in Chicago Neighborhoods, and the Fragile Families and Child Well-Being Project. We conclude with a discussion of challenges for conducting research with observational measures of children's self-regulation and recommendations for future research.

CONCEPTUALIZING SELF-REGULATION IN YOUNG CHILDREN

The complexity inherent within the ability to regulate emotions and behaviors is reflected in the diversity of labels used to describe such capacities, including self-regulation (Kopp, 1982), self-control (Mischel & Patterson, 1979), effortful control (Rothbart, 1989a, 1989b), impulse control (Maccoby, 1980), and behavioral inhibition (Barkley, 1997; see Kochanska, Murray, & Harlan, 2000 for a review). In our work, we use the term *self-regulation* to refer to a multidimensional construct involving affective, cognitive, motivational, and behavioral components (Grolnick & Farkas, 2002). We thus acknowledge the critical nature of internal states and processes, as well as external behavioral manifestations, in the ability to self-regulate (similar to Eisenberg's distinction between emotion regulation and emotion-related behavioral regulation; Eisenberg et al., 2000).

Yet, while recognizing the multidimensional nature of self-regulation, our work has paid particular attention to behavioral components for two reasons. First, we have endeavored to develop *observational* measures of self-regulation for use in naturalistic settings typical of large-scale studies. As behaviors are easy to observe, they represent a natural starting point for these kinds of assessments. Second, our measurement development is based upon extensive self-regulation research, conducted almost exclusively in laboratory or clinical settings, that tends to assess observable features of self-regulatory behaviors. Thus our work builds upon previous studies that have examined behavioral manifestations of self-regulation and extends them for use in homes and classrooms with studies involving large numbers of children.

In focusing on behavioral aspects of self-regulation, we have organized our examination around four capacities prevalent in the existing literature. First, we examine the inhibition of automated, or prepotent, responses in favor of a less dominant behavior. Because this capacity reflects the ability to think before acting, it has often been referred to as cognitive control. Second, we look at motor control. Here we are interested in children's ca-

pacity to control the impulse to go fast and to slow down motor behavior when in an aroused state. Next we consider the ability to delay gratification, a skill that calls upon a child to control impulses in order to wait to a future reward. Finally, we examine sustained attention, a child's ability to filter out extraneous information and focus on a task at hand.

We realize that these capacities are interdependent and that boundaries among them are often fuzzy (Kochanska et al., 2000). Nevertheless, these four particular aspects of self-regulation were deliberately selected because they capture a breadth of self-regulatory behaviors relevant to everyday experiences in homes and classrooms. In addition, three of the areas (cognitive control, motor control, and delay of gratification) parallel the categories of delaying, slowing down motor activity, and suppressing/initiating activity to a signal represented in Kochanska's inhibitory control battery (Kochanska et al., 1996, 2000; Kochanska, Murray, & Coy, 1997) for laboratory settings. Because this battery represents one of the few available for assessing these kinds of self-regulatory behaviors, we have drawn heavily from this work. We added sustained attention to this list because of its importance in real-world settings, especially children's readiness for and performance in school.

LABORATORY AND CLINICAL RESEARCH ON YOUNG CHILDREN'S SELF-REGULATION

Our work expands upon extensive laboratory and clinical research on young children's self-regulation. As these studies and methodologies provide such an important backdrop for our work, we briefly review this literature here.

The Development of Self-Regulation

Tables 24.1 through 24.4 provide an overview of assessments used to examine the four aspects of self-regulation that are the focus of this chapter. Based upon studies using these measures, a great deal of research has examined the development of self-regulation in young children. Kochanska and her colleagues (1996, 1997, 2000) are among the few who have examined multiple aspects of self-regulation at one time. In their series of studies, they examined delay of gratification, cognitive control, and motor control abilities (as part of an inhibitory control battery) in 26- to 56-month-old children. Analysis of composite scores indicated coherence among the tasks and developmental stability in performance. Furthermore, better performance on the battery was positively related to children's internalization of rules and was negatively related to children's displays of joy and anger.

Additional research has focused on more specific aspects of self-regulation. For example, Grolnick's work suggests that active engagement with a substitute object is common behavior among toddlers in a delay of gratification task (Grolnick, Bridges, & Connell, 1996). The use of this strategy is facilitated by the presence of adults and is most common among nondistressed toddlers (focus on the delay object was found to be more common among distressed toddlers; Grolnick et al., 1996). By the preschool years, children make significant progress in choosing appropriate waiting strategies on their own. Children in Mischel's program of research were much more likely to choose to cover a reward while waiting once they had reached age 5 years (Mischel & Mischel, 1983).

Multiple studies (using a variety of tasks such as tapping a wooden dowel and card sorting; see table 24.3) have shown how preschoolers make significant gains in the ability to perform well in cognitive control tasks (Diamond & Taylor, 1996; Jacques, Zelazo, Kirkham, & Semcesen, 1999; Zelazo, Frey, & Rapus, 1996). For example, in a Strooplike task, children between the ages of 3½ and 7 years of age were asked to say "day" to a black picture card with stars and moons and "night" to a white card with a sun (Gerstadt, Hong, & Diamond, 1994). The youngest children, those 3½ to 4 years of age, had much more difficulty with this task than did 5- to 7-year-olds, as indicated by longer response latencies and fewer correct responses. Children reached ceiling performance at 6 years of age. For younger children, performance on such tasks is better when there is a delay before responding, suggesting that younger children need more time to inhibit in-

correct responses (Diamond, Kirkham, & Amso, 2002; Gerstadt et al., 1994).

Young preschoolers also have difficulty with cognitive control in go/no-go activities that require suppressing initiating activity to a signal (such as the Green-red signs game; see table 24.3), even though they seem to understand the task rules. For example, 4-year-olds have difficulty not looking in a box for a toy, even if they have learned under what conditions a toy will and will not be present (Livesey & Morgan, 1991). In research conducted by Zelazo and his colleagues, children were first instructed to sort a deck of cards by one criterion (e.g., color) and then by another (e.g., shape; Jacques et al., 1999; Zelazo et al., 1996). When asked to sort by the second criteria, 3-year-old children were unable to inhibit sorting by the first criteria. These difficulties persist despite children's ability to verbalize the task instructions (Livesey & Morgan, 1991; Zelazo et al., 1996) or to perform control games where prepotent responses do not interfere with responses (Diamond et al., 2002; Gerstadt et al., 1994). For example, in research using a Strooplike assessment, children performed much better when asked to say "day" or "night" to abstract designs (as opposed to sun and moon pictures; Gerstadt et al., 1994).

Motor control abilities have generally been studied in the context of developmental and neurological disorders (e.g., developmental coordination disorder, cerebral palsy) and as outcomes of early risk factors, such as low birth weight and lead exposure (McMichael et al., 1988; Taylor, Klein, Minich, & Hack, 2000; Van Rossum & Laszlo, 1994). In a notable exception to this more clinical work, Maccoby, Dowley, Hagen, and Dergerman (1965) hypothesized that the ability to inhibit motor movements, rather than children's general activity levels, would be positively associated with cognitive test scores. Results indicated that children's ability to inhibit movement on the walk-a-line, telephone poles, and truck tasks (tasks that require the child to slow down motor responses while walking on a line, drawing a line, and moving a truck along a path; see table 24.2) was positively associated with Stanford-Binet test scores, whereas general activity levels (measured by placing a movement detector in-

Table 24.1 Delay of Gratification Laboratory Measures

Measure	Age Range	Procedure[a]	Source
Forbidden Toy tasks			
Telephone task	Toddlers	E brings in toys and demonstrates how to use a telephone. E leaves room to "get additional toys" and says to C, "sit right here and do not touch the phone while I'm gone." C sits for 2.5 minutes or until C touches phone.	Vaughn, Kopp, & Krakow, 1984
NICHD Forbidden Toy	3-year-olds	P and C sit in room, P asked to fill out questionnaire and respond to child's verbalizations with "I am busy right now." E shows a set of toys, which includes a crocodile toy, to C and plays with C for 1 minute. E then tells C that C can play with the toys alone, but that C may not touch the crocodile.	NICHD Early Child Care Research Network, 1998
Alone With Prohibited Toys	Toddlers and pre-schoolers	C left in lab with shelf full of objects that P has prohibited C from touching. C asked to do a dull sorting task.	Kochanska & Aksan, 1995
Snack Delay tasks			
Snack Delay (experimenter absent)	Preschoolers	C taught to summon E by ringing a bell. C asked to choose between two rewards (e.g., toy, snack). C told that C will receive the desired reward if C can wait for E to return, but that C can ring bell for E to return. If C rings bell, C receives the less desired reward (e.g., one cookie, not two). Reward salience can vary (exposed versus obscured).	Mischel, Ebbesen, & Ziess, 1972; similar procedure used by Golden, Montare, & Bridger, 1977, and Grolnick, Bridges, & Connell, 1996 (in this version, child cannot summon E to return to room)
Snack Delay (experimenter present)	Toddlers and pre-schoolers	C has to wait for E to ring bell before retrieving an M&M from under a glass cup. Four trials are administered with delays of 10, 20, 30, and 15 seconds. Halfway through each trial, E lifts bell without ringing it.	Kochanska, Murray, Jacques, Koenig, & Vandegeest, 1996
Tongue M&M	Toddlers and pre-schoolers	Same as Snack Delay above, except that C is asked to hold the M&M on his or her tongue during the delay.	Kochanska et al., 1996

Gift delays

Task	Age	Description	Reference
Gift task (experimenter present)	Toddlers and preschoolers	C, wearing a blindfold, sits on a chair facing E who noisily wraps a gift for the C (60-second delay).	Kochanska et al., 1996
Gift task (experimenter absent)	Toddlers	E shows brightly wrapped gift to C. E leaves room and asks C to not open gift until E returns.	Grolnick et al., 1996 (based on procedure developed by Block & Block, 1980); Vaughn et al., 1984
Gift in a Bag	Toddlers and preschoolers	Similar to Gift task (E absent), except that gift is concealed in a bag while E leaves the room to find a bow for the gift.	Kochanska, Murray, & Harlan, 2000
Surprise in the Box	Preschoolers	C is shown a box and told there is "something really, really special" inside the box that the experimenter "couldn't wait" to reveal. E asks C not to touch the box while the E leaves the room (3 minutes). Keys are left in the room as distraction aid.	Raver, Blackburn, Bancroft, & Torp, 1999
Toy Removal and Weight/Measure	26- to 41-month-olds	E tells P that C has to put down an attractive toy because they must weigh/measure C.	Kochanska et al., 1996
Tower of Patience	Toddlers and preschoolers	C and E take turns adding blocks to a tower. E waits for progressively longer increments before adding a block to the tower.	Kochanska et al., 1996; Lab-TAB (preschooler version); Goldsmith & Rothbart, 1992
Secret from Mom	3- to 6-year-olds	C is instructed not to divulge the location of a hidden toy to his or her caregiver until E counts to 10.	Lab-TAB (preschooler version); Goldsmith & Rothbart, 1992
Whisper	26- to 41-month-olds	C asked to whisper the names of 10 consecutively presented cartoon characters.	Kochanska et al., 1996
Dinky Toys	33-month-olds	C told to look over small toys in a box without touching and to verbally tell the experimenter which toy C wants.	Kochanska et al., 2000

[a] C = child; P = parent; E = experimenter

Table 24.2 Motor Control Laboratory Measures

Measure	Age Range	Procedure[a]	Source
Walk-a-Line	Toddlers and preschoolers	C walks, once at regular speed and twice as slow as possible, over a path marked by a ribbon glued to the floor.	Kochanska et al., 1996; Lee, Brooks-Gunn, & Schnur, 1988; adapted from Maccoby, Dowley, Hagen, & Degerman, 1965
Circle and Star	33-month-olds	C asked to draw a line along two patterns (circle and star). Fast and slow trials are administered.	Kochanska, Murray, & Coy, 1997
Turtle and Rabbit	Toddlers and preschoolers	C moves a same-sex child doll, a "fast" rabbit, and a "slow" turtle from start to finish line along a curved path. Two trials administered for each doll/animal. Doll trials serve as baseline.	Kochanska et al., 1996
Telephone Poles	Preschoolers	C draws lines connecting a picture of two telephone poles in order to allow a squirrel to cross. Three trials are administered: baseline, fast, and slow.	Kochanska et al., 1997; Lee et al., 1988; adapted from Maccoby et al., 1965
Truck task	Preschoolers	C moves a toy truck along a 5-inch-wide path without touching the edges. Baseline and slow conditions are administered.	Maccoby et al., 1965; Lee et al., 1988
Circles	Preschoolers	C asked to draw a round path for a turtle to walk on. One baseline trial and two fast trials are administered.	Kochanska et al., 1996

[a]C = child; P = parent; E = experimenter

strument on children's wrists and ankles during a 2-hour segment of the preschool day) were not related to cognitive test scores. Other research confirms the link between motor control difficulties, generally measured in the context of neurological examinations, and cognitive, learning, academic, and behavioral problems (Dunn et al., 1986, Gillberg & Gillberg, 1989; Lindahl, Michelsson, & Donner, 1988a; Lindahl, Michelsson, Helenius, & Parre, 1988; Losse et al., 1991; Lyytinen & Ahonen, 1988). This comorbidity persists until late childhood (Henderson, 1993).

Evidence about the development of sustained attention comes from a diverse literature about attention in general. Research has demonstrated that, as with many self-regulatory skills, the ability to sustain attention to a task increases between the ages of 4 and 6 (Levy, 1980). Further, research indicates that inattentive behavior may be related to cognitive delays (especially in lan-

guage; Warner-Rogers, Taylor, Taylor, & Sandberg, 2000). Finally, difficulties with continuous performance tasks (CPT; a common measure of sustained attention in which a child presses a button in response to a certain stimulus or sequence of stimuli; Rosvold, Mirsky, Sarason, Bransome, & Beck, 1956) seem to be related to ADHD diagnoses in school-age children (although some researchers have raised doubts about the usefulness of CPTs for ADHD diagnoses; see Corkum and Siegel, 1993).

The Development of Self-Regulation: Nature or Nurture?

Emotional and behavioral self-regulation have long been posited as temperamentally and physiologically based abilities emerging early in life (Gunnar, 1990; Pavlov, 1961; Reed, Pien, & Rothbart, 1984; Rothbart & Derryberry, 1981; see

Rothbart, Ahadi, & Evans, 2000 for a review). In terms of the four self-regulatory capacities that are the focus of this chapter, cognitive control has been linked to the anterior cingulated cortex, the premotor cortex, and the "nonmedial" frontal cortex (Casey, Cohen, Noll, Forman, & Rapoport, 1993; Drewe, 1975; Luria, 1966), while animal models suggest that the medial septum, posterior hippocampus, and orbitofrontal cortex may be involved in the ability to delay gratification (Newman, Gorenstein, & Kelsey, 1983). We also know that the right frontal lobe may be particularly relevant to the ability to sustain attention to a task (Koski & Petrides, 2001).

Despite the numerous studies demonstrating a strong biological component to self-regulation capacities, evidence also suggests that these abilities are susceptible to environmental influences. For example, in an evaluation of Head Start conducted in the early 1970s, researchers found that African American children in Head Start were able to perform more slowly (on tasks such as Walk-a-Line) than children not in Head Start (controlling for a host of family and maternal characteristics; Lee, Brooks-Gunn, & Schnur, 1988). Program effect sizes ranged from 0.27 to 0.32 when comparing Head Start children to children with and without preschool experience.

Further evidence for the malleability of regulatory capacities comes from a diverse literature on parenting. Grolnick has found that when mothers assist their children in regulating emotions during a delay task, without regard to children's actual distress, their children tend to be less able to self-regulate in an independent context (Grolnick, Kurowski, McMenamy, Rivkin, & Bridges, 1998). Similarly, maternal overinvolvement and criticism have also been found to be negatively associated with children's performance on the snack delay task (Jacobsen, 1998). Additional research has found that externalizing behaviors are more prevalent in children who demonstrate low impulse control and have mothers who are low on restrictive control (as opposed to mother who use more prohibitions, warnings, and scolding; Bates et al., 1998). Further, attachment classification has been found to predict children's performance in delay tasks. One study found that attachment classification at 12 and 18 months of age significantly predicted children's

ability to delay gratification at 6 years of age (Jacobsen, Huss, Fendrich, Kruesi, & Ziegenhain, 1997). Children who were classified as insecure-avoidant and insecure-disorganized were 7 and 19 times more likely, respectively, than securely attached children to end the delay prematurely.

Situational variables have also been found to affect children's performance on delay tasks. In a study of children with ADHD, the presence of toys and music during a delay task increased motor activity, which in turn inhibited children's ability to wait for the preferred reward (Schweitzer & Sulzer-Azaroff, 1995). From Mischel's more than 30 years of research on delay of gratification, we also know that a child's ability to delay can be facilitated by increasing psychological distance from the reward (e.g., through distraction and/or affective control techniques; Mischel & Rodriguez, 1993).

Finally, previous research has demonstrated a link between risk factors, such as low income, and self-regulation, especially in the area of attention. Specifically, poor nutrition (caused by a temporary food shortage) was found to be negatively associated with attention (McDonald, Sigman, Espinosa, & Neumann, 1994), and sustained attention difficulties were more likely to occur in children from families with low socioeconomic status (SES) than for those from more affluent families (Warner-Rogers et al., 2000).

HOME AND CLASSROOM OBSERVATIONAL ASSESSMENTS OF YOUNG CHILDREN'S SELF-REGULATION

As the literature presented here suggests, little research includes observations of self-regulatory behaviors in naturalistic settings. We contend that such omissions have led to a knowledge gap in our understanding of the development of self-regulation in young children in three important ways. First, children are often assessed in laboratory or clinical settings that, although they may attempt to simulate the everyday environment, are unnatural settings for the child. Thus a child may not be demonstrating typical behaviors in such studies. We need to explore the development and expression of self-regulation in more

Table 24.3 Cognitive Control Laboratory Measures

Measure	Age Range	Procedure[a]	Source
Simon Says	33-month-olds	C told to perform movement that is verbally requested by model on videotape only if the command has been preceded by "Simon says." 20 "Simon says" trials and 19 non-"Simon says" trials are administered.	Kochanska et al., 1997
Green-Red Signs	33-month-olds	Three series of trials in which a videotape model raises his or her hand, holding a sign. C told to: (1) Raise same hand as model (who is using green sign). (2) Raise opposite hand as model (who is using red sign). (3) Raise same hand to green and opposite hand to red.	Kochanska et al., 1997
Bear and Dragon	Preschoolers	E wears puppet on each hand. C instructed to perform movements requested by the bear (e.g., clap your hands), but not to perform the dragon's requests.	Kochanska et al., 1996; adapted from Reed, Pien, & Rothbart, 1984
Pinball	Preschoolers	For six trials, C instructed to pull a pinball machine plunger until E indicates that C can let go of the plunger by saying "Go!" (delays of 10, 15, 25, 15, 20, and 10 seconds are used). For six additional trials, C instructed to release the plunger when E shows a green sign but hold the plunger in the pulled-out position when E shows a red sign.	Kochanska et al., 1996; adapted from Reed et al., 1984
Windows task	Preschoolers	C and E compete for a chocolate placed in one of two boxes. To obtain the chocolate, C has to deceive E by pointing to the empty box.	Russell, Mauthner, Sharpe, & Tidswell, 1991
Bulb Squeeze	Preschoolers	C has to squeeze a bulb when one colored light is turned on but not squeeze when another colored light is turned on.	Miller, Shelton, & Flavell, 1970
Color/Shape Box	Preschoolers	C has to press one of four (or three) cues to reveal the location of a toy figure hidden under the cue. The cues consist of colored blocks or blocks varying in shape. The location of the figure varies between trials, with the constraint that the figure is not hidden under the same cue in two consecutive trials. To improve performance, C has to learn not to press the cue that concealed the figure in the previous trial (i.e., overcome "position habits").	Bell & Livesey, 1985

Task	Age	Description	Reference
Go/No Go Shapes task	Preschoolers	A toy is concealed in a small well, covered by either a circle or a triangle. C learns that the box will be empty when covered by one of the shapes (negative cue) but will contain a toy when covered by the other (positive cue). Child is told "Your job is to (look/tell me to look) under a shape when you think there is a toy in the well." 20 trials are administered.	Livesey & Morgan, 1991
Shapes task/Stroop paradigm	5–6-year-olds	C shown pictures of large shapes (e.g., animals, geometric figures). Each shape is covered with a design of much smaller figures. C is asked to name the small figures and thus inhibit impulse to name the large figure. "Primer" pictures, in which the large and small shapes are identical, are interspersed with the test pictures. Each presentation is preceded by a picture of the large shape in solid black.	Kochanska et al., 1997; based on Stroop Task (Rothbart, Derryberry, & Posner, 1994); variation using fruit shapes used by Kochanska et al., 2000
Day/Night Stroop	3.5–7-year-olds	C asked to say "day" to a black card with stars and asked to say "night" to a white card with a bright sun.	Gerstadt, Hong, & Diamond, 1994
Tapping	Toddlers and preschoolers	C asked to tap once when E taps a wooden dowel twice and to tape twice when E taps a wooden dowel once.	Luria, 1966; Diamond & Taylor, 1996
Balloon Press	Preschoolers	C asked to press a balloon only twice when a light appears.	Luria, 1959, 1961
Dimensional Change Card Sort (DCCS)	Preschoolers	A set of cards with colored shapes is used (e.g., red triangle, blue circle). C learns to sort the cards by their color, then by their shape. Throughout the task, C is asked to switch between the sorting rules.	Frye, Zelazo, & Palfai, 1995; used in Zelazo, Frey, & Rapus, 1996
Puppet DCCS	Toddlers and preschoolers	C watches puppet perform DCCS task (described above) and is asked to evaluate the puppet's performance on each trial.	Jacques, Zelazo, Kirkham, & Semcesen, 1999
Fruit Distraction test	3 to 15 years	C shown pictures of inappropriately colored fruit (e.g., blue banana) and asked to name the color that the fruit should be (e.g., yellow).	Santostefano, 1988
Number Stroop	3 to 6 years	C presented with groups of numbers (e.g., 222, 11, 3) and asked to say the number of digits, not the numbers within an item (e.g., 3, 2, 1).	Hall, Grant, Lehman, Nolte, & Srokowski, 2001

[a]C = child; P = Parent; E = Experimenter

Table 24.4 Sustained Attention Laboratory Measures

Measure	Age Range	Procedure[a]	Source
Puzzle task	Toddlers	Two puzzles are given to C and P. Both puzzles are chosen to be challenging for the child. P is instructed to allow C to try the first puzzle alone and then to help C if needed. For the second puzzle, P is asked not to help C. Coding examines C's on-task behavior.	Matas, Arend, & Sroufe, 1978
Impossibly Perfect Green Circles	Preschoolers	C asked to draw circles for 3.5 minutes. E points out minor flaws in each circle and asks C to try again.	Lab-TAB (Preschool version); Goldsmith & Rothbart, 1992
Disappointment procedure	Preschoolers	E1 shows a group of toys to C and asks C to identify the most and least desirable toys. As a reward for performance on a separate task, E2 gives the toy that was identified as least desirable to C. E2 then tells C that E2 is going to read and ignores C for 2 minutes. E1 returns to room and gives the most desirable gift to C.	Cole, Zahn-Waxler, & Smith, 1994; Saarni, 1984
Three Box task	4–5-year-olds	E gives P three boxes containing three toys (Etch-a-Sketch, wooden blocks, and a set of puppets) and instructed to allow C to play with the toys on his or her own and then to assist C. P is told that C should play with the toys in order and given instructions for three tasks that C should complete (complete an Etch-a-Sketch maze; stack blocks; free play with puppets).	NICHD Study of Early Child Care (available from http://public.rti.org/secc/)
Computer Cartoon	Preschoolers	C asked to focus on a computer screen displaying randomized cartoon graphics for 2 minutes.	Canfield, Wilkins, & Schmerl, 1991; used in Raver et al., 1999
Transparent Box	Preschoolers	C asked to select one of two toys. E places toy in a locked transparent box. E hands a set of keys to C and says that C can play with toy once C finds the key that opens the lock. However, none of the keys open the lock.	Lab-TAB (Preschool version): Goldsmith & Rothbart, 1992
Exploring Coffee Pot	Preschoolers	C shown a coffee pot and asked to play with it.	Lab-TAB (Preschool version); Goldsmith & Rothbart, 1992
Matching Cards	Preschoolers	C shown cards displaying colored geometric shapes and asked to play with them.	Lab-TAB (Preschool version); Goldsmith & Rothbart, 1992
Perpetual Motion	Preschoolers	C asked to play with a wheel toy that consists of a silver spinner that rests on two tracks.	Lab-TAB (Preschool version); Goldsmith & Rothbart, 1992)

[a]C = child; P = parent; E = Experimenter

ecologically valid settings such as homes and classrooms in order to more fully understand how children regulate in the social world. Second, we know that self-regulation is susceptible to environmental influences, especially those in immediate home and classroom contexts. However, we need a more thorough understanding of how environmental factors such as family income, early childhood education experiences, and even neighborhood characteristics might be related to self-regulation in young children. Large-scale studies, where numerous environmental conditions are often also assessed, provide an opportunity to explore such relationships. Finally, the inclusion of observational self-regulation assessments in multisite studies will enable exploration of normative distributions of such capacities in diverse samples of children.

For these reasons, we believe it is critical for future work to include observational assessments in homes and classrooms. To our knowledge, very little work has been done to create or adapt self-regulation assessments for use outside the laboratory or clinic.[1] Therefore, the first step must be to develop and/or adapt existing measures for this purpose. In this section, we describe two of our projects (Games as Measurement of Early Self-Control [GAMES] and Storytimes) that involved the development and/or adaptation of observational measures for use in homes and early childhood programs. We first provide an overview of each project, including a summary of piloted measures. We then present preliminary data from some tasks, with an emphasis on those particularly well suited to assessing impulse control, cognitive control, motor control, and sustained attention.

Games as Measurement of Early Self-Control

The GAMES project focused on the development and piloting of self-regulation measures in homes and classrooms with diverse groups of children. Working with 116 primarily low-income, Spanish- and English-speaking children, the aim was to adapt and in some cases develop new self-regulation measures for use outside the laboratory. These assessment situations focused on the key regulatory capacities presented throughout this chapter (delay of gratification, cognitive control,

motor control, and sustained attention). The goal was to create three different batteries of measures. The first two included individual assessments either administered by an experimenter with one child and coded simultaneously (Battery 1) or videotaped and coded at a later time (Battery 2). In our third battery, we adapted some of these one-on-one measures for use with small groups of young children. These measures were designed to be implemented with four familiar peers in classroom settings. They were videotaped and coded at a later time.

The majority of children participated in a battery of assessments that lasted approximately 30 minutes and included between six and eight tasks. Assessments were conducted either in the child's home or in a quiet space in his or her early childhood program. A subset of these children ($N = 44$) also participated in group assessments (group assessments preceded individual assessments). Small groups of 4 familiar peers (either same sex or evenly balanced for gender) played six to eight games together with one administrator. All assessments, including those that were coded live, were videotaped. Coding schemes were developed and piloted based on reviews of the videotapes. Further details about coding for individual tasks are provided later in the chapter.

In all, 20 different assessment situations (see table 24.5) were piloted with preschool-aged children ($M = 4.29$ years, $SD = .67$) in individual and group assessments. Children (47% boys) represented a range of racial and ethnic backgrounds (53% Hispanic, 28% Black/African American, 5% European American, 13% Multiracial or other). Assessments were conducted in English (72%) or Spanish depending on the preferences of the child. Families' income level ranged from less than $5,000 per year to greater than $60,000 per year, with the vast majority (78%) of households reporting less than $20,000 per year (McCabe, Hernandez, Lara, & Brooks-Gunn, 2000).

The Storytimes Study

The Storytimes study is an evaluation of language and literacy interactions between parents and preschool-aged children in the context of home visiting programs. Participants in the study were all enrolled in a home-based early intervention

Table 24.5 Description of GAMES and Storytimes Self-Regulation Measures by Construct Tapped

Measure	Procedure[a]	Coding	Project Games	Project Storytimes	Source
Impulse Control/Delay of Gratification					
Dinky Toys	C chooses which toy C wants from a box of small toys by verbally telling E (without using hands).	Latency to choice; ability to choose toy without grabbing or touching it.	X		Essex, 1997; Kochanska, Murray, & Harlan, 1999; Kochanska et al., 1996
Forbidden Toy	C instructed to wait to play with a desirable toy (e.g., stickers or stamps) placed within reach. C is given less desirable toy to play with instead (e.g., crayons).	Regulation techniques; latency to touch.	X		Raver et al, 1999
Gift Wrap	C instructed not to peek while E noisily wraps a gift for C.	Peeking behavior (7-point Likert scale ranging from "no peeks" to "approaches tester"); latency to first peek; regulation techniques.	X		Kochanska et al., 1996; Kochanska et al., 1999
Snack Delay	C instructed to wait to eat snack until signal from tester (0–30 second delays).	Live: success/failure at waiting to eat snack. Video: child impulsive behavior (11-point Likert scale ranging from "waits until signal to eat snack" to "eats snack before signal"); regulation techniques.	X	X	Essex, 1997; Kochanska et al., 1996, 1999
Cognitive Control					
Animal Sounds	C instructed to say "moo" to picture of a pig, and "oink" to a cow; "ruff" to a cat and "meow" to a dog.	Number correct/incorrect.	X		GAMES research team
Bunny Hop	C instructed to follow directions only when told to "hop like a bunny," and not follow any other instructions (e.g., "touch your nose").	Number correct, incorrect, and switching behaviors.	X		GAMES research team

Task	Description	Coding			References
Card Sort	C sorts cards alternatively by color or shape.	Number correct/incorrect.	X		Zelazo et al., 1996
Colors	C instructed to press blue button when red light appears and red button for blue light.	Number correct/incorrect.	X		Drewe, 1975
Drumming	C drums when music plays and stops when music stops.	Stopping behavior coded with 3-point scale (immediate, delayed, or no stopping).	X		GAMES research team
Head and Feet	C instructed to touch feet when E says "head" and touch head when E says "feet."	Number correct, incorrect, and switching behaviors.	X		GAMES research team
Musical Instruments	C instructed to play loudly when E says "soft" and softly when E says "loud."	Child's response coded as loud or soft.	X		GAMES research team
Parrot and Dragon	C instructed to do what the nice parrot puppet says and not to do what the mean dragon puppet says.	Number correct/incorrect.	X	X	Kochanska et al., 1996, 1997, 1999; Reed et al., 1984
Stroop	C presented with large shape covered with pictures of smaller shape. C asked to name the smaller shape.	Number correct/incorrect.	X		Kochanska et al., 1997
Tapping	C taps once when E taps twice. C taps twice when E taps once.	Number correct/incorrect.	X		Diamond & Taylor 1996; Luria, 1996; Kochanska et al., 1996, 1999
Whisper	C asked to whisper the names of food/animals on picture cards.	Child vocalizations coded with 4-point scale (whisper, no response, normal voice/mix, shout).	X		Kochanska et al., 1996, 1999
Motor Control					
Circles	C draws circles as slowly and quickly as possible.	Baseline, fast, and slow trials are timed.	X		Kochanska et al., 1997, 1999
Freeze	C instructed to move to music and stop when music stops.	Game too difficult to administer. Not coded.	X		GAMES research team

(*continued*)

Table 24.5 Continued

Measure	Procedure[a]	Coding	Games	Storytimes	Source
			Project		
Statue (from the Nepsy Battery)	C is asked to close eyes, bend arm, and "freeze like a statue." E attempts to distract child by coughing, dropping item on floor, etc.	Body movement, vocalizations, eye opening for each of 15 trials.	X		Korkman, Kirk, & Kemp, 1998
Telephone Poles	C draws lines connecting a picture of two telephone poles in order to allow a squirrel to cross. Three trials are administered: baseline, fast, and slow.	Baseline, fast, and slow trials are timed.		X	Kochanska et al., 1997; Lee, Brooks-Gunn, & Schnur, 1988; adapted from Maccoby et al., 1965
Turtle and Rabbit	C moves rabbit as quickly as possible and turtle as slowly as possible along a designated path.	2 baseline, 2 fast, and 2 slow trials are timed.	X		Kochanska et al., 1996, 1999
Walk-a-Line	C walks on a 6-foot line once at normal pace and twice as slowly as possible.	1 baseline and 2 slow trials are timed.	X		Kochanska et al., 2000
Sustained Attention					
Make a Card	C makes a card using stamps, crayons, and construction paper.	Latency to first vocalization to administrator; number of vocalizations during trial.	X	X	Essex, 1997
Drawing Game	C instructed to mark pictures that match a target picture.	Number correct/incorrect.	X		Roid & Miller, 1995, 1997
Three Bag	C and P free play with toys from 3 bags.	Sustained attention with objects coded with 7-point scale.		X	NICHD Early Child Care Research Network (available from: http://public.rti.org/secc/)

[a]C = Child; P = parent; E = experimenter

program called Home Instruction Program for Preschool Youngsters (HIPPY) in Bronx and Yonkers, New York (Baker, Piotrkowski, & Brooks-Gunn, 1998). HIPPY helps educationally and economically disadvantaged parents provide educationally stimulating activities and environments for preschool-aged children. Although the primary aim of the Storytimes study was to observe maternal and child language and literacy interactions as they relate to child self-regulation and parent-child interactions, data presented here highlight the piloting of five self-regulation assessment situations for the project (see table 24.5).

Forty parents and preschool-aged children (45% boys) participated in the Storytimes study. Children ($M = 4.37$ years; $SD = 0.34$) were from relatively poor families (mean family income = $25,000), and only 43% of the mothers were high school graduates. Mothers represented diverse racial and ethnic backgrounds (22% Hispanic, 38% Black, and 22% White); 64% of the mothers were born in the United States and 38% were married. Approximately half the mothers were working (59%) and all families were primarily English speaking (although 42% were bilingual). All assessments were conducted and coded live in the home (with reliability calculated from videotape).

Promising Naturalistic Observational Approaches

Across these two projects, we piloted numerous assessments in homes and early childhood settings. What follows is a description of our initial experiences with a variety of measures designed to tap the four aspects of self-regulation included in our work.

Delay of Gratification

As described at the outset of this chapter, delay of gratification has long been a focus of developmental psychologists. Yet the vast majority of our knowledge regarding this ability comes from studies of middle-class, White preschoolers in laboratory settings. Unfortunately, some of the classic paradigms for delay of gratification (e.g., in Mischel's task, children may wait up to 20 minutes before receiving their prize) do not

translate well for large-scale studies with limited time to gather sizeable amounts of data in homes and early childhood programs. Two tasks, however, do show promise. Our experiences are as follows.

Snack Delay

The Snack Delay task was used in both GAMES and Storytimes. Multiple versions of this assessment (adapted from Kochanska et al., 1996) were piloted in each project. In general, the task proceeded as follows. Children were first told that there was going to be special game with M&M's.[2] An M&M would be placed on a mat (or card) in front of the child and the child would have to wait for the experimenter to ring a bell (or blow a whistle) before putting the M&M in his or her mouth. After conducting a practice trial to ensure that the child understood the task, five to six timed trials (ranging between 0 and 60 seconds) were conducted.

In the Storytimes project, 91% of the children were successful in waiting for the bell to ring before eating the M&M for all the trials. Only three children did not wait for the bell to ring on two of the five trials. The GAMES project found similar results in that the vast majority of children (71%) were successful on all six trials (with 82% successful on at least five trials).

Given that an overwhelming majority of children were successful in waiting for the experimenter's signal before eating the M&M, the Snack Delay task, as we administered it, did not seem to capture the expected diversity in children's ability to control impulses in these two studies. The problem of little to no variability in response may lie within the parameters of the task itself or transferring it from a laboratory to a home setting. More specifically, conducting the task itself felt a bit contrived. Storytimes data collectors reported that, compared to the other tasks conducted in the home, Snack Delay felt the most "lablike" or "experimental." It may also be that because the data collector is a relatively unfamiliar person to the child, children are more likely to demonstrate their best behavior and so control their impulses. It could be that if the parent or a sibling administered the task, we might have gotten different results. It is also possible that if the scoring procedure for this task was adapted to go beyond success and failure on each trial to include more subtle signs of impulse control or lack thereof (e.g., inching toward the M&M or self-control strategies), more variability in scores would be obtained. We are currently working on the development of such a scoring technique (based on the work of Welfare and Children: A Three City Study; Brady-Smith et al., 2003) using the videotaped assessments. Finally, Snack Delay may be more appropriate for the youngest preschoolers, as 3-year-olds did show more variability in responses than 4- and 5-year-old children. Specifically, in the GAMES project, 21% of 3-year-olds failed three or more trials (as opposed to 17% of 4-year-old and 0% of 5-year-old children). Longer wait times might be more informative for older children (as was done in Mischel's research; Mischel & Rodriguez, 1993). It should be noted, however, that the children really appeared to enjoy the task, in part because they received a treat at the end of every trial.

Gift Wrap

The Gift Wrap task, based on a laboratory assessment developed by Kochanska and colleagues (1996), is a measure of children's delay of gratification. For this game, which can be administered to individuals or groups, children are told that they will receive a gift, but that it needs to be wrapped before they can have it. They are then asked to "help" the administrator by not peeking while the gift is noisily wrapped behind their backs. (Variations on this procedure were piloted. We found the best procedure was for the administrator to have agift already wrapped in a bag and only pretend to wrap it by crinkling papers. In this way, it was simpler to standardize the wrapping time, and it also enabled the administrator to fully attend to the child to watch for peeks during the assessment.) After 1 minute, the child is given the gift. Coding for this task focuses on the child's peeking behavior while the gift is being wrapped (with a scale ranging from no peeks to child leaving his or her seat to watch the administrator wrap the gift). Directions to the child in the individual and group versions are the same. The only difference is that in the group version, four children (familiar peers) sit together while waiting for their presents.

In the GAMES project, we piloted individual Gift Wrap with 110 children and group Gift Wrap with 44. Results, based on coding from the videotaped assessments, show that older children do much better at this task (i.e., they peek less) than younger children (see figures 24.1 and 24.2). When tested individually, nearly three quarters (72%) of 3-year-old children peeked at least once while waiting for the present. This percentage dropped for 4- and 5-year-old children (to 51% and 28%, respectively). In a group, however, children had a more difficult time not peeking. At age 3 and 4, the vast majority of children peeked at least once (73% and 77%, respectively), while at age 5, 50% of children turned to look at the tester while the present was being wrapped. An examination of the subset of children who participated in the Gift Wrap assessment both individually and with a group of three of their peers shows that of the children who did not peek on the individual assessment, 65% peeked in the group task. Thus, the ability to demonstrate impulse control appears to be much harder in the context of the peer group, especially for children for whom this may be a newly developed skill.

The Gift Wrap assessment, both the individual and group versions, worked very well. Not only did we find variability in children's responses, but it is also an easy assessment to administer in noncontrolled settings and fun for children. With the use of videotape, delay facilitation strategies, such as those used by Grolnick and colleagues (1996) can be examined. This possibility will be explored in future work.

Cognitive Control Measures

Finding an appropriate measure of cognitive control for 3- to 5-year-old children was especially challenging in these projects. Although measures of cognitive control exist for adults (e.g., the Stroop), these measures require skills that are too advanced (e.g., reading) for preschool children. Numerous researchers have attempted to adapt these assessment situations for use with young children (see Diamond & Taylor, 1996; Kochanska et al., 2000). Following the lead of these re-

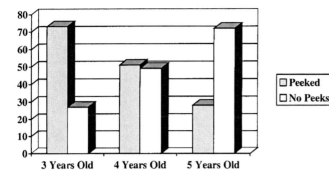

Figure 24.1 Peeking behavior in individual gift wrap assessment.

searchers, the GAMES project attempted to adapt some of these measures for home or classroom use. Tapping, in which the child taps once if the experimenter taps twice and twice if the experimenter taps once, was not a favorite of the administrators in this study. They found that the game did not hold the interest of many of the children. In addition, some children did not understand the task, or chose not to play the game. For example, despite multiple attempts to describe the instructions for the game, one child repeatedly took the "magic stick" used for tapping and slammed it into the table. For these reasons, after only preliminary piloting with this task, we chose not to employ it as a measure of self-regulation.

A child version of the Stroop game (the Shapes task, adapted from Kochanska et al., 1997) also proved to be problematic. In this experimental situation, children were shown pictures of large shapes that were filled with smaller shapes (e.g., a square filled with circles). After seeing a solid "primer" large shape, children were asked to name the small shapes. Though others have had some success with this kind of game (Kochanska et al., 1997), we found that many of the children in our sample did not know their shapes. Attempts to find suitable pictures such as household objects or animals that all children would recognize and that still were identifiable as a solid shape primer (i.e., an outline filled in completely) were difficult. We also had concerns about standardizing the amount of time the children saw the primer picture (as have other groups attempting to use this task; M. R. Gunnar, personal communication, February 22, 1999). Although further work with this task may make it appropriate for 3- to 5-year-old children, we chose to pursue other potential cognitive control games. In this section we therefore present preliminary findings from two other cognitive control tasks, one experimental situation adapted for home use, and one a new measure of cognitive control.

Parrot and Dragon

Parrot and Dragon is a more formalized version of the game Simon Says, commonly played

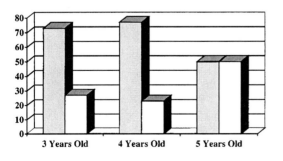

Figure 24.2 Peeking behavior in group gift wrap assessment.

among older preschoolers. In the Storytimes and GAMES studies, we used a version adapted from the work of Kochanska and colleagues (1996) based on pilot testing with a similar-age population. The children were told that they would be playing a game with puppets where they would do what the "nice parrot" asks them to but not what the "mean dragon" asks.[3] After a set of practice trials to ascertain that the child understood the task, 10 to 12 trials were administered. In Storytimes, the average percentage of trials the children got correct was 80%, with a wide range from 27 to 100%. In GAMES, looking at only the seven dragon trials, children got an average of three trials correct (SD = 2.85; range 0–7). Only 16% got all seven trials correct.

Overall, the children really appeared to enjoy the task, and it was easy to administer. A range in the children's success rate was obtained with the trials. However, as a cautionary note, some of the children in both studies had difficulty understanding the game. For example, in GAMES, 47% of children did not pass the practice trials, in part because they were given limited feedback and help to learn to play the game. In future administrations, we would recommend that all children be given a minimum of two practice trials (one each for parrot and dragon puppets) and a maximum of six practice trials (three each for parrot and dragon puppets). Detailed instructions for practice trials (e.g., when additional practice trials should be conducted) should also be given to administrators in order to facilitate consistent administration on practice trials. Such steps ensure standardized administration across children, while still accounting for variation in children's initial ability to understand the task.

In terms of administration of the task, it was important that the data collectors maintained a consistent tone of voice across the parrot and dragon trials, given that changing the valence could influence the children's reaction. A highly animated tone appeared to work the best. It is also recommended that this task be videotaped for reliable scoring. The trials are administered in quick succession, and operating puppets makes it awkward to score trials as they are administered. Even if trials are scored live by an observer (in GAMES, this was the camera person), coding can be problematic. In GAMES, nearly 37% of cases scored live were coded incorrectly (in comparison to coding done by videotape) or not scored at all due to difficulty following the game. Hence, videotaping the trials and scoring them at a later time is probably the best option for accurate and reliable scoring.

Head and Feet

Because of children's difficulty with many cognitive control measures, we developed a new experimental situation appropriate for naturalistic settings. In the Head and Feet assessment, children were asked to touch their head when the administrator said "feet" and to touch their feet in response to a "head" command. Children were first taught to play the game, then were given at least two practice trials (one for each of the two possible commands). Children were given a maximum of six total practice trials. Practice trials were followed by 10 test trials with five "head" and five "feet" commands administered in a standard order. Children who successfully completed at least one practice trial (N = 13), thus indicating that they understood the rules of the game, were included in preliminary analyses of this newly developed assessment.

We developed a coding scheme in which children's behaviors on individual trials were scored as either correct, incorrect, switch to correct (an incorrect response followed by a correct response), or switch to incorrect (a correct response followed by an incorrect response). Because of the small sample size, switch codes were collapsed with correct or incorrect categories, thus forming two broad response categories.

Results indicate that preschool-age children demonstrate a range of ability in successfully completing this assessment. The majority of children (53.8 %) gave correct responses on at least five trials, but the number of correct trials ranged from 0 to 10 (0 correct = 2; 1–2 correct = 3; 4–5 correct = 1; 5–6 correct = 2; 7–8 correct = 2; 9–10 correct = 3). Although sample size is small and findings must be interpreted with caution, results do show a trend toward an increase in the ability to demonstrate cognitive control as children get older, as would be expected based on previous cognitive control research (Gerstadt et al., 1994). Specifically, the mean number of correct responses for the two 5-year-olds who participated was seven. Similarly, both of the 5-year-olds responded correctly on at least half of the trials. In comparison, 3- and 4-year-olds got fewer total trials correct ($M = 4.33$ and 5.14, respectively) and were less likely to get five or more trials correct (33% and 57.1%, respectively).

Though further testing and development is needed, we believe the Head and Feet assessment shows promise as a tool for tapping cognitive control in preschoolers. As it requires no materials, it is easy to implement in diverse settings. It also elicits a range of responses in preschool children, including self-corrective behavior, thus providing researchers with a window into children's self-regulation abilities.

One potential drawback of Head and Feet is that it may be too difficult for some preschoolers. Of the 23 participating in the situation, 13 were able to do the task and 10 children (43.5%) were not. These 10 children failed to independently demonstrate at least one correct response in practice trials, even when the rules of the games were explained multiple times, were demonstrated by the administrator, and incorrect responses were corrected. We would expect that younger children, especially, might have difficulty understanding the game. As very few 5-year-olds were included in this piloting work, however, valid age analyses were not possible. In future administrations, we plan to investigate this issue in more detail.

Cognitive control may be an especially difficult skill for preschoolers to demonstrate. Other tasks developed to assess cognitive control have also proved to be hard for younger preschoolers. For example, in Diamond and Taylor's (1996) work using the Tapping task, nearly 16% of the sample of children were excluded from analyses because of unusable data (8% because they failed the practice trials). Two possibilities may explain this phenomenon. First, cognitive control is a sophisticated skill that may be not be fully developed in young preschoolers. Thus they may not yet have developed the ability to correctly perform tasks that require them to inhibit automated responses. Alternatively, difficulties with task comprehension may mask young preschoolers' abilities to perform such behaviors. Children older than 4 years of age performed better on the Tap-

ping task than the Day/Night Stroop task, suggesting that response modality (i.e., behavioral versus verbal) may influence children's performance on cognitive control tasks. Further measurement development and testing are needed to definitively answer this question.

Motor Control

Motor control represents one of the simplest self-regulatory abilities to measure in young children. Yet far less research has been conducted on this skill in normal developing and diverse groups of children. Given research demonstrating links between motor control and cognition (Lee et al., 1988), future research may want to further explore this connection, especially in large-scale studies. In this section, we present three motor control tasks, two of which are especially easy to implement in diverse settings.

Telephone Poles

In the Storytimes study, the Telephone Poles task (adapted from Maccoby et al., 1965) was administered to 4-year-olds to assess children's motor inhibition and control. For the Telephone Poles game, the child has to draw two straight lines, one fast and one slow. These lines represent telephone wires that squirrels use to climb from one telephone pole to another. The children had no problem understanding the instructions or the activity and appeared to enjoy the task. However, assessing child inhibition and control via timing of the fast trials on the task appeared to pose a major problem. The data collector needed to be extremely adept at timing the task and using the stopwatch, as the fast trials for Telephone Poles at most take a few seconds. To check for possible inaccuracies in timing by the data collector, we timed the trials based on the videotaped observations of the task. However, this second method did not increase the reliability of the results. For this reason, we would not recommend the Telephone Poles task as it was administered in this project.

Circles and Walk-a-Line

The Circles and Walk-a-Line assessment situations (adapted from Maccoby et al., 1965 and more recently used by Kochanska et al., 1997) tap fine and gross motor control, respectively. In each, the child is asked to move (draw a circle in between a larger and smaller circle or walk on a 6-foot line) first at normal speed, then as slowly as possible. The administrator times and records each of the trials. Comparing slow trials to baseline trials gives an indication of how well a child can slow down.

Results from the GAMES project suggest that children perform better on the Walk-a-Line task than on Circles (see figure 24.3). We hypothesize that children may be better able to slow down on the Walk-a-Line task for a number of reasons. First, Walk-a-Line taps gross motor skills while Circles measures fine motor control ability. Second, the Walk-a-Line assessment includes only baseline and slow trials. In contrast, Circles includes a fast trial between the baseline and slow trials (included to look at the ability to slow down after being asked to perform "as fast as you can," theoretically a more challenging task). For pragmatic reasons associated with administration of Walk-a-Line in homes and classrooms, this assessment does not require children to walk as fast as possible (i.e., run) along the path. Without the added challenge of a slow trial following a fast trial, this assessment many be easier to complete successfully.

These motor control tasks are especially useful for large-scale studies because they are quick and easy to implement in naturalistic settings (e.g., homes and classrooms) with diverse samples of preschool-age children. From a practical standpoint, they require minimal equipment, are

straightforward to administer, and do not not require videotaping. For these reasons, we believe large-scale studies of children's development would benefit from inclusion of motor control assessments such as Circles and Walk-a-Line.

Sustained Attention Measures

Sustained attention represents an important skill for early learning, especially in settings such as busy early childhood programs. Despite this fact, very few studies have examined self-regulation in large-scale samples. Therefore, in this section we highlight two experimental situations useful for assessing sustained attention in young children in diverse settings. The first, Make a Card, assesses a child's ability to work independently, and the second, Three Bag, examines sustained attention in the context of a parent-child free play session.

Make a Card

To assess the child's ability to focus attention during solitary work, the Make a Card task was administered. This task was originally developed by the Wisconsin Study of Families and Work (Essex, 1997) as a bookmark-making activity. It was adapted to a card-making activity and used in both Storytimes and GAMES. For this task, the child was handed art supplies (e.g., paper and stamps) and asked to make a card for anyone he or she wanted to, while the data collector worked on filling out some forms. The administrator pretended to be working and responded only minimally (e.g., "I'm working right now") if the child

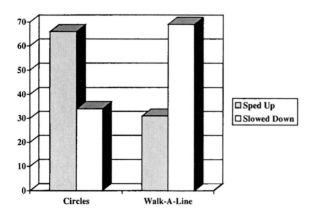

Figure 24.3 Children's behavior on two motor control assessments.

spoke to her. This task was scored in two ways: (1) the number of questions or comments directed toward the data collector; and (2) the latency of first vocalization to the data collector. In Storytimes, children worked for a 3- to 5-minute period, depending on when the child completed the task. On average, two comments or questions were addressed to the data collector. The average latency period of the first question was 1 minute ($SD = 1.26$; range 0–4.57). In GAMES, children worked for a fixed time period (in an attempt to determine whether the length of the game affected children's performance, some children were assessed for 2 minutes and others for 3 minutes). Only the first 2 minutes of each assessment were included for analysis. On average, children vocalized 1.5 times (range 0–10, with 72% of children not vocalizing at all). Latency to first vocalization ranged from 1–111 seconds ($M = 24$ seconds).

In the Storytimes study, the Make a Card task was administered toward the end of the home visit, while in GAMES it was administered first or in the middle of a battery of assessment situations. Later administrations appeared to work better as data collectors reported that implementing Make a Card first was awkward and interfered with establishing rapport with the child. A 2-minute assessment period appeared to be enough time to differentiate children who could work independently from children who attempted to engage the administrator (as well as enough time for most children to finish making a card).

Make a Card appeared to work well in these two studies, both procedurally and in terms of variability in results. The children, for the most part, enjoyed making a card. Given that we did obtain a range in child response both in terms of latency to first vocalization and number of comments or questions addressed to the data collector, we would recommend this task for assessing children's ability to work independently. However, we would also suggest that the content (or intent) of children's vocalizations be taken into account. In some cases, children were obviously trying to engage the administrator ("Look what I made!"), while in others, vocalizations appeared to be more like self-talk (e.g., "I made a butterfly," said while looking at the card). Analyses could then examine child bids (which might include nonverbal communications such as tapping the administrator). Another possibility would be to provide more explicit instructions to the child (such as saying "Draw quietly while I work over here") in order to obtain a more conservative estimate of children's ability to work independently. Finally, because performance on this task is likely influenced by children's interest in making a card, other similar-type games could be implemented in which the child is instructed to work independently in the presence of an experimenter. This strategy would provide a more reliable estimate of children's ability to sustain attention and work independently in a variety of contexts.

Three Bag

Child persistence was also measured via the Three Bag assessment in the Storytimes study. For this assessment, adapted from Vandell (1979) and the "Three Box" used in the NICHD Early Child Care Study (NICHD Early Child Care Research Network, 1998, 1999), the caregiver and child are presented with three closed bags, each containing an age-appropriate toy. To meet the particular needs of this study, we deviated slightly from the traditional model of the Three Bag activity (using three different toys) to include only two activities. The tasks (block building and puppets) were explained to the mothers by one of the data collectors while the other data collector was working with the child in another area. The mothers were told that the activity would take approximately 10 minutes and include a set of interesting blocks followed by free play with puppets. The mothers were given detailed instructions on how to use the different sizes of blocks to build towers. For the puppet play they were told that there was no special game or task, and that they could help the child play with them as they might at home.

Child persistence was coded from videotape using the 54-month Parent-Child Structured Interaction Qualitative Rating Scales (NICHD Early Child Care Research Network, 1998). This seven-point scale measured the extent to which the child was actually involved with the blocks. Lower ratings indicated that the child showed little to no involvement and spent time on off-task activities. Higher scores, on the other hand, indicated that the child was actively involved persistently, either spontaneously or through the parent's mediating suggestions. For the present sample, the mean rating obtained was 4.5 ($SD = 1.5$; range 1–7).

This activity worked very well in homes. Procedurally, it was relatively easy to administer, and the parents and children appeared to enjoy their interaction around the blocks and puppets. The coding for the task, however, was labor intensive, as it is with any coding of videotaped data. The scores reflected a fair degree of variability for the given sample. An advantage of videotaping the Three Bag activity, or other tasks, is that at later points in time they can be coded for several different aspects of parent-child interaction that may not have been planned originally.

In related work at the National Center for Children and Families, coding for child sustained attention in the Three Bag assessment has been further developed since the completion of the Storytimes project (Berlin, Brady-Smith, & Brooks-Gunn, 2002). Details about coding for the sustained attention scale are presented in table 24.6. We would recommend using this recently revised scale in future work using the Three Bag assessment.

Throughout this section, we have outlined potential measures for use in multisite, nonclinical studies. Our summaries, preliminary data, and tips should facilitate the use of such measures in future work. In the next section, we describe some of the first large-scale studies that have included such observational self-regulation assessments.

MEASURING SELF-REGULATION IN LARGE-SCALE, MULTISITE STUDIES

As we have stated throughout this chapter, much of our current knowledge of child self-regulation is derived from studies of small, nonrepresentative samples of parents and children, often with data gathered using laboratory assessment techniques. This dearth in our knowledge base, in combination with reports highlighting the importance of self-regulation abilities for school readiness (Shonkoff & Phillips, 2000), will likely lead to much additional research in this area. In fact, a number of large-scale, multisite national investigations have begun to include home- and child-care-based assessments, using innovative measures, of children's early self-regulation. Three such studies are described vis-à-vis measuring self-regulation in children aged 4 years or younger.

Early Head Start Research and Evaluation Project

The Early Head Start Research and Evaluation Project (EHS) is a national study designed to examine the effectiveness of an intervention program for low-income parents and their infants and toddlers (Brooks-Gunn, Leventhal, Berlin, & Fuligni, 2000; Berlin, O'Neal, & Brooks-Gunn, 2003). Designed as a downward extension of traditional preschool Head Start, Early Head Start provides child development and family services through center- and home-based programs. For the evaluation, approximately 3,000 children (born between September 1995 and July 1998) and their parents from 17 sites across the country were randomly assigned to program or no-program groups. Child assessments and parent interviews were conducted when the children were 14, 24, and 36 months old. These assessments included a number of parent-child interaction measures (e.g., the Three Bag task and the Puzzles task). Coding of the videotaped interaction focused on sustained attention with objects, among other developmentally appropriate aspects of the parent-child relationship (Brady-Smith, O'Brien, Berlin, Ware & Fauth, 1999; see also http://www.mathematica-mpr.com/3rdlevel/ehstoc.htm). In particular, the coding system honed in on the child's ability to explore and play with objects in a focused manner without either jumping quickly from one toy to another or appearing bored, apathetic, or aimless. Given the three time points of data collection, analyses will be able to examine child sustained attention across time from approximately 1 year to 3 years of age and its association to other areas of functioning, including cognitive, motor, and language development. In addition, associations among sustained attention and environmental influences (such as parenting behav-

Table 24.6 Coding Child Sustained Attention in the Three Bag Assessment

Likert Scale Point	Definition
1 (very low)	The child displays no sustained attention with objects. The child moves from one thing to another in a nonsystematic way, without seeming to focus on what the objects have to offer.
2 (low)	The child shows only a few brief moments of sustained attention. During most of the interaction the child is clearly not involved with the toys.
3 (moderately low)	The child is able to sustain attention with objects for brief periods of time, or for a very limited portion of the session. The child may attend to toys, but in a scattered, nonfocused manner.
4 (moderate)	The child displays sustained attention for about half of the session. The child may be distracted at times (e.g., looking around for period of time or leaving the play area for a brief moment), but the distraction is separated by short periods of involvement with the toys.
5 (moderately high)	The child spends sustained periods of time involved with the toys. There are some periods of extended, focused attention, though they may be separated by brief periods of distraction. The child is clearly involved with at least two of the toys or for more than half of the session.
6 (high)	The child displays sustained periods of involved and focused attention for most of the session. There may be a few distractions, but they are brief and immediately followed by focused attention on the toys.
7 (very high)	The child is clearly involved, interested, and focused for almost all of the session. The quality of attention is evident in that there are instances of clear sophistication of play (e.g., child instructs parent in how to "play" with the toys; child creates an imaginary game or constructs an elaborate play sequence). The child is rarely distracted and displays extended periods of sustained attention. Child may show sustained attention with all of the toys or a prolonged period of focused attention with one or two of the toys.

Source: Brady-Smith et al., 1999. Scale developed based on Owen, 1992, and on Spiker, Ferguson, & Brooks-Gunn, 1993.

iors and early child care experience) will be explored.

Project on Human Development in Chicago Neighborhoods

The Project on Human Development in Chicago Neighborhoods (PHDCN) consists of a longitudinal study of children, adolescents, and young adults, along with a community survey and observational study of Chicago's neighborhoods (see also Brooks-Gunn et al., 2000; Leventhal & Brooks-Gunn, 2003). Community survey data include regular, multifaceted assessments of 343 Chicago neighborhoods (approximately 700 census tracts) via neighborhood expert interviews, census data, and systematic observation. Data were collected at two time points, in the mid 1990s with 9,000 respondents and in 2000–2001 to coincide with the 2000 U.S. census.

The longitudinal study focuses on children and youth in 80 neighborhood clusters (about 160 census tracts) throughout the city. The longitudinal study employed an accelerated, longitudinal design with seven age cohorts: 0, 3, 6, 9, 12, 15, and 18 years. Each cohort has approximately 1,000 children, who were followed regularly. In-depth information on child and family development (in addition to neighborhood data) was gathered. In 2001, PHDNC completed its third wave of data collection. With respect to self-regulation, data on emotional competence, delay of gratification, motor control, sustained attention, and self-regulation were collected on approximately 1,200 four-year-old children (wave three of the birth cohort), using the Gift Wrap, Circles,

Walk-aLine, and the Leiter International Performance Scale–Revised Sustained Attention subtask (Roid & Miller, 1995, 1997). These tasks were specifically developed to conform to the constraints of home-based data collection—that is, they are nonintrusive, portable, and easy to administer.

Given the types of data collected, this study is a unique opportunity to address the role of neighborhoods in the emotional development and functioning of young children and their families, while using state-of-the-art methodologies to measure neighborhood processes as well as young children's behavior. In particular, the results from this study will shed light on the nature of the self-regulation abilities among preschool children drawn from a large, urban, and diverse sample interviewed in home-based settings. In addition, associations among self-regulation and child, family, and neighborhood characteristics will be explored. The extent of the mediating role played by self-regulation, at least in part, on associations among individual, family, and neighborhood influences and preschool children's emotional health will also be known. It is expected that results from this study will address potential targets of intervention for programs aimed at improving young children's mental health.

Fragile Families and Child Well-Being Study

The Fragile Families and Child Well-Being Study employs a longitudinal design to follow 1,100 marital and 3,600 nonmarital births in 20 large American cities (see also Brooks-Gunn et al., 2000; Fuligni, McCabe, McLanahan, & Roth, 2003; Reichman, Teitler, Garfinkel, & McLanahan, 2001). This study was designed to learn more about the nature of relationships in nonmarital families, including understanding the forces that pull them together and push them apart.

In-hospital baseline interviews with mothers and fathers occurred between 1998 and 2000. The families, including nonresident fathers, are interviewed by telephone when the children are 12, 30, and 48 months old. In addition, home visits are conducted when children are 36 and 60 months old. Through these phone surveys and

home visits, detailed information is gathered about the mother-father relationship, child development (cognitive, social, and emotional), parenting practices, parental mental health, and family economic circumstances. A child neglect module has been added to the home visits in order to more closely examine the relationship between economic factors (particularly parental resources) and physical and emotional neglect of young children. The parent-child relationship is also a focus of the child neglect module.

The Fragile Families and Child Well-Being Study has elected to include the Walk-a-Line assessment as part of the home visits when the children are 36 and 60 months. Data are presently being collected in 14 out of the 20 sites at the 36-month time point. Analyses will focus on the associations among child self-regulation and parenting practices, early child care experience, and family characteristics.

LIMITATIONS AND CHALLENGES TO HOME- AND CHILD CARE–BASED ASSESSMENTS

As is evident from the measures and studies highlighted here, researchers are beginning to include self-regulation measures for young children that are administered in homes and classrooms as part of diverse research programs looking at child development. While the benefits to such ecologically valid approaches are many, gathering data outside laboratory or clinical settings also has inherent limitations and challenges.

One of the greatest challenges can be the standardization of administration and measures across settings as diverse as homes and classrooms. Researchers must pay careful attention to factors in the environment that may confound the outcome of interest. For example, in adapting the Gift Wrap task from a laboratory to a home or classroom assessment, we needed to take into consideration potential factors in the environment (e.g., presence of a television, toys, or other distractors) that may influence the child's ability to wait for the gift. Thus the protocol for this task included specific instructions about how to position the child for this task, and data collectors were trained to assess the environment and select the most appropriate place for the child to sit (e.g., facing a wall) while playing this game. Similarly, administrators of the Three Bag parent-child interaction measure are trained how to minimize interferences from other family members while the parent and child play for the 10-minute assessment period.

Related to the issue of standardization of administration of tests is the issue of standardizing the environment, to the extent possible. Homes and classrooms pose the problem of being extremely diverse and variable sites for test administration. Adapting measures that were developed for use in more controlled settings to more variable settings is a daunting challenge. Steps need to be taken to minimize the presence of other people, especially parents, and distractors such as the television or radio. McCabe and colleagues (2000) recommend describing the study and discussing the importance of uninterrupted data collection with the parents and teachers as an effective way to control the environment. Additional suggestions were the following: bringing effective distracters (e.g., coloring books or puzzles) for the other children in the home and, if possible, an additional data collector to minimize interruptions from other people or situations.

Perhaps the second greatest challenge to data collection in real-world settings is the need to find measures that adapt well to the rigors involved in bringing the lab to the home or classroom. Thus the measures need to be portable, durable, and nonintrusive (McCabe et al., 2000). Transporting data-collection instruments into classrooms and homes places constraints on the amount, weight, and size of the materials used because of the limitations imposed by traveling conditions. Hence, measures developed in laboratory settings need to be made portable and conducive for travel and transportation.

Nonintrusiveness of measures is an essential criterion for any home- or school-based situational assessments. Oftentimes in homes, especially low-income homes, a limited amount of space is available for data collection. In addition to paying attention to the physical constraints, any disturbances to the family or classroom routine or environment also need to be minimized. These considerations pose a unique set of challenges in adapting measures for real-world settings.

A final challenge for measurement both in home and laboratory settings is the cultural sensitivity and appropriateness of the measures. Given the racial and ethnic heterogeneity within the United States, it is imperative that tasks included in the battery are culturally and linguistically durable (Dumas, Martinez, & LaFreniere, 1998; Geisinger, 1994; Rogoff & Chavajay, 1995). Such measures increase the validity of the results, as they eliminate the influence of confounding factors, such as cultural bias (McCabe et al., 2000). In adapting measures to meet cultural and linguistic demands, it is imperative not to compromise the construct validity of the test. For instance, in the GAMES study, for the Snack Delay task, M&M's were replaced with a sugar-coated cereal for the Latino children in the sample. This substitution was made because in some cuisines, especially Mexican cooking, chocolate is used as an ingredient in main dishes. M&M's could potentially have been seen as a common food as opposed to a special treat. Consequently, in adapting measures to work in home and classroom settings it is important to take into consideration cultural, and in some cases subcultural, differences.

The challenges and limitations discussed here are based on the nascent and unique research that is moving measurement of self-regulation in young children out of the laboratory and into home and classroom settings. However, this is only the tip of the iceberg. As more researchers begin to develop ecologically valid measures of self-regulation, new challenges and limitations are bound to emerge.

FUTURE RESEARCH DIRECTIONS

In this chapter, we have presented results from two projects at the National Center for Children and Families that have used self-regulation measures with diverse families and in multiple settings. Additionally, we have highlighted a few large, multisite investigations that include assessments of early childhood self-regulation. Together, these current efforts suggest some directions for future research.

First, although the GAMES and Storytimes projects provide some preliminary data, additional measurement development is needed. Many questions regarding these assessment tools remain unanswered. Are these assessment situations valid and reliable for larger samples of children? How do home- and classroom-based measures compare to similar assessments implemented in laboratory or clinical assessments? And how do they relate to widely used paper-and-pencil measures such as the Child Behavior Checklist (Achenbach, Edelbrock, & Howell, 1987)?

Second, large-scale studies that examine the ability to self-regulate, as well as factors such as the parent-child relationship, child care experience, or neighborhood characteristics, are relatively rare. As Bates and colleagues (1998) point out, investigations that consider interaction effects are difficult due to the statistical power challenges associated with such work, and the overwhelming number of potential factors to examine. Yet, investigations that consider such multilevel models can perhaps shed the most light on factors related to children's mental health development over time.

ACKNOWLEDGMENTS Support for the writing of this chapter was provided by the Administration for Children, Youth and Families and the National Institute of Mental Health (No. 90YM0001) as part of the Head Start Mental Health Research Consortium led by Cheryl Boyce, Kimberly Hoagwood, Michael Lopez, and Louisa Tarullo. Support also came from the Spencer Foundation, and the Ford Foundation through a Pre-Doctoral Minority Fellowship to the third author. We are grateful to Felton Earls (director) and Kelly Martin (project manager) from the Project on Human Development in Chicago Neighborhoods (funded by the National Institute of Justice and the MacArthur Foundation) for their support of the GAMES project. The authors would like to thank data collectors (Aurelie Athan, Rebecca Fauth, Sandra Lara, Otoniel Lopez, and Eva Medina) and data coders (Aurelie Athan, Helen Rozelman, and Stephanie Tom) for the GAMES project, as well as SueHee Chung, Brenda Morris, and CoriAnn Lupino for their assistance with Storytimes data collection and coding. We are also grateful to Sonja Perteet for suggestions for new assessments, to Colleen O'Neal and Lisa Berlin for contributions to the early stages of the GAMES project, and to Grazyna Kochanska, Marilyn Essex, and Megan Gunnar for their inspirational work on self-regulation. The research projects highlighted in this chapter would not have been possible without the participation of many early childhood programs, families, and children. We appreciate their contributions.

Notes

1. Welfare, Children, and Families: A Three City Study represents a notable exception. Efforts are underway in this project to adapt self-regulation measures for use in homes. For additional information, see http://www.jhu.edu/~welfare/index.html and Brady-Smith, Zaslow, Leventhal, Duncan, and Richter (2003).

2. In some cases (e.g., if a child was allergic to M&M's), an alternative treat such as Goldfish crackers, raisins, or cereal was used.

3. The data collectors were instructed to use an affectively neutral tone of voice while giving the instructions, regardless of whether they were pretending to be the dragon or the parrot.

References

Achenbach, T. M., Edelbrock, C., & Howell, C. T. (1987). Empirically based assessment of the behavioral/emotional problems of 2- and 3-year-old children. *Journal of Abnormal Child Psychology, 15*(4), 629–650.

Aman, C. J., Roberts, R. J., & Pennington, B. F. (1998). A neuropsychological examination of the underlying deficit in attention deficit hyperactivity disorder: Frontal lobe versus right parietal lobe theories. *Developmental Psychology, 34*(5), 956–969.

Baker, A., Piotrkowski, C., & Brooks-Gunn, J. (1998). The effects of the Home Instruction Program for Preschool Youngsters (HIPPY) on children's school performance at the end of the program and one year later. *Early Childhood Research Quarterly, 13*(4), 571–588.

Barkley, R. A. (1997). Behavioral inhibition, sustained attention, and executive functions: Constructing a unifying theory of ADHD. *Psychological Bulletin, 121*, 65–94.

Bates, J. E., Pettit, G. S., Dodge, K. A., & Ridge, B. (1998). Interaction of temperamental resistance to control and restrictive parenting in the development of externalizing behavior. *Developmental Psychology, 34*(5), 982–995.

Bell, J. A., & Livesey, P. J. (1985). Cue significance and response regulation in 3- to 6-year-old children's learning of multiple choice discrimination tasks. *Developmental Psychobiology, 18*(3), 229–245.

Berlin, L. J., Brady-Smith, C., & Brooks-Gunn, J. (2002). Links between childbearing age and observed maternal behaviors with 14-month-olds in the Early Head Start Research and Evaluation Project. *Infant Mental Health Journal, 23*(1–2), 104–129.

Berlin, L. J., O'Neal, C., & Brooks-Gunn, J. (2003). Early childhood intervention research initiatives. In J. Brooks-Gunn, A. S. Fuligni, & L. J. Berlin (Eds.), *Early child development in the 21st century: Profiles of current research initiatives* (pp. 65–89). New York: Teachers College Press.

Block, J. H., & Block, J. (1980). The role of ego-control and ego-resiliency in the organization of behavior. In W. A. Collins (Ed.), *Development of cognition, affect, and social relations: The Minnesota symposium on child psychology* (Vol. 13, pp. 39–101). Hillsdale, NJ: Lawrence Erlbaum.

Block, J., Block, J. H., & Keyes, S. (1988). Longitudinally foretelling drug usage in adolescence: Early childhood personality and environmental precursors. *Child Development, 59*, 336–355.

Brady-Smith, C., O'Brien, C., Berlin, L., Ware, A., & Fauth, R. C. (1999). *30-month child-parent interaction rating scales for the three-bag assessment*. Unpublished manuscript, Teachers College, Columbia University, New York.

Brady-Smith, C., Zaslow, M., Leventhal, T., Duncan, G., & Richter, K. (2003). Welfare-to-work initiatives. In J. Brooks-Gunn, A. S. Fuligni, & L. J. Berlin (Eds.), *Early child development in the 21st century: Profiles of current research initiatives* (pp. 225–278). New York: Teachers College Press.

Brooks-Gunn, J., Berlin, L. J., Leventhal, T., & Fuligni, A. (2000). Depending on the kindness of strangers: Current national data initiatives and developmental research. *Child Development, 71*(1), 257–267.

Campbell, S. B., Pierce, E. W., March, C. L., Ewing, L. J., & Szumowski, E. K. (1994). Hard-to-manage preschool boys: Symptomatic behavior across contexts and time. *Child Development, 65*, 836–851.

Canfield, R. L., Wilken, J., & Schmerl, L. (1991). Speed of reaction, expectancies, and mental processing in young children. Poster presented at the XVIIth Biennial Meeting of the Society for Research in Child Development, Seattle, WA.

Casey, B. J., Cohen, J. D., Noll, D. C., Forman, S., & Rapoport, J. L. (1993). Activation of the anterior cingulate during the Stroop concept paradigm using functional MRI. *Society for Neuroscience Abstracts, 19*, 1285.

Cole, P. M., Zahn-Waxler, C., & Smith, K. D. (1994). Expressive control during a disappointment: Variations related to preschoolers' behavior problems. *Developmental Psychology, 30*, 835–846.

Corkum, P. V., & Siegel, L. S. (1993). Is the Continuous Performance Task a valuable research tool for use with children with attention-deficit-hyperactivity disorder? *Journal of Child Psychology and Psychiatry and Allied Disciplines, 34*, 1217–1239.

Diamond, A., Kirkham, N., & Amso, D. (2002). Conditions under which young children can hold two rules in mind and inhibit a prepotent response. *Developmental Psychology, 38*(3), 352–362.

Diamond, A., & Taylor, C. (1996). Development of an aspect of executive control: Development of the abilities to remember what I said and to "Do as I say, not as I do." *Developmental Psychobiology, 29*, 315–334.

Drewe, E. A. (1975). An experimental investigation of Luria's theory on the effects of frontal lobe lesions in man. *Neuropsychologia, 13*, 421–429.

Dumas, J. E., Martinez, A., & LaFreniere, P. J. (1998). The Spanish version of the Social Competence and Behavior Evaluation (SCBE) Preschool Edition: Translation and field testing. *Hispanic Journal of Behavioral Sciences, 20*, 255–269.

Dunn, H. B., Ho, H. H., Crichton, J. V., Robertson, A. M., McBurney, A. K., Grunaur, V. E., & Penfold, P. S. (1986). Evolution of minimal brain dysfunctions to the age of 12–15 years. In H. G. Dunn (Ed.), *Sequelae of low birth-weight: The Vancouver study* (pp. 249–272). London: MacKeith Press. Clinics in Developmental Medicine, 95/96.

Eisenberg, N., Guthrie, I. K., Fabes, R. A., Shepard, S., Losoya, S., Murphy, B. C., Jones, S., Poulin, R., & Reiser, M. (2000). Prediction of elementary school children's externalizing problems behaviors from attentional and behavioral regulation and negative emotionality. *Child Development, 71*(5), 1367–1382.

Essex, M. (1997). *Procedures manual, part 1: Field, Wisconsin study of families and work.* Unpublished manuscript, University of Wisconsin, Madison.

Frye, D., Zelazo, P. D., & Palfai, T. (1995). Theory of mind and rule-based reasoning. *Cognitive Development, 10*(4), 483–527.

Fuligni, A., McCabe, L., McLanahan, S., & Roth, J. (2003). Four new national longitudinal surveys on children. In J. Brooks-Gunn, A. S. Fuligni, & L. J. Berlin (Eds.), *Early child development in the 21st century: Profiles of current research initiatives* (pp. 326–359). New York: Teachers College Press.

Geisinger, K. F. (1994). Cross-cultural normative assessment: Translation and adaptation issues influencing the normative interpretation of assessment instruments. *Psychological Assessment, 6,* 304–312.

Gerstadt, C. L., Hong, Y. J., & Diamond, A. (1994). The relationship between cognition and action: Performance of children 3½–7 years old on a Stroop-like day-night test. *Cognition, 53,* 129–153.

Gillberg, I. C., & Gillberg, C. (1989). Children with preschool minor neurodevelopmental disorders. IV. Behavior and school achievement at age 13. *Developmental Medicine and Child Neurology, 31,* 3–13.

Golden, M., Montare, A., & Bridger, W. H. (1977). Verbal control of delay behavior in two-year-old boys as a function of social class. *Child Development, 48,* 1107–1111.

Goldsmith, H. H., & Rothbart, M. K. (1992). *Laboratory temperament assessment battery (Lab-TAB): Pre- and locomotor versions.* Eugene: University of Oregon.

Grolnick, W. S., Bridges, L. J., & Connell, J. P. (1996). Emotion regulation in two-year-olds: Strategies and emotional expression in four contexts. *Child Development, 67,* 928–941.

Grolnick, W. S., & Farkas, M. (2002). Parenting and the development of children's self regulation. In M. H. Bornstein (Ed.), *Handbook of parenting: Vol. 5. Practical issues in parenting* (2nd ed., pp. 89–110). Mahwah, NJ: Lawrence Erlbaum.

Grolnick, W. S., Kurowski, C. O., McMenamy, J. M., Rivkin, I., & Bridges, L. (1998). Mothers' strategies for regulating their toddlers' distress. *Infant Behavior and Development, 21,* 437–450.

Gunnar, M. R. (1990). The psychobiology of infant temperament. In J. Colombo & J. Fagan (Eds.), *Individual differences in infancy: Reliability, stability and prediction* (pp. 387–410). Hillsdale, NJ: Lawrence Erlbaum.

Hall, L., Grant, T., Lehman, E. B., Nolte, C., & Srokowski, S. (2001, April). *The number Stroop: A measure of cognitive inhibition in 3- to 6-year-olds.* Poster presented at the biennial meeting of the Society for Research in Child Development, Minneapolis, MN.

Hart, D., Hofmann, V., Edelstein, W., & Keller, M. (1997). The relations of childhood personality types to adolescent behavior and development: A longitudinal study of Icelandic children. *Developmental Psychology, 33*(2), 195–205.

Henderson, S. E. (1993). Motor development and minor handicap. In A. F. Kalverboer, B. Hopkins, & R. Geuze (Eds.), *Motor development in early and later childhood: Longitudinal approaches* (pp. 286–306). New York: Cambridge University Press.

Jacobsen, T. (1998). Delay behavior at age six: Links to maternal expressed mood. *Journal of Genetic Psychology, 159*(1), 117–120.

Jacobsen, T., Huss, M., Fendrich, M., Kruesi, M., & Ziegenhain, U. (1997). Children's ability to delay gratification: Longitudinal relations to mother-child attachment. *Journal of Genetic Psychology, 158*(4), 411–426.

Jacques, S., Zelazo, P. D., Kirkham, N. Z., & Semcesen, T. K. (1999). Rule selection versus rule execution in preschoolers: An error-detection approach. *Developmental Psychology, 35,* 770–780.

Kochanska, G., & Aksan, N. (1995). Mother-child mutually positive affect, the quality of child compliance to requests and prohibitions, and maternal control as correlates of early internalization. *Child Development, 66*(1), 236–254.

Kochanska, G., Murray, K. T., & Coy, K. C. (1997). Inhibitory control as a contributor to conscience in childhood: From toddler to early school age. *Child Development, 68,* 263–277.

Kochanska, G., Murray, K., & Harlan, E. (1999). *Effortful control battery (32–34 months).* Unpublished manuscript, University of Iowa.

Kochanska, G., Murray, K. T., & Harlan, E. T. (2000). Effortful control in early childhood:

Continuity and change, antecedents, and implications for social development. *Developmental Psychology, 36*(2), 220–232.

Kochanska, G., Murray, K. T., Jacques, T. Y., Koenig, A. L., & Vendergeest, K. (1996). Inhibitory control in young children and its role in emerging internalization. *Child Development, 67*, 490–507.

Kopp, C. B. (1982). Antecedents of self-regulation: A developmental perspective. *Developmental Psychology, 18*, 199–214.

Korkman, M., Kirk, U., & Kemp, S. (1998). *NEPSY: A developmental neuropsychological assessment manual.* San Antonio, TX: Pyschological Corporation.

Koski, L., & Petrides, M. (2001). Time-related changes in task performance after lesions restricted to the frontal cortex. *Neuropsychologia, 39*(3), 268–281.

Lee, V. E., Brooks-Gunn, J., & Schnur, E. (1988). Does Head Start work? A 1-year follow-up comparison of disadvantaged children attending Head Start, no preschool, and other preschool programs. *Developmental Psychology, 24*(2), 210–222.

Leventhal, T., & Brooks-Gunn, J. (2003). Neighborhood-based initiatives. In J. Brooks-Gunn, A. S. Fuligni, & L. J. Berlin (Eds.), *Early child development in the 21st century: Profiles of current research initiatives* (pp. 225–278). New York: Teachers College Press.

Levy, F. (1980). The development of sustained attention (vigilance) in children: Some normative data. *Journal of Child Psychology and Psychiatry and Allied Disciplines, 21*(1), 77–84.

Lindahl, E., Michelsson, K., & Donner, M. (1988). Prediction of early school-age problems by a preschool neurodevelopmental examination of children at risk neonatally. *Developmental Medicine and Child Neurology, 30*, 723–734.

Lindahl, E., Michelsson, K., Helenius, M., & Parre, M. (1988). Neonatal risk factors and later developmental disturbances. *Developmental Medicine and Child Neurology, 30*, 571–589.

Livesey, D. J., & Morgan, G. A. (1991). The development of response inhibition in 4- and 5-year-old children. *Australian Journal of Psychology, 43*(3), 133–137.

Losse, A., Henderson, S. E., Elliman, D., Hall, D. B., Knight, E., & Jongmans, M. (1991). Clumsy at six—still clumsy at sixteen? A follow-up study. *Developmental Medicine and Child Neurology, 33*, 55–68.

Luria, A. R. (1959). The directive function of speech in development and dissolution. *Word, 15*, 341–352.

Luria, A. R. (1961). *The role of speech in the regulation of normal and abnormal behavior.* New York: Liveright.

Luria, A. R. (1966). *Higher cortical functions in man.* New York: Basic Books.

Lyytinen, H., & Ahonen, T. (1988). Motor precursors of learning difficulties. In D. J. Bakker & H. Vlugt (Eds.), *Learning disabilities* (pp. 36–43). Amsterdam: Swets and Zeitlinger.

Maccoby, E. E. (1980). *Social development.* New York: Harcourt, Brace, Jovanovich.

Maccoby, E. E., Dowley, E. M., Hagen, J. W., & Degerman, R. (1965). Activity level and intellectual functioning in normal preschool children. *Child Development, 36*, 761–770.

Matas, L., Arend, R. A., & Sroufe, A. (1978). Continuity of adaptation in the second year: The relationship between quality of attachment and later competence. *Child Development, 49*(3), 547–556.

McCabe, L. A., Hernandez, M., Lara, S., & Brooks-Gunn, J. (2000). Assessing preschoolers' self-regulation in homes and classrooms: Lessons from the field. *Behavioral Disorders, 26*(1), 53–69.

McDonald, M. A., Sigman, M., Espinosa, M. P., & Neumann, C. G. (1994). Impact of a temporary food shortage on children and their mothers. *Child Development, 65*(2), 404–415.

McMichael, A. J., Baghurst, P. A., Wigg, N. R., Vimpani, G. V., Robertson, E. F., & Roberts, R. J. (1988). Port Pirie Cohort Study: Environmental exposure to lead and children's abilities at the age of four years. *New England Journal of Medicine, 319*, 468–475.

Miller, S. A., Shelton, J., & Flavell, J. H. (1970). A test of Luria's hypotheses concerning the development of verbal self-regulation. *Child Development, 41*(3), 651–665.

Mischel, W., Ebbesen, E. B., & Zeiss, A. R. (1972). Cognitive and attentional mechanisms in delay of gratification. *Journal of Personality and Social Psychology, 21*, 204–218.

Mischel, W. & Mischel, W. (1983). Development of children's knowledge of self-control strategies. *Child Development, 54*, 603–619.

Mischel, W., & Patterson, C. J. (1979). Effective plans for self-control in children. In A. Collins (Ed.), *Minnesota symposium on child psychology* (Vol. 2). Hillsdale, NJ: Lawrence Erlbaum.

Mischel, W., & Rodriguez, M. L. (1993). Psychological distance in self-imposed delay of gratification. In R. R. Cocking & K. A. Renniger (Eds.), *The development and meaning of psychological distance* (pp. 109–121). Hillsdale, NJ: Lawrence Erlbaum.

Newman, D. L., Caspi, A., Moffitt, T. E., & Silva, P. A. (1997). Antecedents of adult interpersonal functioning: Effects of individual differences in age 3 temperament. *Developmental Psychology, 33*(2), 206–217.

Newman, J. P., Gorenstein, E. E., & Kelsey, J. E. (1983). Failure to delay gratification following septal legions in rats: Implications for an animal model of disinhibitory psychopathology. *Personality and Individual Differences, 4*(2), 147–156.

NICHD Early Child Care Research Network. (1998). Early child care and self-control, compliance, and problem behavior at 24 and 36 months. *Child Development, 69,* 1145–1170.

NICHD Early Child Care Research Network. (1999). Child care and mother-child interactions in the first 3 years of life. *Developmental Psychology, 35*(6), 1399–1413.

Owen, M. T. (1992). *Qualitative ratings of mother-child interaction at 15 months: Prepared for the NICHD study of early child care.* Unpublished manuscript.

Pavlov, I. P. (1961). *The essential works of Pavlov.* New York: Bantam Books.

Pierce, E. W., Ewing, L. J., & Campbell, S. B. (1999). Diagnostic status and symptomatic behavior of hard-to-manage preschool children in middle childhood and early adolescence. *Journal of Clinical Child Psychology, 28*(1), 44–57.

Raver, C., Blackburn, E. K., Bancroft, M., & Torp, N. (1999). Relations between effective emotional self-regulation, attentional control, and low-income preschoolers' social competence with peers. *Early Education and Development, 10*(3), 333–350.

Reed, M. A., Pien, D. L., & Rothbart, M. K. (1984). Inhibitory self-control in preschool children. *Merrill-Palmer Quarterly, 30,* 131–147.

Reichman, N., Teitler, J. O., Garfinkel, I., & McLanahan, S. (2001). Fragile families: Sample and design. *Children and Youth Services Review, 23*(4/5), 303–326.

Rogoff, B., & Chavajay, P. (1995). What's become of research on the cultural bias of cognitive development? *American Psychologist, 50,* 859–877.

Roid, G. H., & Miller, L. J. (1995, 1997). *Leiter International Performance Scale–Revised.* Wood Dale, IL: Stoelting.

Rosvold, H. E., Mirsky, A. F., Sarason, I., Bransome, E. D., Jr., & Beck, L. H. (1956). A continuous performance test of brain damage. *Journal of Consulting Psychology, 20,* 343–350.

Rothbart, M. K. (1989a). Temperament and development. In G. A. Kohnstamm, J. A. Bates, & M. K. Rothbart (Eds.), *Temperament in childhood* (pp. 187–247). New York: Wiley.

Rothbart, M. K. (1989b). Temperament in childhood: A framework. In G. A. Kohnstamm, J. A. Bates, & M. K. Rothbart (Eds.), *Temperament in childhood* (pp. 59–73). New York: Wiley.

Rothbart, M. K., Ahadi, S. A., & Evans, D. E. (2000). Temperament and personality: Origins and outcomes. *Journal of Personality and Social Psychology, 78*(1), 122–135.

Rothbart, M. K., & Derryberry, D. (1981). Development of individual differences in temperament. In M. E. Lamb & A. L. Brown (Eds.), *Advances in developmental psychology* (Vol. 1, pp. 37–86). Hillsdale, NJ: Lawrence Erlbaum.

Rothbart, M. K., Derryberry, D., & Posner, M. I. (1994). A psychobiological approach to the development of temperament. In J. E. Bates & T. D. Wachs (Eds.), *Temperament: Individual differences in biology and behavior* (pp. 83–116). Washington, DC: American Psychological Association.

Russell, J., Mauthner, N., Sharpe, S., & Tidswell, T. (1991). The "windows task" as a measure of strategic deception in preschoolers and autistic subjects. *British Journal of Developmental Psychology, 9*(2), 331–349.

Santostefano, S. (1988). *Cognitive control battery manual.* Los Angeles: Western Psychological Services.

Schweitzer, J.B., & Sulzer-Azaroff, B. (1995). Self-control in boys with attention deficit hyperactivity disorder: Effects of added stimulation and time. *Journal of Child Psychology and Psychiatry and Allied Disciplines, 36*(4), 671–686.

Shonkoff, J. P., & Phillips, D. (2000). *From neurons to neighborhoods: The science of early childhood development.* Washington, DC: National Academy Press.

Spiker, D., Ferguson, J., & Brooks-Gunn, J. (1993). Enhancing maternal interactive behavior and child social competence in low birth weight, premature infants. *Child Development, 64*(3), 754–768.

Taylor, G., Klein, N., Minich, N. M., & Hack, M.

(2000). Middle-school-age outcomes in children with very low birthweight. *Child Development, 71*(6), 1495–1511.

Van Rossum, J. H. A., & Laszlo, J. I. (Eds.). (1994). *Motor development: Aspects of normal and delayed development.* Amsterdam: VU University Press.

Vandell, D. L. (1979). The effects of play group experiences on mother-son and father-son interactions. *Developmental Psychology, 15,* 379–385.

Vaughn, B. E., Kopp, C. B., & Krakow, J. B. (1984). The emergence and consolidation of self-control from eighteen to thirty months of age: Normative trends and individual differences. *Child Development, 55*(3), 990–1004.

Warner-Rogers, J., Taylor, A., Taylor, E., & Sandberg, S. (2000). Inattentive behavior in childhood: Epidemiology and implications for development. *Journal of Learning Disabilities, 33,* 520–536.

Zelazo, P. D., Frey, D., & Rapus, T. (1996). An age-related dissociation between knowing rules and using them. *Cognitive Development, 11,* 37–63

Epilogue

The chapters presented in this book highlight current enthusiasm and progress within the field of infant, toddler, and preschool assessment of mental health. The authors demonstrate that a variety of methods and measures have now been developed to capture the variability of normative and psychopathological social-emotional development, including assessments of behavior problems, competencies, and diagnostic symptoms. Building on theoretical advances and empirical data, methods that have been developed include caregiver report questionnaires and interviews as well as observational tools. Also notable in this compendium of information is the consensus regarding the importance of identifying and assessing the relevant contexts that promote (or at times hinder) early development. Thus, it is crucial to evaluate a young child's functioning within the caregiving contexts that are most proximal to the child (e.g., parents, day care settings) and to examine the contribution of broader environmental influences, including cultural values and beliefs, to ensure adequate understanding of the functions of the child and parent's behaviors. Despite dramatic progress in this area of inquiry over the past 15 years, one of the biggest challenges remaining is the development of systematic strategies for determining clinical caseness. The limits of our current ability to identify those children and families who are experiencing clinical levels of psychopathology restricts our ability to assess the prevalence of disorders in this age group and compromises our capacity to advocate for improved services for families of young children.

Despite considerable advancement in theory and measurement of infant, toddler, and preschool mental health, the scientific evidence regarding the boundary between age-typical functioning and disorder in the early childhood period is very incomplete. For example, although there is consensus about the importance of regulation in early childhood, the demarcation between normal variation in temperament and the presence of a sensory modulation or regulatory disorder or the presence of ADHD prior to age 4 years remains ambiguous at best. Yet, it is clear that many parents and children suffer significant impairment due to children's over- or underreactivity to a wide range of stimuli in the environment. The task of determining clinical caseness is complicated both by an absence of agreement regarding methods to document impairment in the early childhood period and by the necessity of evaluating children within the contexts of their caregiving environments.

As children get older, and particularly as they enter school settings, expectations for daily performance are more consistent across caregivers and settings, making the task of defining impairment easier. Many infants and toddlers are not required to negotiate multiple contexts, and parents vary dramatically in terms of their expectations regarding self-care (e.g., eating, toileting, dressing, self-grooming) and household participation (e.g., chores). Parents also vary with respect to the importance they place on peer exposure as well as in their capacity to provide opportunities for their children to engage with other children in play. Therefore, in many instances there are limited opportunities for young children to demonstrate a decline in functioning (i.e., impairment) within the home or with peers following the development of a psychiatric disturbance. Examination of impairment in the first years of life may be more reliably assessed if expanded to include not only the child's functioning but also the extent to which the child's functioning impacts day-to-day family life. Thus, the family that cannot take the child to the supermarket due to the child' reactivity in the supermarket or the family that cannot find a baby-sitter due to the child's negative emotionality and aggression is suffering impairment that can be quantified. At present, diagnostic systems that address impairment rely on an individual-level impairment construct. However, several researchers are currently gathering data to address the impact of emotional and behavioral symptoms and disorders on family, as well as individual, functioning. Such data will likely inform future definitions of impairment in the early childhood arena.

Determining caseness at the individual level is further complicated due to the reliance of young children on their caregiving contexts. Thus, evaluating the role of extraregulatory support is crucial in evaluating the boundary between regulatory disorders and normative temperamental variations. Specifically, highly attuned caregiver regulatory support may allow a highly reactive child to function adequately in day-to-day activities while in-

sensitive, inconsistent, or intrusive caregiver behaviors may disrupt a moderately reactive child's capacity to function in day-to-day settings. Moreover, the parent's ability to moderate the highly reactive child's experience of potentially stressful and overwhelming stimulation influences the child's acquisition of self-regulation strategies. Thus, the goodness of fit between parenting strategies and a child's underlying temperamental or regulatory substrate is likely to be more important in predicting the onset of psychopathology than either parenting or child temperament/regulation alone. Although the goodness-of-fit model is an extremely valuable heuristic tool in providing families with feedback about their children, more empirical research in community, high-risk, and psychopathological populations is needed to be able to use the concept of goodness of fit in a systematic manner for clinical assessment.

In 1989, Sameroff and Emde published a pivotal book, *Relationship Disturbances in Early Childhood: A Developmental Approach*, that challenged traditional individualistic diagnostic approaches and advocated that in early childhood it was more developmentally appropriate to consider assigning clinical caseness at the dyadic rather than individual level. This strategy was adopted, in part, within the DC:0–3 diagnostic nosology in the form of parent-child diagnoses, which can be used in conjunction with individually assigned child diagnoses. Given the fact that many maladaptive behaviors may have their roots in the young child's efforts to adapt to a maladaptive or ill-fitting nurturing environment, the inclusion of parent-child diagnoses provides an important mechanism for providing early intervention to children who are clearly at risk for subsequent individual disturbance but who may not meet criteria for clinical caseness. Although the DC:0–3 inclusion of relational disturbances is laudable, greater diagnostic specificity is needed to ensure reliable and valid assignment of the parent-child relational diagnostic classifications.

In addition to relationship disturbances, a number of other child, parent, and broader environmental risk factors have been identified and linked with negative child mental health outcomes. Moreover, as documented by Sameroff, Seifer, and McDonough in this text, the accumulation of multiple risk factors appears to be more salient in the prediction of concurrent and later psycho-pathology than the presence of specific individual risk factors. Thus, of major importance for the field of early childhood mental health is the need to emphasize assessment of risk exposure and prevention along with more traditional intervention services that are typically only offered when a child meets criteria for a formal psychiatric diagnosis. As we have gained both in understanding of the long-term consequences of risk exposure and in tools that permit assessment of child, family, and environmental risk factors, it behooves us to advocate for services that can ameliorate risks and buffer families and children exposed to multiple risk factors to promote positive mental health adaptations.

A final challenge that the field of infant, toddler, and preschool mental health faces is systematizing methods for aggregating information across multiple sources and methods of data collection. As infants and toddlers are not capable of providing self-report information, the inclusion of multiple adult informants and observations of both the child and caregiving contexts is crucial. Such systems will not only be highly valuable for assessing very young children, but will also have implications for the assessment of older children and adults. Similarly, expanding our understanding of diagnosis and impairment from the individual to the level of relationships and family context will likely inform our understanding of older child and adult psychopathology and may provide new evaluation methods that will enhance lifespan assessment strategies. Too often, assessment approaches for children have been derived from adult approaches. By adopting developmentally sensitive assessment approaches that recognize the importance of emerging regulatory capacities and the embeddedness of children within their caregiving and cultural contexts, we anticipate that the emerging field of young child mental health assessment will likely offer new strategies that can "filter up" to inform assessment of older child and adult mental health.

Index

LaVergne, TN USA
05 April 2011
222775LV00002BA/2/P